LEO BAECK INSTITUTE
YEAR BOOK

1977

Presidium of the first Jewish Synod at Leipzig in 1869

From left to right: Ritter v. Wertheimer, Vienna (Second Vice-President),
Moritz Lazarus, Berlin (President), Abraham Geiger, Frankfurt a. Main
(First Vice-President)

PUBLICATIONS OF THE
LEO BAECK INSTITUTE

YEAR BOOK XXII

1977

SECKER & WARBURG · LONDON
PUBLISHED FOR THE INSTITUTE
LONDON · JERUSALEM · NEW YORK

EDITOR: ROBERT WELTSCH

OFFICES OF THE
LEO BAECK INSTITUTE

JERUSALEM (ISRAEL) : 33 Bustanai Street
LONDON : 4 Devonshire Street, W.1
NEW YORK : 129 East 73rd Street

THE LEO BAECK INSTITUTE

was founded in 1955 by the

COUNCIL OF JEWS FROM GERMANY

for the purpose of collecting material on and
sponsoring research into the history of the Jewish
Community in Germany and in other German-
speaking countries from the Emancipation to its
decline and new dispersion. The Institute is
named in honour of the man who was the last
representative figure of German Jewry in
Germany during the Nazi period.

The Council of Jews from Germany was established after
the war by the principal organisations of Jews from
Germany in Israel, USA and UK for the protection of
their rights and interests.

THIS PUBLICATION WAS SUPPORTED
BY A GRANT FROM THE
MEMORIAL FOUNDATION FOR JEWISH CULTURE

© Leo Baeck Institute 1977
Published by Martin Secker & Warburg Limited
14 Carlisle Street, London WIV 6NN
SBN 436 24430 6
*Printed in Great Britain by Richard Clay (The Chaucer Press), Limited,
Bungay, Suffolk*

Contents

Illustrations

Introduction

BY ROBERT WELTSCH

When the first volume of this Year Book was published by the Leo Baeck Institute in 1956, we began its introduction with the quotation of a statement from the work of one of the foremost representatives of Jewish learning in Germany, Julius Guttmann, who in his standard work *Die Philosophie des Judentums* said: "Germany is the birthplace of modern Judaism". This fact has in the meantime been widely acknowledged by all those who devoted their studies to the significant transition of Jewish reality from the more medieval former aspects to the stage where the decisive attempt was made both at combining Judaism with the forms of modern European life, and at applying modern scientific and scholarly methods to the study of Jewish history and ways of life. One of the important steps in this process was the evolution in Germany of what was called *Wissenschaft des Judentums*.

This term was coined, as is well known, by the group of young Jewish intellectuals who had gone through the process of assimilation to German culture at the beginning of the nineteenth century, but were still faithful, to some degree, to the values of Judaism and interested in its history. These people established in 1819 an association, officially called *Verein für Cultur und Wissenschaft der Juden*, whose first president was Eduard Gans. (A short history by H. G. Reissner was published in our Year Book.)[1] Something of a programmatic explanation of the intentions of this group was written by one of its members, Immanuel Wolf (Wohlwill), in the usual Hegelian German of the time, a difficult text which was translated into English – as far as we know for the first time – by Lionel Kochan at the initiative of the Leo Baeck Institute and printed in the same second volume of our Year Book.[2] This phenomenon, with all its shortcomings characteristic for the ferment created by the encounter of two worlds, reflected the problems involved in Jewry's entry into the modern era, and it had its influence, in the short as well as long term, on the thought and actions of Jews in other countries. That it occupies the attention of the present generation of Jewish students in America is shown by the contributions of younger American scholars in the present volume of our Year Book. Indeed, the essence of these deliberations which started in 1819 is topical also today, with all the differences, of course, brought about by change of place and time.

The initiative of 1819 was a first experiment and not all the original members remained faithful to it, as we well know. Yet, the idea was in the air and it bore fruit in the work of great and enthusiastic Jewish scholars like Leopold Zunz, Abraham Geiger, I. M. Jost and others. This activity, unavoidably imbued with elements of assimilation, was, however, looked at with suspicion, especially

---

[1]'Rebellious Dilemma: The Case Histories of Eduard Gans and some of his Partisans', in *LBI Year Book II* (1957), pp. 179–193.

[2]'On the Concept of a Science of Judaism (1822)'; *ibid.*, pp. 194–204.

by prominent representatives of East European Jewry whose approach to the whole complex of Jewish revival was, understandably, different, because East European Jewry had an unbroken tradition of Jewish learning, not interrupted by assimilation to the same degree as Western Jewry. In the course of events, German *Wissenschaft des Judentums* became a controversial subject, regarded by many as a sort of evasion and even as a camouflage for assimilation. Among those who dissociated themselves in a strong and passionate manner from these German-Jewish endeavours were such great men as Ahad Ha'am, Chaim Nachman Bialik and others. They had an inherent distrust of the educated German Jew who, according to their view, used Jewish themes only for glossing over their indifference or, at the least, for a scientific analysis of an antiquated past instead of identifying himself with living Judaism.

This controversy seems to us now somewhat outdated, because after the dramatic events of the present century the whole approach to the questions of Judaism has completely changed. A new centre for Jewish studies in the widest sense has arisen in Israel and in some respect also in the United States, and the great institutions of Jewish learning in Eastern Europe were destroyed in the most tragic manner. A new attitude to all Jewish values and also to the problem of Jewish studies has emerged all over the world. Former judgments are in need of revision. A great many studies of considerable interest have been written during the last period in academic institutions of Israel, America and elsewhere, and we may claim that, as far as the German-Jewish position is concerned, the Leo Baeck Institute has also contributed a considerable part; to this many essays in our Year Book – and its growing reputation – bear witness. It is, therefore, of special interest that a modern Jewish scholar and rabbi, Ephraim Shmueli, raised the issue again in an article published in the Hebrew-language American periodical *Hadoar* (12th November 1976), with the intention of doing justice to the founders of *Wissenschaft des Judentums*, and of bringing the situation of nineteenth-century German Jewry into the right perspective. Dr. Shmueli goes back to Immanuel Wolf's above-mentioned essay (that an English translation had been published by us in 1957, apparently escaped his notice), and to the ensuing controversy which according to his view was based on a misunderstanding of the whole dialectical situation in the evolution of different forms of Jewish culture. Shmueli argues that Immanuel Wolf's article deserves attention even after 160 years, because he evaluated *Wissenschaft des Judentums* as a scientific movement for the revitalisation of Judaism. If translated into appropriate Hebrew Wolf's essay would be an equivalent to Bialik's own point of view as expressed in his famous letter to the editors of *Dvir* (1922) which he wrote while in exile in Berlin, of all places.[3] Wolf, too, regarded *Wissenschaft*

[3]In this letter Bialik vehemently attacked Western Jewry and its *Wissenschaft des Judentums* primarily because of its abandonment of the Hebrew language by which it excluded itself from the core of the Nation; he extolled East European Jewry (which actually at that time was already on the brink of destruction) for its faithfulness to Hebrew and Jewish reality. He concluded, however, on a more conciliatory note, expressing the hope for a future reunion of all Jewish "tribes" for creative Hebrew work also in the field of *Wissenschaft* – in his wrath Bialik overlooked the fact that it was not the men of *Wissenschaft des Judentums* who were to blame; the "original sin" which caused the displacing of the Hebrew language was the opening of the

GERSHOM SCHOLEM

Photo: Aliza Auerbach

as necessary in order to bring young Jews back to an intensive preoccupation with Judaism, and in this way to create agreement between its vitalisation and modern spirit. *Wissenschaft des Judentums*, he insists, does not intend to restrict Judaism to abstract spiritualism. As a Hegelian, Wolf explained that by using the concept of Judaism he had in mind a comprehensive spiritual public reality in the widest sense, in the field of religion, philosophy, history, law, literature, civil life and all other human interests, and not restricted to Jewish religion only. It is difficult, says Shmueli, to discern between this interpretation of *Wissenschaft des Judentums* and that of the great masters of East European Jewish learning whom Bialik had praised. In the mid-twentieth century, Gershom Scholem has revived this issue.

Of course, we cannot agree with everything the West European masters of *Wissenschaft des Judentums* did or intended, Shmueli points out; but even the apologetical tendency should not be altogether condemned as long as it does not lead to misrepresentation of documents and achievements of the past which have to be understood according to their own historical context. Every historian judges the past according to his own views; for this Dubnow is an outstanding example. Shmueli concludes with the statement that he does not intend to go all the way in defending *Wissenschaft des Judentums* as it was in its time. His purpose is only to point out that its errors are no worse than those of all other cultural stages in Jewish history, such as the Talmudic period, the philosophy, the mysticism and rabbinism. *Wissenschaft des Judentums* in Western Europe is a product of the culture of emancipation, the sixth stage in the evolution of Jewish culture. What critics found there to object to exists also in the other stages of culture preceding it. Each was determined by the dialectics of contradiction and productivity, and all contributed to the evolution and rejuvenation of Judaism and of the Jewish people, as well as to indifference and/or straightforward defection.

Shmueli's article is a contribution to that debate about Jewish historiography which has never stopped and which was also developed in the United States. Often widely differing views depend on the general attitude of the interpreter, whether more secular or more religious; one sector regards history, in accordance with the Bible, under theological aspects. Against this there arose a modern view, that of laying stress on the social and political factors which contributed decisively to the shaping of Jewish destiny; such factors result mainly from the forces of the surrounding world, not autonomically from Jewish ideas or Jewish will.

Gershom Scholem, in the original version of his attack on the reputation of *Wissenschaft des Judentums*, as printed (in Hebrew) in the Haaretz Almanach 5705 (1944/45), concludes his essay with a galaxy of emphatic rhetorical questions addressed to the contemporary generation in Palestine (as it then was), calling

---

ghetto, a social process which also had many positive sides, to say the least. He measured West and East with a different yardstick, as the future was to show. In Palestine (later Israel), Jewish scholarship was to achieve unprecendented heights and many Western scholars contributed to it; without its close contact with Western science – albeit not in Hebrew – Jewish scholarship in modern times would not have achieved the progress it did.

them to account for the continuing superficiality and dilletantism in their attitude to exploring the essence of Judaism. The nationalist attitude which prevailed after the rise of Zionism and boasted of having replaced the assimilationist
approach, was not less rationalistic and short-sighted than its predecessor, he
argued. Its representatives, too, ignored the creative "anarchistic" forces en-
shrined in what Scholem calls the hidden, or the secret, history. This is not the
place to attempt an answer to these questions in detail, nor is this writer competent to do so. Yet, it cannot be an accident that this passionate appeal for a
thorough revision and a new approach has been eliminated from Scholem's later
treatment of the same subject-matter, especially in the German language version
of 1959. The subject is also omitted in the recent collection of Scholem's Essays
in English translation, published by Schocken Books New York 1976 under the
title *On Jews and Judaism in Crisis*, edited by Werner J. Dannhauser. In this book,
however, the two pronouncements Against the Myth of the German-Jewish
Dialogue, which also gave rise to controversy, are included.

Some of the Jewish writers at that time could not withstand the influence of
the climate of contemporary Jewish aspirations which was primarily determined by the all-pervading quest for emancipation. The dominant spirit of
Jewish public life was that of apologetics, and an inclination to minimise the
importance of Judaism. This situation had a depressing effect even on some of
the most devoted sponsors of *Wissenschaft des Judentums* and led to a mood of
resignation, as illustrated by a – perhaps ironical – remark of Moritz Steinschneider (1818–1907), quoted by Gershom Scholem who had heard it from
Gotthold Weil.[4] The aged Steinschneider (he was then nearly ninety), whom
Scholem calls "one of the greatest scholars the Jewish people has ever produced",
is reported to have said that "nothing is left to the men of *Wissenschaft des
Judentums* but to give the remnants of Judaism an honourable burial". One
may doubt whether this casual remark in a personal conversation justified the
far-reaching conclusions which Scholem draws when he says that the *Wissenschaft des Judentums* had lost contact with Jewish life and the will for a Jewish
future. On the other hand, Scholem himself in this context emphasises the greatness of Zunz.

It seems evident that the thirty crucial years or so which have passed since
Scholem's first provocative challenge, have also provided some material for a
less pessimistic judgment, although some of his arguments have an unshakeable
validity, e.g. the statement that among the masses of European Jews who perished
in Auschwitz and similar places, there must have been a remarkable reservoir of
talent and potential scholarly creativity of a modern kind. Moreover, not a little
of what Scholem demanded and hoped for in his quest for a real scholarly re-
casting of *Wissenschaft des Judentums* according to the principles he formulated

---

[4]Gerschom Scholem, 'Wissenschaft vom Judentum Einst und Jetzt', a lecture given in German
in London on 7th September 1959 at a World Conference of the Leo Baeck Institute, published
in *Bulletin des Leo Baeck Instituts*, 3 (1960), No. 9, pp. 10–20, later reprinted in: Scholem,
Judaica, Frankfurt a. Main 1963, pp. 147–164. The lecture is based on an earlier Hebrew
version printed in *Luach Haaretz* 5705 (1945). Gotthold Weil, orientalist, (1882–1960), was
1918–1931 Director of the Oriental Department of the Staatsbibliothek, Berlin, 1934–1946
Director of the Hebrew National and University Library, Jerusalem.

thirty years ago, has been achieved, not least by himself. At the age of eighty, which he reached this year, he is justly regarded as one of the greatest, possibly *the* greatest Jewish scholar of the age. He could be described as the protagonist and actual master of *Wissenschaft des Judentums* as its idea was originally conceived – albeit then in the Hegelian terms of 1820. He has, however, corrected the original concept and also made good the principal sin of nineteenth-century scholars in one decisive respect, namely by restoring Jewish mystical literature and the world of Kabbala, which had been despised or even ridiculed by some of the greatest Jewish historians, to its proper place in the setting of Judaism. As Jerusalem professor of Kabbala he actually founded a new department of Jewish science, attracting many disciples and gradually changing the traditional outlook. His latest English[5] language opus magnum in this field is the monumental historical biography of Sabbatai Zwi, an enlarged and revised version of his previous Hebrew book of 1957.

As Scholem has also been a member of the Board of the Leo Baeck Institute from its very beginning in 1954 – he was actually one of its founding fathers, – we take the opportunity of saluting him in admiration and friendship on the occasion of his eightieth birthday. At the summit of his scholarly achievement, he, too, appears as one of those demonic figures of whose role in the development of Judaism and *Wissenschaft des Judentums* he has so emphatically spoken.[6]

It is also true that the controversies about *Wissenschaft des Judentums* were inspired by the political or ideological attitude of the disputants more than by matter-of-fact consideration. We have mentioned before the antipathy of Eastern Jews to the Western assimilated Jew who had experienced a secular non-Jewish education. Actually, as we can see today, thanks to outside circumstances Western Jews were only about a hundred years ahead. The Eastern Jews, as soon as they had the chance, could not withstand the same social pressures of assimilation to the surrounding world and its modes of thinking. But such transformation of ways of life in neither case necessarily means the abandonment of Jewish identity and feeling, though this may assume new forms. These were all stages in the evolution of the painful process of combining Jewishness in a changed world with the requirements of modern life, after the walls of the Ghetto had fallen.

---

[5]*Sabbatai Ṣevi. The Mystical Messiah 1626–1676*. Published in England (after the American edition in Bollingen Series XCIII) by Routledge and Kegan Paul London 1973. The author, who does not lack a sense of humour, enjoyed the fact that the printed book ran to exactly one thousand pages. On Scholem's published works in English see also 'Books' in *The New Yorker*, 22nd October 1973.

[6]I am indebted to Dr. Erwin Rosenthal of Cambridge for drawing my attention to an essay by David Biale (University of California) 'Gershom Scholem's Revision of the Wissenschaft des Judentums' which was printed in the *Newsletter of the Association for Jewish Studies* in U.S.A., No. 19, 1977. The author describes Scholem as a "counter-historian" who, while not denying the reality of a "mainstream" history, believes that "the vital elements of history lie in a secret or subterranean tradition; therefore the historian must 'brush history against the grain' " (the phrase stems from Walter Benjamin). It is also significant that Scholem in his German-language writings does not use the term "Wissenschaft *des* Judentums", but prefers to call it "Wissenschaft *vom* Judentum".

It is a fascinating, and from the Jewish historian's point of view a very promising phenomenon that young Jewish historians, who have grown up in the United States in a quite different civilisation, are attracted by the problems connected with the ideas of *Wissenschaft des Judentums* in early nineteenth-century Germany. We have to remember that medieval Judaism was a closed society whose leaders (with some important exceptions) abhorred secular knowledge. This applies not only to Germany but also to Russia (as is known to us through the numerous autobiographical writings of nineteenth-century Russian Jews). Speaking of the situation in Germany, Ismar Schorsch in his essay in this volume points out that some of the sponsors of *Wissenschaft des Judentums* learned the German language at a comparatively late stage of their lives. The introduction of secular education by S. M. Ehrenberg and the ambiguous relation stemming from the vacillation between loyalty to Judaism and hunger for an – earlier tabooed – secular knowledge created a peculiar psychological situation which we post-assimilation Jews, having enjoyed a thorough secular education, should be reluctant to condemn. It was a genuine problem, the result of an irresistible historical process; yet one can easily understand that it gave rise to misunderstandings and misgivings.

In his letter of 1817, published in this volume, I. M. Jost made a mocking remark about the kind of German spoken in the Berlin Reform congregation. But in 1833, Jost stated that in the few intervening years German Jews had made "progress of a millennium" in German culture. It is, of course, a tragic sidelight to be aware today of what was to happen exactly a hundred years after the German patriot Jost had uttered this statement.

But there is no doubt that those first decades of the nineteenth century were a time of considerable ferment in Jewish affairs, caused by the encounter with European culture and the consequences of integration into the economic and cultural life of the environment.[7] The quandary of the first post-Mendelssohn generation, especially those families which had attained the standards of the upper middle class, was how to combine their Jewish existence which they certainly did not want to abandon, with the demands of modern education and of their assumed social responsibilities. One of the most conspicuous cases in point is the family of the wealthy banker Jacob Herz-Beer (1769–1825), three of whose sons at least were to play a more or less prominent role in cultural life: Wilhelm (1797–1850), an important astronomer, Michael (1800–1833), a playwright of noteworthy though transitory success,[8] and Jakob Liebmann Meyer Beer (1791–1864), i.e., the world-famous composer Giacomo Meyerbeer. The Beer family lived remote from the popular Jewish life of the lower strata, although Jacob Beer was a member of the Council (*Älterenrat*) of the Jewish community and an active fighter for emancipation. The momentous work of Heinz Becker, Meyerbeer's Letters and Diaries, the third volume of which

[7]This is the topic of the latest collective volume published by the London Leo Baeck Institute: *Das Judentum in der Deutschen Umwelt 1800–1850. Studien zur Frühgeschichte der Emanzipation*, herausgegeben von Hans Liebeschütz und Arnold Paucker, Tübingen 1977 (Schriftenreihe wissenschaftlicher Abhandlungen des Leo Baeck Instituts 35).
[8]See Lothar Kahn, 'Michael Beer (1800–1833)', in *LBI Year Book XII* (1967), pp. 149–160.

appeared last year,[9] reflects somehow the birthpangs, the tension and mental unsteadiness of this phase of Jewish transformation. The artistic, social and psychological problems involved were discussed in Year Book IX in connection with the centenary of Meyerbeer's death, after the publication of the first volume of Becker's great work.[10] The third volume, dealing with the period when the composer stood at the peak of his glory, shows again Meyerbeer's almost hysterical mania for theatrical success (which was sometimes interpreted as "Jewish" showing-off and anxiety to be accepted) and also his and his family's nervous suspicion directed against what Meyerbeer in his letters from Paris to his wife calls "richesse" (sic!), a phonetic rendering of the Yiddish expression for "malevolence", that is antisemitism, here spelled paradoxically like the French word for riches or wealth. From the human and Jewish point of view, Meyerbeer, a warm-hearted and family-minded man, was a product of the light-hearted optimism of the period. Personally, he was faithful to the Jewish creed though not observant. But he left no Jewish offspring.

His father, as said above, was the man who had founded the first Reform Temple in Berlin, even in defiance of the outspoken prohibition by the Prussian King Friedrich Wilhelm III, who refused to tolerate an additional place of Jewish worship in Berlin. When the proponents argued that the official Service in the community synagogue was conducted in a language (Hebrew) which nobody in the audience understood, the King said the community should be responsible for introducing a translation of the text in the vernacular (German), but must not install a separate place of worship.[11] Nevertheless, Prussian *Kanzler* Hardenberg preserved the existence of Beer's *Tempel,* under a pretext, at least for several years, and later it was allowed to function as a substitute for the main synagogue.

It was in this reform *Tempel* that Jost, one of the more controversial fathers of *Wissenschaft des Judentums,* attended the Rosh Hashanah service in 1817 on which he reported to his teacher S. M. Ehrenberg in the letter reproduced and commented upon by Nahum Glatzer in the present volume of the Year Book. It shows the ambivalent feeling – bordering on disappointment – with which even the radical moderniser regarded the new approach of the assimilatory Jews with its tendency to break with the past and with the traditional cult. This revolutionary action, with its application of the German language and also the institution of the German sermon[12] was one of the reasons why spiritual leaders of East European Jewry, as referred to above, reacted so vehemently against

[9]Giacomo Meyerbeer, *Briefwechsel und Tagebücher.* Mit Unterstützung der Akademie der Künste Berlin in Verbindung mit dem Institut für Musikforschung Berlin. Herausgegeben und kommentiert von Heinz Becker und Gudrun Becker. 3. Band (1837–1845), Walter de Gruyter, Berlin 1975.

[10]Contributions by Heinz Becker, 'Giacomo Meyerbeer. On the Centenary of his Death', and Max Brod, 'Some Comments on the Relationship between Wagner and Meyerbeer', in *LBI Year Book IX* (1964), pp. 178–205; see also Introduction to the same volume, pp. xiii–xix.

[11]For the full text of the King's letter see Becker, *op. cit.,* vol. I, pp. 32–33.

[12]Cf. Alexander Altmann, 'Zur Frühgeschichte der jüdischen Predigt in Deutschland. Leopold Zunz als Prediger', in *LBI Year Book VI* (1961), and also Introduction to the same volume, pp. xiii–xvii.

the disdained type of assimilated German Jew and against the new form of worship. Another cause of anger was the musical innovation which was condemned as an alleged imitation of Christian custom.

Apart from purely musicological aspects, the development of synagogal music is a significant reflection on the many-sided transformation of consciousness and of spiritual tendencies during the stormy period of Jewish integration into the social and cultural European (German) atmosphere. Music and song have always been an indispensable part of Jewish worship, and it is no wonder that in this area, too, the assimilatory inclinations exerted their – conscious or unconscious – impact. From the very beginning it was felt by the fathers of *Wissenschaft des Judentums* that this symptomatic complex must not be neglected. It is therefore a matter of satisfaction that – while these lines were being written – the Leo Baeck Institute in New York produced a scholarly historical work on this subject: *The Sacred Songs of the Ashkenasic Jews*, by one of the most competent experts in this field, Professor Eric Werner.[13] It is not possible here to enter into a full analysis of this recent work, but in the context of this Introduction to a discussion of *Wissenschaft des Judentums* as a phase in the struggle for achieving some kind of synthesis of Jewish and general values, and application of modern scientific methods to Jewish problems, it seems to me imperative to mention it as a contribution to the core of our theme. Even at the first cursory glance one is stunned by the extent of the interplay of mutual influence between Jewish customs and their surroundings, both intentional and automatic, often in a popular mood and, of course, without scientific aspirations. Some examples of this kind were published by the late Eugen Mayer in Year Book III.[14] Melodies of German and even overtly Christian folksongs were adapted to Hebrew texts; according to Mayer this kind of assimilation may have proceeded from the sixteenth century onward, in all kinds of quaint and amusing combinations. On the surface this has not necessarily anything to do with religious service, but as Jewish life at that pre-emancipation era was almost exclusively and intrinsically centred on the synagogue, it is a reasonable assumption that such habits intruded also, officially or unofficially, into the realm of liturgy.

The appearance of well-known melodies, taken mainly from operas which resounded in the ears of a music-loving community, was by no means a rare occurrence at prayers, presented in a perfectly naïve manner, especially in small places and often at improvised Services. I shall never forget a Rosh Hashanah Service of about seventy-five years ago at a small Bohemian resort in a semi-private synagogue attended by summer visitors; when the amateur *Hazan* intoned the "unetaneh tokef", a stir went through the audience and I heard the grown-ups whispering – with smiling satisfaction, mind you – "Norma!" Actually, the *Hazan* sung the famous Hebrew text to the tune of "Mira, o Norma, ai tuoi ginocchi . . ." With the semi-assimilated middle class of that

---

[13]*A Voice Still Heard . . . The Sacred Songs of the Ashkenazic Jews*. A Publication in the Leo Baeck Institute Series. The Pennsylvania State University Press, University Park and London 1976.
[14]'A German-Jewish Miscellany (Migration of Melodies)', pp. 202–210.

generation Bellini and Donizetti were favourites for such purposes; their melodies were also sometimes applied to the recital of portions of the Passover Hagadah. No one took offence; on the contrary, it was considered an imaginative idea, linking the traditional custom with the newly-acquired musical taste. This, too, was characteristic of the good-natured mentality of these "ba'al-battic" newcomers to European civilisation, addicts of Meyerbeer and of Italian opera, who had emerged from the ghetto to fill the central European theatres.[15]

Indeed, one of the principal questions in re-shaping the synagogue service was its musical design. Here, the controversy centred on the use of the organ. For many years the slogan of "organ synagogue" was the shibboleth among the supporters of various forms of service. Dr. Werner dwells exhaustively on this subject, quoting the view of *halakhic* authorities and discussing the pros and cons. There was no final authoritative verdict on whether the organ must be banned.[16] The Jost letter mentioned above seems to show that even such a radical reformer as Jost was not an admirer of Jacob Beer's reform service. His impression was that the enthusiasts for German were not really masters of the language; between the lines of his report one may discover a nuance of contempt for the vulgarity of the nouveaux riches who cared more for money and pretension than for learning or moral standing. Furthermore, Jost considered the seat close to the organ the worst in the whole hall, and his being placed there as a humiliation. He criticises the inferior quality of the old shaky instrument which contrasts poorly with the shouting clumsy choir; in short, if the purpose of reform service was to improve the aesthetics of the Service, it had certainly failed in this respect. Obviously, Jost was in a bad mood and also outraged by the hypocrisy of the promoters, although it is not clear in which direction he would have liked to see improvements made, certainly not in favour of bringing back orthodox attitudes. He admitted, however, the advantages of *decorum* which the Reform service had enforced after many difficulties.

It would be a mistake to regard the Reform as a straightforward uniform movement. There were within this camp many dissensions and controversies and also a clash of personalities, which later were extended to America, the most important region for its unfolding and expansion. This is skilfully demonstrated by the essays of our American authors where the leading figures of reform are contrasted. Dr. Petuchowsky explains the immense divergence between Geiger and Holdheim. Speaking of Jost and Zunz, Dr. Schorsch lets us discover that Jost was the more radical assimilationist while Zunz's scholarly merits are generally admitted even by most critics of *Wissenschaft des Judentums*. On the

---

[15]See also Werner, *op. cit.*, p. 242: ". . . immediately after the Emancipation both hazan and *klezmar* turned to the concert hall, inundating the field of secular music like turbulent waters long dammed up . . . Even today opera exercises a strong attraction for the hazan [in the Ashkenaz community] . . . the oriental hazan never experienced the opera's attraction . . ."

[16]The organ controversy – in *minhag ashkenaz* – has troubled the synagogue until the present day. Although the attitude on both sides was very passionate, the question itself remained undecided. Werner, *op. cit.*, pp. 195–198.

other hand, Georg Herlitz, himself an historian, in his essay in Year Book IX[17] praises Jost as a remarkable pioneer of Jewish historiography because his nine-volume history, notwithstanding its shortcomings, is not only based on internal Jewish intellectual development and on a lachrymose approach but he was also the first to appreciate fully the importance of social and political forces and the influence of outside factors on Jewish life. It could also be added that the *Weltanschauung* revealed in Jost's work was that of the majority of German Jews of that period. Undoubtedly, they were more interested in secular matters and in their relation to the surrounding society than in the purely religious and parochial issues.

This decreasing interest in Jewish affairs – except by the then small circle of professional Jews – was also responsible for the limited response which all endeavours of Jewish scholarship found in Jewish society before the Hitler era changed this attitude. This indifference offended men like Moritz Stein-schneider[18] and brought them to despair. Only with great efforts could a small number of middle-class Jews be persuaded to purchase the scholarly works published, and whether they were read at all is even more questionable.

As stated above, the new attitude of the more or less accultured Western Jews, which gave birth to what Julius Guttmann called "modern Judaism", was vehemently contested by the majority of Eastern Jews (*Ostjuden*) who saw in the Western approach a deviation from genuine Judaism and therefore a sort of defection or even heresy. On the high intellectual level, this was demon-strated, as Rabbi Shmueli recalls, in the hostility of prominent Eastern Jews (like Ahad Ha'am and Bialik) to the Western post-assimilatory tentative steps to initiate a new kind of *Wissenschaft des Judentums*. This was a reflection of the feelings of the Yiddish-speaking masses who did not conceal their aversion against the Western type, although this was sometimes mixed with a touch of admiration for those who had succeeded in the Gentile world. Perhaps one can say that there were two main sources of this antagonism: on the one hand the indignation of the strictly Orthodox at all relaxation of the traditional ways of life and at any alteration of religious customs, on the other hand the ideas of democracy which had seized the secularised sector with its various socialist groupings which had revolted against being dominated or represented by the assimilated "Gvirim" (wealthy ones).

In the period of the great migration which started in 1881, this hostility was transferred to America, where the "German" Jews already there had arrived at the beginning of the century and had quickly achieved prosperity and social standing, especially in the banking and to some extent also in the industrial sector. In their own way, these German Jews, also bound together by family ties, were faithful to their Jewish origin, but in religious matters they followed the ways of the German Reform. They might not have been particularly pleased

[17]'Three Jewish Historians: Isaak Markus Jost – Heinrich Graetz – Eugen Täubler', in *LBI Year Book IX* (1964), pp. 69–90.
[18]On Steinschneider see Arnold Paucker, 'The Letters of Moritz Steinschneider to the Reverend Bandinel', in *LBI Year Book XI* (1966), pp. 242 ff.

by the influx of proletarianised masses of Jewish refugees, with their out-
rageous poverty and the inevitable admixture of vulgarity, but they did not
shirk their responsibility of easing not only the bitter material predicament of
the newcomers but also that of supporting them on the Sisyphean path of
orientation in a completely foreign world. In a recently published comprehensive study of the New York Jewish immigrant society, which reflects the
phenomenal development of present-day American Jewry,[19] the ensuing
antagonism is amply described. The "German" Jews, seeming to appear even
then as one hundred per cent American, were accused of presumption and
condescension, which indeed they had sometimes displayed. They were not to
be accepted as an authority on Jewish conduct. Nevertheless, with their help
and thanks to the devoted work of some great idealistic figures, magnificent
social institutions were established on the East Side including (1893) the so-
called Educational Alliance, depicted by Howe as "a curious mixture of night
school, settlement house, day-care centre, gymnasium and public forum" which
in due course became "for several decades a major source of help to the new
immigrants, as well as a major cause of contention between uptown and
downtown Jews".

We do not want to enlarge on this issue in its many-sided phases, which
is now an indispensable part of Jewish history and had a decisive impact on
Jewish social psychology. The feelings aroused lasted through the period of the
First World War, the inter-war years, and slowly abated only after the Second
World War, when almost seventy years had passed since the beginning of the
Immigration. A new generation had arisen which no longer rejected American-
isation; on the contrary, having enjoyed decades of freedom of a kind unknown
in the former Russian homeland, these Jews had become enthusiastic Americans,
in many respects no less assimilated than the German Jews had been. This also
affected the religious area; the influx of originally East European Jews into the
Reform and the so-called "Conservative" (founded by the great Solomon
Schechter) camps changed the social composition of these groups. From the
historical point of view, this process is, of course, a very instructive phenomenon,
confirming the dependence of Jewish behaviour on surrounding conditions. It
shows the earlier East European criticism of nineteenth-century German Jews
in a new light. Incidentally, whoever was privileged at that time to listen to
Bialik's own story, after his first journey from Berlin to the immigrant Russian
Jews in the United States in 1924, was impressed by the great man's disappointment due to the turn events had taken before the process of acculturation had
achieved its full effect.

In the context of the subject discussed in this Introduction particular interest
attaches to the American scion of *Wissenschaft des Judentums*. In a special chapter
entitled 'The Scholar-Intellectuals', Howe describes the two specific Jewish
cultures emerging in the United States, both a continuation of European

---

[19]Irving Howe (with the assistance of Kenneth Libo), *The Immigrant Jews of New York, 1881 to
the Present*, The Littman Library of Jewish Civilization, Routledge & Kegan Paul, London and
Boston 1976.

conditions: the German-Jewish and the Yiddish.[20] The German Jews set up the Hebrew Union College in Cincinnati (1875), the Jewish Publication Society (1888), the American Jewish Historical Society (1892); the (American) *Jewish Encyclopedia* in the early 1900s issued an impressive compendium of *Wissenschaft des Judentums*, "synthesised for the American reader", containing contributions by such scholars as Kaufmann Kohler, Richard Gottheil, Emil Hirsch, Cyrus Adler and Louis Ginzberg. They erected a fortress of respectable, positive Judaism. Admittedly, this trend had a strong assimilationist tendency. And when at the beginning of the twentieth century a secular Yiddish culture arose among the immigrant community in America, there appeared again this juxta-position of two different kinds of Jewish life and culture.

This duality with all the ensuing frictions and quarrels dominated Jewish life practically until the Holocaust and the emergence of the State of Israel created a completely new all-Jewish mentality and a basis of solidarity. Actually, the Yiddish-speaking community steadily declined while their children joined the Americanised congregations. Mr. Howe pays a warm tribute to the great but transitory experiment of the East Side's Yiddish subculture created by a hard-working courageous and "messianic-inspired" group which gradually overcame its initial disadvantages and succeeded also in the economic field, thanks to its own industrial initiative and organisational skill; meanwhile it had produced an astonishing self-contained ebullient life with a mighty mass-circulation press, with its own literature, theatre, clubs and (sentimental, witty, self-deriding) entertainment which for many individuals provided a step to prominence on the American scene. Although this period, to which Mr. Howe wrote a sort of obituary, is now over, it has left noticeable traces, noticeable primarily in contemporary American fiction. If the New York Yiddish downtown East Side life has vanished, so has – in an overwhelmingly tragic fashion – its great parent in Eastern Europe.

This is the unexpected melancholy aftermath of the split caused in World Jewry by the Enlightenment, which came to the West about a hundred years before it reached the East, and by way of an earlier start gave the Western ("German") Jews the advantage in the process of modernisation. Against this background we have today to see the problems which emanated from German Jewry's involvement in assimilation, political emancipation and cultural Europeanisation in the nineteenth century.

That this epoch, not minimising its shortcomings and negative aspects, has been rich in cultural productivity in both the secular and the spiritual sphere has been widely recognised. When the bell tolled for German Jewry in 1933, it was Leo Baeck who said that the age-long existence of Jewry in Germany can be compared in creativity and brilliance only with the Hellenistic and the Spanish–Arabic period of Jewish history. No wonder that these periods, by their

[20]*Ibid.*, pp. 498 ff.

similarity and their peculiarity, were attracting the attention of Jewish historiography in Germany, as indicated in some of the essays in our present volume. As regards the future, however, a sombre question-mark is hovering over Jewish destiny. What is now called the quest for Jewish identity is nowhere voiced with more intensity than in American Jewry and its prolific literature. This crisis is also the counterpoint to the Epilogue of Irving Howe's book.

*

Once more, I would like to thank Dr. Arnold Paucker who has again taken on the editing of part of the Year Book.

Jews and Socialism

"Between Baden and Luxemburg"
Jewish Socialists on the Eve of the First World War

BY WERNER T. ANGRESS

In August 1910, a few weeks after Baden's Social Democrats had once again voted for the budget in their state's diet,[1] and a month before the *Sozialdemokratische Partei Deutschlands* (SPD) was to meet for its annual party congress, Karl Kautsky, the party's chief theoretician and spokesman for its centrist majority, published an article entitled: 'Zwischen Baden und Luxemburg'.[2] While castigating the *Badenser* for their breach of party discipline, a matter to be taken up by the impending party congress, Kautsky also turned his literary guns against two prominent party members, Rosa Luxemburg and Kurt Eisner. The former was taken to task for her recently stated argument that the breach of discipline committed by the Social Democrats in Baden – of which she strongly disapproved – was nevertheless insignificant *vis-à-vis* the fact that the party majority was not supporting, was indeed suppressing, her efforts to unleash a forceful attack against Prussia's three-class voting system by means of a mass strike.[3] Eisner, Kautsky charged, was supporting Luxemburg, and he quoted him with unconcealed disapproval:

> "If an influential comrade such as Rosa Luxemburg, whose suggestions and advice have justifiably attracted attention, claims that the principal task [*Lebensaufgabe*] of German politics, the Prussian electoral reform movement [*Wahlrechtsbewegung*], has been botched through the party's mistaken tactics, then this raises a question of such seriousness and long-range consequence that nothing of greater importance exists for the entire party, and thus for this reason the antics of the otherwise certainly highly esteemed *Badenser* become utterly immaterial."[4]

---

[1] On the budget vote in Baden and its background see Beverly Heckart, *From Bassermann to Bebel. The Grand Bloc's Quest for Reform in the Kaiserreich, 1900–1914*, New Haven and London 1974, pp. 100–121, 146–153, and *passim*; Jürgen Thiel, *Die Grossblockpolitik der Nationalliberalen Partei Badens 1905–1914. Ein Beitrag zur Zusammenarbeit von Liberalismus und Sozialdemokratie in der Spätphase des Wilhelminischen Deutschlands*, Stuttgart 1976 (Veröffentlichungen der Kommission für geschichtliche Landeskunde in Baden-Württemberg, Reihe B, Forschungen 86), pp. 69–81, 115–140, and *passim*; Carl E. Schorske, *German Social Democracy 1905–1917. The Development of the Great Schism*, Cambridge, Mass. 1955 (Harvard Historical Studies 65), pp. 188–191, 194–195; Dieter Groh, *Negative Integration und revolutionärer Attentismus. Die deutsche Sozialdemokratie am Vorabend des Ersten Weltkrieges*, Frankfurt a. Main–Berlin 1973, pp. 163–165, 167–185. See also note 13 below for additional literature pertaining especially to Ludwig Frank.

[2] Karl Kautsky, 'Zwischen Baden und Luxemburg', in *Die Neue Zeit*, XXVIII (5th August 1910), No. 45, pp. 652–667.

[3] See on this issue especially Schorske, *op. cit.*, pp. 45–48, 171–187, and *passim*; Groh, *Neg. Integration*, pp. 78–79, 129–160, and *passim*. On the Prussian three-class voting system see Bernhard Vogel, Dieter Nohlen and Rainer-Olaf Schultze, *Wahlen in Deutschland. Theorie-Geschichte-Dokumente 1848–1970*, Berlin–New York 1971, pp. 85–94, 125–128.

[4] Kautsky, *loc. cit.*, p. 652 (quoted from Karlsruher *Volksfreund*, 'Das Grosse und das Kleine', no further citation given).

We need not pursue here either Kautsky's polemics or the circumstances which gave rise to them in 1910. What matters for the purpose of this essay is that Kautsky here pointed to the existence of a three-way division within the SPD, a situation which was to bedevil German Social Democracy for years to come.[5] Kautsky summed it all up very neatly in his closing paragraph:

> "When we look on the map at the Grand Duchies Baden and Luxemburg we discover that between them lies Trier, the city from which Marx came. If one goes from there to the left, across the border, one gets to Luxemburg. If one goes to the right, across the Rhine, one reaches Baden. The situation on the map is today symbolic of the situation of German Social Democracy."[6]

This situation did not change basically during the three years which preceded the outbreak of the First World War, a period on which this essay will concentrate. Between January 1912, when the SPD scored an impressive victory at the polls, and August 1914, two and a half years during which the party's course and tactics were hotly contested among its various factions, a number of Jews played an important part in trying to influence their party's stand on several crucial issues. As it is impossible within the restricted frame of this essay to do justice to the many complex problems that faced the Empire in general and the SPD in particular, the following discussion will be largely confined to three issues which confronted the party: its reaction to the election victory of 1912; the army bill of 1913 and the concomitant taxes to cover the cost of this military outlay; and the debate that same year over the application of the mass strike as a suitable weapon against Prussia's anachronistic and class-bound electoral system. In these debates Jews were passionately engaged on all sides.[7]

Of course, Jews had made their voices heard before whenever important questions were debated within the party, and they were to do so during and after the war as well. As the overwhelming majority of them were intellectuals of middle-class origin, men and women with a better education than had been available to most of their non-Jewish peers even among the leading party functionaries, this was hardly surprising.[8] But it was particularly during these

---

[5]Basic for this problem are Schorske, *op. cit.*, and Groh, *Neg. Integration*, both *passim*. I am deeply indebted to the studies of both authors for the discussions of party politics in this article.

[6]Kautsky, *loc. cit.*, p. 667; also quoted in Schorske, *op. cit.*, pp. 185–186; see also Groh, *Neg. Integration*, p. 167 and ff. on the formation of these factions.

[7]On the role which Jews have played in the political life of the Wilhelminian Empire see Ernest Hamburger, *Juden im öffentlichen Leben Deutschlands. Regierungsmitglieder, Beamte und Parlamentarier in der monarchischen Zeit 1848–1918*, Tübingen 1968 (Schriftenreihe wissenschaftlicher Abhandlungen des Leo Baeck Instituts 19); Jacob Toury, *Die politischen Orientierungen der Juden in Deutschland. Von Jena bis Weimar*, Tübingen 1966 (Schriftenreihe wissenschaftlicher Abhandlungen des Leo Baeck Institute 15); and Peter Pulzer, 'Die jüdische Beteiligung an der Politik', in *Juden im Wilhelminischen Deutschland 1890–1914*. Ein Sammelband herausgegeben von Werner E. Mosse unter Mitwirkung von Arnold Paucker, Tübingen 1976 (Schriftenreihe wissenschaftlicher Abhandlungen des Leo Baeck Instituts 33), pp. 143–239. On the reasons why Jews were attracted to the SPD see Hamburger, *op. cit.*, p. 404 and *passim*; Toury, *op. cit.*, pp. 212–229; Pulzer, *loc. cit.*, pp. 198–202.

[8]Hamburger, *op. cit.*, pp. 407–410; Pulzer, *loc. cit.*, p. 204; Erich Matthias and Eberhard Pikart, eds., *Die Reichstagsfraktion der deutschen Sozialdemokratie 1898–1918*, two volumes, Düsseldorf 1966 (Quellen zur Geschichte des Parlamentarismus und der politischen Parteien, Erste Reihe: Von der konstitutionellen Monarchie zur parlamentarischen Republik), I, pp. lxiv–lxvi.

decisive pre-war years that Jewish Social Democrats were ranged in the fore-
front in party disputes, at a time when the majority of the SPD, including its
Executive, stood divided between the "reformist", largely South German wing
on its right – with Ludwig Frank as one of its principal exponents – and Rosa
Luxemburg's radical faction on the extreme left. It is on this aspect that the
essay will largely focus. In between these two wings stood other Jews – Eduard
Bernstein, Hugo Haase, Kurt Eisner, Emanuel Wurm, Gustav Hoch, Arthur
Stadthagen, to name but some of the best known [9] – who took, and frequently
switched, their positions and wrestled, each according to his convictions, for the
soul of their party, for the proper road to choose in an effort to preserve peace
in Europe and to forge inside Germany a society based on equality of rights,
democratic institutions, liberty and justice. That Jews were particularly concerned in achieving these objectives was due to the fact that they were doubly
isolated in imperial Germany, as Socialists and as Jews, and while many of
them were usually loath to emphasise their religious origins,[10] the passion which
they often displayed during the battles of and within the SPD cannot be fully
understood without taking into account their awareness of being second-class
citizens marked as such by the accident of birth.

I

The position of the SPD "between Baden and Luxemburg", as Kautsky had
put it, meant a division into three factions which differed on tactics, priorities,
and often on objectives as well. At the right wing stood those who viewed Social
Democracy essentially as a socialist-democratic reform movement which would
eventually come to power by peaceful means, through the attraction of more
and more voters during elections; through selective and initially tentative
parliamentary alliances with the liberal middle class, notable the Progressives;
and through limited cooperation with the government, both at local and
national level, whenever such a move could benefit the working class. There
were, of course, many diverging views among the right, notably as to tactics
and priorities, and historians of the labour movement have carefully distinguished between Revisionists, Reformists and Practicists.[11] Next to the strong

[9] For biographical sketches of the Jewish delegates here mentioned see Hamburger, *op. cit.*, pp.
455–474 (Bernstein); pp. 426–444 (Haase); pp. 483–485 (Wurm); pp. 492–498 (Hoch); pp.
480–483 (Stadthagen). On Eisner see Franz Schade, *Kurt Eisner und die bayerische Sozialdemokratie*, Hanover 1961 (Schriftenreihe der Forschungsstelle der Friedrich-Ebert-Stiftung), pp.
28–29, 33–37, and Allan Mitchell, *Revolution in Bavaria 1918–1919. The Eisner Régime and the
Soviet Republic*, Princeton 1965, pp. 35–62. For Bernstein also: Peter Gay, *The Dilemma of
Democratic Socialism. Eduard Bernstein's Challenge to Marx*, New York 1952, 1962. On Haase, see the
recently published biography by Kenneth R. Calkins, *Hugo Haase. Demokrat und Revolutionär*,
transl. Arthur Mandel, Berlin 1976.
[10] On the attitude of Jewish Reichstag delegates to their religion see Hamburger, *op. cit.*, pp.
410–413, and *passim*; Matthias and Pikart, *op. cit.*, lxiv–lxvi; Pulzer, *loc. cit.*, pp. 201–203.
[11] Hans-Josef Steinberg, *Sozialismus und deutsche Sozialdemokratie. Zur Ideologie der Partei vor dem 1.
Weltkrieg*, Hanover 1967 (Schriftenreihe des Forschungsinstituts der Friedrich-Ebert-Stiftung),
pp. 87–125.

labour union movement, the *Freie Gewerkschaften*, which wielded a great deal of influence over the party's policies,[12] the strongest single bastion of this wing was the South German Socialists. Until he withdrew from active politics for reasons of health, their principal spokesman for many years had been the Bavarian Georg von Vollmar. Yet during the years immediately preceding the war leadership had passed to Baden's most prominent party leaders, Wilhelm Kolb and Ludwig Frank, with the latter gradually overshadowing the former.

Who was Ludwig Frank? As he is generally less well known than other Jewish Social Democrats such as Luxemburg, Bernstein, Haase *et al.*, and as this essay deals with him extensively, he and his career within the party deserve a brief introduction.[13] Born on 25th May 1874, in Nonnenweier, Baden, a village with a small Jewish community, Frank grew up among the peasants and small tradesmen – his father was one of the latter – of this South German rural region. A heavy-set man with broad hands and a fine head, somewhat resembling Ferdinand Lassalle, Frank loved Baden with its liberal-democratic tradition, its lighthearted and easygoing people and its beautiful landscape. Although he was not a deeply religious man, he was one of the few Jews active in German politics who never tried to conceal his origins.[14] During his last year at the

---

[12]Schorske, *op. cit.*, pp. 88–115, and *passim*; for a somewhat more qualified assessment regarding the predominance of trade-union functionaries within the SPD see Thomas Nipperdey, *Die Organisation der deutschen Parteien vor 1918*, Düsseldorf 1961 (Beiträge zur Geschichte des Parlamentarismus und der politischen Parteien 18), pp. 330–351; see also Matthias and Pikart, *op. cit.*, I, pp. lvii f., lxx–lxxii.

[13]There is as yet no satisfactory biography of Ludwig Frank. Simon Grünebaum, *Ludwig Frank. Ein Beitrag zur Entwicklung der deutschen Sozialdemokratie*, Heidelberg 1924, is very sketchy, as is Rolf Gustav Haebler, *In Memoriam Ludwig Frank. Ein Beitrag zur Geschichte der badischen und der deutschen Sozialdemokratie und des internationalen demokratischen Sozialismus*, Mannheim 1954. By far the most useful source on Frank is still H[edwig] Wachenheim, ed., *Ludwig Frank. Aufsätze, Reden und Briefe*, Berlin n.d. [1924], hereafter Wachenheim, *Frank*. By the same author also 'Ludwig Frank', in *Mannheimer Hefte* (1964), No. 2, pp. 28–40, as well as her discussion of her personal recollections of Frank in *Vom Grossbürgertum zur Sozialdemokratie. Memoiren einer Reformistin*, Berlin 1973, ed. Susanne Miller (Beihefte zur Internationalen wissenschaftlichen Korrespondenz zur Geschichte der deutschen Arbeiterbewegung 1), pp. 25–54, *passim*. See also Theodor Heuss, 'Ludwig Frank', in *Profile. Nachzeichnungen aus der Geschichte*, Tübingen 1964, pp. 236–239; Johannes Timm, 'Reichstagsabgeordneter Ludwig Frank', in *Süddeutsche Monatshefte*, XII, No. 10 (October 1914), pp. 122–127; Carlo Schmid, *Tätiger Geist. Gestalten aus Geschichte und Politik*, Hanover 1964, pp. 141–168; and Hamburger, *op. cit.*, pp. 444–455.

[14]See especially Hamburger, *op. cit.*, pp. 445–446, and Haebler, *op. cit.*, p. 11. Dr. Karl Kaufmann, a lawyer and close friend, wrote in an obituary (*K. C. Blätter*, V, Kriegsausgabe [November/December 1914], vol. I, No. 2, pp. 297–299) that Frank came from a very religious Jewish background, liked to spend the High Holidays at home with his parents whenever he could, and reacted with contempt both to antisemitic comments and to Jews who were baptised. "Wie konnte er . . . gegen feige, von Streberei und Rangsucht geleitete Judentaufen wettern. Wenn er mit solchen Täuflingen den Verkehr vermeiden konnte, tat er es stets." On 3rd February 1907 Frank wrote to another friend, Moritz Pfälzer, about a recent election speech he had delivered in Cologne, and stated: "Es wird Dich gewiss interessieren, dass viele jüdische Wähler da waren, und ich glaube, für sie den richtigen Ton getroffen zu haben. Das Gefühl der Zusammengehörigkeit mit meinen Stammesgenossen wird bei mir mit den Jahren nicht schwächer, sondern stärker und tiefer . . ." 'Moritz Pfälzer Nachlass', Leo Baeck Institute, New York, AR C 4021, item No. 19. Nevertheless, on 12th April 1908 he wrote again to Pfälzer, and this time raised some doubts about the depth of his religious commitment: "Deine temperamentvollen Artikel habe ich mit grosser Freude gelesen. Ich habe bisher als Nicht-

Gymnasium Frank joined the Social Democratic Party because its political and social objectives appealed to him.[15] He saw it as the only existing political movement capable of realising the democratic objectives which the Revolution of 1848 had failed to achieve. His entire political career, brief though it was, was to reflect the idealistic spirit of that revolutionary period which inspired him and held for him lessons and traditions deemed worthy of revival. After studying law at Freiburg and at Berlin, with a break for the requisite year of military service, in Baden's 113th Infantry Regiment,[16] he settled down as a lawyer. He practised his profession, despite his demanding political duties, until the outbreak of the war, and could always be counted upon to defend especially members of his party who were prosecuted for political reasons.[17] In 1903 Frank was elected to the city council of Mannheim. Two years later he founded a socialist youth movement in Karlsruhe which spread rapidly throughout Southern Germany and eventually fused with a similar organisation that had been developing in Northern Germany.[18] In the same year he was elected to the lower chamber of the Baden diet, and in 1907 became a delegate to the *Reichstag.*

The leading role which Frank soon occupied among his party's delegation

---

benützer irgend eines Gebetbuches eine begreifliche Scheu gegen Parteinahme in dieser Sache gehabt. Deine Frage, die zu beantworten ist, wurzelt in dem Problem der Assimilierung. Wer das jüdische Volkstum erhalten will, wird gegen die Änderung ehrwürdiger, wenn auch barocker Ritualien sich wenden müssen. Deine Ausführungen sind klar und warm und haben Überzeugungskraft. Aber [wer] von uns hätte gedacht, dass ein grosser Teil der heranwachsenden Generation wieder konservativ wird? Wie lang ist's her, seit das Schiff unserer Studentenschaft noch mit stolzen liberalen Segeln gefahren ist! Such is life." *Ibid.,* item No. 22. And when Ludwig Geiger, the editor of *Allgemeine Zeitung des Judentums,* asked in April 1912 all "Jewish" *Reichstag* delegates to send the newspaper brief *vitae* which were to include statements on their attitude towards their *Judentum,* Frank merely sent three lines in which he listed place and date of birth, profession, and the dates when he became a delegate to the Baden Diet and the German *Reichstag* respectively. He did not comment on his attitude towards Judaism, an omission duly noted by the editor. See *AZdJ,* LXXVI (5th April 1912), No. 14, pp. 159–160, and *ibid.* (2nd May 1912), No. 18, pp. 208–210. Frank's silence on this point contrasts strongly with the warm feelings he expressed on 12th April 1914 to Hedwig Wachenheim: . . . "Die Sedernächte, die Du wohl nur aus der Oper oder dem Roman kennst, haben auf mich wieder gewirkt, wie ein erlebtes Märchen, das mich mit den Jahrhunderten vor mir verbindet." 'Frank to Hedwig Wachenheim', in Wachenheim, *Frank,* p. 323; see also *ibid.,* p. 324. And on 23rd August 1914 he wrote to Leonie Meyerhof-Hildeck: "Ich bin in der Kaserne einquartiert und schlafe auf dem harten Feldbett wie mein Stammvater Jakob 'zu Häupten den Stein', traumlos von 10 bis 5 . . ."; *ibid.,* p. 356. In short, the available evidence would indicate that Frank's attitude towards his religion was indeed very positive, but that he was not in any way orthodox or dogmatic about it and considered the matter his private concern, a sentiment which he shared with the great majority of Germany's Social Democrats.

[15]For the following brief outline of Frank's career I am indebted to the studies of Hamburger, Wachenheim and Haebler.

[16]According to Hedwig Wachenheim's memoirs, Frank suffered several epileptic attacks while serving his year of military duty, and Haebler assumes that Frank's military year of service remained undistinguished because he was most likely marked down in the regimental records as a "Red". Wachenheim, *Vom Grossbürgertum . . .,* p. 47; Haebler, *op. cit.,* p. 17.

[17]See, for instance, Wachenheim, *Frank,* pp. 239–243.

[18]Rudolf Falkenberg *et al., Geschichte der deutschen Arbeiterjugendbewegung,* Dortmund 1973, pp. 13–14; Schorske, *op. cit.,* pp. 97–108; Wachenheim, *Frank,* pp. 32–48.

in the Baden diet brought him before long into conflict with the party's majority over the question of the budget vote.[19] It was a firm party principle that Social Democrats must not cooperate with any government, be it in a state diet or the *Reichstag*, and this included legislation affecting the budget. Such a policy of opposition made sense in Northern Germany, notably in Prussia, where the SPD's ostracism and isolation were particularly pronounced. Yet the situation was different in Southern Germany. For whereas in the *Reichstag* and the Prussian diet the National Liberals and Progressives had formed between 1907 and 1909 an uneasy alliance with both conservative parties and antisemitic splinter groups in the so-called *Bülow Block* which was pitted against the Catholic Centre Party (*Zentrum*) and the SPD,[20] an altogether different constellation of political forces had developed during the same period in Baden. There, a strong and reactionary Centre Party, supported by a – numerically rather small – Conservative Party was balanced by the National Liberals and Progressives. This situation forced the Social Democrats either to align themselves in the diet with the National Liberals and Progressives, or to refrain from taking sides, thereby running the risk of allowing Baden's Blue–Black coalition to pass legislation detrimental to the interests of the working class. What did not work in Prussia – where the party on account of the three-class electoral system was not even represented in the diet until 1908, and then by only seven delegates out of 443 – proved feasible in Baden. For there the Social Democrats, numbering twelve delegates out of a total of seventy-two, were able to make their weight felt, and in 1905 allied with the liberal middle-class parties in what came to be known as the Baden *Grossblock*.[21]

Frank, who became soon after his election the principal spokesman for the party's Baden branch, defended its position on the question of the *Grossblock* at the SPD's annual congresses in 1908 and 1910 and rejected the charges levied by the Executive that by voting for the budget in alliance with Baden's liberals the Social Democrats of that state had committed an unpardonable sin. Without expanding on the confrontations which have been ably treated elsewhere,[22] it will suffice to state that despite vituperative attacks from especially the radical wing of the SPD Frank stood his ground and refused to make concessions. He did so for two reasons. He was convinced that most of his fellow Social Democrats in the North were unable to appreciate the peculiar political situation which the party's Southern branches were facing, specifically in Baden, where participation in a *Grossblock* yielded advantages for the workers. But beyond the purely pragmatic arguments Frank was also convinced that Baden, alongside Bavaria and Württemberg, could and should serve as a proving ground for subsequent party tactics on the national level. While fully aware of the political differences that existed between North and South, Frank did

---

[19]Besides the accounts of Heckart, Schorske, Thiel and Groh, cited in n. 1, above, see also Wachenheim, *Frank*, pp. 108–125, 170–183, 187–209.

[20]Still one of the best accounts of the Bülow Bloc is Theodor Eschenburg, *Das Kaiserreich am Scheideweg. Bassermann, Bülow und der Block*, Berlin 1929; see also Heckart, *op. cit.*, pp. 44–87.

[21]*Ibid.*, and Thiel, *op. cit.* (on the Baden *Grossblock*).

[22]See the studies cited in n. 1, above.

believe that a policy of selective cooperation with the liberal middle class on the parliamentary level should be expanded to the *Reichstag* as well. But although he collided here head-on with official party doctrine, Frank was aware that the SPD's theories no longer coincided with its practice, that the party's trend was to move away from dogmatic rigidity and towards a more pragmatic and moderate political stance, its public pronouncements to the contrary notwithstanding.[23] If the SPD would finally make an effort to break out of its isolation by seeking positive contacts with the liberal middle-class parties and to cooperate with them on specific issues in parliament, as Baden's Socialists did, in order to curb the influence of Centre and Conservatives, then a more democratic *Reichstag* majority might ultimately emerge, and with it the chance of transforming the Empire, and Prussia with it, along Western constitutional lines.[24]

Frank's views on these matters were deeply rooted in, and coloured by, his South German background, his admiration for the ideas of 1848 which he sought to revive, and his faith in practical and rational solutions, despite the far from favourable political climate which prevailed on the national level. But in addition, his entire political career was marked by a pronounced humanism, a trait which he shared with most of his Jewish colleagues, regardless of where they stood within the party.[25]

More complex than the position of the "Baden Wing" was that of the party's majority, composed of the centre and left centre. The latter included the Executive, which until his death in 1913 was under the leadership of August Bebel. Its principal spokesman was Karl Kautsky whose views – admittedly here over-simplified – were as follows: the SPD was the only party which represented the interests of German labour. Marxist in origin and outlook, its ultimate aim was to capture the power of state through revolution. But revolution would not be "made" by the working class, given the strong political, military and economic position of its opponents in the Empire. Rather than arrive as a result of dubious battle, the revolution would come like a force of nature or, as Bebel liked to put it, in the form of the *grosse Kladderadatsch*, brought on by the inevitable forces of historical development. As the imperial régime and the social élites supporting it were increasingly confronted by mounting armament costs, accompanied by international tensions – in part the result of imperialist ventures – developments which brought the threat of war continuously closer; and as the moral decay of Germany's ruling classes became more and more obvious (e.g., the Eulenburg Scandal of 1907/8), discontent within the nation would grow, and the régime would ultimately be swept away

[23]For these trends see especially Schorske's and Groh's accounts, *passim*.

[24]Wachenheim, *Frank*, pp. 185–186 (speech delivered at the Baden *Parteitag* in Offenburg, 20th August 1910). Frank expressed similar ideas in notes which he made prior to one of his speeches after the *Reichstag* elections of 1912. 'Ludwig Frank Nachlass', Archiv der sozialen Demokratie, Friedrich-Ebert-Stiftung, Bonn-Bad Godesberg, item No. 36. Similar ideas were expressed by Bernstein in 1913. See Eduard Bernstein, 'Politik: Vom sozialdemokratischen Standpunkte', in *Das Jahr 1913. Ein Gesamtbild der Kulturentwicklung*, ed. D. Sarason, Leipzig-Berlin 1913, pp. 8–18, esp. pp. 16–18.

[25]Frank shared this trait notably with Haase, Bernstein, Eisner and, despite her radical stance, Rosa Luxemburg.

by either an economic collapse or by war.[26] In short, the "revolutionary attentism", as Groh has formulated it, meant in effect that the party would continue to tell the masses of the coming revolution, would agitate within the limits dictated by circumstances for specific short-term objectives, but would otherwise wait for "the day" to come of its own accord. As a corollary to this attitude of "Waiting for Godot", the party was expected to concentrate on strengthening its organisation, i.e., the party apparatus, and would place special emphasis on winning elections, which would become a visible indicator of the party's growing strength and, conversely, of the decaying basis of the existing régime and its societal structure. Furthermore, an imposing organisation and electoral victories would also boost the morale of the mass of party members who were living and toiling in a society which denied them equality of rights, exploited and suppressed them, and treated them as pariahs.[27]

The group on the party's extreme left, whose most eloquent exponent was Rosa Luxemburg, rejected not only the views of the right wing but also those of Kautsky. Although she was aware, as were Bebel and Kautsky, that the revolution was not just around the corner, she condemned the SPD's official tactic of revolutionary rhetoric, coupled with passive anticipation, as unworthy of a Marxist party. Rather than sit and wait for the historical process to make up its mind, she wanted to drive it forward by means of radical activism, by means of street demonstrations and, ultimately, by means of the mass strike in order to achieve concrete political objectives while simultaneously educating and preparing the masses for the final and decisive showdown.[28]

As Rosa Luxemburg's life and work are by now well known, she requires no introduction.[29] During the period here under discussion this Polish-born Jewish[30] woman had become an eminent leader in the German and Polish working-class movements, the SPD and the Social Democracy of the Kingdom

[26]Groh, *Neg. Integration*, pp. 57 ff. and *passim*; Schorske, *op. cit.*, pp. 112–113 and *passim*.

[27]On this aspect see especially Dirk Stegmann, *Die Erben Bismarcks. Parteien und Verbände in der Spätphase des Wilhelminischen Deutschlands. Sammlungspolitik 1897–1918*, Cologne–Berlin 1970, and Klaus Saul, *Staat, Industrie, Arbeiterbewegung im Kaiserreich. Zur Innen- und Aussenpolitik des Wilhelminischen Deutschland 1903–1914*, Düsseldorf 1974; see also Peter Domann, *Sozialdemokratie und Kaisertum unter Wilhelm II. Die Auseinandersetzung der Partei mit dem monarchischen System, seinen gesellschafts- und verfassungspolitischen Voraussetzungen*, Wiesbaden 1974 (Frankfurter Historische Abhandlungen 3), and Groh, *Neg. Integration*, all *passim*.

[28]For a succinct summary of Luxemburg's views and those of her followers on mass action see J. Peter Nettl, 'Rosa Luxemburgs Theorie der Massenaktion', in Gerhard Albert Ritter, ed., *Die deutschen Parteien vor 1918*, Cologne 1973 (Neue Wissenschaftliche Bibliothek 61, Geschichte), pp. 358–363.

[29]The bibliography on Rosa Luxemburg is by now so extensive that I shall merely refer the interested reader to the most incisive biography so far written about her: J. Peter Nettl, *Rosa Luxemburg*, two volumes, London–New York–Toronto 1966; an exhaustive bibliography is in vol. II, pp. 864–934.

[30]Although she was throughout her life attacked, insulted and maligned because, even in her appearance, she was so obviously Jewish, Luxemburg herself rarely alluded to her religious origin and treated all matters Jewish with reserve, if not with outright disdain. In fact, she seems to have been attracted to certain aspects of Christianity, admired the historical figure of Jesus, and celebrated Christmas while in prison during the First World War. Helmut Hirsch, *Rosa Luxemburg in Selbstzeugnissen und Bilddokumenten*, Hamburg 1969, pp. 16–18.

of Poland and Lithuania. Her radical stance, coupled with her oratorical powers and her often biting sarcasm had made her a familiar figure in Germany, both among the workers who flocked to the meetings she addressed and among the middle and upper classes who saw in her the archetype of the radical Jewish intellectual. In the SPD and the (Second) International she was highly respected for her political acumen and her journalistic and theoretical writings, although the frequently aggressive style which she adopted during debates had made her enemies in the labour movement too. During the years preceding the war she was without any doubt the most dynamic and effective exponent of the party's extreme left wing, a faction by no means devoid of able men and women, to mention only Karl Liebknecht, Clara Zetkin and Georg Ledebour. Yet it was Rosa Luxemburg who generally took the initiative, devised the tactics and charted the course for the Left.

II

The *Reichstag* elections of January 1912 [31] proved an unprecedented victory for the SPD. The party which in 1871 had sent two delegates into the first imperial *Reichstag* now seated 110, twelve of whom (subsequently thirteen) were Jews. [32] The party owed its success in the first place to the growing discontent among large segments of the nation with the Black–Blue *Reichstag* majority, the two conservative parties and the Centre. This coalition had been formed after the collapse of the *Bülow Block* over the Empire's financial reforms in 1909. [33] These had been carried through at the expense of the working classes and, to a lesser extent, of the commercial middle classes as well, while the Prussian agrarians and heavy industry, whose respective interests were represented in the two conservative parties, had been the beneficiaries. The Centre had supported the conservative parties, mainly in order to break out of the political isolation in which it had found itself throughout the existence of the *Bülow Block*. As the mounting cost of armaments and the country's colonial ventures were borne increasingly by that part of the population least able to afford them, and as the

[31] On the elections see Jürgen Bertram, *Die Wahlen zum Deutschen Reichstag vom Jahre 1912. Parteien und Verbände in der Innenpolitik des Wilhelminischen Reiches*, Düsseldorf 1964 (Beiträge zur Geschichte des Parlamentarismus und der politischen Parteien 28), and for the reaction to the elections on the part of the political Right see Stegmann, *op. cit.*, pp. 257–304, and *passim*.

[32] They were Eduard Bernstein, Oskar Cohn, Georg Davidsohn, Ludwig Frank, Georg Gradnauer, Hugo Haase, Joseph Herzfeld, Gustav Hoch, Otto Landsberg, Arthur Stadthagen, Georges Weill and Emanuel Wurm. In December 1912, Max – actually Emanuel – Cohen, known as Cohen-Reuss, was elected in a by-election. Five of these – Cohn, Davidsohn, Frank, Haase and Wurm – were listed in the register of the *Reichstag* as *mos[aisch]*. Cohn, Cohen, Davidsohn, Landsberg and Weill were elected to the *Reichstag* for the first time. On the Social Democratic *Reichstag* delegates of Jewish origin see Hamburger, *op. cit.*, pp. 399–522 and Pulzer, *loc. cit.*, pp. 201 ff.

[33] For the end of the *Bülow Block* see Eschenburg, *op. cit.*, pp. 203–257; on the financial reform, Peter-Christian Witt, *Die Finanzpolitik des Deutschen Reiches von 1903 bis 1913. Eine Studie der Innenpolitik des Wilhelminischen Deutschland*, Lübeck and Hamburg 1970 (Historische Studien 415), pp. 199–316.

Black–Blue coalition also blocked all attempts to reform the Prussian three-class voting system – including those half-heartedly sponsored by the government – the swing to the left in January 1912 reflected widespread dissatisfaction with the political and economic policies of the prevailing dominant *Reichstag* constellation.

As the SPD had cooperated with the Progressives during the run-off elections whereby both parties had agreed to support each other's candidates in a number of specified election districts,[34] and as the moderate wing of the National Liberal Party had likewise grown disenchanted with the political and economic practices of the Conservatives in particular, there seemed to be at least the chance of a political alignment "from Bassermann to Bebel", thus from the National Liberals to the SPD. This, as it turned out, was not to happen. Yet the mere fact that numerically speaking a potential for such an alignment existed in the *Reichstag* aroused some optimism within the SPD and prompted several leading proponents of closer cooperation with middle-class liberals to steer the party into this direction.

Whereas the right-wing press reacted to the election results with unconcealed anger and violent antisemitic charges,[35] the mood of the SPD was one of jubilation. In an article published in February in the *Sozialistische Monatshefte*, the organ of the party's revisionist wing, Eduard Bernstein expressed cautious optimism that the electoral victory might lead to closer cooperation between Social Democracy and liberal middle-class parties.[36] "A brilliant election result," Bernstein wrote, and then credited the remarkable growth of the labour movement in an era of rapid industrialisation, and the efficiency of Social Democratic organisation, propaganda and press with the outcome of the election. Future victories of the party would now depend on its willingness to adopt flexible policies and on attracting uncommitted voters. What would henceforth be the principal task of the party's strong *Reichstag Fraktion*? Though numerically the largest party, the SPD would still remain in a minority position unless it could build bridges towards the camp of the liberal middle class. Bernstein observed that Germany's political parties now formed roughly two large groups – the SPD, Progressives and National Liberals on the one side, the

---

[34]Bertram, *op. cit.*, pp. 221–234; Groh, *Neg. Integration*, pp. 273–276; Schorske, *op. cit.*, pp. 226–235; Heckart, *op. cit.*, pp. 186–192.

[35]Werner Jochmann, 'Struktur und Funktion des deutschen Antisemitismus', in *Juden im Wilhelminischen Deutschland*, p. 464; Stegmann, *op. cit.*, pp. 257–262. This antisemitic reaction is vividly reflected in numerous editorials and articles which appeared throughout January 1912 in the *Neue Preussische [Kreuz] Zeitung*, the principal organ of the Conservative Party. Here only one example. After lamenting the electoral defeat of the Right, the writer – identified only by the initials H.v.N. – stated: "Wohltuend ist zunächst, dass die Masken überall gefallen sind und dass an Stelle der unsere innere Politik beherrschende Heuchelei und Verschleierungskunst ein klares Für und Wider getreten ist. Es kämpft sich so sehr viel besser mit einem deutlichen und unmissverständlichen Feldgeschrei: Hie deutsches Kaiser- und preussisches Königstum gegen Republik und jüdische Internationale! Hie Gottesfurcht und Christentum gegen Glaubenslosigkeit und Materialismus. Hie Nächstenliebe und ehrliche Arbeit gegen Kommunismus und Mammonismus . . ." *Neue Preussische Zeitung* (27th January 1912), No. 45.

[36]Eduard Bernstein, 'Bedeutung und Aufgaben des Sieges', in *Sozialistische Monatshefte*, XVI (15th February 1912), No. 3, pp. 141–147.

two conservative parties, the Centre and the array of right-wing splinter groups, notably the antisemites, on the other.[37] Would those parties which had won the election be able to cooperate in parliament? Bernstein pointed to the issues which, in his view, divided the victors from the defeated Black–Blue coalition: the attitude towards the authoritarian concepts which governed state and society; (Christian) confessionalism in state and school; the predominance of feudal-agrarian tendencies based on an anachronistic estate system; the existence of a class-based unequal suffrage system in Prussia, Saxony and other states; the bureaucratic form of government, and the right of the workers to organise (*Koalitionsrecht*). To resolve all of these issues in favour of a more equitable, more democratic society would require cooperation between the SPD and liberal middle-class parties in the *Reichstag* and, while the government was doing its utmost to prevent just such a development, Bernstein expressed the hope that the government would find itself on the losing side, provided the National Liberals made no common cause with Conservatives and Centre. The SPD was willing to do its part in cooperating with potential allies to its right, provided the party could do so without having to sacrifice its basic principles. Decisions on which issues to support and which to oppose would have to be made from case to case but, while the SPD was determined to protect its independence, it was willing to work with its respective allies whenever the opportunity to do so should arise. The immediate task would be to maintain a defensive front against the former Black–Blue majority. The future would show whether, from this basis, the still remaining differences dividing the Socialists from the liberal middle class could not be overcome to pave the way for more far-reaching cooperation in achieving common objectives.

On the day that Bernstein's article was published, 15th February 1912, Ludwig Frank outlined his party's position in the *Reichstag*.[38] Criticising the government for its failure to submit a financial reform bill, an omission which Frank considered the more incomprehensible in that the election had clearly indicated the popular resentment of indirect taxation, he prophesied that direct taxes were inevitable, if not sooner then later.[39] Yet even more important than this issue was the question of how to achieve savings for the *Reich*. Frank pointed to the military expenses as the most appropriate area where savings could be realised, especially if the government were to make an effort to improve relations with Germany's neighbours, notably Great Britain. His party, Frank said,

---

[37]Understandably enough, Bernstein's view of the two political camps was an oversimplification. It was harder for a contemporary observer to analyse the situation than it is for the historian who has the benefit of perspective. Modern scholarship sees three political groupings during the pre-war period, groups that were always tentative and in flux: the conservative Right; a middle constellation which included on and off the Centre, National Liberals, Progressives and the Revisionist wing of the SPD; and the SPD Left Centre and extreme Left. See, for example, Gustav Schmidt, 'Innenpolitische Blockbildungen am Vorabend des Ersten Weltkrieges', in *Aus Politik und Zeitgeschichte*. Beilage zur Wochenzeitung *Das Parlament*, B 20/72 (13th May 1972), pp. 3–32.

[38]*Reichstag. Sten. Ber.*, vol. 283, 6th Session (15th February 1912), pp. 25–30.

[39]On the financial situation of the Empire see Witt, *op. cit.*, esp. pp. 316–376, and Volker R. Berghahn, *Germany and the Approach of War in 1914*, New York 1973, *passim*.

would gladly support the government in any peace efforts which it was going to undertake, but would never support a policy of imperialist adventures. What the *Reich* needed was less secrecy on the part of those who governed and greater efforts to win the confidence of all the people rather than merely that of a small clique of Pan-German politicians. "In order to achieve a sound foreign policy, we need democratic institutions and democratic men." The SPD, Frank stated emphatically, was now speaking for four million voters, and the reason why so many people had voted for the party was the result of governmental policies, both on the national level and in the individual German states. In closing, Frank sounded a note of triumph:

> "During the past decades, Germany has developed for the most part into a people of wage and salary earners, and we have become the political expression of this economic fact. For this reason you are also powerless against our growth, that of the past as well as of the future. Five years ago there sat – where today the Herr Chancellor is not sitting – a very clever man . . . Prince Bülow. How he did jeer at the time at our party! . . . Prince Bülow is gone, and we have remained and shall continue to remain! The chancellors are passing phenomena. But Social Democracy fits into the structure of your so-called order like a wedge; and the more you hit that wedge, the firmer it will sit, and the deeper it will penetrate!"

Whereas Bernstein and Frank, both men who were then identified with the party's right wing,[40] interpreted the election as a victory and, explicitly or implicitly, voiced hopes that the SPD would now be able to break out of its isolation, Rosa Luxemburg, speaking for the party's left wing, disagreed. In an address which she delivered in Bremen on 1st March[41] she acknowledged the recent victory at the polls but drew different conclusions from either those of Bernstein or Frank. Gratifying though the outcome of the election was, it now required further action, but action not restricted to the parliamentary level. After a recapitulation of the circumstances which had led to the remarkable achievement at the polls, Luxemburg pointed to the unremittant hostility, oppression and exploitation which had always determined and continued to determine the attitude of the ruling élites and the government *vis-à-vis* the German working class. The election had been held in an atmosphere of international tension, notably the result of the Second Morocco Crisis,[42] for which Luxemburg blamed Germany as well as the other capitalist powers involved in it. Luxemburg attributed the success of the SPD to the people's reaction against rampant imperialism. Thereby the party had been given a mandate

---

[40]Such a classification was, and still remains today, an arbitrary one. Both men, while normally associated with the party's right wing, did at times take positions which were opposed to the views of that wing. See, for instance, below, pp. 26 ff. (Frank), and Groh, *Neg. Integration*, p. 487, n. 101, and p. 553 (Bernstein).

[41]Institut für Marxismus–Leninismus beim ZK der SED, eds., *Rosa Luxemburg. Gesammelte Werke*, three volumes, Berlin (East) 1973, III, *Juli 1911 bis Juli 1914*, pp. 124–133 (hereafter *Luxemburg. G. W.*, III).

[42]On this event see Berghahn, *op. cit.*, pp. 94–98; Fritz Fischer, *Krieg der Illusionen. Die deutsche Politik von 1911 bis 1914*, Düsseldorf 1969, pp. 117–142; Winfried Baumgart, *Deutschland im Zeitalter des Imperialismus (1890–1914). Grundkräfte, Thesen und Strukturen*, Frankfurt a. Main–Berlin–Vienna 1972, p. 108; Wolfgang J. Mommsen, 'Domestic Factors in German Foreign Policy before 1914', in *Imperial Germany*, ed. James J. Sheehan, New York–London 1976, pp. 239–242.

and now would have to show "how to combine the weapon of parliamentarism with the fundamentals of revolutionary class struggle". Was the party prepared to follow that road? Luxemburg indicated that she had doubts and pointed to the party's recent run-off election agreements with the Progressives.[43] In contrast to Bernstein, she rejected any cooperation with segments of the bourgeoisie who, as the run-off elections had shown, were unreliable partners. As the German Right would only be crushed by a large and powerful mass movement, the party's first task after its electoral victory must be to tell its voters: "now that you have demonstrated your power [at the polls] you must learn how to use it. You must henceforth arrive on the field of battle in massed ranks and must fight in the streets for the [reform of] Prussia's electoral law and for the Eight-Hour Day . . ."

Cautious offers of cooperation from the party's right, an exhortation to the masses for militant agitation from its left, these were the initial responses of the two wings to the outcome of the election. As it turned out, the party decided to follow Kautsky's advice that the goal should be "the same as it always was: the conquest of the state power by winning a majority in parliament and by making parliament the controller of government". Though Kautsky's suggested approach did not specifically rule out possible limited cooperation with the liberal middle class, events did. For before very long the National Liberals made it amply clear that they would not be part of a *Reichstag* coalition "from Bassermann to Bebel".[44] Thus the SPD remained in isolation, and labour was put on the defensive by militant employers' organisations, big industry, and demands for "right to work" legislation which were pressed by the right-wing parties in parliament and various economic pressure groups allied with them outside the *Reichstag*.[45]

Nor was 1912 a good year for Rosa Luxemburg's radical activism. Workers' morale was low, and only a few protest demonstrations against the Prussian electoral law were held in Berlin in May and October.[46] All attempts to sway the party's executive to support the agitation by sanctioning the use of a mass strike fell on deaf ears.[47] A sombre mood permeated the SPD, turning by the end of the year into something approaching gloom. This despondency was to deepen in 1913 and led to a number of intra-party debates over the direction which the SPD was to take.

What caused the gloom? The winter 1912/1913 saw the beginning of an economic recession which, although it did not affect all branches of the economy

[43]See above, p. 12, incl. n. 34.

[44]Heckart, *op. cit.*, pp. 186–192, 198–229; Schorske, *op. cit.*, pp. 236–241 and *passim*; Groh, *Neg. Integration*, pp. 276–278, 322–324 and *passim*.

[45]Stegmann, *op. cit.*, esp. pp. 305–338; Schorske, *op. cit.*, pp. 258–259; Saul, *op. cit.*, pp. 322–381, *passim*.

[46]Franz Osteroth and Dieter Schuster, *Chronik der deutschen Sozialdemokratie*. Vol. I: *Bis zum Ende des Ersten Weltkrieges*, Berlin–Bonn/Bad Godesberg 1975, p. 151. Groh, *Neg. Integration*, p. 461, ignores the May protests cited by Osteroth and Schuster and refers only to demonstrations in October.

[47]Groh, *Neg. Integration*, p. 461.

equally, was to last until the outbreak of war.[48] Rising prices, notably those of food, outdistanced wages, and the morale of labour declined still further, affecting both the SPD and the free trade-union movement which was closely associated with the party. Confronted by an unfavourable economic situation, the trade-union leadership tried hard to restrain its members from engaging in strikes, thereby exacerbating unrest without preventing either strikes or lockouts. The leadership of the SPD in turn was distressed by the realisation that growth of membership was rapidly declining, and by the fear that subsequent elections would face a diminishing reservoir of potential voters. In short, German labour entered a period of stagnation. Against this general background, here only briefly sketched, the party was to face several crucial issues on the political scene.

The first one was the military bill of 1913 with its concomitant financial coverage legislation. In December 1912, the German General Staff had submitted to emperor and government an urgent request for increasing the army in order to strengthen the empire's defences in a period of rapidly deteriorating international relations. The first Balkan War in 1912, accompanied by Russian and Austrian mobilisations, served the military as a convenient justification for the suggested army expansion.[49] News of the projected increase in military manpower and armaments was published in the Press as early as January 1913, long before the draft bill was published at the end of March, or before Chancellor Bethmann Hollweg officially submitted it to the *Reichstag* on 7th April.[50] The first half of the year saw a concerted effort on the part of the SPD to defeat the impending bill and, in the process, to force reforms of the entire military establishment upon the Emperor, the Prussian War Ministry and the German General Staff. In its fight against the military bill the SPD stood unified, and two of its principal spokesmen were Hugo Haase and Ludwig Frank. Both men, together with Georg Ledebour, Eduard David, Gustav Noske and Phillip Scheidemann, represented the SPD in the important budget commission of the *Reichstag* where the details of the impending bill were discussed throughout the first months of 1913.[51] Haase, who since 1911 had shared the chairmanship of the party's executive with August Bebel and who in 1912 had become also the chairman of the party's *Reichstag Fraktion*, was a natural choice. But so was Frank, as he had become in 1912 one of the party's four speakers on budget questions[52] which of necessity touched closely on military expenditure. During the secret proceedings of the commission Haase and Frank stressed in particular

[48]Groh, *Neg. Integration*, pp. 461 ff.; Schorske, *op. cit.*, pp. 257–274, also for the following summary.

[49]Fischer, *op. cit.*, pp. 251–257.

[50]Eberhard v. Vietsch, *Bethmann Hollweg. Staatsmann zwischen Macht und Ethos*, Boppard a. Rhein 1969 (Schriften des Bundesarchivs 18), p. 153. Kurt Stenkewitz, *Gegen Bajonett und Dividende. Die politische Krise in Deutschland am Vorabend des Ersten Weltkrieges*, Berlin (East) 1960 (Schriftenreihe des Instituts für Deutsche Geschichte an der Karl-Marx-Universität, Leipzig 6), pp. 96–106 and ff.; despite the partisan approach, this is the most detailed recent account on the issue of the army bill.

[51]Groh, *Neg. Integration*, pp. 416–418, including notes 206–215.

[52]Matthias and Pikart, *op. cit.*, I, p. 259. The others were Scheidemann, Ledebour and David.

the need for a naval agreement with England and improved relations with France. Both objectives would require the abandonment of the projected military expansion programme.[53] Haase pressed also for a reduction of the term of service to one year for the infantry, together with several other reform measures, outlined earlier that year by Max Cohen-Reuss, which the party likewise pressed in the *Reichstag*.[54] On 24th April, when representatives of all parties met with the chancellor and war minister in special session, Frank raised the issue of Belgian neutrality, which he wanted to see publicly confirmed by the German government. He also asked a number of specific questions about German–Austrian military arrangements and suggested that if Germany's military strength was indeed numerically inferior to that of her neighbours, this deficiency could well be offset by raising the morale of the troops through the immediate institution of long overdue reforms.[55]

When the draft bill was introduced for the first reading on 7th April, Haase spoke for the party.[56] The bill, he said, was unprecedented in its dimensions and the sacrifices it required from the people. Nor had the government made a convincing case in justifying the projected military expansion. The international situation had not markedly changed. Balkan quarrels were not new, and the possible emergence of a Slavic coalition posing a threat for Germany was a phantom. Relations with France and England had likewise not changed and the government would be well advised to improve them, especially with England. Germany should not place herself in a situation whereby she might be compelled to fight for Austria-Hungary's dubious adventures in the Balkans. As for the argument that Germany must strengthen her army because France was contemplating the passage of a three-year military service law, Haase said: "Whoever claims this presents counterfeit arguments [*begeht Falschmünzerei*]; for

---

[53]Groh., *Neg. Integration*, p. 416, n. 208. The minutes of the commission were not available to me.
[54]*Ibid.*, p. 417, n. 212 and p. 418, n. 215. For Cohen-Reuss, see Hermann Heidegger, *Die deutsche Sozialdemokratie und der nationale Staat 1870–1920. Unter besonderer Berücksichtigung der Kriegs- und Revolutionsjahre*, Göttingen–Berlin–Frankfurt 1956 (Göttinger Bausteine zur Geschichtswissenschaft 25), pp. 100–101. The programme contained the following main points: 1. Immediate establishment of two years of service for the cavalry and mounted artillery. 2. Immediate establishment of one year of service for all infantry units. 3. Creation of an officer corps from suitable enlisted men. 4. Elimination of all military special courts. 5. All military expenses to be covered by property, inheritance and income taxes. For a succinct treatment of the relations between SPD and the military see Domann, *op. cit.*, pp. 168–195.
[55]Groh, *Neg. Integration*, pp. 427–431; and the same, 'Die geheimen Sitzungen der Reichshaushaltskommission am 24. und 25. April 1913', *Internationale wissenschaftliche Korrespondenz zur Geschichte der deutschen Arbeiterbewegung*, VII (April 1971), No. 11/12, pp. 35–36. It may well have been during this session that Frank asked Wilhelm Groener, then a lieutenant colonel and *Abteilungschef* in the German General Staff, during a private conversation why the army was so "modest" in its demands for an army increase. See Wilhelm Groener, *Lebenserinnerungen. Jugend. Generalstab. Weltkrieg*, Göttingen 1957 (Deutsche Geschichtsquellen des 19. und 20. Jahrhunderts 41), p. 136, and Hamburger, *op. cit.*, p. 452. Groh, *Neg. Integration*, p. 429, writes in this connection that the Social Democrats who participated in this meeting, i.e., Frank, Ledebour and Bebel, "waren sichtlich beeindruckt und beugten sich der militärischen Notwendigkeit und der Autorität des Generalstabs." This private interlude did not, however, affect Frank's subsequent oppositional stand on the army bill when he addressed the *Reichstag*. See below, pp. 18–20.
[56]*Reichstag. Sten. Ber.*, vol. 289, 133rd Sess. (7th April 1913), pp. 4517–4527.

without our army bill, the French government would never have thought of introducing a three-year service bill into parliament."[57] True, France had her chauvinists, but so had Germany, notably the *Wehrverein*, the Pan-German League and similar pressure groups. And did Germany's neighbours really want war? The French and Russian workers at least desired peace, just as Germany's workers did. Haase then turned to German militarism and condemned the army's frequently inhumane treatment of the soldiers under its command, abuses which could only be eliminated once the country adopted the militia system which the SPD advocated.[58] In closing, Haase quoted Fichte: "We want a *Reich* which is genuinely based on law, such as has never before existed in the world; [a *Reich*] where all citizens desire liberty . . . based on the equality of all who bear a human face." If we abide by these words, Haase said, then we shall not need additional armaments, aimed at our neighbours, "for then all our efforts will be directed toward the improvement of civilisation and the establishment of liberty of all the people."[59]

Haase, a member of the party's left centre, was essentially a pacifist, an attitude which he shared with a number of his Jewish colleagues. His speech did not run counter to the party's official views on the matter of international relations, but the fervent tone of conviction was his alone. His arguments were a combination of common sense and deeply felt emotions, devoid of hatred and cheap polemics, a stance which revealed both his strength and weakness as the leader of a "revolutionary" party. Like Bernstein and Eisner, Haase's *Weltanschauung* was largely derived from Kant rather than from Marx,[60] which proved as much of a liability when it came to practical politics as it was an asset in upholding humanistic principles.

Frank addressed the *Reichstag* on the military bill on 9th April.[61] Though he covered essentially the same ground as Haase had done two days before, Frank's speech was tougher, often coloured by irony and interlaced with wit. The government, he began, did not enjoy the necessary authority with the *Reichstag* to justify the immense military outlay demanded by the bill – a judgment which events were to prove wrong. According to Frank, the military bill was a provocation of Germany's neighbours. After discussing the situation in

---

[57]*Reichstag. Sten. Ber.*, vol. 289, 133rd Sess. (7th April 1913), p. 4519. In this last statement Haase may have stretched a point. France's plan for introducing a three-year military service law predated the discussions on the German military reform bill, though these may have speeded up the French decision to introduce a three-year service bill on 6th March 1913. See Adalbert Wahl, *Deutsche Geschichte. Von der Reichsgründung bis zum Ausbruch des Weltkriegs* (1871–1914), four volumes, Stuttgart 1936, IV, p. 610; but cf. Stenkewitz, *op. cit.*, p. 100.

[58]See on this issue Heidegger, *op. cit.*, pp. 93–103, *passim*; Reinhard Höhn, *Sozialismus und Heer*, three volumes, vol. I, *Heer und Krieg im Bild des Sozialismus*, 2nd edn., Bad Harzburg 1961, pp. 258 ff. and *ibid.*, vol. III, *Der Kampf des Heeres gegen die Sozialdemokratie*, Bad Harzburg 1969, pp. 569–570 and *passim*.

[59]*Reichstag. Sten. Ber.*, vol. 289, 133rd Session (7th April 1913), p. 4527.

[60]Schorske, *op. cit.*, p. 209. On the neo-Kantian trend within the SPD see Steinberg, *op. cit.*, pp. 98–100 (though the author does not mention Haase in this context). See also Ernst Haase, *Hugo Haase. Sein Leben und Wirken, mit einer Auswahl von Briefen, Reden und Aufsätzen*, Berlin n.d., p. 26. See now also Calkins, *op. cit.*, pp. 11, 18, 205, 208 and *passim*.

[61]*Reichstag. Sten. Ber.*, vol. 289, 135th Sess. (9th April 1913), pp. 4596–4600.

the Balkans and Austria-Hungary's military strength which, in his opinion, was adequate without the unprecedented increase of Germany's military forces, he turned to an argument, recently advanced by the Conservatives, that the military bill was essential because the army was the "school of the nation" and as such constituted an effective counterweight to future Social Democratic growth. To this argument Frank replied: "Among the 136,000 soldiers [additionally required by the bill] will be, on their entering the barracks, at a low estimate, 50,000 Social Democrats and, on their leaving, 80,000 of them." Would it not be wiser, he asked, to rely instead on a "so-called moral–political" armament, i.e., reforms of the army along democratic lines? These would prove more effective than military and financial defence measures. "Unity within the army is only possible when there is unity among the people, and unity among the people is only possible where the law is administered equally." At the end of his speech, following Haase, Frank called for an understanding with England and France. Talks with England looked promising, [62] and an understanding with France should also be possible, provided that good will and serious efforts prevailed. At the moment, however, hopes for reaching an understanding among the nations were endangered by the military bills pending in Germany and France. A conference of men of good will from both countries would shortly convene in Berne [63] where these questions would be discussed, and Frank expressed confidence that positive results would be achieved there.

> "We Social Democrats hope and wish that we shall not remain isolated in this serious attempt to serve the peace, and that middle class [*bürgerliche*] friends of peace who respect the will of their voters will work together with us. Should this happen, then nobody will be happier than we. But should you fail to join us we shall not panic. We shall then go our way [alone] with the awareness that behind us stands the will of two nations, two working nations. We shall then proceed with the proud certitude that we are citizens of the impending great European cultural community, and that we are serving our fatherland by preparing the way for this community." [64]

Here again, as in Haase's speech, the tone of fervent idealism so frequently struck by Jewish Social Democrats could not be missed. But neither could Frank's open invitation to middle-class liberals to join the Social Democratic efforts in maintaining the peace of Europe.

Two weeks before the final vote on the military bill was taken, Frank spoke once again on the issue of German military abuses. [65] This time he concentrated on the widespread practice of the military boycott whereby the army command placed off limits to all troops certain commercial establishments, notably eating houses and retail stores, if their proprietors either supported the SPD or were at least suspected of doing so. It was part of the party's far-reaching objective to

[62]On Germany's tenuous relations with England during this period see Andreas Hillgruber, 'Zwischen Hegemonie und Weltpolitik. Das Problem der Kontinuität von Bismarck bis Bethmann Hollweg', in Michael Stürmer, ed., *Das kaiserliche Deutschland. Politik und Gesellschaft 1870–1918*, Düsseldorf 1970, pp. 198–200; Konrad Jarausch, *The Enigmatic Chancellor. Bethmann Hollweg and the Hubris of Imperial Germany*, New Haven and London 1973, pp. 132–143 and *passim*; Mommsen, *loc. cit.*, pp. 249–250; Groh, *Neg. Integration*, pp. 401–410, *passim*.
[63]On the Berne Conference see below, p. 30.
[64]*Reichstag. Sten. Ber.*, vol. 289, 135th Sess. (9th April 1913), p. 4600.
[65]*Ibid.*, vol. 290, 165th Sess. (19th June 1913), pp. 5621–5625.

force reforms upon the army, and in this instance the efforts were at least partly successful. When on the following day a vote was taken on a Social Democratic motion that a military boycott could not be enforced against eating houses merely on account of the proprietors' political views or because Social Democrats frequented the premises, it was passed with the aid of liberal middle-class delegates.[66] But another motion to remove the military boycott against Social Democratic barbers, physicians, lawyers *et al.* was defeated.[67]

Despite all efforts on the part of Social Democratic speakers, the army bill was passed on 30th June.[68] Needless to say, Haase and Frank had not been the only delegates who had spoken on the issue; so had Scheidemann and Noske. What distinguished the speeches of the former from those of the latter was the pronounced faith which Haase and Frank repeatedly expressed in the ultimate triumph of common sense and good will, whereby the rule of law, the dignity of man, and a spirit of conciliation and understanding would emerge, both within the national and international spheres. It was not coincidental that during the last two peacetime years Haase and Frank were in the forefront of their party in working for peace on the international level[69] while continuing to fight at home for reforms and a more equitable society.

In conjunction with the army bill, the *Reichstag* also considered the financial sources that were needed to cover the costs of the military expansion programme.[70] The National Liberals and Progressives, for once in agreement with the SPD, wanted to see the costs covered, at least in part, by a national property tax which hitherto had always been turned down by a majority of the *Reichstag*. The Conservatives, as was to be expected, opposed any direct taxation on the national level. The Centre vacillated but entered upon talks with the National Liberals in order to find an acceptable financial solution which would not jeopardise the military bill. In the end, and with the support of the government, a compromise emerged. The *Reichstag* voted – against the Conservatives – for a once only defence levy, to be paid by the wealthier citizens, and also for a permanent capital gains tax (*Vermögenszuwachssteuer*) levied on personal property. While still a far cry from a genuine national income tax, the bill constituted a decided advance over the previous practice of financing national expenses exclusively through indirect taxes and the contributions from the individual states (*Matrikularbeiträge*), customs receipts and related resources.

The position of the SPD on the question of taxation had been consistent over the years: for this system not a man and not a penny. As a large part of the taxes were spent on armaments, the party refused to underwrite what it considered blatant militarism. Thus it had become an iron rule for the SPD to vote

---

[66] *Reichstag. Sten. Ber.*, vol. 290, 166th Sess. (20th June 1913), p. 5648; see also Höhn, *op. cit.*, III, p. 207. On related issues pertaining to SPD sponsored army reforms during these debates see Domann, *op. cit.*, pp. 192–195.

[67] *Ibid.*, vol. 290, 166th Sess. (20th June 1913), p. 5647.

[68] The most detailed account of the entire issue in Stenkewitz, *op. cit.*, pp. 96–119.

[69] See below, pp. 30–32.

[70] This complex story could be only sketched in here. The best accounts are Witt, *op. cit.*, pp. 356–376, and Stenkewitz, *op. cit.*, pp. 96–119 (treated in conjunction with the army bill). See also Schorske, *op. cit.*, pp. 265–267 and Groh, *Neg. Integration*, pp. 407–444.

against every tax measure in the *Reichstag*, and we have noted earlier the party majority's strong condemnation of the South German Socialists who had violated this iron rule when they voted for the budgets in their respective state diets. And yet, when the question of how to cover the costs of the military bill was debated in the *Reichstag* during the first months of 1913, the SPD faced a genuine dilemma. For the first time in the history of the empire the tax proposals contained a substantial levy on the propertied classes.[71] Could the Socialists afford to vote against the proposals – undoubtedly in company with the Conservatives – thereby assuring the bill's defeat and risking the dissolution of the *Reichstag*, and with it new elections? Furthermore, there was the danger that, in order to avoid such a dissolution of parliament, the National Liberals and Progressives might reconsider their position and resolve to vote exclusively for indirect taxes.

The taxation issue led to heated debates within the party. One of the first pronouncements came from Bernstein who by the spring of 1913 had moved closer to the position of the party's Executive.[72] In an interview given to a Paris newspaper, Bernstein stated in February:

> "If the fate of the military bill were to depend on the financial question, then we would vote against it. But the vote on the military bill will come first, and only then will come the question of how to pay for it. The costs for military bills will always be covered . . . Our duty will be to see to it that the new expenses will not be laid upon the shoulders of the workers. For this reason we shall probably agree [to the tax bill] if the money is to be raised by a levy on the propertied. One must choose the lesser of two evils whenever it proves impossible to prevent both."[73]

Bernstein's prediction proved to be ultimately accurate, though until the final vote on the bill was taken on 30th June the debate over which position to adopt, which began in earnest early in April and was not concluded until 25th June, was carried on within the *Fraktion* with passionate intensity.[74] Here, the leading proponent in support of the bill was Ludwig Frank. As a member of the *Reichstag*'s budget commission he was well informed and worked hard and consistently on persuading his colleagues to vote for the bill.[75] The principal opponents of the tax bill within the *Fraktion* were Arthur Stadthagen, Gustav Hoch and Fritz Geyer, all of them supporters of the party's left centre; the two former were Jews. On 25th June, when the question was put to a vote within the *Fraktion*, fifty-two out of ninety-six delegates present indicated that they would support the bill while thirty-five were opposed to it.[76] As the majority decision prevailed, the entire *Fraktion* cast its vote in the *Reichstag* in favour of the bill five days later.

[71]Witt, *op. cit.*, esp. pp. 373–374.

[72]Groh, *Neg. Integration*, p. 419, n. 217.

[73]*Berliner Neueste Nachrichten*, *Tageblatt* (22nd February 1913), as cited in Fritz Klein *et al.*, eds., *Deutschland im ersten Weltkrieg*, three volumes, vol. I, *Vorbereitung, Entfesselung und Verlauf des Krieges bis Ende 1914*, 3rd edn., Berlin (East) 1971, p. 199, n. 140.

[74]Matthias and Pikart, *op. cit.*, I, pp. 291–300, *passim*.

[75]Frank was, of course, not alone, but he assumed a leading position. Schorske, *op. cit.*, p. 266; Groh, *Neg. Integration*, pp. 345–346; Wachenheim, *Frank*, pp. 252–253.

[76]Matthias and Pikart, *op. cit.*, I, p. 300.

The matter did not end here but had an aftermath when the annual party congress met at Jena in September. As the congress had to review all major decisions taken during the preceding year by the party's executive and the *Fraktion*, the vote on the tax bill was high on the agenda. The congress was presented with a resolution, drafted by Emanuel Wurm, which justified the decision taken by the *Fraktion*. Wurm's resolution had the backing of the party's right wing, the Executive and large segments of the centre.[77] Wurm, an expert on financial questions, belonged to the party's left centre and considered himself a "radical". Before the vote on the tax bill had been taken in the *Reichstag*, he had been an outspoken opponent of the bill when the matter was debated within the *Fraktion*.[78] But at the party congress he spent two and a half hours in defence of an issue which he had violently opposed only a few weeks earlier. The reasons for his switch are not known. It is conceivable that after the question had been decided against him, Wurm put party unity before his own partisan views and defended the majority position.

After Wurm, who spoke in all three times, Albert Südekum addressed the congress for another two hours in defence of the *Fraktion*'s vote, and only then did the debate on Wurm's resolution get underway. It was long, heated and acrimonious.[79] Of the twelve speakers, including Wurm and Südekum, who joined the debate, five were Jews, and of these, three – Hoch, Stadthagen and Luxemburg – talked against the resolution. Hoch charged in particular that the property taxes for which the *Fraktion* had voted were not extensive enough to warrant the party's support. In supporting the bill the SPD had abandoned its principle of opposing all forms of militarism.[80] Stadthagen spoke in a similar vein and also stressed the *Fraktion*'s abandonment of principle. "If a conflict arises between our struggle against militarism and that against indirect taxes, then the former must be given preference. For this reason we should reject everything which might benefit militarism, be it through direct or indirect taxation."[81] But the strongest criticism was voiced by Rosa Luxemburg. Weeks prior to the meeting of the congress she had aired the entire question in a series of six newspaper articles.[82] While generously acknowledging both the *Fraktion*'s skilful and determined opposition to the military bill and the tactical successes which the members of the budget commission – including Frank – had achieved in separating the debates on the military and tax bills in the plenum of the *Reichstag*, she did charge the *Fraktion* with inconsistency as their vote in the *Reichstag* had violated the party's basic views on the matter of the military budget. After reviewing step by step the events that had led up to the vote in the *Reichstag*, she stressed especially the inadequacy of the direct taxes when

---

[77]Stenkewitz, *op. cit.*, p. 124.

[78]*Protokoll über die Verhandlungen des Parteitages der Sozialdemokratischen Partei Deutschlands. Abgehalten in Jena vom 14. bis 20. September 1913*, Berlin 1913, p. 485; hereafter *PT 1913*.

[79]*Ibid.*, pp. 419–517. Haase, who was ill at the time, did not attend the party congress.

[80]*Ibid.*, pp. 481–485, esp. p. 482.

[81]*Ibid.*, p. 495.

[82]In the *Leipziger Volkszeitung*, reprinted in *Luxemburg. G. W.*, III, pp. 267–290. The articles appeared on 23rd, 24th, 25th, 26th, 28th and 29th July.

compared to the indirect ones already in existence. The SPD should have fought harder for the elimination of the indirect taxes instead of voting for the direct ones. Then she concluded:

> "It finally follows from all this that neither the financial–political illusions nor the vain hopes that direct taxes might tone down militarism[83] can serve to lighten the struggle of the working class against militarism. On the contrary . . . 'to facilitate our fight against militarism', nothing is as important as the thorough enlightenment of the mass of the people as to the true economic and political roots of the existing militarism as a pillar of exploitation and class domination, under all circumstances and with all financial–political methods of raising money, [and] the fact that in the last analysis, even with direct taxation, it is the working class which in every respect, economically and politically, must pay the bill . . . for this reason we must grant to this system not a man and not a penny."[84]

When she addressed the congress a few weeks later, she briefly summarised the main points previously made in her articles, and then closed with a prophetic warning:

> "Should you support the majority resolution of our *Fraktion* [i.e., Wurm's], then you may find yourself in the position, should war break out and we be unable to change the situation that you may have to face the question whether the costs [for war] should be covered by indirect or direct taxation, and that you then consequently will have to approve the war expenditure."[85]

Shortly before the conclusion of the debate Frank spoke briefly in favour of Wurm's resolution. His was neither a long nor a strong speech but was mainly designed to dispute some technical points raised by Stadthagen and Hoch. Luxemburg he ignored. The sole principal argument which he advanced was that which had made him the driving force behind the *Fraktion*'s vote on the tax bill:

> "Stadthagen has brought out a single fact: Somewhere . . . somebody is said to have stated: 'The bourgeoisie voted for the soldiers and the Social Democrats voted for the means to cover the costs' . . . Be that as it may, it is still better than if it could be said: 'Through the stupidity of the Social Democratic *Fraktion* it has come to pass that the bourgeois parties have voted for the soldiers and the Social Democratic workers must pay for these soldiers.' "[86]

Thus at the congress, "Baden and Luxemburg" faced each other head on, though neither side could have foreseen at the time of the debate that the issue in question was to split the party three years later. Party principle demanded that militarism be fought without any concessions, as Luxemburg had tersely reminded the congress. But could the SPD afford to stand rigidly on principle when tactical considerations, and especially the welfare of the workers, demanded a measure of flexibility? This was the question which Wurm and Frank posed, whereby the latter stressed in addition the cooperation between SPD and

[83]The argument that the wealthy classes would be less enthusiastic about military expenditure if they had to bear the brunt of the costs was frequently advanced as an argument by those members of the party who supported the vote for the tax bill. See, for instance, Witt, *op. cit.*, pp. 373–374, incl. n. 407.
[84]*Luxemburg, G. W.*, III, pp. 285–286.
[85]*PT 1913*, p. 487.
[86]*Ibid.*, p. 505.

the liberal parties which had isolated the Conservatives, had won the Centre over to the majority position on direct taxation, and as a result had relieved the working class of additional financial burdens. On this point Frank, who had been in the forefront during the fight against the army bill, never wavered and most of his Jewish colleagues, some of whom had prominently figured in the debate, found his arguments more convincing than Luxemburg's. When the final vote was taken at the Jena congress, Wurm's resolution was adopted by a large majority – 366 to 144.[87] With the majority, and alongside such stalwart supporters of the party's right wing and centre as Adolf Braun, Max Cohen-Reuss, Ludwig Frank, Georg Gradnauer, Ernst Heilmann, Berthold Heymann, Simon Katzenstein and Georges Weill voted Eduard Bernstein, Oskar Cohn, Paul Levi, Kurt Rosenfeld and Emanuel Wurm; all of the latter were to break with the SPD three years later over the party's stand on war credits. Conversely, of the five Jews who voted against Wurm's resolution – Georg Davidsohn, Joseph Herzfeld, Gustav Hoch, Rosa Luxemburg and Arthur Stadthagen – Davidsohn and Hoch were to remain in the SPD when the break came. In 1913 the lines were not yet clearly drawn. It was to take Verdun and the mounting casualty lists before five of the thirteen Jewish Social Democrats who had then supported Wurm's resolution, including Wurm himself, turned decisively and demonstratively against militarism by voting with their feet.

III

Three months before the party congress had met at Jena, where Frank and Luxemburg took opposing positions on the tax bill vote, they had been briefly aligned on another burning issue, the fight against Prussia's three-class voting system. The issue as such was not new for the party. It had been debated at length in 1905 and 1909,[88] and while there was full agreement that the Prussian suffrage reform was an essential prerequisite for the SPD's long-range objective of breaking the stranglehold of the dominant ruling élites, opinions on how to proceed tactically had been divided in the past, and were to be so again in 1913. The question was revived that year by the outcome of the elections to the Prussian lower house in late May and early June. For months prior to the elections Bernstein, supported by Eisner, had advised in a series of articles in the *Sozialistische Monatshefte* that it would be wise to seek close cooperation with the liberal parties in order to isolate the Conservatives and to increase the representation of the SPD in the Prussian house of delegates.[89] But although the

[87] *PT 1913*, pp. 515–516.
[88] Schorske, *op. cit.*, pp. 45–49, 172–187.
[89] Eduard Bernstein, 'Landtagswahlpolitik in Preussen', in *Sozialistische Monatshefte*, XVI (29th August 1912), No. 17, pp. 1026–1033; 'Chemnitz und die preussischen Landtagswahlen', *ibid.*, XVI (17th October 1912), No. 21, pp. 1276–1282; 'Der Preussentag und die Landtagswahlen', *ibid.*, XVI (27th December 1912), No. 26, pp. 1596–1605; 'Zwischen Wahlmänner-wahl und Abgeordnetenwahl', *ibid.*, XVII (27th May 1913), No. 10, pp. 589–594. Throughout these articles Bernstein urged support, if necessary, for Progressive candidates even without a promise of reciprocity.

party Executive adopted Bernstein's advice, negotiations with the Progressives did not lead very far, and when the votes were counted the SPD had merely gained three additional seats, increasing the number of delegates from seven to ten.[90]

The disappointing outcome unleashed another party debate over tactics. Cooperation with the left liberals, the panacea of the party's reformist wing, had miscarried. Was the SPD to resign itself to future defeats in Prussia, or was it to step up its fight for election reform in that state? To everyone's amazement, and particularly startling to the party's Executive it was Ludwig Frank, the budget voter from Baden, the advocate of moderation and of parliamentary alliances with middle-class parties, who in answer to the question came out with a proposal hitherto strictly associated with Luxemburg's faction – the mass strike.

Two events had prompted Frank to adopt this position. The most immediate one was the party's recent election defeat in Prussia, which convinced him of the need for a more forceful approach to the question of suffrage reform. But he had also been impressed by a general strike in Belgium that spring – from 14th to 24th April – when the Belgian workers had demanded a revision of their country's restrictive suffrage law and had succeeded in receiving assurances from their government that the law would be revised.[91] Although Frank was aware that Prussia was not Belgium, the spirited example set by that country's working class had captured his imagination. On 10th June, a week after the Prussian elections, he addressed a Social Democratic meeting in Berlin-Wilmersdorf and surprised his audience, which included Rosa Luxemburg, with a fire-eating speech:

> ". . . The King has promised an electoral reform [in 1910]; now the time has come to tell the King: 'King, now keep your promise' . . . We demand equality with those who rule and the abolition of the class-based electoral law in Prussia. But the people must also soon revert to the initially so effective method of expressing their will in the streets as well . . . and if all our requests should lead nowhere, then we must finally say: leave the factories, the shops, the offices! . . . Then, when all other means have failed, the day of the mass strike will have arrived . . ." [92]

The struggle, he went on to say, would require sacrifices; undoubtedly, some innocent people would suffer, and a number of employers might go bankrupt in the process. Those who had always wanted the workers to remain quiet should now join them in finally eliminating the prevailing Prussian electoral law. Mass strikes had been effective in the past, Frank said, singling out the Chartist movement in England and the recent strike in Belgium. Why should it not work here? "Prussia and Germany have the best working-class movement and the most extensive working-class press in the entire world. Now we are learning from the international proletariat the mass struggle! . . ." He suggested specifically that the mass strike be applied as a weapon of attrition, starting in

[90]Osteroth and Schuster, *op. cit.*, p. 157. Groh, *Neg. Integration*, pp. 463–464.

[91]Wachenheim, *Frank*, pp. 252, 268; the war delayed the fulfilment of these assurances in Belgium until 6th May 1919.

[92]Wachenheim, *Frank*, pp. 267–268.

one region today, in another tomorrow, thereby depriving the Prussian ruling class of peace and the enjoyment of power. Such a course undoubtedly involved risks, but when had political struggles ever been devoid of them? "There can be no assurances against such risks, nor do we need any . . . Whoever is so afraid of the rocks ahead that he stays in the harbour will not hazard much, but he will never reach the distant shore which is the goal of our ardent desire. Thus to the boats, and forward, forward into battle!" [93]

When he had finished, Rosa Luxemburg rose for her reply. With her customary irony she told her listeners that she had enjoyed both the speaker and the applause which his speech had received. To have heard Frank's words was indeed a sensation, though she could not help wondering whether it was indeed compatible to forge a *Grossblock* in Baden while calling for a mass strike in Prussia. She did not mean to pose this question from a spirit of pettiness, she assured her audience. Frank's speech had revealed to her that even in Baden one had finally come to realise that in the face of an ever-sharpening political conflict the masses of the people must act. "I should have been overjoyed if the party comrades in Baden had heard the speech which Dr. Frank has delivered today." Pointing out that it was she who had been one of the earliest proponents of the mass strike in Germany she also warned that such a strike must not be misdirected. "It is no miracle cure which one may pull out of one's pocket at will; it is closely tied to general politics and cannot be separated from the general party tactics. It is irreconcilable with any kind of cooperation with bourgeois parties; but at least I have now the hope that we shall be spared future escapades on the part of Baden." [94]

Luxemburg's critique that day was still muted, implicit and mixed with left-handed compliments. No doubt Baden had caught Luxemburg by surprise that day in Berlin-Wilmersdorf! Yet two weeks later she launched her first counter-attack in an article published in the *Leipziger Volkszeitung* on 26th June:

> "The concept, for instance, that a mass strike in Prussia can be coupled with the Baden *Grossblock* testifies to a purely mechanical and superficial view of the mass strike . . . If everything fails, then 'we make' a general strike – that is truly the rude concept of anarchism. In reality the mass strike is not a cleverly conceived 'extreme measure', to be resorted to on special occasions . . . when all other weapons have failed. The mass strike as practised by the proletariat is a historical phase of development [*Entwicklungsphase*] of the general class struggle, i.e., the phase of independent action on the part of the proletarian mass, [of] the extreme intensification [*Verschärfung*] of the class struggle as a whole." [95]

On 22nd July, during another meeting which she addressed in Berlin, Luxemburg's attack on Frank grew sharper and more personal. Calling him an opportunist, on account of his general views and policies, notably in connection with his *Grossblock* tactic in Baden, she said:

> "His politics are very simple. One makes politics in the grand style in parliament, with all the means of statesmanlike tactics; one hobnobs with the bourgeois parties; one creates a

---

[93]Wachenheim, *Frank*, pp. 268–269.
[94]*Luxemburg, G. W.*, III, pp. 240–241. For a reaction to Frank's speech and Luxemburg's rebuttal see Wachenheim, *Vom Grossbürgertum* . . ., pp. 40–41.
[95]*Luxemburg, G. W.*, III, p. 247.

large bloc of the entire Left. Yet if the cause of the workers thereby does not advance by one step – to nobody's surprise – well then, workers, go into the street and make a mass strike. Frank's statements are a classic example of how not to look at the mass strike. The mass strike is not something that can be pulled off whenever the politics of the parliamentarian artists have failed." [96]

Luxemburg's arguments were not up to her usual level of astuteness. One cannot escape the impression that she, usually so sure of herself, felt threatened by Frank's unsuspected manoeuvre, and that her vanity had got the better of her. [97] She seemed particularly nettled by the fact that Frank had been given credit for having raised the mass strike issue in the first place, and indicated repeatedly that others had done so before him, implying with barely concealed annoyance that it had been above all she who had done so. Nor did she do justice to Frank's sincerity in the matter but twisted his arguments to serve her own purposes. At the meeting on 10th June Frank had said that despite the policies he pursued in Baden he had never opposed the mass strike. On the contrary, "as long as I have been in politics I have always preferred the politics of action to those of the phrase". He had then defended his *Grossblock* tactics, pointing out that his friends in Prussia never had the opportunity to follow the Baden example because the political circumstances in the two states differed. The Prussian comrades must first create the constitutional basis from which to proceed. And, returning to the mass strike, he had reiterated: "All objections to the mass strike are invalid; whoever knows a simpler or better approach should point this out. [But] since nobody can do so we shall have to take this approach, however steep it may prove to be. I at least lack the courage to be so cowardly as to dispense with the mass strike." [98]

It was a remarkable situation indeed. The principal exponents of the party's two extreme wings had fixed on an identical radical approach for fighting the Prussian electoral law, although the precise tactics they suggested differed, as did their motives. There was as a result considerable perplexity among the party's establishment. "Frank's sudden thrust [*Vorstoss*] is remarkable," Kautsky wrote to Victor Adler on 26th June. "When August [Bebel] read about it, he said: 'he [Frank] presents himself already as my heir'. There is certainly some truth to that. Fortunately, Rosa is even more vain than she is clever and thus does not receive Frank as an ally, but as unfair cut-rate competition." [99]

Bebel's caustic remark which Kautsky alluded to was wrong as far as Frank was concerned, [100] although there existed strong sentiments throughout the party's right wing and centre that he be given a leading post. Already in the summer of 1912 members of the *Fraktion*'s revisionists had urged that if Bebel

[96]*Ibid.*, p. 261.
[97]This was certainly Hedwig Wachenheim's impression; see *Von Grossbürgertum . . .*, p. 40. See also 'Kautsky to Adler, 26th June 1913', in *Victor Adler. Briefwechsel mit August Bebel und Karl Kautsky*, ed. Friedrich Adler, Vienna 1954, p. 573; hereafter *Adler Briefwechsel*.
[98]Wachenheim, *Frank*, pp. 270–271.
[99]*Adler Briefwechsel*, p. 573.
[100]This emerges from a letter which Frank wrote to Leonie Meyerhof-Hildeck on 1st September 1913; Wachenheim, *Frank*, pp. 283–284; there Frank also comments on his good relations with Bebel during the last year of the latter's life.

should resign from the executive for reasons of health, Frank should take his place and with Haase become co-chairman.[101] After Frank's speech on 10th June, his surprise move met with a widely based favourable response within the party[102] which might have indeed boosted him into the position as co-chairman of the executive had he not been – ironically – too much of an activist, too outspoken a man of conviction to suit the leading power brokers of the SPD.[103] These men preferred Kautsky's wait-and-see attitude, the emphasis on first of all strengthening the party's organisational structure, election victories, and cautious political manoeuvres to "politics of action" such as Frank practised in Baden and had recently advocated in Berlin, but also Rosa Luxemburg who, though she proceeded from a very different vantage point than that of Frank, was the party's activist par excellence. Because these two antagonists, each of them heading one of the SPD's extreme wings, were outspoken people who were opposed to the "politics of phrases" and tried hard to have their respective views on objectives and tactics accepted as official policy, neither of them ever attained a position at the top of the party's hierarchy.[104] After Bebel's death in August 1913, when the vacancy thus created in the chairmanship of the party's executive had to be filled, the man who was chosen was the cautious and uncontroversial trade-union functionary Friedrich Ebert.

The mass strike issue, like the military tax bill, was hotly debated at the Jena party congress. The Executive, aware of the growing support which a more activist approach to Prussian electoral reform had gained among the party's rank and file, had submitted a resolution which ingeniously mentioned the mass strike as a potential weapon, but had rendered the wording so ambiguously that any realistic application of that weapon was virtually nullified.[105] Once again, Luxemburg and Frank confronted each other over the issue on which they both agreed and disagreed. Shortly after Bernstein, the only other Jew who participated in the debate at some length, had stated that he had been one of the first party members to advocate the mass strike as a feasible and, under certain circumstances, even inevitable weapon, but then spent the rest of his speech repudiating its practical application with the argument that even a mass strike would not persuade the Prussian government to grant far-reaching reforms,[106] it was Rosa Luxemburg's turn to speak. She had submitted to the congress a counter-resolution to that of the Executive by way of an amendment. Now, ignoring Bernstein, she lashed out at Scheidemann who the previous day had ridiculed the mass strike and, implicitly, both Luxemburg and Frank when he

---

[101]Groh, *Neg. Integration*, p. 479.

[102]*Ibid.*, p. 477.

[103]*Ibid.*, p. 479. Calkins, *op. cit.*, p. 27, referring to an earlier event (the replacement of Paul Singer, who died in January 1911), states that Frank could not become a candidate because of his close ties with revisionism.

[104]*Ibid.*, p. 501.

[105]*PT 1913*, pp. 192–193; for a discussion of the proceedings see Schorske, *op. cit.*, pp. 278–280 and Groh, *Neg. Integration*, pp. 493–499.

[106]*PT 1913*, pp. 284–286.

had spoken in support of the Executive's resolution on this issue.[107] The mass strike, she said, was the only possible means of achieving the objective for which the SPD had been fighting for years in vain, the reform of Prussia's reactionary three-class voting system. To this end the masses must be systematically prepared and educated. "To be sure, the party must stand at the head of the movement, but if it wants to stand at the head it cannot afford just to sit there and wait for the revolutionary situation to arise and then to be dragged along by the masses; it must instead – by shaping the entire tactic and mode of struggle along revolutionary lines – . . . prepare the masses in such a way that they will follow us with full confidence."[108]

If Luxemburg's position on the mass strike remained consistent, Frank's did not. Speaking shortly after Luxemburg had finished, he too delivered a forceful rebuttal to Scheidemann's speech, and with an air of chivalry declared his support of Luxemburg's assertion that the necessary enthusiasm for the mass strike would not come overnight, but required hard work if the masses were to be properly prepared for such action. Turning next to the resolution of the Executive, Frank found it wanting in that it failed to express a strong political will. But when he came to Luxemburg's amendment, Frank surprised his listeners by criticising it for being just as ineffectual and evasive as the resolution presented by the Executive, "and if I want a muted [*gedämpfte*] resolution then I might just as well accept that of the party's Executive". And so he did, for when it came to the vote, Frank joined with the majority in defeating Luxemburg's amendment.[109] The question is, why did he do so? What caused this reversal? Had he been sincere when he said that he found Luxemburg's formulation of the amendment unsatisfactory and therefore would not support it, or had he sensed that the mood of the delegates clearly indicated that a majority favoured the Executive's resolution, and he wanted to be with the stronger battalions?[110] As Frank did not explain his switch, we shall never know. His move is the more surprising in that he had ended his speech with an unequivocal reaffirmation of his original stand on the mass strike. Demanding strongly that the congress must make its collective position clear and leave no doubts, he had closed with the words: "We must stay firm [*es bleibt dabei*], there will be either an electoral reform in Prussia, or a mass strike. That must remain

---

[107]*PT 1913.*, pp. 228–235. Scheidemann had delivered his criticism during his presentation of the "Report of the Executive" (*Vorstandsbericht*).

[108]*Ibid.*, p. 293; the entire speech pp. 288–293.

[109]*Ibid.*, pp. 304–306, 337. Among the Jewish delegates present, the following voted for Luxemburg's amendment (*Antrag* No. 100; *PT 1913*, pp. 194–195): (Adolf) Braun, Cohen-Reuss, Cohn, Herzfeld, Hoch, Katzenstein, (Paul) Levi, Luxemburg, (Kurt) Rosenfeld, (Max) Süssheim and Stadthagen. Against the amendment voted, besides Frank: Bernstein, Davidsohn, Gradnauer, (Ernst) Heilmann, (Berthold) Heymann, Weill and Wurm. Here, too, the lines were by no means defined as yet. Of those who supported Luxemburg's amendment, Braun, Cohen-Reuss, Hoch, Katzenstein and Süssheim remained in the SPD when the party split in 1916. Of those who opposed her amendment, Bernstein and Wurm were to join the secessionists.

[110]This motive was suggested by Georg Ledebour who spoke right after Frank. *PT 1913*, pp. 306–307.

the watchword."[111] Thus he did not retreat from his original position – except when it came to the vote. Yet the vote was decisive, because for all practical purposes it eliminated the mass strike as a viable alternative. Like most politicians Frank, when faced by an unpalatable choice, could be as inconsistent as the next one.

IV

It would be tempting to pursue the story in some detail up to the outbreak of the war, but limited space will only permit a brief sketch.

One of the most important questions which the Social Democrats faced during the period was the preservation of peace. Here again, Jews were in the forefront – Bernstein, Haase, Frank and, in her own inimitable way, also Rosa Luxemburg.[112] It was Frank who in March 1913 took the initiative for convening a conference of German and French parliamentarians, socialists and liberal middle-class delegates, who met in Berne to discuss ways and means for achieving better relations between the two countries. Four of the twenty-five Social Democratic members who attended the conference, which met on 11th May, were Jews – Frank, Haase, Weill and Bernstein.[113] The Berne meeting ended on a note of harmony. A general resolution was adopted which proclaimed the desire of all participants to work towards "clearing up and preventing misunderstandings" between the two nations, and an interparliamentary commission was created with the express purpose of fostering closer relations between France and Germany. It was designed to follow up the work of the conference.[114] Both Frank and Haase were designated permanent members of the commission.[115]

Another joint conference, though restricted to members of the permanent commission, met at Basle in May 1914. There it was agreed to continue with a programme of holding joint conferences in an effort to work for peace.[116] Luxemburg was sceptical as to the efficacy of the conferences and severely criticised the bourgeois delegates who had attended the Berne conference for having subsequently voted in both countries for the respective military bills.[117]

[111]This motive was suggested by Georg Ledebour who spoke right after Frank. *PT 1916*, p. 306.

[112]On the roles which Bernstein, Haase and Luxemburg played – the author omits Frank altogether – see Georges Haupt, *Socialism and the Great War. The Collapse of the Second International*, rev. edn., Oxford 1973, *passim*. For Luxemburg's views on imperialism and its implications and consequences, Schorske, *op. cit.*, pp. 243–245.

[113]Haupt, *op. cit.*, pp. 118–119; Roger Chickering, *Imperial Germany and a World without War. The Peace Movement and German Society, 1892–1914*, Princeton 1975, pp. 281–282; Wachenheim, *Frank*, pp. 254–256, 264–267; Matthias and Pikart, *op. cit.*, I, p. 292; *PT 1913*, pp. 7, 370; Philipp Scheidemann, *Memoiren eines Sozialdemokraten*, two volumes, Dresden 1928, I, pp. 227–230; *Haase, op. cit.*, p. 23. All accounts differ on the total number of German Social Democrats who attended. It might be pointed out, in addition, that among the six Progressive *Reichstag* delegates who attended the Berne Conference was one Jew, Ludwig Haas.

[114]Haupt, *op. cit.*, p. 118.

[115]Wachenheim, *Frank*, p. 251.

[116]*Ibid.*, pp. 334–335; Chickering, *op. cit.*, p. 283.

[117]*Luxemburg, G. W.*, III, p. 444.

As far as she was concerned, the Basle conference was equally disappointing in its result, and she referred to it as an "improvisation of parliamentarianism".[118]

During the winter months 1913/1914, when the empire was rocked by the Zabern incident,[119] both Luxemburg and Frank resumed their attacks on German militarism, Luxemburg in two scathing articles, Frank in an impressive speech which he delivered on 23rd January 1914 in the *Reichstag*.[120] In these instances, both reflected the position of the party as a whole. Luxemburg continued her fight against German militarism in the spring of 1914 and up to the outbreak of war. She had stated earlier, in September 1913 when she had addressed another meeting, that "if they think we are going to lift the weapons of murder against our French and other brethren, then we shall shout: 'We will not do it.' "[121] This remark led to a trial, and on 20th February 1914 she was sentenced to one year in prison. But as the appeal procedure took months, she was freed on bail and used the opportunity to carry her campaign to the masses in a series of speaking engagements throughout the country. During these speaking engagements she was accompanied by her two (Jewish) defence counsels, Paul Levi and Kurt Rosenfeld,[122] who defended her again in a second

---

[118]*Ibid.*, p. 460 (the entire article pp. 460–463).

[119]The best treatment of the Zabern incident so far is Hans-Ulrich Wehler, 'Symbol des halb-absolutistischen Herrschaftssystems: Der Fall Zabern von 1913/14 als eine Verfassungskrise des Wilhelminischen Kaiserreichs', in *Krisenherde des Kaiserreichs 1871–1918. Studien zur deutschen Sozial- und Verfassungsgeschichte*, Göttingen 1970, pp. 65–83; all contributions in this book are by Wehler.

[120]*Luxemburg, G. W.*, III, pp. 367–371, 385–388; *Reichstag. Sten. Ber.*, vol. 292, 198th Sess. (23rd January 1914), pp. 6730–6740. See also Vietsch, *op. cit.*, p. 172 and Domann, *op. cit.*, pp. 181, n. 24, and pp. 183–184.

[121]Nettl, *Rosa Luxemburg*, II, p. 481; see also ff., *passim*, for her subsequent campaigns against German militarism.

[122]Both men were to figure prominently, though for the most part as high-minded mavericks, in working-class politics and as lawyers after the war. Levi was from March 1919 until his expulsion from the KPD in the spring of 1921 chairman of the German Communist Party's *Zentrale*. After a brief sojourn in political limbo as the leader of a small group of followers who together with him had been expelled from the KPD in the aftermath of the disastrous March Uprising of 1921, Levi first rejoined the USPD and, after that party merged with the SPD in the autumn of 1922, thereby returned to the party which he had left in 1916 and within which he was to remain an outsider until his tragic and untimely death in 1930. To the end of his life he also continued his legal practice and became best known during the Jorns trial of 1929 when he defended Josef Bornstein, an editor of *Das Tagebuch*, against the plaintiff, the *Reichs-anwalt* Paul Jorns who a decade earlier had "prosecuted" the men then on trial for the murder of Rosa Luxemburg and Karl Liebknecht. Bornstein had charged that Jorns had conducted that trial in such a way as to protect the defendants, and Jorns had sued for libel.

Rosenfeld, like Levi, had left the SPD in 1916, became a member of the USPD when it was founded in April 1917, was during the revolution briefly at the head of the Prussian ministry of justice, rejoined the SPD in the autumn of 1922 and, again like Levi, remained an outsider on the party's left wing. In 1931 he broke again with the SPD to found the *Sozialistische Arbeiterpartei Deutschlands* (SAPD) and became its co-chairman. He, too, continued his legal practice, worked closely with the *Deutsche Liga für Menschenrechte* and, in 1931, defended Carl von Ossietzky, publisher of *Die Weltbühne*, in a celebrated case whereby Ossietzky was tried for treason after his journal had allegedly published "military secrets". On Levi, see Charlotte Beradt, *Paul Levi. Ein demokratischer Sozialist in der Weimarer Republik*, Frankfurt a. Main 1969, and on his Communist phase Werner T. Angress, *Stillborn Revolution. The Communist Bid for Power in Germany*, 1921–1923, Princeton 1963, pp. 38–174, and *passim*. There is as yet no

trial, held in Berlin from 29th June to 3rd July 1914, when she was accused of having besmirched the honour of the German corps of officers and non-commissioned officers in her speeches.[123]

We cannot treat here the complex events of the July crisis in 1914, and the involvement of Jewish Social Democrats in attempts to prevent the impending conflict. Here it was above all Haase who tried, virtually up to the last minute, to forestall the outbreak of hostilities by working closely with the International Socialist Bureau in an attempt to rally the workers of all potential belligerents behind the International's peace efforts.[124] When these efforts failed, Haase faced what was probably the most trying moment in his political career when he, as chairman of his *Fraktion*, had to read in the *Reichstag* on that fateful 4th August 1914 his party's resolution to vote for war credits.[125]

Haase, the disciple of Kant, faced the coming of the war with grave forebodings. Frank, though he did not welcome it, greeted its outbreak with a mixture of resignation and optimism. When he became convinced, by the end of July, that the war which he had tried so hard to prevent was inevitable, he accepted it, though he still delivered a rousing anti-war speech in Mannheim on 29th July. But while he condemned the German government for not having done enough to secure the peace, he indicated in his speech that should hostilities commence, the empire's stepchildren, the Social Democratic workers, would do their part and stand by their fatherland.[126] This remark indicated clearly where Frank would stand once war broke out. During the following days he worked actively and passionately to persuade the *Fraktion* that they must vote for the war credits,[127] thereby confirming how right Luxemburg had been when she had predicted a year earlier that those who had supported the military tax bill would also vote for the war budget once hostilities were about to begin.[128] On 5th August Frank enlisted as a volunteer, and on the 13th joined his unit, the reserve battalion of the 110th Infantry Regiment. Two weeks later he wrote to a friend: "I am happy that I can actively experience all this. The international idea has been set back for a long time to come by the reality of the national

---

biography of Rosenfeld, though a brief sketch of his life is in *Biographisches Lexikon des Sozialismus*, vol. I, *Verstorbene Persönlichkeiten*, ed. Franz Osteroth, Hanover 1960, p. 255. On the SAPD see Hanno Drechsler, *Die Sozialistische Arbeiterpartei Deutschlands (SAPD): Ein Beitrag zur Geschichte der deutschen Arbeiterbewegung am Ende der Weimarer Republik*, Meisenheim am Glan 1965.

[123]Nettl, *Rosa Luxemburg*, II, pp. 484–485. Luxemburg was on trial for having accused the officer and non-commissioned officer corps of mistreating soldiers under their command.

[124]See esp. Haupt, *op. cit.*, pp. 183–265, *passim*, and Susanne Miller, *Burgfrieden und Klassenkampf. Die deutsche Sozialdemokratie im Ersten Weltkrieg*, Düsseldorf 1974 (Beiträge zur Geschichte des Parlamentarismus und der politischen Parteien 53), pp. 37–41, 44–46. Luxemburg, like Haase, also attended the last meeting held prior to the war by the International Socialist Bureau which met at Brussels on 29th and 30th July 1914. She attended as a delegate of the Polish Social Democracy.

[125]Haase, *op. cit.*, pp. 27–29; Miller, *op. cit.*, pp. 51–74, esp. pp. 65–66; Calkins, *op. cit.*, pp. 59–60.

[126]Wachenheim, *Frank*, pp. 348–354, esp. pp. 353–354.

[127]Miller, *op. cit.*, pp. 46–48; Wachenheim, *Frank*, pp. 348, 354 and, by the same author, *Vom Grossbürgertum . . .*, pp. 50–51.

[128]See above, p. 23.

working-class movement. Instead of a general strike we shall fight a war for the Prussian election reform [*Wahlrecht*]."[129] Frank fell in battle on 3rd September 1914, at Noissoncourt, near Baccarat, shot through the head by a French bullet. It was a tragic end for the man who had tried, probably harder than most, to work for peace and cordial relations with France while combating the militarism of both countries.

V

By an ironic twist of history it was in accordance with Kautsky's rather than with Frank's or Luxemburg's political concepts that responsibility of government fell to Social Democracy in November 1918. The revolution, Bebel's *grosser Kladderadatsch*, came indeed like a natural catastrophe, and in the wake of military defeat toppled thrones and swept away a discredited political system without encountering resistance. But it was not the revolution which Rosa Luxemburg had envisaged, and the disappointment she suffered as she watched its course poisoned the few remaining weeks of her life. Nor was it Frank's "Baden" solution, a political alliance of Social Democracy with liberal middle-class parties, which led to the collapse of the empire, although such an alliance had existed since 1917 and was to enjoy a brief, albeit brittle, revival during the post-war years. And yet, their respective efforts during the last years of peace in guiding the party's course, trying to head it into the direction each of them conceived as the correct road to a new and better society, constituted a unique phase in the history of the SPD.

To be sure, Jewish socialists of both the SPD and USPD as well as Luxemburg's Spartacus League – soon to be transformed into the German Communist Party (KPD) – participated actively in the revolution, some of them in unprecedented governmental posts. Yet it was a brief and passing episode.[130] By the autumn of 1919, most Jews had already withdrawn from the prominent positions they had held so briefly. And while some of them occupied temporarily leading positions in the young Communist Party and the short-lived USPD, neither of which represented the bulk of German labour, those who joined the KPD were either murdered, like Rosa Luxemburg and Leo Jogiches, or were eventually expelled as the party under the growing pressure from Moscow became subject to Bolshevisation, a trend which led by the mid-twenties to the virtual elimination of most Jewish functionaries from the KPD.[131] The USPD,

[129]Wachenheim, *Frank*, p. 158.

[130]Werner T. Angress, 'Juden im politischen Leben der Revolutionszeit', in *Deutsches Judentum in Krieg und Revolution 1916–1923*. Ein Sammelband herausgegeben von Werner E. Mosse unter Mitwirkung von Arnold Paucker, Tübingen 1971 (Schriftenreihe wissenschaftlicher Abhandlungen des Leo Baeck Instituts 25), pp. 137–315.

[131]On the Bolshevisation of the KPD – a process in which initially a number of Jewish functionaries participated – see Hermann Weber, *Die Wandlung des deutschen Kommunismus. Die Stalinisierung der KPD in der Weimarer Republik*, two volumes, Frankfurt a. Main 1969, I, esp., pp. 53–238, and the biographical sketches of individual functionaries, *ibid.*, II, pp. 58–353, *passim*.

after Haase's assassination in 1919, saw likewise a decline of Jewish leaders, and those who ultimately rejoined the SPD remained for the most part isolated and in fruitless opposition. For the SPD which emerged from the war and revolution was no longer the same party it had been prior to 1914. It had lost most of its left-wing followers, and the few who remained or rejoined it in 1922 were alienated by the party's mounting bureaucratisation, inflexibility and "respectability".[132] Although Jews had still a place in such a party, theirs was no longer the role of challenging intellectuals and initiators, but that of solid functionaries harnessed to the party's bureaucratic routine. Men like Levi, Rosenfeld and Oskar Cohn, more impatient and idealistic than the average run of party leaders during the Weimar Republic, found themselves on the fringes of the SPD, crying in the wilderness. Nor was the prevailing antisemitic climate of the Weimar Republic conducive to prompt Jews into the foreground, be it in exposed positions of government or within the party.[133] Finally, the SPD no longer depended on the services of Jewish intellectuals to the same extent that it had done before the war, for the party was no longer an outcast, was on and off represented in the government of the *Reich* (and until 1932 of Prussia), and could dispense with the array of Jewish lawyers and publicists who in the past had at times been resented as troublesome, albeit indispensable, gadflies. For better or for worse, the heyday of Jewish influence within the SPD was over after the Guns of August had begun to speak. And although Jews within the party continued to figure in a variety of important functions until 1933, they never again played so eminent, and often decisive, a role in party affairs as they had done prior to August 1914 when its two major wings – Baden and Luxemburg – had challenged the majority of the SPD to choose between alternative tactical approaches to politics.

[132]On the post-war SPD and its various weaknesses see esp. Richard N. Hunt, *German Social Democracy 1918–1933*, New Haven and London 1964 (Yale Historical Publications, Miscellany 79).

[133]On this and related problems see Donald L. Niewyk, *Socialist, Anti-Semite and Jew. German Social Democracy Confronts the Problem of Anti-Semitism, 1918–1933*, Baton Rouge 1971; Hans-Helmuth Knütter, *Die Juden und die deutsche Linke in der Weimarer Republik*, Düsseldorf 1971 (Bonner Schriften zur Politik und Zeitgeschichte 4), esp. pp. 153–224; and the contributions by Werner E. Mosse, E. G. Lowenthal, Hans-Helmuth Knütter and Arnold Paucker in *Entscheidungsjahr 1932. Zur Judenfrage in der Endphase der Weimarer Republik*. Ein Sammelband, herausgegeben von Werner E. Mosse unter Mitwirkung von Arnold Paucker (Schriftenreihe wissenschaftlicher Abhandlungen des Leo Baeck Instituts 13), all *passim*.

Anti-Capitalism or Antisemitism?
The Case of Franz Mehring

BY ROBERT S. WISTRICH

The Marxist labour movement in Wilhelminian Germany viewed the Jewish question as an inseparable aspect of the crisis of modern bourgeois society. It also recognised that Jewish emancipation had been brought about by capitalism but considered that the process could only be completed in a new, classless society. By the end of the 1870s it was already evident that economic liberalism was on the defensive in Germany and one of the symptoms of its fading hegemony was the deflection of social tensions against the Jewish minority.[1] Discontented groups in German society who opposed the liberal status quo now began to focus their offensive against the Jews who were depicted as a domineering and privileged clique. This led to the formation of a number of antisemitic political parties which achieved temporary electoral successes in the early 1890s, only to subside again in the first decade of the twentieth century.[2]

It has long been considered that the Social Democrats proved more resistant than any other political party to the impact of antisemitism in Wilhelminian Germany.[3] The evidence for and against this assumption has been documented elsewhere and it is not intended here to challenge its general validity.[4] However, a detailed examination of the relevant literature, especially during the 1890s, reveals that the German labour movement adopted a more equivocal attitude towards the Jewish question than is widely believed. A case-study of one of the leading publicists of the labour movement, the revolutionary socialist and historian Franz Mehring, is particularly illuminating in this respect. No other German socialist wrote so extensively on the Jewish question in this period. Hence an examination of Mehring's writings on this topic can tell us a great

---

[1]Reinhard Rürup, 'Emanzipation und Krise. Zur Geschichte der "Judenfrage" in Deutschland vor 1890', in *Juden im Wilhelminischen Deutschland 1890–1914*. Ein Sammelband herausgegeben von Werner E. Mosse unter Mitwirkung von Arnold Paucker, Tübingen 1976 (Schriftenreihe wissentschaftlicher Abhandlungen des Leo Baeck Instituts 33), pp. 1–56; Hans Rosenberg, *Grosse Depression und Bismarckzeit*, Berlin 1967, pp. 88–117.

[2]See Richard S. Levy, *The Downfall of the Anti-Semitic Political Parties in Imperial Germany*, New Haven–London 1975, for the most recent account.

[3]See for example Robert Michels, *Political Parties*, New York 1959, p. 262, 2nd English edn. translated by Eden and Cedar Paul (the first German edition, a sociological classic, appeared in 1913). Michels claimed that "the consciousness of all that the party owes to Jewish intellectuals" was as important in its resistance to antisemitism as any "theoretical socialist aversion for 'nationalism' and racial prejudices". Eduard Bernstein, writing in a Dutch socialist periodical, was more emphatic. "In the German Social Democratic Party an outspoken antisemite is an impossibility. One can find some anti-Jewish sentiment here and there in the party or the socialist trade unions but this does not influence the distribution of positions or privileges." See Eduard Bernstein, 'De Joden in De Duitsche Sociaal-Demokratie', *De Socialistische Gids*, No. XI, November 1921 (Jg. VI), p. 984.

[4]For a detailed discussion of this whole problem, see Robert S. Wistrich, *Socialism and the Jewish Question in Germany and Austria 1880–1914*, University of London, Ph.D diss. 1974.

deal about the tactical and ideological dilemmas which confronted the labour movement with the rise of *völkisch* antisemitism in the 1890s. More than any of his contemporaries in the German labour movement, Mehring exhibited attitudes which illustrate the difficulty in clearly demarcating the Marxist from the antisemitic critique of liberal capitalism.

Franz Mehring was born into a middle-class Pomeranian family in 1846. Nothing in his early journalistic career suggested that seventy years later he would, together with Rosa Luxemburg and Karl Liebknecht, become one of the co-founders of the German Communist Party. His road to Marxism followed a long and painful detour which necessitated a sharp break with his class, culture and family background. Along with Engels, Kautsky and Wilhelm Liebknecht, Mehring was one of the few Gentiles in nineteenth-century German society ready to abandon bourgeois comforts and status and devote himself wholeheartedly to the cause of the working class. Mehring combined a rebellious and artistic temperament with a chivalrous sympathy for the oppressed masses. More than any other German socialist he sought to transmit the heritage of German classical philosophy, poetry and drama to the proletariat. In the words of Rosa Luxemburg, who hailed him on his seventieth birthday as ". . . der Vertreter der echten geistigen Kultur in all ihrem Glanz und Schimmer", Mehring had taught the German workers "through every line from your wonderful pen, that Socialism is not merely a knife and fork question, but a civilising movement, a great and proud Weltanschauung".[5]

Nevertheless, Mehring did not finally commit himself to the labour movement until 1890, when at the age of forty-four he became the Berlin correspondent of the Marxist review, *Die Neue Zeit*. By this time his views on the Jewish question had already crystallised. If, therefore, his writings after 1890 clearly reflect the ideological bias of historical materialism they also express pre-Marxist attitudes which had taken shape at least a decade earlier.

Franz Mehring had first encountered the Jewish question in Berlin at the end of the 1870s when as an independent young journalist in his early thirties he witnessed at first hand the rise of a new literary antisemitism. The embittered social climate which gave rise to this trend also produced a temporary convergence of conservative and radical critiques of the dominant liberal–capitalist order. Conservative publicists like Rudolf Meyer and Hermann Wagener as well as *Kathedersozialisten* such as Gustav Schmoller, Lujo Brentano and Adolph Wagner sharply attacked the laissez-faire ethos of German liberalism.[6] Christian "socialists" like Rudolf Todt and Adolf Stoecker joined in this assault from the Right, while espousing the principles of a Prussian monarchical socialism. On the Left, socialists like Eugen Dühring and the neo-Lassalleans led by Wilhelm

---

[5]Quoted from Rudolf Lindau, *Franz Mehring zu seinem 100. Geburtstag am 27. Februar*, Berlin (Ost) 1946, p. 11. See also Clara Zetkin, *Rosa Luxemburg. Karl Liebknecht. Franz Mehring. Den Führern des Spartakusbundes und Gründern der Kommunistischen Partei Deutschlands*, Moskau–Leningrad 1934, p. 64.

[6]See in particular Rudolf Meyer, *Politische Gründer und die Korruption in Deutschland*, Leipzig 1877, a work which Mehring much admired. Also Fritz Stern, 'Money, Morals and the Pillars of Bismarck's Society', *Central European Affairs*, III (1970), pp. 49–72.

Hasselmann were no less severe in their critique of "Manchesterism".[7] Not all the opponents of free-trade liberalism were antisemites. But the prominence of Jewish names among the entrepreneurs, stockbrokers and money-changers implicated in the *Gründungsschwindel* of the early 1870s, inevitably led to unfavourable comment. Petty-bourgeois pamphleteers of radical tendencies like Otto Glagau and Wilhelm Marr made Jewish participation in the swindles the starting-point of an antisemitic indictment of the new Bismarckian *Reich*.[8] They presented their campaign as an *Abwehrkampf* to defend the interests of the "little man" against the domination of a Jewish financial clique which had succeeded in gaining control of German society.

Mehring who had become personally embroiled in 1876 with the proprietor of the liberal *Frankfurter Zeitung*, Leopold Sonnemann, himself of Jewish origin, was undoubtedly influenced by this current of anti-capitalist antisemitism. It had even infiltrated into the German labour movement where the Lassalleans openly attacked the "Marxist" Eisenachers as *Judenknechte* for their alliance with Sonnemann and other liberal democrats.[9] Mehring shared the antipathy of the Lassalleans towards "Jewish liberalism" and specifically accused Sonnemann of having accepted bribes and of involvement in the feverish speculation of the *Gründerjahre*. His accusations were not supported by the Social Democratic leaders, Bebel and Liebknecht, which led to a rift between the young Mehring and the labour movement that took fifteen years to heal. Much of the suspicion and distrust of labour leaders towards Mehring relates back to this period. Equally it is in the Sonnemann Affair that one can find the origins of Mehring's intransigent hostility to what he scathingly called the "Frankfurt stock-exchange democracy".[10]

The anti-Jewish strand in Mehring's writings was not unconnected with his early Lassallean sympathies and with his hatred for what he regarded as the cringing servility, philistinism and cowardice of the German bourgeoisie. Though he did not share the admiration of the Lassalleans for Bismarck's *Realpolitik* he echoed their contempt for the middle classes and for Jews. Indeed his favourable treatment as a historian of the Lassallean contribution to German Social Democracy remains a feature of Mehring's writing that is invariably subjected to criticism in contemporary communist historiography.[11] Nevertheless, this has not prevented him from being widely cited in East German, Polish

---

[7]See Franz Mehring, *Geschichte der deutschen Sozialdemokratie*, Stuttgart–Berlin 1921, 2nd edn., Bd. III, pp. 14, 70, 86. Also Eduard Bernstein, *Sozialdemokratische Lehrjahre*, Berlin 1928, p. 26.

[8]Otto Glagau, *Der Börsen und Gründungsschwindel in Berlin*, Leipzig 1876.

[9]See Bernstein, *Sozialdemokratische Lehrjahre, op. cit.*, p. 26.

[10]Thomas Höhle, *Franz Mehring. Sein Weg zum Marxismus 1869–91*, Berlin (Ost) 1956, pp. 109, 113, 119. Also Franz Mehring, 'Über Geschäfts- und Prinzipblätter', *Die Neue Zeit* (1892–1893), Bd. 1, pp. 329 ff., where he wrote that the Frankfurt *Börsendemokratie* was among "the most effective levers of antisemitism".

[11]See the standard biographies by Höhle, *op. cit.*, and Josef Schleifstein, *Franz Mehring. Sein Marxistisches Schaffen 1891–1919*, Berlin (Ost) 1959, which faithfully reflect the communist standpoint. Also Walter Kampmann, 'Franz Mehring als Vertreter des Historischen Materialismus', *Veröffentlichungen des Osteuropa-Institutes*, München 1966, Bd. XXIX, pp. 150–152 especially.

and Soviet literature as an exemplary exponent of historical materialism.[12] Needless to say, this same literature does not discuss the ambivalence in Mehring's position on the Jewish question.

This ambivalence was already apparent in 1881, a decade before he had become the guardian of philosophical and historical materialism. Writing in the *Weser-Zeitung*, Mehring blamed the anti-Jewish riots in his native Pomerania on the philosemitic *Hetze* (sic) of the liberal press in Berlin.[13] By its mania for denunciation and its desire to stifle any criticism of Jews, it had allegedly provoked an antisemitic climate of opinion. The most insignificant street-brawl or casual remark was inflated into a threat against the established order. Mehring not only considered that the Berlin press was dominated by Jewish interests but that its intolerance and paranoia was a major factor in provoking the anti-Jewish backlash.

In a pamphlet, published in 1882, he claimed that the situation in the Eastern provinces of Germany had been blown up out of all proportion.

> "As for the antisemitic riots, it so happens I was visiting my Pomerania home when they took place. I looked into the matter carefully and can only say that the reporting of them was in part wholly fabricated, and that in more than one small town, the trouble started solely because of the fuss made over the affair."[14]

Mehring may well have been correct about this but he was too shrewd an observer not to realise that the *Judenfrage* in Germany was created and manipulated by powerful interest-groups as well as enjoying a broad-based popular support. In 1882 he devoted twelve pages to this theme as part of a hard-hitting tract for the times directed against the Christian-Social leader Adolf Stoecker.[15] Mehring made a clear distinction between the inflammatory exploitation of racial and religious prejudice by ambitious agitators like Stoecker and the seemingly calm, dispassionate analysis of the Jewish question by historians like Heinrich von Treitschke.

What was unacceptable in Stoecker's approach was his open appeal to the passions of the mob, his deliberate *Entfesselung der Bestie* which could only exacerbate a complex problem. When the Protestant Court-preacher declared that modern Jewry was "... ein Volk im Volke, ein Staat im Staate, ein Stamm für sich unter einer fremden Rasse",[16] it was clear to his lower-middle-class audience that Stoecker was questioning the premises of Jewish emancipation. Their enthusiasm was not a response to Stoecker's theological interpretation of the *Judenfrage* as a "socio-ethical problem" but to his unleashing of what Mehring called "the three most potent sources of hatred known in history: a

[12]For the most recent assessments see Annelies Laschitza, 'Franz Mehring. Ein Lehrmeister der marxistischen Biographie', and Hans Jürgen Friederici, 'Historiker, Journalist, Revolutionär. Franz Mehring', in *Beiträge zur Geschichte der Arbeiterbewegung*, I (1976), Jg. 18, pp. 58–69 and pp. 120–129.

[13]Significantly, Mehring's watchword at this time was "Weder Judenhetze, noch Judenherrschaft". See Franz Mehring, *Kapital und Presse. Ein Nachspiel zum Falle Lindau*, Berlin 1891, pp. 83–84.

[14]Franz Mehring, *Herr Hofprediger Stöcker der Socialpolitiker. Eine Streitschrift*, Bremen 1882, p. 67.

[15]*Ibid.*, pp. 64–76.

[16]Adolf Stöcker, *Christlich-Sozial. Reden und Aufsätze*, Bielefeld–Leipzig 1885, p. 151.

religious, a racial, and a class conflict".[17] What Mehring found so "unspeakably depressing" in this demagogic approach was the long-term consequences which it might have on the Jewish minority and on German society as a whole. The Jewish question was already peculiarly difficult in Germany because as Mehring put it "the fusion of the Germanic and Semitic elements has not yet proceeded far enough and at the same time too far";[18] the fanaticism of a Stoecker could therefore only act as a further obstacle to the integration of the Jews in German society. With considerable sensitivity and insight, Mehring glimpsed into the abyss and saw perhaps further than he knew. "No man of feeling", he wrote, "can think without the deepest pangs of those many honourable and high-minded fellow citizens who, hurt to the quick, must become obsessed by the devilish thought that their life and work among the German people, the best and deepest part of their earthly existence, is after all nothing but a snare and a delusion."[19]

This was the only occasion on which Mehring took into account the impact of German antisemitism on the Jews themselves. Moreover his harsh judgment on Stoecker in 1882 was to change drastically a decade later, when he depicted the *Hofprediger* as more akin to a "second Luther" who had lacked "the revolutionary period in his life", than to a miserable demagogue.[20] But even in 1882 it was evident that Mehring's critical assessment of Stoecker's Berlin movement was not based on any real sympathy for German Jewry. This is clear from his complete identification with Treitschke's strictures against Jewish behaviour, which he still considered as the main cause for the emergence of German antisemitism.[21] Like the Berlin Professor of History, Mehring felt strongly about what he called the "alien, unpleasant, or at least unaccustomed features of the Jewish character" which had become painfully evident to the majority of Berliners in the 1870s. The *Judenfrage* was largely a consequence of "Jewish vulgarities and ill-manners"; the tactless and ignorant criticism of the Christian churches by the "Jewish" press during the *Kulturkampf*; and the stock-market swindles of the *Gründerzeit* brought about by the "more mischievous elements of Berlin Jewry". Each day, Mehring concluded, "produced new evidence of that strange lack of *verecundia* which Schopenhauer rightly or wrongly attributes to the Jewish people".[22]

These were extremely severe criticisms which, like those of Treitschke, tended to shift the responsibility for antisemitism back to the Jews. Even as a Marxist

[17]Franz Mehring, *Herr Hofprediger Stöcker . . .*, *op. cit.*, p. 69.
[18]*Ibid.*
[19]*Ibid.*, pp. 75–76.
[20]Franz Mehring, 'Das Ende eines Demagogen', *Die Neue Zeit*, (1892–1893), Bd. II, p. 545.
[21]On the controversy over Treitschke and the Jewish reactions, see Hans Liebeschütz, 'Treitschke and Mommsen on Jewry and Judaism', in *LBI Year Book VII* (1962), pp. 153–182; Wanda Kampmann, *Deutsche und Juden*, Heidelberg 1963, pp. 265–279; Michael A. Meyer, 'Great Debate on Antisemitism. Jewish Reactions to New Hostility in Germany 1879–1881', in *LBI Year Book XI* (1966), pp. 137–170; Hans Liebeschütz, *Das Judentum im deutschen Geschichtsbild von Hegel bis Max Weber*, Tübingen 1967 (Schriftenreihe wissenschaftlicher Abhandlungen des Leo Baeck Instituts 17), pp. 212–219; and Ismar Schorsch, *Jewish Reactions to German Anti-Semitism 1870–1914*, New York–London 1972.
[22]Franz Mehring, *Herr Hofprediger Stöcker . . .*, *op. cit.*, pp. 64–65.

historian, Mehring many years later made it clear that he regarded the anti-semitism of the late 1870s as a natural reaction to the parvenu tactlessness of *Das Geldjudentum*: ". . . monied Jewry had given itself airs which inevitably made it a centre of unpleasant attention; Judaisation of public life (*die Vermauschelung des öffentlichen Lebens*), especially in Berlin, had reached proportions such as to make the most uninhibited enthusiasts of Nathan the Wise uncomfortable."[23] In his pre-Marxist phase Mehring did not ignore the historical forces which had contributed to exacerbating the Jewish question in German society. For centuries the Jews, through no fault of their own, had been forced "into an unnaturally narrow channel" which had bottled up their energies. As members of a "gifted, shrewd, tenacious race", they had inundated German society once the artificially constructed dykes had been removed. But the tone of this analysis, behind the mask of objectivity, was sharply disapproving.

Hence it is not surprising to find that Mehring like Treitschke strongly attacked the German liberals for ignoring the "historical fact of Judaism" and the negative effects of Jewish emancipation. At the same time he was openly contemptuous of those critics who accused Treitschke of antisemitism when he had simply ventilated the "deep animosity against the Jewish character" felt in all cultivated circles of Berlin society.[24] The aim of the liberals was to suppress free speech when it came to the Jewish question. For Mehring this was a "wretched attempt at intellectual terrorism" designed to procure for the Jews an unjustified immunity from criticism. "It is an ironic fact that one may publicly speak and write about God and the world, about Church and State, about everything between heaven and earth – except the contemporary effects of Jewish emancipation, or rather its bad effects. For enthusiastic praise of its good effects is considered the highest flower of 'liberalism' in certain circles. Some of these people seem to believe in good faith that, once Jewish civil emancipation has been written into our laws, the historical concept and the historical fact of Judaism had thereby ceased to exist and that it would be a grave mistake to revive them."[25]

What Mehring most admired in Treitschke's exposition was the fact that he had broken through the curtain of silence and made explicit what lay dormant in the hearts of most educated Germans. This was his "great and unforgettable service" performed with "courage", "manly frankness" and "scientific seriousness" according to Mehring. This verdict altogether ignored the fact that Treitschke, no less than Stoecker, had unmistakably branded the Jews as an "alien" element in the Christian-Germanic State.[26] It passed over the even more

[23]Franz Mehring, *Geschichte der deutschen Sozialdemokratie*, Stuttgart 1913, Bd. IV, p. 96.

[24]See *Der Berliner Antisemitismusstreit*. Herausgegeben von Walter Boehlich, Frankfurt a. Main 1965, which includes Treitschke's original articles in the *Preussische Jahrbücher* (November/December 1879, January and December 1880, January 1881) and replies by Heinrich Graetz, Harry Breßlau, Hermann Cohen, Ludwig Bamberger and Theodor Mommsen.

[25]Franz Mehring, *Herr Hofprediger Stöcker . . .*, *op. cit.*, p. 66.

[26]See especially Heinrich von Treitschke, 'Unsere Aussichten', *Preussische Jahrbücher*, November 1879, reproduced in Boehlich (ed.), *op. cit.*, p. 11, where he calls the antisemitic agitation a natural reaction ". . . des germanischen Volksgefühls gegen ein fremdes Element, das in unserem Leben einen allzu breiten Raum eingenommen hat."

disturbing implication that antisemitism had for the first time in Germany received the halo of academic respectability, when the most prestigious of Prussian historians could publicly declare that "the Jews are our misfortune". Among the younger generation of the educated middle classes (to which Mehring himself belonged) Treitschke's "scientific" approach inevitably had a far greater appeal than the noisy agitation of a Stoecker or the hysterical Judeophobia of Marr and Dühring. Moreover, Treitschke was no racialist in spite of his obsession with the homogeneity of the German nation, its political unity and strength. As a nationalist he demanded that the Jews totally surrender their historic identity and group cohesion in order to become completely absorbed by the Gentile majority. Although Mehring did not share Treitschke's views on other issues (e.g., his antipathy to materialism, atheism and enlightenment) he approved of this extreme assimilationist position.[27] Hence, only those critics of Treitschke such as Hermann Cohen (described by Mehring as a serious, "high-minded" and patriotic Jew) who sought a complete integration of the Jewish minority into German society, were given a respectful hearing.[28] The remainder were accused of "disgusting vilification" and intolerance of any criticism that threatened their privileges.

Already in 1882 it was characteristic of Mehring that he distinguished sharply between assimilated Jewish writers, scholars and revolutionaries and the Jewish community as a whole. To the former he was often bound by ties of friendship and mutual esteem. The latter he identified with *Judentum*, exploiting in a fashion reminiscent of the young Marx, its dual connotation of Judaism and commerce. In his pamphlet against Stoecker, he had suggested that Jewry emerged as a conquering force in German society, thanks to its money-power, "the mightiest weapon of your time". Increasingly, Mehring came to equate *Judentum* not only with unsavoury swindling, or unscrupulous stock-exchange dealing but with the material and intellectual pretentiousness of the *nouveaux riches* in German society. Through the use of this term Mehring could express his aristocratic aversion to the vulgarity and philistinism of the German bourgeoisie which had adopted the mercenary values of "monied Jews".

The second feature of Mehring's antipathy to Judaism was his preoccupation with the quality of modern journalism and his resentment at its subordination to purely commercial criteria. Mehring was not a *Sprachmystiker* like Karl Kraus in Vienna, but he was equally concerned with the corruption of the Press by business interests and its responsibility for the "cretinisation of the masses".[29]

---

[27] For Mehring's socialist appraisal of the great Prussian historian, see 'Heinrich von Treitschke', *Die Neue Zeit* (1896), Bd. II (Jg. XIV), pp. 193 ff.

[28] Hermann Cohen, *Ein Bekenntnis in der Judenfrage*, Berlin 1880, is reproduced in Boehlich (ed.), *op. cit.*, pp. 124–179. For a discussion of Cohen, see Uriel Tal, *Christians and Jews in the 'Second Reich'* (1870–1914), Jerusalem 1969, pp. 33–36, 141–148. This Hebrew edition has now been translated into English by Noah Jonathan Jacobs as *Christians and Jews in Germany. Religion, Politics, and Ideology in the Second Reich, 1870–1914*, London 1975.

[29] See Franz Mehring, *Kapital und Presse . . .*, *op. cit.* On Karl Kraus, see Wilma Abbeles Iggers, *Karl Kraus. A Viennese Critic of the Twentieth Century*, The Hague 1967; and Robert S. Wistrich, 'Karl Kraus: Jewish Prophet or Renegade?', *European Judaism*, vol. 9, No. 2 (Summer 1975), pp. 32–38.

It was not for nothing that Mehring greatly respected Maximilian Harden, the Jewish-born editor of the *Zukunft*, a self-appointed "Censor Germaniae" who conducted a relentless guerilla war against the modern press.[30] At the same time it was probably significant that Harden, like Kraus, was an antisemitic Jew who sharply attacked the influence of his co-religionists in the Press while indulging in the aesthetic idolisation of such radiant Germanic figures as Bismarck.[31] Their masochistic self-hatred notwithstanding, satirists like Harden were infinitely wittier and more penetrating in their criticism than the antisemites who blamed all the evils of modern urban culture on the *Judenpresse*. Mehring was obviously closer in spirit and sophistication to a Harden than to the obscene ravings of the nationalist gutter-press. But bitter experiences with influential Jewish personalities in the newspaper world were scarcely guaranteed to transform him into a philosemite. In 1886 he was removed from his post as editor of the *Berliner Volkszeitung* as a result of intervention by a Jewish millionaire and co-proprietor of the rival *Berliner Tageblatt*, Emil Cohn. Mehring's protest against the application of the anti-socialist laws (which landed him in difficulties with the authorities and threatened the continuation of the newspaper) was one factor leading to his resignation. A second was his vendetta against Paul Lindau, an extremely influential Jewish theatre critic whose unscrupulous behaviour towards an actress he had ruined aroused Mehring's anger.[32]

Mehring not only detested individuals like Sonnemann, Cohn or Lindau – he regarded the role played by Jewish press-magnates such as Rudolf Mosse and his chief editor on the *Berliner Tageblatt*, Artur Levysohn, as socially harmful. In his eyes their influence indicated to what extent the popular press had become an appendage of commercial advertising, financial interests and "stock-exchange democracy".[33] In this respect, Mehring's attitudes were virtually indistinguishable from the refined antisemitism associated with a whole trend of conservative cultural criticism. Mehring's sophisticated intellectual tastes did not make his transition from the bourgeois to the proletarian camp any easier. Nor were his harsh earlier criticisms of the labour movement readily forgotten.[34] For many of his new comrades, Mehring was not only an outsider, a *Heimatloser*, but a "psychological riddle", whose hypersensitivity and capacity for irrational feuds made close personal contact difficult. In a letter to Engels in March 1892, the German party leader August Bebel touched on

---

[30]Mehring played for a time with the idea of regular collaboration with Harden. See Ursula Ratz, 'Aus Franz Mehrings marxistischer Frühzeit' (Ein Briefwechsel Franz Mehrings mit Lujo Brentano 1891–93), *Internationale Wissenschaftliche Korrespondenz zur Geschichte der deutschen Arbeiterbewegung*, No. 19/20 (December 1973), p. 40.

[31]Erich Gottgetreu, 'Maximilian Harden: Ways and Errors of a Publicist', in *LBI Year Book VII* (1962), pp. 205–246.

[32]Franz Mehring, *Kapital und Presse . . .*, *op. cit.*

[33]On these points see the articles by Ernst Kahn, 'The Frankfurter Zeitung', in *LBI Year Book II* (1957), pp. 228–235; and Werner E. Mosse, 'Rudolf Mosse and the House of Mosse 1867–1920', in *LBI Year Book IV* (1959), pp. 237–259, which provide a valuable corrective to this simplistic view.

[34]See Karl Kautsky, 'Franz Mehring', *Die Neue Zeit* (1903–1904), Bd. I, pp. 103 ff.

some of those traits which made Mehring an isolated figure in the labour movement: [35]

> "Mehrings Arbeiten sind allerdings ausgezeichnet, aber trotzdem lässt sich kein intimeres Verhältnis mit ihm herstellen; man befürchtet immer wieder, er bekäme einen Rückfall; und ausserdem muss man sich fürchten, mit ihm sich vertraulicher einzulassen, weil der Verdacht besteht, er notierte alles, was er hört. Das sind fatale Eigenschaften, die seine Person nicht zur Geltung kommen lassen."[36]

Nevertheless, his polemical talents were so highly regarded by Karl Kautsky, editor of the *Neue Zeit*, that he was almost immediately appointed its Berlin correspondent in 1891. This gave him an excellent vantage-point from which to report on the mushrooming antisemitic movement in Wilhelminian Germany. No other contributor to the review was to make the *Judenfrage* so frequently his starting-point for a general critique of capitalism. None so consistently took the essay of the young Marx (written in 1844) on the same theme, as his model and inspiration.[37]

Mehring's admiration for this essay is certainly one touchstone in attempting to assess the anti-Jewish element in his writings. Marx's *Zur Judenfrage* evidently provided an unbreakable alibi for his own (pre-Marxist) negative judgment on Jews and Judaism. If the founder of scientific socialism had virtually equated *Judentum* and *Kapitalismus* then this offered the perfect ideological justification for the long-standing emotional resentment of Mehring. There was no doubt that Marx's opinions were acceptable to antisemites and that Socialists with antisemitic inclinations eagerly accepted his verdict.[38] At the same time the essay offered what Mehring once called an "Olympian" perspective from which to view the "Jewish question" as a symptom of the death-agony of capitalist society. "Today, a single look at the anti-philosemitic war enables one to grasp all the depth of these sentences. From this secure bulwark of knowledge one may watch with a calm smile how the furious fighters in both camps storm against and beat each other."[39]

Mehring not only considered that Marx's analysis was completely applicable to German society in the 1890s, he made every effort to popularise it in the working-class milieu.[40] This was in significant contrast to other leading German socialists like Kautsky, Bernstein, Bebel and Liebknecht, who rarely, if at all, mentioned *Zur Judenfrage* and certainly never justified it.[41] Even Friedrich

---

[35] Bebel–Engels, 20th March 1892, in Werner Blumenberg (Hrsg.), *August Bebel. Briefwechsel mit Friedrich Engels*, Den Haag 1965, p. 527.

[36] *Ibid.*

[37] See in particular his introduction to Marx's essay in Franz Mehring, *Aus dem literarischen Nachlass von Karl Marx, Friedrich Engels und Ferdinand Lassalle*, Stuttgart 1902, Bd. I, p. 356: "Jeder Kommentar würde diese grundlegende Untersuchung nur abschwächen; die wenigen Seiten wiegen die thurmhohe Literatur auf, die seitdem über die Judenfrage erschienen ist."

[38] See Eduard Bernstein, 'Die Joden in De Duitsche Sociaal-Democratie' . . ., *loc. cit.*, p. 970. Also Robert S. Wistrich, *Revolutionary Jews from Marx to Trotsky*, London–New York 1976.

[39] Franz Mehring, 'Kapitalistische Agonie', *Die Neue Zeit* (1891–1892), Bd. II, p. 548.

[40] See note 37 and also his commentary in *Karl Marx. Geschichte seines Lebens*, Leipzig 1923, 4th edn., pp. 71–78.

[41] On this point see Robert S. Wistrich, 'Karl Marx, German Socialists and the Jewish Question 1880–1914', *Soviet Jewish Affairs*, vol. 3, No. 1 (1973), pp. 92–97.

Engels refrained from trying to adapt Marx's terminology to the post-emancipation "Jewish question" and warned the labour movement against any flirtation with anti-capitalist antisemitism.[42] This silence of German labour leaders with regard to the essay of the young Marx may perhaps explain why Mehring felt obliged to free the founder of scientific socialism from any taint of antisemitism. Without this apologia, the essay would scarcely be usable in a political movement that was dedicated to eliminating all forms of racial, religious and class discrimination. In that case, Mehring's own alibi for expressing an anti-Jewish nuance in his writings would disappear.

Moreover, it was easier for Mehring to engage in this apologetic operation precisely because he was a historian with philosophical interests who was well equipped to place Marx's intellectual development in its social and historical context. This was the case in his introduction written for a Polish edition of *Zur Judenfrage* (published by the PPS in 1896) where he asserted: "Marx has nothing in common with antisemitism. He not only says this but also proves how the Jew has an unassailable claim to political emancipation and to the enjoyment of general human rights."[43] Similarly in another commentary on the essay in 1902, Mehring sought to explain the profundity of Marx's analysis in relating Jewish political emancipation to the development of capitalism. The Jews were entitled to civil equality because it was part of the rights and freedoms guaranteed to the individual in modern bourgeois society. But as Marx had argued, the social essence of Judaism already permeated the ethos of commercial capitalism. In other words bourgeois society was already "judaised". In this context the issue was not political emancipation (the expression of human self-alienation, egoism and materialism) but the emancipation of the Jews from capitalism and of society from *Judentum*.[44] "Beseitigt den Schacher, und ihr seid den Juden los,"[45] as Mehring put it in an article of 1894, that touched on the Young Hegelian roots of Marxism.

On the philosophical level, Mehring tried to emphasise the difference between the "idealism" of the Young Hegelians and the "materialism" of Marx and Engels, as being crucial to their subsequent political development. Bruno Bauer and the Young Hegelians had ended in the cul-de-sac of antisemitism and political reaction because they neglected economic factors. With regard to the "Jewish question" Bauer's perspective had remained purely theological and was predicated on an élitist disdain for the masses. Hence his subsequent decline into racial chauvinism and his collaboration with Hermann Wagener (the ideologist of the East Elbian Junkers) was no surprise to Mehring.[46]

[42]Friedrich Engels, 'Über den Antisemitismus', *Arbeiter-Zeitung* (Vienna), 19th May 1890.

[43]The introduction, obviously translated from the German, prefaced a pamphlet entitled Karol Marks, *W Kwestyi żydowskiej*, Biblioteka politycznospołeczna, t. IV, London 1896, p. xxvi.

[44]For an extended analysis of this dialectical paradox see Chapter I of Wistrich, *Revolutionary Jews from Marx to Trotsky, op. cit.*, pp. 30–38.

[45]Franz Mehring, 'Drillinge', *Die Neue Zeit* (1894), Bd. II, p. 582.

[46]*Ibid.* See also Nathan Rotenstreich, 'For and against Emancipation. The Bruno Bauer Controversy', in *LBI Year Book IV* (1959), pp. 3–36; Zvi Rosen, 'The Anti-Jewish Opinions of Bruno Bauer (1838–1843). Their Sources and Significance', *Zion* (1968), vol. XXXIII, pp. 59–76, (in Hebrew); and Ernst Barnikol (ed.), *Bruno Bauer. Studien und Materialien*, Assen 1972.

"Bauer brauchte einen Sündenbock, auf den er die kapitalistische Masse abladen konnte, und er fand ihn im Juden. Bei ihm versetzte sich der Kapitalismus als Antisemitismus, wie er sich bei Stirner als Anarchismus versetzt hatte."[47]

Marx on the other hand was led by his materialist philosophy to link the Jewish question to its social and economic bases in the relationship between civil society and the State.[48]

This has always been the standard socialist apologia for Marx, and Mehring's chief originality was in being one of the first to develop a coherent defence along these lines. What was perhaps more significant was that Mehring elsewhere also offered an implied apologia for Bruno Bauer's antisemitic writings on the *Judenfrage*. Thus he agreed with Bauer that German Jewry demanded emancipation in the 1840s, not to achieve civil equality but to reinforce their special status. According to Mehring, they had shown themselves ". . . always ready to abandon liberal principles as soon as these contradicted a special Jewish interest".[49] It was a characteristic of Jews that they would "betray democracy and liberalism as soon as it obstructed their own domination".[50] Mehring went still further in a passage which betrays a deep-rooted antipathy beneath the thin Marxist veneer. "We have lived through enough examples during the last fifty years and still experience it every day, that Jewish fellow-citizens, whom we have even admired as unshakeable flagbearers of bourgeois democracy, become corrupt reactionaries if the result of civil legislation harms any specifically Jewish interest. This phenomenon is as old as the participation of Jewry in political struggles and precisely this provoked Bruno Bauer's works on the Jewish question."[51]

Once again Mehring implied that liberalism and democracy were merely a camouflage which "Jewish" interests deserted if it no longer suited their purposes. The image of the Jew conveyed in such passages was that of the *Schutzjude* who seeks double privileges, the gratification of enjoying wealth and a special claim to protection *because* he is a Jew.[52] His preoccupation with exposing this manoeuvre doubtless explains why Mehring devoted so much energy to denouncing the hypocrisy of liberal newspapers in the face of antisemitism. He was particularly severe on Rudolf Mosse and his colleagues who "defend in Judaism the possibility and the presuppositions of huckstering on which the glamour of the capitalist world stands: hence they happily close both eyes when a Jew is crushed because his Judaism obstructs capitalism in some way, but equally they raise a wail of lamentation if an anti-capitalist movement comes too near a Jew on account of his Judaism".[53]

The word-play and the bitter, sarcastic tone are reminiscent of the young

---

[47]Franz Mehring, 'Drillinge', *loc. cit.*, p. 581.
[48]*Ibid.*, p. 582.
[49]Franz Mehring, *Karl Marx. Geschichte seines Lebens*, *op. cit.*, p. 94.
[50]Franz Mehring, *Aus dem literarischen Nachlass . . .*, *op. cit.*, Bd. I, pp. 354–355.
[51]*Ibid.*
[52]See the perceptive comments by Paul Massing, *Rehearsal for Destruction. A Study of Political Anti-Semitism in Imperial Germany*, New York 1959, p. 187.
[53]Franz Mehring, 'Kapitalistische Agonie', *Die Neue Zeit* (1891–1892), Bd. II, p. 546.

Marx, whose analysis was interpreted by Mehring to mean that no socialist could be "philosemitic" without betraying his class principles.[54] In order to avoid any confusion, Mehring stressed that there was nothing in common between contemporary liberal–capitalist philosemitism and the *Judenfreundschaft* of eighteenth-century *philosophes* like Lessing.[55]

The Lessing legend of the German bourgeoisie had been fabricated to serve venal capitalist interests and to counter the claim that all great Germans from Luther to Bismarck had been antisemites. In fact, Lessing's defence of Jews was no different from his attitude to other persecuted and oppressed groups and he had never ignored the "shadowy sides of the Jewish character".[56] It was therefore as mistaken to see in *Nathan der Weise* a eulogy of the Jew as to imagine that it was intended to downgrade Christianity.[57] Moreover, the social situation in Germany at the end of the nineteenth century precluded any comparison with the position taken up by Lessing.

In Mehring's terminology, "philosemitism" was identical in the 1890s with the apologetic defence of rich Jews and the dishonest whitewashing of capitalistic injustices. Hence he considered "artificially bred philosemitism" as more repugnant and also more dangerous to the labour movement than the "spontaneous Jew-hatred of peasants and artisans".[58]

The most representative figure of "artificial" philosemitism was the (non-Jewish) leader of the liberal *Freisinn* party, Eugen Richter – "no more a glaring satire of Lessing, than is Herr Stöcker of Karl Marx".[59] By the early 1890s Mehring had come to regard Stoecker as "a model of truthfulness in comparison with an Eugen Richter".[60] Philosemitism, in terms of Marxist class analysis, represented the worst form of *Schacherpolitik*, a solidly entrenched front of wealth and privilege – "the last ideological disguise of exploiting capitalism".[61] Seen in this context it is not surprising that a violently anti-liberal socialist like Mehring could consider it as much more of a threat than the hysterical, but impotent rhetoric of noisy, semi-literate Jew-baiters. "In considering the brutalities which antisemitism with words rather than deeds commits against the Jews, one should not overlook the brutalities which philosemitism with deeds rather than words is committing against everyone, be he Jew or Turk, Christian or pagan, who opposes capitalism."[62]

---

[54]Franz Mehring, 'Anti- und Philosemitisches', *Die Neue Zeit* (1890–1891), Bd. II, p. 587.

[55]Franz Mehring, *Die Lessing-Legende*, Stuttgart 1893, p. 7. This study, highly thought of by Engels, was a pioneer effort to apply historical materialism to the domain of literary criticism.

[56]Franz Mehring, *Aufsätze zur deutschen Literaturgeschichte*, Leipzig–Berlin 1960, p. 76.

[57]*Ibid.*

[58]Franz Mehring, *Geschichte der deutschen Sozialdemokratie*, Berlin (Ost) 1960, Bd. II, p. 451.

[59]"Aber Herr Stöcker ist keine grellere Satire auf Karl Marx als Herr Eugen [Richter] eine grelle Satire auf Lessing ist." 'Anti- und Philosemitisches', *Die Neue Zeit* (1890–1891), p. 587.

[60]Franz Mehring, *Geschichte der deutschen Sozialdemokratie*, Stuttgart 1913, Bd. IV, p. 131.

[61]Franz Mehring, 'Das erste Wahlergebnis', *Die Neue Zeit* (1892–1893), Bd. II, p. 389: "Diesen Philosemitismus, der nichts als die letzte ideologische Verkleidung des ausbeuterischen Kapitalismus darstellt, rücksichtslos zu brandmarken, ist doch wohl recht eigentlich die Aufgabe der sozialistischen Presse . . ."

[62]Franz Mehring, 'Anti- und Philosemitisches', *loc. cit.*, p. 587.

Such was Mehring's obsession with the iniquities of philosemitism that he even accused those Germans who had taken up a public collection for the Jewish butcher, Buschhoff (accused of ritual murder in Xanten, 1891), of humbug and cheap publicity-seeking "at the expense of human misery".[63] In his commentary on the episode Mehring appeared more concerned with mocking the "idiotic fanaticism" of Buschhoff's liberal defenders than with the barbaric superstitions of the antisemites. It is not surprising, therefore, that some colleagues of Mehring in the SPD, notably Eduard Bernstein, challenged his one-sided emphasis on the philosemitic spectre threatening the labour movement. In an essay published in the *Neue Zeit* in 1894 Bernstein pointed out that it had become difficult to differentiate between the use of the term "philosemitism" by socialists or by antisemites. Both equated it with sycophantic subservience to capitalist interests.[64] There was a danger that as a result antisemitism might come to be regarded as the "lesser evil" by the labour movement (a position implicit in Mehring's writings despite his denials).

Mehring's reply to Bernstein's criticisms disclaimed any desire to minimise the importance of antisemitism, if only because its progress would ultimately benefit Social Democracy. But it was inconceivable that a Marxist proletarian party could support the "brutal capitalistic interests, politically organised in the *Freisinn* party" against the antisemites. Did not the latter "in its way also represent a social rebellion"?[65]

There could only be one answer to a set of alternatives phrased in these terms,[66] an answer which was all the more effective because it appealed to a powerful belief in the German labour movement during the 1890s concerning the imminent collapse of capitalist society. Mehring presented his analyses of the Jewish question within this framework. Both philo- and antisemites represented two poles of a moribund society engaged in a sham battle that was a vulgar but "particularly instructive" parody of the class struggle.[67] Their grotesque skirmishes, however superficial, might none the less prove to be "a powerful midwife to accelerate the birth of a new society".[68]

This analysis was reflected in many statements that appeared in the German socialist press during the 1890s. For example, in an editorial of 26th June 1893, *Vorwärts*, the central organ of the SPD, described antisemitism as the "cultural manure for socialism in the truest sense of the word".[69] Party newspapers rejoiced over antisemitic successes in the 1893 elections as they appeared to strike a blow at the capitalist parties and herald the imminent victory of

---

[63]Franz Mehring, 'Kapitalistische Agonie', *loc. cit.*

[64]Eduard Bernstein, 'Das Schlagwort und der Antisemitismus', *Die Neue Zeit* (1893–1894), Bd. II, p. 233.

[65]Franz Mehring, 'Das erste Wahlergebnis', *loc. cit.*, p. 389.

[66]*Ibid.*

[67]Franz Mehring, 'Kapitalistische Agonie', *loc. cit.*; "In dem Verwesungsprozess des Kapitalismus spielt das anti-philosemitische Fieber eine ganz besonders hässliche und widerwärtige, aber auch ganz besonders lehrreiche Rolle."

[68]*Ibid.*

[69]*Vorwärts*, 26th June 1893. For a detailed examination of this trend, see Robert S. Wistrich, 'The SPD and Antisemitism in the 1890s', *European Studies Review* 7 (1977), pp. 177–197.

socialism.[70] Heinrich Braun, editor of the *Archiv für soziale Gesetzgebung und Statistik*, wrote in 1893 that antisemitism was "the seed of Social Democracy", a view shared by most party ideologists and leaders. Braun asserted that through their brutal demagogy, the antisemites were overcoming the "rural idiocy" of the peasants and other backward strata in Germany. "Its rapid growth is not unlike that of Social Democracy . . . there can be no doubt that in antisemitism we are faced with a strong social movement and that together with the attacks upon Jewry, a radical anti-capitalist trend of a general kind is more and more openly and consciously seeking to affirm itself." [71]

Braun, like Mehring and other Marxist theorists, was convinced that antisemitism was essentially an anti-capitalist movement which would be tactically useful for Social Democracy. This assumption to a large extent explains the benevolence with which labour leaders at that time looked upon the new movement.

It also partly explains how Mehring could so drastically revise his assessment of an antisemitic demagogue like Adolf Stoecker, whom he had pitilessly exposed in 1882 as an ambitious charlatan and megalomaniac. Ten years later, long since outflanked by more radical, plebeian agitators like the Pomeranian schoolmaster, Hermann Ahlwardt, and Otto Böckel, the Hessian "peasant-king", Stoecker had been transformed by Mehring into a man of "native wit, with the gift of ready repartee, quickness of thought, and indestructible good humour".[72] The *Hofprediger* was now depicted as a "bold and God-fearing man" destroyed by liberal wickedness and the ungrateful "howling mob of his own followers". It was true that Stoecker had always tended to light-headedness on points of fact, but "it was this aspect of his character," Mehring complained, "that was exploited to the utmost by the hired scribblers of monied Jewry to present Stoecker as a scarecrow of mendacity. His admirers came much closer to the truth when celebrating him as a 'second Luther'." [73]

Through the prism of historical materialism, even Stoecker's antisemitism now demonstrated a truly "proletarian" instinct to Mehring, though it lacked the populist, anti-clerical appeal of Böckel and Ahlwardt. The new *völkisch* demagogues who had taken on the mantle of the fading Court-preacher, were more able to win support from impoverished peasants, shopkeepers and artisans

[70]Robert S. Wistrich, *Socialism and the Jewish Question in Germany and Austria . . .*, *op. cit.*, pp. 223–231.

[71]Heinrich Braun, 'Zur Lage der deutschen Sozialdemokratie', *Archiv für soziale Gesetzgebung und Statistik* (1893), pp. 513–514. Braun, the brother-in-law of Victor Adler, leader of the Austrian socialist party, was a converted Jew who played an important role in the "revisionist" wing of German Social Democracy. At one time on friendly terms with Mehring, their relations soon soured. In a letter to Lujo Brentano (26th November 1891) Mehring wrote: "Braun ist arm an eigenen Gedanken und ein schlechter Stilist, aber der richtige Wiener Geschäftsjude, findig, rührig, zähe, und wie Sie ganz richtig sagen, besonders geeignet, andere für sich arbeiten zu lassen." Quoted in Ursula Ratz, *op. cit.*, p. 37. After Braun's criticisms of his *Lessing-Legende*, Mehring confided in Kautsky: (1st October 1893, *Kautsky Nachlass*, I.I.S.H. Amsterdam) ". . . und läuft mir dieser 'talentvolle' Geschäftsjude nochmals über den Weg, dann gnade ihm Gott!"

[72]Franz Mehring, 'Das Ende eines Demagogen', *Die Neue Zeit, loc. cit.*, p. 545.

[73]*Ibid.*

who identified capitalism with Jewish cattle-dealers, money-lenders and middlemen.[74] In 1892 Ahlwardt had defeated the Conservative Party candidate in the rural district of Arnswalde-Friedeberg, east of Berlin, with a populist campaign that depicted Jews, Junkers and clerics as enemies of the people. Mehring saw in this agitation a genuine protest movement against the establishment, against big business, anonymous exploitation and the remote metropolis.[75] The *völkisch* Jew-baiters expressed the spontaneous, blind fury of oppressed strata in German society at financial corruption and the domination of oligarchical capitalist cliques. Sometimes, as in Ahlwardt's hysterical pamphlet, *Judenflinten* (which accused the liberal Jewish industrialist Ludwig Loewe of deliberately supplying the German army with defective rifles on the orders of the Parisian *Alliance Israélite Universelle*) the antisemites were a long way off the mark. But Mehring saw no need to moralise about their failings, since as long as financial corruption existed – "the Ahlwardt type remains a Siegfried against whom the capitalist world vainly seeks the place where he can be struck down by a deadly spear".[76]

Moreover, Ahlwardt and his followers had demonstrated that antisemitism was a two-edged sword for the Junker ruling class. In the long run it would help to sweep them away along with all the other débris of bourgeois society. "In Berlin," Mehring observed, "it has taken half a man's lifetime for pampered and adored antisemitism to become a fire that all the extinguishers of society can state no longer put out."[77] From a Marxist perspective one could only welcome the fact that this movement was proving such an acute embarrassment to its original sponsors, the Junker and capitalist establishment.

Mehring's interpretation of antisemitism was in line with the prevailing opportunist trend in German Social Democracy during the 1890s. It was only distinctive when taken in conjunction with his treatment of philosemitism, at which point it becomes evident that Mehring's selectivity expressed a personal bias. This is perhaps even more evident in his historical writings, precisely because they were less subject to the distortions inherent in purely polemical journalism. It may be useful, therefore, to look briefly at Mehring's depiction of Jewish personalities and issues in his more scholarly works.

Particularly revealing in this respect were his comments on the Jewish background of Karl Marx and Ferdinand Lassalle, the founding-fathers of the German labour movement, and also Mehring's main intellectual and political guides. Although Mehring noted that the adolescent Lassalle at one time dreamed of leading the Jews to their independence[78] he felt little empathy for his Jewishness, emphasising instead the "civilising" influence of German culture upon his hero. Mehring equated Lassalle's Judaism with medieval obscurantism and usury.

---

[74]Franz Mehring, *Geschichte der deutschen Sozialdemokratie* . . . Bd. IV (1913), p. 96.
[75]Franz Mehring, 'Sauve qui peut!', *Die Neue Zeit* (1892–1893), pp. 161–164.
[76]Franz Mehring, 'Sic vos, non vobis', *Die Neue Zeit* (1892–1893), p. 361.
[77]*Ibid.*, p. 363: "In Berlin hat es ein halbes Menschenalter gewährt, bis der gehätschelte und geliebkoste Antisemitismus zu einem Brande geworden ist, den alle Spritzen von Gesellschaft und Staat nicht mehr löschen können."
[78]Franz Mehring, *Zur deutschen Geschichte*, Berlin 1931, p. 186.

"Und indem sich Lassalle von dem Schacher abwandte, wandte er sich auch von dem Judentum ab; die fleissige Beschäftigung mit den deutschen Klassikern öffnete seine Augen für die Geistesschätze der modernen Kultur."[79]

Elsewhere he spoke of the unfavourable influence which the Russo-Polish (sic) family milieu exercised on Lassalle's character, though his birthplace was in Breslau.[80] Mehring claimed that Lassalle's parents "belonged to East European Jewry, which was still deeply stuck in huckstering and usury".[81] In fact this was inaccurate since Lassalle's father belonged to the reform community in Breslau and was a supporter of Abraham Geiger's efforts to synthesise Judaism with the most progressive achievements of modern European culture.

A similarly "enlightened" bias can be found in Mehring's biography of Karl Marx, long considered to be a classic in the field. Mehring devoted a few pages only to the Jewish background of the founder of scientific socialism, yet they reveal much about his preconceptions concerning Judaism. In the first place he felt obliged to emphasise that Karl Marx's father, Heinrich, did not convert to Lutheranism for opportunistic reasons, but purely as a result of his convictions. As a man of the enlightenment, a follower of Rousseau and Voltaire, he could not be expected to feel anything in common with the synagogue. Nor could he have sympathised with the Jews of the Rhineland who had aroused the deepest antagonism among the local peasantry by the "murderous usury" which they practised at their expense.

According to Mehring, German Jewry in the 1820s was still languishing in "the depths of medieval barbarism".[82] In spite of the solitary efforts of Moses Mendelssohn they had not participated in the great cultural achievements of the German enlightenment. In this context, *die Lossagung vom Judentum* was a progressive step, an act of social emancipation. The conversion to Christianity of "free spirits" like Heinrich Heine, Ludwig Börne, Eduard Gans and Heinrich Marx was therefore a sign of "civilised progress".[83] Missing altogether from Mehring's account was any mention of the reactionary social pressures to conform, instigated by the Prusso-Christian State in the aftermath of the Napoleonic wars, which left little alternative to Jews such as Heinrich Marx who wished to practise their secular profession. Nor did Mehring appear to be aware that "free spirits" like Heine and Börne bitterly regretted their "conversion" or that Karl Marx's Jewish self-hatred was not unrelated to his position as a convert.

It is also interesting to note that in his eagerness to dejudaise Marx's background, Mehring emphasised the *echtdeutsche* quality of the letters from Heinrich

---

[79]Franz Mehring, *Zur deutschen Geschichte*, Berlin 1931, p. 186.

[80]*Ibid.*, p. 207. Mehring referred to the contradictions in his character, " . . . die er im Kampf mit dem niederziehenden Erbe einer unterdrückten Rasse noch nicht ausgeglichen hatte; in seinem elterlichen Hause hatte noch ganz und gar der fade Dunst des polnischen Judentums geherrscht."

[81]*Ibid.*, p. 186. See also Eduard Rosenbaum, 'Ferdinand Lassalle. A Historiographical Meditation', in *LBI Year Book IX* (1964), pp. 122–130; and Chapter 2 of Wistrich, *Revolutionary Jews from Marx to Trotsky, op. cit.*

[82]Franz Mehring, *Zur deutschen Geschichte, op. cit.*, p. 148.

[83]Franz Mehring, *Karl Marx . . ., op. cit.*, p. 25.

to Karl which betrayed not a trace "von jüdischer Art oder Unart".[84] The father had evidently been liberated "from all Jewish prejudices" by his humanistic culture which he had transmitted as a "valuable heritage" to his gifted son.[85] It is more than a little amusing that after this extended apologia which contains a microcosm of Mehring's subconscious prejudices, he concluded that it was unnecessary to justify or excuse Heinrich Marx's conversion! Mehring's difficulties with this theme indicate the dilemma confronting a socialist historian fundamentally out of sympathy with the national, religious and economic characteristics of Jewry. For Mehring, it was a necessity to sever the elusive link that bound "progressive" Jews like Heine, Börne, Gans, Marx or Lassalle to those of their co-religionists who remained within the Jewish fold. The former were eulogised as fighters for humanity while the latter were dismissed as ethnic obscurantists or denounced as parvenu "monied Jews".

Franz Mehring, like Karl Marx, accepted that Jewish emancipation was a necessary consequence of social development, though he also considered that as a result of their history the Jews had become "the representatives of money-power and hence an anti-social element".[86] Mehring strenuously denied that this position was antisemitic. In a polemic in 1910 defending his left-wing comrade Rosa Luxemburg against the accusations of Polish antisemites, he asserted that Marxism had adopted a standpoint towards the Jews which was "completely free of prejudice". In Mehring's interpretation, the Marxist attitude was "as far removed from anti- as from philosemitism".[87]

In the light of the evidence which we have put forward it is difficult not to regard this claim with some scepticism. Even before his conversion to Marxism, Mehring had viewed the Jewish minority as a privileged rather than a vulnerable and oppressed group in German society. Increasingly he came to see in this community an embodiment of the worst features of capitalistic behaviour. This one-sided standpoint was reinforced by his reliance on the anti-Jewish stereotypes contained in Karl Marx's *Zur Judenfrage*. Taken together, these factors precluded Mehring from achieving a more objective and balanced treatment of the Jewish question.

---

[84]*Ibid.*, p. 26.
[85]*Ibid.* ". . . und diese Freiheit hat er seinem Karl als wertvolles Erbe hinterlassen."
[86]This formulation, like so much of Mehring's writing on the Jewish question, is a paraphrase of the young Marx.
[87]Franz Mehring's intervention on behalf of Rosa Luxemburg occurred after the Polish antisemite Andrzej Niemojewski had attacked her Polish Social Democrats (the SDKPiL) as anti-national and "judaised" and further claimed that Western socialists from Marx to Kautsky (and Mehring) were all antisemites. On the background to this affair see *Revolutionary Jews from Marx to Trotsky*, *op. cit.*, pp. 83–90, and Georges Haupt/P. Korzec, 'Les socialistes et la campagne antisémite en Pologne en 1910: un épisode inédit', *Revue du Nord*, Université de Lille, No. 225 (Avril–Juin 1975), t. LVII, pp. 185–194. Mehring's reply concentrated mainly on the historical background to Marx's essay and denied that it had anything in common with the standpoint of Niemojewski. It appeared as an open letter in *Mlot*, No. 15 (12th November 1910) a socio-political review in Warsaw which was the official organ of the SDKPiL. Apart from Rosa Luxemburg, the contributors to this review included Karl Radek, Leo Jogiches (the editor) and Adolf Warski, the first three being Polish–Jewish revolutionaries active in the German labour movement.

Emancipation and Assimilation

Types of Jewish Municipal Rights in German Townships
The Problem of Local Emancipation

BY JACOB TOURY

I. HISTORICAL ROOTS AND TYPOLOGY

When the world-shattering occurrences of the French Revolution brought freedom and equality also to the French citizens of Jewish faith, it was widely assumed that the pattern set by these events was the one and only logical way to a general emancipation of the Jews. And indeed, the French emancipatory paragraph of 28th September 1791 was understood to contain not only the Jewish citizens' rights within the framework of the state but also the full rights of "local" citizenship. This understanding found its legal expression in the French Law of Municipalities of 1795, which pronounced the full identity of municipal burghers' rights with state-wide citizens' rights – the former being no more than the local application of the latter, with regard to any and all regular inhabitants of a given community.[1]

However, no such identification took place in Germany before 1871. Until then there prevailed a variety of local rights, emanating from diverse sources and not at all coinciding with the constitutional rights within the framework of the State. Thus, one might even be justified in introducing the term "municipal emancipation" as denoting the struggle for local citizens' rights which was waged quite separately from the widely publicised efforts at attaining state-wide political equality.

Yet, as general political emancipation in Germany did not develop in a straight line but had its ups and downs between 1791 and 1871, the main interest, perhaps rightly, concentrated upon legislation with regard to Jewish rights as citizens of the state, while the local stage remained more or less in obscurity. Moreover, as the manifold intermediate steps leading to the goal of absolute equality were often disregarded as falling short of that ultimate aim, the variegated stages in the development of Jewish local citizens' rights and the diverse sources from which they emanated could scarcely demand special attention.

Nevertheless, Jewish efforts to attain local rights in German towns have had a far longer history than the general political concept of emancipation, which was not known before the middle of the eighteenth century,[2] and their beginnings may even be traced back to the Middle Ages.

---

[1]Robert Heuser, *Die Bedeutung des Ortsbürgerrechts für die Emanzipation der Juden in Baden*, Diss., Heidelberg 1971 (Mimeographed). Thanks are due to my esteemed colleague, Professor Reinhard Rürup, for calling this dissertation to my attention.

[2]If one wants to go back to the (then) Dutch colony of New Amsterdam in 1654/1664 for a non-German early starting point, one should bear in mind that the efforts to attain civic rights there bore a distinctly local character.

There were medieval towns in which Jews were regarded as "burghers",[3] or – as the difference between "burgher" and "inhabitant" (*Beiwohner, Bei-* or *Hintersasse*) was not yet definitely established – were accorded at least certain rights similar to those of the burghers.[4] This assumption is strengthened by the fact that during the fourteenth century Jews in some towns still participated in the defence of the city walls. Moreover, even so late a list as that of the Jews in Braunschweig from the year 1400 (or thereabouts) contains against the individual names remarks such as: "est b[urgher]", "sunt burgeri borin", or: "non sunt b[urgeri]".[5] Thus, it is evident that certain Jews enjoyed a local standing above and beyond that of a *Schutzjude*, whereas others had to be content with the latter status. It stands to reason and is proven by the case of Worms that Jews – in order to be received as "burghers" – had first to be accepted by the heads of the Jewish community as members of the *Kehillah*, but that their sons succeeded automatically to the status of burgher. As yet it has not been established to our satisfaction whether such rights as the Jews attained in the various townships emanated from imperial prerogative, either from the emperor himself or from territorial lords who had appropriated such regal prerogatives, or whether they stemmed from the local power of the autonomous city authorities.

These scanty remarks on Jewish citizenship in medieval towns are not meant to further the discussion of a still quite controversial problem, but rather to show that the question of Jewish municipal rights was not a new-fangled ramification of emancipatory developments and that already before the onset of modern times it was conceivable that Jews might achieve – in one form or another – civic status in German townships.

From the precedents mentioned so far, and from logical inference, it can be deduced that the civic rights attainable by Jews were of different origins and of a different nature. As to their origin, they might be granted by the towns, or by the territorial lords, or by the central authority of the State. As to their nature, they might be individual rights, granted by any of the aforementioned agencies to select applicants, either before or after state-wide political emancipation. But individual local citizens' rights might also be granted to the public at large in so far as its members fulfilled the other requirements of municipal citizenship (i.e., local emancipation by a general State-Law either before, or together with, or after state-wide political emancipation).

Yet the above-mentioned precedent of Worms, where Jews were accepted as citizens only after being scrutinised by the *Kehillah* authorities, points to quite another kind of local status: to corporative rights, granted not to single applicants, but rather to the *corporate body* of the Jewish community, the latter also taking part in their realisation, being in itself a political body among the other corporations of the town and exercising certain decentralised functions of self-government within its precincts.

---

[3]So Guido Kisch, *Forschungen zur Rechts- und Sozialgeschichte der Juden in Deutschland während des Mittelalters*, Stuttgart 1955, p. 98 ff.
[4]". . . den Bürgerrechten ähnlich", Anna-Dorothee v. den Brincken, 'Das Rechtfertigungsschreiben der Stadt Köln', in: *Mitteilungen aus dem Stadtarchiv von Köln*, 60. Heft, Köln 1971, p. 309.
[5]Stadtarchiv Braunschweig, *Juden: Bürger und Nichtbürger, 1400*, Kastenkatalog.

Such a corporate status could be granted to the Jews by the magistrate of the town or by a territorial lord, as will be shown below; yet there were certain German states, such as some small Thuringian principalities, and especially the largest German Kingdom – Prussia – in which corporate tendencies were upheld even by the central governments, either as a relic from times past, or as an outcome of political reasoning on an imaginary impasse in the development of the so-called "Jewish question".

As this diversity in the origins and the nature of local civil rights may seem bewildering, they may be arranged, together with suitable examples to be treated later on in the text, in the scheme of reference which we show in the table below.

Types of Local Citizens' Rights

Local Rights	Granted To Select Persons			Granted To All Qualified Persons (Full municipal emancipation)		
	Before any kind of emancipation		After attainment of individual citizenship by Central Governments	By State-Law before General Political Emancipation	Together with General Political Emancipation	After General Political Emancipation
	By Towns	By Territorial lords				
Individually Granted	Upper Silesia Middle- and North German towns (origins not always ascertainable)		Berlin 1792. Palatinate/ Baden since 1799/1809. Württemberg since 1817.	Prussia 1808 (Anhalt 1852) while political emancipation was again cancelled. Bavaria 1861/69	Brunswick, Hesse– Darmstadt, Hesse– Homburg, Nassau Oldenburg Saxonia S.-Weimar Waldeck (all during or immediately after the Revolution of of 1848)	Baden 1862 Württemberg 1864
	by Towns	by Feudal Lords	by Central Governments	by State-Law before General Political Emancipation		
Corporatively Granted	Fürth	Thuringian Principalities; Laupheim (Würtbg.); Floss (Bav.); Hürben? (Bav.); Sulzbürg? (Bav.); Ichenhausen (Bav.)	S.-Weimar until 1823 S.-Meiningen until 1856	New South- and East Prussia 1797 Prov. Posen-Bromberg 1833, 1838/40 Prussian Jew-Law 1841, 1847 (draft)		

It goes without saying that only one type of local rights listed in this table can be regarded as full emancipation in modern understanding, viz. in the sense of equal rights and equal duties for all; these are the rights granted to all otherwise qualified persons by state-wide legislation. Yet the table shows clearly that such rights were not attained simultaneously in all German towns, nor were they automatically linked with state-wide political emancipation. Therefore, it would seem worthwhile to scrutinise the various precursory forms of local emancipation that began to emerge in the German territories as early as the seventeenth century.

II. CORPORATIVE RIGHTS GRANTED BY
MUNICIPALITIES – FÜRTH

The tradition of corporative rights is probably older than that of individual rights and thus it would be appropriate to begin with a survey of those corporative remnants which were still discernible at the end of the eighteenth and the onset of the nineteenth century.

Although the autonomous towns may have been one main source of Jewish corporate municipal rights in the late Middle Ages, only one example remained extant until the nineteenth century. It was the city of Fürth, where Jews were granted corporate municipal rights when they began settling there after their expulsion from Nuremberg (1498). The Fürth magistrate accorded them not only the right to be represented in the municipal assemblies but theoretically even the right of being elected as burgomasters. Although they soon were "liberated" from this burden [6] by the municipal statutes of 1652, Fürth Jews continued to serve as members of the municipality until 1806, when the town came under the Bavarian crown. Moreover, during the long period from their settlement to their becoming Bavarian subjects, there emerged, even within the Jewish corporation of Fürth, a class distinction between Jewish *Kehillah*-burghers and Jewish *Kehillah-Beisitzer*, the latter being deprived of representation in the councils of the *Kehillah* and also otherwise discriminated against by the Jewish *Kehillah*-burghers. [7]

Naturally enough, when after 1806 the question of Bavarian local and state-wide citizens' rights for Jews – and particularly the question of their enrolment as local citizens in the township of Fürth – came under discussion, the magistrate of that town would adduce the fact of their being a corporation in the town, but not of the town. As late as 1823 they were regarded by the townspeople as a separate entity with autonomous rights, but without a claim to the status of citizens of the town. [8] The magistrate – although well aware of the declared policy of the government to dissolve all Jewish corporations [9] – held that the administration of Jewish legacies and endowments for benevolent institutions and schools had remained exclusively in Jewish hands and that therefore the Jews could not demand participation in the administration of non-Jewish funds belonging to the town. This hair-splitting argument of the magistrate was brought forth in answer to a previous Jewish complaint lodged with the King,

---

[6]A yearly payment of 2 guilders was extracted from them in lieu of the "duty". Otto Gebhard, *Die Verwaltung des Fleckens Fürth zur Zeit der Dreiherrschaft*, Erlangen, n.d. (1941?), pp. 32, 110.

[7]Cf. Jacob Toury, *Der Eintritt der Juden ins deutsche Bürgertum. Eine Dokumentation* (henceforth: Toury, *Dokumentation*), Doc. VII a2. There is only one known instance of similar collective municipal rights outside Germany: in 1780 the Jews of Livorno were granted corporate municipal representation by the Grand Duke of Toscana.

[8]Stadtarchiv Fürth, Fach 19, Nr. 20: Draft of a petition by the magistrate to the Ministry of the Interior, dated 20th October 1823.

[9]Edict 10th June 1813, § 20: "Alle in dem Königreiche noch bestehenden Judencorporationen werden aufgelöst . . ." It must however be stressed that this referred mainly to religious corporations, which should be replaced by "Gemeinden".

namely that since 1806 no Jewish councillors or magistrates had been elected in Fürth.[10]

It ought to be noted that the orthodox elements of Fürth were utterly reluctant to relinquish their previous corporate status and tried hard to have it both ways: to become individual citizens of the town and to remain a corporation with autonomous internal jurisdiction.[11] One can in a way understand the sharp reaction of the magistrate, but in the end both sides had to yield and the Jews finally became accepted as individual citizens and had to pay the price of relinquishing their autonomy.

Although the Jewish collective citizens' status of Fürth appears to be quite singular, it was indeed exceptional only inasmuch as it was granted by the township itself. There were other localities in which Jews enjoyed full or partial local citizens' rights as early as the latter part of the seventeenth century, but the traces of such extraordinary precedents have almost been obliterated – probably because the Jews themselves lost interest in them or even found them harmful to their cause during their struggle for state-wide equality after 1815. They began to spurn the principle of a separate collective existence, like the one enjoyed by the Jews of Fürth; emancipation, in the eyes of an ever-increasing majority, became tantamount to individual freedom and equality. Anyhow, no other instance has so far come to light in which Jewish local rights could be attributed directly to the legislative power of a city-magistrate.

III: CORPORATIVE RIGHTS GRANTED BY TERRITORIAL LORDS: BAVARIAN TOWNSHIPS

On the contrary, the prevalent sources of early citizens' rights accorded to Jews seem to have been diametrically opposed to the singular instance of Fürth. As a rule, they stemmed from the prerogative of "Territorial Lords". Some of these *Mediatherren* tended to grant a certain amount of autonomous local rights to people under their protection, even if they were newcomers to the locality under their sway and did not comply with the magistrates' requirements for acceptance as fully-fledged local citizens.

Thus a corporate autonomy on a local level for a Jewish settlement within or besides an existing township or village was the usual outcome. The measure of that municipal autonomy and the mode of its operation might vary from place to place; but the fact of its existence in various parts of Germany can be amply verified, although up to now only the case of the Bavarian settlement of Floss in Upper Palatinate has been commented upon.

[10]Cf. the King's answer, dated 5th October 1818, StdA Fürth, Fach 19, Nr. 26, reprinted in Toury, *Dokumentation*, III h5.

[11]Cf. the report of the Commissioner of Police on a Jewish petition of 1815, which asked that the Jews of Fürth be exempted from the edict of June 1813 in order to preserve their corporation. StdA Fürth, Fach 19, Nr. 6.

The inhabitants of the *Judenberg* alongside Floss formed a local political community, separate in every respect from the adjacent township and administering its local affairs in quite an autonomous way.[12] The Jews were entirely forbidden to dwell in the town itself. This total separation might have been facilitated by the fact that the *Judenberg* had originally been a part of the Monastery of Waldsassen.[13]

Even when, in accordance with the Bavarian Jew Law of 1813, the Government ordered the abolition of Jewish corporations and, in the case of Floss, also the incorporation of the Jews into the township, both sections of the population obstructed the execution of the necessary measures. The Jews demanded representation in the town-council and permission to live in the town proper, whereas the townspeople absolutely refuted precisely these demands by pointing out that as far as they understood the *Judenberg* had always been a separate local entity. The government then halted the execution of its order (1824) and for twelve years left everything as it was, except for the policing of the *Judenberg*, which was handed over to the police department of the town. In 1836 a new proposal was made by the government: the Jewish community should be regarded as a private society, but it should be allowed to choose a local agent (*Gemeindepfleger*) in charge of communal property, with a seat and vote in the town-council of Floss. As the latter condition was again rejected by the municipality, no further step towards reconciliation of the two communities was taken, and the *de facto* Jewish township of the *Judenberg* continued to exist until the abolition of the Bavarian matricle-laws in 1861, or perhaps even until the implementation of the new Bavarian Local Legislation (*Gemeindeordnung*) of 1869. By then the Jewish population of Floss, which until 1840 had constituted something over 20 per cent of the inhabitants of both parts of Floss, had already decreased to about 9 per cent.[14]

Less well known than the precedent of Floss, in fact a riddle up to now, has been the municipal status of the Jews of Ichenhausen (Swabia). The riddle was posed by the eminent liberal Professor Alexander Lips of Erlangen. In 1819 Lips appended a footnote to one of his books,[15] in which he stated that the market town of Ichenhausen was the only Bavarian community whose inhabitants – swayed more by the spirit of the law than by intolerance – elected one half of their aldermen from among their Jewish neighbours.

Yet this statement was based upon a double error: the local election laws of Bavaria[16] did not envisage a proportional representation of different parts of the local population, nor did the inhabitants of Ichenhausen elect aldermen before the year 1819, not to speak of Jewish aldermen. For the market town – up to

[12]M. Weinberg, *Geschichte der Juden in der Oberpfalz*, vol. V, München 1926, pp. 75 ff.; Stefan Schwarz, *Die Juden Bayerns im Wandel der Zeiten*, München–Wien 1963, pp. 87 ff.; Toury, *Dokumentation*, Ch. III h, introduction and document III h6.

[13]Weinberg, *op. cit.*, p. 75.

[14]Central Archives for the History of the Jewish People (CAHJP) Jerusalem, Inv. 835.

[15]A. Lips, *Über die künftige Stellung der Juden in den deutschen Bundesstaaten*, Erlangen 1819, n. to p. 83 f.

[16]Edict concerning constitution and administration of the communities (15th May 1818); Ordinance concerning communal elections (5th August 1818).

1806 in the hands of the baronial family Marquard von Stein – remained under feudal administration even after its incorporation into the Kingdom of Bavaria and only after the promulgation of the local laws mentioned above did it receive a municipal organisation according to the official Bavarian pattern of local self-government. Moreover, only in 1824 were the Jews of the town sworn in as burghers.[17] Thus, they could not have participated in municipal elections before that date. The chronicler of the town even states quite naïvely that there lived *two* communities in that place, with separate tax-rolls, and their assessments were worked out separately, Christians by themselves and Jews by themselves. He even states that the establishment of one single unified civic community was accomplished only in 1869. But it is at least probable that already before the year 1869, and possibly even immediately after the taking of the burghers' oath in 1824, the main obstacle to unification had been removed, so that Jews could take part in local elections. Only the separate tax-assessments seem to have lingered on for about another forty years.[18]

Ichenhausen was also rather typical in another respect, already encountered at Floss and still to be encountered in other settlements that had been granted local autonomy by feudal Lords: In 1811 the Jewish population amounted to more than 45 per cent of the total population. In 1838 the proportion between the Jewish and the Christian community of Ichenhausen was still about 44:56.

How do these facts affect the statement of Professor Lips on Jewish aldermen? It ought to be assumed that until 1819, or even until their reception as burghers in 1824, the Jewish community functioned not only as a religious but also as a political body, that their *Parnass* was regarded as mayor of the Jewish sector of the market town and that the deputies (*Repräsentanten*) of the religious community also took part in the mundane administration of their separate sector, and especially in the assessment of taxes. The number of the representatives – by chance or on purpose – may have been similar to that of the aldermen in the Christian sector. By this interpretation, Lips's statement does not seem to have been devoid of a certain factual basis. What he did not grasp was the curious fact that two separate civic communities existed side by side in the one township. In years to come, some Jews of Ichenhausen were indeed elected by their (Jewish and Christian) neighbours to municipal honours. An archival entry regarding just such a case leads to a further quest for other Bavarian places where Jews might have held some autonomous local rights. The document in question was occasioned by a Jewish protest in 1836 against the exclusion of Jews from municipal offices in Regensburg. The petitioner pointed out that Jews had been chosen "electors, and even been elected to local offices in several places, e.g., in Sulzbürg, Hürben and Ichenhausen".[19] Although some materials

[17]Heinrich Sinz, *Geschichtliches vom ehemaligen Markte und der nunmehrigen Stadt Ichenhausen*, 1926, pp. 68, 261.

[18]*Ibid.*, p. 177. The following population-figures: *ibid.*, p. 70; B.Z. Ophir, *Pinkas Kehilloth, Germania/Bavaria* (Hebrew), Jerusalem 1972, p. 598.

[19]Bayerisches Hauptstaatsarchiv München, Allgemeines Staatsarchiv, Staatsrat 3370, fol. 1–10, containing the governmental attitude towards the Jewish petition (by Jacob Guggenheimer, Regensburg). Although the exclusion from municipal offices is de facto upheld, the quoted facts about Jewish municipal officers are recapitulated without comment.

exist on the history of the Jews at Sulzbürg,[20] no facts pertaining to their
municipal rights have so far been established, and it is a moot point whether their
local constitution might have been similar to that of the Ichenhausen Jews. In
any case, the Jews of Sulzbürg constituted more than 30 per cent of the local
population[21] and corresponded at least in this respect to the circumstances prevailing in the former place.

Some more particulars have come to light with regard to Hürben, the third
place mentioned in the above petition. Yet, even so, no clear-cut picture of
municipal autonomy emerges. The Jews of Hürben began to increase in numbers after the middle of the seventeenth century, when the Counts of Liechtenstein
settled a considerable number of newly immigrated families between the township of Krumbach and their domain at Hürben. Forty Jewish families were then
counted in the locality, constituting about 80 per cent of the inhabitants.[22] The
increase in the local population continued even after the domain had reverted
to Upper-Austria (1718), but now not only Jews but also Catholics were settled
at Hürben.[23] Thus in 1751 there were fifty-one Jewish and forty-nine Christian
families living side by side in Hürben.[24] But the Jews then owned only ten
houses, whereas the Christians had almost five times that number. Nevertheless,
the Jews must still have amounted to at least 30 per cent of the total population,
as the Jewish dwellings generally were far more crowded than those of the non-
Jews. But what in our context is more important than the number of souls is
that fact that eight Jewish and forty-seven Christian houses were endowed with
the *Gemeinds-Gerechtigkeit*,[25] meaning that their owners had local citizens' rights.

This was the case before Hürben became a Bavarian village in 1806. As the
quoted document from 1836 speaks of active and passive Jewish participation
in local elections,[26] it is possible, but by no means proven, that in analogy to
Ichenhausen and Floss, an autonomous local tradition had lingered on from the
times of the granting of privilege by the feudal landowners until the establishment of Bavarian rule.

IV. THE CASE OF LAUPHEIM-WÜRTTEMBERG

If it seems rather curious that one continues to speculate on autonomous Jewish
municipal rights, one must take into account the peculiar geographic fact that

---

[20]Weinberg, *op. cit.*; Ferdinand Koeppel, 'Die Judenfrage in der Oberpfalz im 17. und 18.
Jahrhundert', in *Zeitschrift für bayerische Landesgeschichte*, Bd. 1–3, 1941.

[21]Ophir, *op. cit.*, p. 163 arrives at 32 per cent for the year 1810.

[22]Ernst Vogel, *Kampf um Krumbach*, Krumbach 1933, p. 11: "Hirben, ein Dorf vom 50 Feuer-
stätten . . . allhier befinden sich 40 jüdische Haushaltungen . . ."

[23]J. Kahn-Krumbach, 'Geschichtliches von Hürben-Krumbach', *Bayerische Israelitische Gemeinde-
zeitung*, 1925/1926, No. 5, p. 139 f. Another (and better) source for the local history has been
excerpted by Otto Landauer, *Chronik der Firma M.S. Landauer* (mimeographed). This volume is
kept in the Collections of the Leo Baeck Institute, New York, No. C. 229. Unfortunately
Landauer's source has so far not been identified.

[24]*Landauer*, as in the previous note, p.T.8.

[25]*Ibid.*, p.T.7. In the first half of the nineteenth century the Jewish population again amounted to
40 to 50 per cent of the total.

[26]Cf. n. 19 above.

not very far from Hürben or Ichenhausen, in the Württembergian part of Swabia, another well-documented case exists of feudal endowment of a Jewish community with municipal autonomy. This is the instance of Laupheim.

There is ample documentary evidence that in the year 1811 the Jewish community of Laupheim repeatedly petitioned the provincial authorities, and even the central government, to be freed from the communal dues of the Christian township, pointing out that the Jews constituted "a corporation quite distinct" from the town.[27] Nor did the Jewish inhabitants lack proof for their contention: in 1730, the first Jewish families had been settled by the feudal Lords of Gross- and Klein-Laupheim on their baronial lands and under their special protection, outside the township proper. The treaty of protection was duly registered by the Austrian authorities of Freiburg (1734). The payment of the protection dues absolved the Jews *inter alia* from the defrayment of local taxes (*Gemeinde-Prästationen*). Because of this tax exemption they were not allowed to put their horses to graze on the village common or to draw water from the public well at Laupheim.[28]

When the treaty came up for its second prolongation (1784), twenty new families were received under the protection of the baronial Welden family and settled in Laupheim. They were allowed to build new houses on the so-called *Judenberg*. Moreover, old and new Jewish houses alike were now declared as freehold of their inhabitants, until the expiration of the treaty (thirty years).[29]

The old Jewish houses, adjacent to the domain, and the newly built quarters on the *Judenberg* now formed an almost regular quadrangle, a township alongside the existing town of Laupheim, standing between it and the manorial domain.[30] It is independently attested that the Jewish community had separate local rights as a corporation and was represented and led by a *Judenschultheiss* or *Parnass*.[31]

Long before the expiration of the third treaty between the manorial Lords and the Jews of Laupheim, the implementation of the decrees of the Diet of Regensburg put an end to the baronial autonomy of the *Reichsritterschaft*. The newly created Kingdom of Württemberg claimed all political rights over the former subjects of the Welden family, stipulating that the Jews and the two branches of the Weldens settle their private claims among themselves.[32]

But there remained the question of the municipal status of the Laupheim Jews. In 1810 the magistrate had ordered the assessment and registration of the tax-value of the Jewish "civic property", i.e., their houses, and immediately afterwards demanded payment of the rates due. The Jews at once protested that they never had been and were not now part of the town. The magistrate re-

---

[27]Württembergisches Staatsarchiv Ludwigsburg, E 212/78 (old No. 214/78).

[28]Johann Gottfried Brigel, *Statistisch-geschichtliche Beschreibung des Ortes Laupheim*, Laupheim 1845, p. 10 f.

[29]*Ibid.*, p. 12.

[30]Johann Albert Aich, *Laupheim 1570–1870*, 3.–4.Aufl., Laupheim 1921, p. 99.

[31]Utz Jeggle, *Judendörfer in Württemberg*, Tübingen 1969, p. 19 and n. 35.

[32]This was done in 1812 and 1813, when the Jews agreed to pay to the former Lords of Gross- and Klein-Laupheim 2,700 fl. and 1,900 fl. respectively for transferring all property-rights unconditionally to the Jews. Brigel, *op. cit.*, p. 14.

torted: "If civic property is to be free from communal payments, who shall pay them?" Moreover, the Jews had "no magistrate" of their own and "would never constitute a [civic] community by themselves". On the contrary, they participated in the civic services, such as the provision of roads, bridges, police- and fire-protection, and if their huge number were to be exempted from pay- ments, "the Christian community would be greatly oppressed".[33] The outcome of the Laupheim dispute was never in question, as Württemberg did not over- much heed the local Jewish traditions. Although it can only be ascertained that at some unspecified time after 1811 the Jews received grazing rights on the Laupheim commons,[34] this fact alone seems to justify the conclusion that their aspirations to a separate municipal status came to nothing.

Nevertheless, in Württemberg, like everywhere else in Germany, the demand for separate Jewish settlements became for a time, especially from 1815, an anti- semitic slogan[35] – probably conceived in order to forestall general legal emanci- pation in the various German principalities.[36] During the deliberations on the Jew-Law of 1828 there appeared at least two anti-emancipatory tracts, one from Ulm[37] and the other from Stuttgart,[38] that expressly proposed the establishment of separate Jewish colonies. Moreover, the law promulgated on 8th May 1828 contained a special paragraph that "permitted the Jews to associate for the foundation of separate colonies with separate boundaries and communal ad- ministration".[39] It is most probable that whoever drafted the law had been aware of the peculiar status of the Laupheim Jews who in Württemberg had come nearest to the realisation of the quoted paragraph.

But what in 1811 still looked desirable to the Laupheim Jews did not at all induce the Württembergian Jews of 1828 to comply with the right to form separate settlements bestowed upon them by the discriminatory Jew-Law. They longed for individual emancipation and integration into the general civic society, and the mere thought of collective local corporations must in this light have seemed to them reactionary and indeed hostile. In any case, no more was heard of autonomous Jewish settlements in Württemberg.

---

[33]Württembergisches Staatsarchiv Ludwigsburg E 212/78. As to the "huge number" – Jeggle, *op. cit.*, p. 328, gives the number as 464 Jews for the year 1824. Twenty years later, Brigel (*op. cit.*, p. 8) mentions 121 Jewish families with 710 souls among 2,747 Christians, almost all of them Catholics. The Jewish percentage was therefore about 25 p.c.

[34]Aich, *op. cit.*, p. 102. The other particulars there seem to be incorrect.

[35]Cf. the present author's paper: ' "Jewish Colonies" as part of the first deliberations on the "Jewish Question" ', *Hazionuth, V*, Tel-Aviv 1977 (Hebrew).

[36]E.g., in Hesse, where Carl Edler von Kuchen from Ems presented a plan for the foundation of a Jewish town, near Frankfurt and in competition with its trade. Staatsarchiv Marburg, Abt. 16, Rep. XIV, Kl. 1, Nr. 64, fol. 2,3.

[37]D. Schultes, *Eingabe des Handels- und Gewerbs-Standes in Ulm an die Stände-Versammlung etc.*, Ulm 1828.

[38]Rudolf Moser, *Die Juden und ihre Wünsche*, Stuttgart 1828. Here, the colony was proposed only for those Jews who could not be coerced into emigrating.

[39]Art. 20, *Gesetzblatt Württemberg*, 8th May 1828.

V. AUTONOMOUS COMMUNITIES IN THURINGIAN VILLAGES

But more was heard, even up to 1856, from some Thuringian villages. We now know for certain that – as in Laupheim and places in Bavaria – the Jews of the Thuringian village of Aschenhausen formed a separate corporation, quite apart from the village-community.[40] They originally had been forced upon the inhabitants by the *Mediatherr* v. Spesshardt, and in 1806 were incorporated into the Grand-Duchy Sachsen-Weimar-Eisenach. When in 1823 the Grand-Duke accorded to his Jewish subjects (although conditionally) local and state-wide citizens' rights, the question of their feudal dues to the estate of the Spesshardt family as well as that of their relations with the local village-community was the cause of lengthy litigation, to be finally settled only shortly before the Revolution of 1848.

It seems that Aschenhausen was not the only place in the Thuringian principalities harbouring autonomous and separate Jewish communities settled there by feudal landowners, and the above-mentioned first emancipatory law of Sachsen-Weimar, dated 20th June 1823, bears witness to it. One paragraph expressly states that "wherever they have been accorded a separate local district for their residence, it shall remain so".[41] This passage does not refer to the existence of a closed ghetto, but to certain colonies of Jews, originally settled by local lords in villages under their sway, similar to the instance of the Jewish settlement at Aschenhausen.

Proof for this contention may be adduced from another Thuringian principality – Sachsen-Meiningen. There, too, certain traces of separate and autonomous Jewish dwellings have been preserved in the statute-book: a law from the year 1856 concerning Jewish local enfranchisement in the Duchy of Sachsen-Meiningen-Hildburghausen contains the pronouncement that "henceforth they shall not be allowed to form separate civic communities ('keine besondern bürgerlichen Gemeinden bilden'), but shall be incorporated in the communal structure of their dwelling place".[42] This means that in Sachsen-Meiningen, too, separate Jewish corporations with municipal rights had previously existed and were now to be abolished. Apparently, nobody outside the Duchy knew about their existence, for the editor of the leading Jewish paper of the day, Ludwig Philippson, added a personal remark to the above text in his *Allgemeine Zeitung des Judentums*: "Where and how did they constitute in Meiningen a separate civic community?!!"[43]

---

[40] The present author has extensively described the circumstances in his paper 'Probleme jüdischer Gleichberechtigung auf lokalbürgerlicher Ebene', in *Jahrbuch des Instituts für deutsche Geschichte*, II, Universität Tel-Aviv 1972, pp. 267 ff., where the sources are partially reprinted.

[41] "Wo ihnen ein eigner Bezirk des Ortes zum Aufenthalt angewiesen ist, soll es dabei bleiben". 'Übersicht der bürgerlichen Verhältnisse der Juden in den deutschen Bundesstaaten', Beilage E to the Prussian Memorandum *Denkschrift zu dem Entwurf einer Verordnung, die Verhältnisse der Juden betreffend*, Berlin 1847, p. 415.

[42] Quoted in *Allgemeine Zeitung des Judentums*, 1856, p. 256.

[43] *Ibid.*, editor's note.

However, traces of an answer to this question concerning the autonomous local status of Jewish villagers in Sachsen-Meiningen-Hildburghausen may be found in some archival sources, now housed in the collections of the Leo Baeck Institute, New York.[44] Thus the owner of one of the largest textile works in central Germany, stemming from the community of Walldorf in the vicinity of Meiningen, commented upon the history and the communal status of the Jews in that place:

> "The Jews . . . were induced to settle . . . under the protection of the baronial land-owners, in whose hands the patrimonial jurisdiction was placed . . . Three baronial families divided between themselves the authority over Walldorf (v. Diemar; v. Bibra; v. Marschallk). Each local inhabitant belonged only to the patrimonial court of his special lord . . . When in the year 1808 Walldorf reverted to the Ducal House of Meiningen, the Jewish population that (in 1688) consisted of only nine families, had by then gradually increased . . . for every additional protected soul was an additional source of revenue – for the always overstrained nobles . . ."[45]

And indeed, in 1833, some 537 Jews lived in Walldorf, constituting about 36 per cent of the local population of that place.[46] This rather extraordinary concentration of Jews seems to be characteristic for Jewish settlements on the lands of most *Mediatherren* and can be verified also for other Thuringian places outside Walldorf.[47] The one remarkable trait of the last-mentioned place was that until the end of the eighteenth century the Jews living there were organised in three separate religious communities, just as they were dependent upon three different lords of the manor. Similar circumstances may have prevailed before 1808 in other villages of Meiningen.[48]

In any case, after their reception into the Principality of Sachsen-Meiningen, the Jew-Ordnance of January 1811 commanded them "to form their own communities, without regard to former jurisdiction . . . so that in every place there should exist only one Jewish community".[49] It must be pointed out that the term "Community" (*Gemeinde*) in this context is quite ambiguous. If only the religious community is meant, then the term "their own communities" is redundant. Thus, it may be assumed that the law pointed to political communities and to the abolition of the former pluralistic congregations under feudal tutelage. The political intention is made clearer by the paragraph of the same law which declared the former Jewish "Elders" (*Parnasse*) to be henceforth the heads and spokesmen of the now unified local communities: "The functions of

---

[44]Cf. n. 45. It is to be regretted that it was impossible to look for additional material in the archives of the German Democratic Republic.

[45]Handwritten memoirs by Moritz F. Siegel (1843–1923), Collections of the Leo Baeck Institute, New York, No. C. 373, 4 vols. The above quotations from vol. 1. (pages not numbered).

[46]A. Human, *Geschichte der Juden im Herzogtum Sachsen–Meiningen–Hildburghausen*, Hildburghausen 1898, p. 14.

[47]Other villages with an outstanding percentage of Jews were: Bibra and Simmershausen: 20 per cent; Marisfeld: 24 per cent; Bauerbach: 31 per cent; Gleicherwiesen: 42 per cent (*loc. cit.*). Therefore it may be assumed that in these places too, they were protected by *Mediatherren*.

[48]Cf. previous note.

[49]Human, *op. cit.*, p. 67: "eigene Gemeinden zu bilden . . . und aller Orten nur eine Juden-gemeinde gebildet werden sollte".

the village-mayor should be conferred upon them, insofar as the prevailing circumstances warrant it."[50]

In other words, the Jews in some villages of Sachsen-Meiningen continued even after 1811 to form local political corporations quite separate from the village-communities, just as in the village of Aschenhausen in Sachsen-Weimar.

If so, the Meiningen Law of 1856 – which aroused Philippson's mocking comment[51] – was quite logically pronouncing the abolition of the last traces of Jewish local autonomous self-government as a preparatory step to the granting of full individual local citizens' rights to all the Jews of the principality.

VI. TRACES OF CORPORATIVE INFLUENCES ON PRUSSIAN MUNICIPAL LEGISLATION

Ludwig Philippson's apparent dismay at the traces of corporate legislation in Meiningen had perhaps an additional motive: he, a Prussian Jew of Magdeburg, had lived through a period when his King, Friedrich Wilhelm IV, had tried to regulate the basic status of Prussian Jewry on corporative principles – and had fought against this tendency until a successful conclusion was reached.

Nor was Friedrich Wilhelm IV the first and only Prussian ruler to favour a corporative train of thought with regard to the Jews. Such ideas had first found expression in Friedrich Wilhelm II's legislation for the newly acquired Polish provinces of South- and New-East-Prussia, which in turn might have been an adaptation to Prussian patterns of Catherine II's municipal legislation with regard to White-Russian Jews.[52]

The relevant paragraph of the administrative directives for the new Prussian provinces expressly states[53] that a proportionate number of Jewish councillors be elected in every locality in accordance with the Jewish quota of the general population. These councillors should participate in municipal matters as representatives of the Jewish sector, and should at the same time carry out the administration of the Jewish community and its property. However, it is doubtful whether this directive was ever implemented. Not only were the Jews not happy with the whole of the Statute, which compared unfavourably with former Polish laws, but the election of these new town-councillors was to have taken place only after the demission or the demise of the then-serving Elders and, as in the peace of Tilsit (1807) the territory in question was again taken from

---

[50]*Ibid.*, "die Funktionen der Dorfschultheissen insoweit übertragen, als es die bestehenden Verhältnisse gestatten".

[51]Cf. above, n. 42 and 43.

[52]Catherine II ordered the enrolment of Jewish inhabitants of the White-Russian townships (acquired in 1772 from Poland) in the general citizens' rolls, according to their economic position. They were accorded, without regard to religion, the same municipal rights as those granted to the non-Jewish citizens belonging to a similar economic stratum. From 1778 Jews participated for a time in the municipal administration of White-Russian towns. Cf. Simon Dubnow, *Weltgeschichte des jüdischen Volkes*, VII, p. 258 ff.

[53]General-Judenreglement für Süd- und Neuostpreussen, 17th April 1797, Ch. IV, § 12 – according to L. v. Rönne und Heinrich Simon, *Die früheren und gegenwärtigen Verhältnisse in den . . . preussischen Staaten*, Breslau 1843, p. 301 (henceforth: *Rönne-Simon*).

Prussia, there seems to have been only scanty opportunity for holding elections in accordance with the above-mentioned §12, and no evidence for it has so far come to light.

This instance of corporate thinking in Prussian governmental circles was in abeyance between 1806 and 1814. But it again came to the fore in the subsequent period of reaction. A striking example may be adduced from the Grand-Duchy of Poznań that roughly corresponded to the former territory of South- and New-East-Prussia. The "Preliminary Ordnance" of June 1833, which, *i.a.*, was intended to put the municipal status of naturalised Jews on an equal footing with the status of non-Jews, contained in §20a a proviso excluding Jews from the chairmanship of the magistrates.[54] But this exception was only the beginning: during the Poznań municipal elections of 1838 a rather impressive number of Jewish town-councillors had been elected in various localities – the Jews constituting in certain places 30 per cent and more of the inhabitants. This caused a certain apprehension in government circles as to the future preponderance of the Jewish element in local administration. Thus the Ministry of the Interior empowered the provincial authorities[55] to enact a numerus clausus for the election of Jews, "of a third or a quarter [of the total to be elected] . . . if so proposed by the municipal authorities". This step, which seems to have been implemented in a number of townships (*i.a.*, Birnbaum, Strzelno and Rogasen),[56] practically amounted to the setting-up of a Jewish autonomous "curia" for municipal purposes. Thus, not only was the corporate character of the Jewish electorate preserved for some decades in certain Poznań townships but its influence made itself felt throughout the whole of the province, where until 1863 Jews had tended to regard themselves on certain occasions as a separate division of electors. An instance from Naklo has been recorded elsewhere,[57] and some more examples of a similar kind may be added.[58]

True, the province of Poznań with its Jewish masses was a special case. But even with regard to the Western parts of Prussia, corporative tendencies re-entered the scene with the Cabinet Order of Friedrich Wilhelm IV of 13th December 1841, initiating the preparation of a new Jewry-Law for the whole of Prussia. In his order the King renounced all attempts of his predecessors "to assimilate . . . the Jews individually". They should, therefore, "be organised as a political entity", side by side – but not within – the political framework of Prussia.[59] This intention met with strong opposition, not only from Jewish

[54]*Rönne-Simon*, p. 307.

[55]In fact, an order of the Oberpräsident to this effect was drafted (7th October 1838) before the official ministerial authorisation of 17th February 1840 had been published, *Rönne-Simon*, p. 330.

[56]Rogasen: *Allgemeine Zeitung des Judentums*, 1869, p. 1004; Strzelno and Birnbaum: *Der Israelitische Lehrer*, 1862/139.

[57]Jacob Toury, *Die politischen Orientierungen der Juden in Deutschland. Von Jena bis Weimar*, Tübingen 1966 (Schriftenreihe wissenschaftlicher Abhandlungen des Leo Baeck Instituts 15), p. 106.

[58]E.g., the attempts at electing Ludwig Philippson or Moritz Veit as Jewish representatives to the Prussian Diet. On Philippson's candidacy, cf. Toury, *Die politischen Orientierungen*, p. 105; on Veit: Bulletin des Leo Baeck Instituts, 8 (1965), No. 29, p. 83.

[59]Horst Fischer, *Judentum, Staat und Heer in Preußen im frühen 19. Jahrhundert. Zur Geschichte der staatlichen Judenpolitik*, Tübingen 1968 (Schriftenreihe wissenschaftlicher Abhandlungen des Leo Baeck Instituts 20), p. 155 ff.

quarters but also from the Ministry of the Interior, and was in the main abandoned. But some influences in that direction lingered on and found expression in the draft-proposal for the Prussian Jew-Law of 1847, when corporate representation was to be granted to the Jews on a municipal level. Paragraph 15 of the draft contains the following modus for the municipal representation of the *Judenschaft*: [60] if there are in a township so many Jews that, in proportion to the entire population, at least one councillor might be elected by them, the Jews who have the vote may be allowed to elect one or – if the proportion allows it – more councillors from *among themselves.*

Both houses of the Prussian Diet rejected the proposed modus and indeed the whole scheme of a renewed corporate *Judenschaft*, perhaps less in consequence of a liberal concept of emancipation than because of their general critical attitude to Friedrich Wilhelm IV's policies.

It goes without saying that the Prussian Jews in their entirety were violently opposed to these corporate tendencies and greeted their rejection as a victory in the struggle for emancipation.

VII. INDIVIDUAL CITIZENS' RIGHTS, GRANTED TO SELECT PERSONS

So far, all the cases surveyed consist of corporative rights granted to the Jews as a community by a township or by territorial lords. Only in the Prussian example (or the Württemberg Law of 1828) did a Central Government envisage plans for the establishment of Jewish local corporations as a generally applicable political measure, which however was hardly ever realised in practice. In other words, governments as a rule recoiled from the underlying conception of "towns within towns". The quest for unification and even uniformity characterised their modern image of statehood. Thus they tended to prefer the "educational" way of bettering the individual Jew and rewarding him for his attainments with individual citizens' rights.

Some of the territorial lords, as early as the seventeenth century, might have had the same attitude towards one or more of "their" useful Jewish subjects, but it remains doubtful whether they could prevail upon the magistrates of the towns under their sway to grant citizens' rights to individual Jews. It is still more doubtful whether towns of their own free will accorded individual burghers' rights to certain Jews in the eighteenth century because their economic activities were beneficial or perhaps even crucial to the development of the township. Yet, as there exist records of citizens' rights conferred upon Jews in the eighteenth century, without appropriate steps being enacted by Central Governments, it has to be assumed that in certain cases territorial lords forced

[60] This appellation "Jewry" alone is sufficient to remind one of the corporate legislation of former centuries. The following extract of the law – as printed in the *Reform-Zeitung*, Berlin 1847, No. 7 – contains the parallel text of the draft and of the final law of 23rd July 1847. The central passage in the original: "kann den jüdischen wahlberechtigten Bürgern gestattet werden, einen oder nach dem angegebenen Verhältnisse auch mehrere Verordnete . . . aus ihrer Mitte zu wählen . . ."

their will upon some towns and that in others magistrates on their own decided to award citizenship to Jews. So far it has not been possible to ascertain in every case the moving force behind each conferment of individual burghers' rights, and it can only be stated that those rights emanated partly from the Central Authorities and partly from local and/or feudal considerations, but were in fact bestowed upon individual Jews many years before the onset of governmental emancipatory tendencies.

This individual form of Jewish municipal citizenship is dimly remembered from Upper Silesia, which until 1740 had belonged to the Hapsburg Monarchy and came at this date under Prussian rule. If one is to believe the testimony of a Jewish amateur historian of that region a Jewish citizen existed in Myslowitz as early as the seventeenth century! [61] How could he have become a citizen, if not by a momentous decision of the magistrate – or what seems more likely – by the influence of the local landowner? And precisely from one of these local gentry comes confirmation regarding the civic rights of Upper Silesian Jews, even before the onset of general emancipatory tendencies: one of the scions of the Henckel v. Donnersmarck family, who were among the most affluent and influential of the local magnates, remarked that even before the Municipal Law of 1808 (to be treated later on) Upper Silesian Jews had "in most townships enjoyed the right to become citizens". [62] Some instances of the realisation of this right – e.g., in Guttentag – are also mentioned in modern research on Jewish local citizenship [63] and they round off the surprising picture of individual local "emancipation" in Upper Silesia on the eve of the nineteenth century.

Some similar cases of local enfranchisement of certain affluent Jews have been reported from Segeberg (Schleswig-Holstein) since the middle of the eighteenth century. [64] More have been vouched for immediately after with regard to some townships in the small principalities of Schwarzburg-Sondershausen, Mecklenburg and Schaumburg-Lippe. [65] But the latter instances should rather be ascribed to the grace of the territorial rulers themselves and not to local causes, for the local population and the nobility in these regions were well known for their anti-Jewish bias and the Jews as a whole were still far removed from attaining equal rights.

[61]The late Justizrat W. Immerwahr of Beuthen, an eminent lawyer and town-councillor of long standing, remarks on this case in his contribution: 'Zur Geschichte der Juden in Oberschlesien', in: *Oberschlesischer Heimatkalender*, Ratibor 1933, p. 57 ff. A transcript of this essay has been made for me by Dr. Lotte Weissmann, Haifa, and I hereby express my sincere thanks for her helpfulness.

[62]L. V. F. Henckel v. Donnersmarck, *Darstellung bürgerlicher Verhältnisse der Juden im preussischen Staate, unmittelbar vor dem Edikt vom 11. März 1812*, Leipzig 1814, p. 46 f.

[63]Stefi Wenzel, *Jüdische Bürger und kommunale Selbstverwaltung in preussischen Städten*, Berlin 1967, p. 89 f.

[64]Written communication by Studiendirektor Dr. Horst Tschenscher, Stadt Segeberg, dated 17th August 1975, to the Diaspora Research Institute, Tel-Aviv University. It is probably the Danish influence that made itself felt there. Thus citizens' rights for Copenhagen Jews are mentioned as early as the third decade of the seventeenth century, municipal rights for the Portuguese Jews of Altona since 1719. Cf. Günter Marwedel, *Die Privilegien der Juden in Altona*, Hamburg 1976, p. 108, n. 374, and document no. 43, p. 205 f.

[65]Specifications on these instances and sources for them: Toury, *Dokumentation*, p. 70 and n. 2–4.

However, the first individual municipal rights emanating from a Central Government and granted to select persons seem to have been established in Berlin by those few Jewish families who in 1791 had been granted individual naturalisation as Prussian subjects and a year later were accepted as burghers of the Prussian capital.[66]

In Berlin, such local application of an enlightened monarch's grace towards some favoured subjects went more or less unnoticed and was then regarded almost as a matter of course. Not so in Königsberg. Two of the scions of the new Berlin-Jewish citizens settled in the East-Prussian capital (1795), giving rise to immediate protests by the local patricians, who felt encroached upon by the imminent "danger" of being forced to grant the freedom of the city to Jews.[67] In short, the overall Prussian concept, in conformity with the concept of most of the other German states, was still rather far removed from the French revolutionary model of an indivisible citizens' status in State and Municipality alike, although the Berlin precedent did somewhat resemble it.

The discrepancy between the French and the German approach to local emancipation is strikingly reflected by the circumstances prevailing in Baden and the Palatinate on the right bank of the Rhine which in 1803 was incorporated into the Grand-Duchy of Baden. Since 1798 there had emerged in the towns of that region an absolute dichotomy between local and state-wide citizens' rights. It all started in the Palatinate (then still under nominal Bavarian administration). In some towns on the right bank of the Rhine, the first Jews had acquired either citizens' rights in the state but expressly without municipal rights, or local citizens' rights, without becoming enfranchised in the state.

It seems that the remarkable development in the former direction stemmed from the particular wishes of those Jews who asked for naturalisation but did not want to be burdened with municipal taxes or become dependent upon the town-magistrates and be subjected to the local Courts of Justice, preferring to remain under the jurisdiction of their princely protectors. Thus, on 30th September 1798, the Negociant Joseph Lallement, formerly a French subject and now proposing to settle in Mannheim, was received into the "Christian burghers' rights", not of the town, but under "immediate Protection of His Highness" (the Palatine Elector).[68] In a similar manner Aron Seeligmann was granted naturalisation in the Palatinate (1799), without being enfranchised in one of the townships.[69] Needless to say that both Lallement and Aron Seeligmann acted as purveyors for the Elector and felt relatively safe under his protection, but had little truck with town-authorities.

Yet such considerations were rather short-lived. The weakening of governmental power during the political and military upheavals in the Palatinate

---

[66] Jacob Jacobson, *Die Judenbürgerbücher der Stadt Berlin*, Berlin 1962, pp. 5, 6. Their names are listed, *ibid.*, nos. 1*–16*.

[67] M. Toury, *Dokumentation*, p. 66 and Document III a 1.

[68] "der ohnmittelbare Höchstschutz, dann Christlich bürgerliche Rechte und Befreiung Chur-mildest" gewährt. Quoted: Adolf Lewin, *Geschichte der badischen Juden*, Karlsruhe 1909, p. 64.

[69] GLA Karlsruhe, 206/2206, containing a confirmation on his naturalisation, dated Mannheim, 1st September 1808. Cf. J. Toury, *Dokumentation*, p. 26, n. 38 and p. 72. The spelling "Seeligmann" is preferred to "Seligmann", as all the documents down to 1822 use the first form.

during the years 1798–1802 stripped protection by an insecure and unstable government of much of its worth, while local citizenship again began to prove itself of some value. The central government in the Palatinate came in abeyance, then changed hands, and those Jews who wanted citizens' rights asked explicitly – from 1801 on – for *municipal* enfranchisement. In fact, even before the establishment of Badenian sovereignty, two Jewish families were received as local citizens in Mannheim [70] and Schwetzingen. [71] But when in the same year (1802) four families of Heidelberg applied for local citizenship in that town they were turned down, [72] partly because of the fierce resistance of the Heidelberg magistrate, partly because of the impending change in sovereignty. Probably all the municipal and governmental agencies first wanted to establish the intentions of the incumbent ruler Carl Friedrich of Baden with regard to the Jews. They soon became clear: a general law on the "organisation of the Jews" should be quickly enacted, and until then all requests for enfranchisement should be deferred. [73]

General regulations regarding Jewish status in Baden were indeed promulgated in 1808/1809, whether as part of the constitution of 1808, or in the form of a separate Jew-Law (1809). These constitutional edicts confirmed in theory the Jewish claim to full citizens' rights in the state, [74] but made their admittance to full local rights dependent upon the grace of the ruler. Some eminent Jewish families (then and also in later years) were indeed enfranchised in their dwelling places, but most of the Jews had to be content with the secondary position of *Hintersassen* or *Schutzbürger*. [75] True, the legal distinction between full citizens and the status of *Hintersassen* lost much of its discriminating character when the latter were granted the right to participate in local elections (1819). Nevertheless, especially after a new municipal ordinance had been drawn up in 1831, Jews remained the last *Schutzbürger* in Baden, if they were not locally enfranchised by the grace of the Grand-Duke.

Similar to Baden, and even a little worse, were matters in the neighbouring Kingdom of Württemberg. Since 1806 and until the Jew-Law of 1828, the Jewish "subjects" (*Untertanen*) were declared to be and treated as protected individuals (*Schutzgenossen*), who had been allocated their dwelling places by the government, but whose legal connections with the other local inhabitants had not been exactly defined. They paid local taxes and in some places – against

---

[70]Badisches Generallandesarchiv Karlsruhe 77/7266, fol. 8, 11, 17 ff.

[71]*Ibid.*, fol. 29, 41.

[72]*Ibid.*, fol. 53 ff. They were the families of Moses Fuld, Moses Flehinger and of David and Löw Zimmern.

[73]*Ibid.*, old pagination fol. 92, marginal decree, dated 11th March 1803.

[74]But in practice they were made dependent upon equal professional status with non-Jews. All the problems of the gradual development of state-wide emancipation in Baden are fully treated by Reinhard Rürup, 'Die Judenemanzipation in Baden', in, *Zeitschrift für die Geschichte des Oberrheins*, vol. 114, 1966, pp. 241 ff. Now reprinted in Reinhard Rürup: *Emanzipation und Antisemitismus. Studien zur "Judenfrage" der bürgerlichen Gesellschaft*, Kritische Sudien zur Geschichtswissenschaft, *Band 15*, Göttingen 1975. (The following source references are to the original article.)

[75]R. Heuser (as above, n. 1), pp. 25–28, 41 ff.

certain payments – could even participate in the benefits accruing from communal property. But in legal terms they were not even *Hintersassen*, although their status of natives of the place was recognised. As such, they could acquire real estate, be accepted into craft-guilds and were even drafted into the army.[76] Moreover, since 1817, the King granted certain well-to-do Jews local citizens' rights, if and when they agreed to "build a new house . . . on a site appointed by the police-authorities".[77] In this respect Württembergian Jews then enjoyed a similar position to that of the Jews of Baden.

When the Württemberg constitution of 1819 pronounced the principle (§62) that every citizen of the state should also belong, either as burgher or as *Beisitzer*, to a local community – thus establishing in theory the French principle of the identity of local and state-wide rights – it was immediately understood hat with regard to the Jews the paragraph was inapplicable. For the Jews were not then recognised as citizens of the state.

Such a recognition was not even unconditionally accorded to them by the Jew-Law of 25th April 1828, although the term "subjects" (*Untertanen*) was again applied to them and the mode of their enrolment as burghers or *Beisitzer* in the dwelling places was mentioned. But it was by no means automatically granted, not even to such of them who had addressed themselves to "useful" occupations and refrained from peddling and hawking. Thus, the local self-governing bodies became arbiters of Jewish municipal rights, and they, as true representatives of petty local interests, were quite averse to accepting Jews as co-citizens[78] and agreeing to their participation in local elections,[79] or – above all – to according them a share in the communal benefits.[80]

Their legal arguments against Jewish municipal rights culminated in the sentence that the Law of 1828 had not explicitly granted them local citizenship, and thus they did not attain them until "the actual admittance of an Israelite to burgher's rights".[81]

The problem of full local citizenship *for all* the Jews in Württemberg and Baden was not even alleviated by the fact that during the following decades ever-growing numbers of them were admitted individually as burghers in various towns, and especially in the commercial and governmental centres. Nor did the political emancipation of the Jews of Baden in 1849, or that of the Württembergian Jews in 1861, solve the municipal problems and in both countries the process of emancipation had to be crowned by separate laws settling the question of local citizenship, which remained the final step to be taken on the long road to full emancipation.

---

[76]Paul Tänzer, *Rechtsgeschichte der Juden in Württemberg*, p. 44 f.

[77]Württembergisches Hauptstaatsarchiv (HStA) Stuttgart, E 143/3226, No. 10.

[78]Cf. Toury, *Dokumentation*, III e 3. Refusal to grant citizens' rights to a Jewish physician at Rottweil.

[79]*Ibid.*, III e 4, Neunkirchen.

[80]Buchau/Federsee, HstA Stuttgart E 143/3226, No. 10. Long-drawn-out litigations accompanied Jewish endeavours to attain local citizens' rights there. *Allgemeine Zeitung des Judentums*, 1846, p. 480.

[81]HStA Stuttgart, as in n. 77.

VIII. FULL MUNICIPAL EMANCIPATION GRANTED
BEFORE STATE-WIDE POLITICAL EMANCIPATION

This fact in itself is already sufficient to prove our contention that, unlike France, the attainment of full local citizens' rights in Germany constituted a separate complex of problems which was not automatically solved together with state-wide emancipation, but adhered to certain causalities of a historical, socio-economic or psychological and even regional character. If so, it can easily be understood why there were German States which granted full municipal emancipation to all Jews otherwise qualifying for local citizenship, even before realising state-wide political emancipatory legislation.

The first, and perhaps the most striking, example of a municipal emancipation in advance of general political emancipation was given by the Kingdom of Prussia.[82] In the course of vigorous inner reforms after Prussia's defeat in the war against Napoleon there emerged the well-known Prussian *Städteordnung* of 1808, in which the enrolment of all qualified applicants in the citizens' lists was not made dependent upon a religious criterion. It opened the way to municipal enfranchisement to all Prussian Jews otherwise qualified for local citizenship. Thus, the first full emancipation on the municipal level was coincidentally the best of all: no specific mention of Jews was made, and their rights were implicitly anchored in a general law. Moreover, this law – unlike the so-called emancipatory edict of 1812 – was not later on restricted to the "old" Prussian provinces, but remained in force for the whole of the Kingdom.

Nevertheless, there were some attempts at curbing the general provisions of the Law of 1808, in order to discriminate against Jewish citizens also on a local level. In 1831 a revision of the law was enacted which disbarred them from the posts of Mayor or of *Dorfschulze*. The declared intention was to preclude non-Christians from being in authority over Christians.

In 1844 some additional restrictions were imposed on the confirmation of Jewish members of the magistracy and on their conduct of office. Some regional exceptions were also practised.[83] Certain restrictions continued until 1861[84] and served as an expression of the reactionary mood then prevailing in Prussian governmental agencies. But as a whole the *Städteordnung* of 1808 with its implicit principle of local emancipation was never seriously attacked as long as the Prussian monarchy lasted – in counter-distinction to the so-called "Emancipation-Law" of 1812, or even to the emancipatory paragraph of the Prussian constitution of 1849 (§ 12), that was soon countermanded by paragraph 14 of 1850, postulating the Christian character of the Prussian monarchy.

Similar were the latter stages of the struggle for emancipation in the Anhalt principalities. There, general and local emancipation was enacted during the Revolution of 1848/1849; but while the state-wide political rights were again

---

[82]The German territories under temporary French occupation, like Westphalia, may remain outside this study.

[83]E.g., in Poznań, cf. above, § 6.

[84]The highest municipal honour, that of becoming mayor, was withheld from them even longer.

abolished during the reactionary period,[85] local citizens' rights remained in effect and were even expressly incorporated in the *Gemeinde-Ordnung* that became the law of the land in Dessau, Coethen and Bernburg alike (1852/1859). Thus, final local emancipation preceded the final enactment of general political emancipation by ten years and more, as full political equality in Anhalt was not restored before the emancipatory Law of the North German Confederation (3rd July 1869).

The same holds true for the South German Kingdom of Bavaria. There, not even the Revolution of 1848 could bring into being a general emancipatory law, and only after the unification of Germany, when the constitution of the North German Confederacy with its above-mentioned emancipatory paragraph was recognised as binding also for Bavaria (22nd April 1871), did Bavarian Jews enjoy full civil and political equality.[86] But on a municipal level the repeal of the infamous Matricle-Law in 1861 could be regarded as the main step towards the fulfilment of Jewish aspirations towards untrammelled local citizens' rights.[87] The final removal of secondary obstacles was carried out by a series of general (and not specifically Jewish) laws during 1868/1869, viz. the *Gewerbe-Ordnung*, dated 30th January 1868, the Law concerning Homesteads, Marriage, etc. (25th April 1868), the Law concerning Social Services (29th April 1869) and the *Gemeindeordnungen* of 29th April 1869.[88] Thus in the last phase of local emancipation Bavarian Jews had arrived at the same stage of implicit municipal rights which the Prussian *Städte-Ordnung* had granted to their brethren in Northern Germany sixty years earlier. But, apart from chronological considerations, local emancipatory legislation in Bavaria as well as in Prussia preceded state-wide emancipation and had no direct connection with it.

IX. FULL MUNICIPAL EMANCIPATION GRANTED TOGETHER WITH STATE-WIDE POLITICAL EMANCIPATION

As already stated, the emancipatory model of the great French Revolution had coordinated the bestowing of state-wide and local citizens' rights to the Jews. It is, therefore, rather significant that those German states in which Jews were accorded general political rights together with local citizenship usually took the

[85]Yet Coethen had been one of the first few German principalities that of their own free will had granted emancipation to its Jews as early as 1810. Also Bernburg had pre-revolutionary Jewry-laws that nearly approached emancipation. Anhalt-Dessau, under whose rule the smaller principalities reverted after the Revolution of 1848, was the mainstay of reactionary policies towards the Jews.

[86]Even so some residuary discriminatory dues had to be abolished separately, which was done in 1881: Bayerisches Hauptstaatsarchiv München, Allgemeines Staatsarchiv/Staatsrat No. 1292.

[87]*Gesetzblatt des Königreichs Bayern*, No. 10, München, 18th November 1861, p. 70, § 15. On the Matricle-Law cf. Jacob Toury, 'Jewish Manual Labour and Emigration. Records from some Bavarian Districts (1830–1857)', in *LBI Year Book XIV* (1971), p. 48 f.

[88]On this phase of Bavarian legislation see now: Horst Hesse, *Die sogenannte Sozialgesetzgebung Bayerns Ende der sechziger Jahre des neunzehnten Jahrhunderts*, in Neue Schriftenreihe des Stadtarchivs München, 1971. Ample archival sources are adduced.

decisive step as the outcome of a revolutionary situation. In Hesse-Kassel it happened in 1831/1833, as an aftermath of the revolutionary mood of 1830, while in other states the Revolution of the years 1848/1849 brought about emancipation of the Jews, both as municipal burghers and as citizens of the state. States that then enacted coordinated emancipatory laws and even maintained them during the years of reaction following the revolution included Brunswick, the Grand-Duchy of Hesse (Darmstadt), Hesse-Homburg, Nassau, Oldenburg, the Kingdom of Saxony, the Grand-Duchy of Weimar and the Principality of Waldeck.[89]

Yet the revolutionary movement in Germany did not bring about the full emancipation of *German* bourgeoisie, and hence it is easily understood why Jewish emancipation did not attain an unconditional breakthrough. Not only did some states revoke Jewish state-wide and municipal emancipation granted during the Revolution – e.g., Hanover, Mecklenburg-Schwerin and Hesse-Kassel (where it had been in force since 1833) – but some governments, even under the impact of revolutionary events, still refrained from enacting emancipatory legislation – e.g., Bavaria, the Hohenzollern States, Mecklenburg-Strelitz and most of the Thuringian States.[90]

Even Baden and Württemberg, in other respects priding themselves on their liberal spirit, did not during the revolution arrive at a coordinated local and general political emancipation of Jews. While both granted their Jews state-wide citizens' rights in 1849, they continued to withhold from them, at least in principle, the full local enfranchisement.

Moreover, the realisation of state-wide political emancipation in Baden during the Revolution of 1848/1849 – which in any case was not devoid of repercussions on a municipal level[91] – expressly deferred the regulation of local rights until "the stormy excitement so inimical to the Israelites" should have abated.[92]

But while in Baden at least the principle of equal political rights was upheld, notwithstanding oppositional clamours, Württemberg even abrogated the state-wide political emancipation of the Jews (1855) and had to enact it anew in 1861.

Yet, in any case, in Baden and Württemberg local emancipation was established only after the realisation of political equality.

---

[89]In some of them the appropriate legislation was even ratified as late as 1852.

[90]Not mentioned here are the city-states, Hamburg, Lübeck, Bremen, Frankfurt, where the dichotomy between local and state-wide emancipation was not relevant; and the principalities of Lippe that followed the Prussian pattern of granting rights and then curbing them by administrative measures.

[91]Serious outbreaks against the Jews had occurred during the spring of 1848, some of them expressly aimed at deterring the Jews from their quest for local benefits, cf. Toury, *Dokumentation*, p. 89 and Doc. III d 8. And see now Michael Anthony Riff, 'The Anti-Jewish Aspect of the Revolutionary Unrest in Baden and its Impact on Emancipation', in *LBI Year Book XXI* (1976), pp. 27ff.

[92]Quoted by Rürup, *loc. cit.*, according to n. 198.

X. FULL LOCAL EMANCIPATION GRANTED AFTER STATE-WIDE POLITICAL EMANCIPATION

In Baden and Württemberg the situation was in so far remarkable, as the Jews were indeed enfranchised as citizens of the state (in Württemberg with an interruption from 1855 to 1861), but were devoid of an automatic claim to full local citizens' rights. Although many Jews had been enfranchised over the years, especially in the larger towns, they were still debarred from settling wherever they pleased and/or restricted to the status of *Hintersassen* without claim to the benefits accruing from communal property: pasture, wood, fishing, use of the local baking facilities, *et al.*

Baden and Württemberg and most of their townships had, in the main, retained their agricultural character. These benefits constituted, therefore, no mean part of a citizen's livelihood, one which he did not wish to share with the Jews. But there was a far more serious point in the day-to-day relations between Jews and their local neighbours. Very many Jews in the small communities were rather poor. As long as they had not been fully enfranchised, they were not able to insist that their needy be relieved out of the communal chest, and the non-Jews dreaded the time when they would be obliged to share all and everything with their Jewish co-inhabitants. There were still more difficult questions – those of local hospitals, school funds and in some instances also of allocations for religious purposes. These questions arose not only in Baden and in Württemberg but in very many states. But as the Jews themselves did not overly stress these points, being themselves interested in a certain degree of religious, educational and social independence, they remain outside the scope of this study.

But even so, the destitution of very many of the Jewish communities in Baden and Württemberg, at least before 1848, was a main stumbling-block to the unification of the local social services, while for instance even in the poor communities of Poznań the problem had not only been raised but had already begun to be solved – at least after the Prussian Jew-Law of 1847. However, it must be remarked that in Poznań, as by and large in the whole of Prussia, the communal benefits (*Gemeindenutzungen*) either were not of any economic importance to the bulk of the inhabitants or were made dependent upon a special payment (*Einkaufsgeld*).[93]

It is evident that the communal benefits in the rural communities of Baden and Württemberg had retained a somewhat higher value. For Baden the yearly top yield was officially assessed in 1860 for two places at 95 fl., although generally it was far lower and only in twenty-two communities did it reach a value of 20 fl. or more.[94] It may be assumed that the state of affairs in Württemberg was

[93]Not to be associated with the *Einzugsgeld* that was demanded from every stranger settling in a place. One of the points of local emancipation was the Jewish contention that they were not strangers and were not liable to pay *Einzugsgeld* in lieu of their enfranchisement. This was generally upheld by the government, but for the enjoyment of local benefits they were asked to pay the purchase-price (*Einkaufsgeld*). Staatsarchiv Koblenz, 403, Nr. 15226, betr. Vallendar, Reg. Koblenz, Abt. d.I., 9th July 1849.

[94]*Protokoll der 60. öffentlichen Sitzung d. II. Badischen Kammer*, 27th July 1860, Beilage p. 4 f., n. 2.

not dissimilar. It stands to reason that such additional income was desirable, but even in poorer communities its sharing with ten or more Jewish families hardly made a decisive difference. Moreover, Jews lived only in 191 places in Baden and 73 in Württemberg, while the majority of villages had nothing to fear.

Or did they fear that local emancipation, as tantamount to freedom of movement and settlement, would bring them a big influx of Jews? From the petitions against local emancipation in Baden, it might almost seem so.[95] If it were, one should even in this respect bear in mind that the main financial burden seemingly inherent in local emancipation must have been the expected increase in local expenditure on social payments.

There exists some evidence from Württemberg for the validity of such an assumption. When in 1855 a first draft of a local emancipatory Law for the Kingdom was deliberated in various governmental branches, the highest Jewish organisation with official standing (*Oberkirchenbehörde*) came up with a remarkable proposal: it was prepared to content itself with a law burdening the local authorities with only two-thirds of the social expenditure for the Jewish sector, while the Jews themselves would cover the remainder, if it "proved impossible to induce the political community to accept total responsibility for the expenditure of keeping the destitute Israelites".[96]

A moot point in the allocation of social funds was the question of the use of local endowments with a specific religious (Jewish or Christian) character. Could they, or should they, be used for interconfessional social services? But this was a secondary question of local character and no overall solution was offered.[97]

In the final process of steering the local emancipatory laws of Baden and Württemberg through the legislative assemblies both questions – the burghers' benefits and the welfare expenditure – were raised during the debate. But there seems to have been a marked difference of approach and of public mood between the two states.

In Baden, the draft-law for local emancipation, as tabled in the chambers, expressly provided for a transitory period of five years until the Jews could fully participate in the common benefits and the social services. These issues also took precedence over others during the parliamentary deliberations, which as a whole proceeded sedately and without many differences of opinion on the principle of emancipation. But there was a bombardment of petitions, sent in mostly on lithographed duplicate forms, and in some places there were even threats of violence against the Jews, decisively and quickly curbed by the government.[98]

---

[95]Rürup, *loc. cit.*, n. 222: From 194 petitions against the emancipatory law of 1862, 126 came from districts that were only sparsely settled by Jews.

[96]HSt Stuttgart, E 201 c/4, Opinion of the Secret Council, 31st October 1862. The Jew-Law of 1828 included a parallel, though inverse, ratio: Only if the Jews could not keep their poor should the local community be obliged to take over responsibility for up to two-thirds of the total.

[97]In the kingdom of Hanover most local communities, even in 1848, objected to Jewish participation in social services, as their funds were purportedly of confessional origin: Hauptstaatsarchiv Hannover: Hann. 80, Hann. I A, No. 478; Hann. 80, Hildesheim I N, No. 145.

[98]*Allgemeine Zeitung des Judentums*, 1862, pp. 114, 118, 125, 149, 242.

On the whole, these occurrences did not impress the legislators as really serious or especially well organised. Nevertheless, the final draft of the emancipatory law, unanimously approved in the Second Chamber and with only three dissenting votes in the Upper House (12th June 1862), differed from the first by the significant provision that the transitory period for the full acceptance of the Jews to all the civic benefits and social services was extended from five years to ten.[99] And this fourteen years after the attainment of state-wide emancipation!

The deliberations on the local emancipatory law of Württemberg proceeded in quite another vein. It may be that the chronological sequence played a part in it – state-wide emancipation having been finally enacted only in December 1861, while already a week before that date the Second Chamber had decided to petition the King for the speeding up of local emancipation[100] – and it is quite certain that the new professional legislation (*Gewerbeordnung*, 17th February 1862) did much to pre-empt the solution of questions pertaining to local economic competition. But it seems that the main difference stemmed from the formulation of the local emancipatory law itself. It consisted of a single paragraph, promising the Jews equal civic rights against equal civic duties. Not even a specific formula for a Jewish oath was mentioned, and during the deliberations on the proposal in the State Council it was explained that – as the old form of the oath *more judaico* was thus not explicitly abolished – it could be reimposed by mere administrative measure, if it should prove necessary.[101] In the main, one should now desist from discriminating against the Jews, as "the former restrictions had only strengthened their specific character and hampered their amalgamation with their co-citizens".[102]

The State Council opposed special legislation with regard to the Jewish poor with similar arguments, since now "the Israelites have to participate in all civic dues . . . on the same footing as the Christians . . . and anyway it must be conceded that they have never yet lacked a charitable spirit". Moreover, in mixed Protestant–Catholic localities the whole of the social burden was carried by the political community, and one should not exempt the Jews from such a state of affairs.[103]

But the draft-law did add one – seemingly self-explanatory or even inconsequential – passage. With regard to the religious practice and to the marriage-laws certain provisions of the Jew-Laws of 1828 and 1831 were to remain in force.[104] Yet, from this starting-point there arose, even during the preliminary deliberations in the Council, the question whether it was not appropriate to take this opportunity to establish the civic character of Marriage-Law and to enact a form of civil marriage pertaining also to the Jews with a view to legalising interconfessional marriages between Christians and Jews.

---

[99]Rürup, *loc. cit.*, p. 294, 298 and notes.
[100]HstA Stuttgart, E 33/664, No. 85.
[101]As in n. 96.
[102]*Ibid.*
[103]*Ibid.*
[104]§ 37, No. 2 and 38–40 (from 1828) and § 48–61 (from 1831). The reason was that these provisions were not of a civic but of a religious nature.

Although these additions were not included in the draft-law, the commission set up by the Lower Chamber expressly added a new and general formula for the oath (so help me God – so wahr mir Gott helfe) and a special *passus* for the legalisation of mixed civil marriages between Jews and Christians. The commission could point to the fact that it had been petitioned in this sense by various Jewish communities and bodies. But there were also counter-petitions, Jewish and non-Jewish alike, and it so happened that during the discussion in both Houses the question of civil marriage and of the general oath usurped the centre of the stage, whereas the principle of local emancipation with its inherent problems of social services and civic benefits did not arouse a significant controversy.[105]

Finally, both Württembergian Chambers threw out the provisions for mixed marriage and ratified the local emancipatory law, which also, by the abolition of the oath *more judaico*, signified the conclusion of the long process of general emancipation in this country. Only with this last step did the Württembergian legislation succeed in bridging the gap between local and state-wide emancipation that had characterised the emancipatory processes in Württemberg from its very beginnings almost up to the time when the emancipation of the Jews was to be fully enforced.

[105]The interest of the general public in the former questions is reflected in the reporting of the deliberations in '*Schwäbische Kronik*' *des Schwäbischen Merkur*, No. 287, 288 (4th, 5th December 1863), where civil marriage, the oath formula and the closing of Jewish shops on Sundays took precedence over the principle of local emancipation.

German Nationalism and Jewish Assimilation
The Bismarck Period

BY GORDON R. MORK

Among the greatest and most tragic ironies of the history of western civilisation is that of the Jews of Germany.* As German nationalism grew in strength during the nineteenth century, Jews were among its leading advocates. Then, in the twentieth century, it developed a wild perversity which utterly destroyed German Jewry. The unfolding of this sobering irony was of massive significance to Jews and to Germans. And its reverberations can yet be felt in current news reports. But its significance goes beyond the history of Germans and Jews and extends to that of any society which faces problems of ethnic or cultural diversity.[1] These reconsiderations will introduce the reader to no startling new documentation, recently unearthed from the archives; it is hoped, however, that the interpretive framework may add a new dimension to our understanding of the subject.

The paradox of German nationalism and Jewish assimilation can be studied in microcosm during the Bismarck period. Most politically active Jews supported the nationalist policies of Otto von Bismarck after 1866. Full civil emancipation came to North Germany with the *Reich* law of 1869 and was extended to Baden, Württemberg and Bavaria with the Imperial constitution of 1871. Bismarck's chief political support during the early 1870s came from the National Liberal Party, in which a number of Jews were prominent. Indeed, the association between Jews and the German chancellor was so close that when antisemites began their agitation after the economic crash of 1873, their targets included Bismarck as well as such well-known Jews as Ludwig Bamberger, Gerson von Bleichröder and Eduard Lasker.[2] As the agitation grew during the next few years, involving Court-preacher Stoecker, Heinrich von Treitschke and the petition entitled 'The Emancipation of the German People from the Yoke of Jewish Rule', Jews began to wonder if the German national state which they had helped to create would indeed accept them as equal citizens. Berthold Auerbach, the popular Jewish novelist and storyteller, who was devoted to the

---

*An earlier version of this paper was read at the meetings of the American Historical Association in 1973. The author wishes to thank Dr. Marjorie Lamberti and Dr. Herbert Levine for their helpful comments.

[1] The author once wrote a brief review of Ismar Schorsch's excellent monograph, *Jewish Reactions to German Anti-Semitism, 1870–1914*, New York 1972, and commented in closing that the book should be required reading in college level Black Studies courses. The book review editors evidently thought he was playing a prank on their readers and exercised their option of deleting the remark. See *Library Journal*, 15th June 1972.

[2] For example, the so-called "Era Articles" in the *Neue Preussische Zeitung*, June and July 1875, especially No. 149, 30th June 1875.

ideal of assimilation, responded to the situation with an anguished outcry: "My life and my work has been in vain."[3]

This is neither the time nor the place to review the recent literature on German-Jewish history.[4] Suffice it to say that much of that literature has added significant details to our knowledge of the subject, while remaining within the standard interpretive patterns, be they liberal, religious or ethnocentric. Now, in the 1970s, it may be time to try to place the topic of Germans and Jews into a larger framework of economic, social and institutional history. Marxists, of course, have long favoured this approach, though not without partisan motive.[5] At an American Historical Association symposium in 1971, which was later published in a previous Year Book, Paul Duggan suggested that the "sociology of interest groups" be applied to the topic, while more recently it has even been proposed that German Jews were "psychologically dependent" on a "myth" of the German Enlightenment.[6] This paper is offered as quite another interpretive direction. The author makes no claim of exclusive validity for his interpretation; yet he suggests that its comparative approach may have greater meaning for generations not personally touched by the searing experiences of the 1930s and 1940s than standard interpretations.

American historians and sociologists have devoted much effort to the study of the immigration of Europeans into the United States and to the interrelationships of the immigrants and the so-called native born Americans brought about by that phenomenon. This paper will suggest that an important new dimension in our understanding of Germans and Jews will result if we try to think of Jews as *cultural immigrants* into German society during the nineteenth century and the reception which they received from the German Gentile population as essentially a nativist welcome.[7]

In his influential book, *Strangers in the Land,* John Higham has told the story of American responses to European immigrants, "an internal minority" distinguishable by its foreign connections. "Specific nativist antagonisms may, and

---

[3]"Vergebens gelebt und gearbeitet". In a letter to his cousin Jakob Auerbach (Berthold Auerbach, *Briefe an seinen Freund Jakob Auerbach, Ein biographisches Denkmal,* Frankfurt a. Main 1884, vol. II, p. 442). On the disappointed Auerbach see now Margarita Pazi, 'Berthold Auerbach and Moritz Hartmann. Two Jewish Writers of the Nineteenth Century', in *LBI Year Book XVIII* (1973), pp. 215–218.

[4]The literature is extensive, as seen in the ongoing bibliography in this *Year Book* and the series: Schriftenreihe wissenschaftlicher Abhandlungen des Leo Baeck Instituts, the latest volume of which available to the author was *Juden im Wilhelminischen Deutschland 1890–1914.* Ein Sammelband herausgegeben von Werner E. Mosse unter Mitwirkung von Arnold Paucker, Tübingen 1976 (Schriftenreihe wissenschaftlicher Abhandlungen des Leo Baeck Instituts 33).

[5]The approved Marxist–Leninist view may be represented by Walter Mohrmann, *Antisemitismus. Ideologie und Geschichte im Kaiserreich und in der Weimarer Republik,* [East] Berlin 1972.

[6]See Duggan's comments on papers by Marjorie Lamberti and Werner T. Angress, in *LBI Year Book XVII* (1972), pp. 43–54, and Sidney Bolkosky, *The Distorted Image: German Jewish Perceptions of Germans and Germany, 1918–1935,* New York 1975.

[7]Conceivably this analysis might be pushed to a still higher level of generalisation, but conceptualisation of general migration theory is not yet well advanced. See J. J. Mangalam and Harry Schwarzweller, 'General Theory in the Study of Migration: Current Needs and Difficulties', *International Migration Review,* 3 (1968), pp. 3–18.

do," he says, "vary widely in response to the changing character of minority irritants and the shifting conditions of the day . . . [But] the nativist's most characteristic complaint runs against the loyalty of some foreign (or allegedly foreign) group. Seeing or suspecting a failure of assimilation, he fears disloyalty." [8] The resemblance of this description of American circumstances to the German situation is readily apparent. Indeed, the liberal German Jew Ludwig Bamberger pointed out in 1880 that there was great similarity between German antisemitism and the American Know-nothing movement.[9] The major difference, he argued, was that Jews were *not* immigrants to Germany, but had rather lived there for many centuries.

Let us pose our major question this way: was the position of Jews in Germany during the period of Bismarck's lifetime in some sense analogous to the position of European immigrants to the United States during the same period? To answer the question we might find it useful to divide German Jews into three groups: foreign-born Jews, Prussian-Polish Jews, and central and west German Jews.

The first group would include all Jews who were in fact born outside the boundaries of the several German states and who took up residence in the German *Reich*. It is interesting that a number of well-known German Jews came from such families. For example, Albert Ballin's father emigrated from Denmark, Karl Marx's mother was Dutch and Sigmund Freud's family emigrated from Galicia to Leipzig, moving on to Vienna when young Sigmund was only four years old.[10] The overwhelming majority of the Jewish immigrants came from Eastern and Southeastern Europe. To some observers, their number was increasing during the 1870s. "Over our eastern borders," wrote Heinrich von Treitschke in 1879, "presses year after year, from the bottomless Polish cradle, a herd of pushy pants-selling youngsters, whose children and grandchildren will some day dominate Germany's stock exchanges and newspapers. The immigration is rising steadily, and the question becomes ever more serious: how can we blend this foreign people with our own?"[11]

Specific immigration statistics are difficult to find, and those which are available are subject to varying interpretations. In 1880 less than three per cent of the 560,000 Jews in the German *Reich* were foreign-born, hardly a large proportion. On the other hand, the number of Jews in the *Reich* rose by some

---

[8]New Brunswick, N.J. 1955, p. 4.

[9]In his *Deutschthum und Judenthum*, Leipzig 1880, reprinted in Walter Boehlich (ed.), *Der Berliner Antisemitismusstreit*, Frankfurt a. Main 1965, p. 158.

[10]Lamar Cecil, *Albert Ballin*, Princeton, N.J. 1967, p. 15. Oscar J. Hammen, *The Red '48ers*, New York 1969, p. 9. Freud's *Autobiographical Study*, quoted in Marthe Robert, *The Psychoanalytic Revolution. Sigmund Freud's Life and Achievement*, New York 1966, p. 13; Oscar Handlin, 'Jews in the Culture of Middle Europe', *Studies of the Leo Baeck Institute*, New York 1967, p. 164. Similarly, the first Jewish students admitted to German universities (in 1678) were foreign-born; Monika Richarz, *Der Eintritt der Juden in die akademischen Berufe. Jüdische Studenten und Akademiker in Deutschland 1678–1848*, Tübingen 1974 (Schriftenreihe wissenschaftlicher Abhandlungen des Leo Baeck Instituts 28), pp. 33, 53, 71. During the eighteenth century, foreign-born Jews made up a high proportion of Jewish students at the universities of Königsberg and Frankfurt a.d. Oder, and the medical college at Berlin.

[11]In *Preussische Jahrbücher*, November 1879, reprinted in Boehlich, *op. cit.*, pp. 4–5.

41,000 between 1875 and 1880 (nearly 8 per cent in five years). And the concentration of Jews in certain urban areas added to the *impression* of a surge of foreign immigration. Between 1856 and 1871, for example, the number of Jews resident in Berlin rose from some 13,000 to 36,000 and by 1880 the number had risen to 54,000. About 3,000 foreign-born Eastern Jews were listed as resident in Berlin in 1880, a large enough group to be fairly conspicuous when concentrated in certain areas of the city. The situation in Dresden and Leipzig was even more pronounced.[12] In a pamphlet arguing that the so-called mass immigration of Jews to Germany was only a myth, one observer pointed out quite correctly that more Jews were emigrating from Germany than were immigrating into the country in the 1850s, 1860s and 1870s. His figures, however, are not detailed enough to demonstrate how many of those Jews who left Germany were recent immigrants or individuals virtually in transit, and how many were Jews who had lived within the German states for a generation or more.[13] Those who claimed there was a mass immigration of foreign-born Jews were exaggerating, but there was enough apparent truth in their claims to elicit a resonance in oversensitive inhabitants of some of the major German cities.

What of the great majority of German Jews, then, who were born and raised within the geographical boundaries of the several German states? Clearly they cannot be legitimately called immigrants in the geographical or legal sense. However, a large proportion of them were born and raised in a milieu which was recognised as foreign to German culture by Jew and Gentile alike. And their movement from one culture to another was usually accompanied by geographical movement as well. Thus their circumstances were clearly analogous to those of the immigrants literally defined. This, the second category of the analysis, is the Jewish population of the Polish provinces of Prussia. These people had been acquired by the Hohenzollern monarchs during the partitions of Poland only a century earlier, lost during the Napoleonic wars, and re-acquired at the Congress of Vienna in 1815. These Jews were not granted the civil rights extended to other Prussian Jews in 1812, and they were generally considered to be more akin to the Jews of Russian Poland than to the Jews of Berlin and points west. In the early nineteenth century their vernacular was Yiddish, their reli-

---

[12]Detailed figures on the religious background of immigrants were not published. Nor were systematic figures published on the origin of the population of given towns, districts, etc. Census data is from *Die statistischen Tabellen des preussischen Staats . . . 1843*, Berlin 1845, pp. 16–17; *Vierteljahrshefte zur Statistik des Deutschen Reiches . . .*, Bd. II, Heft I, Berlin 1873, pp. 188b–188c; *Die Volkszählung im Deutschen Reich . . . 1880*, Bd. LVII, *Statistik des Deutschen Reichs*, Berlin 1883, pp. 248–249. Further statistics are available from Stefan Behr, *Der Bevölkerungsrückgang der deutschen Juden*, Frankfurt a. Main 1932; Jakob Segall, *Die beruflichen und sozialen Verhältnisse der Juden in Deutschland* (Veröffentlichungen des Bureaus für Statistik der Juden, Heft 9), Berlin 1912; Klara Eschelbacher, 'Die ostjüdische Einwanderungsbevölkerung der Stadt Berlin', *Zeitschrift für Demographie und Statistik der Juden*, 16. Jhrg. (1920), 2–23. See the discussion in S. Adler-Rudel, *Ostjuden in Deutschland, 1880–1940. Zugleich eine Geschichte der Organisationen, die sie betreuten*, Tübingen 1959 (Schriftenreihe wissenschaftlicher Abhandlungen des Leo Baeck Instituts 1), pp. 19–23. Evidence that a concern about the number of foreign-born Eastern Jews extended to the Jewish community is offered by Schorsch, *op. cit.*, pp. 26–27.

[13]S. Neumann, *Die Fabel von der jüdischen Masseneinwanderung*, Berlin 1880, pp. 14–15 *et passim*.

gious observances were strict, and they were in every way ethnically distinct from the Polish and German Christians who formed the majority of the population of the area. When limited citizenship began to be granted in the 1830s, according to a complex formula involving both *Bildung* and *Besitz* (in the German sense), only a minority of families could qualify.[14]

The urbanisation of the nineteenth century stimulated large numbers of these Prussian-Polish Jews to leave the little towns of their birth and move to great cities like Breslau or Berlin. Between 1843 and 1880 the Jewish population of Berlin increased from 8,400 to 54,000 (more than six times) while the overall population of the city increased by a factor of only three. Meanwhile the number of Jews in Prussian Poland fell from 79,000 to 56,000.[15] When these Jews left the little towns of their birth, they left behind them a traditional society ethnically distinct from that of Germany, where learning meant the Talmud, where religion meant strict observance of ritual law, where bright young men were supposed to study solely for the rabbinate, and where contact with the non-Jewish world was limited to necessary commercial and occasional political intercourse. When they moved to cities like Breslau and Berlin they mastered the German tongue, they turned from the study of sacred to profane subjects, and they sought to integrate themselves into every aspect of German culture. Sometimes they changed their names. They were not always welcomed, and their staunch proclamations that they were as much German-born as anyone from another part of Prussia were met with some scepticism. Many Germans simply placed all Jews from Polish areas (be they ruled by the Hohenzollern, the Habsburg or the Romanovs) in a single category, and made no distinctions among the various "Eastern Jews". When Ludwig Bamberger responded to the charge of mass immigration of Russian Jews with the argument that the majority of those so labelled were in fact of Prussian origin, he was recognising that in the popular mind there was little distinction made between the two. They were all seen as immigrants.[16]

If a case can be made that these first two groups, foreign-born and Prussian-Polish Jews, were either literally or figuratively immigrants to the new Germany, what of the Jews of the Western and Central part of the country, whose forefathers had lived in German-speaking territories for generations, indeed for

---

[14]Ernest Hamburger, *Juden im öffentlichen Leben Deutschlands. Regierungsmitglieder, Beamte und Parlamentarier in der monarchischen Zeit 1848–1918*, Tübingen 1968 (Schriftenreihe wissenschaftlicher Abhandlungen des Leo Baeck Instituts 19), p. 15; Gordon R. Mork, 'The Making of a German Nationalist. Eduard Lasker's Early Years', *Societas*, I (1971), pp. 23–32. Technically, the reference is to the *Regierungsbezirke* Posen and Bromberg: see *Statistischen Tabellen . . . 1843*, pp. 16–17. See also Robert Weltsch, 'Die schleichende Krise der jüdischen Identität – Ein Nachwort', in *Juden im Wilhelminischen Deutschland*, pp. 494–495.

[15]*Volkszählung . . . 1880; Statistischen Tabellen . . . 1843*; and Neumann, pp. 12–15. Describing the situation, Peter Gay said, "Berliners, the familiar cliché had it, are from Breslau, and many Jews were from Breslau and beyond." *The Berlin-Jewish Spirit. A Dogma in Search of some Doubts*, The Leo Baeck Memorial Lecture 15, New York 1972, p. 6.

[16]Reprinted in Boehlich, *op. cit.*, p. 63. See also George L. Mosse, *Germans and Jews, The Right, the Left, and The Search for a 'Third Force' in Pre-Nazi Germany*, New York 1970, pp. 71–72, and Pinchas E. Rosenblüth, 'Die geistigen und religiösen Strömungen in der deutschen Judenheit', in *Juden im Wilhelminischen Deutschland*, p. 552.

centuries? Depending on how and when one counts them, these German-born Jews comprised up to seventy per cent of the Jewish population of the Bismarckian *Reich*.[17] They form the third group. Is there any sense in which these Jews were immigrants to Germany?

Their situation, it may be argued, was directly parallel to that of the Prussian-Polish Jews, except that their assimilation into German society took place one or two generations earlier. During the old régime the Jews of the Holy Roman Empire held a position among the estates of society similar to that of resident aliens. The onerousness of their legal burdens varied from state to state, but nowhere did Jews have a civic position equal to that of Christians of similar economic standing. Jews throughout the German states spoke the vernacular dialect we know as Yiddish and lived their lives either literally or figuratively separated from their German Christian neighbours by stout ghetto walls.[18] When Moses Mendelssohn began to encourage the use of German as a common language for intellectual and even religious discourse in the late eighteenth century, he met with as much resistance from the Jewish traditionalists as from Christians. After Mendelssohn and under the stimulus of the Napoleonic period, Western and Central German Jews rapidly began to acculturate themselves to their German environment. Jacob Katz, who has studied the process in detail, refers to the Prussian Jews emancipated by the decree of 1812 as "newly-born" free citizens of the state. He quotes David Friedländer, one of the leaders of the Berlin community, as follows:

> "I am a Prussian citizen. I have sworn solemnly to promote and support my Fatherland. Both duty and gratitude demand that I achieve this with all my might. First of all, I must endeavor to join with my fellow citizens, to approach them in custom and habit, to enter with them into social and personal connections; for the bonds of sociability and love bind more closely and strongly than the law itself. And only through these bonds can I achieve the aim of living with my fellow citizens in harmony, peace, and friendship."[19]

Friedländer's approach to assimilation parallels almost exactly the first phases of the model sketched by the sociologist Milton Gordon in analysing the situation of European immigrants to the United States. The first step Gordon calls "cultural or behavioural assimilation" or "acculturation". It was, as Friedländer put it, to approach his fellow citizens "in custom and habit". Gordon's second step is "structural assimilation", i.e., the large-scale entrance

---

[17]Hamburger, *op. cit.*, p. 7.
[18]The question of Yiddish is complex. Some authorities like to distinguish between *Judendeutsch*, the ghetto language of German Jews, and *Jüdisch-Deutsch*, the language of the Eastern Jews. Other authorities, including such well-informed scholars as Jacob Katz, *Out of the Ghetto*, Cambridge, Mass. 1973, p. 81, contend that all Ashkenazic Jewry shared the same Yiddish vernacular prior to the emancipation, though of course with many local variations. This is also the view of Herman Pollack, *Jewish Folkways in Germanic Lands, 1648–1806*, Cambridge, Mass. 1971, p. xv, and S. A. Birnbaum, 'Institutum Ascenezicum', in *LBI Year Book XVII* (1972), pp. 243–249. The cultural pattern of Jews in the Germanic lands during the old régime is nicely summarised by Richarz, *op. cit.*, pp. 1 ff. As Peter Gay points out, acculturated Jews were usually quick to dissociate themselves from Yiddish in order to put a respectable distance between themselves and the newly arrived immigrants; 'Begegnung mit der Moderne. Deutsche Juden in der deutschen Kultur', in *Juden im Wilhelminischen Deutschland*, pp. 255–256.
[19]In *Studies of the LBI*, pp. 74–75.

into the cliques, clubs and other institutions of the host society. His third step is intermarriage. Friedländer, similarly, saw the next steps for him in "sociability and love". Gordon's other four steps are "identificational assimilation", i.e., the sense of "peoplehood" based exclusively on the host society, and three steps involving the acceptance of the immigrant: the absence of prejudice, of discrimination, and of power and value conflict.[20] Some of the "new-born" Jewish German citizens, including several of Mendelssohn's own children, took the ultimate step of converting to Christianity to symbolise their acceptance of the majority culture. Many intermarried. The vast majority saw in German nationalism and in the outlook of the *Centralverein* Gordon's "identificational assimilation".[21] Gordon's final three steps were partially achieved during the Weimar Republic, before the process was irrevocably reversed by National Socialism.

During the late eighteenth and early nineteenth centuries, therefore, Western and Central German Jews went through a process which closely parallelled that of Prussian-Polish Jews a few decades later. Even the Jews of Baden, that relatively enlightened state in Germany's Southwest corner, were widely viewed as members of a foreign nation during the early nineteenth century. Berthold Auerbach, a fully assimilated Jew who was born in a village in Baden in 1812, planned a novel in the 1880s which would have illustrated this process of cultural immigration of Western German Jews. He planned to deal with three generations of a German-Jewish family. The hero was to be the representative of Auerbach's own generation, which saw in Germany not only its physical but also its spiritual home, and which fought to secure its position. The hero's father was to represent those orthodox Jews who saw in Jewry a nation as well as a religious group. The hero's son was to be the representative of the new age for which Auerbach hoped, in which tensions between Jew and German would hardly be noticeable (Gordon's final steps). Auerbach died before he could write the novel, but his idea suggests that to become part of the German cultural nation was a migration of some significance even for a Western German Jew.[22]

It appears, therefore, that the analogy holds: Western and Central German Jews were cultural immigrants to Germany. The major differences between them and their cousins whose origin was east of Berlin was that they "arrived" a generation or so earlier. The steps towards full assimilation into Germany were similar for all three of the groups identified. And in each case the steps were analogous to those faced by a newly arrived immigrant in the United States.

Now let us turn to the reception of the cultural immigrants by the German Christian population. As in the case of the responses of the American-born

[20]Milton M. Gordon, *Assimilation in American Life*, New York 1964, pp. 70–71.
[21]See Arnold Paucker, 'Zur Problematik einer jüdischen Abwehrstrategie in der deutschen Gesellschaft', in *Juden im Wilhelminischen Deutschland*, especially the material quoted on p. 488.
[22]Ludwig Geiger, *Die Deutsche Literatur und die Juden*, Berlin 1910, pp. 241–242. On Baden see also Schorsch, *op. cit.*, p. 3. Writing of the situation in Frankfurt a. Main following 1815, Saemy Japhet says that the youth left the ghetto and "migrated into the world". 'The Secession from the Frankfurt Jewish Community under Samson Raphael Hirsch', *Historia Judaica*, 10 (1948), p. 102. See also Goethe's perception of Frankfurt in Mosse, *op. cit.*, p. 46.

population to immigrant groups, attitudes varied widely, from active recruit-ment of immigrants, through apathy and indifference, to several degrees of hostility. Those who welcomed the Jews as cultural immigrants, beginning in the late eighteenth century, argued that they should be granted civil rights to encourage and to facilitate their assimilation as Germans.[23] Those who viewed the cultural immigration with hostility based their argument partly on religion, and partly on the broader grounds that the Jews were fundamentally "un-German" and that lowering legal barriers to integration would therefore undermine and weaken the essence of the German nation. This latter trend be-came stronger after 1869. The new antisemitism, argued Treitschke defensively, was "a natural reaction of Germanic folk consciousness against a foreign ele-ment". Treitschke saw himself as a moderate during the controversy which reached its apex around 1880. He publicly maintained that full assimilation was possible for German Jews and he turned his polemics against those "immi-grants" who seemed unwilling or unable to follow that course.[24]

The antisemitic petition circulated in 1880 and 1881, which claimed 300,000 signatures, dwelt on the same themes. It claimed that Jews were second or third generation immigrants who wanted to impose "a kind of foreign domination" on Germany. Two of its demands were remarkably similar to those of American nativists: the petition called for a special census of the Jews and for strict limitation of Jewish immigration.[25]

The analogy between German and American conditions would not be pushed too far if one pointed out that racialist justifications for nativist feelings arose in both countries at about the same time and from virtually the same historical and pseudo-scientific sources. John Higham, Oscar Handlin and Hans-Ulrich Wehler all note that those who claimed superiority for the Anglo-American way of life emphasised its roots in the virtues of the Germanic tribes described by Tacitus and in the liberties proclaimed by the Protestant reformers. The same linguistic, biological and anthropological thought was adapted to nativist propaganda in both countries.[26]

One of the most striking similarities between German and American develop-

---

[23]For example, Christian Wilhelm Dohm, who published *Über die bürgerliche Verbesserung der Juden* in 1781 at the behest of Mendelssohn in order to aid the Jews of Alsace-Lorraine; Arthur Herzberg, *The French Enlightenment and the Jews*, New York 1968, p. 185. Uriel Tal deals with the complexities of the attitudes of the liberal intellectuals in *Christians and Jews in the 'Second Reich'* (*1870–1914*), Jerusalem 1969, a work now made available to a wider audience by Noah Jonathon Jacobs's translation from the Hebrew into English as *Christians and Jews in Germany. Religion, Politics, and Ideology in the Second Reich, 1870–1914*, London–Ithaca 1975. See pp. *31–34 et passim* of the English version.

[24]In Boehlich, *op. cit.*, p. 11. Treitschke's personal attitudes were shot through with social anti-semitism. A comparison of his letters in the *Deutsche Staatsbibliothek*, East Berlin, with *Heinrich von Treitschkes Briefe*, Max Cornicelius, ed., Leipzig 1920, shows that many of his antisemitic remarks were expunged before publication. Treitschke used the verb "verschmelzen" to describe the complete assimilation he favoured. Hermann Cohen agreed that "verschmelzen" should be the goal. See P. E. Rosenblüth, in *Juden im Wilhelminischen Deutschland*, pp. 559–560.

[25]In H. Schulthess, *Europäischer Geschichtskalender*, 21 (1880), p. 240.

[26]Oscar Handlin, *The Uprooted*, New York 1951, pp. 272, 275, 279; Higham, *op. cit.*, pp. 135–157; Hans-Ulrich Wehler, *Bismarck und der Imperialismus*, Köln 1969, p. 473.

ments was that which students of immigration refer to as "second generation" behaviour. Studying the lives of Ferdinand Lassalle and Eduard Lasker, this author came to the conclusion that their careers exhibited a greater break with their fathers' worlds than is represented by that "generation gap" which has lately become such a cliché. Both aggressively asserted their independence from their parents and the cultural milieu of their parental homes. As young men both changed their names – Lassal to Lassalle and Jizchok Lasker to Eduard Lasker – after educational experiences away from home. The two families were at different stages of acculturation, however. It was Lassalle's grandfather who was immersed in traditional Yiddish culture, while in Lasker's case it was his father.[27]

Writing of Europeans newly arrived in the United States, Handlin says: "The life of the immigrant was that of a man diverted by unexpected pressures away from the established channels of his existence. Separated, he was never capable of acting with the assurance of habit; always in motion, he could never rely upon roots to hold him up. Instead he had ever to toil painfully from crisis to crisis, as an individual alone, make his way past the discontinuous obstacles of a strange world."[28] Surely this passage could apply as well to German Jews as they faced the opportunities and uncertainties of emancipation.

The alienation of the "newly arrived" Jew, his marginality, his ambivalence towards those who had "arrived" before him and who "arrived" later, can all be appreciated within the analogy suggested here. His desire for acceptance, his creativity, his sensitivity to criticism as well as his sometimes bitter self-criticism, all gain new significance and meaning if one views him as a "cultural immigrant". Karl Marx's published commentary 'On the Jewish Question' and Walther Rathenau's essay 'Hear, O Israel!' make more sense if they are viewed in this context.[29] So does the ambivalence among Jewish notables towards the attempts to form a Jewish political bloc in the late nineteenth century, or even the extremely right-wing statements of Max Naumann in the early 1930s.[30]

Finally, one should consider the limitations and the advantages of the analogy suggested here. The author has carefully avoided terms like *model* and *paradigm*, which appear so frequently in the social sciences. The word analogy is preferable, since we will all agree that every analogy has its limits. In comparative history differences are as important as similarities, and if this paper has dwelt on the latter to the exclusion of the former, it is primarily because of the author's

---

[27]See Shlomo Na'aman, *Lassalle*, Hannover 1970, and Mork in *Societas, loc. cit.* Lassalle was born in Breslau in 1825; Lasker was born in Jarocin in 1829. Handlin suggests the "second generation" theme in *Studies of the LBI*, p. 171. Perhaps the Rathenaus, Emil and Walther, should be studied within the same context; cf. Ernst Schulin, 'Die Rathenaus. Zwei Generationen jüdischen Anteils an der industriellen Entwicklung Deutschlands', in *Juden im Wilhelminischen Deutschland*, pp. 128–130.

[28]*The Uprooted*, p. 304.

[29]Karl Marx, 'Bruno Bauer, *Die Judenfrage*' (1844), and 'Bruno Bauer, "Die Fähigkeit der heutigen Juden und Christen, frei zu werden" ' (1844), trans. in Karl Marx, *Early Writings*, New York 1963, pp. 3–40; 'Höre, Israel!', *Die Zukunft*, 6th March 1897, reprinted in Walther Rathenau, *Schriften*, Berlin 1965, pp. 89–93. See Robert A. Pois' analysis, 'Walther Rathenau's Jewish Quandary', in *LBI Year Book XIII* (1968), pp. 120–134.

[30]Marjorie Lamberti, 'The Attempt to Form a Jewish Bloc', *Central European History*, 3 (1970), pp. 73–93; Bolkosky, *op. cit.*, p. 163.

desire to stimulate rather than to blunt critical discussion of the suggested thesis.

In any case, the analogy is probably a significant and useful one.[31] One of its major strengths would be to act as a counterweight to that stream of Anglo-American historiography which views the German experience with a certain air of condescension. The argument goes like this: We, on this side of the Atlantic (or the English Channel, or the Rhine River, as the case may be), have created a flexible and tolerant type of nationalism which has kept the doors of opportunity wide open and set the tone for the creation of a harmonious national whole. But the Germans, with their inflexible ethnic nationalism, set their country on the pathway to genocide.[32]

Such a dichotomous interpretation might have made sense for men and women who personally felt the impact of the 1930s and 40s. But for those who live in the generation whose perceptions are formed by recollection of the My Lai massacre rather than that of Auschwitz, the dichotomy can no longer be so clear-cut. Moreover, I think there is documentary support for the thesis presented here. Let us close with two quotations, one exhibiting nativist anti-semitism, the other a more tolerant attitude.

First:

> "The Russian Jews and the other Jews will completely control the finances and Government of this country in ten years, or they will all be dead . . . The hatred with which they are regarded . . . ought to be a warning to them. The people of this country won't be starved and driven to the wall by Jews who are guilty of all the crimes, tricks, and wiles that have hitherto been unknown and unthought of by civilized humanity."[33]

And secondly:

> "In an unexpected and deeply shameful manner, . . . the racial hatred and the fanaticism of the Middle Ages has been resurrected and turned towards our Jewish fellow citizens. Forgotten is how much of value and honour they have brought to our nation in industry and trade, in the arts and sciences. Broken is that rule of law and of honour which maintains that all [our citizens] are equal, in rights and in duties."[34]

It is the first of these documents which stems from the United States of America and the second from Imperial Germany.

[31]One attempt to apply the thesis is Gordon R. Mork, 'Out of the Ghetto', *Integrated Education*, 12/3 (1974), pp. 46–48.

[32]See Otto Pflanze's article 'Nationalism in Europe, 1848–1871', *Review of Politics*, 28 (1966), pp. 129–143, and the literature cited therein; Pflanze sets forth the dichotomy but also recognises its limitations.

[33]A working man's letter to the editor of the New York *Sun*, 24th March 1895, quoted in Higham, p. 93.

[34]*Erklärung* of seventy-five liberal notables, Berlin 12th November 1880, in Boehlich, p. 203.

Jewish Thought

Aspects of Hebrew Enlightenment Satire
Saul Berlin: Involvement and Detachment

BY MOSHE PELLI

The name of Naphtali Herz Wessely, the 250th anniversary of whose birth fell in 1975/1976, is generally well known as one of the exponents of Hebrew Enlightenment in Germany at the end of the eighteenth century. He is especially known for the four pamphlets, *Divrei Shalom Ve'emet* [Words of Peace and Truth], which he published in 1782–1785, advocating changes in the old-fashioned, traditional Jewish education. Following the publication of the first pamphlet, a controversy ensued between the traditionalists and the *Maskilim* [enlighteners].[1] This controversy had a silent participant, a rabbi turned *Maskil*. Rabbi Saul Berlin, a controversial figure in his own right, came to the aid of Wessely.[2] He wrote a satiric work, probably in 1784, but did not allow it to be published during his lifetime. The satire, *Ktav Yosher* [An Epistle of Righteousness], was published immediately after Saul Berlin's death (on 16th November 1794), towards the end of 1794 or early in 1795. The *Maskilim* who published the pamphlet apparently used a manuscript that had been circulating among them some ten years before.[3] Although there was no apparent indication as to the intention of the publishers, it is quite clear that they had wished to set it in print as a token memorial to the deceased *Maskil*. For otherwise it would seem rather strange that they should publish an out-of-date satire which aimed at a controversy that had been long forgotten. Wessely's "sins" by that time had been forgiven, and he continued on his moderate Enlightenment course which had been interrupted by his *Divrei Shalom Ve'emet*. Nowhere in the pamphlet

[1]On the controversy see Moshe Samet, 'Mendelssohn, Weisel, and the Rabbis of Their Time', in *Studies in the History of the Jewish People and the Land of Israel*, Haifa, Israel 1970, pp. 249–253 [in Hebrew], and Charles L. Ozer, 'Jewish Education in the Transition from Ghetto to Emancipation', in *Historia Judaica*, IX (1947), No. 1, 2, pp. 75–94, 137–158. See also my article 'Naphtali Herz Wessely's Attitude toward the Jewish Religion as a Mirror of a Generation in Transition (During the Early Period of Hebrew Haskalah in Germany)', in *Zeitschrift für Religions- und Geistesgeschichte*, XXVI (1974), No. 3, pp. 222–238.

[2]On Saul Berlin see my studies: 'Some Notes on the Nature of Saul Berlin's Writings', in *The Journal of Hebraic Studies*, I (1970), No. 2., pp. 47–61; 'Hareformah Hadatit Shel Harav "Haharedi" Saul Berlin' [The Religious Reforms of 'Traditionalist' Rabbi Saul Berlin], in *Hebrew Union College Annual*, XLII (1971), pp. 1–23 [Hebrew section]. The most comprehensive bibliography of and on Saul Berlin was published by Moshe Samet, 'R. Saul Berlin Uchtavav' [Rabbi Saul Berlin and His Writings], in *Kirjath Sepher*, XLIII (1968), pp. 429–441. See also Samet's ' "Besamim Rosh" Shel R. Saul Berlin' [R. Saul Berlin's "Besamim Rosh"], in *Kirjath Sepher*, XLVIII (1973), pp. 509–523. A comprehensive, annotated bibliography of sources dealing with *Ktav Yosher* and a discussion of this satire appears in my essay 'Saul Berlin's Ktav Yosher. The Beginning of Satire in Modern Hebrew Literature of the Haskalah in Germany', published in *LBI Year Book XX* (1975), pp. 109–127.

[3] Cf. Israel Zinberg, *Toldot Sifrut Yisra'el* [The History of the Literature of Israel], V. Merhavyah, Israel 1959, p. 122 [Hebrew]; Ben-Zion Katz, *Rabanut, Hasidut, Haskalah* [Rabbinate, Hasidism, Haskalah], I, Tel Aviv 1956, p. 240.

do the publishers cite the author by name, neither do they acknowledge his having died. As a matter of fact, they published the manuscript as it was, intact, leaving even the misleading chronogram, alluding to the year 1784, the date of its writing, as if it were the date of publication.[4]

It may be safely said that the *Maskilim* who were responsible for the publication were indeed very much aware of the timeless value of *Ktav Yosher* both as a satiric work of art and as a satire which could be used to enhance the cause of Enlightenment beyond the limits of the *Divrei Shalom Ve'emet* controversy. No longer were the editors of *Hame'asef*, the journal of Hebrew *Haskalah* [Enlightenment] in Germany, adhering to the Enlightenment oracle's instructions not to publish satiric works. Ironically, it was none other than Wessely who insisted that the young Hebrew *Maskilim* should not utilise the form of satire to further the objectives of *Haskalah*.[5] Indeed, it was one of the reasons why Berlin had not issued his satire in print.[6] By this time the moderate line of the journal had undergone a metamorphosis, as had the editorship of *Hame'asef*. In the first years of the journal, the editors resorted to fables and parables as a means of advocating their enlightenment objectives and of criticising and lampooning their adversaries. However, this policy had not been pursued by the more militant editors. In 1790, Euchel – the first editor of the journal, who became a regular contributor – published a work of satire, '*Igrot Meshulam ben 'Uriyah Ha'eshtemo'i* [The Letters of Meshulam . . .].[7] The editor himself, Aharon Wolfssohn, contributed his share to early Hebrew satire by publishing a closet-drama of his entitled *Sihah Be'erez Hahayim* [A Conversation in the Land of the Living, i.e., in the afterlife].[8] Thus Saul Berlin's work of satiric fiction ought to be viewed against the growth of modern Hebrew satire as an artistic endeavour, culminating in the Galician school of Hebrew *Haskalah* with the satiric works of Joseph Perl and Isaac Erter.

Indeed, *Ktav Yosher* is a cornerstone of Hebrew satire, a testimony to Saul Berlin's artistic achievement, almost a unique one, in fiction. It is a highly sophisticated work, in which the author utilised very clever and witty techniques of the satiric art, and employed the Hebrew language with a skill rarely seen in *Haskalah* literature before, as I have tried to show elsewhere.[9] The literary

[4]I elaborated on this subject in Appendix 1 of my article in *LBI Year Book XX*.

[5]See Wessely's letter published in the prospectus *Nahal Habsor* [The Brook 'Besor', or, Good Tidings] (1783), p. 8 [bound with *Hame'asef*, I (1784)]. Wessely reiterated his opposition to the use of satire in 'Ma'amar Hiqur Hadin' [An Essay (on) Search of Justice], in *Hame'asef*, IV (1788), pp. 97, 98, 165. This article was published also in book form and saw several editions.

[6]The other reasons: a. His father, Rabbi Zvi Hirsch Levin's opposition to Wessely's *Divrei Shalom Ve'emet*; Saul Berlin did not want to come out in public against his father. b. Berlin was apprehensive lest the figure of the traditionalist rabbi in *Ktav Yosher* might be identified with his father. c. Since there was a criticism on Wessely implied, if not overtly stated, he did not want to make it public.

[7]*Hame'asef*, VI (1790), pp. 38–50, 80–85, 171–176, 245–249. On Euchel, see my articles 'Isaac Euchel: Tradition and Change in the First Generation Haskalah Literature in Germany (I)', *Journal of Jewish Studies*, XXVI, No. 1–2 (Spring–Autumn 1975), pp. 151–165; part II, *JJS*, XXVII, No. 1 (Spring 1976), pp. 54–70; 'Jewish Identity in Modern Hebrew Literature', *Judaism*, XXV, No. 4 [100] (Fall 1976), pp. 447–460.

[8]*Ibid.*, VII (1794–1797), pp. 53–67, 120–153, 203–228, 279–298.

[9]See my article in *LBI Year Book XX*.

critics and historians who ignored Saul Berlin as a creative writer deprived
Hebrew literature of one of its best writers. A reversal of this trend is, I believe,
a debt that we owe to Hebrew literature as part of its overall re-evaluation.

The present study will undertake to examine three important components of
this satire, namely, the role of the narrator, inner structures and motifs, and the
overall ideological objectives of the writer and their artistic unity as an inte-
grating tool in this work.

I. THE NARRATOR

A significant insight into the unique nature of Berlin's satire may be gained
through an analysis of the dominant "persona" in *Ktav Yosher*. It is the first-
person narrator who assumes the person of a rabbi, thus creating the impression
that the renowned rabbi-author – "Migdolei Hador", one of the great persons
in this generation – as mentioned on the title page, is no other than Saul Berlin
himself,[10] although his identity is not revealed by name.

Berlin's predicament was indeed unique, being a practising rabbi himself and
related to a well-known rabbinic family. In Saul Berlin's portrayal of the character of the first-person narrator-rabbi one can discern that out of necessity the
author had to resort to very sophisticated satiric devices. On the other hand,
however, the careful student of *Ktav Yosher* may further find in the character
of the first-person narrator the projection of Berlin's own self-image. Beneath
the façade of the narrator-rabbi we find its contrasting image – that of a *Maskil*.
Under the mask we see a committed enlightener who is charged with a sense of
mission and duty beyond the mere defence of Wessely. Thus it will be helpful
to distinguish in *Ktav Yosher* between the narrator-rabbi and the satirist-
enlightener.[11]

---

[10]*Ktav Yosher* [An Epistle of Righteousness], [Berlin? 1794–1795?], on the title page. While no
name is used on the title page, a pseudonym does appear inside the book: 'Avdon ben Hillel
Hayid'oni (pp. 13a, 16b).

[11]By "satirist" I refer here to the author who is disguised behind the figure of the narrator-rabbi.
Kernan uses the designation "satirist" to refer to the protagonist (Alvin Kernan, *The Cankered
Muse*, New Haven 1959, pp. 7–8; published also in his *Modern Satire*, New York 1962, p. 167).
The literature discussing *Ktav Yosher* did not make any distinction between the narrator and the
author. Some writers even used the identical phrase "a conversation between the author and a
melamed" (Simḥah Asaf, *Meqorot Letoldot Haḥinuch Beyisra'el*, I, Tel Aviv 1925, p. 242; Raphael
Mahler, *Divrei Yemei Yisra'el Dorot 'Aḥaronim* [The History of Israel, Latter Generations], II,
Merḥavyah, Israel 1954[2], p. 78; Ben-Zion Katz, *Rabanut, Ḥasidut, Haskalah*, I, p. 240; Joseph
Klausner, *Historiah Shel Hasifrut Ha'ivrit Haḥadashah* [History of Modern Hebrew Literature], I,
Jerusalem 1960[3], p. 133.). That phrase could be traced to its apparent originator, Simḥah Asaf.
However, the identification of the narrator as "author" ("meḥaber") could be traced to the
first reviewer of *Ktav Yosher* in *Hame'asef*, VII (1796), No. 3, p. 268; the reviewer, D-A, is
Dov Ottensosser, according to Steinschneider. In 1861 Eliakim Carmoly picks up the term as he
quotes verbatim from the first review in *Hame'asef*. See his *Ha'orvim Uvnei Yonah* [Ravens and
Pigeons], Rödelheim 1861, p. 41. Later on the term is used by Zinberg, *Toldot Sifrut Yisra'el*, V,
p. 123 [all sources cited above are in Hebrew]. The only writer who does not identify the author
with the narrator is C. Duschinsky, *The Rabbinate of the Great Synagogue, London*, London 1921,
p. 21. But strangely enough, he identifies the narrator as "a modern youth". Duschinsky

Berlin writes from within the Jewish community as a narrator-rabbi. The satirist-enlightener, too, would have it no other way. He writes *ex cathedra*, as a rabbi, regarding himself as "one of the great persons in this generation". And his alter ego – the satirist – revels in it. In his authority as a spiritual leader and a religious scholar, he is on a par with his rivals.[12] He speaks their language, uses their sources for his argumentation, and employs their talmudic and rabbinic methodology. In other words, he plays their game, and plays it very well indeed. As far as the satirist within him is concerned, he is strategically superior to his adversaries.[13]

Berlin does it mainly by portraying the narrator as being objective in the controversy. In the opening lines of the book, where he describes the commotion among the people upon the publication of Wessely's controversial pamphlet, the dominant role of the narrator is as one who serves merely as a recorder, taking no sides in the dispute. By presenting himself as taking an objective stand, the narrator would like to appear to the reader as a mediator, who would listen to the two sides in order to seek the truth, and pass judgment on Wessely. He must persuade the reader that he is sincere and authentic.[14] In addition, by pretending to be objective, not knowing what the controversy is all about, the narrator prepares the background for the surprising denouement about the Kabalistic nature of Wessely's *Divrei Shalom Ve'emet*. To be sure, this record has been tampered with by the clever satirist. In the "quoted" enunciations by the people, one can hear the ironic echo planted by the satirist.

Consider the following sentence: "We were meritorious in having this *honour* [of being] a *unique* nation and a priestly kingdom."[15] One would find it quite difficult to dispute the authenticity of such a declaration as befitting the mentality of the traditionalist people. Undoubtedly, that is the best compliment one can pay to a satirist. However, this phrase must be examined against the background of the Hebrew Enlightenment ideology. Moses Mendelssohn – the guide and master of Hebrew Enlightenment – argues in his writings that the Jewish nation was selected by the deity to convey and perpetuate the idea of monotheism among the nations. The Jewish people – Mendelssohn implies – is no better than any other people,[16] but indeed not inferior (as far as its rights are

---

apparently sensed the dichotomy that exists between the author and the protagonist, but erred in his identification of the latter, unless he considered "a modern youth" to be synonymous with "*maskil*".

[12] *Ktav Yosher*, p. 8b: "that he [the rabbi] speaks to a man like himself". The title page establishes the author-narrator as "one of the great persons of the generation" ("Migdolei hador"). The term is being applied also to the fictional rabbi ("gadol" and "gedol hador" – *ibid.*, pp. 8b, 10b, 11b), thus putting the two as equals.

[13] The satirist must be desirous to portray himself as superior to his adversaries so as to achieve his satiric objectives. Cf. Arthur M. Clark, 'The Art of Satire and the Satiric Spectrum', in *Studies in Literary Modes*, London 1946, p. 47. See the ensuing discussion in n. 32–33 below, and their related text.

[14] The narrator states it emphatically: "[. . .] to crown the truth among my people" (*Ktav Yosher*, p. 13a). Cf. Clark, *Studies in Literary Modes*, p. 36.

[15] *Ktav Yosher*, p. 2a: "ki 'al ken zachinu lechol hakavod hazeh [,] 'am sgulah umamlechet kohanim" (italics, in the English translation, are mine).

[16] Moses Mendelssohn, *Jerusalem*, New York 1969, pp. 89, 93, 117–119.

concerned). Mendelssohn and his writings were no strangers to Saul Berlin. He refers to Mendelssohn's *Be'ur* in this satire,[17] and if my interpretation is correct, Berlin even alludes to Mendelssohn's philosophy of Judaism – Enlightenment Judaism, that is – in this satiric work.[18] Importantly, prior to the Wessely controversy, Berlin wrote an approbation of Mendelssohn's monumental translation into German and exegesis of the Pentateuch.[19]

In addition, there are some intrinsic proofs in *Ktav Yosher* as to Berlin's stand on the alleged utter disregard for European culture and its secular knowledge among traditionalist Jewry.[20]

Thus the ironic implication of the quote is quite obvious. The narrator is very careful to allude to unquestionable *Haskalah* beliefs – cited in the negative as quotes – which serve as guidelines for revealing the narrator's covert stand.

Gradually, Saul Berlin builds up the underlying ironical tone in his introductory chapter where the legend for the correct reading is covertly presented to the reader. He further employs certain accepted Enlightenment concepts intended as guides, or criteria, for the deciphering of his covert intentions. Speaking of Wessely's alleged heretical tendencies, the narrator quotes the complaining people as follows: "For this is the manner of heresy which attracts man's heart by advising him to listen to wisdom, and to turn his heart [be tempted] toward reason, and the little children are attracted by the ideas, which are planted in reason given as a godly gift."[21] The narrator, reporting objectively, incorporates within the quote which is critical of Wessely some positive terms – wisdom and reason – so as to present the reader with the key to the irony. Thus if wisdom and reason are positive concepts in the enlightener's eyes, Wessely's alleged heresy is no heresy at all. The narrator further intensifies his positive allusions by stating that reason is God-given.

The narrator also employs some sophisticated biblical allusions in order to hint as to his covert stand in his all-important introductory chapter. Citing the people complaining about Wessely's alleged heresy, he quotes them as follows: "all the *mizvot* [commandments] and customs and the yoke which are on our neck [and] are as a snail which melts away and is no more".[22] The last part of the citation – the use of the simile – is a quote from Psalms 58:9, which is the narrator's own contribution; for it is inconceivable that the people would use this rare and difficult verse. Indeed its rarity and difficulty attest to its authorship, and it is part of the double play of the narrator as the satirist, which Berlin is thus highlighting. The narrator – playing here his role as a satirist – is already showing his attitude by using the word "yoke" in reference to the *mizvot*, which

---

[17]*Ktav Yosher*, p. 7b; the rabbi refers to Mendelssohn and to his translation into German of the Pentateuch.

[18]*Ibid.*, pp. 11a, 12a–b, ch. 8; and see relevant discussion below.

[19]'Haskamot Harabanim' [Rabbis' Approbations] in *Netivot Hashalom* [Paths of Peace], I, *Bereshit*, Berlin 1783, p. 2b.

[20]*Ktav Yosher*, pp. 2a, 4b, 5b.

[21]*Ibid.*, p. 2b: "ki chen darkah shel minut moshechet lev 'adam be'omrah lehaqshiv laḥochmah ulehatot lev latvunah, vehayeladim rakim nimshachim 'aḥar hara'yonim, hanatu'a basechel matat 'elodim netunah."

[22]*Ibid.*, p. 2a.

is his declared stand throughout this pamphlet.[23] The simile in the Psalms verse is given originally in a negative context: this is the fate of the wicked, that they would melt away just as the snail appears to melt as it crawls along. Therefore, the comparison to the *mizvot* adds a negative tone to it. Furthermore, the snail, as one of the unclean creatures, indeed does not contribute positively to the image of *mizvot*. The figure of the snail carrying its shell adds to the notion that the *mizvot* are a burden, yet an aimless and an endless burden. Significantly, Berlin added to the original Psalms verse his ending of the quote, "Ve'enenu" – and is no more. The voice of the people here is none other than the satirist's voice covertly expressing his view on the *mizvot* in Judaism.

In order to make his position clear to the reader, the narrator uses exclamatory phrases such as "ḥalilah" (God forbid!).[24] At times he puts these exclamatory phrases within parentheses, as in: "(has milehazkir)" (mum's the word!).[25] Both ways, the interjections are overdone to serve as satirical clues for the reader to note. These clues are interwoven with the many other ironic clues in the same paragraph and in the introductory scenes in general. This technique is applied also within a monologue of the *melamed* [religious teacher], where a phrase in parentheses might be attributed to either the speaker or the narrator. To the sophisticated reader, this ambiguity does not exist, for in the *melamed* he can hear his master's voice, as it were. In one such instance Berlin brings to the fore the whole issue of the overemphasis on the study of Torah, to which some rabbis allegedly objected, citing the exact phraseology which had been used by both *Maskilim* and rabbis.[26] This technique is further developed in the Hebrew satire in Isaac Erter's writings.[27]

II. THE NARRATOR'S INVOLVEMENT AND DETACHMENT

It has been observed previously that the narrator endeavours to appear objective in the controversy. However, at the end of the introductory scenes in chapter one, one notes certain developments in the narrator's stand: there are some overt signs as to the narrator's true opinion of Wessely. The narrator is not as yet ready to come out openly in favour of Wessely. For by so doing he would destroy the whole momentum gained by "discovering" Wessely's righteousness after the long tirades of both the *melamed* and the rabbi against

[23]*Krav Yosher*, p. 3b – the many superstitious customs; p. 4a – the *melamed* praising the abundance of *mizvot*; also: pp. 5a, 9a, etc.
[24]*Ibid.*, p. 3b.
[25]*Ibid.* Both expressions appear within five lines; they are repeated in the same sentence in p. 13a.
[26]*Ibid.*, p. 4a: "ki 'asur lilmod harbeh miqra [. . .] min'u bnechem min hahigayon." Cf. my article 'Mordechai Gumpel Schnaber: The First Religious Reform Theoretician of the Hebrew Haskalah in Germany', in *The Jewish Quarterly Review*, LXIV (1974), No. 4, p. 312.
[27]The author elaborates on this subject in his study of Erter which is to be published shortly in the *Proceedings of the Sixth World Congress of Jewish Studies*. It is entitled 'Narrative Techniques of Isaac Erter's Satire "Gilgul Nefesh" [Transmigration of a Soul]' (Hebrew). Another paper, 'Satiric Modes in Isaac Erter's "Gilgul Nefesh" ' (Hebrew) was also submitted for publication.

him. His technique is that of an objective reporter describing his physical reaction upon learning of the people's accusations against Wessely: "I began to tremble." His physical reaction is clearly an external expression of his mental reaction which is also described in the apparently objective reporting style: "my thoughts became confused". The explanation given by the narrator attempts to carry on the ostensible air of factual, objective statements, yet it is intentionally opinionated in Wessely's favour: "For I have known previously the man and his converse, his righteous heart and his pure spirit." [28]

The narrator goes on to cite Wessely's works in a highly euphuistic language in which rhymes are also used. Both are a characteristic of a learned *Maskil*, whose language is clear and poetic, and of a positive attitude towards the subject discussed.[29] By contrast, both the *melamed* and the rabbi are characterised by the grammatically faulty language. There is no doubt as to where the narrator's sympathies lie.

Gradually, the narrator introduces the possibility that there has been a misunderstanding and that the hitherto righteous Wessely could not have turned heretic. Berlin does this by having the narrator express his doubt in the form of "who knows [. . .] perhaps [. . .]." [30] The purpose of this approach is to maintain the narrator's credibility as an unbiased bystander. In order to strengthen the narrator's impartiality, he is led to reassure the *melamed*: "do not fear, for I am like you".[31] Of course he is not, and even the *melamed* acknowledges the narrator's superiority,[32] for indeed the satirist must be – and endeavours to be – superior to his adversaries.[33] In order to maintain the narrator's ostensible objectivity in the controversy, yet to hint as to his preference, the *melamed* is made to recognise the narrator's sympathy towards Wessely. He tells the narrator: "I saw that you love him [Wessely]." [34] The narrator does not, and would not deny it.

At the encounter with the rabbi, too, the narrator achieves an air of objectivity by having the rabbi state: "I have known your ways, for you desire grace even for the one who does not deserve it." [35] The narrator's apparent tolerance is acknowledged and accepted by the rabbi. The rabbi is being portrayed as somewhat more progressive than the *melamed* in preparation for, and anticipation of the former's final conversion and his recognition of the satirically twisted, Kabalistic [mystical] interpretation of Wessely's *Divrei Shalom Ve'emet*.

[28] *Ktav Yosher*, p. 2b.

[29] *Ibid.*, pp. 2b–3a. Occasionally the *melamed*, too, speaks briefly in rhymes (p. 3a). See also the beginning of chapter 6.

[30] *Ibid.*, p. 3a.

[31] *Ibid.*, " 'Al tira ki keficha 'ani." Berlin uses a unique biblical expression to show the narrator's erudition and scholarship. The phrase appears in Job 33:6. There is also a touch of irony, which Saul Berlin, a master of the Hebrew language, utilises for his satire. The idiom "keficha" – like you – is ambiguous because of its rarity, for it literally means: [I am] "like your mouth". Indeed, the two are different in their language and style; the narrator's reassurance is pungently ironic.

[32] *Ibid.*

[33] Cf. Clark, *Studies in Literary Modes*, p. 47.

[34] *Ktav Yosher*, p. 3a.

[35] *Ibid.*, p. 8b: "Va'ani yada'ti derachecha ki ḥafeẓ ḥesed 'atah, va'afilu lemi she'eno hagun."

Furthermore, the rabbi is the one who stamps the narrator as belonging to the traditionalist camp by saying, "I know that you would be the first to lay your hand on him" [Wessely, if found guilty].[36]

The first direct, overt expression of involvement on the part of the narrator takes place then. He relates his wish to suggest to the rabbi that "we and the rest of the sages of the generation" should communicate with Wessely. Although he associates himself with the traditionalists ("we") – or appears to be doing that in preparation for his satirical defence of Wessely – the narrator in effect proposes to do what Wessely himself had requested in his pamphlet, namely, that the rabbis should write to him and start a dialogue with him, a request which they ignored.[37] However, before he is given the chance to speak up, the rabbi puts his hand on the narrator's hand to stop him.[38] There is an apparent ironic, symbolic twist in this play of hands after the rabbi had told him before that he, the narrator, would surely be the first to lay his hand on Wessely; now the rabbi is the one who holds him back from his attempt to reach Wessely and settle the controversy.

The narrator's involvement becomes stronger as he seeks to obtain Wessely's book, but is unable to. The motif of the search for an anti-traditionalist book which everybody is talking about, yet no one, or few, have actually seen or read, is later developed in the satiric work of Joseph Perl, *Megaleh Tmirin*.[39] Significantly, the book is given to him by the rabbi; indeed, the rabbi is being portrayed as possessing the potential for being "converted". The narrator describes in detail his reactions after having read Wessely's book,[40] and at this juncture we see him as completely involved in the controversy. He no longer wears any mask. Like many a narrator in the *Haskalah* literature, the narrator in *Ktav Yosher* cannot remain aloof. He is involved in this controversy of *Haskalah*; he is committed, and he can no longer remain a bystander as he was in the beginning of *Ktav Yosher*. Filled with a sense of mission and with the notion that the fictional realia which he has created is as true, real and obligatory as reality itself, the *Haskalah* narrator would tend to re-create these in his fiction. In many instances it will be manifested in the way the narrator is commissioned – in his own story – to spread the new truth which he had discovered and which is part of the *Haskalah* ideology. Thus as soon as the rabbi is "converted", realising Wessely's innocence, he commissions the narrator to write a book on the controversy and to put in it his persuasive defence of Wessely. He is instructed to further circulate the book among the Jews so as to spread the word of Wessely's righteousness.[41] Significantly, the rabbi is employing the phrase God said to Gid'on upon his mission to save the Israelites: "and now go in this your might,

[36] *Ktav Yosher*, p. 8b.

[37] *Ibid.* See 'Rav Ṭuv Levet Yisra'el' [Great Goodness for the House of Israel], *Divrei Shalom Ve'emet*, Berlin 1782–1785, p. 39a–b.

[38] *Ibid.*, p. 9a: "Vayasem yado 'al yadi."

[39] *Ibid.*, p. 8b. See Joseph Perl's *Megaleh Tmirin* [Revealer of Secrets], Wien 1819; Isaac Erter, 'Gilgul Nefesh' [Transmigration of a Soul], in *Hazofeh Levet Yisra'el* [Watchman for the House of Israel], Wien 1858, p. 48.

[40] *Ibid.*, pp. 10b, 11b.

[41] *Ibid.*, p. 12b. Cf. Joseph Perl, *Boḥen Ẓadiq* [Trying the Righteous], Prague 1838, pp. 118, 120.

and you shall save this honourable, wise and wonderful man [Wessely]".[42] The narrator's mission is likened to the saving of Israel. Of course, within the context of this satire, the commission by the rabbi serves as a justification for the ostensibly objective narrator to side with Wessely in the controversy. It is further an indication – within the satire – of the rabbi's complete conversion. Thus Berlin's success in his mission to find the truth is underlined within the development of the plot.

It should be pointed out that Perl and Erter exhibit the same literary phenomena in their satiric writings; however, it is by no means limited to satire.[43]

III. INNER STRUCTURES AND MOTIFS

In spite of the apparent disorder and the chaotic presentation of reality with which a work of satire is generally characterised,[44] the artistic work of satire must have a unified concept of reality as well as a clear point of view or ideology. The satirist-artist is not content with merely attacking his adversaries, out of which attack his *Weltanschauung* may be deduced by the reader. Neither is he satisfied by the mere assumption that the reader would resort to reversing his ironies in order to find out the underlying message in the satire. The satirist-artist would attempt to convey his truths – all-encompassing truths – throughout his work, using very subtle devices. Those are not merely devices which highlight one technique of the satirist – as I have elaborated upon elsewhere[45] – but there are some underlying concepts which serve as the core of a given artistic work of satire. These concepts nurture the totality of his work which is connected to them and dependent on them.

The title of this satire, *Ktav Yosher*, is of import in this regard. It strikes a number of chords. Berlin employs a phrase used also by Wessely in the second of his series of four pamphlets, *Divrei Shalom Ve'emet*.[46] It is indeed ironic, yet quite meaningful, that a work of satire is called "An Epistle of Righteousness", thus alluding to the nature of the book. It is a further irony that in the final analysis, although Wessely is proven innocent of heresy, the message is that he was not destined "to clear the road" for *Haskalah*.[47] Definitely, it is the purpose of Saul Berlin to employ this title as an allusion to its biblical origin. It is based on the verse in Ecclesiastes 12:10: "The preacher sought to find out acceptable words: and that which was written was upright, even words of truth." The author assumes the role of Qohelet; he "taught the people knowledge" (verse 9) as does the author of Ecclesiastes, and he "set in order many proverbs" [or,

---

[42]*Ktav Yosher*, p. 12b: "ve'atah lech bechohacha zeh vehosha'ta 'et ha'ish hanichbad hehacham hanifla." Cf. Judges 6:14.

[43]See M. D. Brandstaedter, *Kol Sipurei M. D. Brandstaedter* [The Complete Stories of M.D.B.], I, Krakau 1895, p. 69.

[44]Cf. Kernan, *The Cankered Muse*, pp. 7–8; same is published in his *Modern Satire*, p. 167.

[45]In my study in *LBI Year Book XX*.

[46]Wessely, 'Rav Ṭuv Levet Yisra'el,' *Divrei Shalom Ve'emet*, on the title page.

[47]*Ktav Yosher*, p. 16b.

parables] (*ibid.*); *Ktav Yosher* is indeed a parable of Enlightenment, its ideological struggle and its desired success.[48] But above all, he conveys the idea of "Havel havalim [. . .] hakol havel" (vanity of vanities [. . .] all is vanity) (verse 8). It is the notion of scepticism, abundant in the book of Ecclesiastes, that is the hub of this work. The world of stability, of certainty and of one definitive religious truth no longer exists. All events in the story are geared to indicate this metamorphosis. Wessely turns out to be not what he appears to have been; his *Divrei Shalom Ve'emet* is not as simple as it looks, but is a mystical work of Kabalah; and the religious leader, symbol of the traditional, uncompromising views, does change his outlook about Wessely from one extreme to the other. Words and concepts, which were clear and meaningful till then, not only become ambiguous and ambivalent, but may even reverse their meaning altogether. Thus "heresy" is turned to "the words of a living god", according to the narrator's concept of Kabalah, and derogatory and ugly enunciations about the deity are the exact reverse in the Kabalah, as it is able to contain contradictions.[49] The logically impossible becomes possible through Kabalah.

The underlying relationship to the book of Ecclesiastes is not only inferred, but is stated openly by the narrator who attempts to equate the methodology employed by King Solomon, the traditionally accepted author of *Qohelet*, with the one allegedly used by Wessely in his controversial book.[50] The scroll ("Megilah") of *Qohelet* is said to be a work of Kabalah – very much like Wessely's book – and the seven vanities in its first verse refer to exalted and sublime lights. At this point the narrator states that he [too] writes this scroll (Megilah), "*written upright*, words of truth and peace". This phrase, highlighting in bold type the title of the book, is intended to relate the book of *Qohelet* to *Ktav Yosher*.[51]

The critical spirit of *Qohelet* is the spirit of *Ktav Yosher*; it accepts no authority, no God-given, infallible truths, no accepted set of values which are indispensable. Very much like some of the European enlighteners, and like a colleague of his, Isaak Satanow, Saul Berlin introduces scepticism – in the core of his book – as the only sure and stable value in the modern world.[52] Undoubtedly, it is a paradox; but that is the epitome of Berlin's personality and phenomenon. The paradox is further the very representation of Berlin's concept of the world, a world of paradox, a world in paradox.

One other device which Saul Berlin uses to implement this overall structural theme is foreshadowing; as in the other devices and techniques employed here by the author, it is used in an ironical fashion so as to serve his satirical goals. He does it especially in the first chapter, and mainly in the first paragraph. Two examples will suffice to illustrate this point.

---

[48]The Hebrew "Mashal" means both proverb and parable. "Qohelet" is the book of Ecclesiastes as well as the author.

[49]*Ibid.*, pp. 14a, 13b.

[50]*Ibid.*, p. 13a.

[51]*Ibid.*, "Katuv Yosher" citing the verse, as different from "Ktav Yosher" the title of the satire.

[52]See my study 'Isaac Satanow's "Mishlei Asaf" As Reflecting the Ideology of the German Hebrew Haskalah', in *Zeitschrift für Religions- und Geistesgeschichte*, XXV (1973), No. 3, p. 242.

The narrator speaks of "our customary practices which are pleasing to and acceptable by God in heaven".[53] This opening remark sets the ironic tone for the whole work, right from the start. For in the following pages Berlin goes on to illustrate what are the customary practices which please God; namely, the many, many superstitions, nonsensical and meaningless activities deemed by the people as religious acts.[54] This covert ridicule of superstitions turns out to be a leitmotif in *Ktav Yosher*, serving as an ironic unifying element in the story.

Similarly, the narrator expounds in the opening paragraph on the chosenness of the Jewish people, as follows: "We were meritorious to have this honour [of being] a unique nation and a priestly kingdom."[55] It has been already observed that this sentence must be read in an ironic tone. It should be construed as a foreshadowing device for Berlin's leitmotif throughout the satire. He keeps repeating the same idea, in a few instances, using language that alludes to his ironic statement in the first paragraph.[56] The ironic concept is closely related to the expressed utter contempt for the non-Jews and their culture on the part of the traditional protagonists in this story, and to their concept of themselves. The typology of the *melamed* and the rabbi, neither of whom is given any personal identity (the only exception is perhaps the narrator), their thinking, their mentality, the contents of their monologues and the validity of what they say, are indeed a continuous play on the assumption that the reader has in mind the repeated ironic statement as to the uniqueness and holiness of the Jewish people.

Berlin uses this technique of foreshadowing in a meaningful way also with regard to his ironic interpretation of Kabalah. Departing from the *melamed*, the narrator speaks of "the depth of things", alluding to the forthcoming elaboration on the Kabalah of which he also speaks in the same terminology.[57] Speaking of the rabbi's wisdom, he calls it "deeper than hell", and subsequently demands that each act should be examined "in depth".[58] All these enunciations are in preparation for the final, "in-depth" analysis of Wessely's *Divrei Shalom Ve'emet*, and they are scattered throughout the satire as a leitmotif, and as a structural device leading to the crux of the satire.

In addition, Berlin is using two metaphors for the same purpose. The first is the metaphor of "ẓon", flock, which the narrator employs in reference to the Jewish people. He takes the biblical expression "poor of the flock" (Zechariah 11:7) and reduces it to its literal meaning. Thus the narrator alludes to his attitude towards the people: they are indeed sheep.[59] The same usage is to be

---

[53] *Ktav Yosher*, p. 2a: "Hanhagoteinu hanirẓot lelodei me'onah."

[54] *Ibid.*, pp. 3b, 4a, 5a, 8a.

[55] *Ibid.*, p. 2a. See discussion above in the text related to n. 15.

[56] *Ibid.*, p. 2a. See also p. 5a–b: "There is no nation and language [cultural entity] which is crowned with as many innumerable commandments and righteous customs as we are crowned, for we are a kingdom of priests and a holy people"; p. 8a: "We should be happy that we merited to be such a holy people."

[57] *Ibid.*, p. 8b. On the Kabalah as containing "deep, deep things", see p. 11a.

[58] *Ibid.* For a similar use see also p. 10a, an example of a mystical interpretation of a biblical verse that is employed as preparation for the general Kabalistic theory of Wessely.

[59] I discussed Berlin's debasement of the sacred idiom at length in my paper in *Year Book XX*.

found towards the end of the book where Berlin intensifies his intention and attitude by referring to the people of Israel in the traditional term "Zon Qedoshim", a holy flock, which is led by the shepherd each one in his own way.[60] This positive term is based on Ezekiel 36:38. It is a derivation from the flock designated to be sacrificed on the altar before God, and is applied to the holy flock of God. However, in connection with "the poor of the flock", which Berlin employs in the beginning of the satire, flock becomes a leitmotif, and a satiric device, which intensifies Berlin's total attack on and criticism of the Jewish milieu.

Against this negative leitmotif he places a positive one – the metaphor "light". He associates it with Kabalah, and with the teaching of his mystical, Kabalist teacher, "Mori". Once the Kabalistic interpretation of Wessely is accepted, and once Wessely's innocence is acknowledged, light will reign in their dwelling places.[61] Although there is a twist of irony in his conceptualisation of Kabalah and therefore of this light associated with it, the overall implication is of a positive term related to the light of *Haskalah*.[62] A positive aspect of the satiric "Kabalah" is to be found in the figure of the mystical teacher, as discussed below.

IV. STRUGGLE ON BEHALF OF IDEOLOGY

Saul Berlin never intended this work of satire to be merely a defence of Wessely. Indeed, the end result is to some extent a criticism of Wessely who, in Berlin's view, was not intended to carry the torch of *Haskalah* as was his "teacher". Believing that defence (of Wessely, that is) is the best form of attack, Saul Berlin used his book as a springboard to advocate his enlightenment views concerning contemporary Judaism. He ridicules superstitious beliefs and practices; he derides and criticises the abundance of secondary and trivial religious injunctions and ordinances and the casuistic manner in which they have been deduced; he lampoons the religious teachers and religious education in toto; and he mocks at the Kabalah, especially in its far-fetched interpretation of the sacred texts. To be sure, these four general categories are based on Wessely's discussion in *Divrei Shalom Ve'emet*.[63] Significantly, these four subjects recur also in the writings of Hebrew Enlightenment of the time. Thus Berlin's work of fiction must be viewed against, and considered as part of the Hebrew *Haskalah* campaign in its endeavour to introduce changes within Jewish society.

As an author of a work of and for Enlightenment, Berlin does not restrict himself solely to the subjects which were raised by Wessely, but has indeed the

[60]*Ktav Yosher*, p. 15b.
[61]*Ibid.*, pp. 11a, 12b, 14a, 15b, 16a. Based on Exodus 10:23.
[62]On the metaphor 'light' and its instrumentality in the Haskalah literature see Yehudah Friedlander, 'Livḥinat Mahutah Shel Hameṭaphorah "Or" Beshirat Hahaskalah Ha'ivrit' [A Probe into the Essence of the Metaphor 'Light' in the Poetry of Hebrew Haskalah], in *Biqoret Ufarshanut*, IV–V (1974), pp. 53–63 [Hebrew].
[63]Although in a different order and a different emphasis of importance.

whole scope of *Haskalah* and its ideology in mind. Through the satire, and after deciphering the ironies, one should be able to note Berlin's views about Ḥoch-mah, human wisdom, as an ultimate authority,[64] his anthropocentric concept of God and man,[65] his criticism of the rabbis,[66] his anti-*Galut* [state of exile] attitude,[67] and his allusions on borrowing from Christianity.[68] I have dwelled extensively on these themes in Berlin's writings elsewhere.[69]

Neither did Berlin set himself to the defence of Wessely *per se*. Quite sur-prising for a work of defence, Berlin reproaches Wessely for attempting to clear the road of *Haskalah* of stones when he was neither capable of nor destined for it.[70] A thorough examination of the text in this perplexing phenomenon is rewarding. Using Kabalah terminology, Berlin suggests that Wessely was in-fluenced by "the writings of my teacher the godly Kabalist, the great rabbi, may God protect him and bless him". But Wessely has not fully comprehended the Kabalist and has taken from him only some of his secondary views. The intention of the Kabalist-teacher, according to Berlin, was "to rid the vineyard first of the thorns, and only then to replant the vineyard anew. And he fenced it, and gathered out the stones thereof, and (only) later will he plant it with the choicest vine." [71] The vine, or the vineyard, are interpreted in the Kabalah as symbols of Kneset Yisra'el [the people of Israel].[72] Thus that mysterious teacher, called "Mori", my teacher, had in mind, according to the narrator, the re-shaping and re-forming of Judaism and the Jews.

The identity of the teacher who greatly influenced Wessely can be deduced from the text and its context. The narrator speaks of him as being anointed by God with "the holy oil of the purity of idea [—] to examine everything which has been accepted and established, and is careful to do everything according to [the dictates of] time and place".[73] Beneath the metaphors we are confronted here with *Haskalah* terminology which alludes to the ideological association of

---

[64]*Ktav Yosher*, pp. 2b, 5b.

[65]*Ibid.*, p. 4b.

[66]*Ibid.*, p. 7b.

[67]*Ibid.*, p. 4b, 5a. There is a very interesting theme which Berlin cites, regarding the suffering of the Jews in exile, which is repeated in modern Hebrew literature by Ḥayim Hazaz in his story "Hadrashah" [The Sermon], that is, that the Jews who suffered persecutions were in effect desiring them. While Berlin says it tongue-in-cheek, Hazaz' Yudqeh is quite serious about his view.

[68]*Ibid.*, p. 16b.

[69]See my article on Saul Berlin cited above in n. 2 ('Hareformah Hadatit' . . .), especially pp. 4–10.

[70]See above n. 47 and related text.

[71]*Ktav Yosher*, pp. 11a, 16b. The activities around the vine are based on Isaiah 5:2. "Mori", my teacher, is the term which Rabbi Ḥayim Vital used to refer to his teacher, Rabbi Isaac Luria, Ha'ari. (See, for example, his ' 'Eleh Toldot Yizḥaq' [This is the Life story of Isaac], in *Sefer Toldot Ha'ari* [The Book of the Life story of Ha'ari], Jerusalem 1967, ed. Me'ir Bnayahu, pp. 247 ff. See also pp. 315 ff.)

[72]*Zohar* to the Pentateuch, *Bereshit*, Judah J. Rosenberg's edition, New York (reprinted, Jerusalem 1966–1967), Parashat Vayeḥi, p. 199, to the verse "Oseri Lagefen 'iro . . .": "What is [the] vine? This is Kneset Yisra'el."

[73]*Ktav Yosher*, p. 12a: "[. . .] mibal'adei mori 'asher meshaḥo hashem beshemen qodesh ṭehor hara'yon, lehavi bechur habḥinah kol 'asher yimaẓe natun lemunaḥ qayam, venoten libo la'asot bechol davar lefi ha'et vehamaqom."

the teacher. Furthermore, in the context of the discussion of the Kabalist-teacher, the name of Moshe Rabenu [our master, Moses] is mentioned a number of times;[74] however, only in the last four lines of the book do we get the clear hint: "And see what the Zohar said about Moshe and Messiah, and you shall find out that a man like him was prepared [capable] to clean the road and to clear it of stones."[75] Checking what the *Zohar* – that work of Jewish mysticism – said about Moshe and Messiah is not an easy task, yet is most enlightening. I did find Berlin's allusion in the *Zohar* in Genesis 49:10; "The sceptre shall not depart from Judah, nor a lawgiver from between his feet, until he come to Shiloh." *Zohar* has it as follows: "Lo yasur shevet mihudah. This is Messiah ben David. Umeḥoqeq miben raglav. This is Messiah ben Yoseph. 'Ad ki yavo shiloh. This is Moshe." For the numerical value of the letters "Shiloh" and "Moshe" are identical.[76] Indeed, it is in the figure of Moshe ben Menaḥem, Moses Mendelssohn, the teacher of the Hebrew Enlightenment, that Berlin finds the dual representation of Moshe and Messiah; Berlin depicts Moshe Mendelssohn as the modern saviour of his people. The phraseology of clearing the road of stones is applied quite often in the Hebrew *Haskalah* to express Mendelssohn's Enlightenment efforts.[77] Berlin relates the "vineyard" metaphor to the metaphor "road", both of which signify Mendelssohn's *Haskalah*, by using the verb "SaQaL" (clear of stones) in both. By identifying Mendelssohn with the figure of Moshe, Berlin was only following a trend which prevailed among the Hebrew *Maskilim*.[78] However, the comparison of Mendelssohn by way of *Zohar* to Moshe-Messiah is indeed Saul Berlin's contribution to the image of Mendelssohn as seen by the *Maskilim*. Thus Berlin is saying that Wessely was trying to follow in Mendelssohn's footsteps even though he was not destined to do so. "Only a man of his stature" is capable of such a messianic task.

The image of Moses Mendelssohn as seen by the Hebrew and Jewish *Maskilim* in Germany has been investigated in the past. It is enough to mention here the monumental work of Alexander Altmann on Mendelssohn,[79] and the insight on

---

[74]*Ktav Yosher*, p. 11a, 16b.

[75]*Ibid.*, p. 16b.

[76]*Zohar*, p. 199. The *Zohar's* text further alludes to Moshe and his ancestors. It is striking that Berlin's allusion to the vine as being Kneset Yisra'el (n. 72) is to be found right next to this allusion about Moshe.

[77]See my study 'Dmuto Shel Moshe Mendelssohn Kefi Shehi Mishtaqefet Bereshitah Shel Sifrut Hahaskalah Ha'ivrit Begermanyah (*Hame'asef*, 1784–1797)' [The Image of M.M. As Reflected in the Beginning of Hebrew Haskalah Literature in Germany], in *Proceedings of Fifth World Congress of Jewish Studies*, III, Jerusalem 1972, pp. 269–282.

[78]Isaac Euchel uses the expression "the road which he cleared [Hebrew: 'Siqel'] for them" in his biography of M.M., *Rabenu Heḥacham Moshe Ben Menaḥem* [Our Wise Sage M.B.M.], Berlin 1788, p. 112 [Hebrew]. Berlin uses the same verb: 'ulesaqel hamesilah'. Euchel uses other metaphors and similes of "road" in relation to Mendelssohn's Enlightenment (*ibid.*, pp. 5, 111–113). In *Hame'asef* the same terminology is used: "This man Moshe cleared the road ['Siqel Hamesilah'], lifted obstacle from the path of his nation, and he showed the right (righteous) way [. . .] and he said to them behold I cleared the road before you [. . .]" (*Hame'asef*, V [1789], p. 188). See also *Hame'asef*, VI (1790), pp. 57–58.

[79]Alexander Altmann, *Moses Mendelssohn. A Biographical Study*, University of Alabama–London 1973.

Mendelssohn's role in shaping the German *Haskalah* as viewed by Barzilay.[80] I made a modest contribution to the understanding of Mendelssohn's image as seen by the Hebrew *Maskilim* in my Hebrew book on Mendelssohn.[81] A recent article, published in this Year Book, by Lehmann, ought also to be mentioned in this regard.[82] The image of Moses Mendelssohn as a "Moshe-figure" has already been established in the above studies.

It is for the first time, as far as I know, that the figure of Moses Mendelssohn is subtly associated with the image of the Messiah. This new, daring conceptualisation of Moses Mendelssohn could not have been overtly or even covertly delineated lest the orthodox, traditional elements come out with accusations of heresy. Hence the very subtle use of Kabalah, not easily understood, made by the erudite Rabbi Saul Berlin. Berlin's use of Kabalah is partially for satirical purposes, but significantly also for a message of *Haskalah* by keeping in the background the figure of Moses Mendelssohn as a great teacher to be followed. The unnamed Mendelssohn serves also as a unifying element in this satire, very much like the metaphors discussed previously. His writings, too, serve as an Enlightenment criterion. It adds a serious, meaningful dimension to an artistic, well-constructed and well-presented work of satire, the first of its kind in the early *Haskalah* literature. Undoubtedly, it is one of the best works in Hebrew letters of its time.

Very skilfully, this satire reflects and preaches the ideology of *Haskalah*. Moreover, *Ktav Yosher* achieved an intensified projection of the spirit of the time. I find it principally in scepticism and in the ambiguity and contradiction, or paradox, which the author conceptualised as the banners of the modern times of Enlightenment. Those are contrasted with the stable, meaningful world of the past. Ironically, Berlin uses the tools of the past, the sacred literature of the Jewish people, the books of *Qohelet* and *Zohar*, to make his satiric comment on Jewish experience.

---

[80]Isaac Eisenstein-Barzilay, 'The Treatment of the Jewish Religion in the Literature of the Berlin Haskalah', *Proceedings of the American Academy for Jewish Research*, XXIV (1955), pp. 49–55.

[81]Moshe Pelli, *Moshe Mendelssohn: Bechavlei Masoret* [Moses Mendelssohn: Bonds of Tradition], Tel Aviv 1972, pp. 88–114 [Hebrew]. A version of this chapter appeared as a study cited in n. 77 above.

[82]James H. Lehmann, 'Maimonides, Mendelssohn and the Me'asfim. Philosophy and the Biographical Imagination in the Early Haskalah', in *LBI Year Book XX* (1975), pp. 87–108.

From Wolfenbüttel to Wissenschaft
The Divergent Paths of
Isaak Markus Jost and Leopold Zunz

BY ISMAR SCHORSCH

I

From 1803 to 1807 Isaak Markus Jost (b. 1793) and Leopold Zunz* (b. 1794) languished as orphans in the decrepit Samson Talmud School (*Bet ha-Midrash*) of Wolfenbüttel in the Duchy of Brunswick. Amid poverty, filth and disorder, they endured a heartless regimen of talmudic studies, interspersed with three hours of weekly instruction in German and one in mathematics. On Thursdays and Fridays, the Pentateuch with Mendelssohn's translation was added. But the reading of German books was forbidden, and with the language of instruction being "the most frightful jargon", most students could scarcely understand spoken high German. At the age of eleven, aside from a small mathematics book, Zunz had not read a single book in German, and Jost was not to write his first German letter until the age of seventeen. Intellectual curiosity could be satisfied only through the reading of Hebrew books. Lonely and stifled, the two boys found affection and stimulation in their friendship with one another.[1]

*I should like to express my gratitude to those institutions and individuals whose gracious assistance has aided my work immeasurably: The Memorial Foundation for Jewish Culture for its subvention of my larger project, a social and intellectual history of the first phase of the *Wissenschaft* movement, of which this essay constitutes the first fruits; Professor Nahum N. Glatzer and The Franz Rosenzweig Archive for making available to me the rich collection of Jost letters to Ehrenberg, which has since been transferred to the archives of The Leo Baeck Institute; The Central Archives for the History of the Jewish People and The Jewish National and University Library in Jerusalem for placing their rich archival holdings at my disposal during my sabbatical (1974–1975); The Leo Baeck Institute for use of the Ehrenberg correspondence to Jost; Professor David Weiss Halivni for reading and criticising an earlier draft of this essay; Professor Michael A. Meyer for inviting me to read that earlier draft at the Seventh Annual Conference of the Association for Jewish Studies in Boston in December 1975 and for sharing with me his reactions; and Chancellor Gerson D. Cohen for finding the time to read my final draft and to enhance it with his counsel.

Throughout the footnotes of this essay I have used the following abbreviations:

LBIA   Leo Baeck Institute Archives, New York.
JJGL   *Jahrbuch für jüdische Geschichte und Literatur.*
CAHJP   The Central Archives for the History of the Jewish People, Jerusalem.
JNUL   The Jewish National and University Library, Jerusalem.
ZWJ   *Zeitschrift für die Wissenschaft des Judentums*, Berlin 1822–1823.

[1]The biographical data is culled from the following sources: LBIA, letter by Jost to Philipp Ehrenberg dated 12th May 1843; I. M. Jost, 'Vor einem halben Jahrhundert', *Sippurim*, III (1854), pp. 150–157; L. Zunz, 'Mein erster Unterricht in Wolfenbüttel', *JJGL*, XXX (1937), pp. 131–140. In a note to his *Geschichte der Israeliten*, IX (Berlin 1828), p. 64, Jost included himself among those Jewish teachers who had learned their German from Mendelssohn's translation of the Pentateuch.

Release from this repressive setting came unexpectedly in April 1807 when Samuel Meyer Ehrenberg, a thirty-four-year-old educator who had himself been a student at the Samson School from 1789 to 1794, became the director. For years Ehrenberg had struggled to acquire the secular education of which he was deprived as a child, and now as director he moved swiftly to modernise the curriculum and humanise instruction.[2] He also quickly enriched the intellectual fare of his two gifted students and thereby opened the way to *Gymnasium* and university. Years later Zunz observed that on the day that Ehrenberg assumed the directorship of the school, its students had literally passed from the Middle Ages into the modern era, and looking back in 1833, Jost implored the hostile Prussian bureaucrat Karl Streckfuss not to forget how far his generation had come.

> "All of us who were still children thirty years ago can testify to the incredible changes that have occurred both within us and outside us. We have traversed, or better still, flown through, a thousand-year history."[3]

The trek from Wolfenbüttel to *Wissenschaft* bespoke a psychic transformation that had compressed the passage of a millennium into less than a lifetime.

The magnitude of this achievement stands out still more fully when we compare the disordered youth of Jost and Zunz to the secure childhood and adolescence of Leopold Ranke, who was born in 1795 into a respected old Lutheran family in a prosperous Thuringian valley. As the eldest son among nine children and destined for the ministry, Ranke received the finest humanistic classical education available at the famous *Gymnasium* of Schulpforta. At the University of Leipzig, where he had matriculated as a theological student, religious doubts cooled his ardour for the ministry though not his piety. History would soon replace the Bible for him as a text for the study of God's word and will. After finishing his dissertation on the political doctrines of Thucydides, he accepted a position teaching Latin and Greek at a *Gymnasium* in the Prussian town of Frankfurt on the Oder, where he remained until 1824, when the publication of his first history (*Geschichte der romanischen und germanischen Völker von 1495 bis 1514*) earned him a coveted invitation to teach at the University of Berlin.[4] The contrast in backgrounds was to be matched by the contrast in careers. In 1824 Jost who had already completed four volumes of his *Geschichte der Israeliten* was running a private Jewish boarding school in Berlin, and Zunz was dissipating most of his strength on the *Haude- und Spenersche Zeitung*, where he worked as an editor in the mornings.[5]

---

[2]L. Zunz, *Samuel Meyer Ehrenberg. Ein Denkmal*, Braunschweig 1854, pp. 9–15.

[3]Zunz, *JJGL*, XXX, p. 136; I. M. Jost, *Offenes Sendschreiben an K. Streckfuss*, Berlin 1833, p. 65.

[4]Theodore H. Von Laue, *Leopold Ranke. The Formative Years*, Princeton 1950, pp. 9–10, 31; Ernst Simon, *Ranke und Hegel*, München and Berlin 1928, pp. 1–15.

[5]In the autumn of 1816, after lengthy delays, the Minister of Interior finally granted Jost permission to open a Jewish *Mittelschule*. The recommendation of the Berlin municipality had apparently broken the log-jam. While it certainly was desirable to have Jewish children attend Christian schools, the memorandum pointed out that this eventuality was unlikely for the foreseeable future. Consequently, to prevent Jewish children from attending the traditional institutions of Jewish education, the government should encourage the opening of enlightened Jewish schools (CAHJP, P17-498). The Prussian edict of September 1819, which forbade

II

Despite their common hardships and early friendship, Jost and Zunz went on to produce such different types of scholarship that later generations saw fit to honour Zunz alone as the founder of *Wissenschaft des Judentums*. But the accolade is not quite as self-evident as it may appear. From a chronological point of view, by 1832 when Zunz finally found the time to complete his *Gottesdienstliche Vorträge der Juden*, Jost had already published a nine-volume history of the Israelites from the Maccabean era to 1815 and a subsequent two-volume compendium which added an uncritical and tedious survey of the biblical period.[6] But the novelty of Jost's achievement is not to be gainsaid. It bore all the earmarks of the new medium: a secular spirit, source criticism, philological method and extensive utilisation of non-Jewish sources. Not only was Jost the first Jew since Josephus to write a comprehensive history of his people, but more important, he was also among the first since Azariah de Rossi to risk using Josephus for the study of Jewish history.

Moreover, his broad synthesis was not always constructed at the expense of penetrating analysis. At times Jost anchored his narrative in the kind of source criticism which became the trademark of German historiography. Perhaps the most original example was his seminal analysis of the reliability of Josephus for the events in which he participated. Jost contended in a long excursus that the first-century historian had intentionally blamed the rebellion against Rome on brigands and their like in order to absolve the Jewish masses in Roman eyes.[7] No less important was Jost's recognition of and attempt to reconcile Josephus's conflicting accounts of his career in the Galilee during the early stages of the rebellion in *The Jewish War* and *The Life*.[8]

Christian children from studying in Jewish schools, put Jost's school out of business. (LBIA, Jost to Ehrenberg, 22nd December 1819.) It took him more than eighteen months to recover his economic equilibrium. (LBIA, Jost to Ehrenberg, 15th April 1821.) By 1825 both his school and pension were flourishing again. (LBIA, Jost to Ehrenberg, 6th June 1825.) Regarding Zunz's career as editor, see S. Maybaum, 'Aus dem Leben von Leopold Zunz', *Zwölfter Bericht über die Lehranstalt für die Wissenschaft des Judenthums*, Berlin 1894, p. 12. While Zunz could not compete with Ranke in terms of status, his annual salary of 800 taler certainly compared favourably with Ranke's official salary of 500 taler. (LBIA, Jost to Ehrenberg, 16th January 1824; Max Lenz, *Geschichte der Königlichen Friedrich-Wilhelms-Universität zu Berlin*, 4 vols., Halle 1910–1918, I, pp. 257–258.)

[6]I. M. Jost, *Geschichte der Israeliten*, 9 vols., Berlin 1820–1828; *idem, Allgemeine Geschichte des Israelitischen Volkes*, 2 vols., Berlin 1832. Why Jost should have immediately followed his nine-volume opus with another two-volume survey is cleared up by his correspondence with Ehrenberg. Even before he had finished volume nine, it was suggested that at 600 taler it would be well worth his while. He eventually sold it for 640 taler. (LBIA, Jost to Ehrenberg, 8th March 1828; 6th March 1829; 28th May 1829.) In the summer of 1841 Jost took a sixteen-day trip to London to explore the prospects for an English edition, but nothing came of the venture. (LBIA, Jost to Ehrenberg, 1st November 1841.)

[7]*Geschichte der Israeliten*, II, Anhang, pp. 63–64.

[8]Shaye J. D. Cohen, *Josephus in Galilee and Rome. His Vita and Development as a Historian*, Columbia University doctoral dissertation, 1975, pp. 43–45.

Of course, in retrospect it is easy to point out the price that Jost was to pay for daring to write a general history of the Jews prematurely. While Jost hurried to assemble an uneven and faulty narrative out of sources long published, Zunz patiently recovered, collected, dated and analysed the fragments of lost works preserved in known sources and the manuscripts of countless others buried in archives and private libraries. Nor could Jost begin to match Zunz's appreciation of new types of sources such as legal and exegetical commentaries, place names and personal names, homiletical literature, liturgy, tombstones and coins to illuminate the recesses of the Jewish past. In fact, Zunz was among Jost's harshest critics, as Jost confided to Ehrenberg in a letter on 14th March 1830. He reproached him "for having immaturely put out such a long-winded work", whose deficiencies he must have realised. In response Jost insisted that the state of the field precluded perfection and scholarship stood to benefit even from his errors. Perfection had eluded far greater scholars, whose works were nevertheless superseded by later research. This difference in style and standards certainly contributed to turning their former adolescent intimacy into a strained and fluctuating relationship. [9]

But Zunz's criticism may also have been tinged with envy and many contemporaries disagreed with his appraisal. Among the most important was Jost's former teacher at Göttingen, the biblical scholar and historian Johann Gottfried Eichhorn. In a reserved but favourable review of his first two volumes, Eichhorn praised Jost for emphasising the universal aspect of his subject at the expense of its national dimension and for wisely omitting the biblical period, which required a different set of tools. Eichhorn acknowledged that to open a new field with a comprehensive history was unorthodox. Yet despite the paucity of sources and the dearth of specialised studies, he urged Jost to continue. The merit of his work would be to clarify what has to be done.

"How long has the scholarly world waited in vain for these preliminary studies! Why should we not try the reverse: to arouse enthusiasm for such monographs by an overview

[9]LBIA, Jost to Ehrenberg, 14th March 1830. Jost reiterated his defence to Ehrenberg in a letter dated 10th March 1833. To be sure, there is ample evidence in the Jost–Ehrenberg, Zunz–Ehrenberg and Jost–Zunz correspondence (JNUL, 4° 792/G-15) to document the ticklish relationship between the two men. But a unique and precious description by a third party is offered by Philipp Ehrenberg, the son of Samuel Meyer, to his brother Moritz in a letter dated 20th November 1829 (LBIA, 4025/272a). That autumn Philipp had joined his cousin Meyer Isler in Berlin to study at the university. As a frequent guest in the home of his father's former students, he quickly penetrated the façade of civility which masked their true feelings. "The longer and more closely one gets to know him [i.e., Zunz] the more learning he reveals. Without a doubt he is a man of great feeling, a quality he strangely seeks to hide, usually tucking it away behind his wit. In this way I could live with these people [i.e., the Zunzes] quite comfortably and contentedly, except that the rivalry with Jost gets in the way, involving the mutual acquaintances and close friends of both families, so that we are almost the only ones [i.e., Philipp and his cousin] who remain completely neutral, not paying much attention to either side or party. The worst is that when they visit each other they are excessively polite and exchange compliments, especially the wives. Indeed, no *friendship* [underlined in the original] can exist between them; they can merely socialise. This, dear brother, is my opinion. I may see some things too grimly, but this is the truth, and Berlin would certainly be intolerable for me, especially during this first semester, if I did not have Meyer . . ."

of the scattered sources, as far as one diligent scholar can bring them together, even though from the viewpoint of method they should first be worked over piecemeal by individual scholars?"[10]

Certainly in terms of immediate impact, as far as this elusive factor can be measured, Jost's nine-volume history fared no worse than Zunz's one-volume *Gottesdienstliche Vorträge*. To be sure, neither became a best-seller, but at least by 1841 some 950 sets of Jost's work had been sold, whereas the 760 copies of Zunz's book printed in 1832 would not be sold out till 1851.[11] Likewise in terms of personal correspondence, each man became the centre of a far-flung network of scholarly correspondents. In an undated letter from 1830, Jost told Ehrenberg that in the preceding six weeks he had sent out some seventy-five letters, mostly of a scholarly nature, and in 1841 he bemoaned that he was composing about 500 letters a year in five different languages.[12] That staggering quantity certainly compares favourably with the rich correspondence preserved in the Zunz Archive.[13] After 1832 aspiring young scholars and rabbis turned to Zunz for guidance, encouragement and approval. They shared their insights and plans, sent along copies of their first published works, and longed for a review in print from the master. During the 1830s Zunz became the scholarly mentor of men as different as Geiger, Frankel, Sachs, Dukes, Holdheim, Fürst, Herzfeld, Beer, Samuel Hirsch and Steinschneider. But there is little reason to assume that the non-extant correspondence of Jost with students and colleagues would not reveal the same respectful relationships.

In sum, Jost's achievement transcended its faults and earned him at least passing recognition. What eventually cost him his rightful place in the pantheon of the *Wissenschaft* movement was not the quality of his scholarship so much as its programmatic intent. Beneath a veneer of historical objectivity, he restated the older programme of the radical wing of the Berlin *Haskalah* in a new medium.[14]

[10]*Göttingische gelehrte Anzeigen*, 1821, vol. I, pp. 137–141. The quotation is on p. 141. Although the review was published anonymously, Eichhorn had written Jost in advance that it was coming (LBIA, Jost to Ehrenberg, 25th July 1820), and on 2nd February 1821 Ehrenberg informed Jost that it had just appeared. (LBIA, 4025/121.) The Jost–Ehrenberg correspondence from the 1820s is rich in references to favourable reviews of and reactions to Jost's work. Among Jost's early admirers was Salomo Rapoport, who became disenchanted with Jost only in the 1840s. (Isaac Barzilay, *Shlomo Yehudah Rapoport and his Contemporaries*, Israel 1969, pp. 106–115.) Although Geiger's estimate of Jost also soon declined, his early letters do display an affirmative attitude towards his work. (Abraham Geiger, *Nachgelassene Schriften*, V, Berlin 1878, pp. 76, 81, 90.) On the other hand, Samuel Luzzatto was outraged from the very beginning by Jost's biblical criticism and treatment of rabbinic literature. (Eisig Gräber, ed., *S. D. Luzzatto's hebräische Briefe*, Przemysl 1882, reprinted Jerusalem 1967, pp. 178–180, 190–193.)

[11]LBIA, Jost to Ehrenberg, 1st November 1841; 'Das Buch Zunz', JNUL, 4° 792/C-13, p. 73d.

[12]LBIA, Jost to Ehrenberg, 1830; 1st November 1841. See also Jost's letter dated 25th February 1827.

[13]JNUL, 4° 792. For a description of the contents of this unique collection see Gotthold Weil, 'Das Zunz-Archiv', in *Bulletin des Leo Baeck Instituts*, 2 (1959), No. 7, pp. 148–161.

[14]In 1928 Salo Baron in a perceptive analysis of Jost's *Geschichte der Israeliten* argued that he still belonged primarily to the Enlightenment. My own assessment, as will become clear, confirms that thesis, though for very different reasons. That essay has been reprinted in Baron, *History and Jewish Historians*, Philadelphia 1964, pp. 240–262. See also the somewhat less critical but informative essay by Reuwen Michael, 'I. M. Jost und sein Werk', in *Bulletin des Leo Baeck Instituts*, 3 (1960), No. 12, pp. 239–258. The older biography by Heinrich Zirndarf, *Isaak Markus Jost und seine Freunde*, Leipzig and New York 1886, is still useful.

In his harsh and tendentious critique of nineteenth-century *Wissenschaft*, Professor Gershom Scholem has stressed the grave doubts among its practitioners about the prospects of Jewish survival beyond emancipation and pointed out with gusto the presence of a strong destructive intent. But to substantiate such a sweeping charge with the chance remark of an aged Steinschneider to a student is dubious method at best, akin to writing a biography of Zunz on the basis of his despondent letters to the young David Kaufmann, written in the years of unconsolable bereavement which followed the death of his beloved Adelheid.[15] If the motive of giving Judaism a decent burial is verifiable anywhere in the *Wissenschaft* movement, it is only in the early work of Isaak Jost, where the mood fluctuates between animosity and ambivalence. It is this pervasive antagonism towards so much of the Jewish experience, which is so conspicuously absent from the work of Zunz, and not merely the difference in method and substance that curtailed Jost's long-term impact and destined his achievement for oblivion.

III

Thanks to the extensive and revealing Jost–Ehrenberg correspondence which has survived, it is possible to reconstruct the state of mind in which Jost turned out the volumes of his history at a truly incredible pace. Personal emancipation came during three exhilarating semesters that Jost spent at the near-by University of Göttingen in 1813–1814, where he matriculated as a "pauper" free of charge and from which he would receive a doctorate in 1828 upon the completion of the ninth and final volume of his history.[16] Two long unpublished letters by Jost to his "dearest friend" Zunz, who was still teaching for Ehrenberg back in Wolfenbüttel, provide a rare glimpse of his social, academic and intellectual transformation. New Year's eve was spent in rowdy celebration with fellow students, to the dismay of many townspeople. Through the study of Arabic and the Old Testament, Jost drew quite close to Göttingen's renowned Professor of Theology, J. G. Eichhorn. Above all, his views on Judaism were subjected to rapid modification, as he reported at the end of his letter on 1st January 1814.

> "Frequent, reasonable, non-partisan debates with my friends on religion constantly enlighten my own ideas and increasingly motivate me to devote my greatest attention to this important subject. Therefore I am now carefully studying the sources of our religion and reading the Talmud. Two days ago I finished *Berachot* . . . Also I am now busy working out something on the purity of our religion and the proper method to study and teach it."

[15]Gershom Scholem, *Explications and Implications. Writings on Jewish Heritage and Renaissance* (Hebrew), Tel Aviv 1975, pp. 385–403; *idem*, The Messianic Idea in Judaism, New York 1971, pp. 304–317. The Steinschneider story appears in both essays. The Zunz-Kaufmann correspondence was published in part by Markus Brann, *JJGL*, V (1902), pp. 159–209 and VI (1903), pp. 120–157.

[16]Monika Richarz, *Der Eintritt der Juden in die akademischen Berufe. Jüdische Studenten und Akademiker in Deutschland 1678–1848*, Tübingen 1974 (Schriftenreihe wissenschaftlicher Abhandlungen des Leo Baeck Instituts 28) p. 124.

In his next letter exactly three months later, Jost set forth his new attitude towards Hebrew, a language which both friends loved and wrote fluently. Jost now rejected the goal of reviving and modernising Hebrew as utterly futile. The study of Hebrew should rather be directed to illuminate the obscurities of the biblical text and to correct the ideas of Judaism accordingly.[17] Forty years later Jost still spoke with enthusiasm of his liberation at Göttingen, a formative period in which he had scraped off the grime of the ghetto and embraced the thought patterns and civic virtues of his adopted fatherland.[18]

In 1814 Jost switched to the University of Berlin to join his benefactor Israel Jacobson who had settled in the Prussian capital the year before, after the fall of Westphalia. According to his own later testimony, Jost was quickly inspired by the encouragement of Friedländer and Bendavid to undertake a history of the Jews, and by 16th September 1815 he could proudly report to Ehrenberg that

> "My compilation (*Bearbeitung*) of Jewish history excites the young scholars and many have sought my company out of curiosity. Everything inspires me to continue this project diligently." [19]

Ehrenberg's unpublished letters to Jost from this early period display a deep interest in the character and saleability of the work in progress. When Jost surprised him by effusively dedicating the first volume to his teacher and friend, Ehrenberg was overcome with emotion, but recovered quickly enough to chide him for having wasted the opportunity of currying favour with some important public figure.[20]

Jost used the introduction to declare his intentions. He had worked with three types of reader in mind: Christian intellectuals and government officials who respected truth and justice and Jews intent on self-improvement. With the arrival of an enlightened age, the objective study of the origin and development of Judaism could begin with a view to understanding its character and improving its condition.[21] But despite the calm and dispassionate pose, Jost wrote in a mood beset by grave doubts over the worth and viability of his subject. The very year in which volume one appeared, he admitted to Ehrenberg his

[17] JNUL, 4° 792/G-15.

[18] Jost, *Sippurim*, p. 161.

[19] I. M. Jost, *Geschichte des Judenthums und seiner Sekten*, 3 vols., Leipzig, 1857–1859, III, p. 319. Despite the prominence of universal history in the Göttingen tradition (Kurt Hunger, *Die Bedeutung der Universität Göttingen für die Geschichtsforschung am Ausgang des achtzehnten Jahrhunderts*, Berlin 1932, pp. 37–43.) including a *Weltgeschichte* published by Jost's favourite professor, J. G. Eichhorn, in 1799 (p. 41), I have found no evidence to support what I had conjectured earlier (Heinrich Graetz, *The Structure of Jewish History and other Essays*, trans. by I. Schorsch, New York 1975, pp. 6–7) that Göttingen may have prompted Jost to try his hand at a Jewish version of a world history. Moreover, if that had been the genesis of his work, why should Jost have seen fit to conceal the fact in 1859 by crediting two *Maskilim* whose radicalism had long been discredited? The quotation in the text is taken from LBIA, Jost to Ehrenberg, 16th September 1815.

[20] LBIA, 4025/100, Ehrenberg to Jost, 7th April 1820. The dedication read in part "to his revered and beloved foster-father, educator, teacher, and friend" and was followed by a two-page expression of gratitude.

[21] *Geschichte der Israeliten*, I, Vorwort.

preference for pristine Christianity. The comment came in the context of a long and often critical description of the conversion activities of a recently founded and flourishing English missionary society.

> "I am far from admiring clerical Christianity (*Pfaffenchristentum*), although I cannot with-hold my approval from New Testament Christianity, because it is a pure and purged Judaism and our Judaism only a debased Christianity."[22]

Two years later, with more than a third of his history completed, Jost gave vent to his mood of resignation in a remarkably candid letter to Ehrenberg, which alludes again to the same missionary efforts.

> "Furthermore the Jews stand today in the midst of a dilemma. University students simply can not find employment and only baptism saves them for mankind. If we don't push the crafts, our entire next generation will turn Christian. And rightly so, for what should tie them to the religion of their fathers? Only childhood memories still hold us together, no more. Our children live in another world, and they have no reason to give up their entire life just to be called Jews, when they no longer are. Why do we vex ourselves? All efforts in this regard remain fruitless. The proselytisers here are fools because they try to achieve with lots of money and noise a goal which will come of its own. The state can not recognise Jews as legitimate as long as they will not marry the inhabitants of the country. The state exists only by virtue of its people and its people must constitute a unity. Why should it elevate an association whose main principle is that it alone possesses the truth and there-fore must avoid all integration with the inhabitants of the country? . . . This is the way our children will reason and they will gladly abandon a coercive church to gain freedom, a sense of belonging to the Volk, love of the fatherland and service to the state – the highest possessions of earthly man . . . I am no friend of desertion but the history of our day makes it general and justifies it."[23]

That outburst with its grim prognosis was written in the context of a bitter attack against the *Verein für Cultur und Wissenschaft der Juden* and what Jost considered its presumptuous programme of revitalisation. Jost himself had withdrawn from the *Culturverein* on 14th May 1820 out of personal pique when the members voted after seven sessions of debate to reject his lengthy memoran-dum on what form the *Verein's* scholarly journal should take.[24] Two years later on 22nd August 1822, just six days after his profuse denunciation to Ehrenberg quoted above, he curtly rejected an invitation from the *Verein's* scholarly seminar headed by Zunz to become a member.[25] In short, Jost had chosen to divorce

---

[22]LBIA, Jost to Ehrenberg, 25th July 1820. On 21st August 1820 Ehrenberg registered his disagreement. "What you say regarding Judaism and Christianity is partially true. But there is in the Christian world just as little pure Christianity etc. [*sic*] and the New Testament contains even more nonsense than the Old. Even the good stuff in it is to be found in the Old, if one only takes the trouble to look for it. As desirable as a reformation might also be for us, it must not lead through Christianity. The reformed Jew, as I envisage him, will be far more precious than a Christian." (LBIA, 4025/108.)

[23]Nahum N. Glatzer, ed., *Leopold and Adelheid Zunz. An Account in Letters 1815–1885*, Publications of the Leo Baeck Institute, London 1958, pp. 34–35.

[24]JNUL, 4° 792/B-1. See also Zunz's letter to Adolf Strodtmann, the biographer of Heine, dated 6th March 1863. (JNUL, 4° 792/G-27.) In an article in the *Allgemeine Zeitung des Judentums*, 1859, p. 176, Jost claimed he had withdrawn because of the demands of his scholarship, but the minutes of the *Verein* do not bear out his version of the event.

[25]JNUL, 4° 792/B-13.

himself from every single action taken by that small circle of idealistic young intellectuals to salvage and rehabilitate Judaism both inside and outside the synagogue, preferring instead to restrict himself to his small Jewish school which he had received permission to open in the autumn of 1816. Thus in an age pulsating with change, Jost opted for the *vita contemplativa*, while his former friend Zunz plunged with near messianic fervour into the *vita activa*.

The stance of observer, however, did not mean that Jost succeeded in elevating his history above the concerns of the day. On the contrary, it was permeated by the same sense of worthlessness and futility openly acknowledged in the letters to Ehrenberg. Far more fatal than the inelegance of style, which prompted Zunz to quip after the appearance of volume one that perhaps it was so abominably written in order to make subsequent volumes look good, was a consistent lack of empathy for the subject matter.[26] Jost dwelt at length on what he regarded as the flaws and defects of Judaism. As Mendelssohn in part, and Friedländer and Bendavid in full, he had internalised much of the secular critique of Judaism, which derived from Spinoza and gained currency and enrichment through the polemics of the deists and philosophes.[27] His history amounted to a pedantic and passionless plea for the interment of rabbinic Judaism.

Several related themes loosely strung together formed an inchoate theory of history intended to vindicate the radical programme of the Friedländer–Bendavid wing of the German *Haskalah*. To begin with, Jost retained the prevailing periodisation which posited a basic discontinuity in Jewish history. Like Spinoza, Mendelssohn, Friedländer and Bendavid before him, he contended that the destruction of the First Commonwealth, and not that of the Second, constituted the fateful turning point in antiquity.[28] Since Spinoza, the Enlightenment had come to evaluate the achievement of Moses in primarily political terms. As the founder of a state and author of its constitution, he had used religion to further his political ends.[29] The *Maskilim* were thus compelled to counter by assuring their Christian audience that Judaism had abandoned its political character millennia ago. The year 586 B.C.E. marked the end of Judaism's political experiment. Jost merely expanded the argument. The pious Jews of the Second Commonwealth never produced a religious replica of the First. On the contrary, they differed radically in the spirit of their constitution,

---

[26]The source for Zunz's opinion is Heine's letter to Zunz, dated 2nd June 1823, in which Heine cleverly applied what Zunz had said of Jost's first volume to the first volume of the *ZWJ*. (JNUL, 4° 792/G-27.)

[27]For the most recent contribution to the study of this secular critique, see Jacob Katz, 'Judaism and Jews in the Eyes of Voltaire' (in Hebrew), *Molad*, new series, V, 1973, pp. 614–625.

[28]B. Spinoza, *A Theologico-Political Treatise*, translated by R. H. M. Elwes, New York 1951, pp. 72, 236, 247–248; Moses Mendelssohn, *Jerusalem and other Jewish Writings*, translated by Alfred Jospe, New York 1969, pp. 99–104; David Friedländer, *Sendschreiben an . . . Teller*, Berlin 1799, pp. 26–43; Lazarus Bendavid, *ZWJ*, I (1823), p. 208.

[29]Spinoza, *A Theologico-Political Treatise*, pp. 218–236; Julius Guttmann, *Religion and Knowledge* (in Hebrew), translated by Saul Esh, Jerusalem 1955, pp. 195–196; Shmuel Ettinger, 'Jews and Judaism as Seen by the English Deists of the 18th Century' (in Hebrew), *Zion*, XXIX (1964), pp. 182–207.

the means of administration, the rites for gaining divine favour, their ethical norms and language.[30]

Periodisation is rarely a value-free exercise. Just as the needs of emancipation dictated focusing on the year 586 B.C.E., so the needs of survival, as the century progressed, evoked another periodisation. By the middle of the century the emphasis had shifted to the destruction of the Second Temple, a calamity which Jewish historians now proceeded to invest with the mandate of the mission theory. To the preparatory but negative stage of 586, they added a powerful affirmative climax which not only justified the lands of exile as the proper locus of Jewish life but bestowed universal significance on Jewish survival.[31] It is no accident that Jost never embraced the mission theory.[32] As a disciple of Fried- länder and Bendavid, his theological thinking never progressed much beyond their negative terms. With age his fatalism intensified and he scoffingly dis- missed the futile illusions of a Jewish mission.[33]

Aside from these broader implications, the insistence on a total break in Jewish history served immediate ends. It cleared the way for Jost to portray the Pharisaic–Rabbinic Judaism created out of the rubble of Israelite religion as a vast historical aberration. Taking his cue from a famous passage in Spinoza, Jost declared at the very outset of volume one: "If the charge that the Jews destroyed themselves is true, then the Pharisees bear the greatest guilt."[34] In line with this thesis, Jost traced the rise to power of an arrogant and ambitious class of clerics, indifferent to the dictates of life and obsessed with the sanctity of religious law. The steady expansion of that law obstructed the pursuit of an honest livelihood and rendered secular learning abhorrent. In an outburst worthy of Voltaire, Jost depicted the early sages not as philosophers but as teachers who like merchants disperse the wares that come their way without ever creating anything themselves.[35] In volume one, Jost held the Pharisees respon- sible for the death of Jesus and closed with the plea that the time might soon come when "the Pharisaism of all religious parties will cease".[36] Two volumes later he pointedly placed a chapter on the rise of Christianity on the heels of a lengthy indictment of Rabbinism, opening the chapter itself with a diatribe against the Pharisees.[37] Thus Jost's repeated assault on Rabbinism signified the

---

[30] *Geschichte der Israeliten*, I, pp. 39–48; III, pp. 18–33; *Allgemeine Geschichte*, I, pp. 438–450. Like his mentors, Jost also spoke of Moses's work in political terms. "Moses did not give his people a religion, but a political constitution. At that time, all peoples tied religion to the constitution with unbreakable bonds." (*Geschichte der Israeliten*, I, p. 40.)

[31] Graetz, *The Structure of Jewish History*, pp. 15–16.

[32] In fact, he publicly rejected it as speculative and unnecessary. (Jost, *Culturgeschichte der Israeliten der ersten Hälfte des 19. Jahrhunderts*, Breslau 1846, p. 270.)

[33] Nahum N. Glatzer, 'Aus Unveröffentlichten Briefen von I. M. Jost', in *In Zwei Welten. Siegfried Moses zum Fünfundsiebzigsten Geburtstag*, edited by Hans Tramer, Tel Aviv 1962, p. 404.

[34] *Geschichte der Israeliten*, I, p. 57. The passage in Spinoza (p. 56) reads: "Nay, I would go so far as to believe that if the foundations of their religion have not emasculated their minds they may even, if occasion offers, so changeable are human affairs, raise up their empire afresh, and that God may a second time elect them."

[35] *Geschichte der Israeliten*, III, p. 64.

[36] *Ibid.*, I, pp. 297–300.

[37] *Ibid.*, III, pp. 145–160.

Jewish counterpart to the Enlightenment's campaign against the "infamy" of Christianity.

Within the medieval world, Jost's conspicuous preference for Sephardic culture fully reflected the prevailing prejudice of emancipation spokesmen. Since the debates provoked by the English Jew Bill of 1753, proponents of amelioration had emphasised the existing economic and social differences that distinguished Sephardim from Ashkenazim, tending to appeal only on behalf of the former.[38] To project this contemporary disparity back into the past provided inferiority-ridden Ashkenazic intellectuals with an effective critique of their own tradition and a respectable cultural claim for political equality. Just two weeks before Jost pulled out of the *Culturverein*, Eduard Gans, its president, had read at a meeting a lengthy memorandum that he intended to submit to the Ministry of Interior, in which he underscored the different historical experience of Sephardic Jewry and cited its cultural integration into Moslem society in order to allay the fear of many that Jews were congenitally or religiously unfit for citizenship. Even after 1492, he contended, this cultural legacy prevented the uprooted Sephardic Jews who resettled in France, Holland, Italy and England from ever becoming as unlike their Christian neighbours as their Ashkenazic co-religionists.[39] Jost wrote in the same spirit. The secure legal status, economic diversity and intellectual stimulation enjoyed by Spanish Jews relieved the one-sidedness and fanaticism of their religion. These same factors, Jost asserted in a typical subjective flare, also rendered the trauma of expulsion so much more painful for Spanish Jews than for the restricted, isolated and ignorant Jews of France.[40]

When it came to the treatment of medieval Ashkenazic Jewry, Jost lost all restraint. To move from Spain into Northern Europe was to enter a world of insecurity, oppression, persecution, narrow-mindedness, ignorance and moral depravity. Again Jost read back into history the concerns of the day. Uncritically, he accepted the unrelieved condemnation of the Jewish masses by both sides of the emancipation debate and projected the stereotypes on to their ancestors. A legal status that excluded Jews from society, rendering them less than men, had created a condition in which all the inherent flaws of Rabbinism could flourish. Jost applauded the noble intent of diverting Jews away from their useless preoccupation with talmudic study which lay behind the burning

---

[38]Thomas W. Perry, *Public Opinion, Propaganda, and Politics in Eighteenth-Century England*, Cambridge, Mass. 1962, pp. 11–12, 14, 16, 21, 111; Antoine Guénée, *Letters of Certain Jews to Monsieur de Voltaire*, translated by Philipp Lefanu, 2 vols., Dublin 1777, I, pp. 21–77. Among these letters (pp. 29–57) is also the translation of Isaac de Pinto, *Apologie pour la nation juive*, Amsterdam 1762.

[39]JNUL, 4° 792/B-10.

[40]*Geschichte der Israeliten*, VI, pp. 84–85, 122–123, 257, 285, 291–292, 327. This Jewish preference for Sephardic Jewry, I think, has little to do with the enthusiasm generated by the romantic movement for Moorish Spain. It was fed by indigenous Jewish factors, though no doubt reinforced by the cultural climate. The convergence of both set the stage for the extraordinary role played by Jewish scholars in the development of Islamic studies in the nineteenth century. (See Bernard Lewis, *Islam in History. Ideas, Men and Events in the Middle East*, New York 1973, pp. 20–21, 123–137.)

of the Talmud in 1240. That the Church failed was due only to the ill-chosen violence of its means, which proved counterproductive.[41] Jost considered the transference to Spain of the Ashkenazic brand of Rabbinism with its "brutal" legal system by R. Asher ben Yehiel at the end of the thirteenth century as an unmitigated tragedy.[42] About the most favourable thing that he could say about Ashkenazic Jewry was that it was not entirely to blame for its ethical and moral depravity. Jost systematically employed the already well-developed emancipation argument that a steady diet of oppression and persecution had inflicted untold damage on the character and religion of the Jews.[43]

Enough has been said to warrant the contention that not only was Jost's *Geschichte der Israeliten* inspired by Friedländer and Bendavid but also that it was consistently written in their spirit. A decade after Mendelssohn's *Jerusalem*, Bendavid had proclaimed an alternate Jewish approach to the prospect of emancipation. Whereas Mendelssohn had reasserted the divinity of Jewish law and dismissed the idea of a trade-off, Bendavid called for a wholesale repudiation of the law and a return to the pure teachings of Moses, the Jewish version of natural religion. Only then would the state be ready to extend equality and integration. The alternative would be death by attrition: the loss of the wealthy, the educated and the young.[44] Six years later in his well-known letter to Teller, Friedländer deepened the pragmatic argument of Bendavid with a skeletal and speculative theory of Jewish history, though the universe of discourse remained predominantly rationalistic.[45] It was Jost's achievement to legitimise the programme of total assimilation with an elaborate historical argument. Twenty-three hundred years of Jewish history were shown to be an egregious mistake, a period deformed by a religious monstrosity. Never again in the history of the *Wissenschaft* movement would a study be produced with so little sympathy for its subject.

As a historian, however, Jost never shared the simplistic belief in the possibility of a return to a disembodied Mosaism. As he made clear in 1830 to Chiarini, the purported French authority on Polish Jewry, Mosaism must be conceived of as that religious core articulated ideally in the Bible but developed by later generations. Nevertheless, in its pure state Judaism is "nothing else than Mosaism in the idea".[46] It was this attraction to the Mosaic core which may have induced Jost into the indefensible decision to call his work a history of the Israelites, with the obvious biblical allusion, when in fact he was writing nothing

[41]*Geschichte der Israeliten*, VI, pp. 285–286.

[42]*Ibid.*, pp. 334–339.

[43]*Ibid.*, pp. 220–225.

[44]Mendelssohn, *Jerusalem*, pp. 61, 106–110; Lazarus Bendavid, *Etwas zur Charackteristick der Juden*, Leipzig 1793, pp. 45, 56–66. It is worth noting that already in 1793 Bendavid bemoaned the many lacunae in the knowledge of Jewish history (p. 11).

[45]Friedländer, pp. 25–43.

[46]Jost, *Was hat Herr Chiarini in Angelegenheiten der europäischen Juden geleistet?*, Berlin 1830, pp. 87–88. See also *Geschichte der Israeliten*, III, Anhang, p. 158, where Jost declared: "It probably is not advisable to break lightheartedly the chains of religion adopted long ago. But certainly the time has come to convene assemblies which would erect a truthful structure on the basis of holy Scripture in which the Mosaist (*der Mosait*) could live with dignity faithful to the principles of his synagogue."

but a history of the Jews. What is beyond dispute is that like Friedländer and Bendavid, Jost harboured a strong aversion for the epithet "Juden". When Gabriel Riesser in 1832 audaciously called his ephemeral periodical *Der Jude*, Jost was sufficiently distressed to write him so.[47]

Equally clear from Jost's intimate correspondence with Ehrenberg is that he never mustered much faith in the future of Judaism. While the intemperate tone of his early scholarship subsided, his basic views remained unchanged. Despite his investment of several years into the editing of a punctuated text and German translation of the Mishnah, Jost continued to express nothing but contempt for the corpus of rabbinic literature.[48] One volume of Goethe, he declared in 1848, contained more genuine learning and healthy reason than 300 talmudic folios.[49] The efforts to reform Judaism earned only his scorn. The bitter truth, he wrote in 1852, was that the once unique character of Judaism had been irreparably damaged. Only the experiences of childhood, he confessed, still tied him to Judaism. The formative influence of European civilisation on his development could not offset the weight of having experienced the world first as a Jew. But the children of the next generation would lack such Jewish roots with the inevitable result that they would abandon Judaism. With all its imperfections, the world was still immensely attractive, and the Jewish component in their lives too shallow to enable them to resist its lure or endure its wrath.[50] What is remarkable about Jost's later scholarship is the extent to which it belies the dark prognosis of his own correspondence. What eventually emerged in the 1840s in three parts as the tenth volume of his *Geschichte der Israeliten* covering the developments of the first half of the nineteenth century was a balanced, incisive and sanguine panorama with a profound sense for the whole.[51]

IV

Influence, like education, can work two ways, either positively or negatively. In the case of the young Zunz the model provided by Jost proved unacceptable.

[47]David Friedländer, *Akten-Stücke die Reform der jüdischen Kolonieen in den Preussischen Staaten betreffend*, Berlin 1793, p. 8; Ludwig Geiger, 'Aus Zunz's Nachlass', *Zeitschrift für Geschichte der Juden in Deutschland*, V (1892), p. 261; LBIA, Jost to Ehrenberg, 12th July 1832. In his review Eichhorn had already questioned the propriety of Jost's title. (*Göttingische gelehrte Anzeigen*, 1821, vol. I, p. 139.)

[48]Published in Berlin in six volumes from 1832 to 1834, it was officially put out by a "society of lovers of Torah and science in Berlin, the capital". But the last volume as well as Jost's correspondence leave no doubt that Jost was the editor. With its German translation printed in Hebrew characters, the project has all the earmarks of a mishnaic parallel to Mendelssohn's translation of the Pentateuch. Ehrenberg chided Jost for its innumerable printing errors. (Glatzer, *Leopold and Adelheid Zunz*, p. 79.)

[49]LBIA, Jost to Ehrenberg, 9th February 1848. See also the Jost letters of 14th March 1830 and 2nd June 1844.

[50]Glatzer, in *In Zwei Welten*, pp. 400–413.

[51]Jost, *Neuere Geschichte der Israeliten von 1815 bis 1845*, 3 vols., Berlin 1846–1847. In a deeply felt obituary, Raphael Kirchheim, who lived in Frankfurt and was on intimate terms with Jost during his last years, indicated a basic shift in Jost's orientation to Judaism. (*Allgemeine Zeitung des Judentums*, 1860, pp. 720–721.) It is difficult to reconcile this opinion with the sombre letters to Ehrenberg in 1852.

Though the two men were to live in the same city from 1815 to 1835, when Jost left Berlin for Frankfurt a. Main to teach at its Philanthropin school, the physical proximity only exacerbated their estrangement.[52] For Zunz, *Wissenschaft* never became a tool for interment. To read *Die Gottesdienstlichen Vorträge* today, with its awesome command of the primary sources, its refined sense for structure and its spirit of empathy, is still an inspiring experience. In a single stroke Zunz had provided his bewildered generation with an astonishing display of the power of *Wissenschaft* to steer Judaism through the shoals and rapids of emancipation. A meticulous and unprejudiced study of the past could become a force for revitalisation. On each of the themes which made up Jost's anti-rabbinic diatribe, Zunz eventually took a different tack, and it is hard to avoid the impression that his final stance was not at least in part adopted in protest to the spirit to which Jost's early scholarship was subordinated.

The absence of that spirit is the more remarkable because Zunz too was battling the ogre of Rabbinism. In 1819, for example, he lent his hand to the composition of an elaborate programmatic statement published by L. L. Hellwitz designed to enlist government support to break the hegemony of the rabbis. The Talmud was described as a late body of literature of human authorship whose exclusive authority in Jewish life could be reduced only through the convening of a Sanhedrin and the formation of a consistorial system. The revision of Jewish law and the creation of an enlightened rabbinic leadership, on which the prospects of emancipation depended, required government intervention.[53] Zunz's letters to Ehrenberg also bristle with antagonism and convey a sense of urgency. On 5th January 1821 he reported that most of his energy was now directed towards toppling the entire edifice of Rabbinism.[54]

But by Rabbinism Zunz meant primarily what passed for it in his day. His fury was vented against the vulgarisation of rabbinic Judaism brought on by more than two centuries of narrow-minded and sophistic study of the Talmud. He had specifically identified his enemy as early as 1818 in the essay on rabbinic literature, and he never committed the mistake Jost did in projecting that animosity back into history.[55] It was not the Talmud itself that Zunz abhorred, but its contemporary representatives. Until their control was broken and they

---

[52]LBIA, Jost to Ehrenberg, 17th April 1835; 29th July 1835. Jost left Berlin without even saying good-bye. Nahum N. Glatzer, ed., *Leopold Zunz. Jude – Deutscher – Europäer. Ein jüdisches Gelehrtenschicksal des 19. Jahrhunderts in Briefen an Freunde*, Tübingen 1964 (Schriftenreihe wissenschaftlicher Abhandlungen des Leo Baeck Instituts 11), p. 182.

[53]L. L. Hellwitz, *Die Organisation der Israeliten in Deutschland*, Magdeburg 1819, pp. 48–65. Although Zunz never claimed full credit for this pamphlet (unlike Luitpold Wallach, *Liberty and Letters. The Thoughts of Leopold Zunz*, Publications of the Leo Baeck Institute, London 1959, p. 145. See Zunz, *JJGL*, XXX, p. 166), the terse, direct style and rich historical insight confirm the extent of his contribution.

[54]Glatzer, *Leopold Zunz*, p. 117. See also, for example, *idem.*, *Leopold and Adelheid Zunz*, pp. 22–23.

[55]Zunz, 'Etwas über die rabbinische Literatur', *Gesammelte Schriften*, 3 vols., Berlin 1875–1876, I, p. 29, n. 1. It is noteworthy that in the curriculum revision for the Berlin teachers' seminary (*das jüdische Seminar Talmud Torah*), which Zunz submitted in December 1838, he proposed to devote eight of the thirty hours of weekly instruction in each year of the four-year programme to the study of Talmud. Aside from Bible, which was allotted four hours per week, no other subject merited even half that amount of time. (Ludwig Geiger, 'Zunz und das Berliner Provinzialschulkollegium', *Liberales Judentum*, VII [1915], pp. 107–113.)

were replaced by learned but enlightened leaders in tune with the times, no significant improvement in Jewish life could be effected. Unlike Jost, Zunz threw himself into the revolt of young intellectuals. From the autumn of 1819 to the beginning of 1824 he stood in the forefront of a small, self-conscious élite who toiled with a sense of mission and incredible zeal to transform the face of Berlin Jewry through the twin institutions of the *Culturverein* and the "deutsche Gottesdienst". Paradoxically, his deep engagement in the issues of the present sharpened his perception of the past.

The opening salvo was fired in 1818. Read in the context of the emancipation imbroglio, *Etwas über die rabbinische Literatur* was a political tract calling for a change in Jewish leadership.[56] A radical redefinition of an accepted term is usually put forward for a purpose. Rabbinic literature, Zunz contended, was not confined to the Talmud and its expositors and codifiers, but covered the whole vast range of literature written by Jews in Hebrew in the Middle Ages. The authentic spokesmen for Judaism, therefore, could only be its historians, who had explored its cultural diversity, and not its contemporary rabbis, who had restricted themselves to but a single branch of its literature. Without denigrating the Talmud or maligning its students, Zunz had undercut the legitimacy of the ruling rabbinic class to speak for Judaism. Nor did the demise of Hebrew signal the end of Judaism; it merely underscored the urgency of studying its long Hebraic phase historically. And Zunz made it quite clear that he did not expect his generation to be the last to study the subject.

> "For even equipped with all the requisite ability, knowledge, and tools, we always produce in the study of ideas new ideas and new subject matter. Bibliography, critical method, and history are produced not only by scholarship but also by history itself. And thus as we seek to incorporate objectively into the world of scholarship material already available which once was the subjective treatment of an older idea, so our own manner of mastering the world of scholarship will be rendered for us and posterity into new material to be reworked again."[57]

In sum, *Wissenschaft des Judentums* was born in the battle to unseat the rabbis who stood in the way of emancipation. Only those who understood the past were qualified to lead the way into the future.

Towards the end of this first essay, the twenty-four-year-old Zunz also exhibited the prevailing preference for Spanish Jewry. He announced his intention to publish a scholarly Latin edition of the only known manuscript of *Sefer Ha-Ma'alot* (*The Book of Ethical Degrees*), a thirteenth-century ethical treatise by the Spanish philosopher and poet Shem Tob ben Joseph Palquera, plus a separate Hebrew synopsis. His objective, he said, was twofold: to encourage others to join in salvaging the treasures of Rabbinic literature from oblivion and to rehabilitate that literature in the eyes of the world by publishing its finest examples.[58] By implication Zunz was conceding that these were to be found in the Sephardic and not the Ashkenazic world.

In his next major essay in 1822 on the Spanish place-names in Hebrew literature, Zunz delivered a veritable encomium on the uniqueness of Spanish Jewish literature. He chose to begin the arduous task of recovering the data to

[56]*Gesammelte Schriften*, I, pp. 1–31.   [57]*Ibid.*, pp. 26–27.   [58]*Ibid.*, pp. 29–30.

date and place books and authors in Spain, because compared to the cultural desert in Germany and Poland it was simply an oasis. There Jews had achieved a cultural level they had not known since the loss of political independence and which often left Christian Europe far behind. When they sought refuge in Germany from the Inquisition they enriched Ashkenazic culture in the process.[59]

On the issue of discontinuity in Jewish history the young Zunz likewise still saw eye to eye with Jost. In the same essay on Spanish toponyms, Zunz emphasised the break that had occurred with the end of the First Commonwealth. The Jews may have been the lineal descendants of the former inhabitants of Judah, but with a closed codex in hand they differed fundamentally in speech, morals, orientation and theology.[60] Thus up to 1822, on the key issues of Sephardic superiority and the discontinuity of the Jewish past, Zunz and Jost were in complete agreement, while on the historical assessment of Rabbinism their deep differences were submerged beneath their mutual antagonism towards its contemporary exponents. The disparity in their historical method was as yet unaccompanied by an equal disparity in historical interpretation.

With the publication of his essay on Rashi that same year, Zunz struck out boldly in an unexpected direction. Indeed, a biography of Rashi was certainly a strange topic for a man who detested the present generation of rabbis and who preferred the oasis of Sephardic culture. Instead of publishing his doctoral dissertation on Palquera and the single manuscript of *Sefer Ha-Ma'alot*, neither of which incidently were ever to be published by Zunz, he abruptly turned now to study a figure who epitomised both rabbinic Judaism and Ashkenazic culture.[61] Still more significant, Zunz never used his subject as a foil to attack either. His purpose was not to debunk or denigrate, but on the contrary to strip off layers of legend and to get at the historical reality by using data drawn only from Rashi's own writings. With amazing empathy, Zunz was able to reconstruct the specific quality of a Franco-German Jew of the twelfth century. Rashi was not a northern mirror of a Spanish Jew. He was neither worldly nor multi-lingual. At most he knew the French of his day, for which he remains a major source of information. As a witness of the First Crusade, he harboured no love for Christianity. But Zunz neither blushed nor apologised. Rashi's creativity could be understood and measured only within the world of rabbinic Judaism, which constituted his immediate and primary environment.

To appreciate the full import of the Rashi biography, it must be remembered that aside from a few exemplary contemporaries no Ashkenazic Jew from the past had ever merited treatment by the *Maskilim* in the pages of *Hame'asef* and *Sulamith*.[62] The *Maskilim* made use of the biographical genre mainly for didactic

---

[59] *ZWJ*, p. 128.

[60] *Ibid.*, pp. 114–117.

[61] Zunz, 'Salomon ben Isaac genannt Raschi', *ZWJ*, pp. 277–385. *Sefer Ha-Ma'alot* (*Das Buch der Grade*) was eventually published in Berlin, 1894, by Ludwig Venetianer on the basis of four manuscripts.

[62] During the first years of *Hame'asef*, when biography received much more attention than later, essays appeared on such Sephardic luminaries as Abravanel (1784), Yoseph Shlomo Delmedigo (1784), Moses Raphael de Aquilar (1785), Maimonides (1786), Menasseh ben Israel (1788), Isaac Orobio de Castro (1788) and Jacob Yehudah Leon (1788). The biographies of Mendels-

purposes, to provide the young with exemplars whose piety did not preclude worldliness.[63] Moreover, the models they projected were not always constructed with an adequate respect for facts. In their biographies of Maimonides and Abravanel the *Maskilim* were quite ready to bevel the rough edges which they found offensive.[64] It is true that in 1810 *Hame'asef* published the opening section of Jacob Emden's autobiography in which he described his saintly father, Zevi Hirsch Ashkenazi, at length, but then the famous Hakham Zevi had spent much of his life in the Sephardic orbit.[65] Thus Zunz's essay on Rashi with its rigorous method, immense learning and fierce honesty was not only a harbinger of *Wissenschaft* methodology at its best but also a declaration of independence from the tendentious spirit which distorted the research and restricted the horizon of *Haskalah* historiography.

Years later in his *Zur Geschichte und Literatur*, a volume of essays likewise devoted to the study of Ashkenazic literature, Zunz explained what prompted him to write the biography of Rashi. Troubled by the prevailing ignorance of Christian scholars of medieval Jewish literature, Zunz felt that the *Haskalah* with its exclusive concentration on the luminaries of the Spanish milieu was partly to blame. It was neither the brilliance of the Spanish period nor the lack of manuscripts which blinded the *Maskilim* to the literary achievements of Franco-German Jewry, but rather their aversion to everything specifically Jewish. They were also offended by the comprehensiveness of Judaism in the North. In Moslem society in the South a neutral, non-religious sector had prevented Judaism from attaining the all-embracing character which distinguished both it and Christianity in the rest of Europe.[66] Jost's later unequivocal endorsement of this pro-Spanish bias could only have reinforced Zunz in the justice of his cause. He was destined, however, to remain for decades the lonely and embattled expositor of the more particularistic mode of medieval Jewish culture.

The essay on Rashi should not be construed to mean that Zunz had abandoned his commitment to religious reform. Since its writing coincided with his controversial and abortive career as a *Prediger*, this hardly seems likely. What the essay did represent was a major effort to show how far rabbinic Judaism had deviated and degenerated from the cultural creativity it had achieved in the

---

sohn and Wessely were published in 1788 and 1809 respectively. *Sulamith*, which carried both the spirit and programme of *Hame'asef* into the first half of the nineteenth century, likewise devoted its historical biographies to model Sephardic figures. (Siegfried Stein, 'Die Zeitschrift *Sulamith*', *Zeitschrift für die Geschichte der Juden in Deutschland*, VII [1937], pp. 217–218.)

[63]See the programmatic statement which introduced the series entitled 'Histories of the Great Men of Israel', *Hame'asef*, I (1784), pp. 25–30.

[64]See the penetrating essay by James H. Lehmann, 'Maimonides, Mendelssohn and the Me'asfim. Philosophy and the Biographical Imagination in the Early Haskalah', in *LBI Year Book XX* (1975), pp. 87–108.

[65]*Hame'asef*, 1810, pp. 79–97.

[66]Zunz, *Zur Geschichte und Literatur*, Berlin 1845, pp. 158–159. In his review of this book, Zunz's close friend, Bernhard Beer, stressed Zunz's determination to rectify the imbalance by rehabilitating the image of Franco-German Jewry. (*Zeitschrift für die religiösen Interessen des Judentums*, III [1846], pp. 347–348.)

twelfth century. After briefly tracing the path of its decline in the centuries which followed the Reformation, Zunz summed up his case.

> "Neither the religious (rabbis) nor the civil (Parnasim) leadership maintained itself on the level of the best of Rabbinism, let alone the best of the age."[67]

It is thus apparent that historical research could attack the present in two ways: by denigrating its pedigree or by exalting what preceded it. Either technique effectively impugned the legitimacy of what existed. While Jost had set out to demolish Rabbinism by smearing its origins, Zunz sought to reform it by confrontation with the wholesomeness of an earlier age. Both men were in search of a usable past. The merit of Zunz's method was that it struck much closer to the historical truth.

The collapse of the *Verein* in January 1824 left Zunz exhausted and demoralised. Its intense idealism and ambitious programme had utterly failed to elicit the support or even the interest of Berlin Jewry. Historically, it clearly had anticipated the major intellectual and religious developments of the next half-century, but at the time it died it was almost unknown and certainly unmourned.[68] For Zunz, the years that followed were to be among the most arduous, lonely and depressing of his long life. But while he despaired of the Jews who denied him generosity or recognition, he never lost his faith in the survival of Judaism and the power of *Wissenschaft*. During that dark decade he continued to emancipate himself from the biases of *Haskalah* historiography.

The culmination of that process came in 1832, with the publication of *Die Gottesdienstlichen Vorträge der Juden*, a book which unfurled *Wissenschaft* for the first time in all its power and potential. It faced in a constructive and feasible way the major issue of the emancipation era, namely, what was to be done with the legacy of the past. A programme like Jost's that called for the interment of rabbinic Judaism and the eradication of twenty-three hundred years of Jewish history was the petulant folly of a Jewish philosophe. It stood about as much chance of success as Robespierre's cult of the Supreme Being. In contrast, Zunz, despite his deep-seated political liberalism and penchant for rationalism, shared with the romantics of his day a healthy respect for the restricting reality of the past. In place of Jost's unrelieved emphasis on denigration, Zunz introduced the polyphonic theme of organic growth. With the concept of development, Jewish historiography had come of age.

The message of the book was that Rabbinism could not be wiped out nor, properly understood, need it be. Central to his argument was the repudiation of Jost's insistence on the discontinuity between Mosaism and Rabbinism. To begin with, the basic exegetical instrument of rabbinic Judaism was as old as the Canon itself. With deep insight, Zunz showed the process of reinterpretation already in evidence in the work of the Chronicler at the beginning of the third century B.C.E. The instrument of Midrash eventually gave rise to three types of literature: translations, laws and homilies. But Zunz insisted that the latter

---

[67] *ZWJ*, p. 380.

[68] This was also Zunz's estimate of the historical significance of the *Verein*. (See his letter to Strodtmann dated 4th May 1864 in JNUL, 4° 792/G-27.)

two – Halacha and Aggada – represented a continuation of the regimen of biblical law and the freedom of prophecy, and together they constituted the two basic strands of Jewish national life. Zunz portrayed Aggada as the voice of the people, an anonymous, patriotic expression of the deepest national sentiments. The relationship between rabbinic Judaism and Israelite religion, therefore, bespoke an underlying unity, which Zunz would never relinquish.[69]

It was not fortuitous, of course, that Zunz chose to concentrate on the dimension of freedom. His design was to project a new image of Rabbinism that challenged the existing caricature. What emerged from this prodigious learning and rigorous analysis was the vision of a vibrant religious culture responding creatively to the dilemmas posed by each new age. Without special pleading, Zunz marshalled the irrefutable evidence: like any living organism Judaism exhibited flexibility, experimentation and development. With customary vigour he summed up the first 1,500 years of rabbinic literature:

> "This is the nature of the terrain from Chronicles to European Jewish literature: not a desert whose sudden forms – Talmud, Midrash, Targum, Masorah, Kabbalah – frighten the traveller rather than guide him, but an extraordinary road of development strewn with countless works and ruins, testimonies to intense passion, fighting concern, and inspiring ideas." [70]

The decay and rigidity which marked the present was a travesty of rabbinic Judaism brought on by the ever increasing isolation and oppression of Ashkenazic Jewry during the last few centuries.[71]

The understanding and warmth of Zunz's portrait were the achievement of disciplined engagement. Zunz's lifelong personal mission was to revitalise the synagogue, the one institution which, he felt, expressed the essence of the Jewish people and guaranteed its existence. In his very first essay in 1818 he had underscored the immediate usefulness of a historical study of the liturgy based on the sources.[72] His brief career as a *Prediger* merely shifted the approach; the goal remained the same. In 1832 Zunz took recourse to the métier in which he was most effective. *Die Gottesdienstlichen Vorträge* delivered a mountain of precedents to legitimise enriching the service with the introduction of the spoken word. In the 1850s and 1860s he culminated his commitment with a trilogy which effected the vision conceived at the very outset of his career. The national theatre of the Jews, the synagogue, had found its historian, a man whose selfless perseverance was testimony to his deep faith in its future.

In the final analysis, what distinguished Zunz from Jost was the impact of Herder, who was to teach so many alienated intellectuals to rediscover the

---

[69]Zunz, *Die Gottesdienstlichen Vorträge der Juden*, Berlin 1832, pp. 1, 3, 36, 98, 311, 321–322. In 1855 Zunz elaborated his perception of the inherent unity of Jewish history. The genres of prophecy and psalmody constitute the basic forms of Jewish expression. As the prophets brought the wisdom of God to the people so the psalmists gave wings to their pain and prayers. In the post-biblical era these contrasting functions were assumed by the rabbis and the poets, who converged on the synagogue to intensify the religious experience of the entire nation. (*Die synagogale Poesie des Mittelalters*, Berlin 1855, pp. 1–8.)

[70]*Die Gottesdienstlichen Vorträge*, pp. 307–308.

[71]*Ibid.*, pp. 436 ff.

[72]*Gesammelte Schriften*, I, p. 8.

beauty and value of their different national traditions. Jost continued to write in the spirit of Voltaire, that is, judgmentally rather than empathetically. Like Voltaire, who was conscious and proud of being a member of the French bourgeoisie, he measured the past in terms of the present. The spokesman of reason in its eternal conflict with unreason, the historian came to judge, to condemn errors and to applaud anticipations. Consequently, neither Voltaire nor Jost could muster much sympathy for the field of religion. In his rebellion against the Enlightenment, Herder stressed the uniqueness of the individual. There were no universal standards of beauty and good, because every historical collectivity was inimitable. In the challenging words of Herder: "Every nation has in itself its own centre of happiness, just as every sphere has its centre of gravity." The function of the historian is only to understand, and the method, that of sympathetic identification, was an idea so revolutionary that Herder had to invent the term *Einfühlung* to convey its meaning.[73]

Jost may have read Herder, but the young Zunz alone applied his teaching, as early as 1822, to be exact, in his biography of Rashi which he concluded with a cryptic reference to Herder.[74] His treatment of Rabbinism was an achievement of extraordinary self-transcendence, given his animosity for its nineteenth-century form. Where the Jewish philosophes could see only error and degeneration, Zunz revealed creativity and growth. The sustained empathy of his work not only served to uncover the nature of the past, but also to influence the shape of the present. The mood and tone in which he wrote transformed *Wissenschaft* from an esoteric discipline into a powerful social force.

[73]Friedrich Meinecke, *Historism*, translated by J. E. Anderson, London 1972, chapters on Voltaire and Herder. The quotation is on p. 340.

[74]*ZWJ*, p. 381. The correspondence suggests that Herder was regarded highly in the Zunz household (Glatzer, *Leopold and Adelheid Zunz*, p. 82; *idem, Leopold Zunz*, p. 178.)

On an Unpublished Letter of Isaak Markus Jost

BY NAHUM N. GLATZER

One of the most active men on behalf of Jewish synagogal and liturgic reform in the beginning of the nineteenth century was undoubtedly Israel Jacobson (1768–1828). His endeavours were motivated by the desire to remove from Jewish life all that was reminiscent of generations of isolated, segregated existence and to introduce a style that would make the Jew appear "modern", enlightened and as little dissimilar from his Gentile neighbour as possible. Such a transformation of the old type of Jew into an "acculturated Israelite" would, Jacobson and his fellow reformers believed, foster a better understanding of the Jew on the part of the Christian and imbue the Jew with the consciousness of being part of the extended family of man. A medal ordered by Jacobson to celebrate the emancipation of the Westphalian Jews pictured two angels, representing Christianity and Judaism, united in the kingdom ruled over by Jerome, Napoleon's brother (1808).

Jacobson, who became president of the Jewish consistory of Westphalia, established a school in Cassel (the seat of the consistory), to which a chapel for reformed services was attached. In 1810 he dedicated a temple in Seesen, complete with bell ringing, an organ, choir and German hymns. Jacobson, in clerical robes, conducted the services at what was called the "Festival of Jewish Reformation". When the Kingdom of Westphalia came to an end and the consistory ceased to exist (1813), he transferred his activities to Berlin, where he converted a part of his house into a synagogue. Some prayers were read in German, others in Hebrew, for which the Sephardic pronunciation was used. Central to the service was the German sermon, in most cases delivered by Jacobson himself (whose German was far from perfect). Emphasis was on decorum, good taste and orderliness.

On the Feast of Weeks, 1815, the "confirmation and consecration" of Jacobson's son Naphtali was celebrated; the journal *Sulamith* published a report of the occasion.[1] It stressed the fact that several Christian dignitaries and high officials had attended, in addition to some 400 Jews. To accommodate such large numbers, the congregation was to move (1817) to the house of the banker Jacob Herz-Beer.

Again, the German sermon was used for the cultivation of the new spirit, the religious "feeling", the elevated mood, devotion, ethics, universal humanism, progress, confidence in the future. (Here the reader may be referred to the exhaustive study on the subject written by Professor Alexander Altmann in 1961.)[2]

The preacher, or rabbi, though well acquainted with the subject of his particular sermon (and its Christian prototypes) was, with some exceptions, no

[1] IV, No. 2 (1815).
[2] 'Zur Frühgeschichte der jüdischen Predigt in Deutschland. Leopold Zunz als Prediger', in *LBI Year Book VI* (1961), pp. 3–59.

longer the scholar in the Hebrew tradition. What counted now was rhetoric. "The German expression of the speaker was pure, free of artificiality, strong, the pronunciation correct, the voice strong and elastic," reads a report.[3]

The pulpit in the Beer synagogue was occupied by Isaak Levin Auerbach, Eduard Kley and Carl Siegfried Günzburg, "men", according to Graetz, "of mediocre talent and mediocre oratory".[4] Isaak Markus Jost was offered a position as preacher but refused. Leopold Zunz (1794–1886) was appointed preacher in August 1821, preached a number of sermons, a selection of which he published in 1823,[5] and resigned in September 1822.

Zunz came to Berlin in October 1815, a few days before the Day of Atonement. He attented the services in Jacobson's house and shortly afterwards reported on the occasion to his friend and former teacher, Samuel Meyer Ehrenberg in Wolfenbüttel. He found men who after twenty years of alienation from Judaism spent the entire day at the services; men thought to be above religious feeling shedding tears of devotion; the majority of the young keeping the fast. The three preachers, he stated, would be an asset to the largest congregation: Herr Auerbach speaks with philosophical clarity and inner solidity; his voice has a mellow tone; his character is pure; his articulation of Hebrew is beautiful and he is a noted poet in that language. Kley is vital and daring, his imagery excites the imagination. Zunz compares him with Ezekiel, Auerbach with Jeremiah. The third preacher (Günzburg) Zunz hoped to hear on the following holiday.[6] In another letter to Ehrenberg (12th November 1815), he notes that among the varied groups of the Berlin population, were "enlightened persons who spent the whole Day of Atonement in Jacobson's temple".[7]

Isaak Markus Jost (1793–1860), Zunz's schoolmate in Wolfenbüttel, came to Berlin to accept the directorship of the Bock private school (1816) where both Jewish and Christian boys were educated. Jost, too, attended services at the reform group, after its transfer to the house of Jacob Herz-Beer. After the Day of Atonement, 1817, he wrote a long letter to S. M. Ehrenberg in Wolfenbüttel, here published for the first time.

It gives a detailed description of the institution and some of its personalities. The view is personal, rather irreverent, unfriendly and biased, but in keeping with Jost's well-known critical attitude towards Judaism, even in its reform garb. Note the contrast to Zunz's almost enthusiastic report on the Day of Atonement service two years prior to Jost's.

In his letter, Jost informs his former teacher that the new German form of service is causing a sensation but that the greater part (of the prayers) is recited in Hebrew; "the preachers, however, preach in German, true, not in accordance with the accepted rules of grammar but nonetheless that is what their auditors

[3]*Sulamith*, VIII, No. 7 (1819).
[4]*Geschichte der Juden*, Leipzig 1870, XI, p. 415.
[5]*Predigten gehalten in der neuen Israelitischen Synagoge zu Berlin von Dr. Zunz*, Berlin 1823.
[6]Cf. Nahum N. Glatzer, ed., *Leopold and Adelheid Zunz. An Account in Letters 1815–1885*, Publications of the Leo Baeck Institute, London 1958, p. 4.
[7]Nahum N. Glatzer, ed., *Leopold Zunz. Jude – Deutscher – Europäer. Ein jüdisches Gelehrtenschicksal des 19. Jahrhunderts in Briefen an Freunde*, Tübingen 1964 (Schriftenreihe wissenschaftlicher Abhandlungen des Leo Baeck Instituts 11), p. 77.

believe". The idea (of reform) is a healthy one – if properly executed, Jost continues. The congregation is about to elect seven men to reorganise the service. By now everyone is weary of the old, scarred, out-of-tune organ and the new, clumsy, shrieking choir, composed of pupils of the Heinemann school. Much therefore depends on this election, Jost adds. He calls the congregation fanatic, citing a member who, about to betroth his daughter to another member, made the primary condition of his consent observance of the Sabbath by the young man. "O tempora", exclaims Jost.

Planning to bring some of his pupils and boarders to the forthcoming Day of Atonement service, he requested that they be included in his ticket of admission. He pointed out to Ruben Samuel Gumperz, the man in charge, that it was the duty of the congregation to admit his, Jost's, boarders, since non-admission could be interpreted as favouring Jeremias Heinemann's institute. Gumperz promised to take up the matter with the banker J. A. Muhr, who was in charge of the seating arrangements. To provide Ehrenberg with a clear picture of the situation, Jost attached a sketch of the synagogue, which consisted of three large, interconnected rooms in Beer's house.

The central room housed the holy ark, "the altar", the pulpit, the canopy (for weddings), the organ and choir, and the seats for wealthy leaders of the congregation. The room to the right was for the men, the one to the left, with its own entrance, was for the women. The central room was "romantically" adorned, abounding in golden tassels, gold-covered columns, silken gold-embroidered curtains, golden crowns, etc. Jost found the separation between the wealthy and others offensive and quoted his friend Günzburg (or Günsberg), the co-preacher, who took the liberty of remarking that such an arrangement could only serve to make all of them look ridiculous. This remark led to the decision to include the scholars among the rich. Jost was counted among the scholars, though, he adds, without his consent. As such, he received a ticket of admission "with a number denoting an honoured seat", under the window, near where the women sat.

Now, Jost continues his report, having heard that only persons with tickets were to be admitted and that others would be sent away by the police, he wondered why nothing had been done about his students. He wrote to J. A. Muhr, who conferred with Mr. Gumperz; both decided to honour his request, for, if this request were not granted, he threatened to absent himself completely. He returned his ticket, which was amended to read "and four boarders". (As we would expect of Jost, he noticed a grammatical error in the amendment.) However, in the synagogue, he found that his number had been changed and that the newly assigned seat was next to the organ, i.e., it was the worst seat in the room. He realised that he was evidently considered as an opponent of the cause (of reform) and as such treated with a certain disdain.

On the Day of Atonement, he and his pupils appeared quite late, at 8.30 a.m., whereas the service had started at 8 o'clock. The man at the door refused the pupils entry; Jost tried to push them in and quietly insisted on his right. The doorman pretended to have explicit orders from Mr. Muhr to turn the pupils away. At this moment, he says, a "pork-eater" (*Schweinefleischfresser*), who was fasting that day "to relieve himself of the sins of the year by means of a general purgative", stood up from his seat and shouted: "You deserve to be thrown out if you are such a teacher and train your pupils to come late to Shul, such a teacher should be thrown out neck and crop." (This is a rather polite rendering of vulgar, boorish jargon.) This procedure, Jost continues, could be answered either with one's fists or not at all; he chose the latter, took his pupils, left quietly and went to a small prayer group (*minyan*) where he witnessed with deep piety the auctioning off of ritual honours.

The next day he complained to Gumperz and Muhr about the treatment accorded not to his person, but to a man of his position, adding that he would take measures which would be unpleasant for everyone concerned. The gentlemen were frightened, invented a web of contradictory lies to excuse themselves and "that ruffian", regretted his (Jost's) absence on the Day of Atonement, and promised to restore his original seat and grant uncontested admission to his pupils.

As for the issue (of reform), Jost returns to a previously expressed opinion: it is based on a good idea that, however, has not yet been very well worked out. The Jew is rightly embarrassed at not being able to answer the Christian who asks: "What is your faith? What makes you a Jew?" It is this embarrassment, rather than a religious need, that has led to the steps taken to improve the form of worship – which is why the leaders act not out of principle, but institute matters in such a manner as to preclude the old-type Orthodox Jew from accusing them of heresy, or the Christians of mere deism. It is for this reason that they soft-pedal their steps towards reform; this explains the feeling of unease that the issue will be misunderstood by the government even after consent has been granted. Hence the concern with mere externals . . . Only after they realise what nonsense this is will they elect these seven leading men. To Berlin's shame it must be said that the men eligible to vote are in a dilemma; it is difficult to find seven capable men with sufficient learning.

The following will illustrate such embarrassments, Jost continues. Kley and Günzburg edited the reform service, called *The German Synagogue*. Kley wrote a preface in which he criticised the Berlin Jews. The leaders of the congregation were upset; they feared the King would read these truths and wished to announce in the Press that the book was written without authorisation. Kley let it be known that he would publish a rebuttal. This frightened the leaders and they desisted from the intended announcement. Jost notes that Kley left for Hamburg to organise a German form of worship and expressed the hope that Hamburg would display greater firmness than Berlin.

Returning to the Berlin situation, Jost complains that people pray for the King and talk about the Fatherland, while in all prayers the Messiah plays a major role; prejudices are being eliminated and yet spirits are being chased away with the *lulav* (on the festival of booths). Men shave, do business on the Sabbath, opt for German prayers for lack of knowledge of Hebrew, yet from the pulpit one hears: "Sacred is the Law, sacred the oral tradition, sacred and unshakeable all the teachings of the men who gave stability to our religion. This is the spirit of truth that must move you if you wish to be blessed, if you hope to

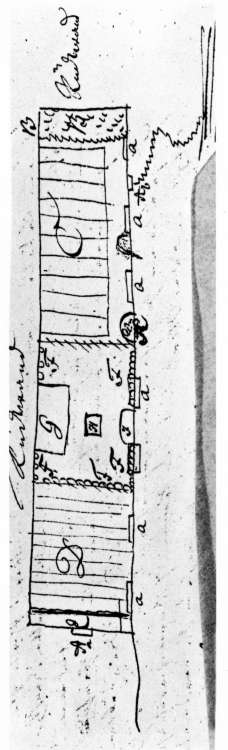

Original sketch by Isaak Markus Jost in his letter of 30th September 1817

By courtesy of the Franz Rosenzweig Archive, Boston

partake in the blessing, promised to Israel, etc." Jost is outraged by this hypocrisy, labelling it "playing games with religion". "Such orthodoxism (Jost's term) cannot and must not prevail." It may well lead to cooling the zeal for the cause (of reform) and the present enthusiasm may change into lethargy. As one more example of hypocrisy Jost cites a confirmation service, wherein two boys took an oath to sanctify the Sabbath and the festivals in the manner of their forefathers. "In this way the boys are taught to commit perjury. Kley would not do this," Jost concludes. The rest of the letter concerns an incident of a different order and is not included here.

The criticism of the twenty-four-year-old Jost may have been too sharp and the pettiness which he so keenly observed a bit out of focus. But he was right in sensing that the type of reform undertaken in Berlin offered no solution to the real problems of enlightened Jews living in a period in which enlightenment was no longer the prevailing doctrine. In addition, the opposition of Orthodoxy was strongly felt. It was this opposition that led to the closing of the reform synagogue in 1823. Jacobson died a deeply disappointed man.

The letter published here is one of 221 letters addressed by Jost to his friend and former teacher, Samuel Meyer Ehrenberg and his son, Dr. Philipp Ehrenberg, in Wolfenbüttel. The collection of letters spans the years between 1815, shortly after Jost's departure for Berlin, and 1860, the year of his death. It was preserved by the Rosenzweig family (S. M. Ehrenberg was a great-grandfather of Franz Rosenzweig) and was a part of the Franz Rosenzweig Archive in Boston before being transferred to the Archives of the Leo Baeck Institute in New York. Seven of the letters were published in the present writer's above-mentioned edition of *Leopold and Adelheid Zunz*[8] and two in a Festschrift in honour of the late President of the Leo Baeck Institute, Dr. Siegfried Moses.[9]

[8] See n. 6.

[9] 'Aus unveröffentlichten Briefen von I. M. Jost', in *In Zwei Welten. Siegfried Moses zum Fünfundsiebzigsten Geburtstag*, ed. by Hans Tramer, Tel-Aviv 1962, pp. 400–413.

APPENDIX

Letter by I. M. Jost to S. M. Ehrenberg in Wolfenbüttel

Berlin den 30ten Sept. 1817

Sehr geliebter Herr Inspector!

Bei meinen unendlichen Arbeiten kann ich selten den Genuss haben mich mit Ihnen schriftlich zu unterhalten, und doch sind *Sie mir* Antwort schuldig! Ein Beweis dass Sie nicht minder beschäftigt sind. Da indess mein Hausmeister jetzt mit meinen Zöglingen, deren schon 12 da sind einen Spaziergang macht, so will ich den Augenblick benutzen. Sie erhalten in der Beilage einige Exemplare meines neuen verbesserten Schul-Plans, die Sie gütigst unter meine Ihnen bekannten Freunde vertheilen werden. Wir befinden uns alle wohl. Meine Hochzeit[10] muss noch immer verschoben bleiben, bis wir ein grösseres Lokal haben; was in Berlin äusserst schwer ist. Aufsehen macht hier jetzt der neue *deutsche* Gottesdienst, dessen grösster Theil aber in *hebräischer* Sprache gehalten wird! Die Prediger reden aber deutsch, zwar nicht nach Heinsius,[11] aber doch nach der Ansicht ihres Publikums. Die Idee ist übrigens heilsam, wenn sie gehörig ausgeführt wird. Die Gemeinde wählt jetzt nach der Mehrheit der Stimmen 7 Männer, welche ihn gänzlich organisiren sollen; denn bisher hat die verstimmte, löcherige, alte, verrunzelte Orgel, und der neue, ungeschickte, schreiende Chor, und die zehnmal ungeschicktere Gemeinde jedes Mitglied gelangweilt. Auf diese *Wahl* kommt sehr viel an. Sie wird in diesen Tagen entschieden sein. Der Fanatismus dieser Gemeinde geht so weit, dass ein *Neumodischer* der seine Tochter einem andern aus derselben Gemeinde zur Frau geben will, als erste Bedingung aufstellt, dass er am Sonnabende den Laden verschliesse! O tempora! Die Schüler der Heinemannschen Anstalt[12] bilden den Chor. *Mich* hat man dazu nicht aufgefordert, weil man voraussetzte ich würde mich dazu nicht verstehen wollen. Man hatte Recht. Dennoch benutzte ich die Gelegenheit, um darauf einige Ansprüche zu gründen. Da nämlich jeder Platz in diesem Tempel 5 Th. Cour kostet, und ich gern auf meine Einlasskarte noch einige Pensionäre mitbringen wollte, so wendete ich mich an H. Gumperz,[13] der den Vorsteher dieser Sache spielt, und bewies ihm, wie es die Pflicht der Gemeinde sei meine Pensionäre einzulassen, indem man sonst sich für Heinemann partheïsch zeigen würde, welches ich nicht zugeben dürfte. Er erwiderte mir, er wolle mit H. Muhr,[14] einem Banquier, der das Departement der Plätze in der Synagoge hat reden. - Um nun das Folgende zu verstehen muss ich Sie mit dem Lokale dieses Gotteshauses bekannt machen. Es gehört

[10]Jost married a Miss Wolf, a niece of Isaac Euchel, on 8th June 1818.
[11]Theodor Heinsius (1770–1849), German grammarian, author of *Neue deutsche Sprachlehre*, 1801–1802.
[12]Jeremias Heinemann (1778–1855), inspector of the Jewish Teachers Seminary in Berlin.
[13]Ruben Samuel Gumperz (or Gumpertz, 1769–1851), a leader of the Berlin Jewish community and a distant relative of Leopold Zunz.
[14]J. A. Muhr, a banker and leader in the Berlin Jewish community.

einem reichen Banquier Herz-Beer,[15] der es in seinem Hause mit 7000 Th. Unkosten einrichten lies. Es besteht aus 3 grossen Zimmern in seinem Hause, deren Fenster in den Hof gehen.[16]

Aa. Eingang für Frauen.
Ab. Eingang für Männer.
a.a.a. . . . . Fenster.
B. Orgel und Chor.
C. Sitze der Männer.
D. Sitze der Frauen.
F. Sitze der *Magnaten*, d.h. der *reichsten*.
G. Baldachin zur *Chuppe*, feststehend über Säulen.
H. Altar.
I. Ohren hakaudesch.
K. Kanzel.
nnn sind *Stühle*.
§ durchbrochene Wände.

Der mittelere Theil ist romantisch ausgeziehrt, strotzend von goldenen Troddeln, goldbedeckten Säulen, seidenen, goldgestickten Vorhängen, goldenen Kronen, etc. Diese Sitze glaubten sich die Reichen wählen zu können, während alle andern Sitze verloost wurden. Mein Freund Günzburg,[17] jetzt Mitprediger, hat sich aber die Freiheit genommen, die Bemerkung zu machen, dass eine solche Anordnung nur dazu dienen könnte, sie alle lächerlich zu machen. Das sahen sie ein, und beschlossen, nächst den Reichen auch die *Gelehrten* da zu placiren. Unter diese rechnete man auch mich, ohne meine Zustimmung abzuwarten. Man schickte daher meiner Wenigkeit ein Billet, mit der ehrenvollen Nummer eines Platzes, unter dem Fenster, dicht an der Damen Sitzen. Ich, der ich mit dem Lokal unbekannt war, und von der ganzen Anordnung keine Sylbe wusste, nahm meine Charte hin. Da ich aber hörte, dass *nur* Personen mit Charten versehen, eingelassen, alle andern aber durch Polizei abgewiesen würden, so wunderte ich mich, dass man auf meine Zöglinge keine Rücksicht genommen hatte, und schrieb daher an Herr *Muhr* deshalb. Dieser conferierte darüber mit Gumperz, und beschloss endlich, weil ich sonst ganz auszubleiben gedroht hatte, mein Verlangen zu befriedigen. Er schrieb mir daher, ich möchte die Charte zurücksenden, damit er darauf (mit grammatischer Lizenz) *nebst vier Zöglingn* schreiben könne. Das geschah. Ich erhielt meine Charte zurück. Aber als ich in der Synagoge meinen Platz 133 einnehmen wollte, fand ich unvermuthet meine Nummer radirt, und dafür 112 stehen, welche Nummer *neben der Orgel* ist, also die schlechteste Stelle. Ich stutzte, lies es aber gelten um keinen Zank zu beginnen. Jedoch nahm ich mir vor, nach Jom Kippur[18] nie

---

[15]Jacob Herz-Beer, banker, advocate of synagogal reforms; father of the composer Giacomo Meyerbeer.
[16]For Jost's original sketch see illustration opp. p. 132.
[17]Carl Siegfried Günzburg (or Günsberg, 1784–1860), preacher in the Beer synagogue. In 1819 he moved to Breslau.
[18]Yom Kippur, Day of Atonement (in the original letter written in Hebrew characters).

diesen Tempel wieder zu besuchen, weil ich nun voraussetzte, dass man mich als den Gegner der Sache betrachtete und mit einer gewissen Zurücksetzung behandelte. Am grossen Versöhnungstage erschien ich sehr spät, das h[eisst] um 8 1/2 Uhr, da der Gottesdienst schon eine halbe Stunde gewährt hatte, mit meinen Kindern an der Thür. Der Pförtner wies jene ab, ich drängte sie vor, wollte mein Recht ohne Geräusch behaupten; jener schützte einen ausdrücklichen Befehl des H. Muhr vor, meine Zöglinge abzuweisen; ich erwies mein Recht; da stand plötzlich ein Schweinefleischfresser, der an diesem Tage fasten musste, um die Sünden des Jahres durch eine Hauptpurganz abzuführen, von seinem Sitze auf, und sprach laut:

> Mer geheert Ihnen mit araus sse schmeissen, wenn Sie sohn Lehrer sin, un Ihre Schieler gewehnen an so spät kommen in der Schul, solch an Lehrer muss me mit araus schmeissen, dass er Hals un Bein bricht.

Eine solche Satire verdiente eine handgreifliche, oder gar keine Antwort. Das Letzte war meine Wahl. Ich nahm meine Zöglinge bei der Hand, ging still ab, und begab mich in ein Minjan,[19] wo ich mit vieler Andacht der Mitzwess Auktion beiwohnte. Am andern Morgen beklagte ich mich bei H. Gumperz, in Gegenwart des Herrn Muhr über diese unwürdige Behandlung meines *Standes*, nicht meine Person, die solche Dinge nicht der Berücksichtigung werth erachte, indem ich hinzufügte, dass, wofern mir nicht Genugthuung geschehe, ich *Maassregeln* treffen würde, die nicht jedem angenehm sein würden. Sie erschraken; ersannen ein Gewebe von sich widersprechenden Lügen, um sich und jenen Grobian zu entschuldigen, bedauerten meine Abwesenheit am Jom Kippur[20] da man mich gewiss hätte rufen lassen, wäre mein Platz leer bemerkt worden, und versprach mir zum Beweise von Ehre und Achtung meinen alten Platz unter den Magnaten, und unbedingten Eintritt meiner Zöglinge ins Gotteshaus. - Was die Sache betrifft, so liegt ihr eine gute Idee zum Grunde, die aber noch nicht gut ausgeführt ist. Der Jude schämt sich mit Recht dem Christen nicht antworten zu können, was ist denn Dein Glaube? Was macht Dich denn zum Juden. Diese falsche Schaam, nicht Bedürfniss der Religion ist es, die sie zu dem Schritt leitete, den Gottesdienst zu verbessern. Daher sie auch durchaus nicht nach Grundsätzen hierbei handeln, sondern stets darauf bedacht sind, alles so einzurichten, dass weder der alte, orthodoxe Jude sie der Ketzerei, noch die Christen sie des blossen Deismus beschuldigen können. Daher die Geräuschlosigkeit, mit welcher ihre Tritte schleichen, daher ihre Angst, dass die Sache noch bei der Regierung selbst nach erhaltener Erlaubniss, in ein falsches Licht gestellt werde. Daher auch der Anfang mit dem Äussern, ehe noch festgesetzt ist, *wie* soll es geschehen? Erst nachdem man den Unsinn fühlen *musste*, werden 7 Männer gewählt. Und zur Schande Berlins muss man erzählen, dass ein jeder Stimmfähige in Verlegenheit ist, 7 fähige Köpfe mit hinlänglicher Gelehrsamkeit aufzufinden. Zum Beweise dieser Aengstlichkeit mag folgendes dienen. Kley und Günzburg haben die Ordnung der Gebete herausgegeben, die bei Jacobson[21] Statt fand, unter dem Titel: *Die deutsche*

[19]Minyan, prayer group (written in Hebrew characters).
[20]See n. 18.
[21]Israel Jacobson: see Introductory Note above.

Synagoge. Kley[22] lieferte dazu ein *Vorwort*, worin die hiesigen Juden ziemlich mitgenommen werden. Dies verdross die Anführer der jetzigen Sache so sehr, weil sie fürchteten der König[23] möchte diese Wahrheiten lesen, dass sie in die Zeitung einrücken lassen wollten, das Buch sei ohne Autorisation geschrieben. Kley erfuhr dies noch zur rechten Zeit und liess ihnen sagen, er werde, wofern dies geschehe, gleich dahinter 3 Fragen als Erwiderung einschalten lassen, über welche Fragen er sich jedoch weislich nicht erklärte. Dies setzte sie abermals in Furcht, und sie unterliessen die Bekanntmachung!- Kley ist übrigens abgereist, um in Hamburg die Realschule zu übernehmen, die ihm von der Gemeinde übertragen ist. Es heisst, er soll dort auch den deutschen Gottesdienst organisiren. Ich bin überzeugt, dass er besser den Character der Bestimmtheit an sich tragen werde, als der hiesige. Man betet hier für den König und redet vom Vaterland, während der Messias in allen Gebeten eine Hauptrolle spielt; man schafft Vorurtheile weg und doch vertreibt man noch die Geister mit dem Lulav. Man rasirt sich, man handelt am Sonnabend, man trägt sein Schnupftuch an Festagen vor dem Thore, man will deutsche Gebete aus Unkunde des Hebräischen, und doch lässt man von der Kanzel reden: ,,Heilig ist das Gesetz, *heilig die mündliche Ueberlieferung,* heilig und unerschütterlich alle Lehren *jener Männer die unsrer Religion ihre Festigkeit gaben!* Dies ist der Geist der Wahrheit, der in euch ruhen muss, wenn ihr selig werden wollt; so ihr hofft theilhaftig zu werden des Segens der Jisrael verheissen ist, etc." - Meines Erachtens heisst dies mit der Religion sein Spiel treiben. Ein solcher Orthodoxismus kann und darf nicht bestehen! Es ist auch leicht vorauszusehen dass der Eifer für die Sache, dadurch selbst erkalten, und der gegenwärtige Enthusiasmus in eine Lethargie ausarten müsse. - Samsons[24] *Moritz* und *Herrmann* sind auf diese Weise eingesegnet, und haben den *Eid* abgelegt, alle Sonnabende und Festtage nach der Weise ihrer Väter zu heiligen! So lehrt man die Knaben auf der Stelle *meineidig* zu werden!- So handelt *Kley* nicht!- . . .

Indem ich wünsche dass Sie die Feiertage vergnügt beenden mögen empfehle ich mich, samt meiner Braut, Ihrer ferneren Liebe und Freundschaft, und bin wie immer ganz der Ihrige

I. M. Jost

[22]Eduard Kley (1789–1867), preacher in the Beer synagogue; in 1817 he became first preacher in the reform temple in Hamburg.
[23]King Frederick William III of Prussia (1797–1840).
[24]Samson: influential Berlin Jewish family.

Abraham Geiger and Samuel Holdheim

Their Differences in Germany and Repercussions in America

BY JAKOB J. PETUCHOWSKI

I. LEFT, RIGHT AND CENTRE

There seems to be a socio-psychological law which enables all human groupings – organised for political, philosophical or religious purposes – to be broken down into Left, Right and Centre.* Thus in contemporary American Judaism we have Orthodoxy on the right, Conservative Judaism in the centre and Reform Judaism on the left. But the picture is even more complicated, since each group, within its own organisational structure, has its own Right, Centre and Left.

When German Reform Judaism had passed its first and primarily aesthetic phase, and had, in the forties of the nineteenth century, entered upon its ideological phase, its thinking was dominated by three outstanding personalities. All three of them recognised the need for reform, appreciated the demand for change and saw the necessity of adjusting the Judaism of tradition to the totally changed circumstances of post-Emancipation Jewish life. Of the three, Zacharias Frankel (1801–1875) represented the Right, Samuel Holdheim (1806–1860) the Left and Abraham Geiger (1810–1874) the Centre.

Frankel, by withdrawing from the Frankfurt Rabbinical Conference of 1845 on the issue of Hebrew as the language of prayer,[1] and by espousing a far greater concern for traditional Jewish practice and sentiment, disappeared from the Reform Jewish scene, and is now remembered as the founder of the Conservative movement in modern Judaism. This left the field to Geiger and Holdheim, who, agreeing on many aspects of Reform Judaism, yet differed to a considerable extent on others. Henceforth, Geiger would represent the right wing of the Reform movement, and Holdheim the left.

II. ABRAHAM GEIGER

So much has been written by and about Geiger[2] that we can be relatively brief in singling out the salient features of his theological position. Geiger had a distinguished rabbinical career in Wiesbaden, Breslau, Frankfurt a. Main and Berlin. He always combined his rabbinical duties with pioneering work in the field of the *Wissenschaft des Judentums*; and his scholarly work went hand in hand with his Reform perspective. Indeed, Geiger may be regarded as the first real

---

*This essay is based on a lecture given at the Leo Baeck Institute, New York, on 12th April 1976.
[1] Cf. David Philipson, *The Reform Movement in Judaism*, 3rd edn., New York 1967, pp. 190–192.
[2] See the bibliography of Geiger's works in Ludwig Geiger, *Abraham Geiger. Leben und Lebenswerk*, Berlin 1910, pp. 413–470; and Michael A. Meyer's 'Bibliography of Secondary Literature', in Jakob J. Petuchowski, ed., *New Perspectives on Abraham Geiger*, Cincinnati 1975, pp. 55–58.

theologian of Reform Judaism, the first one to outline the theological foundations on the basis of which the work of Reform could proceed.

But Geiger endeavoured to be a Reformer within the total Jewish community,
and not the leader of a peripheral sectarian group. As he saw it, progress and
development were not a new demand made on Judaism. Judaism, from its very
beginning, had been a developing and progressive phenomenon, undergoing
various stages of transformation in response to environmental and historical
challenges. The very concept of "tradition" was a progressive concept, enabling
the latter-day Reformer to be guided by the past. The present evolved out of the
past organically, not through radical and revolutionary breaks with tradition;
and the future will have to evolve in the same way out of the present. Yet this
evolution is a process which is undergone by the Jewish community as a whole;
and it is, therefore, the task of the Reformer to work with and within the entire
Jewish community.

Geiger's convictions in this respect were put to the test three times. The first
test occurred shortly after Geiger, in the face of strong opposition from Rabbi
Solomon Tiktin and Tiktin's followers, had established himself as the Second
Rabbi of the Breslau Jewish community in 1840. Geiger insisted on shouldering
the full load of rabbinical functions, including participation in the administering
of Jewish Law. Tiktin, the older rabbi of the community, and a staunch up-
holder of unbending traditionalism, refused to serve together with Geiger.
Looking for a way out of the impasse, the officers of the community approached
Geiger and suggested to him that he confine himself henceforth to the homiletical
and educational aspects of spiritual leadership, leaving the *beth din* (the Rabbinical Court) and the *halakhic* (legal) functions to Tiktin. Geiger refused the
offered compromise. He wanted to be as much the rabbi and the *halakhic*
authority of the total Jewish community as was his more traditionalist senior
colleague.

> "Geiger claimed that the division of Judaism into two parts, the one quick and the other
> dead, which this arrangement presupposed, harmed the religion incalculably in the
> estimation of its own followers. It made the formation of two parties inevitable, the one,
> following the leadership of the rabbi, must look upon the preacher as an unbeliever, while
> the other, adhering to the preacher, would consider the rabbi an ignorant obscurantist.
> Such states of mind must lead without fail to a schism in fact as well as in thought, and
> Judaism would be in a sorrier condition in the end than it had been at the beginning."[3]

The two other tests emanated from one and the same source, the Berlin
Jewish Reform Congregation. That congregation had been founded in 1845 on
a pronounced and radical Reform basis. It emphasised universalism at the
expense of particularism. The so-called Ceremonial Law was no longer considered binding. The use of Hebrew in the service was all but abolished. The use
of head covering and prayer shawl was discontinued. Unlike the minor changes
in the liturgy which had been introduced in the Hamburg Temple since its
establishment in 1818, and unlike the occasional liturgical reforms which had
found their way into the services of some other German-Jewish communities,
the Berlin Jewish Reform Congregation was, as it were, "all of one piece".

[3]Philipson, *op. cit.*, p. 56.

Here Reform Judaism could flourish in a completely unhindered way, with no need to pay attention to the religious susceptibilities of Jews with a more traditionalist bent. It was this congregation which turned to the foremost Reform theologian, Abraham Geiger, and invited him to become its spiritual leader. Indeed, that invitation was extended to Geiger twice. Both times he refused. As Caesar Seligmann put it:

> "Twice he declined an urgent call to serve that congregation – primarily because he did not want to be the rabbi of a private congregation, which had separated from the total community. He did not want Reform to separate from the totality of Jews, and to organise separatist congregations. He wanted to avoid a schism in German Judaism. At the very least, he wanted to prevent Reform from initiating such a schism." [4]

In the evolution of Judaism, Geiger discerned four different periods.[5] The first period was the period of *Revelation*, i.e., the period when the Bible came into being. It should be pointed out in this connection that Geiger did not hold the Orthodox belief in a supernatural Revelation, but that, like several of the Reform thinkers of the nineteenth century, he conceived of Revelation in terms of the special "genius" of the Jewish people for religious and ethical perceptions.[6]

The second period, lasting until the completion of the Babylonian Talmud, is the period of *Tradition*. Tradition, as we have noted, is a positive value for Geiger. It proves that the ancient Rabbis felt free to adapt the provisions of the Bible to the changing circumstances of Jewish life.

Rigid Legalism is Geiger's name for the third period, which lasted from the sixth century until the eighteenth century. This period took over the teachings of the Bible as modified by the talmudic Rabbis. But it was a period of rigidity in which the liberties which the ancient Rabbis had taken in bringing the Law up to date were no longer taken. Anything and everything handed down from the past was rigidly codified and adhered to. Geiger's name for that period implied a value judgment. Yet Geiger readily admitted that, within that particular setting, i.e., during the Dark Ages, it may indeed have been necessary for the survival of the Jewish spirit that it clothe itself in the garments of rigid legalism.

But that period was over now, and Geiger knew himself to be living in a new phase of Jewish existence, the period of both *Liberation* and *Criticism*. He defined its tasks as follows:

> "The loosening of the fetters of the previous period through the use of Reason and historical investigation – without interrupting the connection with the past. It is a period of attempts at self-renewal, of bringing the historical process into flux again, a period of criticism." [7]

Geiger's insistence on organic evolution must not be misunderstood. It is indeed "organic" and not revolutionary, but it is no less of an "evolution" for all that. The past is the past, and it will never return. And to that past, and only

---

[4] Caesar Seligmann, 'Zum hundertjährigen Geburtstag Abraham Geigers', in *Liberales Judentum*, vol. II (1910), pp. 97–104.
[5] Abraham Geiger, *Nachgelassene Schriften*, ed. Ludwig Geiger, vol. II, Berlin 1875, pp. 63 ff.
[6] Cf. Abraham Geiger, *Das Judentum und seine Geschichte*, 2nd edn., Breslau 1910, pp. 28–37.
[7] Geiger, *Nachgelassene Schriften*, vol. II, p. 64.

to that past, belongs the national phase of Jewish existence. "Jerusalem," he wrote in 1868,

> "remains for us the holy source whence, in the past, sprang the teaching of truth . . . The present heap of ruins, Jerusalem, is, for us, at best a poetic and melancholy memory, but no nourishment for the spirit. No exaltation and no hope are associated with it."[8]

The movement of Judaism had to be towards greater universalism, but it also had to be a movement of the Jewish community of faith as a whole. Geiger was prepared to dispense with some of the particularist trappings of the past, but not with those elements making for group cohesion which could still be harmonised with an enlightened and rational faith.

There were radical elements in Geiger's Reform Jewish theology. But the average American Reform Jew today, when shown a copy of Geiger's prayer-book without being told the name of its editor, is very likely to pronounce it "Conservative".

III. SAMUEL HOLDHEIM

In terms of ultimate commitments to universalism, and in the recognition that the medieval phase of Judaism had come to an end, there was probably very little difference between Geiger and Samuel Holdheim (1806–1860),[9] the rabbi who accepted the pulpit of the Berlin Jewish Reform Congregation which had been offered to, and turned down by Geiger. Indeed, attempts have been made by Holdheim's disciples to show that Geiger sympathised far more with the aspirations of Holdheim and of his congregation than he is normally given credit for.[10] Nevertheless, Geiger and Holdheim differed – both in their temperaments and in their reading of Jewish history.

So far from seeing that history in terms of organic development, as Geiger did, and choosing the path of evolutionary change for Judaism's entry into the modern world, Holdheim called for a revolutionary break with the past. He did so because, according to his reading of the facts of Jewish history, the whole of Rabbinic Judaism was based on a serious mistake, on a misunderstanding of

[8]Abraham Geiger, *Unser Gottesdienst*, Breslau 1868, p. 18.

[9]The following books have been consulted in writing this paper. The listing here is not meant as a complete bibliography of Holdheim's writings: *Über das Gebetbuch nach dem Gebrauche des neuen Irsaelitischen Tempelvereins zu Hamburg*, Hamburg 1841; *Verketzerung und Gewissensfreiheit. Ein zweites Votum in dem Hamburger Tempelstreit*, Schwerin 1842; *Über die Autonomie der Rabbinen*, Schwerin 1843 (hereafter referred to as *Autonomie*); *Über die Beschneidung*, Schwerin 1844; *Das Ceremonialgesetz im Messiasreich*, Schwerin 1845, (hereafter referred to as *Ceremonialgesetz*); *Gemischte Ehen zwischen Juden und Christen*, Berlin 1850; *Predigten über die jüdische Religion*, vol. II, Berlin 1853; *Jüdische Glaubens- und Sittenlehre*, Berlin 1857; *Ma'amar Ha-ishuth*, Berlin 1860; *Predigten über die jüdische Religion*, vol. IV, Berlin 1869. Among the books about Holdheim, the following are useful: David Philipson, *op. cit.*; David Philipson, *Samuel Holdheim. Jewish Reformer*, Cincinnati 1906; Immanuel Heinrich Ritter, *Samuel Holdheim. Sein Leben und seine Werke*, Berlin 1865 (=vol. III of *Geschichte der jüdischen Reformation*); Max Wiener, *Jüdische Religion im Zeitalter der Emanzipation*, Berlin 1933.

[10]Cf. Karl Rosenthal, 'Abraham Geigers Stellung zum Reformjudentum', in *Mitteilungen der Jüdischen Reformgemeinde zu Berlin*, New Series, vol. 18, No. 4, 2nd April 1935, pp. 60–63.

the events of the year 70 C.E., when the Jewish State and the Jerusalem Temple were destroyed. The task of the nineteenth-century Jew, therefore, was to get back to the Bible – or, at any rate, to those parts of the Bible which, according to Holdheim, were meant to have eternal validity, by-passing, as it were, some eighteen centuries of post-biblical development.

What makes Holdheim's approach so ingenious and remarkable is the fact that Holdheim himself was essentially a Talmudist of the old school. He is said to have received his own rabbinic ordination from no less an authority than Rabbi Moses Schreiber, the famous *Hatham Sopher* (1763–1839).[11] Moreover, in an extant responsum, addressed to him while he was still the Orthodox rabbi of Frankfurt a. d. Oder, his respondent, Rabbi Ephraim Eliezer Zevi Harlap of Mezeritch, calls Holdheim, *harav hagadol*, "the great rabbi" – no negligible encomium, considering its source.[12]

Basic to Holdheim's understanding of the Bible – and, in terms of the super-natural, revelatory character of that Bible, Holdheim, throughout his career, seems to have retained a far more traditionalist position than Geiger – is the assertion that the Pentateuch contains two different kinds of law, the religious and the political.

> "That which is of an *absolutely religious* character and of a *purely religious* content in the Mosaic legislation and in the later historical development of Judaism – whether we call it a divine tradition or human progress – and which refers to the relationship of man to God, his Heavenly Father, that has been commanded to the Jew by God for eternity. But whatever has reference to inter-human relationships of a *political*, *legal* and *civil* character was originally meant to apply only to the given conditions of such a political and civil existence – as Scripture states innumerable times. Yet it must be totally deprived of its applicability, everywhere and forever, when Jews enter into relationships with other states, or, at any rate, when they live outside the conditions of the particular state for which that law was initially given."[13]

That particular state was, of course, the theocracy envisaged by the Mosaic legislation. That legislation, according to Holdheim, knew of three such kinds of holiness: the holiness of the people, the holiness of the priesthood and the holiness of the land. All three kinds of holiness were inter-related, and they were basic to the many laws of the theocracy which were derived from them.

> "If one were to trace the source of most of the biblical ceremonial laws, one would find that they have been given solely with a view to the existence of the other nations, and that their purpose was to separate Israel from those other nations. If Israel had been the only nation in the world, those laws would never have been given, or given in a totally

[11]Cf. Geiger's *Wissenschaftliche Zeitschrift für jüdische Theologie*, III (1837), pp. 430 f. But note the letter by Holdheim which was published in *Allgemeine Zeitung des Judentums*, 62 (1898), No. 2, p. 19. It is the letter which Holdheim wrote on 19th June 1833, when he applied for the rabbinical position in Hohenems. In that letter, Holdheim mentions a number of rabbinic authorities from whom he had obtained "Qualifikationszeugnisse", but he does not mention Moses Schreiber. He does, however, say that he had also obtained similar documents "from several others". Perhaps Schreiber was covered by that phrase. Otherwise, the note in Geiger's *Wissenschaftliche Zeitschrift* must be considered erroneous.

[12]Cf. Jekuthiel Judah Greenwald, *Letoledoth Hareformatziyon Hadathith Begermaniyah Uve-ungariyah* (in Hebrew – On the History of Religious Reform in Germany and Hungary), Columbus, Ohio 1948, p. 46n.

[13]*Autonomie*, pp. 49 f.

different form – just as there would have been no special laws for the priesthood, if that tribe had not been especially chosen. There would only have been a simple, universal Moral Law."[14]

But, just as the holiness of the soil of Palestine was bound to the holiness of Israelite peoplehood, so it is impossible to think of the holiness of Jewish peoplehood, in its original integrity, once that peoplehood is deprived of its connection with the holy soil.[15]

Yet the Jewish people was deprived of its connection with the holy soil through the events of the year 70 C.E. Moreover, it was not just the Romans who destroyed Temple and State. God Himself, according to Holdheim, was responsible for that destruction, indicating thereby that Israel's national and theocratic phase – the two are identical for Holdheim – had come to an end. In this way, too, Holdheim comes to terms with Moses Mendelssohn's insistence that the Ceremonial Law had to be observed until God would abolish it as publicly and as spectacularly as He had originally given it. Holdheim argues that, by letting Temple and State be destroyed, God had done precisely that, and had removed the preconditions for the Law's observance.[16]

Now, Holdheim concedes that the early Rabbis did have an inkling of this when, in *Mishnah Kiddushin* 1:9, they made a distinction between the commandments which can only be observed in the Land of Israel, and the commandments which are not dependent upon the Land of Israel for their observance. However, according to Holdheim, that Rabbinic distinction is neither quite consistent nor does it go far enough.[17]

When it comes to certain ceremonial laws, Rabbinic Judaism declares them to be postponed but not abolished (*aufgeschoben und nicht aufgehoben*), when they should have been declared abolished and not postponed. "History does not move in a circle. We shall never return to the infancy stage of our religion, when such things were essential."[18] Indeed, says Holdheim, even for the messianic age, the Talmud, at best, envisages an up-dating of the Ceremonial Law, but certainly not its abolition.[19]

In short, Holdheim seems to be saying that, if the ancient Rabbis had only seen things as clearly as he, Holdheim, was now seeing them, they would have declared the ceremonial and the political laws of the Pentateuch, the "constitution" of the Hebrew theocratic State, abolished once that state had disappeared. They would then have based the religion of Judaism solely on the moral laws of the Torah, the eternal validity of which was whole-heartedly affirmed by Holdheim.[20] The Rabbis, however, did nothing of the sort. They acted as though the old "constitution" were still in force after the destruction of Temple and State; and, doing so, they managed to mislead the Jews until the dawn of the modern age. That dawn came, said Holdheim, when the governments of various German *Länder* abolished the autonomy of the rabbis and the special jurisdiction of the Jews. Henceforth, Jews will no longer have to fear Haman's

---

[14]*Ceremonialgesetz*, pp. 24 ff.   [15]*Ibid.*, pp. 33 ff.
[16]*Ibid.*, pp. 55 ff.   [17]*Autonomie*, pp. 25 ff.
[18]*Ceremonialgesetz*, p. 7.   [19]*Ibid.* pp. 46 ff.
[20]Cf. Holdheim in *Der Israelit des neunzehnten Jahrhunderts*, VI (1845), pp. 405 f.

accusation (Esther 3:8) about the Jews' being governed by their own different legislation.[21]

So rigorous and consistent was Holdheim in his understanding of the time-bound nature of the civil and the ceremonial laws of the Torah that, in his view, those laws would not be applicable again even if, perchance, Jews were given an opportunity of returning to Palestine.

"Whether, if the Jewish State were suddenly to arise again, the Jew would be obligated to *become* a citizen of it, is a question which, in our opinion, must be answered in the negative. For there is no religious law which commands him to enter the Jewish polity against his will. All such laws refer exclusively to the relationship which has *already* been entered, and to the fulfilment of the citizen's obligations obtaining in the same. The Lost Ten Tribes of Israel – which, by the way, strikingly prove the Jew's ability, so often denied, of acquiring foreign nationalities – and the overwhelming majority of Jews who did not think of returning from the Babylonian Exile demonstrate the truth of our assumption."[22]

"The Bible speaks only of a theocracy, and thinks solely of an independent national existence and the life of a State. The Rabbis have everywhere omitted to prove that, even without all of those inner conditions of life and the necessary preconditions, those laws must be practised. I maintain, on the contrary, that, if all the Jews were to live in Palestine under Turkish rule, they would be obligated, according to the Bible, to observe the laws of the present-day Turkish governments, and not those of the former Palestinian theocracy."[23]

It makes little difference whether, in a given context, Holdheim speaks of the Ceremonial Law or of the Civil Law of the ancient theocracy. The two are inter-related, both of them having had the function of keeping Israel as a distinctive and holy people at a time when such a distinctive existence was still called for in the divine scheme of things.

While the validity for the Jew of the *secular* Civil Law of the country in which a Jew lives has been asserted by traditional Jewish authorities long before the time of Holdheim,[24] it was left to Holdheim to break up the intricate texture of religious and civil elements which had always governed various areas of Jewish life, and to insist that those areas were actually areas of Civil Law alone, and, therefore, outside the domain of post-theocratic religious legislation.

Thus, in his book, *Gemischte Ehen zwischen Juden und Christen* (Berlin 1850), Holdheim defends the thesis that the prohibition of mixed marriages had nothing to do with the marriage partners' differences in religion. In spite of all the nice homilies about Jewish marriage, marriage, in Rabbinic Judaism, is essentially a civil matter. Marriage with non-Jews was prohibited in order to maintain the racial purity of the Jews as long as, in the divine scheme, the Jews were still required to be a separate and distinctive holy nation, living in a theocracy. But that time is long gone!

Holdheim was as good as his word. He not only officiated at mixed marriages, but a sermon he preached on one such occasion was actually published.[25]

[21]*Autonomie*, pp. 4 f.
[22]*Ibid.*, pp. 15 ff.
[23]*Ceremonialgesetz*, p. 35n.
[24]Cf. Leo Landman, *Jewish Law in the Diaspora. Confrontation and Accommodation*, Philadelphia 1968.
[25]Cf. Samuel Holdheim, *Predigten über die jüdische Religion*, vol. IV, Berlin 1869, pp. 211–214.

Again, in the case of the Saturday Sabbath, Holdheim argued that the weekly day of rest was indeed an eternally binding religious commandment of the Torah. But the binding character extended only to the institution of the Sabbath as such, not to the particular day of the week on which it is to be observed. In the ancient Hebrew theocracy, the constitution designated Saturday as the weekly day of rest. According to nineteenth-century German law, the weekly day of rest was Sunday; and German Jews would, therefore, have to celebrate their Sabbath on Sunday – as, in fact, Holdheim's *Reformgemeinde* did.[26]

Whatever, then, within the totality of Judaism, could be shown to have had any kind of relation to the ancient Jewish State or to its Temple cult and priestly legislation was *ipso facto* considered by Holdheim to have lost its validity already with the destruction of Temple and State, and most certainly with the entry of the Jew into the modern era.

Yet, far from regarding this sacrifice of Jewish particularism as a mere accommodation to the need for Emancipation, Holdheim waxed eloquent in bringing this abolition of Jewish uniqueness into relation with Israel's messianic hope:

> "Even though all Christian peoples and states may prevent us from participating in the life of their nations and states, because *they* regard us as foreigners, we must not forget that, because of this, we nevertheless do not constitute a separate people – least of all the former Jewish people. That is why such concepts as that of a Chosen People, with all the particularist laws connected with it, must be given up by us, if only in the interest of the purity of our Mosaic religion – if we are to see in the *fall* of our former peoplehood the *beginning* of the messianic kingdom, in the destruction of legalistic particularism the foundation-stone for the building of a universalism founded upon a pure humanity. Let the daughter-religions, therefore, seek to undergo the purification process as they see fit. Let them remain in their own modified particularism as long as they desire. Let them exclude us from the life of their nation and their state because we lack that Christian particularist element. We, for our part, if we properly understand our own point of view, must not speak of any ceremony which would set us apart. As proclaimers and harbingers of the messianic epoch, we must not destroy our own work. Every human being must be able to find his brother in us. We may trust in the power of truth that it will, of its own accord, win the victory over prejudice. But we may not, through our own narrow-minded example of clinging to a remnant of a legalistic particularism, which was destroyed forever by God Himself, make the victory of truth and love more difficult by interfering with the building of the messianic kingdom."[27]

It was, then, a messianic kind of enthusiasm which impelled Holdheim to espouse his antinomian position – even as messianic enthusiasm and antinomianism had gone hand in hand before in the course of Jewish history. The example of the Apostle Paul comes readily to mind; and, in spite of the criticisms levelled against Heinrich Graetz by Reform Jews, Graetz may not have altogether missed the mark when he said about Holdheim:

> "Since Paul of Tarsus, Judaism had not known such an enemy in its midst, who shook the whole edifice to its very foundation."[28]

Somewhat more dispassionately, the late Max Wiener noted that Holdheim's kind of Reform bore an unmistakable resemblance to the Protestant-Lutheran

---

[26]Cf. Immanuel Heinrich Ritter, *Samuel Holdheim. Sein Leben und seine Werke*, Berlin 1865, pp. 195 ff.

[27]*Ceremonialgesetz*, pp. 73 f.

[28]Heinrich Graetz, *History of the Jews*, vol. V, Philadelphia 1895, p. 680.

type of Reform.[29] Wiener also made the point that Holdheim's attempt to reform on the basis of a uniform principle might indeed have been a theoretical possibility, but that, when it came to a practical attempt which would have involved German Jewry as a whole,

> "it became evident soon enough that not much was to be gained by the distinguishing marks of the 'national–political' and the 'purely religious' elements within the infinite complexity of Jewish life."[30]

But it was not only Jewish life which had its complexity. Holdheim too was, as a person, far more complex than the passages we have quoted from his writings would seem to indicate.

Shmuel Joseph Agnon has recorded an anecdote about Holdheim, according to which Holdheim was in the habit of spending the long break between the Day of Atonement Morning and Concluding Services – which was customary in the Berlin *Reformgemeinde* – at a near-by café. Yet, contrary to what might have been expected, Holdheim did not repair to the café in order to eat. Instead, he would sit there in order to read all the prayers and *piyyutim* which had been omitted from the liturgy of his congregation![31]

One might be justified in doubting the literal truth of that story, and yet recognise that there was also another aspect to Holdheim, that his overt antinomian view of Judaism does not tell us all there is to be known about the man.

Holdheim may have said, as we have seen, that "we do not constitute a separate people – least of all the former Jewish people". But, in a sermon preached in 1852, he also said this:

> "If one were to think that our religious faith is to be separated from every form of Jewish nationality, also in the sense of its having to be uprooted from the soil of the history of the Jewish people out of which it gradually evolved, and that it could exist as a healthy and strong stem all by itself, or that it could flourish when transplanted into a foreign soil – if one were to think that, then this would be a great and dangerous error. Jewish faith never hovered in the air . . . but always lived rooted in the spirit and in the heart of the Jewish people . . . Judaism is not the acknowledgment of the existence of the One God, the way an occasional philosopher might arrive at such a concept, but Judaism is this acknowledgment of the One God as it has been demonstrated and testified to by almost four thousand years of history in the spirit and in the life of the Jewish people."[32]

Elsewhere, when expatiating upon Judaism's universal messianic hope, Holdheim is careful to stress that this universalism does not entail uniformity among mankind. Judaism

> "does not want to destroy the peculiarities of the peoples, to extinguish the spiritual and emotional directions of their historical life, and to impose upon them those of the Jewish people. Rather does it want to espouse them with its spirit, to fructify, to ennoble and to sanctify them."[33]

[29] Wiener, *op. cit.*, p. 97.

[30] *Ibid.*, p. 98.

[31] Sh. Y. Agnon, in *In Zwei Welten. Siegfried Moses zum Fünfundsiebzigsten Geburtstag*, ed. by Hans Tramer, Tel-Aviv 1962, Hebrew Section, p. 10.

[32] Holdheim, *Predigten*, vol. II, pp. 148 f.

[33] Holdheim, *Jüdische Glaubens- und Sittenlehre*, p. 124. Cf. *Ceremonialgesetz*, p. 72.

This much might be attributed to Holdheim's striving for Emancipation, to his desire not to alarm the non-Jewish world with the prospect of a universal messianic conversion to Judaism. But Holdheim is forced by his own logic to affirm also the survival of the "spiritual and emotional directions" of the historical life of the Jewish people. And so, he continues:

> "But least of all does Judaism want to extinguish the peculiarities of the Jewish people, and to destroy those phenomena of life which were produced by the inter-action between the Jewish spirit and the destiny of the Jewish people – so that Judaism, as a philosophical monotheism, denuded of all of its historical garb, could become the property of all mankind. Israel must never cease to be a *historical* people. Judaism must never cease to be a *historical* religion!" [34]

Again, notwithstanding his constant polemics against the Talmud, Holdheim's sermons are profusely illustrated with talmudic materials – the *halakhic* and *aggadic* passages being quoted in their original Aramaic and Hebrew.

Finally, we have to consider Holdheim's relationship to the Hebrew language itself. He was fully aware of, and he frequently stressed the talmudic permission to pray in the vernacular. Modern Orthodoxy's unwillingness to avail itself of that permission he attributed to the fear prevailing in modern Orthodox circles as to what would happen if people really understood the contents of the traditional prayers. Modern Orthodoxy, after all, was no longer naïve in the way in which talmudic antiquity was naïve. That is why, unlike the Talmud, modern Orthodoxy would see the preservation of the Hebrew language as a precondition for the preservation of Judaism. [35]

In 1845 Holdheim voted with the majority of the Frankfurt Rabbinical Conference against the "objective necessity" of having Hebrew as the language of prayer. In his own Berlin Reform Congregation, only the weekly Torah pericope, the *Shema'*, the *Kedushah* responses, and the Priestly Benediction were retained in Hebrew, while the service as such was, to all intents and purposes, entirely in German.

But when, towards the end of his life, Holdheim was writing his monograph dealing with the development of Jewish marriage law, *Ma'amar Ha-ishuth*, which was published posthumously, he wrote in Hebrew. The following sentences from his Preface convey to us something of the pathos and the ambiguity of Holdheim's self-consciousness:

> "Even though I am not acceptable to the majority of my brethren, many are those who accept my authority and who come to hear the Word of the Lord from my mouth . . . I have not tried to speak to you in the Holy Tongue [before], for I am slow of speech and of a slow tongue, not having been accustomed to do so for more than thirty years. Nevertheless, dear reader, accept from me the first-fruits of my soil which I have placed in the basket as a gift for you." [36]

It would seem, then, that Samuel Holdheim, the *yeshivah bahur* from the East who became Germany's most radical and revolutionary Reform rabbi, had not,

---

[34]Holdheim, *Jüdische Glaubens- und Sittenlehre*, p. 125.
[35]Holdheim in *Der Israelit des neunzehnten Jahrhunderts*, VI (1845), p. 388n. Cf. also his *Predigten*, vol. II, pp. 293–296.
[36]Holdheim, *Ma'amar Ha-ishuth*, Preface (no page number).

in the final analysis, severed all of his connections with the Judaism of history and tradition. Torn between his profound Jewish learning, on the one hand, and his interpretation of the needs of the hour, on the other, not to mention the messianic aura in which he perceived Emancipation, his trained talmudic mind forced him into positions the full logic of which his Jewish heart was unable to accept. This, perhaps, is the profound truth contained in the anecdote, retold by Agnon, about Holdheim's repairing to a café on the Day of Atonement in order to read the prayers and the synagogal poems which, with his sanction, had been omitted from the liturgy of his own congregation.

IV. GERMAN AND AMERICAN REFORM

Reform Judaism was a German-Jewish product. When it was exported to America, it remained for a long time confined to the circles of German-Jewish immigrants. Even the one instance, in the nineteenth century, of a "native" American Reform congregation, "The Reformed Society of Israelites", founded in Charleston, S.C., in 1824, evidences, at least in part, a conscious emulation of the strivings for Reform in Germany, in general, and of the Hamburg Temple prayerbook, in particular.[37] In the later and more pervasive attempts to establish Reform Judaism on American soil, under a German-trained leadership, the influence of the German pattern was, of course, still more in evidence.

Yet, different courses of development marked the progress of Reform Judaism in Germany, on the one hand, and in America, on the other. In Germany, the initial revolutionary burst of Reform stabilised itself with the evolution of *Liberales Judentum*, a modernised form of the Jewish tradition which, on the whole, manifested a greater similarity to what, in America, ultimately became known as "Conservative Judaism" than to the American Reform Judaism of the so-called "classical" period.

It has often been argued that this difference in development was related to the failure of the European revolutionary movements of the 1840s and the subsequent reaction which set in not only in political life. This, it is argued, accounts for the loss of reforming fervour on the part of the Jews in Germany. America, by way of contrast, was spared that reactionism, and Reform Judaism could progress in an unhindered way.

No doubt, political circumstances affected this phenomenon as they affect most other phenomena. But the invocation of the political scene is not sufficient to account for the differences which marked the development of Reform Judaism on the two continents. We also have to bear in mind the profound differences in the structures of the Jewish communities. German-Jewish communities were recognised as such by the State. If one was born a Jew, one automatically belonged to them; and it was not until 1876, when the "Prussian *Landtag*" passed the appropriate enabling law, that a Jew could terminate his membership of the local Jewish community without, at the same time, having to declare

---

[37]Cf. Philipson, *op. cit.*, pp. 329 ff; and W. Gunther Plaut, *The Growth of Reform Judaism*, New York 1965, pp. 3 ff.

his apostasy from Judaism as such. And it was the majority of a given local Jewish community which decided whether that particular community would abide by the traditional ritual in an unchanged manner or whether it would introduce such reforms as instrumental music in the synagogue, an abbreviated liturgy and some prayers in the vernacular.

Besides, many of the German-Jewish communities could look back upon a history of centuries – sometimes even of almost a millennium – a history in the course of which *minhagim* (local ritual customs) were developed, customs to which the Jews adhered possibly with an even greater tenacity than was shown for those provisions of Rabbinic Law which applied to all Jews. That loyalty to local tradition was so deeply entrenched that even non-Orthodox Jews gloried in it. When, for example, in 1929, the Liberal Jews of Germany finally produced their "Union Prayer Book" (*Einheitsgebetbuch*), that supposedly common liturgy had to appear in three different editions – one for Frankfurt a. Main, one for Berlin and one for Breslau!

This, then, was the setting of Reform Judaism in Germany. With two exceptions – the Hamburg Temple, founded in 1818, and the Berlin Reform Congregation, founded in 1845 – such Reform as was achieved in Germany was a Reform which was fought for and achieved within the total Jewish community.[38] It was a Reform which aimed, successfully on the whole, at avoiding a schismatic split within the local Jewish community, and which was also rather cautious in its approach to cherished local traditions. If, therefore, we find that prior to the destruction of German Jewry, most of the major, and many of the smaller German cities could boast of official synagogues in which a reformed liturgy had been introduced, then, contrary to what some American Jewish historians assert, we would have to admit that Reform Judaism was eminently successful in its native land. But it was a Reform Judaism geared to the needs and the requirements of its particular setting – as, by definition, any Reform Judaism should be.

It was, of course, an entirely different setting in which American Reform Judaism flourished. There were no old-established Jewish congregations on American soil – with the exception of a handful of synagogues established in the Colonial period. There was no ancient tradition to be reckoned with, or to be broken. Above all, the absolutely voluntary basis of religious association was guaranteed by the American Constitution. The government took no interest in the affairs of local Jewish communities – any more than it had a right to concern itself with the religious affiliation of the individual citizen.

Thus, conceivably, ten Jews could get together in a small Kentucky town, rent a warehouse and read the Quran in a Chinese translation. If those Jews chose to call what they were doing "Judaism", then this, to all intents and purposes, was Judaism in that small Kentucky town. If, later on, ten other Jews decided that they would rather recite the prayers of the Rödelheim *siddur*, then they would rent another warehouse, and establish the town's second Jewish congregation, *Kehillah Kedoshah Benei Frankfort*. That is how Jewish congregations came into being on American soil. It was a setting which held no restric-

[38] Cf. Jakob J. Petuchowski, *Prayerbook Reform in Europe*, New York 1968, pp. 31–43

tions for religious radicalism and extremism. In such a setting, Radical Reform Judaism could succeed and flourish.

When, in 1869, the Reform rabbis of America held their Philadelphia Conference, Abraham Geiger, in Germany, felt that that Conference contrasted favourably with the Leipzig Synod, held in the same year. But Geiger knew what it was that accounted for the difference. He noted that the Philadelphia Conference was attended exclusively by "men sharing a common conviction – one of decisive Progress". That, of course, was not the case in Germany, where delegates to the Synod came as representatives of local Jewish communities rather than as spokesmen for "denominational" Reform congregations.[39]

The fact that Geiger took an interest in the Philadelphia proceedings also shows that, in spite of the different courses which the development of Reform Judaism took in Germany and in America, there existed a keen interest on either side of the Atlantic in what was going on on the other. Considering the length of time it took ships to get from one continent to the other, it is indeed remarkable how the two branches of Reform Judaism managed to keep in constant touch.

Ludwig Philippson's *Allgemeine Zeitung des Judenthums* was avidly read by David Einhorn in Baltimore and by Isaac Mayer Wise in Cincinnati. Wise's German-language *Deborah* and even his English-language *Israelite* were read in Germany. Einhorn would reprint some of Philippson's editorials,[40] Holdheim would make frequent appearances in Einhorn's *Sinai*[41] and Isaac M. Wise would publish a *halakhic* problem in Geiger's *Jüdische Zeitschrift für Wissenschaft und Leben*, eliciting Geiger's favourable comment.[42]

V. WISE AND EINHORN

Given those frequent transatlantic contacts as well as the German provenance of the leaders of American Reform Judaism, it should not be surprising that the differences between the theological positions of Geiger and Holdheim should also find their repercussions on American soil. *Mutatis mutandis*, Geiger's *evolutionary* concept of Reform, of a Reform growing *organically* out of the previous stage of Jewish religious development, was championed in America by Isaac Mayer Wise (1819–1900) who came to America in 1846.[43] It should be noted, however, that Wise was both a greater organiser and far less of a scholar than Geiger – quite apart from the entirely different challenges which faced Geiger in Germany, and Wise in America.

[39]Cf. Abraham Geiger in *Jüdische Zeitschrift für Wissenschaft und Leben*, III (1870), pp. 6–27.

[40]See Einhorn's *Sinai*, I (1856), pp. 20–25. Philippson's editorials commented negatively on the Cleveland Conference of 1855, on which see below.

[41]Cf. for example, *Sinai*, III (1858), pp. 901 ff.; IV (1859), pp. 365 ff.; V (1860), pp. 10 ff., 37 ff., 70 ff., 100 ff., 133 ff., 173 ff.

[42]*Jüdische Zeitschrift für Wissenschaft und Leben*, I (1862), pp. 163–164.

[43]A full bibliography of writings by and about Wise is given in James G. Heller, *Isaac M. Wise. His Life, Work and Thought*, New York 1965, pp. 677–692. See also Andrew F. Key, *The Theology of Isaac M. Wise*, Cincinnati 1962.

There may have been some fleeting personal contacts between the two men. Wise is said to have been a "spectator" at the Frankfurt Rabbinical Conference of 1845, which was dominated by Geiger, and to have been so profoundly impressed by the proceedings there that "nearly all the reforms approved at that conference were eventually introduced by him in America".[44] It has also been claimed that, in 1846, on his way from Bohemia to Bremen, where he took ship for America, Wise stopped over in Breslau to meet Geiger.[45] Much later, in 1871, Wise meant to attend the Augsburg Synod. He was unable to do so; and Geiger read a letter to the assembly, in which Wise said: "I intended to visit the synod, but I am unfortunately *eved olam* (a perpetual slave)." He went on to describe the interest manifested in the synod by American Jews.[46]

Like Geiger, Wise held that

> "Reform must be doing something for the common cause of Judaism and not only for the minority. Reform can not be disconnected with [*sic*] the historical development of Judaism."[47]

Also, like the later Geiger,[48] Wise regarded Hebrew as the main language of the synagogue service:

> "The individual must pray in the language he knows best, but these services must be conducted in Hebrew not merely to maintain the union of Israel in the synagogue, but to maintain the language of the Bible in the mouth of Israel. Hymns, prayers, sermon in English, but the main portion of the divine service must remain in Hebrew *kedé shelo tishtakaḥ torah miyisrael* (so that the Torah may not be forgotten in Israel)."[49]

Again, like Geiger, Wise saw the struggle for Reform as taking place within the total Jewish community, not on the periphery of it. He was a convinced Reform Jew who believed in necessary changes; but those changes were not to be made unilaterally. They had to be sanctioned by Tradition, and they had to win the consent of the Jewish community as a whole. If only all American Jews could be united, then, so he believed, Reform would be the direction in which such a united Jewry would inevitably move. To bring about such a united American Jewry, Wise was ready to make all kinds of compromises with the more traditionalist elements of American Jewry. Note that none of the institutions he founded – the Union of American Hebrew Congregations, the Central Conference of American Rabbis, the Hebrew Union College – carries the adjective "Reform" in its title. And just as Geiger's prayerbooks of 1854 and 1870 were called *Israelitisches Gebetbuch*, without any further "denominational" specification, so did Wise's 1859 *Minhag America* describe itself as the "Divine Service for the American Israelites" – without specifying on its title-page that

---

[44]Cf. Max B. May, *Isaac M. Wise. A Biography*, New York 1916, pp. 38 f. If Wise was indeed present at the Frankfurt Conference, "spectator" is certainly the right word, since no indication of his presence is given in the *Protokolle und Aktenstücke der zweiten Rabbiner-Versammlung.*

[45]Cf. May, *op. cit.*, pp. 41 f.

[46]Heller, *op. cit.*, pp. 403 f.

[47]*The Israelite*, II (9th May 1856), p. 356.

[48]Cf. the quotation from Geiger in Jakob J. Petuchowski, ed., *New Perspectives on Abraham Geiger*, Cincinnati 1975, p. 49.

[49]*The Israelite*, IX (14th November 1862), p. 148.

certain liberties, based on reformist theological considerations, had been taken with the traditional liturgical texts.

James G. Heller is, therefore, correct in saying about Wise that

> "in his general attitude toward Reform he did not differ greatly from the more moderate group in Germany, men like Abraham Geiger, who believed that progress had always been the rule in Judaism, and that change was no less valid or imperative in our day than it had been under the *Tannaim* or *Amoraim*."[50]

Holdheim's position was known to Wise. He even translated some of Holdheim's articles for publication in *The Asmonean*.[51] But his judgment on Holdheim's position was brief and unequivocally negative: "The Berlin pattern means no religion."[52]

If Geiger's influence on Wise was remote and indirect, Holdheim's relationship with Einhorn (1809–1879)[53] was both personal and intimate. It is true that Holdheim and Einhorn first "met" as antagonists in print. In 1844, after the Braunschweig Rabbinical Conference voted unanimously for the abolition of the *Kol Nidré* formula, Holdheim had published an article in which he justified that decision, and in which he also made the claim that, according to Rabbinic Judaism, not only *some*, but *all* vows can be annulled. Holdheim saw in this an additional argument for breaking with Rabbinic Judaism.[54] Einhorn, in an opposing article,[55] accused Holdheim of misrepresenting the teaching of Rabbinic Judaism on the subject of vows, and of mounting "groundless attacks on the innocent *Kol Nidré*".

Sixteen years later, Einhorn, after Holdheim's death, reminisced about that controversy:

> "In the heat of discussion, I let fall many a harsh word which, without withholding respect for the opponent, nevertheless hurt him, and which I later bitterly regretted. This notwithstanding, it was *he*, then standing on the summit of his reputation, who gladly rushed towards me, who had only recently made my first public appearance, and, offering me his hand, said: 'After all, we both fought *leshem shamayim* (for the sake of God).' "[56]

The two men did indeed become close friends, and, when Holdheim accepted the pulpit of the Berlin Reform Congregation, in 1847, Einhorn became his

[50]Heller, *op. cit.*, p. 239.

[51]*Ibid.*, p. 223.

[52]*The Israelite*, I (23rd November 1855), p. 164.

[53]The following works by Einhorn have been consulted: *Das Princip des Mosaismus und dessen Verhältniss zum Heidenthum und rabbinischen Judenthum*, Leipzig 1854; *Sinai – Ein Organ für Erkenntniss und Veredlung des Judenthums*, vols. I–VII, Baltimore 1856–1863; Kaufmann Kohler, ed., *Dr. David Einhorn's Ausgewählte Predigten*, New York 1880. The following works about Einhorn have been helpful: Bernard N. Cohn, 'David Einhorn. Some Aspects of His Thinking', in *Essays in American Jewish History* (American Jewish Archives Tenth Anniversary Volume), Cincinnati 1958, pp. 315–324; Eric L. Friedland, '*Olath Tamid* by David Einhorn', in *Hebrew Union College Annual*, XLV (1974), pp. 307–332; Kaufmann Kohler, 'David Einhorn, the Uncompromising Champion of Reform Judaism', in *CCAR Yearbook*, XIX (1909), pp. 215–270; David Philipson, *op. cit.*; Martin B. Ryback, 'The East–West Conflict in American Reform Judaism', in *American Jewish Archives*, IV, (1952), pp. 3–25.

[54]*Der Israelit des neunzehnten Jahrhunderts*, V (1844), pp. 277–280.

[55]*Ibid.*, V (1844), pp. 375–378.

[56]*Sinai*, V (1860), p. 293.

successor as Chief Rabbi of Mecklenburg-Schwerin. Holdheim called Einhorn his "most powerful comrade in conviction" (*mächtigster Gesinnungsgenosse*),[57] and added that Einhorn's

> "energetic intervention into the religious conditions of the Jews of America as well as the periodical, *Sinai*, which he edits, entitle us to great, great expectations."[58]

Einhorn, for his part, saw in Holdheim "the great master in Israel, the high-priest of Jewish theological scholarship, the lion in the battle for light and truth."[59]

Einhorn also shared Holdheim's occasional misgivings about Geiger. Holdheim, while recognising Geiger's great scholarly ability, nevertheless felt that Geiger

> "was compelled more to conceal than to reveal Reform's *ultimate* aims. While, in his scholarly work, he laboured ever more intensively towards the breach between the older view of religion and the contemporary religious consciousness, thereby encouraging those of his colleagues living under more favourable conditions than himself, he sought, in actual life, to stand in front of the breach, and to fill the gap with his own *personality*. As the rabbi of a whole community, he regarded it as his duty to stand above the parties like a constitutional monarch. By only *half* lifting the veil of Reform in front of the party of progress, he anticipated the thanks of Orthodoxy, for not removing the veil altogether."[60]

More specifically, Holdheim accused Geiger of a blatant inconsistency between Geiger's plea, at the Frankfurt Rabbinical Conference, for prayer in the vernacular and his insistence, in the Preface to his 1854 prayerbook, that the language of the public worship service should be Hebrew.[61]

For Einhorn, too, Geiger did not seem to evince enough enthusiasm for advancing the cause of Reform Judaism. Appending his own remarks to a negative review of Geiger's book *Leon da Modena* (Breslau 1856) Einhorn wrote:

> "We, too, have been as unsatisfied by this monograph as we have been by everything else Geiger has written of late. At one time, the lion roared; but, for many years now, he has been slumbering. Every once in a while, he opens his eye and winks a little at the reform of Judaism. But then he immediately closes it again, full of literary-historical bliss."[62]

But Einhorn adds that a report "from the most reliable source" about the forthcoming publication of Geiger's *Urschrift*

> "makes us hope that the *helel ben shaḥar* ('day star, son of the morning' – Isaiah 14:12) will shortly rise again in his full might to expel the night owls."[63]

The alignment, then, is clear. If Wise was, to some extent, the protagonist in America of Geiger's position, Einhorn, to an even larger extent, was the American apostle of Holdheim's doctrines. Like Holdheim, he regarded the so-called Ceremonial Law of Judaism as no longer applicable to the post-biblical

[57]Samuel Holdheim, *Geschichte der Entstehung etc.*, p. 79.
[58]*Ibid.*, p. 140, n. 1.
[59]*Sinai*, V (1860), p. 288.
[60]Holdheim, *Geschichte der Entstehung etc.*, pp. 68 f.
[61]*Ibid.*, p. 197, n. 1.
[62]*Sinai*, II (1857), p. 435.
[63]*Ibid.*

age, in general, and to modern Jewish life, in particular. Also, like Holdheim, he saw in the Moral Law the only eternally binding element of Judaism. And just as Holdheim, with all of his rejection of the Ceremonial Law, did not deny that it originally constituted a part of divine Revelation, so did Einhorn argue that

> "one can very well believe in the divine origin of the Ceremonial Law, and nevertheless be thoroughly convinced that God had ordained it as a mere pedagogical device – both for a certain group among mankind and for certain times and places." [64]

At that, Einhorn was probably somewhat more radical in his concept of Revelation than Holdheim was; for Einhorn did not regard divine Revelation "in any way as an external Revelation". He identified "the rational divine spirit within man, Reason", as the sole "organ of Revelation with respect to the totality of the truths and the laws of Judaism".[65]

But there were also areas in which Einhorn found himself closer to the Judaism of tradition than to the position of Holdheim. Liturgy was one of them. Einhorn's prayerbook, *Olath Tamid*, published in 1858, though "radical" by the standards of its time and borrowing some material from Holdheim, was far more in accord with the rubrics and arrangement of the traditional *siddur* than with the liturgy of Holdheim's Berlin Reform Congregation. Also, while much of the service was in German, Einhorn retained Hebrew for many of the classical prayers which he included in his prayerbook.[66]

It was, above all, in the matter of mixed marriages that Einhorn took a position diametrically opposed to that of his friend Holdheim. The latter, as has been noted, not only considered such marriages as permitted by Judaism, but he also officiated himself at such ceremonies. Einhorn, on the other hand, stated that "such marriages are to be strictly prohibited even from the standpoint of Reformed Judaism". He also said:

> "To lend a hand to the sanctification of mixed marriage is, according to my firm conviction, to furnish a nail to the coffin of the small Jewish race, with its sublime mission." [67]

Holdheim and Einhorn may have shared the same enthusiastic faith in universalism. But, for Holdheim, that faith entailed the demolition of all barriers between Jews and monotheistic non-Jews, whereas Einhorn's concept of the Jews as God's "Priest People" with a mission to all mankind necessitated the survival of the Jews as a distinct group; and he, therefore, saw in mixed marriage a danger to universalism itself.

Einhorn came to the United States in 1855. That was the year in which the Cleveland Conference took place, a conference in which Isaac M. Wise collaborated with the traditionalist Isaac Leeser (1806–1868) – another American

---

[64] *Sinai*, III (1858), pp. 796 f.
[65] *Ibid.*, II (1857), p. 401.
[66] Cf. Eric L. Friedland, *op. cit.*
[67] The bibliographical references to Einhorn's repeated arguments against mixed marriage are given in Moses Mielziner, *The Jewish Law of Marriage and Divorce*, Cincinnati 1884, p. 52.

Jewish leader of German provenance – for the purpose of uniting all the Jews
of America. That conference adopted a "platform" which declared:

> 1. "The Bible, as delivered to us by our fathers, and as now in our possession, is of im-
> mediate divine origin, and the standard of our religion.
> 2. The Talmud contains the traditional legal and logical exposition of the biblical laws,
> which must be expounded and practiced according to the comments of the Talmud." [68]

Wise could all the more readily subscribe to that statement about the Talmud
because of his conviction that the Talmud itself warranted changes and abroga-
tions of a number of biblical laws, and because he saw his own reforming efforts
as being in line with talmudic developments. But many of the Reformers on the
Eastern Seaboard of the United States regarded the Cleveland Platform as sheer
treason to the cause of Reform.

Foremost among the critics of the Cleveland Platform was David Einhorn.
In the very first issue of his periodical, *Sinai*, he launched a bitter attack on the
Cleveland Conference, in general, and on Isaac M. Wise, in particular. [69]

> "Your Union is that of the men of the Tower of Babel. The volumes of the Talmud are
> to be brought out of your lumber-room, to serve as a pedestal for your 'Minhag America'
> and your 'Zion College'. And they, in turn, are to serve *you personally* as the summit of
> the lofty structure, and elevate you unto heaven. But God has confused your language, so
> that one might know in good time what kind of Judaism and what kind of Jews your
> *Minhag* and your Jewish Faculty are going to produce. No! A Babel can never turn into
> a Zion." [70]

The lines were drawn. Throughout the years, Einhorn attacked Wise, and
sought to frustrate Wise's plans for a union of congregations and for a rabbinical
seminary in America. For the differences between Wise and Einhorn were not
confined to matters of doctrinal and ceremonial import. The two differed also
in their very concepts of Reform's constituency.

Wise's primary aim, as we have seen, was the unification of all American
Jews. His ultimate aim was to steer them in the direction of Reform. Another
aim, not inferior in Wise's hierarchy of values, was the creation of a distinctively
American Judaism, adapted to the needs of the American environment. German
was to give way to English when it came to prayers, sermons, hymns and publications. Above all, the religious education of the young was to be conducted
in English. That is why the creation of the English-speaking rabbi, trained in
an American setting, became the keystone of Wise's whole enterprise.

Einhorn, on the contrary, was so uncompromising in his espousal of Radical
Reform that, so far from envisaging Reform Judaism as the religion of a united
American Jewry, he wanted to see Reform confined to a – German-speaking –
cultural élite.

> "Take away from Reform Judaism the German spirit, or what is the same thing, the
> German language, and you have torn away from it the mother soil and it must wither
> away, the lovely flower. The English sermon can have for its mission nothing else than to
> utilize the treasure of the German spirit and German literature for our religious life and
> therewith enrich it. In a word, where the German sermon is banned, there the reform of
> Judaism is nothing more than a brilliant gloss, a decorated doll, without heart, without
> soul, which the proudest temples and the most splendid theories cannot succeed in
> infusing with life." [71]

[68]Philipson, *op. cit.*, p. 353.   [69]*Sinai*, I (1856), pp. 4–10.
[70]*Ibid.*, p. 10.   [71]Quoted in Friedland, *op. cit.*, p. 321.

The friendship which, in spite of ideological and practical differences, marked the relationship between Geiger and Holdheim in Germany gave way to open and bitter animosity in the case of their respective disciples, Wise and Einhorn, on American soil. Wise went so far as to call Einhorn "a Deist, a Unitarian and a Sadducee and an Apostle of deistical rationalism", and he urged Einhorn to leave the fold of Judaism.[72]

Only towards the end of Einhorn's life did the relations between the two men become somewhat less strained. By then, however, both of them had achieved their victories. Wise had succeeded in creating his Union of American Hebrew Congregations and his Hebrew Union College, while Einhorn had managed to enunciate what was to become the official ideology of American Reform Judaism.

It was Einhorn who was instrumental in bringing together the Philadelphia Conference of Reform Rabbis, in 1869, and it was Einhorn who dominated the proceedings.[73] The resolutions adopted at that conference reflected the spirit of Einhorn and the theology of Holdheim. They included the following:

> "The Messianic goal of Israel is not the restoration of the old Jewish state under a descendant of David, involving a second separation from the nations of the earth, but the union of all men as children of God in the confession of the all embracing unity of God, so as to realize the unity of all rational creatures and their call to moral sanctification."

> "We do not regard the downfall of the second Jewish State as a punishment for Israel's sinfulness, but as a result of the divine purpose, revealed in the promise to Abraham and manifesting itself more and more in the course of world history, to disperse the members of the Jewish race to all parts of the earth in order to redeem their lofty priestly task of leading the nations to true knowledge and reverence of God."

> "The Aaronic priesthood and the Mosaic sacrificial cult were preparatory steps to the real priesthood of the whole people, which began with the dispersion of the Jews, and to the sacrifices of sincere devotion and moral sanctification which are pleasing and acceptable to the Most Holy. These institutions, preparatory to higher religiosity, were consigned to the past, once for all, with the destruction of the Second Temple . . ."[74]

The proceedings of the Philadelphia Conference were, needless to say, in German. Perhaps that is the reason why the resolutions adopted at that conference are not quite as well known in America today as are the resolutions adopted sixteen years later, in 1885, and which are known as the "Pittsburgh Platform". Yet a close study of the "Pittsburgh Platform"[75] reveals that document to be little more than a restatement and amplification of the resolutions adopted in Philadelphia in 1869.

Einhorn had been dead for six years by the time the Pittsburgh Conference met. But the impetus for that conference came from Kaufmann Kohler (1843–1926), a native of Fürth (Bavaria), Einhorn's son-in-law and ardent disciple.

Ever prepared to enter new alliances for the sake of greater Jewish unity – within the Reform camp itself, seeing that an over-all unity of American Jews

---

[72] *The Israelite*, II (15th February 1856), p. 1. On that whole dispute, primarily as reflected in the columns of *The Israelite*, see Ryback, *op. cit.*

[73] Cf. Sefton D. Temkin, *The New World of Reform*, London 1971.

[74] Cf. Temkin, *op. cit.*, p. 116.

[75] For the text, see Philipson, *op. cit.*, pp. 355–357.

had not been achieved – Isaac M. Wise was in attendance at both the Philadelphia and the Pittsburgh gatherings. His heart cannot have been very much in it, though. Both conferences made dogmas of Einhorn's radical theology, and, via Einhorn, of Holdheim's.

Wise created the institutions for which he had been striving. But, ideologically, he suffered defeat. And that ideological defeat was, before long, to manifest itself in Einhorn's ideology being imposed upon Wise's institutions. When, in 1894/1895, the Central Conference of American Rabbis, one of Wise's own creations, produced the *Union Prayer Book,* that prayerbook was based on Einhorn's *Olath Tamid,* and not on Wise's *Minhag America.* And in 1903, only three years after Wise's death, Kaufmann Kohler assumed the presidency of the Hebrew Union College, an office he held for eighteen years. During that time, he raised generations of rabbis who preached the Holdheim–Einhorn version of so-called "classical" Reform Judaism. The one victory over Einhorn which Wise achieved posthumously was the fact that this "classical" American Reform Judaism did become an English-speaking one.

Writing in 1928, Willy Cohn noted that "Holdheim's endeavours were overcome in a relatively short time" – an observation which is true only in view of Cohn's further remark that "the orientation of the Berlin Reform Congregation was unable to gain additional acceptance anywhere else in Germany".[76] Cohn's observation applies to Germany alone. It does not deal with the short-lived existence of a Radical Reform congregation in Hungary, which was very much under Holdheim's influence, and which was ministered to by David Einhorn when the latter was still in Europe.[77] Nor does it refer to the crucial and far-reaching effects which Holdheim's teachings had on the beliefs and practice (or *lack* of practice) of American Reform Judaism – Holdheim's teachings, rather than Geiger's.

In his Hebrew history of Reform Judaism, published in 1900, Simon Bernfeld was no doubt a little premature when he dismissed the whole of American Reform Judaism in the following lines:

> "Various attempts were made afterwards in America, where 'rabbis' assembled time and again to 'reform Judaism' and to make it compatible with the requirements of life. But those attempts have no place in a history of *Judaism.* We do not mean to imply that the Jews of America are not a part of the Jewish nation . . . But we do believe that only that can be called 'Reform' which, to a greater or lesser degree, desires a relationship to historical Judaism. American Judaism has no history; and those who come from abroad consciously suppress the memories of the past. And since this is a new settlement, it pays no attention at all to any previous traditions; and its tie to the Judaism of history is very loose indeed." [78]

Bernfeld may have been too hasty in his judgment. He did, however, see very clearly the significance of setting and environment in the evolution of a religious movement. It was the German setting which set limits to the spread of Hold-

---

[76]Willy Cohn, 'Holdheim, Samuel', in *Jüdisches Lexikon,* vol. II, Berlin 1928, column 1653.
[77]Cf. Philipson, *op. cit.,* pp. 270–283.
[78]Simon Bernfeld, *Toledoth Hareformatziyon Hadathith Beyisrael* (in Hebrew – History of Religious Reform in Israel), Cracow 1900, p. 234.

heim's radical ideas, and which enabled Geiger to be the major influence in the shaping of German Liberal Judaism. It was the American setting which permitted Holdheim's ideas to take root in America, under the loving care of his disciples and of the disciples of his disciples.

But even settings and environments do not remain constant. The constellation and the composition of American Jewry in the first third of the twentieth century were to be altogether different from what had been taken for granted in the second half of the nineteenth century. Besides, political developments in Europe were to cast a dark shadow on the easy optimism which had been the stock-in-trade of the nineteenth-century Reformers. In addition, the remarkable development of the Jewish National Home in Palestine called into question the very destiny which the nineteenth century had envisaged for the Jewish people.

The Pittsburgh Platform of 1885, with its Holdheimian overtones, gave way to the Columbus Platform of 1937, which, among other things, stressed the importance of Hebrew and ceremonies, the fact of Jewish peoplehood, and the duty of Reform Jews to help in the development of Palestine, both as a haven of refuge for persecuted brethren and as a cultural and spiritual centre.[79] These tendencies have become intensified in the wake of the Holocaust and of the creation of the State of Israel. American Reform Judaism is now as conscious as any other branch of Judaism of its relationship to Jewish history and destiny, and of its partnership in *kelal yisrael*, the total world Jewish community. In this respect, at least, Isaac M. Wise seems to have superseded David Einhorn as the dominant influence on American Reform Judaism in the second half of the twentieth century.

Not that this influence has remained unopposed. The inevitable tripartite division into Left, Right and Centre is coming into view again; and there are those who attempt to salvage and to restore the main emphases of "classical" Reform Judaism. At issue is the basic question whether Reform Judaism is predicated on organic growth and development, that is, on evolution, or whether it stands for revolution and the radical break with the Jewish past. Particular terms of reference may have changed, and some problems may be differently construed; but the old dialectics between Wise and Einhorn – and, beyond them, between Geiger and Holdheim – still shape today's discussion.

[79]For the text, see Louis Finkelstein, ed., *The Jews. Their History, Culture, and Religion*, vol. IV, Philadelphia 1949, pp. 1344–1347.

From Relativism to Religious Faith
The Testimony of Franz Rosenzweig's Unpublished Diaries

BY PAUL R. MENDES-FLOHR AND JEHUDA REINHARZ

On the evening of 7th July 1913 Franz Rosenzweig, author of a recent doctoral dissertation on Hegel and an unabashed agnostic in matters of religious faith, engaged in a heated discussion with Eugen Rosenstock, a young lecturer at the University of Leipzig and a deeply believing Christian. Their discussion that evening was the culmination of months of intent debate in which Rosenzweig defended the relativism sponsored by the regnant philosophical and historical perspectives, while Rosenstock affirmed the absolute grounding of human existence provided by religious faith. In the end Rosenzweig conceded the strength of his friend's position. On that July evening he parted from Rosenstock resolved to adopt a faith in God who reveals himself to man, a faith in the sovereign Lord of Creation who manifests an abiding concern for man and who enters human time to speak to man in agapeic love.

Thus Franz Rosenzweig began to turn from *Kulturgeschichte* to theology, initially considering the Church as the only possible modality for his newly acquired piety, but soon he sought to establish that piety in his ancestral Judaism. He discovered within Judaism – and not only for himself but for many Western Jews estranged from the tradition of their fathers – the possibilities of a deeply meaningful life of theocentric faith.

Rosenzweig's dramatic *volte-face* from modern agnosticism to *Offenbarungsgläubigkeit* – faith based on revelation – has become the subject of legend. Legend, however, suggests the extraordinary, the atypical, indeed, the ahistorical. While Rosenzweig's affirmation of faith may have been atypical, this affirmation emerged from a dilemma that he shared with modern, secular men of his age and culture. Rosenzweig's unpublished diaries,[1] the subject of this essay, poignantly indicate his struggle with the relativism and subjectivism that plagued German thinkers from Goethe to Nietzsche; it is this relativism that lies behind his eventual adoption of *Offenbarungsgläubigkeit*.

The unpublished diaries of Franz Rosenzweig offer a rich tapestry of aphorisms and short disquisitions, recording the reflections of a *gebildeter* young man.[2]

[1]The diaries are deposited in the Archives of the Leo Baeck Institute in New York. A typewritten transcript is also found in the Franz Rosenzweig Archive in Boston. The latter manuscript was made available to us through the kindness of Professor Nahum N. Glatzer, to whom we would like to express our sincere gratitude.

[2]Excerpts from the early sections of the diaries with brief comments are given in N. N. Glatzer, 'Frank Rosenzweig in his Student Years', in *Paul Lazarus Gedenkbuch. Beiträge zur Würdigung der letzten Rabbinergeneration in Deutschland*, ed. by Schlomo Rülf, Jerusalem 1961, pp. 143–153. Citations from the diaries are also found in *Franz Rosenzweig. His Life and Thought*, presented by N. N. Glatzer, 2nd, revised edn., New York 1961, pp. 1–31, *passim*.

He discusses *inter alia* Mozart's operas; Shakespeare and the problem of Hamlet; Hegel, Schelling and historiosophy; Schiller and Fichte and their relation to Goethe. The diaries, to which he gave the title *Hemerai kai nuktes* (Days and Nights), are more a collection of *Pensées* than a record of personal, biographical details. Indeed, the diaries hardly contain anything which may be considered intimate. His published *Briefe* offer far greater autobiographical material. None the less, the diaries are "autobiographical". As Rosenzweig himself observes in his journal: "You believe you are philosophising, but you are only writing your own biography" (11th February 1906). A year later he copies this sentence verbatim, and adds: "Indeed" (21st February 1907). In the diaries – which cover the larger part of his student years, 14th December 1905 to 22nd June 1908, and then continue from 7th September 1914 to 18th April 1922 – we witness Rosenzweig grappling with ideas and issues that were central to his thought. In the first part of the diaries, which will be the focus of the present essay, the *leitmotif* is subjectivism and relativism. This is of significance, for Rosenzweig characterised his adoption of *Offenbarungsgläubigkeit* in that fateful July evening of 1913 as the overcoming of his "relativism".[3] But relativism bears many faces, and being bereft of specification Rosenzweig's confession remains somewhat obscure.[4] The diaries serve to illumine the nature and depth of the relativism that so intensely preoccupied Rosenzweig and from which *Offenbarungsgläubigkeit* "redeemed" him.

The diaries begin with a romantic teenager of eighteen pondering the core of his own identity, his "personality and genius". The young Rosenzweig observes that genius – sovereign, self-enclosed personality – is primed by imagination (*Phantasie*), "our most sovereign component", independent even of will. In pursuit of their imagination "some geniuses caught fatal pneumonia". He lists such instances as Kleist, Hölderlin – and Herostratos, he who represents the criminal lust for fame and who will serve the role of alter-ego in the diaries[5] (14th December 1905). From Goethe – who has been referred to as "the prince of youth, [and] standard bearer . . . of ephemeral geniuses"[6] – Rosenzweig learned to see the problem of the Self as an incessant struggle between subjectivism and objectivism. He muses that "the tendency to adopt one or the other view may only be a matter of mood" (11th January 1906). The mild cynicism expressed here points to a mounting intellectual and spiritual uneasiness.

Philosophy, which he apparently understood at this stage as metaphysics, he held, cannot obtain objective truth. To believe it can, "one either has to be naïve or a mathematician . . . I am a sceptic and unmathematical." Therefore, he continues, "philosophy for me is only an expression of personality" (2nd May

---

[3]Cf. Franz Rosenweig, *Briefe*, ed. Edith Rosenzweig in collaboration with Ernst Simon, Berlin 1935, p. 72.

[4]Rosenzweig's relativism is briefly discussed in Glatzer, *Franz Rosenzweig. His Life and Thought*, pp. xiii ff.

[5]Rosenzweig on one occasion refers to Herostratos as "the schoolmaster of one's ego" (24th June 1906).

[6]Giuseppe Antonio Borgese, 'The Message of Goethe', in *Goethe and The Modern Mind*, ed. by Arnold Bergstraesser, Chicago 1950, p. 4.

1906). "Why do we philosophise? Just as we pursue music or literature or art, for no other reason. Here, too, in the final analysis it is the cultivation of the individual personality" (1st April 1906). Commenting on the development of Goethe, he concludes, "le style c'est l'homme" (24th April 1906). In this early period of his thought, according to his own observation, Rosenzweig develops from "within Goethe" (24th May 1908). His understanding of the problem of subjectivism and objectivism is defined by his intense reading of Goethe. Indeed, the young Rosenzweig could endorse Hegel's statement to Goethe: "When I survey the course of my spiritual development, I see you everywhere woven into it and would like to call myself one of your sons; my inward nature has . . . set its course by your creations as by signal fires." [7]

In an inchoate, fragmentary form Rosenzweig sketches a scheme of European thought. This was prompted by a lecture given by August Horneffer, the Nietzsche scholar, who contended that modern culture was heir to the Greek as opposed to the Judaic world-view. "The Greek," Rosenzweig quotes Horneffer, "knows science, unconditional striving for knowledge (*Erkenntnis*); the oriental knows only revelation (*Offenbarung*)." The Greek world-view rests on a belief in man, a belief that man should be the focus of all contemplation. For the Greek "man is the beginning", Rosenzweig paraphrases Horneffer, "God *could* be the goal, but *not necessarily so*" (Gott *kann* das Ziel sein, *muss* es nicht sein). Rosenzweig is dissatisfied with Horneffer's formulation, and offers his own: "The Greek proceeds from the Self; the Jew from the godhead, the totality of the world" (der Grieche geht von sich aus; der Jude von der Gottheit, vom Weltganzen). Rosenzweig apparently wishes to suggest that the Greek worldview locates the axis of knowledge and being in the individual. The Judaic world-view, on the other hand, is grounded in divine revelation which gives immediate and total knowledge of the cosmos. Here where ultimate truth is manifest the individual, who is defined by a never ceasing quest for knowledge, is eclipsed. In Rosenzweig's terminology, Greek "individualism" is the diametric opposite of Judaic "totalism" (*Totalismus*). As a proof text Rosenzweig points to the theophany in the Book of Job, where God speaks entirely as *deus sive natura*: "[here] the position of man is in a totalistic manner determined by the totality of the world (*das Weltganze*)" (1st April 1906). Rosenzweig admits that he is vague about all this, that in truth his knowledge of both Jewish and Greek culture is too exiguous to address Horneffer's question, "Griechentum oder Judentum?", nor is he certain whether the question is properly formulated. In the light of his mature thought, what is significant is his summary rejection of revelation. As Nahum Glatzer has observed,[8] it is noteworthy that Rosenzweig singles out the Jobian theophany as representative of theistic revelation. (Rosenzweig does not distinguish between Judaism and Christianity here.) He, of course, turned to the Book of Job in order to underscore his proposition that theistic revelation violates the dignity of the individual as an autonomous,

---

[7]Letter to Goethe, 24th April 1825. Cited in Walter A. Kaufmann, 'Goethe and the History of Ideas', in *Ideas in Cultural Perspective*, ed. by Philip P. Wiener and Aaron Noland, New Brunswick, New Jersey 1962, p. 281.
[8]Glatzer, 'Franz Rosenzweig in his Student Years', *loc. cit.*, pp. 148 ff.

thinking being. *Mutatis mutandis,* this is a typically deistic viewpoint – the individual has an inalienable right (and postulated ability) to seek knowledge unaided by divine revelation.[9] With Rosenzweig's adoption of faith, revelation is a special order of knowledge – knowledge not accessible to the unaided individual, and, furthermore, knowledge which is indispensable for the affirmation of individuality, namely, the knowledge of divine love. But this re-assessment of revelation would have to wait until he exhausted the possibilities of "deistic" individualism.

With reference to Goethe, he distinguishes between two types of individualism. The Renaissance heralded "a return from Christian totalism to the naïve subjectivism of Greece" (27th April 1906). "Naïve subjectivism" (echoes of Schiller) is "personally interested, affective contemplation" (*ibid.*). It is marked by a "soulful", "eternal striving" of the subject for self-expression and truth (6th May 1906). This "youthful" orientation has been opposed to that of "old-age" – "objective, sensate (*erfahrungsvolle*), passionless contemplation" (27th April 1906). In the latter the subject, the Self, is irrelevant. Age denies youth; the objectivism of maturity precludes child-like subjectivism. But, recalling his Goethe, Rosenzweig notes there is a form of objectivism that permits the subject to gain expression. The "classic objectivity" taught by Goethe does not seek disinterested knowledge of the objective world of phenomena. Knowledge is according to Goethe "subjectivity projected onto objectivity" (*ibid.*). In a separate entry, but with apparent reference to Goethe, Rosenzweig contends that "the balance of the external and the inner, the sensuous and the spiritual nature of man that would characterise the perfect man is in truth less a matter of balance than a mutual penetration of these elements – the spiritual becomes sensual, the sensuous spiritualised. Further, the world enters him [as] he enters the world" (4th September 1906). Rosenzweig may have quoted Goethe's comment to Eckermann: "Every healthy effort . . . is directed from the inward to the outward."[10] The classical Goethe, who is Rosenzweig's reference, according to Ernst Cassirer,[11] was dominated by the idea of inherent form: of modulating subjective freedom of the form's objective necessity, not only of the external, natural world but also of the inner world of spirit and aesthetics. Indeed, only objective law can give freedom. And here, as Cassirer has observed, "the circle of the subjective and objective was closed" for Goethe.[12]

The "unbounded striving" (*unendliches Streben*) of naïve subjectivism is replaced by the "circumscribed striving" (*begrenztes Streben*) of Goethe's classical objectivism (6th May 1906). Rosenzweig sees this best expressed in *Faust.* In the beginning of the drama Faust is "a man of storm and stress. In Part II he becomes obsessed by Helena; only with the start of Act 4 does his yearning

---

[9]In contradistinction to classical deism, Rosenzweig is uncertain about the omniscience of *ratio.* But in consonance with deism – so it seems the diaries must be read – he asserts the exclusive prerogative of the subject, *ratio-cum-irratio,* to obtain without divine aid knowledge and truth.

[10]*Gespräche,* ed. by Flodoard Freiherr von Biedermann, Leipzig 1910, III, p. 254.

[11]Ernst Cassirer, *Rousseau, Kant and Goethe,* trans. James Gutmann, *et al.,* New York 1968, pp. 86–92.

[12]*Ibid.,* p. 91.

cease, and the drama proceeds to present a Faust of fulfilled, circumscribed striving" (*ibid.*). This conforms with standard interpretations of *Faust*. It is interesting to note that the Romantic Goethe of *Sturm and Drang* affirmed genius, the underived Self, as a law unto itself. In this perspective nature was a mere reflection of man's soul. After his sojourn in Italy Goethe sought to bound the striving of the soul by a regard for nature, the realm of objective forms. Goethe thus studied science in order to free himself from utter subjectivity. It is then perhaps noteworthy that Rosenzweig, the student of medicine and the natural sciences, showed a keen interest in the mature Goethe's conception of objectivity and "circumscribed striving for self-fulfilment".

Classical objectivity in Rosenzweig's view is in effect an aesthetic exercise. "Aesthetic contemplation", which for him is clearly a correlate of classical objectivity, seeks to grasp the object under consideration in its unity (*Einheit*); in contrast, "theoretical contemplation" seeks to analyse, to sunder into parts. Analysis can never lead to comprehension of the whole, whereas aesthetic contemplation despite its admitted "one-sidedness" has a Platonic quality. To be sure, "the individual contemplation (*Anschauung*) will only result in a one-sided picture of the object: but, while all theories about the object will never add up to *the* theory about the object, the sum of possible contemplations will grow to the contemplation of the object in the highest sense, to the Platonic" (20th March 1906). In another entry, Rosenzweig affirms "particulars [to be] a reflection (*Gleichnis*) of the universal" (12th February 1906). Again Rosenzweig's reference in these discussions is Goethe, and in them we clearly hear the echo of Goethe's famous epigram: "Am farbigen Abglanz haben wir das Leben." [13]

In its search for causes, theoretical contemplation, according to Rosenzweig, is obliged to postulate an ultimate cause. Thus, theoretical contemplation perforce assumes an untenable metaphysical position (16th February 1906). In the history of ideas, the concept of ultimate cause has led to the assumption that the world enjoys a teleological design. In contradistinction, Rosenzweig emphatically declares that nature has no purpose. "Nature follows neither an external, purpose-serving power nor an inherent, purpose-serving principle, but solely an inner necessity" (8th August 1906). Aesthetic contemplation, he would undoubtedly say, avoids the fallacious proposition that nature has purpose. Both Kant, whom Rosenzweig cites in this regard (*ibid.*), and Goethe rejected the teleological argument. Goethe acknowledged his debt to Kant on this score in a most illuminating manner: "It is an unbounded service of our old Kant to the world, and I may add to myself, that in his *Critique of Judgment* he effectively placed art and nature side by side, and granted them both the right of acting in accordance with great principles without purpose . . . Nature and art are too great to aim at ends, and they don't need to either. There are relations everywhere, and relations are life." [14] *En passant*, we may note that Rosenzweig's rejection of teleology, together with his conclusion that the natural universe is indifferent to man, contrast sharply with his later theological view of the world

[13]*Faust* II, Act 1, Scene 1.
[14]Letter to Zelter, 29th January 1830. Cited in Cassirer, *op. cit.*, p. 68.

as Creation: to the man of faith the world is an aspect of divine providence.[15] Moreover, with the continuing graciousness of God, the world *qua* Creation assures the success of man's prayer and righteous deeds. In the diaries, the young Rosenzweig is cynical about the notion of "purposeful, rational action". It is a "confusion" maintained by the "mediocre". "*Homo primitivus* and the *summus homo* (*sive* 'genius') know nothing of it" (8th July 1906).

The post-classical Goethe – "der alte Goethe" – has been alternately interpreted as a sanguine optimist or a tormented sceptic. Rosenzweig's Goethe seems to be the latter. His reading of Goethe and abiding scepticism might reflect the influence of Nietzsche, to whom he frequently refers in the diaries and whom he acclaims as "our last great prophet" (25th May 1906). He compares without comment Nietzsche's "scepticism and doubt" with Goethe's method of "wonder and intuition (*Anschauung*)" (9th February 1905). In the light of Walter Kaufmann's observation that Nietzsche was "almost the first German writer to realize and emphasize the greatness of the old Goethe",[16] it is of interest to read in the diaries: "It is noteworthy how often Nietzsche quotes the old Goethe" (14th November 1906). This suggests that Rosenzweig's appreciation of Goethe may have been informed by Nietzsche. The prophet of Zarathustra, according to Erich Heller, admired Goethe's realism, his conviction that "what really is is not a dream or shadow, nor the meaningless agony of the Will, nor the abstractions of Reason, but the living revelation of the unfathomable".[17] In particular, Nietzsche saw in the "old Goethe" a confirmation of his vision which leads through scepticism and despair to a glorification of the here and now. But this journey was to be traversed not by mere contemplation, but by one's actions. According to this vitalist criterion, Rosenzweig deprecates his own "quietism", which he attributes to his "aesceticism" (24th June 1906). In a long dialogue with "his old friend Herostratos" (his alter-ego), he focuses on the latter's inhibitions. Rosenzweig excoriates Herostratos with these words: "And furthermore, you are forever an *Augenmensch* – that is precisely what we two have in common and why we understand each other. Did you not at all enjoy the magnificent scenes (*Bilder*) last night [at the celebration of the summer solstice] as everyone – colourful and enraptured – raged about the flames, and as the sparks and smoke spread so far that one could hardly discern the starry sky above? And the exultation and dancing. Regardless whether as participant or spectator I would have been intoxicated by [those scenes]." And Herostratos retorts: "Oh be quiet. *Augenmensch!* 'To look on enrapturedly' (*berauscht zuschauen*) – that atrocious phrase behind which uselessness hides . . . 'Aesthetic man' – how destructive. Life wants to be lived (*das Leben will gelebt werden*)." The dialogue ends with Rosenzweig citing a novella by Paul Heyse: " 'Every man must make the decision whether to enjoy or perceive life' (*das Leben geniessen oder erkennen*) – according to your terminology, to live or contemplate life (*leben oder anschauen*)." Herostratos: "Quietist!" (24th June 1906). In an entry a few weeks later, Rosenzweig observes that the man of action is a "fanatic",

[15]Cf. Rosenzweig, *The Star of Redemption*, trans. by William W. Hallo, New York 1970, pp. 94–97.
[16]Kaufmann, *op. cit.*, p. 280.
[17]Erich Heller, *The Disinherited Mind*, New York 1959, p. 108.

one who believes in what he says; a "weakling" is gripped by doubt (16th July 1906). Previously, he has recorded his envy of Nietzsche – a lonely "mountain climber", whom no ordinary man would dare follow. "Who is conceited enough?" (5th February 1906). Rosenzweig dared not follow. He remained a student of medical science and Goethe's classical objectivism.

After one of his frequent peripatetic conversations with his cousin Hans Ehrenberg, in which "Achilles, Homer and the essence of Greece" was discussed, Rosenzweig recorded in his diary: "An idea flashed through my mind: history after the pre-medical boards (*Physikum*). All indications are there: the direction of my thinking, my passions, my writing ability . . ., my habit of seeing everything in an historical light; [my predilection] to comprehend particulars as reflections of the whole . . ., *my scepticism which, in this case, would not render me unproductive*" (12th February 1906; italics added). History would render his scepticism productive in that a scrutinising, critical eye is requisite for good historical judgment.[18] His cousin provided an additional reason. History would correct the flaws in his objectivism, would make his judgment more objective, that is, history would oblige him to distinguish his Self from the world. History, "to use Hans's expression, means to become 'more pluralistic'; for the subject is singular, the object plural" (22nd May 1906).

Rosenzweig's formal historical studies did not begin until after he had successfully completed his *Physikum* in August 1907. Even before the completion of his medical studies he did, however, attend various courses in history and philosophy. In the winter semester of 1906/1907 he participated in a seminar on Kant's First Critique given by Professor Jonas Cohn.[19] This, his first encounter with academic philosophy, was to prove decisive in his intellectual development. A diary entry from 24th May 1908, reads: "The following has a place in this book: From the autumn of 1900 to autumn 1906, continuous development: from then to autumn 1907, negation of that development. At first I developed 'within Goethe'; then I went beyond him, moving along his boundaries – [a venture] expressed with one word: *Critique of Pure Reason*. Finally, starting with the autumn of 1907, contact [with Goethe] is renewed: the thesis, Goethe, and the antithesis, Kant, have been followed by a synthesis for which as yet I have no name . . ."

In December 1906, when he had just begun to absorb the principles of transcendental logic, Rosenzweig reformulated his scepticism. "Perfect scepticism, which no longer believes in anything objective, in any 'value', leads by necessity to the proclamation of the subjective as the highest value for the subject, [in other words] to the proclamation of individualism . . . For, without a centre man as enduring and effective is unthinkable". The individual "wrestling" with scepticism has lost objectivity – "he has to recreate it [objectivity] anew from that which scepticism has left untouched, namely, the subjective: the subjective has to be objectified" (2nd December 1906). Classical objectivity is then perhaps no more than a solipsistic re-definition of objective reality. In any event,

---

[18]Cf. "An historian must be a sceptic as the natural scientist must, in accordance with his vocation, be a materialist" (9th May 1907).

[19]Cf. *Briefe*, p. 30.

the Self as the centre of that reality now seems to Rosenzweig arbitrary, pragmatically determined. "The subject is the only component, unimpaired by scepticism, that could become the centre. But is it of itself indeed capable of being the centre? That is the question and, as such, I would have to answer in the negative. However, the question as posed would never have been asked by a sceptic. He would only ask: 'Are you there, you individual [subject], capable of being your own centre? If so, good. If not, then you will have to look for another centre, and look for it according to your liking, in another person, an institution, a pursuit, in at least something . . . !' " This leaves the question "resolved" but not, Rosenzweig admits, "solved". A genuine solution would require a belief in objective truth. A radical sceptic is then incapable of solving the question. But given a belief in the existence of objective truth, a solution should be sought by the adoption of a "scientific, critical" procedure: "Which of the objective components [of reality] might be best suited as the centre?"

There is a decidedly Kantian flavour to these remarks. But as Rosenzweig remarked in a letter dated 6th March 1907 to Hans Ehrenberg, his understanding of the critical method had until recently been rather imprecise.[20] Now, suddenly the principles of the transcendental dialectic have become clear to him. From this deeper understanding of Kant he acquired an epistemological modesty. On 20th March 1907 he observes in his diary that scepticism stems from an inordinate nominalism. "Only he who assumes too much reality will become a sceptic. Only when he relinquishes *in toto* the postulated 'objectivity' of objects will he cease to be a sceptic and become an 'idealist' – to become more positive than he ever believed possible." A sceptic derives pain and pleasure in destroying particular objectivities, but never does he challenge the principle of empirical objectivity itself. A sceptic may doubt the objectivity of the perceiving subject, but never does he question the objectivity of the world. Idealism turns scepticism upon its head, securing the objectivity of the perceiving subject. But Kant, Rosenzweig was soon to protest, leads us to a new form of relativism (26th December 1906). Moreover, Kant denies a role to the concrete, existential Self. Hence Rosenzweig's annoyance with Georg Simmel, the Kantian sociologist, who stressed the *a priori* forms of sociation and interaction. Simmel, he exclaims, renders the real self (*das wirkliche Ich*) into a border-concept, a negative concept marking the boundaries of effective knowledge and therefore having at the most noumenal value (20th May 1908, 24th May 1908).[21] In a letter to his mother of the 18th November 1908, Rosenzweig advised her not to study Kant.[22] Kant's philosophy, he tells his mother, is only truly necessary for students of the medical and natural sciences. Kant teaches them the limits of their access to truth. We learn from Kant that we are unable to determine whether the world had a beginning and that we are not to consider ourselves "wiser than others". Kant's philosophical message might "sound paradoxical", namely, it is inadmissible to philosophise. But, he continues, "I have no idea why an artist, a practical man, a businessman, an historian (if he does not pretend to treat history as a natural scientist) and finally a woman need read Kant – they already know what Kant has to teach them." With filial warmth and sincerity, he tells

[20]Cf. *Briefe*, p. 31.   [21]Cf. *ibid.*, pp. 152 ff.   [22]*Ibid.*, pp. 33–35.

his mother that her metaphysical interests regarding "inner truths" will best be met by the "philosophical poetry" of, say, Plato.

Dissatisfied with the limitations of Kant, Rosenzweig makes his way back to Goethe. He now argues that self-objectification need not be incompatible with transcendental logic. He demonstrates this by elaborately indicating the parallels between Kant and Goethe. The basic affinity between these two thinkers, according to Rosenzweig, is established in the border-concept (*Grenz-begriff*). Accordingly, both affirm a "naïve realism" – Kant "justifies" the phenomenal world, Goethe "transfigures" it (19th February 1908). Ernst Cassirer also finds the affinity between Kant and Goethe to lie in their shared realism. "What Kant aimed to set forth in the *Critique of Pure Reason* was the limits of pure reason. He has to solve this problem by logical means . . . All this Goethe could accept without reservation. Kant laid down the limits which the human mind is capable of attaining, and he did not touch on insoluble problems. The same sense of human limitation was strong in Goethe; but he felt and spoke as an artist . . . This is Goethe's sense of humility and limitation . . . Goethe had no desire to lay bare the secret of life; he rejoiced in life's infinitely rich surface." [23] Both agreed that this surface is governed by objective laws – and both held that epistemological judgment and artistic expression should abide by these laws. Hence, Rosenzweig asks, "is not 'antimetaphysics' something comparable to the cry for 'nature' in the arts?" (29th February 1908). Art and transcendental logic are not only compatible, they are, in Rosenzweig's view, interdependent. In perceiving the world the Kantian philosopher "rationalises the irrational" (*Rationalisierung des Irrationalen*); the Goethean artist, on the other hand, "irrationalises the rationalised" (*Irrationisierung dieses Rationalisierten*) – that is, he reintroduces "the non-logical, the wonder-ful" back into objectified reality (20th May 1908).

Previously, Rosenzweig had recorded in his diary that although he regarded his subjectivity to be sound, he found the "flaws" in his objectivity to be distressing (22nd May 1906). In a letter to Gertrud Oppenheim dated New Year's Eve 1907/1908, he informs her that after much struggle he has learned to anchor his subjectivity in objectivity. "Men desire objectivity and know the subjective only in its objective manifestation." [24] Apparently his encounter with Kant helped him clarify the nature of objectivity. But although he continues to work with what he believes to be his successful synthesis of Kant and Goethe, he remains uneasy regarding his objectivity. In an entry in his diary of 20th May 1908, he ponders whether there is not something tyrannical about the activity of *ratio*, about the "rationalising of the irrational". "To comprehend something means: to express it in rational form at all cost; the [*a priori*] concept of substance must be conceived . . . in order to make [nature] comprehensible; it is but an expression of our desire to comprehend" (20th May 1908). In *The Star of Redemption*, Rosenzweig will identify this compulsive desire to comprehend as a salient feature of paganism. Here in the diaries that which he understands to be the tyranny of *ratio* cast doubt on the objectivity of the perceiving mind.

[23]Cassirer, *op. cit.*, p. 79.   [24]*Briefe*, p. 32.

The study of history did not rescue Rosenzweig from his scepticism. Cryptically, he remarks in his diary that "Nietzsche was a bad philosopher because he was a good historian" (29th February 1907). Nietzsche, we surmise he meant, did not illumine ontological truths, but disclosed the axiological underpinnings of assumed truths. Nietzsche cast a relativistic light on culture.[25] Following the above comment on Nietzsche, we read: "People of the past did not live as consciously as we do; they did not know whether they were living in the 5th or 4th century B.C." (*ibid.*). History gives one consciousness of one's position in time, and, if we may extrapolate, consciousness of one's position in relation to truth. History relativises. Not insignificantly, Rosenzweig began his historical studies as the "crisis of historicism" was beginning to take shape. In the winter semester of 1908 at the University of Freiburg he commenced his doctoral studies with two of the protagonists of the debate over the meaningfulness of history, Heinrich Rickert and Friedrich Meinecke. The former has been frequently referred to as "the father of historical relativism".[26] Although he heatedly rejected what he deemed to be a dubious honour, this philosopher of historical method undeniably fostered a relativism with his concept of *Wertbezogenheit* – values as they are manifest in history are not timeless, but are culturally bound. It is the task of the historian, Rickert taught, to ascertain the values of a particular society and to determine the relation of these values to its cultural history.[27] Rickert held that methodologically such an approach was justified, but he readily admitted – as early as 1904 – that should it be raised as a *Weltanschauung* it would be "a monstrous thing (*Unding*), a form of relativism and scepticism" which carried to its logical conclusion can lead only to complete nihilism.[28] In the diaries Rosenzweig often mentions Rickert. In one instance, he refers to his teacher's "distinction between methodological and constitutive forms" and his caveat that the latter is not applicable to the study of history (23rd May 1908). The next day he observes that Hegel committed the error of confusing constitutive and methodological forms in that he treated the regulative principles of Kant's moral philosophy as "constitutive to historic perception". "Values," he adds in a spirit somewhat critical of both Hegel and Rickert, "should be rescued from history as well as from the natural sciences: space and time are coffins" (24th May 1908).

When Rosenzweig came to Freiburg, Meinecke had just published his monumental *Weltbürgertum und Nationalstaat*.[29] Rosenzweig was thoroughly enamoured of Meinecke the teacher and of his book. He shared this enthusiasm with his

---

[25]Cf. Arthur Danto, 'Nietzsche's Perspectivism', in *Nietzsche. A Collection of Critical Essays*, ed. by Robert Solomon, New York 1973, pp. 29–57.

[26]Cf. Georg G. Iggers, *The German Conception of History. The National Tradition of Historical Thought from Herder to the Present*, Middletown, Connecticut 1968, p. 152.

[27]*Ibid.*, pp. 152–159.

[28]Rickert, 'Geschichtsphilosophie', in *Festschrift für Kuno Fischer*, Heidelberg 1904–1905, pp. 101 f. Cited in Iggers, *op. cit.*, p. 158.

[29]The volume was first published in 1907. For a brief discussion of Meinecke's impact on Rosenzweig, see Alexander Altmann, 'Franz Rosenzweig and History', in *Between East and West. Essays dedicated to the Memory of Bela Horovitz*, ed. by A. Altmann, London 1958, pp. 194 f., esp. fn. 3.

mother, to whom he wrote: "Meinecke more than pleases me";[30] "to write such a book [as *Weltbürgertum und Nationalstaat*] I would give ten years of my life."[31] Rosenzweig's doctoral dissertation, later published with the assistance of Rickert as a book,[32] *Hegel und der Staat*, was inspired by a chapter in Meinecke's *magnum opus*.[33] Appropriately, Rosenzweig dedicated his study to Meinecke. Methodologically, Meinecke's work had a two-fold significance. In it he introduced the new concept of *Ideengeschichte*, the treatment of ideas as inseparable from the lives in which they take shape and the institutions which they affect, and the use of this method to strengthen the view of history known as ethical historicism.[34] Starting with perhaps Herder it was a dominant tendency in German thought to attribute a positive ethical significance to the unfolding of history. The emergence and retrenchment of the particularistic nation-state, however, seemed to contradict the cosmopolitan ethical vision expressed by so many of Germany's leading spirits. In *Weltbürgertum und National-staat*, Meinecke sought to demonstrate that the existence of the nation-state was consistent with this vision and, indeed, was envisaged as the most effective setting for the realisation of universal human values.[35]

In the midst of the horror, death and myopic nationalism wrought by the First World War, Meinecke's ethical historicism weakened considerably, although he continued to resist relativistic conclusions.[36] His student, Franz Rosenzweig, began to doubt his teacher's faith even before the war. In a long letter to Hans Ehrenberg dated 4th August 1909, Rosenzweig contends that any ideational history of the German *Reich* should also consider the *Allzeit-mehrerdesreichs-Politik*.[37] Such an enquiry, he is certain, will indicate that although "[it was] not at all apparent [at its founding] that the German *Reich* was already more than merely one nation alongside other nations, more than a body that sought the *suum esse conservare* and nothing else, even if the Imperium was [viewed] only in cultural terms". "Von der 'Kultur' zur 'Kanone' ist ein kleiner Schritt."[38] None the less, he wrote his dissertation, completed under Meinecke's supervision, on the ethical premises of Hegel's concept of the state. The dissertation was written – as Rosenzweig says in the preface of the book (published in 1920) that emerged from it – with the hope of checking in its modest way the parochial tendencies then regnant in the Bismarckian state. The Hegelian concept of the state, "which became the dominant concept in the foregoing century

[30]*Briefe*, p. 41.
[31]*Ibid.*
[32]Cf. Rosenzweig, *Hegel und der Staat*, München–Berlin 1920, p. xiii.
[33]Cf. *ibid.*, Meinecke refers to this fact and warmly praises Rosenzweig: "Franz Rosenzweig, der durch das Hegelkapitel in meinem Weltbürgertum angeregt, [hat] das subtile Buch über Hegel und den Staat geschrieben ..." Meinecke, *Strassburg, Freiburg, Berlin, 1901–1919. Erinnerungen*, Stuttgart 1949, p. 97.
[34]Cf. Iggers, *op. cit.*, pp. 195–228.
[35]Cf. Meinecke, *Cosmopolitanism and the National State*, trans. Robert B. Kimber, Princeton, New Jersey 1970, ch. I, esp. pp. 21 f.
[36]Cf. H. Stuart Hughes, *Society and Consciousness. The Reorientation of European Social Thought, 1890–1930*, New York 1958, pp. 236–248.
[37]*Briefe*, p. 44.
[38]*Ibid.*

and which 'like a bolt of lightning from the clouds' appeared on 18th January [18]71 as a world-historical fact – this idea as it unfolds in the life [of Hegel] was to place before the eyes of the reader the internal and external prospects of Germany's auspicious future" (eine nach innen wie aussen geräumigere deutsche Zukunft).[39] These prospects, Rosenzweig laconically notes in his preface of 1920, were, alas, not realised. "A field of ruins marks the place where formerly the *Reich* stood."[40]

Rosenzweig's published letters indicate that his doubts regarding ethical historicism were manifest even prior to the war. Unfortunately the diaries do not extend beyond 22nd June 1908, and they resume only in September 1914 until 18th April 1922, containing much interesting material on Schelling, Hegel and theology in particular, but virtually none on historicism or other matters we have discussed in this essay.[41] The early diaries do contain one long essay (thirty-five pages) of some relevance. Dealing with *Kulturgeschichte*, it was written in June 1907, just prior to Rosenzweig's transfer to the University of Freiburg. Although he had not yet begun to study with Meinecke, the essay, entitled "Baroque", reflects the method of *Ideengeschichte*. "In this discussion," he points out, "I do not wish to 'explain' men in terms of the time in which they were born, but the time in terms of those men. As long as men and time have not grown together into one unified picture we will [have not] comprehended the time. From Mozart we derive what constitutes Rococo; however, we can never comprehend from the concept of the Rococo what Mozart is." Ideas have an autobiographical grounding in the life of their authors. The essay proceeds to treat Baroque as an antithesis to the Renaissance. This approach gives Rosenzweig a cultural–historical perspective on the subjective/objective issue. "Whereas we conceive the essence of personality to be something eternal – the viewpoint of the Renaissance, we conceive the 'true face' of nature to be its

[39] *Hegel und der Staat*, p. xii.

[40] *Ibid*. The volume was prepared before the war, and only reluctantly did he agree to publish it in 1919. "Dies Buch, das ich heute nicht mehr geschrieben hätte, konnte ich genau so wenig umarbeiten. Es blieb nur übrig, es so herauszugeben wie es einmal war, in Ursprung also und Absicht ein Zeugnis des Geistes der Vorkriegsjahre, nicht des 'Geists' von 1919" (*ibid.*, p. xiii). He did, however, include one minor change in the published text. To the original motto that he inscribed on the manuscript in 1909, he added a second. "Hölderlin, *An die Deutschen*. 1800. 1909: 'Aber kömmt, wie der Strahl aus dem Gewölke kömmt/Aus Gedanken vielleicht geistig und reif die Tat? Folgt der Schrift, wie des Haines/ Dunkelm Blatte, die goldne Frucht?' 1919: 'Wohl ist enge begrenzt unsere Lebenszeit, Unserer Jahre Zahl sehen und zählen wir, Doch die Jahre der Völker, Sah ein sterbliches Auge sie?'" Also cf. "Wir glauben an einem Anfang zu stehen und haben in einem Ancien Régime gelebt." Attributed to Rosenzweig by Siegfried A. Kaehler, in a letter to Meinecke of 22nd January 1919. Meinecke, *Ausgewählter Briefwechsel*, Stuttgart 1962, p. 329. Rosenzweig's profound disappointment with ethical historicism as a *Weltanschauung* perhaps explains the extreme ambivalence to the nation-state evidenced in *The Star of Redemption*.

[41] Of some relevance are the following citations from the diaries: "Characteristically 19th century is [Hermann] Cohen's concept of a federation of states. The nation-state is to him so matter of fact that he conceives of peoples only as a federation of states, not as a state of peoples" (11th December 1915). And: "The transformation of the Church in accordance with St. John [meaning its growing missionary activities] brought about by the Enlightenment, has only become apparent in *this* war which embraces all of the Christian world and which is leading to supra-Christian politics" (14th January 1916).

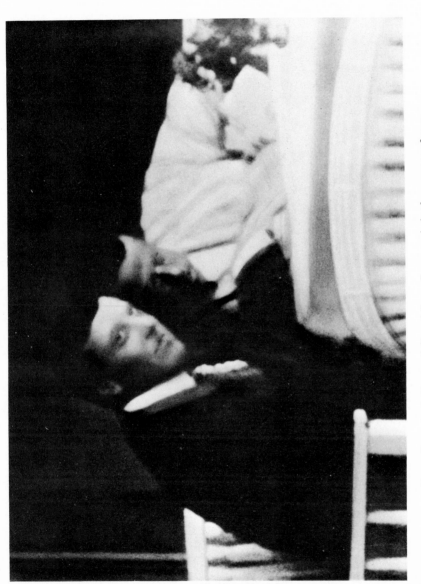

Eugen Rosenstock-Huessy (*left*) and Franz Rosenzweig in the summer of 1913

By courtesy of Argo Books Inc., Norwich, Vermont

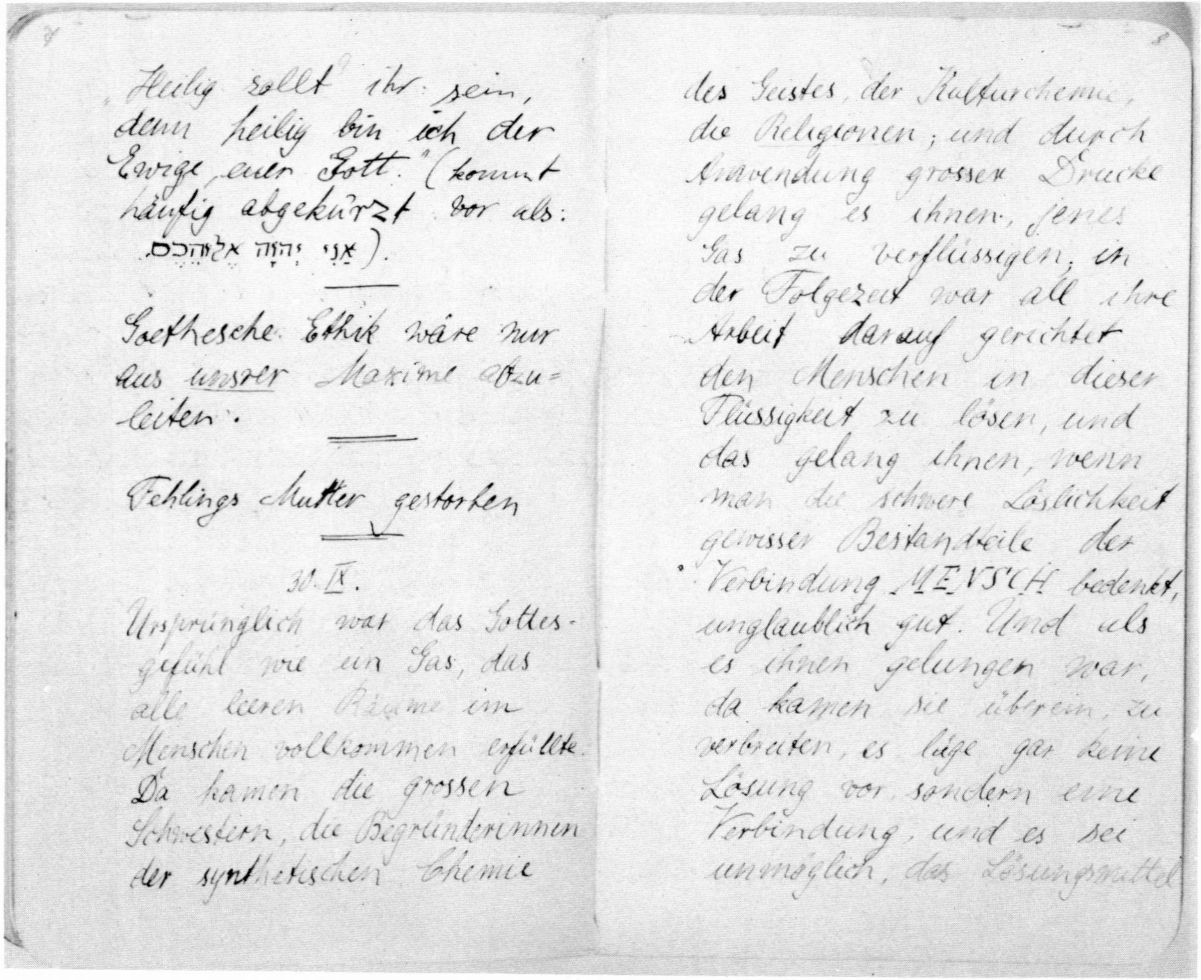
„Heilig sollt ihr sein, denn heilig bin ich der Ewige, euer Gott." (kommt häufig abgekürzt vor als: אֲנִי יְהוָה אֱלֹהֵיכֶם).

Goethesche Ethik wäre nur aus unsrer Maxime abzuleiten.

Fehlings Mutter gestorben

30. IX.

Ursprünglich war das Gottesgefühl wie ein Gas, das alle leeren Räume im Menschen vollkommen erfüllte. Da kamen die grossen Schwestern, die Begründerinnen der synthetischen Chemie des Geistes, der Kulturchemie, die Religionen; und durch Anwendung grosser Drucke gelang es ihnen, jenes Gas zu verflüssigen, in der Folgezeit war all ihre Arbeit darauf gerichtet den Menschen in dieser Flüssigkeit zu lösen, und das gelang ihnen, wenn man die schwere Löslichkeit gewisser Bestandteile der Verbindung MENSCH bedenkt, unglaublich gut. Und als es ihnen gelungen war, da kamen sie überein, zu verbreiten, es läge gar keine Lösung vor, sondern eine Verbindung, und es sei unmöglich, das Lösungsmittel

Two Pages from the Diaries of Franz Rosenzweig

momentariness, its actuality – the Baroque viewpoint." This historistic under-standing of the subjective/objective dilemma could only compound Rosen-zweig's scepticism.

On 9th January 1910 Rosenzweig and a group of young historians and philosophers met in Baden-Baden to establish a society that would seek "to make contemporary culture a subject of historical contemplation".[42] From the historical perspective and the objectivity obtained thereby, the proposed society hoped to forge a new subjectivity, not a mere consciousness of one's own sub-jectivity (as the nineteenth century sought), but rather a consciousness of the self *qua* subject of the *Zeitgeist*.[43] Furthermore, historical consciousness of the present will provide men with a new unity, not the false unity of Bismarck's *Reich* or of Wagner's Bayreuth festivals.[44] In the unity that Rosenzweig and his friends wished to foster one will cease to worship his "private God" for he "will find himself more or less objectively conscious of the time, and herein he will revere something greater, the God who reveals himself in measure in the here and now".[45] Heard here are strong echoes of Meinecke's insistence that an understanding of the present requires an historical perspective on the ideas and spiritual forces immanent within it. But the aspirations of the Baden-Baden conference reflect even more emphatically the impress of Hegel's *Heilsgeschichte*.

The society envisaged by the Baden-Baden conference failed to materialise. In Rosenzweig's case at least, this failure was accompanied (if not prompted) by a disaffection with Hegel's religious "intellectualism". In a letter to Hans Ehrenberg of the 26th September 1910 he declares that Hegel had erred in ascribing to history an ontological status. History is not the unfolding of Being, rather it is but the discrete act of men (*Tat der Täters*). "We see God in every ethical event, but not in one complete Whole, not in history."[46] Indeed, history which takes shape in the phenomenal world cannot serve as a vessel for divinity. "Every human act becomes sinful as it enters history" – although the actors intended otherwise the morality of an act is neutralised by the material world of necessity.[47] We are hence left with only one possible conclusion: God re-deems man not through history but – "es bleibt nichts andres übrig" – through religion.

This is not a statement of faith, but a philosophical proposition, a logical deduction. Rosenzweig would adopt a living religious faith, and at long last abandon his scepticism, only after his later encounter with the testimony of faith given by a co-participant in the Baden-Baden conference, Eugen Rosenstock. On a summer evening in 1913, as noted in the introduction to this essay, the two men (together with Rudolf Ehrenberg) entered into a heated discussion on relativism and religion.[48] Rosenzweig, as Glatzer reports, asked Rosenstock: " 'What would you do when all answers had failed?' Rosenstock replied, with the simplicity of faith: 'I would go to the next church, kneel and try to pray.' "

[42]*Briefe*, p. 47, n. 1.   [43]*Ibid.*, p. 48.   [44]*Ibid.*, p. 51.
[45]*Ibid.*   [46]*Ibid.*, p. 55.   [47]*Ibid.*
[48]Eugen Rosenstock-Huessy, 'Prologue to the Letters. Fifty Years Later', in *Judaism Despite Christianity. The Letters on Judaism and Christianity Between Eugen Rosenstock-Huessy and Franz Rosenzweig*, ed. by H. Stahmer, New York 1969, pp. 72–74.

"These simple words" as Glatzer observes, "did more than all previous discussions concerning reason and faith, history and revelation, Hegel and Nietzsche, to convince Rosenzweig" of the power of faith.[49] Four months later, Rosenzweig wrote to Rudolf Ehrenberg: "In that night's conversation Rosenstock pushed me step by step out of my last relativist positions that I still occupied, and forced me to take an absolute standpoint. I was inferior to him from the outset, since I had to recognise for my part too the justice of his attack ... Any form of philosophical relativism is now impossible to me."[50] Rosenzweig became a man of faith. From the perspective of his newly adopted *Offenbarungsgläubigkeit* he began to reassess the philosophical issues that occupied him in the diaries. *The Star of Redemption* may be deemed *inter alia* a record of this reassessment. Therein the point of departure is the individual existentially considered, unique and with his own biography. Yet Rosenzweig still recognises the need for "the objectivity of science". And "the bridge," Rosenzweig now affirms, "from maximum subjectivity to maximum objectivity is formed by theology's concept of revelation."[51]

[49]Glatzer, *Franz Rosenzweig. His Life and Thought*, p. xv.
[50]*Briefe*, p. 71. Cited by A. Altmann, 'About the Correspondence', in *Judaism Despite Christianity*, pp. 32 f.
[51]*The Star of Redemption*, p. 106.

Yitzchak Baer: A Reappraisal of Jewish History

BY PINCHAS E. ROSENBLÜTH

I

Few areas of research have suffered as much from misunderstanding and distortion as Jewish historiography. There are special reasons for this – the collapse of the traditional Jewish world and the aspiration to equality with other peoples. Most modern Jewish historians with the exception of Krochmal and to some extent Graetz, tried to place less stress on the idea of the uniqueness of the Jewish nation during the ages, and to explain its history by general standards. Jost and Dubnow were opponents of the world of Jewish tradition. Jost (1783–1860) saw Jewish history as a gradual release from national segregation and as a process of emancipation and submersion among the nations.[1] It was to refute him that Graetz (1817–1891) planned to write his *History of the Jews*. In his view the Jews were the bearers of the idea of the One God, battling continually against idolatry. Graetz's main intention was to describe the sufferings of the people and their spiritual creativeness, although sometimes his emotions got the better of him, leading him to biased judgments. He failed to understand *halakhic* concepts and the irrational and popular movements in the Jewish people.[2] As for Dubnow (1860–1941), he tells us that he started his career as an opponent of the traditional religion and as its reformer, after he had rebelled against the *cheder* and had become a *Maskil*.[3] Under the influence of the positivism of men like Comte and Spencer, he saw all the mysteries of Jewish history in the light of the struggle for survival. According to this school, Judaism, like every national culture, is merely the result of the nation's growth and its adaptation to special conditions, and the task of the historian is to describe this process.

II

In contrast to this trend, Yitzchak (Fritz) Baer endeavours to clarify the fundamental inner forces acting in the various periods of history. He stresses the religious character of Jewish history and the continuity between the generations, along with their setting in the history of mankind.[4] In order to understand his

[1]Reuwen Michael, 'J. M. Jost und sein Werk', in *Bulletin des Leo Baeck Instituts*, 3 (1960), No. 12, pp. 239–258; Georg Herlitz, 'Three Jewish Historians, Isaak Markus Jost – Heinrich Graetz – Eugen Taeubler. A Comparative Study', in *LBI Year Book IX* (1964), pp. 74–76.

[2]Herlitz, *loc. cit.*, pp. 76–80.

[3]Simon Dubnow, *Weltgeschichte des jüdischen Volkes*, Berlin 1925–1930; *History of the Jews*, New York 1967–1973; B. Z. Dinaburg, 'J. Dubnow on his 75th Birthday', *Zion*, 1936.

[4]Yitzchak Baer, *Principles in the Study of Jewish History*. Opening Address at the Hebrew University, Jerusalem 1931, p. 14; *idem.*, *A History of the Jews in Christian Spain*, Philadelphia 1966, vol. I, p. 4; *idem.*, 'The Historical Unity of Israel', in *World Congress of Jewish Studies*, vol. 1, Jerusalem 1952, p. 337.

personality and his work, we have to consider the background in which he grew up. He was born in Halberstadt, a German community barely touched by the storms of emancipation. There every householder was capable of studying Torah but there was also a spiritual openness to their surroundings.[5] The house of the Baer family stood between two synagogues and the Jewish school, separated from them by the farmstead of a non-Jewish neighbour. Yitchak Baer went to the Jewish elementary school which had been in existence since the end of the eighteenth century; when, later, he went to the local Gentile *Gymnasium* he continued his Jewish studies, as he did in Berlin when he attended the University there. His home and his community were pervaded by traditional unbigoted Judaism and at the same time by European culture. Baer was drawn to German literature and to classical and modern art,[6] and in his youth he was already corresponding with his sisters in Hebrew. As Zionists they seem to have been influenced by Izchak Feuerring, a grandson of Rabbi Cohen, the head of the 'Klaus', a well-known *Beth-Midrash* in Halberstadt. Rabbi Cohen was assisted by Rabbi Nobel, the father of Rabbi Nehemia Nobel, who was to become one of the early leaders of the Mizrachi and the teacher of Franz Rosenzweig in Frankfurt. Rabbis Cohen and Nobel had joined the Zionist movement from its beginnings, in contrast to Rabbi Auerbach, Chief Rabbi of the community. Yitzchak Baer developed a deep attachment to the prayers and traditional melodies, and to the beauty of the *mitzvot*. Yet from his childhood on he was familiar, too, with Greek and Roman literature.

In his attachment to history and classical studies Baer was deeply influenced by his uncle Hermann Dessau (1856–1931), the pupil and assistant of Mommsen. Baer described him in terms which apply no less to himself: his personality combined spiritual nobility and genuine modesty. By his mastery of historical research and of the Talmudic sources, Dessau tried to achieve a new evaluation of the Second Temple period and to understand its original values.[7] No less important in his influence on Baer was Eugen Taeubler (1879–1953), founder and director of the *Gesamtarchiv der deutschen Juden*. Like Dessau, he later joined the *Akademie für jüdische Wissenschaften* which had been founded in 1919 on the initiative of Franz Rosenzweig. In his lecture on the principles of Jewish historical research,[8] Baer pointed out that Taeubler first reopened for him the true path to a revaluation of Jewish history.[9] Taeubler wanted to free the history of the Jews in the Diaspora from the fetters of theology and apologetics. It was not to be studied as a martyrology, panegyric or spiritual movement. Not these specific aspects but the complex network of economics and politics, of social, religious and cultural forces determined Jewish life and its interaction with the general history of the surrounding world. Thus the great fields of Jewish and

[5]H. B. Auerbach, 'Die Halberstädter Gemeinde 1844 bis zu ihrem Ende', in *Bulletin des Leo Baeck Instituts*, 10 (1967), Nos. 38–39, p. 40.

[6]M. Calvary, *Das Neue Judentum*, Berlin 1936, p. 6.

[7]Y. Baer, *Hebrew Encyclopaedia*, vol. 12, p. 920. His programmatic and wide-ranging article 'The Historical Foundations of the Halacha', in *Zion*, 17 (1952), Nos. 1–4, is dedicated to Dessau's memory.

[8]Baer, *Principles*.

[9]*Ibid.*, p. 7.

general history intersect. Taeubler and his colleagues regarded themselves as members of an ascetic sect which was to reshape Jewish studies.[10] In consonance with that plan, so it would seem, Baer devoted his dissertation to the history of the Jews in the Kingdom of Aragon in the thirteenth and fourteenth centuries. He was sent to Spain (1925–1926) as a research worker by the *Akademie* to gather source material relevant to the history of the Jews in Christian Spain. This study and his further book, *A History of the Jews in Christian Spain*[11] revealed a new, wide insight into Jewish history based on detailed and profound knowledge of the sources.

In 1922 Baer published the minute book of the communities of the Cleve district near his home-town. In a detailed introduction he notes that Taeubler had a decisive influence on his scholarly method.[12] He clarified the understanding of the general forces at work in moulding this federation of communities which coincided with ancient Jewish foundations, although their integration into the medieval feudal state gave them a special character. At that time he also analysed the sources contributing to Ibn Verga's work *Shebet Yehuda*, which discusses the reasons for the expulsion from Spain and incorporates stories of persecutions of the Jews in various periods. Here, too, Baer attaches great importance to the social conditions of the Jews in Spain.[13] In his view, this is the first book in Hebrew to deal with the problem of the Jews among the nations of Christendom.

III

In his opening address at the Hebrew University, Baer propounded for the first time a set of principles for the study of Jewish history, particularly in relation to the Middle Ages.[14] He maintained that historians had hitherto disregarded this period because, in their evaluation, the Jewish people at that time were only a passive adjunct to the development of nations rather than an active component of history. Challenging this view, Baer argued that medieval Jewry was conscious of its historical destiny and of its special character. Ranke's principle that every epoch stands immediately before God holds well for the Jewish people. "Jewry is one of the forces of general history, influenced by them and influencing them." No event in Jewish existence can be explained without understanding the underlying world culture; but just this understanding

---

[10]Herlitz, *loc. cit.*, pp. 73–83. Cf. also Baer's eulogy of Prof. Taeubler, delivered at a memorial meeting in Jerusalem in November 1953, *Zion*, 19 (1954), Nos. 1–2, p. 71. On Taeubler see also Selma Stern-Taeubler, 'Eugen Taeubler und die Wissenschaft des Judentums', in *LBI Year Book III* (1958), pp. 40–59.

[11]Hebrew, 1945; English translation, Philadelphia 1966, 2 vols.

[12]Fritz Baer, *Das Protokollbuch der Landjudenschaft des Herzogtums Kleve*, Erster Teil, Berlin 1922. Cf. also Fritz Baer, 'Gemeinde und Landjudenschaft Ein Beitrag zur Geschichte des jüdischen Organisationswesens', in *Korrespondenzblatt des Vereins zur Gründung und Erhaltung einer Akademie für die Wissenschaft des Judentums*, II (1921), pp. 16–23.

[13]Fritz Baer, *Untersuchungen über Quellen und Komposition des Schebet Yehuda*, Berlin 1923. Cf. also Baer's contribution to *Jüdisches Lexikon*, vol. V, Berlin 1930, coln. 1181–1182.

[14]*Principles*, p. 6.

accentuates the special character of Jewish development. The historian must above all recognise from within the internal tendencies of his subject. Baer thus arrives at a conclusion which distinguishes him from all his predecessors, that the public and social order of the Jews in the Middle Ages and their political condition was a result of organic forces, faith being the most sublime expression of the will in the nation's life. It is likely that this was said in opposition to Dubnow, who has interpreted the faith in terms of the needs of national survival. Baer, however, suggests that the past generations were first and foremost concerned not with the survival of the nation, but with those things for the sake of which the nation was created. The contemporary historian must simply describe the forces of religion as they were, as they arose and became effective. The developing community of the early Second Temple period under Ezra is an archetype for all the medieval communities and their ordinances. The supremacy of the internal forces of the Jewish people induced and attracted the outside factors and thus grew into the idea of the "Eternal People".[15] While Baer – in contrast to those other historians whose main aim is to seek the similarities – emphasises the unique character of the life and ways of thinking of the Jewish people it is he who deals more objectively and thoroughly than his predecessors with the relationship between Israel and the nations. The Jewish people, which in his view has a religious destiny of universal content, is integrated into the general history of mankind, encountering and indeed clashing with other world cultures.[16]

Baer sees "wandering and united" Israel going its way without central direction. All political and religious authority was vested in the local community by a fusion of religious and *halakhic* tradition with the corporate law of the European nations. In this respect he is again in opposition to Dubnow, in whose description every age produced a dominant centre which guided the other Diaspora communities.[17] Baer sees in this autonomy of local communities one of the great historic achievements, comparable in import to the laws of the Torah and the Mishnah.[18] He extols particularly the medieval German communities on which circles of the Hasidic movement headed by Rabbi Yehuda Hasid (author of *Sefer Hasidim*) and Rabbi Eliezer (author of *Harokeach*) had made their mark. Their political and economic situation was more limited than that of Spanish Jewry, which was nourished by rationalist Arab culture. Yet German Jewry developed social and religious forms which reinvigorated its life. This process was parallel with certain Christian movements, such as the Franciscan, and made direct contact with them, but it also involved the renewal of Jewish traditions as ancient as the Mishnah period.[19] There was thus

[15]*Principles*, p. 17.

[16]*The Historical Unity*, p. 337.

[17]*Ibid.*, p. 341. Cf. Baer's description of the Jewish Community in 'Gemeinde', *Encyclopaedia Judaica*, Berlin 1931, vol. 7, p. 191, and his excellent article on 'The Origins of the Organization of the Jewish Community of the Middle Ages', *Zion*, 15 (1950), pp. 1–41.

[18]*The Historical Unity*, p. 341.

[19]Y. F. Baer, 'The Religious and Social Tendency of *Sepher Hasidim*', *Zion*, 3 (1937), No. 1, pp. 1–50; *idem.*, 'Theory of Equality of Early Man According to Ashkenazi Hasidim', *Zion*, 32 (1967), Nos. 3–4, pp. 129–136.

created a religious and social type not restricted to observance of the *mitzvot* but accepting additional stringencies in order to sanctify public and private life. At the hour of trial most German Jews were thus prepared to become martyrs for their faith. The German communities were of a more democratic nature than others, partially under the influence of the Christian township, which at that time was beginning to free itself from the authoritarian fetters. In contrast to the later Hasidic movement and to the Christian ideal, the Hasidim of Germany prized highly the study of Talmud and *Halakhah*. Indeed, Baer emphasises, the Talmud is more ascetic and less optimistic in spirit than the rationalists of our day believe. The study of the Talmud is intended to remove a man from worldly affairs, but if he cannot achieve this, then he is to strive for integrity in his dealings. Rather like the monastic movements of its day, this Hasidic movement projected the early ideals of equality, brotherliness and modesty, extolling frugality and poverty. The importance which has been attached to *hazkarat neshamot* (the annual remembrance of the departed) especially since the persecutions and down to the present day may be traced to the Christian factor. The same trend is stressed even more strongly by the mystics of thirteenth-century Spain, there, too, in parallel with movements in Christendom.[20] Their books are replete with criticism of the wealthy and of the courtiers, who, allied to the Court, oppressed the poor; this philosophy estranges them from simple faith and sometimes even leads them into heresy. In Baer's opinion, these movements renew the social and religious aims of the Prophets and the Tannaim. The description of the social and historical background of these currents he sees as supplementary to the researches of Gershom Scholem, to which he attaches great importance for the understanding of Jewish history.[21] The educated pleasure-seeking courtier, the aggressive and unscrupulous politician of Arab Spain, stands contrasted with the Hasid of Northern Christian Spain, a burning mystic and ascetic.[22] For Baer the rationalist trend is always blemished, being associated with oppression and injustice in Jewish society. Also in Spain, there arose a reaction, "mystically national and popularly ascetic" against an aristocracy which had become estranged from the principal national values. The Hasidim of Germany were the only religious movement in the history of the Diaspora which managed to create a perfect harmony between theory and practice, between tradition and the demands of the heart and reality. They tried to return the *Halakhah* to its natural foundation in the hearts of men and the soul of the people.[23] Their leaders understood better than the philosophers and mystics of Spain what was essential for Diaspora Jewry.[24]

Thus we understand Baer's comprehensive critique of Salo Baron's work, *A Social and Religious History of the Jews*.[25] According to Baron, Jewish monotheism was to be detached from the soil. Therefore the destruction of the First Temple

---

[20]*Idem.*, 'The Historical Background of the Raya Mahamina', *Zion*, 5 (1939), No. 1, pp. 1–44.
[21]*Ibid.*, p. 1.
[22]Y. F. Baer, *A History of the Jews in Christian Spain*, I, p. 188.
[23]*The Historical Unity*, p. 432.
[24]*Zion*, 1937, *loc. cit.*, p. 50.
[25]Y. F. Baer, *Zion*, 3 (1938), No. 4, pp. 277–299.

provided the first decisive test for the vitality of the idea of a Jewish people beyond state and territory. Baer calls this conception artificial, abstract and unhistorical. According to Baron, the Talmud received its authoritative formulation on foreign soil, with a view to Jewish life in foreign lands; the result of this "constitution" has been the "intellectualisation of Jewish life". Baer, however, suggests that Baron failed to understand the anti-rationalistic, anti-secular and anti-capitalistic tendencies prevailing in Jewry from the times of the prophets via the Pharisees and up to the Jewish writings of the seventeenth century, that first era of capitalism. These have conservative, or rather, strongly ascetic tendencies. Baer criticises the "lachrymose conception" entertained by Jewish historians in contrast to his own. These historians assumed that there were prolonged periods of Christian tolerance towards the Jewish religion, and the Diaspora was by no means solely a history of travail and humiliation. Against this Baer argues that Jewish history in the Middle Ages is one of continuous persecution and insecurity, even during those periods in Spain normally regarded as tranquil.[26] It is not, in Baer's view, a mere coincidence that Baron ends the first volume of his work with a glowing description of the enlightened Jewry of the centres of Islam: a Jewry settled in the capitals of world culture; a rich and civilised Jewry with wide commercial and political connections; a generation of poets and philosophers. This picture Baer regards as distorted and certainly incomplete. The high rank achieved by the Jews in commerce and royal service is the high rank attained by exiles and vassals.[27] The true representatives of Jewry were not the philosophers and the wealthy classes, but really the poor ordinary folk, humiliated, tortured and desperate, longing for redemption in their own land. The Jewish period of Islamic Spain was far from being a "Golden Era". Arbitrariness and cruelty were the hallmarks of political life at that time.[28] "The original national and religious aspirations were tending to return to their populist source, in order that the community as a whole should carry forward the national-religious values."[29]

Baer wrote these books during the first years of Nazi tyranny in Germany. This throws light on his preoccupation at that time with the meaning of Diaspora.[30] Unlike his colleague, B. Z. Dinaburg (later Dinur), who emphasised the exiled people's unstinting attachment to the Land of Israel,[31] Baer did not ignore the fact that the people did not always want to leave the Diaspora.[32] Exile has a religious and ascetic meaning and is an atonement. The wandering Jew advances the prestige of the true faith wherever he establishes its tent and delves into its laws and fundamentals.[33]

[26]Y. F. Baer, *Zion*, 3 (1938), No. 4, p. 291.
[27]*Ibid.*, p. 289.
[28]*A History of the Jews in Christian Spain*, I, pp. 37–38.
[29]*Ibid.*, p. 189.
[30]Y. Baer, 'Erez Israel and the Galuth in the View of the People in the Middle Ages', *Zion*, 6 (1934), pp. 149–171; Yitzchak Baer, *Galut*, New York 1947; *idem.*, Introduction to *Persecutions in Germany and France*, ed. by A. M. Habermann, Jerusalem 1946.
[31]Ben Zion Dinaburg (Dinur), *Israel Bagola*, Jerusalem 1926, 1, part 1, introduction, p. 11.
[32]*Zion*, 1934, p. 164.
[33]Introduction to *Persecutions*, p. 1.

Summing up, Baer merits being the first among the historians to describe the Jewry of Germany and of Christian Spain on the basis of comprehensive source research. He has in particular increased our understanding of the role of the local community as an institution guiding its public, and he has revealed the popular and mystic currents in German and Spanish Jewry.

There are, however, some reservations. Baer himself has pointed out[34] that every value judgment is subjective, and he, too, cannot refrain from discussing historical phenomena by standards taken from outside. He often contrasts "naturalness" and "natural" condition and law with artificiality and intellectualism. So, for instance, the Hasidim of Germany "clung to those natural roots from which no man can ever quite be severed".[35] Baron, writing in the United States, sees Judaism liberated from local conditions. He believes that a permanent Diaspora is centred on a community in Eretz Israel and invigorated by national and religious forces radiating from there.[36] For Baer, the inner trends of history are directed at a return to a "natural" socio-political structure, i.e., a return to the motherland and to the nation's original religious and social destiny. Neither of them can prove or verify his thesis on the strength of historical material alone, as it depends on his own outlook and personal decision. There is no doubt that Baer has been influenced greatly by the atmosphere, as described above, in which he grew up, and by the time and place in which he was active. Contrasting with the trends that dominated the previous century, irrational and mystical moods have come into the ascendancy, and this particularly after the recent overthrow of the world-order and the Holocaust. Judaism as described by Baer is radically different from that discussed by Hermann Cohen, for example, and he is fully aware of the influence on himself of Martin Buber and Gershom Scholem. He maintains that the inner foundations of society must rest on the simple bases of "nature, brotherliness and cooperation".[37] One may argue that these concepts as well as that of "natural law" are borrowed from Stoic philosophy and from the spirit of the enlightenment, where they mean those laws which human reason has laid at the foundation of legal systems. Yet Baer uses these concepts to express the permanent qualities of the soul of the nation, that is in an irrational sense.[38] The *Sefer Hasidim* and the *Raya Mehemna* are for him the true representatives of the original Jewish spirit. In the latter work, Messianic redemption is essentially spiritual – the triumph of the Tree of Life over the Tree of Knowledge of Good and Evil (representing Talmudic Law).[39] These ideas had found expression in the philosophy of Kabbala, and particularly in attitudes which dominated the movement of Sabbatai Zwi. Moreover, they bear some resemblance to the modern *Weltanschauung* with all its dangerous implications.[40] One wonders, furthermore, whether an ideal which seeks to remove a

[34]*Principles*, p. 3.
[35]*A History of the Jews in Christian Spain*, I, p. 37.
[36]*Zion* (1938), p. 297.
[37]*A History of the Jews in Christian Spain*, I, p. 4.
[38]Yacob Fleischmann, 'On the Problem of Objectivity in Jewish Historiography', in *Contemplations*, dedicated to M. M. Buber, Jerusalem 1958, p. 114.
[39]Baer, *Zion* (1939), p. 29.
[40]Georg Lukacz, *Die Zerstörung der Vernunft*, Neuwied 1973, vol. II, p. 101.

man from worldly affairs and bring him close to the Kingdom of Heaven, as Baer so often postulates,[41] is really natural to man. Baer's description of the Middle Ages as a period of unbroken persecution contradicts somewhat his own claim that this period saw a lively spiritual contact and interaction between the Jews and their surroundings.

IV

Baer was intensely involved with the spiritual image of German and Spanish Jewry and the Hasidic and Kabbala movements. With his wide knowledge of the Tannaitic and Amoraic worlds, he was able to appreciate that those same movements were, despite external Christian influences, not foreign to Judaism. According to him, they are principally a return to authentic roots, as revealed in the period of Ezra, the Hasmoneans and the Tannaim. They attempt to perfect an enterprise in religio-national romanticism and ascetic religious reformation.[42] The organic unity of Jewish history was ever clear to him.[43] Hence "that which the fathers envisaged and desired, whether consciously or not, happened to the sons".[44] To him, it was obvious that we must again examine the opening chapters of our history which tell of simple folk life, of just commandments and laws, of yearnings for nature.[45] There were similarities of circumstance between two epochs so widely separated in time. Jewry of the Second Temple reacted to the perils of Hellenism with a *Halakhah* permeated with mysticism, just as the German and Spanish Jews did when they were confronted with the impoverishment of Judaism on the part of nationalistic philosophy. The same tendency characterised these two epochs: to return to the original social and religious trends which had been shaped in the period of the Second Temple and of the Mishna. For that reason, from the beginning of the 1950s Baer concentrated on the problems of that epoch.

Baer suggests that "there was a single unified period, covering the history of our people from the early Pious Jews of the Second Temple up to the beginning of the modern Enlightenment". Throughout this long period, the people were governed by religious, social and historical concepts, decisive for the building of our inner world. The Jewish nation enters the gates of history as a community aspiring to fulfil specific religious-social ideals in this world. The character of the nation was determined for ever from its very beginning.[46] Consequently Baer regards the consolidation of the *Halakhah*, and not Prophecy or Aggadah, as the characteristic expression of these ideals, and the period of the Mishnah, rather than that of the Second Temple, as the decisive period up to the Middle Ages. From the days of Alexander to the Arab conquest, the religious and social

[41]Baer, *Zion* (1938), p. 282.
[42]*Zion* (1939), p. 35, n. 73; *A History of the Jews in Christian Spain*, I, p. 189.
[43]*Principles*, p. 13.
[44]*Ibid.*
[45]*Zion* (1938), p. 299.
[46]Y. F. Baer, *Israel Among the Nations*, Jerusalem 1955, p. 12.

concepts were created and then maintained up to the modern age. A model natural society of the Pious (Hasidim) and the Sages, was destined to implement the human ideals of justice, equality and simplicity, which had to struggle against inner obstacles and outside influences. The *Laws of Heaven*, as opposed to the laws of man, are those of the simple society of peasants which set up the Hasmonean Kingdom, and laid the foundations of the *Halakhah*. This society created a new organisation, the *Knesset*, which extended beyond territorial limits, and formed the link between the Eretz Israel and the Diaspora. It became a guarantee for the continued maintenance of the national body after the Destruction of the Second Temple, and served as a model for the establishment, later, of the "Ecclesia", the Christian Church.

As we see, Baer was concerned not only with the Jewish world but with its place in general history. "From its earliest days, the Jewish people has been involved with great political powers and with foreign cultures, from which it has received many external values; but at the same time it has known that a deep antagonism separates it from them, in spite of their political power and cultural wealth."[47] The connection with Greece had an enormous influence on the development of ideas, customs and institutions, long before the rise of the "Hellenisers", as proved by the names of persons and institutions, and by various *Halakhot* and Midrashim. The Sanhedrin is on the one hand similar to the Areopagus in Athens, and on the other hand related to the school and fraternities of Greek philosophers, such as those of the disciples of Pythagoras and Plato, who also aspired to set up a form of government in their image and their ideal structure.[48] In almost all the periods and in most of the centres there was contact with the neighbouring people and its culture. But there is reason to doubt if similarities can always be taken as proof of common origin or of direct outside influences.[49] Nevertheless, Baer infers that parts of the Mishnah and the *Halakhah* are of early origin, and – contrary to other views – are not a late construction, not a product of Exile and political dependence on foreign powers.

In comparison with parallel groups in Greece, particularly with Socrates, Plato, the Cynics and the Stoics, Baer regards our Sages and Pious as prototypes of the later Christian monks and ascetics, divinely inspired. They – as opposed to the early Christians – can take the credit for having established a whole society and having educated a whole nation for its historic destiny. Their teaching was based on critical self-education, on love of fellow-men, on extreme equality and on poverty. In Baer's view, the early Hasidim are to be identified with the *Essenes*, counted along with the Pharasees who were the first founders of the *Halakhah* as "Comrades" in the language of the Mishnah. The early Sages of the Mishnah – like the *Essenes* – were opposed in principle to commerce and to gold and silver coinage. Their lives in common came near to complete abolition of private property, and they were accustomed to hand over part of

---

[47] Y. F. Baer, *A History of the Jews in Christian Spain*, I, p. 4.

[48] *Zion* (1952).

[49] E. E. Urbach, *The Sages. Their Concepts and Beliefs,* Jerusalem 1975, pp. 12, 74. Saul Leibermann, *Greek in Jewish Palestine*, New York 1942; *idem.: Hellenism in Jewish Palestine*, New York 1950. Benjamin de Vries, 'Israel Among the Nations', *Bechinot* 10, 1956, p. 23.

their land to public ownership, trying to live in the spirit of freedom and equality. Baer interprets the maxim of Simeon the Just, denoting *Gemilut Hasadim* (acts of loving-kindness) as one of the three Pillars of the world, as follows: "A man should share with his neighbour all that he possesses, in order to counteract in this way the inequality prevailing in the world. This is how the maxim was understood by the Christian fathers, and there is good reason to assume that their interpretation was derived from a Jewish source. 'Torah, Worship and Acts of Loving-Kindness' – this was the early ascetic teaching, in the spirit of religious monotheism." [50] Baer suggests that these Pious peasants set out to fulfil the Torah of Moses and the Prophets, with the help of organisational and theoretical instruments borrowed from the Greeks. There was a confluence of Torah with the ideals of Lycurgus, Pythagoras, Plato and the Stoics, as evidenced by the parallelism between many customs and ideas. This shaped the future form of Western-Christian civilisation. Contrary to the current approach of modern scholars, according to which the influence of the Jewish people ceased with the completion of the Bible, it was precisely the Sages of the *Halakhah* and the Mishnah who played an important part in the development of European culture, Baer concludes.

V

We know little about the origins of the *Essene* Sect. But, in spite of some external similarities, its affinity to Plato's Republic and to Sparta cannot be assumed – contrary to Baer's view, based on letters and correspondence with Sparta in the Hasmonean period. For the spirit of their laws and way of life are utterly different. Baer's theory that Greek culture had a considerable influence on Jewish ideas is noteworthy but are we really to regard the founders of the *Halakhah* as prototypes of the Christian monks and ascetics? It would seem that Baer is trying here – though with reservations – to anticipate ideas of the Middle Ages and to introduce them into the ancient period. Contrary to Baer's view, one may say that the laws of the Torah, the words of the Prophets and the rules of the Mishnah are not intended to abolish the separate existence or property rights of the individual. Property and capital in themselves – so long as they were not extravagant, but were the product of a man's own labour – were not regarded as a sin or a moral defect as in Christianity. On the contrary, the aspiration was to abolish poverty. A man must attend to his own needs first of all: "Beware of poverty – for your (need) comes before that of any other man." This is the rule, but one must not be content with it, for "whoever thus deals with himself, will himself ultimately come into need". [51]

The concept of "Pharisees" (from the Hebrew "Parush" – "separated"), Baer explains from the assumption that Orphic-Pythagorean and Platonic teachings on the baseness of the material world, had a decisive influence on the

---

[50] Y. F. Baer, *Israel Among the Nations*, pp. 41, 51.
[51] Baba Metsia 33a, and see Rashi there.

Sages; as though, in their view: "God is separated from this base world below and its defilements, and, like Him, the pious man too must separate himself from this world."[52] True, Baer partly dissociates himself from this as a principle, adding that "perhaps" our forefathers did not accept the system of complete separation of body and soul, as did the Greeks. But in the view of the Sages, the term "Parush" (separated) – as Baer himself testifies – served as a more detailed exposition of the term "Kedushah" (holiness) – "A holy nation is separated from the nations of the world and their abominations" (Mechilta).[53] But there is no intention here of separation from life as worthless, or of abstinence in general. The Sages intended on the contrary – in the spirit of the Torah and the Prophets – to exalt and sanctify life as "a Kingdom of priests and a holy nation" (and not to separate matter and spirit, as in other nations).

As against the Greeks, who did not eschew worship of the human body, or on the other hand, going to the opposite extreme, sometimes despised it, and as against Christianity and other religions of the East, the Sages made no separation of body and soul, of matter and spirit, and by no means exalted asceticism. If indeed almost all the ideas of early Christianity find their expression in the various Midrashim, that is because Judaism was sufficiently broadminded and variegated to contain these ideas also.

It is difficult to avoid the impression that Baer – perhaps under the influence of his studies of the Middle Ages and those of his colleagues at the Hebrew University on Kabbalah – may have overestimated the irrational and mystical factor in the *Halakhah*. Rationalism is not only the product of Greek influence – for the currents of Greek thought which, according to Baer, influenced the Sages of the Mishnah were precisely those of mysticism and of secret sects – but it is already evident in the Torah and the Prophets, although the generation of Enlightenment and Reform may have exaggerated its importance. The objection (of the Sages) to prophecy as a factor in determining *Halakhah*, and their desire to base it on a majority decision (of the Sanhedrin), was derived from a rational approach.

VI

Baer stresses the common element in Judaism and Christianity also in later periods. He tries to prove that in the third century (C.E.) the Jewish people were in the same condition of being persecuted as the Christian communities. One of the letters of Tertullian "is one of the most sublime documents in the history of human martyrdom, and it has much of the gentle simplicity of the tales of Jewish martyrs in the period of persecution".[54] Jews, Christians and Polytheists were all three ascetics, longing for their home in the world to come, yet the Jewish settlements in Palestine were the only ones which continued to fulfil the sacred ideals of the ancients, both of Israel and of Greece – the same ideals that Christian monks tried to practise subsequently in lives of seclusion.

[52] Y. F. Baer, *Israel Among the Nations*, p. 53.
[53] Mechilta, Jithro. See his article in *Zion* (1952), p. 47, n. 42. Ramban, Commentary on Leviticus, 19:2.
[54] *Zion* (1956), p. 13, n. 57.

The time was ripe then for common observances, had Christianity not betrayed its original ideals and, from being a persecuted sect had turned into an oppressive persecuting power.[55]

In this writer's view, Baer's far-reaching comparison between the two religions, derived from his ascetic concept of Judaism, is exaggerated, in the light of the fundamental theological differences between Judaism and Christianity. Some also question his statement that Jews were persecuted together with Christians by the Romans as not being based on factual evidence.[56] We may assume that his hatred of Christianity when it was in power can be explained by his sense of spiritual affinity to early Christianity, and consequently by his fury with its treachery.

VII

Baer's approach becomes increasingly rigid – and obviously inspired by contemporary motives – in his comprehensive essay on 'Jerusalem in the Times of the Great Revolt'.[57] He arrives at the conclusion that Josephus distorted and falsified the facts. By transferring to Palestine constitutional conceptions of Athens, Josephus – according to Baer – constructed a false image of a cruel struggle between the parties in Jerusalem. Baer relies on the findings of H. St. John Thackeray[58] and others. But these showed that Josephus imitated only the style and the phrases of the classical Greek writers[59] – as was then usual – whereas Baer claimed that these imitations brought with them tendentious analogies to the events in Athens. But Baer's attitude is itself based on preconceived suppositions, as he himself clearly indicates.[60] He believes that the Talmudic legend of the fall of Jerusalem, the internal quarrels and the flight of Rabbi Yohanan ben Zakkai, are untrustworthy and only based on Josephus's tales. How could such horrors as described be possible? It could not have happened. Nor can it be imagined that a revered leader such as Rabbi Yohanan ben Zakkai should have behaved so disgracefully as to flee from the beleaguered town.[61] These examples show quite clearly how patriotic and mystic feelings overcame Baer, and decisively shaped his judgment. This is very strange, as elsewhere Baer refers to Talmudic texts as reliable historic material. But when such material contradicts his assumptions, he disqualifies it. And as for Josephus [62] Baer gives no basis for his extreme criticism.[63] Recent archaeological excavations lend support to the reliability of Josephus.

[55]Zion (1968), p. 118; Zion (1956), pp. 31, 49.

[56]Saul Liebermann, 'The Persecution of the Religion of Israel', in Salo W. Baron, *Jubilee Volume*, vol. III, New York 1975, pp. 235, 242.

[57]*Zion*, 36 (1971), Nos. 3/4, pp. 127–190.

[58]H. St. John Thackeray, *Josephus. The Man and the Historian*, 1929.

[59]*Zion*, 36 (1971), Nos. 3/4, pp. 129, 136, n. 31.; p. 144.

[60]*Ibid.*, pp. 164, 166.

[61]*Ibid.*, pp. 177, 180, 185.

[62]*Ibid*, 36 (1971), Nos. 3/4, pp. 141, 162. Baer admits that his evaluation here is contrary to that of most scholars. See p. 186, n. 206.

[63]*Cathedra for the History of Eretz Israel*, Yad Izchak Ben Zvi, Jerusalem, 1 (September 1976), pp. 57, 59.

Baer's conjecture by no means fits the sources we possess concerning these events. The view according to which the Jewish State is a preparation for the Kingdom of Heaven served in the hands of Augustine as a basis for emphasising the conflict between the Kingdom of Heaven and "civitas diaboli".[64] Baer's belief in the unity of the Jewish community at that period brings him to the view that the Qumran texts were of later origin, and their authors were members of a Jewish-Christian sect.[65] Most of these texts, in his opinion, were written at the beginning of the Second Century (C.E.) and bear obvious signs of Christian influence.

VIII

There is reason to suppose that Baer's deep involvement and identification with his subject outweighed his balanced judgment in this last essay. He has been rightly called a follower of Ranke in the sphere of Jewish history.[66] Like Ranke, Baer saw the value of a period not in its results, but in its own right.[67] Consequently, he tried, more than any historian before him, to understand the essential quality of Jewish history from within.[68] Nevertheless no event, not even a single page of Talmud, could be properly interpreted without an understanding of contemporary world-culture.

Thanks to his broad historical outlook and accuracy in details Baer is thus able to regard Jewish history, in all its branches and varied circumstances of time and place, as a "continuous, organic unity". According to Baer, the Jewish people, from the period of the Bible, and through that of the early Hasidim and the Mishnah, wished to erect a complete religious-social structure, "whose base was in this world, but whose aim and plan were directed towards the world above".[69] Consequently the modern revival of the nation had its origin in an ancient holy nationalism, and not in the national movements of modern times.[70]

This attempt to understand the singularity and significance of Judaism throughout the generations argues that the Jewish nation came into being "essentially in order to create the image of a society whole in all its parts, and to educate it to faith in the one and only true God".[71] Baer thus comes near to Hermann Cohen, in spite of the profound differences between them. For Cohen derives his religion from the sources of Reason, and almost identifies it with moral socialism;[72] whereas Baer, along with his positive appreciation of the "land", sees the life of the individual and of society only as a preparation for the

---

[64]Baer, *Zion* (1971), pp. 166, 190.
[65]Y. F. Baer, '*The Manual of Discipline*. A Jewish-Christian Document from the Beginning of the 2nd Century, C.E.', in *Zion*, 29 (1964), pp. 1–60; Y. Baer, '*Pesher Habakuk* and its Period', *Zion*, 34 (1969), pp. 1–42.
[66]A. E. Simon in *Historians and Historical Schools*, Jerusalem 1962, pp. 69, 71.
[67]*Ibid.*
[68]Baer, *Galut*, p. 119.
[69]Baer, *Zion* (1962), p. 155.
[70]Baer, *Galut*, p. 119.
[71]Baer, *Zion* (1968), p. 124.
[72]Hermann Cohen, *Die Religion der Vernunft*, Frankfurt a. Main 1919, pp. 305, 313 ff.

world to come. But both of them regard the poor as the truly pious, and humility as the quality characterising the Jew more than all other virtues. Samson Raphael Hirsch, the leader of Orthodox Jewry, was here in direct opposition to Baer, for in his view, "the essential Presence resides below, in the implementation of Judaism in this world",[73] and "Judaism is the highest stage of Humanism."

Baer anticipates that the historic unity of the Jewish People will be fulfilled in the future, if the transitional period in which we now live leads to a rejuvenation with "the same longings for a transcendental world, without which there can be no life or survival for any nation".[74] This continuity may unexpectedly give birth to a new creation linked to the old,[75] and so to a fulfilment of the hopes of the fathers for their children.[76]

In this way, the historian of the past becomes an interpreter of the present and seer of the future of his nation.

[73]S. R. Hirsch, *Der Pentateuch*, I. Teil, Frankfurt a. Main 1920, p. 374; Mordechai Breuer, *The Torah im Derech Eretz of S. R. Hirsch*, Jerusalem–New York 1970, pp. 19, 23 ff.; Pinchas E. Rosenblüth, 'Die geistigen und religiösen Strömungen in der deutschen Judenheit', in *Juden im Wilhelminischen Deutschland 1890–1914*. Ein Sammelband herausgegeben von Werner E. Mosse unter Mitwirkung von Arnold Paucker, Tübingen 1976 (Schriftenreihe wissenschaftlicher Abhandlungen des Leo Baeck Instituts 33), p. 586.
[74]Baer, *The Historical Unity*, p. 343.
[75]Simon, *op. cit.*, p. 70.
[76]*Principles*, pp. 12, 19.

Bankers and Financiers

Three Chapters of German-Jewish Banking History

BY KURT GRUNWALD

Editorial Note

The three chapters given here are part of a larger manuscript of *Studies in the History of German Jews in Global Banking*. (Another chapter of the same manuscript, 'Lombards, Cahorsins and Jews', was published in the *Journal of European Economic History*, Rome, vol. 4, No. 2, Autumn 1975.) In this study the author seeks to show the uninterrupted process from the moneylenders and moneychangers of the Middle Ages via the Court Jews of the emerging national state to the modern bankers up to the time of Hitler, and the spreading, particularly since the end of the eighteenth century, of German-Jewish bankers to practically all countries of the globe. This "macro-economic" part, which deals with the group experience in German-Jewish history, is followed by a number of "micro-economic" histories of Jewish banking dynasties, to which the third chapter belongs.

The purpose of these Studies is to stimulate further research in this hitherto insufficiently explored chapter of Jewish economic and entrepreneurial history.

A. The Age of the Court Jew

In Memoriam Edgar Salin

The question as to the original sources of capital of the Jews in the Middle Ages, and of its renewed accumulation after repeated confiscations was one which seemed to have greatly intrigued the late Professor Edgar Salin. He referred to it twice in recent years in his letters to the present writer. He complained that[1] ...

"[We still lack] ... an explanation of where the Jewish money which first permitted the rise of the non-Jewish capitalism actually came from."[2]

"In none of the literature on the economic history of the late Middle Ages, Sombart included, can one find an answer to the question as to the actual source of repeated renewal of Jewish capital. As soon as Jewish wealth is noted, confiscations, expulsions, *auto da fés* take place. What was the source of the capital of the early communities? Even assuming that a substantial part of it came from Byzantium, the question becomes the more difficult and urgent: from where, after all the confiscations at the same or other places, did the accumulation of capital, sufficiently big to make it interesting for princes and towns, to negotiate for loans, and to confiscate it thereafter, come."[3]

In the following pages, dedicated to the memory of Edgar Salin, an attempt is made to answer his question, at least in part.

I. THE COURT JEWS

By the end of the sixteenth century Jewish wealth had become marginal. A powerful upper middle class had risen in the towns like Augsburg and Nuremberg whose political power impinged on that of the princes whose feudal rights

---

[1]Translated from the German original.
[2]Letter of 13th December 1973.
[3]Letter of 25th August 1973.

and prerogatives continued in the countryside only. The outstanding examples of this rising plutocracy were the Fuggers and the Welsers. "Fuggers" soon became a synonym for the large trading companies, and "fuggern" for usurious trading; it almost took the place of "Judaicare". But the Fuggers' was a short-lived glory. Anton (the "Great") Fugger's successors could not restrain the insatiable demands of the Habsburgs for loans, and the subsequent bankruptcies in Spain and the Netherlands in the sixteenth and seventeenth centuries spelled the end of this house, just as the repudiation of debt by Edward III of England had caused the bankruptcy of the Peruzzis and Bardis in 1343/1344 and severely affected the once so strong position of the Lombards.

The Thirty Years War changed the economic and political structure which had prevailed at the end of the sixteenth century. The War – 1618–1648 – was disastrous for the citizens and yeomen. Few cities escaped major damage. But the material damage, great as it was, was not all. The civic corporations, the yeomen farmers' meetings – the "democratic institutions" of those days – were swept away, and the innumerable princelings re-established their absolute rule, confirmed under the Treaty of Westphalia in 1648. Now the country was ruled by 350 odd petty autocrats – secular and/or clerical – each with his little court attempting to vie with the splendour of Versailles. The "Grace of God", by which these princelings claimed to rule, did not, however, provide the considerable means required for the maintenance of court, administration and army, particularly not in their war-impoverished territories. They thus, as in the by-gone days, turned to the Jews. From the Emperor down to the pettiest "Serenissimus", each ruler had to have his Court Jew.[4] There was, actually, nothing new in this. There had been Jews employed in the past centuries by emperors, kings and princes as bankers, financial administrators and masters of the Mint, and not only in the German lands; but, as it is asserted, never before and nowhere else was the "Court Jew" officially part of the Establishment, and in such numbers. They were listed in the staff-lists, as for instance in the *Chur-Pfältzischer Staats- und Stands-Calendar, 1734, nebst einem Verzeichnis Aller Hohen Hof-Dignitaten*,[5] which lists under "Hoff-Factoren": seven Jews, down from Jud Michael May, Ober-Hoff- und Militz-Factor to those of lesser rank.

The Middle Ages was a period of protracted struggles for power, between Emperor and Pope, between Emperor and princes (Otto II had created the prince-bishoprics as a counter-weight to the tribal dukedoms) – between the

---

[4]Although a number of monographs had been published on some of the individual Court Jews, such as Oppenheimer, Wertheimer and the most dramatic figure among them, "Jud Süss", in the earlier years of this century, comprehensive studies appeared only in more recent years, i.e., Selma Stern, *The Court Jew*, Philadelphia 1950, and the monumental six volume opus of Heinrich Schnee on *Die Hoffinanz und der moderne Staat*, Berlin 1953/1967. An excellent correctivum to both these important contributions, both written somewhat *cum ira et studio*, one with a Jewish, the other with an anti-Jewish bias, was supplied by F. G. Carsten in his essay on *The Court Jews. A Prelude to Emancipation*, in *LBI Year Book III* (1958), pp. 140–156 It is noteworthy that in the *Propyläen Weltgeschichte* the volume *Das Zeitalter des Absolutismus*, Berlin 1930?, of the Court Jews only Jud Süss is referred to briefly, but neither the institution of the Court Jews, nor the name "Hofjude" is mentioned therein.
[5]See illustration between pp. 196–197.

princes and the estates, the rising urban patricians and sometimes the proletarians and peasants. The Jews were deeply affected by these struggles. They got along well, on the whole, with emperors and princes, even those of the church with secular powers, such as in the bishoprics along the Rhine. Some of them protected the Jews out of broadmindedness, some for economic or fiscal reasons, for the wealth their commerce and their credit brought to the land, or the taxes they brought to the treasury.

It was this mixture of broadminded lack of anti-Jewish prejudice and of material self-interest which formed the basis of collaboration between ruler and Jew also in the years that followed the Thirty Years War. The attitude of the rising bourgeoisie was different. They saw the Jews as competitors, and tried to expel them from their cities, once they themselves were established in commerce. They re-admitted the Jews when they needed their credit, but expelled them again when their own capital accumulation had made them independent of Jewish funds. As in the case of Vienna in 1670, they promised the emperor compensation for the loss of taxes from the expelled Jews, but rarely paid up.

The Jews were equipped for the collaboration with the princes through two skills which their forefathers had acquired and developed in the Middle Ages: the ability to procure goods and services even if in short supply, and to provide the funds needed for acquiring them. The rulers of the newly risen "national" states were badly in need of both, and thus a new function for the Jew emerged in the establishment of these states, that of the Court Jew, the Royal Merchant Banker.

It was their marginal position in the money market, and possibly also a higher liquidity preference in anticipation of the difficult days ahead, which enabled the Jews to enter the period of the Thirty Years War in a more advantageous position than their more powerful competitors. The latter's claims on their princely debtors were frozen; their stores filled with valuable merchandise and their houses full of costly luxuries, often meant to be "stores of value", were ransacked; their landed estates, in which they had invested heavily, laid waste by the armies moving to and fro. The Jews with ready cash on hand were soon able to make themselves indispensible as suppliers of provisions for the armies, and thus enjoyed the protection of the war-lords, like Wallenstein. Restricted, as they had been for centuries, to trading in secondhand goods, they were thereby well equipped for the advantageous disposal of war-booty. Though the Jews, too, suffered from the deprivations of the war, they did so less than their neighbours, and many of them emerged from the war with their financial resources preserved or substantially increased. It was from their ranks that the Court Jews arose.

The student of Jewish economic history in the Middle Ages, and even thereafter, must be impressed by the remarkable power of economic recuperation which the Jewish communities and their individual members showed after arbitrary acts of the rulers, such as fiscal extortions, cancellation of claims or confiscation of their immobile property and expulsions. In the absence of documentary evidence we can only find some indirect explanation for this phenomenon.

The individual businessman seems to have followed a wise policy of spreading the risk. In his loan, say, to the King of Bavaria, he had his relative in Prague as a partner, and vice versa, he participated in the loan which his relative granted the King of Bohemia. And not all claims of this kind turned sour at one and the same time. Moreover, there was a traditional system of mutual help; individuals and communities in distress were helped by their brethren in happier circumstances till they were on their feet again. Also many apparently migrant beggars carried, hidden beneath their rags, bills and jewels for their principals to places of safety.

And one may wonder whether sometimes the silent non-Jewish partners of the Jews, often in elevated position, were not able to help their Jewish partner to recover, at least partly, his, and thereby their own property. Such action became more open in the eighteenth century when for instance the emperor pressed the Bavarian ruler to pay his debt to Wertheimer so that he could repay his aristocratic creditors. Thus, as Jacob Katz put it: "Notwithstanding the expulsions and ever-recurrent confiscations and impositions, a fund of capital remained and was handed down from generation to generation." [6] In any event, here is a wide field open for research and speculation.

The Court Jews, in the evolution of economic institutions, were no innovation. There was not much difference, as far as economic organisation and function is concerned, between them and their predecessors in the rise and progress of early capitalism, the Medicis and Fuggers whose place in the German economy they were now taking. What was different, however, was their status and their emergence as a "mass-phenomenon". This latter fact, indeed, was to result and to be reflected, at a later period, in the proliferation and prominence of Jews in the evolution of modern banking, not only in the German lands, but wherever the scions of the Court Jews went.

Their status resulted, in a way, from an adaptation of the institution of the "servus cameri", the *Kammerknecht*, of the feudal state to the concepts of the new absolutistic state, with its administration by professional officials and a standing army. The (Court) Jews who by virtue of the previously mentioned socio-economic circumstances had become the principal, if not the only, competitors for filling the manifold needs of the new state machinery – i.e., court, administration and army – had to be fitted into this machinery by titles indicating their function and position, sometimes accompanied by corresponding emoluments. These titles were manifold, and usually indicated a specific function. In the previously mentioned staff-list of the Chur-Pfaltz we find Hoff-factor, Cabinets-factor, Militz factor, Hoff-Crämer und Militz Livrant, and, on top, the Ober-Hoff und Militz factor. There were also the Masters of the Mint and other functionaries. As "Hoff befreite", i.e., freeman of the Court, they were exempt from municipal jurisdiction and the restrictions on lodging and dress in force for the rest of the Jewish population.

Selma Stern in her book on the Court Jew reviews his functions under the captions: "The Commissary; the Court-Contractor; the Financial Agent and Resident; the Cabinet Factor; the Commercial Agent; the Master of the Mint;

[6] Jacob Katz, *Tradition and Crisis*, New York 1971, p. 47.

and the Shtadlan, the spokesman for the Jewish communities." Many of these positions were frequently held by one and the same person simultaneously.[7]

The first contacts which the Jews usually established with the authorities were as suppliers of food, fodder, horses and, more rarely, arms to the army, or of jewels to the courts, a business gradually extended to cover all the requirements, not only of luxuries like material for the outfitting of the princely household, but even of the larder and cellar.

The credits required not only for these ever-increasing supplies, not always easily available, but also for soldiers' pay, the cost of diplomatic missions, the purchase of higher princely ranks and crowns, soon exceeded the resources of the individual Court Jew. He had to rely on the cooperation of his "correspondents", his friends and relatives, who, scattered over a wide area, were able both to act as buyers of the supplies needed and as financiers. Some, like the greatest of them, the Imperial Oberhof Faktor Samuel Oppenheimer of Vienna, had silent partners in the ranks of the high aristocracy, who refrained from lending money directly to the emperor, but did not disdain doing so indirectly. To secure and repay these credits, the Jews obtained liens on specified state revenues, the taxes from selected provinces, or customs duties. They became Masters of the Mint, for which they procured the precious metals, and they were blamed for the deterioration of the coins, a popular measure by which some of the rulers, like Frederick the Great, financed their campaigns. The Jews obtained monopolies on the sale of tobacco and salt, sometimes resented by the population; persuaded or forced by the ruler, as in Prussia, they engaged in manufacture and, thus, became pioneers of industrial enterprise, from which non-Jewish capital still shied away. Through these activities the Jews became the financial advisers of the princes, always looking for new sources of revenue. In exceptional cases, they were appointed ministers of finance, which did not help their popularity with the overtaxed population. But they were engaged not only in fiscal but in diplomatic services as well. As "Residents" they served in their home-town as suppliers of information to some foreign government, much like honorary consuls in our days. And the purchase of Poland's crown for Saxony's king by Leffman Behrens is probably the most outstanding example of the "extra-curricular activities" in which the Court Jews were engaged. We find them reflected, in a later generation, in the services which the Rothschilds, Bleichröder and Cassel rendered to Disraeli, Bismarck and Churchill.

Like the merchant bankers in the nineteenth century who acted as issue-houses for more than one government, some of the Court Jews acted as bankers

[7]This acceptance into the hierarchy of the Jew – despised not so long before as a pariah – is indeed surprising. It was facilitated by a combination of political and intellectual developments. The estates, guilds, civic corporations who had used their influence to have the Jewish competitor kept down, if not eliminated altogether, had lost their power – at least temporarily – in the absolutistic state. And so did to a great extent "the only salvation promising church" since the Reformation. The princes who even in medieval times had, on the whole, been tolerant towards the Jews, if not pressed too hard by guilds and corporations into anti-Jewish measures, now imbued with the ideas of mercantilism and an incipient enlightenment, were keen to attract to their war-depopulated countries new manpower of a high economic development potential, regardless of their religion. The economic *raison d'état* was probably the over-riding consideration.

and/or suppliers "by appointment" to several ruling houses. Quite a number of these resided in Frankfurt a. Main.

In view of the often remarkable services these Court Jews rendered to their lords it is not surprising to see them often in positions not only of confidence but intimacy with them, enjoying unprecedented honours and privileges. But their elevated position meant also dangerous living. Samuel Oppenheimer's house in Vienna was not protected by his position from the mob bent on plunder, nor was he protected from bankruptcy through the malfeasance of the Imperial Treasury. The dramatic end on the gallows of his relative Jud Süss has become an often told drama. The Jew-hatred of the masses, the envy of Christian competitors, the resistance to change by those who had lost standing under the new régime – economic and political – were but contributing factors. Basically it was the ire of the population, overtaxed directly, or indirectly, as by inferior coinage, who saw in the Court Jew the cause of their misery: he it was who collected the taxes, and not the prince who spent them lavishly. The prince was not averse to being covered in this way by the Jew whom occasionally he could sacrifice as a scapegoat. He was in a luckier position than his "cousin" on the throne of France whom the same social tensions were to bring to the guillotine.

The story of the Court Jews ends, just as did the political framework within which they operated, the Absolute Régime, with the Napoleonic Wars. But the economic institution which they represented continued adjusting itself to the new needs of industrial capitalism. Modern banking, in fact, was largely based on this predecessor. Names like Eichthal (Munich, Paris), Arnstein and Eskeles (Vienna), Bleichröder (Berlin), Hirsch (Munich, Brussels), Kann (the Hague), Kaulla (Stuttgart), Rothschild (Frankfurt, London, Paris, Vienna, Naples) and Speyer (Frankfurt, New York, London) refer, indeed, to scions of Court Jews. These few names indicate that the Court Jews survived the age of courtly absolutism. With the change in the form of the régime his rank in the establishment became replaced by honorific titles; the *Hofjude* became *Hof-Bankier*, the *Resident* became *Consul*, and some became elevated to the nobility with a knighthood or barony.[8] Many Court Jews had used their position at Court to act also as spokesmen for the Jewish communities, over which they often presided – sometimes dictatorially in the style of the absolutistic age. They had used their wealth for the furtherance of Jewish learning. But their offspring were often lost to the Jewish community by conversion and by intermarriage with the German and other nobility. If anything, this was the tragedy of the Court Jew.

The family pattern of the Court Jew deserves special attention. They wanted their children to marry the offspring of learned fathers, but seem to have been equally eager to establish family ties with their business friends. Thus the leading houses of Court Jews, the Gumperts, Leffmann, Lehmann, Liemann, Oppen-

---

[8]It is wrong, in our opinion, to see, as Selma Stern does (*op. cit.*, p. 267), in "the life and death of the Court Jew . . . a symbolic significance for the fate of the Jew in all ages . . .", because the Court Jew (except for a few cases like Jew Süss) did not die, but adjusted himself to a changing world. His history was not a closed chapter, but a passing phase. What is true, however, is that many of the offspring of the Court Jews ceased to be Jewish.

Chur-Pfältzischer Staats- und Stands-Calender

Auf das gemeine Jahr
1734

Nebst einem Verzeichnuß
Aller Hohen Hof-Dignitären
und
Chur-Pfältzischen
Dicasterien.

Cum Privilegio Electorali speciali.

Zu finden bey Jacob Simon, Universitäts-Buch-Händler in Heydelberg.

30

Hoff-Capplâne.
Herr Jacobus Bernardus Bellen.
Herr Johann Jacob Binner
Herr Sigismund Heinrich Fergher.
Herr Johann Jacob Gobr.
Herr Johann Reinhard Linden.
Herr Henricus Trippelfues, Ceremoniarius.
Herr Joseph Weibel.

Capell-Priester.
Herr Carolus Philippus Linnenborn.

Capell-Diener.
Johann Melchior Fröschel/ mit zwey Acolythen

Hoff-Medici.
Herr Philippus Ludwig Limberg.
Herr Johann Conrad Moeller.
Herr Wilhelm Bernard Rebel.
Herr Heinrich Einzheim.
Herr Johann Christoph Zehner.

Hoff-Apothecker.
Herr Ferdinand Bader.

Hoff-Balbierer.
Herr Johann Ehrenreich/ Hoff-Zahn-Artzt.
Herr Johann Arnold Engel.
Herr Johann Georg Nozel.
Herr Georg Philipp Wilßheim.

Hof.

31

Hoff-Bibliothecarius.
Herr Johann Büchels.
Herr Franciscus Aleß, Adjunctus.

Hoff-Kriegs-Auditor.
Herr Flender.

Hoff-Mahlere.
Herr Johann Philipp von der Schlichten/ Cabinets-Mahler.

Hoff-Ballet-Director.
Herr Paul de Floris.

Hoff-Tantzmeister.
Herr Sebastianus Scio.

Hoff-Ballhauß-Director.
Herr Johann Wilhelm Vils.
Herr Friedrich Sozer.

Hoff-Statuarius.

Hoff-Jubelierer.
Herr Johann Hartmann Roth.

Hoff-Gold-Arbeiter.

Hoff-Bildhauer.
Herr Christion ...

Hoff-Uhrmacher.
Herr Franciscus Busat.

Hoff-Seidenstücker.
Herr Daniel Klein.

Couriere.

32

Couriere.
Herr Zacharias Hermanns.
Herr Matthias Niesemann.
Herr Simon Steinberger.
Herr Wilhelm Tummeler.

Hoff-Factoren.
Jud Michael May, Ober-Hoff- und Militz-Factor.
Jud Jacob Ullmann/ Hoff-Cammer-und Militz Livrant.
Jud Emanuel Meyer, Cabinets-Factor.
Jud Wolff Wertheimer/ Hoff-Factor.
Jud Marx und Moyles, Schlesinger.
Jud Samuel Levi.
Jud Moyses David Oppenheimer/ Hoff-Factor und Garde meubles Livrant.

Unter diesen Stab gehören auch alle andere Hoff-befreyete Persohnen.

Obrist.

Court Calendar of 1734 listing Court Jews

Steel engraving showing Samuel Oppenheimer's mansion in Vienna

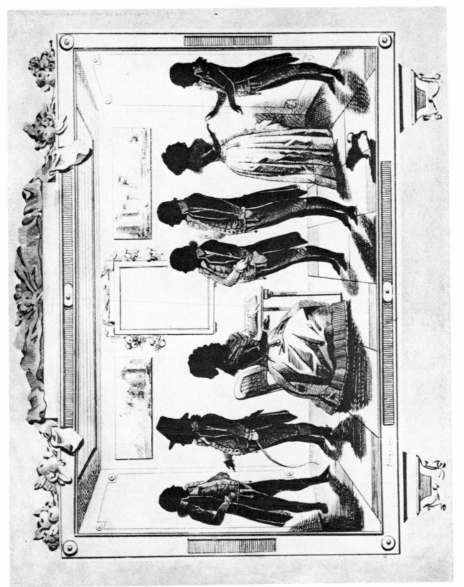

The Kaulla family, Stuttgart
Etching by Goog, 1795

heimer, Wertheimer, Hirschel, Michael, Geldern, Reinganum, Beer, Drach, Kann, Wulff, Itzig, Ephraim and David were all related in one way or another. They came from Berlin, Breslau, Brunswick, Dessau, Dresden, Frankfurt, Hanover, Leipzig, Vienna and many other German principalities.[9] These family ties were reflected in their business organisation, as shown in that of the biggest operator of his time, Samuel Oppenheimer in Vienna.[10] In Vienna, his son Emanuel was his general representative in the Empire, assisted by his nephew Samson Wertheimer. In Frankfurt his two sons-in-law, Emanuel Drach and Loeb Dentz worked for him as well as his grandson Moses Samuel Oppenheimer, his cousin Hertz Oppenheimer, and the Resident Aron Beer. Others in the clan were: in Heidelberg his brother Moses, the Court Agent of the Elector of the Palatinate; in Hanover his son Wolf and his relative Leffman Behrens; in Italy his grandson Loeb Oppenheimer; and in Amsterdam and Cleve his relatives the Gumperts. Also connected with his business transactions were Loew Sinzheim, Court Purveyor of the Elector of Mayence; Moyses Isaac, Court Jew of Bamberg; Lazarus Hirschel, Imperial Court Purveyor, Vienna; the Models, Court Agents of Anspach; and his most important correspondent, Samuel Ullmann, Court Purveyor of Bavaria, residing in the Free City of Augsburg.

This family pattern repeats itself *mutatis mutandis* later with the Five Frankfurters and other Frankfurt houses, spread over the continent and overseas, by the Bischoffheims and others, apparently without a parallel in non-Jewish banking.

II. SOME QUESTIONS OF HISTORIOGRAPHY

In his essay on 'The Court Jews' F. L. Carsten[11] poses the question why there were no Court Jews before and after the seventeenth and eighteenth centuries in Germany (and Austria), and why in no other country did they, as a distinctive group, play a similar distinctive role.

Another who views the Court Jew as a unique German phenomenon seems to be H. K.[ellenbenz] who in his article in the *Encyclopedia Judaica*[12] sees them as a feature limited in time and location (which includes Poland as well). But in another article in this Encyclopedia[13] the same author recites an impressive list of Jews in Christian Spain in the thirteenth and fourteenth centuries, who as *Almoxarijes* (revenue collectors), treasurers, controllers over bailiffs and supervisors of tax farmers were apparently no less "Court Jews" than their brethren in Germany in a later period. They were, like the latter, part of the "Establishment". And it was in a Spain torn by wars and divided by disparate kingdoms, with some resemblance to Germany after 1648 with its multitude of petty

[9]Stern, *op. cit.*, pp. 27–28.
[10]*Ibid.*, p. 28.
[11]*Loc. cit.*, p. 140.
[12]H. K[ellenbenz], Article: 'Court Jews', *Encyclopedia Judaica*, Jerusalem 1972.
[13]*Idem*, Article: 'Banking and Bankers', *ibid.*

sovereignties. H. Beinart,[14] therefore, with some justification, speaks in an essay of "the Features of the Court Jews in Christian Spain", who, we believe, had their antecedents in Moorish Cordova.

And in the seventeenth century, Egypt, according to Manasseh ben Israel (1656), every viceroy had his Jewish Zaraf bashi (treasurer), apparently a permanent feature of the Establishment.

The question, therefore, arises as to what the features are which entitle us to designate certain individuals or groups as Court Jews, which political, social and economic conditions favoured their rise and fall.

As Hans Liebeschütz,[15] referring to the Court Jews, put it most recently: "The age of Absolutism with its increasing interest in military power and monarchical representation found it necessary to produce economic growth with forces outside the conventional framework. In this way the *avant-garde* of the outsiders obtained a special function in their German environment." Thus, according to this definition, the Court Jews were an instrument in the pursuit of economic aims of the absolutistic state, i.e., of the Mercantilist system. They were a substitute, they filled a gap created by the retarded rise in Germany after the Thirty Years War of an actively enterprising bourgeoisie capable of linking Central Europe with the expansion of the economy in the West.[16] But the privileged position which the Court Jews thus enjoyed was not a unique one in German economic history. In the tenth century when the terms Jew and merchant were practically synonymous, they were a privileged class. And, as Pirenne[17] states: "The merchant . . . seems to have been not only a freeman, but a privileged man to boot. Like the cleric and the noble, he enjoyed a life of exception. Like them he escaped the demesnial and seignorial authority which continued to bear down upon the peasants." In fact, in the charter given by Emperor Otto I to the town of Magdeburg in 965 the Jews were placed even before the Christian merchants. And in 1084 Bishop Rüdiger of Speyer tried to attract the Jews to his town by offering them a secure quarter and ample economic privileges, "for the major glory" of his town, i.e., for its economic importance as a commercial centre.

These privileges, thus, were early "mercantilistic" measures for furthering this first process of urbanisation. But barely a century later the Jewish share in long-distance trade, hitherto a near-monopoly, had become marginal. The Gentile burghers of the towns the Jews had helped to develop into commercial centres had taken their place in the trade with commodities and left them the trade with money – though for the time being only.

Just as previously in the long-distance trade, so now in the money trade, i.e., as providers of credit, the Jews had become indispensable for the economic development, for trade and treasury alike. While condemned by the church

---

[14]H. Beinart, in *Élites and Leading Groups* (in Hebrew), Historical Society of Israel, Jerusalem 1966.

[15]Hans Liebeschütz, 'The Relevance of the Middle Ages for the Understanding of Contemporary Jewish History', in *LBI Year Book XVIII* (1973), p. 22.

[16]*Ibid.*

[17]H. Pirenne, *Medieval Cities*, Princeton 1969, p. 129.

and the scholastic school as usurers, they enjoyed, though only temporarily, the protection of the emperor. The struggle between Sacerdotum and Imperium from the eleventh century onward seems to have had its bearing also on the position of the Jews, as did the subsequent struggle for power between the emperor and the rising corporations and local lords. It was under the strong emperors, Frederick Barbarossa (1132–1190) and Frederic II (1212–1250), that a new system was devised, meant for the protection of the Jews as a privileged group of *Kammerknechte*, servants of the Treasury. "Mercantilistic" too, in intent this measure made the Jews, like in the previous privileges, exempt from any local jurisdiction and subject to the imperial court only. This institution of the *Kammerknecht*, not yet sufficiently explored, seems to have had in its original concept some connotation of civil service, as it provided the imperial chamber with a personnel of undivided loyalties, able to perform the tasks required by the imperial treasury. Only under the weaker successors of these emperors did this system deteriorate into an oppression rather than a protective privilege, when local lords or free cities acquired by grant or by purchase the right to hold Jews as servants of their treasury.

These strong emperors, incidentally, attempted to achieve, and temporarily succeeded in achieving that strong, centralised régime, unhampered by the vested interests of the church, local lords, cities and corporations which marked the political system in the age of Absolutism five centuries later.

It thus seems that in space, as well as in time, in German economic and political history, situations and conditions existed, not unlike those which produced the Age of the Court Jews. The uniqueness of this period, claimed, as we saw, by some authors, thus seems to have been a consequence of the numbers involved, of the quantity rather than the quality of their achievements.

B. *The Jewish Contribution to the Evolution of American Banking*

I

"The history of the Jewish migratory movements – as H. A. Shulvas claims – has not been fully explored in Jewish historiography."[1]

The validity of this claim is proven, for instance, by the many lacunae in the history of the migration of Jews from German lands to the United States, its impact on the American economy and its various branches, such as banking, a subject to which the following pages are devoted.

C. C. Aronsfeld in his impressive essay on 'German Jews in Victorian England'[2] makes the important observation that most of the Jewish immigrants to England from Germany "hailed from Northern Germany, Hamburg, Hanover, and Cologne, also from Berlin and what was then the Grand Duchy of Posen (now Western Poland). By contrast, Jewish emigrants from Southern Germany, especially Bavaria, usually chose the U.S.A., the watershed being the city of Frankfurt. It is probable that proportionately as many Frankfurt Jews went to England as to America."[3] Between these two migratory movements there were, however, considerable differences in quantity, in quality and motivation.

As Aronsfeld states, between 1830 and 1930 no more than 250,000 Jews are believed to have left Germany. Those who went to Britain never exceeded a few thousand, the vast majority settling in America.[4] In this respect Jewish migration followed the general German pattern. Of a total of 2,635,819 *Auslandsdeutsche*, i.e., natives of the German lands united in the *Reich* living abroad in 1910, 2,501,333 were settled in the United States, but only 56,476 in the United Kingdom and Ireland.[5]

From Baden, Württemberg and Bavaria an endless stream of emigrants started flowing to the United States in 1816/1817. The "epidemic of emigration"[6] reached its highest figure during the years 1820–1845 in Southern Germany, while Prussia and Saxony registered a net immigration over the period 1824–1848.

It was a mass flight from poverty to a new Promised Land, a poverty of small peasants and landless farm workers brought about by an inheritance law permitting the unrestricted divisibility of land, over-population and years of crop failure and aggravated by heavy taxation, political dissatisfaction and severe

---

[1]H. A. Shulvas, *From East to West*, Detroit 1971.
[2]C. C. Aronsfeld, 'German Jews in Victorian England', in *LBI Year Book VII* (1962), pp. 312–329.
[3]*Ibid.*, p. 313. Recently attention has been drawn to this observation by Vivian D. Lipman in her essay on 'The Anglo-Jewish Community in Victorian Britain' (p. 167, n. 28), in *Studies in the Cultural Life of the Jews in England*, Jerusalem 1975.
[4]*Ibid.*, p. 312.
[5]*Handwörterbuch der Staatswissenschaften*, Jena 1924, vol. II, p. 40.
[6]M. Walker, *Germany and the Emigration 1816–1883*, Cambridge 1964.

restriction on marriages. The Jews living in these parts were largely "primitive village Jews" (*Dorfjuden*) who in addition to the plight of the general population suffered from their special civic disabilities. No wonder then that they too, particularly the young ones among them, joined the stream of emigrants.

While it was, thus, the pressure of the economic and political conditions in their homelands which prompted these *Dorfjuden* to emigrate, it was the attraction of the City of London, the financial centre of the world, and the rising industrial centres like Manchester, Bradford and Birmingham with their new opportunities, which drew the gifted and adventurous, on the whole well-educated sons of a Jewish "settled" middle class. Antisemitism, if at all, was a very minor factor in their decision to go and settle abroad. But it became a motivation, especially for some academics, in the second half of the century in the declining years of the Age of Liberalism, when the pressures gradually equalled, if not outweighed, the considerations of a more attractive future, particularly during the two decades of depression following the boom of the early seventies.

By contrast, the success of the South-German Jewish emigrant made the United States an enticing destination which exercised a strong pull, outweighing often the greatly improved economic and political conditions at home. But the following waves of immigration do not seem to have had the same creative impact on the American economy as did their predecessors in the earlier decades of the century. It is largely on these latter that our attention will be focussed in the following pages.

II

The story of the Jewish contribution to the evolution of commercial banking in the United States has so far remained unwritten. It was largely the story of "America's colonial merchants (who) had combined the roles of importers, exporters, bankers, middlemen and shopkeepers." [7] A respectable number of these merchants had come from Germany in the early part of the nineteenth century. Some had set out as pedlars in the Middle West and the Wild West, and found it the Golden West. Some were to sire Macy's and Gimbel's, others found themselves in Wall Street. The stories of these families have been recorded in memoirs and re-written in books, such as *Our Crowd*. But little is known about the legion of others who did not make their way to Wall Street, but sold out and retired or lost, in the failure of their banks, the fortune they had previously made. Only a few of these stories have been told, such as the one of the Spiegelbergs of New Mexico, 1844–1890, originally from Frankfurt, who had set up a merchandising firm in Santa Fe and eventually the Second National Bank of New Mexico, [8] or of the "banking empire" which Samuel Hermann, coming from Rödelheim

[7] M. Friedman, *Pilgrims in a New Land*, Philadelphia 1948, p. 280.
[8] Floyd S. Fierman, *Merchant Bankers of Early Santa Fe*, Southwestern Studies, No. 4, Texas Western College, El Paso 1964.

near Frankfurt, had built and lost in New Orleans,[9] or of F. Strong, the founder of the Bank of Louisville, Kentucky.

And there was the merchandising enterprise of the Jacobs brothers in Tucson, Arizona, first established as a kind of branch of their father's, Mark J. Jacobs's business in San Francisco in 1867. (He was born in Poland (Posen?) in 1814, went to Prussia and England before following, in 1851, the gold-rush to California.) By 1879 its ancillary exchange operations had become sufficiently profitable to justify its separation from the commodity trade as the Pima County Bank, Tucson's first banking institution. By a series of mergers and consolidations it had become in 1935 the Valley National Bank, controlled and directed till that time by members of the Jacobs family.[10]

On the whole, it was the General Store in the rising little towns of the American Mid-West and South of the mid-nineteenth century, frequently owned by Jews of German origin or descent, which provided the modest banking services of the population of the rural hinterland, and frequently these banking departments of general stores were eventually converted into the early commercial banks.

In Glasgow (County of Barren, Kentucky), the general store of "Squire Frederick Morris" engaged in banking in the 1850s, as his grandson, Arthur Krock of the *New York Times* tells us.[11] Morris's parents had come from Prussia and Bavaria to Louisiana, which he had left as a lad of eighteen for Southern Kentucky, with a pedlar's pack on his back. While others of his compatriots, after a similar career, eventually arrived in Wall Street, Morris became a wealthy landowner in the South, but was ruined by the consequences of the Civil War. His story is probably only one of many which together form the early history of American commercial banking.[12]

Numerous as these local banks must have been which Jews set up in the South and West, only a few remained in the founder families' hands by the turn of the century. And with them shrunk the Jewish share in commercial banking.[13] The *Grossbanken* had taken over also here.

From Frankfurt, too, had come some such well-known figures in American banking and finance as George Blumenthal (1858–1941), Felix Fuld (1869–?) and Paul Baerwald (1871–1961), the latter not only prominent as a partner in Lazard Bros. but as a Jewish community leader. Before them Gustav Speyer in New York (b. 1845) and Jacob H. Schiff (1847–1920) had started making their mark in Wall Street.

[9]Bertram Wallace Korn, *The Early Jews of New Orleans*, Philadelphia 1969.

[10]Gerald Stanley, 'Merchandising in the South-West', *American Jewish Archives*, XXIII/i (April 1971).

[11]Arthur Krock, *Memoirs*, New York 1968, p. 4.

[12]In a recent issue of the *American Jewish Archives*, November 1973, we learn of David Mayer of Atlanta (p. 131), a confederate Civil War hero and banker who was one of those responsible for the establishment of the Atlanta Board of Education in 1872, and of Edmund Wells, lawyer, farmer and banker (p. 164) who in 1891 became Assistant Justice at Arizona's US District Court and a candidate for the governorship.

[13]According to Rufus Learsy's sources (*The Jews in America*, New York 1954, p. 294) of the 93,000 directors and executives in 1935 of US commercial banks, a mere 600 were Jewish.

From Eppelsheim came the Greenebaum brothers, Eliaz (1822–1919), Michael (1824–1894) and Henry (1833–1914), bankers in Chicago, and from Darmstadt, Benjamin Altheimer (1850–1938), a banker in St. Louis.

Most impressive, however, is the story of Isaias W. Hellman (1842–1920)[14] who had come from Reckendorf in 1859. Opening a dry-goods store in 1865, he soon provided banking services, the first in Los Angeles, in a corner of his store. In 1868 he formed with partners the Bank Hellman, Temple & Co. which in 1871 was converted into the Farmers & Merchant Bank (in 1956 it was sold by the family to the Security National Bank of Los Angeles). In 1890 Hellman, by now a recognised civic and economic leader, was invited to head The Nevada Bank at San Francisco, which later on merged with the noted Wells Fargo Bank, of which Hellman became president. It is still principally owned by his descendants.

On leaving Los Angeles, he entrusted his brother Herman (1843–1909) with the Farmers & Merchant Bank, which, however, the latter left after disagreements with his brother and bought the Commercial Trust & Savings Bank. In 1906 his sons Marc and Irving changed its name to Hellman Bank, which had thirty-three branches till 1930, when during the Great Depression it had to sell out to the Bank of Italy, now the Bank of America.

Other banking pioneers in Southern California were Lewis Jacobs, who started a bank in San Bernadino as early as 1858, and Achilles Levy (1853–1922)[15] of Mommenheim in Alsace, a dealer in produce whose "Bank of A. Levy", now managed by his descendants, had sixteen branches in the Ventura County. The Union Bank of California was founded by Kaspare Cohen in 1914. Also in Fresno, San Luis Obispo, San Diego (Baer & Lucien Blochman) and elsewhere Jews were prominent in the development of commercial banking.

From Bavaria came Ephraim Hart (1747–1825), who served on the council of New York's young stock-exchange and the New York State senate, and from Buttenhausen Nathan Hofheimer (1848–1920). The legendary Bernard Baruch (1870–1965), though American born, was the son of a doctor from Schwersenz in Posen.

These now partly forgotten names constitute a selection only from the great number of German-Jewish immigrants who had contributed to the growth of American commercial banking. Many of them had come with the same wave of immigration which had brought to New York "Our Crowd",[16] the "Business Élite" of German-Jewish financiers in the last century.[17] Most of them, as Supple points out, had come to the United States in the late 1830s and early 1840s, usually in their late teens or early twenties, often single, with little money and practically no financial experience. And very few of them went straight to

---

[14]Norton B. Stern, 'Towards a Biography of Isaias W. Hellman, Pioneer Builder of California', *Western States Jewish Historical Quarterly*, vol. II/1, October 1969.
[15]W. M. Kramer and N. B. Stern, 'A. Levy of the Bank. From Beans to Banks in Ventura County', *Western States Jewish Historical Quarterly*, vol. VII/2, January 1975.
[16]Stephan Birmingham, *Our Crowd*, New York 1964.
[17]B. E. Supple, 'A Business Élite. German-Jewish Financiers in Nineteenth-Century New York' *The Business History Review*, vol. XXXI, No. 3 (1957), pp. 141–178.

Wall Street. Most of them had started out as pedlars and petty tradesmen, gradually advancing to store-keeping and wholesaling and local "banking" before arriving there. And almost all, with few exceptions, had come from a very small corner of Europe: the South-West of Germany – the Munich–Frankfurt axis, one might say – and particularly the small villages of Bavaria. This veritable "explosion" of Jewish banking talent, this "group experience" seems to indicate the need for a more thorough socio-economic historical analysis.

III

Civil and economic pressures, as mentioned previously, were apparently also the motivation for the move of most, though not all the future members of "Our Crowd" to the more promising shores of the New World. Their names and places of origin appear in the table below as listed by Supple[18] (with minor additions).

German-Jewish Immigrants

	Date of Entry	Age at Entry	Marital Status	Origin
Bache Semon	1845	under 20	Single	Bavaria (Mississippi store)
Belmont August	1837	21	,,	Prussia (Alzey)
Goldman Marcus	1848	27	,,	Bavaria (Pad./Store)
Guggenheim Meyer	1848	19	,,	Switzerland
Hallgarten Lazarus	1849	?	Married	Hesse
Heidelbach Philip	Pre-1850	under 20	Single	Bavaria (Peddl. Ohio, Clothing, loc. bank)
Schalheimer Isaac	?	?	,,	Frankfurt
Kuhn Abraham	1839	20	,,	Bavaria
Lehman Henry	1844	22	?	Bavaria
,,　Emanuel	1847	20	Single	,,
,,　Mayer	Pre-1848	20(?)	,,	,,
Lewisohn Leonard	1865	22	,,	Hamburg
Loeb Salomon	1849	19 or 20	,,	?
Sachs Joseph	1848	?	Married	Bavaria
Schiff Jacob	1865	18	Single	Frankfurt
Scholle William	1841	19	?	Bavaria
Seligman Joseph	1837	17	Single	,,
,,　7 brothers	1839–43	4–17	,,	,,
Speyer Philip	1837	23	,,	Frankfurt
Straus Lazarus	1852	?	Married	Bavaria
Thalman Ernst	1868	17	Single	Rhenish Palatin.
Warburg Felix	1897	23	,,	Hamburg
Wertheim Baruch	1850s	in 20s	,,	Cassel
Kahn Otto Hermann	1893	26	,,	Mannheim
Speyer Gustav	1845	?	?	Frankfurt

[18]*Ibid.*

This migration resulted in the establishment of the following finance houses on Wall Street, many of which are still among the leading American investment bankers:

August Belmont & Co.	Hallgarten & Co.
James Speyer & Co.	Heidelbach, Jekelheimer & Co.
J. & W. Seligman & Co.	Asiel & Co.
Kuhn, Loeb & Co.	J. S. Bache & Co.
Goldmann, Sachs & Co.	Albert Loeb & Co. (later
	L. F. Rothschild & Co.)
Lehmann Bros.	Scholle Bros.
Ladenburg, Thalmann & Co.	Adolf Lewisohn & Sons

Not all of them had started as merchants. August Belmont, whose father Simon had been a merchant, moneylender and loan collector at Alzey in Southern Hesse,[19] had been sent by his employers, the Rothschilds, to New York to look after their interests there, and in due course set up his own most successful business, becoming a leading figure in New York society. (As it was believed that he had converted to Christianity, he was not included in *Our Crowd*.) The Speyers, too, came from an old-established Frankfurt banking family, which had branched out to London as well.

And then there was a second generation. While Abraham Kuhn and Salomon Loeb had started as merchants before becoming bankers, it was Jacob H. Schiff, scion of an ancient Frankfurt family, and trained in banking, who raised the house to its eminent position. And of his juniors, Otto Kahn and Felix Warburg, the latter was the son of the old Hamburg banking family. (We may mention here his brother Paul, who had been one of the fathers of the Federal Reserve system, and from 1914 to 1918 a member of its Board. In 1918 he became the founder and chairman of the International Acceptance Bank, in which he had Sir Ernest Cassel's support.)

As one contemporary source stated . . . "The fourteen greatest private banking firms in Wall Street in 1894 were of either German-Jewish or Yankee origin."[20] And nearly all these major investment houses prior to the First World War conducted a general banking business as well.

In more recent years, with Hitler's coming to power, the flow of banking talent into Wall Street was renewed, but was largely absorbed by the existing houses. An exception, perhaps, was the transfer from Berlin of the distinguished house of Arnhold & S. Bleichröder, which reopened in New York.

The foregoing pages do not claim to be more than a modest blueprint, a suggestion for the story still to be written, one hopes in the not too distant future, of the Jewish contribution to the evolution of American banking in general, and commercial banking in particular, within an all-embracing economic history of American Jewry, a field sadly neglected hitherto.

---

[19]Cf. Rahel Liebeschütz, 'The Wind of Change'. Letters of Two Generations from the Biedermeier Period, in *LBI Year Book XII* (1967), pp. 227–256.

[20]V. P. Carosso, *Investment Banking in America*, Harvard 1970, p. 26.

C. *The Josephs of Michelstadt*

The study of Jewish entrepreneurial history is not an easy task. Rarely have family and business archives been preserved over several generations, and the few that had been so preserved were lost in the Holocaust. It is fortunate, therefore, that in some cases one may come across a pamphlet which a reverent son has dedicated to the memory of his parents and family which, incidentally, tells us something of their economic background and business life. And, if one is fortunate, one might find some other source, enabling one to follow the history of such a family into the more recent past or up to our own day.

It was, therefore, a lucky chance to find, in the catalogue of the National and University Library, Jerusalem, *Familie Abraham S. Joseph. Ein Denkblatt* by Leopold Joseph, published (in German), in London in 1912, sixty-five years ago. The name of the author sounded familiar. Not only is it listed in *The Banker's Almanack* as that of a firm of merchant bankers in London, but we remembered a small but excellent book by him on *The Evolution of German Banking*,[1] which can still hold its own today. And thus we were able to trace the story of three generations in the banking business on both sides of the Channel.

The story starts in *ca.* 1860 when Abraham Salomon Joseph (1827–1892) added a banking department to his wholesale business in grain, wool and cotton which he had gradually built up in his native Michelstadt, a small county-town in Hesse. He was a supplier of raw materials to the local industries, including some belonging to the noble family which had ruled the district in feudal days. It was at their suggestion that Joseph added banking to his business. Their complete confidence in him, sustained even after his later move to Frankfurt a. Main, recalls the unique relationship of trust between ruler and Jew which had made the preceding two centuries those of the Court Jew.

As in most other cases where banking started as an ancillary to another business, whether wine, grain or forwarding, the ancillary soon became the main business. Joseph eventually left the trading side to a relative and in 1874, looking for a larger field of activities, opened the office of A. S. Joseph in Frankfurt. The times, however, did not favour such a move. With the annexation of Frankfurt by Prussia in 1866 this once proud Free City gradually lost its importance as a financial centre to Berlin, since 1871 the capital of the new *Reich*. And the newly established large joint-stock banks started to squeeze out even the old-established family banks. Thus the success of the new house was only moderate. About 1890 the ageing A. S. Joseph retired from the management of the bank, leaving his wife's nephew and junior partner Arthur Abenheimer in charge. His son Leopold, who had worked in the bank from 1884 to 1887, joined him as a partner in 1891. But in view of the prospects, so unpromising for private banks, its liquidation was decided upon in 1895.

Abraham Salomon's oldest son, Salomon (1860–1899), the third of his seven children, who had proved a sound scholar at the *Gymnasium*, started his banking

[1]London 1912.

career in 1877 as an apprentice to the Frankfurt firm of A. L. Schwartzschild Söhne, where he soon became entrusted with responsible tasks. To gain wider experience he took employment in 1879 in the Parisian bank – Ancien Maison Leon & Dreher, but soon changed over to the Amsterdam house of Philipp Meyer. Finally, in 1882, he entered the service of the recently established Union Bank of Spain & England (1881–1897), in which, much appreciated by the London board, he achieved managerial rank in their Madrid office within two years. Rejecting attractive offers from other institutions, he stayed with the bank until 1894 when he retired for reasons of ill-health. His retirement, as his London directors predicted, meant the end of the bank, which, in fact, ceased operations a year later. Salomon himself died two years thereafter, only thirty-nine years old.

The next of Abraham Salomon's children, Leopold (1863–1943), the narrator of the family saga (which takes us to 1912), had worked in the paternal bank, on and off, from 1884 till its liquidation in 1895. A first visit to London, in 1887, seems to have determined his future course of action. While modestly reticent about himself in his story, which is dedicated to the deceased members of the family, we learn that in 1895, i.e., the year of the liquidation of A. S. Joseph, he joined Reuter's Bureau in London and since then had contributed articles on economic and financial subjects to numerous journals, in particular to the *Frankfurter Zeitung* – famous for its economic section – whose economic correspondent in London he was from 1896 to 1910. (A few samples of this literary production are appended to the pamphlet.)

Thus far his story, which we must now supplement from other sources. Paul H. Emden in his classic *Money Powers of Europe in the Nineteenth and Twentieth Centuries* [2] shows that Leopold Joseph's activities at Reuters were apparently not restricted to journalism and that his financial talents were given an equal chance. In this book we are told that:

> "Amongst the many concessions which Reuter had acquired was one from Greece for the construction of a railway from the Piraeus to Larissa, which also lay dormant for a long time. Leopold Joseph, who had joined Reuter's in 1895, and is now the head of the highly respected merchant bankers, Leopold Joseph & Sons, saw a favourable opportunity for exploiting it in 1897 when the Graeco-Turkish War was over and the Bank of England, together with the Bank of France and the Bank of Russia made a loan to Greece at 2½ per cent. With the co-operation of Pauling & Co., who were closely associated with Erlanger's, the necessary funds were raised, and the railway was built. The proceeds of the Greek 4 per cent. Railway Loan of 1902–1904, offered by Hambros and Erlanger's at 83½, were used to reimburse the money advanced by Reuter's and by the banks." [3]

Joseph left Reuters in the early years of this century to join the London office of the Swiss Bank Corporation as its manager, a position he held until 1917, when he started preparations for opening his own bank.

As for his bank, which Emden mentions as a house of respected merchant bankers, we now turn to *The Banker's Almanack*. Here we learn that the house of Leopold Joseph, merchant bankers, was established in London in 1919, changing the name to Leopold Joseph & Strauss in 1921, to L.J. & Sons in 1929 and

[2]London [1938].   [3]*Ibid.*, p. 402.

to Joseph (Leopold) & Sons Ltd. in 1956. Here three of his sons joined him, a fourth one became a member of the London Stock Exchange. But, since there was no succession, outside interests were brought in in 1963, and the Joseph brothers subsequently retired in 1966. On the board of this private company today we do not see any of the members of the family, apart from Karl Ernst Ruge (b. 1912), a grandson of Leopold's younger sister Mathilde, representing the fourth generation. (All the other names of the Company's officers are strictly Anglo-Saxon, except for Louis Heymann and Prince Rupert Loewenstein, a name familiar from the days of refugee rescue activities during the Hitler period.)

On another page of *The Banker's Almanack*, however, we discovered the names of two of Leopold's sons: Edward Walter Joseph, O.B.E. (b. 1909) as Managing Director, and Henry Oscar Joseph, O.B.E. (b. 1901), a noted philanthropist, as a member of the board of the Anglo-Israel Bank, now Bank Leumi of Israel (London) Ltd. They retired in 1972.

German and Austrian Jews in the Financial
Modernisation of the Middle East

BY JOACHIM O. RONALL

INTRODUCTION

A discussion of the role of German and Austro-Hungarian Jews in the financial modernisation of the Middle East during the imperialist era calls for some justification.[1] Although the number of these Jews was small, their role was significant in the political, economic and social development of the area.

The beginning of financial modernisation in the Middle East coincided with the end of the Crimean War (1854–1856), and the process continues today. Technically speaking, *development* means quantitative change ("growth") plus structural change such as technical, institutional or social innovation. An illustration of the development process is the introduction of Western financial institutions and methods into the Middle East to be discussed here.

In the specific context of the Middle East – a predominantly Moslem area – financial innovation assumes a particular aspect which requires a few historical remarks. The structure of the Ottoman Empire, which occupied the larger part of the Middle East during the period under review was militaristic, feudal and bureaucratic. From medieval Islam the Ottoman Turks inherited the classical islamic attitude of utmost self-confidence and self-sufficiency. The islamic tradition knew only four occupations: government, war, religion (which included law) and agriculture. Due to this exclusivity and to the Koranic prohibition of giving and taking interest, business and finance were left to minorities and foreigners. Moslems disdained commerce and finance, and their contempt was extended to those who engaged in these occupations. This situation opened the way for the growing economic influence in the Ottoman Empire (and, by the same token, in Persia and the rest of the Middle East) of both foreigners and those minorities possessed of financial and business talents.

At first the financial needs of the Ottoman Empire were met by Italian, Levantine, Ragusan, Armenian, Greek and Jewish bankers, who as a group became known as "The Bankers of Galata".[2] Modern Western banking entered the Middle East in the wake of the Crimean War, but for almost half a century was mainly represented by British and French interests. However, even before central European Jews, as officials or collaborators of German and Austrian banking institutions, participated in the financial modernisation of the Middle East, some members of this group had been working in the field as individuals.

[1]The author of this paper is an economist with the Federal Reserve Bank of New York. The views presented here are his own and not necessarily those of the Bank. The paper benefited from Mr. Tom Draper's editorial advice. It was originally delivered as a lecture at the Leo Baeck Institute, New York.

[2]See K. Grunwald and J. O. Ronall, 'Die Bankiers von Galata', in *Tradition. Zeitschrift für Firmengeschichte und Unternehmerbiographie*, vol. VIII, No. 4 (August 1963).

Jewish private bankers in Europe and in the Western hemisphere played a significant role in the formation of, and participated to a large extent in, the new banking and financial institutions which were required for the mobilisation and distribution of the unprecedented sums needed to finance the industrial revolution and its aftermath. However, the attempt at specifically investigating the part played by German-speaking Jews in this process in the Middle East reveals that their operations in that area must be considered as an offshoot of their overall activities and that modernisation of the Middle East seems unrelated to the accidental facts of their Jewish ancestry and their birth in German-speaking Central Europe. Naturally, one could go even further and contend that such an investigation may even offer an instructive lesson in the possible pitfalls of group history. This is a complex question which goes far beyond the scope of this short survey though I may touch on it again in my concluding remarks.

Germany was a latecomer to the Middle East. Napoleon's arrival in Egypt in 1799 was the beginning of European penetration of the Middle East, but it took Germany almost a century to enter the Western competition for political and economic influence in that area. The Danube monarchy, although directing much of its political and economic activity towards the Balkans, did not itself become conspicuous in the Middle East. But a number of individual Austro-Hungarian subjects performed signal services in the financial modernisation of the area.

In order to arrive at a realistic appraisal of the role of German-speaking Jews as financial innovators in the Middle East, the definition of that group must be extended to include those who, at the time of their Middle East operations, were no longer resident in Germany or the Austro-Hungarian empire.

THE ROAD BUILDERS

A convenient starting point for the present discussion is the role of Baron Maurice de Hirsch (1831–1896) in linking the Middle East to Europe through his *magnum opus*, the railway link between Vienna and Constantinople. In 1869 he obtained the necessary concession from the Ottoman government, and on 12th August 1888, almost twenty years later, the first train left Vienna for Constantinople.[3] Since the detailed story of Baron Hirsch has recently been told by Kurt Grunwald,[4] it will suffice here to recall the highlights. Hirsch was born in Munich, the scion of orthodox Bavarian court bankers and a descendant of Samson Wertheimer (1658–1724) of Vienna. After an apprenticeship with the Brussels banking firm of Bischoffsheim & Goldschmidt, he began to pursue his own business interests which culminated in the oriental railway project. It was financed through the famous *Türkenlose*. These were bonds carrying 3 per cent interest, payable over ninety-nine years, and participating in a bi-monthly draw of lottery prizes, three of which were as high as 600,000 francs. On account of

[3]The service was suspended in 1977. After ninety years it had become unprofitable.
[4]K. Grunwald, *Türkenhirsch. A Study of Baron Maurice de Hirsch*, Jerusalem 1966.

his business acumen, these highly speculative bonds and other business practices, Hirsch became a man who was both admired and vilified. This presentation is only concerned with his outstanding role as the entrepreneur who first linked the Ottoman Empire to Europe by rail.

One of Baron Hirsch's closest assistants in the Oriental Railway venture was a young banker from Bohemia, Karl Morawitz (1846–1914). Born in Iglau, he joined Ludwig Bamberger's *Banque de Paris et des Pays Bas* in Paris; later he became chief comptroller at the Paris office of the *Banque Ottomane*, and the principal aide to the bank's president, Charles Mallet. Compelled by the outbreak of war to leave France in 1870, Morawitz became the financial manager of Hirsch's oriental railway. In 1885 he moved to Vienna and was coopted to the board of the Anglo-Austrian Bank in which both Ernest Cassel and Hirsch were interested. From 1906 to his death he served as the bank's president. Shortly before his death he was knighted. Morawitz was an expert in international finance, and his wide experience and many relationships made him an influential adviser. He frequently wrote and lectured, and his study *Les Finances de la Turquie* (published 1902 in Paris) is a standard work on the financial history of the Ottoman Empire during the nineteenth century.

PERSIA

Turning from those who were instrumental in linking the Middle East to Europe through modern means of transportation to those involved in the Eastern part of the area under review, we find among the first representatives of German-speaking Jews, or their direct descendants, in Persia, the Paris house of Erlanger which originated in Frankfurt. In 1866 the Erlangers applied for a concession to establish a modern bank in Teheran. The negotiations with the Persian government were broken off when the Shah refused to guarantee the inviolability of deposits against arbitrary seizure by the authorities – a pledge required by the Erlangers as a condition of operating the bank.[5] During the latter part of the nineteenth century the entire Middle East, the Ottoman Empire including Egypt, and Persia, rapidly became theatres of competition by the Western powers for political and economic influence. On 25th July 1872, when British prestige had risen as a result of the Franco-Prussian war of 1870–1871, Shah Nasr-ed-Din granted Baron Julius de Reuter (1816–1899) a concession which actually constituted a monopoly over Persia's entire economy, including the construction of railways and the formation of a national bank. Baron Reuter was born Israel Bar Josaphat, in Kassel. He began to work as a clerk in his uncle's bank in Göttingen, where his acquaintance with Karl Friedrich Gauss familiarised him with telegraphy. He later moved to London where he opened his famous telegraphic agency. He was created a baron by the Duke of Saxe-Coburg-Gotha and permitted by Queen Victoria to retain this privilege in England.

[5]Karl Helfferich, *Georg von Siemens. Ein Lebensbild*, Berlin 1923, vol. I, p. 132.

Soon after the Shah had granted the Reuter concession he went on his first European tour, during which he was surprised and disappointed to find the European governments not only indignant over the terms and the scale of the concession but also unresponsive to the venture's financial attractions. London considered investment in Persia a poor risk; some Persian concessions granted to British interests had come to grief, and funds for the Reuter venture were not forthcoming. In particular, the Russian government strongly opposed the Reuter concession. Therefore, the Shah upon his return to Teheran annulled the concession, but retained Reuter's performance bond of £40,000 sterling. However, the concession to establish a bank in Teheran was eventually granted to Reuter in 1889 as *amende honorable* for the anulment of its predecessor with the active support of Sir Henry Drummond Wolff, the British minister in Teheran. Sir Henry was the son of the Reverend Joseph Wolff (1795–1862) who had been born at Weilersbach in Franconia, the son of a rabbi. A convert to Christianity, Joseph Wolff became a minister of the Anglican Church and a widely travelled missionary. His son, Sir Henry, was an eminent member of the British diplomatic service and became deeply involved in Middle Eastern developments. The bank concession was the basis for the formation of the Imperial Bank of Persia (later of Iran) which served as a central bank until the 1930s. Its successor institution today is the British Bank of the Middle East, a member of the Hong Kong and Shanghai Banking group.

Some years later, another German Jew became active in Persian banking affairs. Towards the end of 1905 the German legation in Teheran informed Berlin of Persian interest in financial ties with Germany. This approach coincided with the expansion of German ambitions in the Middle East, which were reflected in the *Baghdadbahn* project. The German Ministry of Foreign Affairs approached the *Deutsche Orientbank*, a 1906 venture of the *Dresdner Bank, National Bank für Deutschland*, and *A. Schaaffhausenscher Bankverein*, to investigate the possibilities of opening a German bank in Teheran. In April–May 1907, Herbert Gutmann,[6] the manager of the *Deutsche Orientbank*, visited Teheran. His negotiations with the Iranian authorities resulted in a banking concession for Germany, but a combination of circumstances prevented its being taken up. Internal developments in Persia, which then went through the aftermath of the 1905 revolution, domestic hesitations on the part of the *Orientbank* and its partners over the risk of investment in Persia, and a combined Russian–British front against German penetration into Persia were obstacles which the ambitious German diplomats found impossible to overcome. Gutmann realised that under these circumstances the German venture had no prospects, and the *Deutsche Orientbank* decided against taking up the Iranian concession. Urged by the legation in Teheran and German traders active in Iran, in 1908 the German Ministry of Foreign Affairs again suggested to the *Orientbank* that they take up the concession, since the Persian government had become critical of German procrastination. But the bank again most definitely declined. In 1910 the German authorities once more proposed taking up the concession, this time to

---

[6] 1879–1942, the son of Eugen Gutman n, one of the founders of the *Dresdner Bank*.

the *Deutsche Bank*, but also unsuccessfully. The First World War, the British presence and the subsequent rise of Iranian nationalism eliminated the country as a field of financial activities for others.[7]

THE OTTOMAN EMPIRE

The *Deutsche Bank* which in April 1970 celebrated its one hundredth anniversary was the first major German financial institution to be directly active in the Middle East. Instrumental in bringing the bank to the area was Alfred von Kaulla (1852–1924), a board member of the *Württembergische Vereinsbank* and a descendant of a family of Court Jews and bankers documented in Southern Germany since the seventeenth century.[8] In 1877 he was in Constantinople soliciting orders for the *Mauserwerke*, one of Germany's leading arms manufacturers, in which the *Württembergische Vereinsbank* had a financial interest. That was at a time when, in the words of the British ambassador to Constantinople, "every few weeks a new plan to construct a Turkish railway emerged".[9] These plans referred to the extension into Asian Turkey of Baron Hirsch's oriental railway which, as mentioned before, linked Turkey with the rest of Europe. The first direct train from Vienna reached Constantinople in August 1888; but by the end of the 1880s, there existed in Asian Turkey, that is South and East of Constantinople, only four short lines all of which represented British interests. Kaulla saw himself in a situation where several powerful international groups were competing savagely to obtain a concession from the Ottoman government to extend Hirsch's railroad from Haidar Pasha (just South of Constantinople) into Anatolia and possibly further into Mesopotamia, with the eventual terminal at the Northern end of the Persian Gulf. One of the competing groups was the Imperial Ottoman Bank. At that time it mainly represented French interests, but also maintained contacts with the *Diskonto Gesellschaft* and with Bleichröder[10] for the purpose of financing the Anatolian railway project in case the group should obtain the concession. Kaulla, always alert for new business, first entered the race on behalf of the *Württembergische Vereinsbank*, whose board chairman showed but little inclination to become entangled in oriental adventures. He referred Kaulla to Georg von Siemens of the *Deutsche Bank*. Siemens found the idea interesting, explored the views of the German government concerning the project, and obtained from Bismarck a low-keyed approval coupled with the warning that the government would not assume or guarantee any

---

[7]An interesting contemporary example of German-Jewish activity in Iran was the work of Miss Goldenberg with the Iranian Ministry of Finance during the 1930s and 1940s, and her subsequent affiliation with the *Bank Bazargani* which had taken over the assets of the Imperial Bank of Iran when the latter had to liquidate its operations in Iran under the *Mossadegh* régime in the early 1950s. Her brother was for many years the representative of the *Deutsche Bank* in Istanbul.

[8]Heinrich Schnee, *Die Hoffinanz und der moderne Staat*, Berlin 1953/1967, vol. IV, p. 148.

[9]*Deutsche Bank, 1870–1970. 100 Jahre*, Frankfurt a. Main 1970, p. 63.

[10]Bleichröder also represented German interest at the *Dette Publique Ottomane* and the Tobacco Monopoly whose revenue formed a collateral for Turkish public commitments.

financial risks of the venture.[11] However, the Chancellor authorised the German embassy in Constantinople to support Kaulla in his negotiations, since without such an official backing any approach to the Ottoman authorities was sure to fail. Kaulla's correspondence with the *Deutsche Bank* has been preserved and reflects a fascinating picture of diplomatic, business and engineering planning, plotting and counter-plotting in Sultan Abdul Hamid's Constantinople. On 4th October 1888 Kaulla cabled to Berlin that he had obtained the Sultan's *Irade* (the law confirming the concession). Siemens, who realised the financial dimensions of the project, hesitated to be the sole underwriter. He looked for partners but all of those whom he approached remained cool, including Salomonsohn of the *Diskonto Gesellschaft*, Carl Fürstenberg of the *Berliner Handelsgesellschaft*[12] as well as Sir Ernest Cassel of London. The *Deutsche Bank* was left alone to carry out Kaulla's initiative. Construction began immediately, proceeded quickly, and in July 1896 the Anatolian railway reached Konia, with a branch to Ankara. During the construction the project had grown, once its importance had become clear to the many interested parties. German traders and shippers were looking forward to the completion of the line and a possible extension further South as the backbone and basis of their expansion in the entire area. One of the major promoters of the German Middle East railway programme was Albert Ballin (1857–1918),[13] manager of the *Hamburg-Amerika Linie*, who was thinking of a German transportation network throughout the world, and saw in the Turkish railway network a major support and feeder for his ships. From the beginning it had been clear in the Anatolian project that the lines to Ankara and Konia would only be torsos and would therefore not be left to remain for long as unfinished undertakings. While construction of the line was going on, the concessionaire was consolidating his position by incorporating the *Bank für Orientalische Eisenbahnen* in Zürich and also acquired a controlling interest in more than a thousand miles of rail track in the Balkans by purchasing the holdings of Baron Hirsch in the Oriental Railway Company. As a result, the *Deutsche Bank* in carrying out Kaulla's plan soon appeared on the international scene as a giant. The extension to Baghdad and the Persian Gulf of the Anatolian railway as an intrinsic part of the entire project, which was discussed during the construction years of the Anatolian part, became a political liability to Germany since Britain, France and Russia saw in the project a threat to the spheres of influence which they had created for themselves in the Ottoman Empire. It has been contended that this German penetration was a major factor in bringing together the members of the Triple Entente. To Germany, however, it appeared differently. The *Alldeutsche Blätter* of 17th December 1899, complimented Kaulla by writing:

> "The idea of this railway was conceived by German intelligence; Germans made the preliminary surveys; Germans overcame all the serious obstacles which stood in the way of its execution . . ."[14]

[11]Quoted in *100 Jahre Deutsche Bank*, p. 67.
[12]Carl Fürstenberg, *Die Lebensgeschichte eines deutschen Bankiers 1870–1914*, Berlin 1931, p. 240.
[13]Lamar Cecil, *Albert Ballin*, Princeton 1967, p. 87.
[14]*100 Jahre Deutsche Bank*, p. 159.

Wilhelm II had become a fervent supporter of the orient railway project. He expressed himself in a letter to Arthur von Gwinner of the *Deutsche Bank*, dated 25th October 1904:

> "From your communication of the 20th I noted with great satisfaction that today, on the birthday of my illustrious friend, his Majesty the Emperor of the Ottomans, the first part of the Baghdad railroad from Konia to Burgurli has been completed. I am glad that it has been possible to promote to its present important stage this significant venture of German entrepreneurial spirit and German engineering skill despite the many obstacles that arose. I cannot refrain from expressing to you as well as to all other participants in the great undertaking my unqualified recognition of what has been achieved so far, and my warmest wishes for the subsequent prosperous continuation and completion of the Baghdad railroad venture."[15]

The Emperor's trip to the Orient in 1898 was the point of departure for a new line in German diplomacy. Contrary to Bismarck's reluctance to commit the government to commercial projects, the German Foreign Ministry under Wilhelm II began to urge the *Deutsche Bank* to underwrite the project of the *Bagdadbahn*, i.e., the extension of the Anatolian railway. The bank hesitated, partly because of the financial magnitude of the project, and partly because it was apprehensive of antagonising British and French interests. When the German government finally agreed to the bank's suggestion that the project should be internationalised,[16] it was too late. British interest in cooperation could alone be solicited, and that only during the summer of 1914.

The *Baghdadbahn* was eventually completed during the Second World War.

One of the major influences in securing British interests in the Ottoman Empire between the turn of the century and beginning of the First World War was that of Sir Ernest Cassel of Cologne (1852–1921). Again we are indebted for details to the work of Kurt Grunwald.[17] Cassel has been previously mentioned as one of those who had been unsuccessfully approached by the *Deutsche Bank* for cooperation in the Anatolian railway project. During 1912–1914 he was soliciting British interest in participation in the financing of the *Baghdadbahn* project, in order to prevent the Turkish railway system from becoming a German monopoly. However, rail networks were not Cassel's only interest in the Ottoman Empire. In 1909 he was instrumental in forming the National Bank of Turkey which, according to the intentions of the Young Turks, the revolutionaries of 1908, was to counteract the predominant positions of the French (through the *Banque Ottomane*) and the Germans (through the *Deutsche Bank*) in Turkey. Subsequent developments, including French pressure on the British to subordinate financial intrusion into Turkey to the larger objective of the *entente cordiale*, led to the decline of the National Bank of Turkey, the sale of its assets and to its subsequent liquidation.

One of the basic ideas of Kaulla's original Turkish railway project was that the construction of such a railway was justified to a large extent by the concomitant exploitation of adjacent natural resources which would supply the freight.

[15]*Ibid.*, p. 149.
[16]"Der Traum der deutschen Baghdadbahn bis zum Golf ist ausgeträumt", as Helfferich wrote to Arthur von Gwinner on 30th November 1908.
[17]' "Windsor-Cassel" – The Last Court Jew', in *LBI Year Book XIV* (1969), pp. 119–161.

Attempts by Dutch and British groups to obtain mineral – mainly oil – mining concessions in Mesopotamia, originally held by the Anatolian Railroad Company, had failed. Cassel was successful in arranging an understanding with the *Deutsche Bank* according to which the Turkish Petroleum Company was established. British, German, Dutch and other interests shared the capital stock of the company, but the outcome of the First World War radically changed the petroleum situation in the Middle East.

During the First World War German and Austrian banks excluded other Western banks from the Ottoman Empire. The German group included the *Deutsche Orientbank* (of which Herbert Gutmann was a leading executive) and in addition to its previously mentioned parent institutions: S. Bleichröder, Salomon Oppenheim and M. M. Warburg. Leader of the Austrian group was the *Österreichische Kreditanstalt*, a Rothschild affiliation under the leadership of Julius Blum Pasha to whom we shall revert. This grouping reflected the intention of the German and the Austrian governments to provide Turkey's wartime finance not through competing individual banks, but rather through centralised and coordinated groups amenable to executing government policies according to a master plan. An unforeseen factor in the formation of these two monolithic banking groups was the resulting ease with which (at the end of the First World War) the Allied Powers could eliminate German and Austrian influence in the former Ottoman Empire by simply suspending the operations of these two groups instead of having to deal with numerous individual banks.

EGYPT

The last geographical section of this survey deals with Egypt, which since the middle of the nineteenth century had become semi-independent under Ottoman suzerainty. Two representatives of the group are important in Egypt, though neither of them active on behalf of German or Austrian interests. The first, Julius Blum Pasha (1843–1919), was an Egyptian government official, and the second, Sir Ernest Cassel, was a British citizen when he began his Egyptian operations.

Julius Blum was born in Budapest. In 1862 he joined the *Credit Anstalt*, first at its branch in Trieste, and two years later he was transferred to the bank's newly opened offices in Egypt. After the liquidation of these offices in 1876 he entered Egyptian government service where he remained until 1890, when he was recalled to Vienna to join the management of the *Credit Anstalt*. In 1913 he became its president. Julius Blum became an Egyptian government official a few months after the Egyptian Treasury suspended payments on its bonds (April 1876). The country was bankrupt and ruled by the Debt Commissioners, representing British and French bondholders. In order to sketch the background of Blum's activities in Egypt, a brief summary of the major events of the period is in order: In 1869 the Suez Canal had been opened; in 1875 the British government acquired a controlling interest in the Suez Canal Company; in 1876 the country went bankrupt; in 1879 the Sultan deposed the Khedive whose son was then installed; in the summer of 1882 the British occupied Egypt in the wake of Arabi Pasha's revolt. From the beginning of the British occupation until the end of his work in Egypt in 1890, Blum, who had become a Pasha in 1878, was preoccupied in balancing Egypt's need to meet its foreign commitments with its need to regain a sound financial structure. In achieving this major objective Blum rendered signal service in modernising the structure of the Egyptian budget and in mobilising the foreign support necessary for the country's financial rehabilitation. He was a key figure since he had acquired the confidence of both Egyptians and British. His expertise in Egyptian and international finance, and his talent for reaching a compromise, were probably decisive in lessening the frequent tensions between Egyptians, British, the other creditor countries and the representatives of the Ottoman government. It seems safe to say that Blum Pasha's familiarity with Egyptian conditions, his financial experience, his reliability and his consequent reputation were major factors contributing to the success of Lord Cromer's reform.[18]

After the consolidation of British power in Egypt Sir Ernest Cassel appeared on the scene. His interest in the country probably stemmed from earlier experiences with French and British banks which, together with many others, had lent money to the Egyptian government. In 1898 the foundation was laid for the (first) Aswan Dam. The need to increase the country's productivity required not only the creation of new technical facilities but also the formation of modern financial institutions. Since law and order had been restored in Egypt, foreign capital readily flowed in, but British investments had remained below those of France. The British authorities, who still competed with the French for influence in Egypt, became apprehensive lest French finance should undermine British political positions. Cassel helped to realise three major projects, all considered essential to Egypt's economic expansion. The first was the financing of the Aswan Dam and the Assiut Barrage. The second was the sale of the Khedive's private holdings (Daira Sanieh) for the liquidation of a major part of Egypt's public debt for which these assets served as collateral. Cassel's third and lasting contribution was the formation in that same year of the National Bank of Egypt which until 1962 served as Egypt's major commercial bank and its central bank. A year after its establishment the bank introduced a department for agricultural loans, the first modern institution of this kind in Egypt, which in turn became independent in 1902 as the Agricultural Bank of Egypt.

Thus far this brief and of necessity selective survey. At the outset some doubts were expressed as to whether the activities of German-speaking Jews as financial modernisers in the Middle East (exclusive of Palestine) justify the treatment of the topic as a separate chapter of economic history. And one may well raise the broader question as to what warrants the treatment of Jews, or of Jewish subgroups, as entities in economic history, or what such treatment can accomplish.

[18]For details of Blum Pasha's Egyptian activities see J. O. Ronall, 'Julius Blum Pasha', in *Tradition. Zeitschrift für Firmengeschichte und Unternehmerbiographie*, vol. XIII, No. 2 (April 1968).

A selective approach certainly has its dangers, as it may lead to the temptation to exaggerate the role of one's selected group in its interaction with others. While acknowledging that this has certain objectionable aspects, the realities of Jewish existence do justify a group approach to history. Groups are best studied while remaining aware of the fallacies on the way and at the same time keeping in mind that a group (or community) is, in the words of MacIver, a matter of degree.

Aspects of Jewish Existence

Jewish Surnames – Further Researches

BY WILLIAM STERN

INTRODUCTION

The results of my investigations into Jewish surnames, as published in *Year Book XIX* of the Leo Baeck Institute, must not be taken as finalising the work, especially where a number of the more "difficult" names are concerned. In a field like this, where historical, sociological, geographical, etymological, religious and other influences interact, further researches are always indicated, and frequently the results – particularly when proofs are lacking – can only be provisional ones. Since the conclusion of the above-mentioned essay I have continued to interest myself in this subject, and I have been able to elucidate some of the questions which then remained unanswered as well as make several new discoveries. In many respects I had relied on the standard work by Kessler,[1] the findings of which I quoted many times, though constrained to be critical of a few of them in the analysis. For his part, Kessler on numerous occasions draws on articles which had appeared in the periodical journal *Jüdische Familien-Forschung*, published in Berlin between 1924 and 1938. In the meantime I have been fortunate in obtaining a complete set of this journal.[2] I have studied all its articles which deal with the origin or explanation of Jewish surnames and, wherever appropriate, compared these with my own findings. The arguments on the following pages are based on those *JFF* contributions to a great extent. In addition, I have received letters from many parts of the world during the last few years; various correspondents who evinced an interest have put forward a number of suggestions or, on occasion, theories about names. Several of these opinions of private individuals have commended themselves, also, for incorporation in the present essay. Finally, in a few cases other sources have become available.

The structure of the present article will be as follows: in its first part, a certain number of names with which I had dealt previously, either briefly or more extensively, will be considered again, while in the second part various "new" surnames will be investigated, viz., those in relation to which I came across novel or otherwise fascinating explanations. Once again, it must be emphasised that conclusive and fully substantiated results should not be expected in every case; actually, researches of this nature can never be completed (even though, for myself, I must now envisage an end to it, at least for the time being). Moreover, as far as possible repetitions ought to be avoided, and for this reason I shall assume that all the material contained in my essay in *Year Book XIX* has been

---

[1]Gerhard Kessler, *Die Familiennamen der Juden in Deutschland*, Leipzig 1935.

[2]Throughout this essay, as well as in the footnotes, whenever reference is made to the journal, *Jüdische Familien-Forschung*, this source will be abbreviated as *JFF*, followed by specification of issues and pages.

read and is presently known.[3] This must apply in particular also to the classification list of the derivation of Jewish family names, which means that in the following, without any further definition of the terms, reference will be made to "names of origin", "patronymics", "allegorical names" and all the other categories.

In general, it must *not* be assumed that I have as yet accepted all the cited hypotheses, theories or opinions, in the absence of further corroboration. In those instances, the sources or the learned authors must speak for themselves. A quotation as such, therefore, does not automatically imply that I agree with the view thereby put forward. Where I do feel that I can agree, the letters "acc." (acceptable) will be added in brackets.

I

May I reiterate at the outset that the explanation of many hundreds of surnames has for a long time been well known and agreed. It is quite unnecessary to deal with these; the relevant information is available in the sources quoted in my previous essay.

Bär (p. 228): Gustav Samuel[4] considers this name, in its frequent connection with Issachar, "evidently a symbol for a 'strong-boned' person ('*Starkknochiger*')". One of my correspondents, Mrs. Hanna Nehab, Kibbutz Hazorea, tentatively suggests that "Bär" ("Behr") could be understood as an abbreviation of "Ben Harav" ("Son of the Rabbi"). This might not be far-fetched, since according to tradition the Tribe of Issachar consisted of scholars who used to sit in the academies and to study.[5] Another correspondent, John J. Thal, New York, writes: "I feel that to the names from Jacob's blessing[6] the name *Hammer* could be also added," as a cognomen for Issachar, because in that blessing Issachar is described as a "Chamor" ("ass"), from which, according to this hypothesis, "Hammer" would be colloquially derived. Heinrich Flesch[7] considers that Issachar, consequent on this very verse from Jacob's blessing, was nicknamed "Bär" for the reason that "the bear is the symbol of the inert". This, however, is contradicted by Rashi's description of the bear in his commentary to Genesis 49, 14, and more especially still by Rashi's description of the bear in Genesis 39, 6; cf. there also the remarks of the supercommentary "Sifte Chachamim": "The bear is always restless, he is continuously on the move to and fro." This would show that he is certainly *not* inert!

Falk (p. 227): According to Heinrich Flesch[8] the connection with Joshua might be based on the notion that "Falk" ("falcon") is possibly "the symbol of

---

[3]The page numbers after individual names in the following Part I refer the reader to the page(s) of my essay 'On the Fascination of Jewish Surnames', in *LBI Year Book XIX* where the particular name has previously been dealt with or explained.
[4]*JFF*, Issue 34, p. 542.
[5]Cf. Deuteronomium 33:18 and Rashi *ad loc*.
[6]Genesis 49:14
[7]*JFF*, Year II, No. 1, p. 112.
[8]*Ibid*., p. 111.

the hero". Gustav Samuel,[9] while not offering an explanation for this connection, points to its presumed historical origin: The family name was adopted to "honour the Talmudic scholar Josua ben Alexander Hakohen (1550–1644), who became famous, above all, for his commentary on the *Shulchan Aruch* and called himself Josua Falk in brief". This may well be so, but it must come as no surprise that the combination of "Joshua Falk" (or "Walk") may be found in documents and books already prior to the sixteenth century. Our own hypotheses, as put forward in *Year Book XIX*, have so far remained uncontradicted.

Gimpel, Gumpel (pp. 223 ff.): Gustav Samuel,[10] too, derives this group of names from "Gundbert", meaning "famous in battle", as a cognomen of Mordecai, but does not vouchsafe any reasons for this link. Heinrich Flesch[11] similarly establishes this combination with Mordecai, again without explanation. Mrs. Hanna Nehab, already quoted above, offers the following intriguing hypothesis: A "Gimpel" – as such a jester at fairs – could at one time have been the jester at Jewish weddings; again, he could have played such a role at Purim celebrations, and this would establish a connection with Purim and thus with Mordecai. Since the kin of the Gumpels is, at the outset, traceable back to Jülich near Cologne, Mrs. Nehab even envisages a possible connection with the mirth of the Cologne carnival. As regards the alternative, viz., that names like "Gumpel" or "Gimpel" also occur in combination with Ephraim, she points to the famous verse from the Book of Jeremiah[12] where Ephraim is called "Ben Yakir Li" ("My dearly beloved son"); she submits that due to sloppy Ashkenazi pronunciation this could have been transmuted into "Ben Joker" ("son of the jester"), which would close the circle, bringing us back to "Gimpel" as a jester.

Süsskind (p. 228): Heinrich Flesch[13] expresses the opinion that "Süsskind" developed out of "Israel"; and he refers to the Jewish troubadour of the thirteenth century, Süsskind von Trimberg. At the same time, he rejects the possibility of equating "Süss" with "horse" ("horse" in Hebrew is "ssuss"). But this very hypothesis would, as far as I am concerned, be the first known link with Alexander, as in "Alexander Süsskind" or "Alexander Süsche", because this twin-name would then mean "Alexander, the Horseman". According to historical tradition, Alexander the Great of Macedonia (to whom "Alexander" as a Jewish first name does indeed go back) was a famous rider and horseman.

Lamm (pp. 225 ff.): While the relationship between "Lämmle" and "Asher" has been investigated in our previous essay, some observations must now be made about *Lamm* as a name "on its own". John J. Thal, New York, writes in his letter: "A particularly peaceable and easy-going business friend bore the nickname of Lamm (i.e., lamb)." Additionally, he mentions an anecdote which may be found, also, in the *JFF* where Heinrich Loewe[14] relates it thus: "In Buttenwiesen, there had lived for a long time a family named Lammfromm. In front of the commission for the allocation of names two Jews appeared, of whom the one bore this name whereas the other had no name at all, and so the all-powerful official decided: 'One of you has two names, the other no name at all.

[9] *JFF*, Issue 34, p. 542.
[10] *Loc. cit.*
[11] *JFF*, Year II, No. 1, p. 111.
[12] Jeremiah 31:19.
[13] *JFF*, Year II, No. 1, p. 111.
[14] *JFF*, Issue 12, p. 276.

He who has too much will, therefore, hand over part of it to him who has nothing. Lammfromm will henceforth be called Lamm, and the other will be allotted the name of Fromm.' Thus the anecdote. But besides Lamm and Fromm there continues to exist (the name of) Lammfromm, too." It may be stated that these names were also to be found among Jews in Fischach, which is not far from Buttenwiesen. Additionally, a highly intriguing suggestion of Dr. Hans Lamm, Munich, ought to be quoted; he is inclined to think that his surname could be an abbreviation of the Hebrew letters "Lammed-Mem". But which word would in this manner be abbreviated? That question remains. Finally, a reader's letter in the *JFF*[15] is worth quoting: "The name *Lamm* does not always describe an animal, but in Boskowitz (Moravia) it demonstrably stemmed from 'lahm' ('lame'), a physical defect; similarly in Hollenschau *Schiff* was demonstrably not a house-sign, but developed out of 'schief' ('lop-sided'), equally indicating a physical defect." So there it is.

Schachne (pp. 232–233): It should be mentioned that Heinrich Flesch in the *JFF*[16] sees this as a colloquial name for "Schalom". The same opinion is put forward by R. Aharon ben Meir Gordon in his *"Sefer Even Meir"*:[17] "According to common opinion this is a cognomen ('Kinnui') for Schalom." "Schachnowitz", of course, is "Schachne's Son".

Moellin (p. 234): In *Year Book XIX* I had briefly quoted the generally current views about this name. It is now necessary, however, to refer to the *Jewish Encyclopedia*,[18] entry under "Moelln (Molin)": "One of the sons of Maharil is called simply 'Molin', after the name of his grandfather. 'Molin' is usually considered to be a pet name for 'Moses'; the correctness of this theory, however, is doubted by Salfeld ('Martyrologium', p. 406)." The father of the "Maharil" was indeed named Moses, and according to the theory now cited "Moellin" would be a patronymic. The diminutive suffix "lin" is, after all, to be found elsewhere, too, thus in Aberlin (little Abraham) or Isserlin (little Israel). For his part, Adolf Kober points out in *Jewish Names in the Era of the Enlightenment*[19] that (not only during the period of the Enlightenment but already much earlier) it had been Jewish usage to combine a person's name with that of his father in the manner that Jacob ben Moses simply became Jacob Moses' (genitive). On the basis of the material so far accessible, I am personally not in a position where I can prefer one opinion to the other.

Lehmann (p. 226): I had dealt with this name only in so far as it took the place of "Lämmle" in one specific case. Now, however, some more general observations are called for: Kessler explains this name, on the one hand,[20] as a derivation from "Levi" and, on the other hand,[21] as an "Exchange Name during the

---

[15] *JFF*, Issue 47, p. 888.

[16] *JFF*, Year II, No. 1, p. 111.

[17] Aharon ben Meir Gordon, *Sefer Even Meir al Sh'mot Gittin*, Pietrkow 1909.

[18] *Jewish Encyclopedia*, New York and London 1925, vol. VIII, p. 652.

[19] Adolf Kober, *Jewish Names in the Era of the Enlightenment*, in *Historica Judaica*, vol. V, No. 2, New York 1943. I am indebted to Professor Dr. Guido Kisch, Basel, one-time editor of *Historia Judaica*, for drawing my attention to this article.

[20] *Op. cit.*, pp. 24 and 97.

[21] *Op. cit.*, p. 107.

Period of Assimilation and Emancipation", the "exchange" suggested by him being for "Hanau", the historical or etymological reason for which he does not, however, give. Arthur Bab in the *JFF* [22] derives the name from "Lehnsmann" ("vassal"). As for myself, I had toyed with the idea that it was related to *Lachmann*, which I was inclined to consider a professional name, originating from "Lechem" ("bread"), consequently: a "bread merchant" or indeed a "baker". But this name *Lachmann* is so interesting that further views should be quoted. Arthur Bab writes in the *JFF* on two different occasions [23] that this was originally a person who lived near the "Lache", i.e., near the boundary or border, but definitely not someone who would always be prone to "lachen" ("laugh"). Rabbi Dr. Bernhard Brilling, however, in an essay published in *Yeda-Am*,[24] proves conclusively that in very many instances this name derived from "Nachman" (a Hebrew first name), the change from "N" to "L" having occurred because of a wrong pronunciation by a non-Jewish neighbour or official (acc.). Kessler[25] links "Lachmann" with Isaac and thus indeed with "laugh", because the Pentateuch[26] relates that the announcement of Isaac's birth and his birth itself were greeted with laughter.

Götz (p. 229): As regards this name, it is right to add that many authorities – including Kessler[27] – consider this a colloquial name for "Eljakim", developing out of "Gottschalk" as a translation of this particular Hebrew name. This is supported by Heinrich Flesch in the *JFF*.[28] Elsewhere, Kessler[29] lists "Götz" also under the heading of "Names sounding like Nobility" ("People giving themselves Airs"). As regards the surname *Gottesmann*, however, two contributions in the *JFF*[30] see this as a paraphrase for "Moses" ("The Man of God"), together with "Cosman" and "Coss"; and this is confirmed by Kessler.[31] But "Cosel" is considered by the latter[32] to be a place-name from the East German-Slavonic region.

Budge (p. 229): By way of supplement, reference may be made to the cognomen *Butche* which occurs among the Frankfurt family of the Schwarzschilds. Siegfried Schwarzschild comments on this as follows in the *JFF*:[33] "It might be difficult to substantiate this name etymologically. Neustadt is inclined to trace it back to the English 'butcher', the more so since this branch (of the family) was for a long time engaged in the privileged trade of butchers." As for myself, I am unable to come to a definite conclusion.

Bloch (pp. 230 and 234): Whereas Kessler[34] confirms the origin from the

---

[22] *JFF*, Issue 13, p. 22.
[23] *JFF*, Issue 11, p. 271, and Issue 14, p. 51.
[24] *Yeda-Am*, Tel Aviv, Issue 14/15 (1954), p. 233 (cf. also his note in *Yeda-Am*, Issue 11 [1953], p. 14 top).
[25] *Op. cit.*, pp. 20 and 62.
[26] Genesis 17:17; 18:12; 21:6.
[27] *Op. cit.*, p. 20.
[28] *JFF*, Year II, No. 1, p. 111.
[29] *Op. cit.*, p. 92.
[30] *JFF*, Double Issue 30/31, p. 473; and Issue 34, p. 543.
[31] *Op. cit.*, p. 21.
[32] *Op. cit.*, p. 40.
[33] *JFF*, Issue 18, p. 134.   [34] *Op. cit.*, p. 57.

Wallachei, Arthur Bab in the *JFF* [35] explains this name as an abbreviation for "Ben Levi Cohn"!

Wessely (p. 230): John J. Thal, New York, already quoted earlier, writes in his letter: "Vessely is 'merry' in Czech, and the surname 'Lustig' ('merry'), as well as Vessely or Wessely, is not a rare one in Bohemia and Austria." Kessler [36] traces the name back to an East German-Slavonic place-name, but he does not state what the place is actually called. As against this, he definitely derives [37] *Wessel* from the town of Wesel on the Lower Rhine. Louis Lamm in the *JFF* [38] thinks that the connection between *Wessely* and Wesel (as cited by us in *Year Book XIX*) is probable.

Schragenheim (p. 231): I have found a confirmation of the explanation for this name (as offered in *Year Book XIX*) – being a combination of Schragai and Chayim – in an article by Max Markreich in the *JFF*. [39]

Abt (p. 233): Gustav Samuel, in a specific essay, [40] derives this name from the town of Abterode in Westphalia. He adds that under a law dated 1808 the Jews in the then Kingdom of Westphalia were not permitted to choose place-names, and so they resorted to the subterfuge of changing these somewhat. (As another example for this "trend" he instances the "adaptation" of the town of Soest into names like "Sostheim" and "Sostberg". Incidentally, Kessler [41] merely lists "Sostmann" and "Soestmann", both of which he links with Süssmann and Süsskind.)

Munk (p. 229): As to the origin of this name I had quoted Japhet's and Kessler's alternative suggestions; the one traces it back to the town of Munkacs, the other to "Menachem" as a first name. Another correspondent, Dr. Julius Pfeiffer, Montreal, writes: "Many years ago, Michel Munk told me that this name goes back to the Greek 'Monachos', meaning 'monk', and therefore indicates that the holder is a Cohen." It is a fact that the Munks are Cohanim, and in reference to this point Gustav Samuel writes in the *JFF*: [42] "Since this cognomen is first mentioned in Prague non-Jewish documents, about the year 1500, as 'Munka', it is assumed that it is identical with the Slavonic word 'monk', thus also meaning a 'priest'. In any event, the origin of the name is non-Jewish." This view is, however, later contradicted in a reader's letter, [43] where the theory is upheld that it derives from "Menachem", because in Bohemia and Slovakia "the Jewish personal name of Menachem was commonly vulgarised to read Munko or Menko". Many Munkos, so the letter goes on, can be proven to be descendants of Akiba Kohen, who died about 1500 in Prague and who, according to an

[35] *JFF*, Issue 14, p. 53.

[36] *Op. cit.*, p. 42.

[37] *Op. cit.*, p. 52.

[38] *JFF*, Issue 24, p. 320.

[39] *JFF*, Issue 20, p. 204.

[40] Gustav Samuel, 'Die Namensgebung der westfälischen Judenschaft', in *Zeitschrift für die Geschichte der Juden in Deutschland*, VI (1935), pp. 47–51.

[41] *Op. cit.*, p. 20.

[42] *JFF*, Issue 46, p. 844.

[43] *JFF*, Issue 47, pp. 887–888.

existing document, was wont to sign his name thus: Akiba ben *Menachem* HaCohen.

Rappaport (p. 230): The interpretation as quoted in my earlier essay, namely, "Rofe miPorta" ("Physician from the Port"), is the one generally accepted. An alternative, viz., "Raven at the Port", has been rejected by most authorities. Dr. Julius Pfeiffer, Montreal, writes that he had, by chance, come across an article in *Jahrbuch für die Geschichte der Juden* (vol. 2, Leipzig 1861) by Livius Fuerst, 'Beiträge zur Geschichte der jüdischen Ärzte in Italien'. This mentions (pp. 347 ff.) a Jewish medical family named Porta Leone, four generations, who "from the father down to the great-grandson were the pride and the example of all their contemporaries and who made the name of Porta Leone one of the most honoured in Jewry". This correspondent poses the question whether Porta Leone might ultimately have been shortened simply into Porta, which could then have led to "Rappaport".

Sander (p. 229): As regards this name we had quoted the *Jüdisches Lexikon*, which considers it to be an abbreviation for "Syndikus". This point is taken up in a letter to me by Rabbi Dr. Bernhard Brilling, Münster: "In one case, in any event, the interpreter of names as cited by you has presumably been a victim of a printer's error. In my view, Syndikus had actually nothing to do with Sander at all, but related to *Sandek*, and the person concerned must have misread this."

II

For a fair number of names with which I was not concerned in *Year Book XIX* it has since been possible to discover interesting explanations, partly after following up individual enquiries, partly "fortuitously". In each case the results are now being reported; in part these are, yet again, only considered provisional ones.

Lewin: I was asked for an explanation of this name where its bearers are not Levites; in any event, it is a fact that many families Lewin do not belong to the Tribe of Levi. Kessler[44] understands this name, together with "Levin" and "Levien", as indeed deriving from "Levi" and makes no observations about non-Levites (though it must be remembered that "Levi" is also a *"general" first name*). The *JFF*[45] has two relevant readers' letters. According to the first of these, "Lewin" in the case of non-Levites would be equated with "Leib" (which statement needs only to be supplemented by the information that "Leib", together with "Löb", "Löwe" and similar names, is, on the basis of Jacob's blessing in Genesis, chapter 49, an allegorical cognomen for "Jehuda"). The second *JFF* contribution suggests a connection with the Talmudic scholar and "Stadt- und Oberlandrabbiner" of Berlin, Zwi ben Arye Löb Berlin (1721–1800). It goes on: "It is possible that colloquially 'Löb Berlin' was contracted into 'Lewin' (*Enc. Judaica*)." On the other hand, I once received the verbal

---

[44]*Op. cit.*, p. 55.
[45]*JFF*, Issue 47, p. 887; and Issue 48, p. 911.

"hint" that the name could go back to an Eastern place- or district-name, but Dr. Brilling[46] rejects this, in any event for Silesia.[47]

Lewek: Allied with this, an investigation of the surname *Lewek* suggests itself. A reader's letter in the *JFF*[48] refers to the thirteenth-century Jewish family name of "l'Eveske" = "Episcopus" ("Bishop"). It opines that this could, on the one hand, be a tribal name (of Levites) or, on the other hand, indicate a communal leader, because the term "Episcopus-Parnas" was used in an "old Cologne document". Contrasting with this view, a further reader's letter[49] states: "Leweck (with 'ck'), as an Eastern-Jewish name, is identical with 'Jehuda Loeb' in Polonised form" – which would establish a relationship to one of the explanations for "Lewin" as quoted above. Finally, Gustav Samuel in an article in the *JFF*[50] derives the name from "Levi", for "corresponding to the German diminutive syllables . . . chen, . . . lein are the Slavonic . . . ek, . . . ko: Lewek, Lewko" (acc.). Kessler does not list *Lewek* at all; he enumerates "Lewes", "Lewess" and "Lewitz",[51] all of which he links with "Levi"; besides these, he shows, separately,[52] "Levis" and "Lewis" as names in the genitive form (meaning: "of Levi"), together with dozens of other genitives, such as Abeles, Isserles, Jacobs, Jeiteles, etc.

Rosenbaum: Kessler[53] includes this name in his group of "Artificial Names patterned on Ancient Jewish Mothers' Names," together with many others which all start with "Rosen" (this mother's name would be "Rose" or "Rosa"). In a reader's letter in the *JFF*[54] it is considered "noteworthy that the bearers (of this name) are all Levites", and the question is put: "Was there perhaps a general designation, meanwhile fallen into oblivion, for the first-born of the Levites – possibly Rosh B'Am?" "Rosh B'Am" would mean "First among the People", but to me personally it seems an artificial term and somewhat far-fetched. Be that as it may, that particular correspondent declines to acknowledge any botanical connotation of "Rosenbaum". His assertions led to several further readers' letters.[55] One of these observes that certain Rosenbaums who come from Moravia and Bohemia bear the additional name of "Letsch" as a name of origin and are all Levites; on the other hand, it finds that this is also a house-name, viz., "House with the Rose-Tree". Another letter reads: "I know of many Rosenbaum families who are not Levites. I also am acquainted with Christians called Rosenbaum." Both these last statements are correct.

Ballin: It is fascinating to register the views concerning the origin of this name. Jakob Moritz Ballin writes in the *JFF*[56] that its original Hebrew spelling

---

[46]Bernhard Brilling, 'Schlesische Ortsnamen als jüdische Familiennamen', in *Zeitschrift für Ostforschung*, XV, Marburg 1966, p. 62: "Equally, the well-known Jewish name of Lewin has nothing to do with the township of the same name in the Earldom of Glatz."

[47]It is of some interest to note how Basil Cottle, *The Penguin Dictionary of Surnames*, Harmondsworth 1967, p. 167, explains the *British* family name "Lewin": He derives it from an Old English first name meaning "dear/loved friend". In German, the corresponding term would be "Lieber Freund", "Lieber Mann" or simply "Lieber".

[48]*JFF*, Issue 27, p. 404. [49]*JFF*, Issue 28, p. 427.

[50]*JFF*, Issue 46, p. 845. [51]*Op. cit.*, p. 97.

[52]*Op. cit.*, p. 62. [53]*Op. cit.*, p. 88.

[54]*JFF*, Issue 25, p. 348. [55]*JFF*, Issue 26, p. 375.

[56]*JFF*, Year II, No. 1, pp. 113–114.

(unvocalised) Beth-Lammed-Yud-Nun could be read either as "Ballin" or as "Blin". He traces the name back to the township of Belin in Southern France, not far from Bordeaux, because "Jewish families used to live there". At the same time, he opposes the idea of any connection with the city of Berlin. Confirmation is forthcoming in a later article by Gustav Samuel;[57] he, too, derives the name from the township in Southern France and considers it "a good example of the transformation that place-names underwent when written in Hebrew letters". According to him, all bearers of this name are Levites, but "the branch of the family that remained in Worms spells its name as 'Bluen' or 'Blün' ". Kessler differs from this; he writes:[58] "It has been widely assumed that 'Ballin' is a Polish or a Southern French place; both explanations are disputable, the more so since the family is to be found – already in the seventeenth century – in North-Western Germany, including Hamburg-Altona." How does Kessler, then, explain the name? With a big question-mark he catalogues it[59] under "Professional Names – Eastern Jewish Trades", as devolving out of the (late) Hebrew word "Balan" as a translation of "Bader" (public baths' attendant).

Berlak: This Jewish family name may serve almost as a test-case to show how widely opinions can diverge or how quite different circumstances attending the origins could eventually lead to the same surnames. Kessler[60] spells it with "ck" ("Berlack") and offers this explanation: "A buffoon, according to Karl Buecher, *Die Berufe der Stadt Frankfurt im Mittelalter*, p. 28: berlocker." However, Paul Kalisch in the *JFF*[61] puts forward the theory that the name is an abbreviation of "Ben Reb Leib Kalischer"; as he writes, his ancestor, R. Jehuda Löb Kalischer, was a well-known scholar and Talmudist. None the less, it is necessary to make this qualification here: it is feasible that this abbreviation does not go back to the named Jehuda Loeb (eighteenth and nineteenth century) but rather to the earlier R. Arye Löb Kalischer, author of the learned work *Gur Arye*, who had died in Amsterdam in 1709. A third possibility must also be considered, namely, a derivation from "Berl"; and so far as this name "Berl" itself is concerned, Kessler[62] contradicts himself: On the one hand, he postulates a diminutive form of "Bär" and thus of "Issachar" (see our own remarks, above, about "Bär"), on the other hand he holds that it is an abbreviation of "Ben Rabbi Leser". This would close the circle again, for instead of "Rabbi Leser" one might just as well postulate "Rabbi Leib". Finally, "Berles" – in order that no chances are ignored – is shown by Kessler[63] as a genitive form of "Bär" or "Berl", together with "Berels".

Brann: All opinions coincide that this is an abbreviation: "Ben Rabbi N. (Nachman, Nathan, etc.)".[64] On this point it is of considerable historical interest to quote from a reader's letter by Julius Brann in the *JFF*:[65] "According to oral tradition . . . the name 'Brann' is an abbreviation – initials of 'Bnei Reb Nechemje Nemirow' ('Sons of Reb Nechemje from Nemirow'). This Reb

[57]*JFF*, Issue 46, p. 846.   [58]*Op. cit.*, p. 52.
[59]*Op. cit.*, p. 69.   [60]*Op. cit.*, p. 67.
[61]*JFF*, Issue 40, p. 715.   [62]*Op. cit.*, pp. 20 and 61.
[63]*Op. cit.*, p. 62.   [64]Kessler, *op. cit.*, p. 61.
[65]*JFF*, Issue 22, p. 264.

Nechemje is said to have fled, as the sole survivor of Nemirow, from the Cossacks' pogrom of 1648 and to have sought safety in the monastery at Rawitsch. There he received permission to engage in trade and to settle."

Bunem: Evidently, this is a Hebrew male first name; as a surname it is rare. It frequently goes together with "Simcha". I was of the opinion that this was a mutilated "Benjamin", and this is indeed the explanation put forward by Kessler [66] and by Walther Meyer in the *JFF*.[67] But it is contradicted by other contributions in the *JFF*. For one, Heinrich Flesch [68] considers it to be literally a nick-name for "Simcha", as a derivation from "bon homme" ("good man"). Secondly, the same Walther Meyer (!) writes elsewhere in the *JFF*: [69] "'Simcha' in Hebrew means joy or something joyous, something good. The Latin word 'bonum' has the same meaning. In Judaeo-German, Bonum becomes Bunem or Bunim . . . There is no reason to derive 'Bunem' from the French 'bon homme'; French was at that time not yet the *lingua franca* of Europe's intelligentsia, this was Latin." In this way the theories once again clash, and still more striking is the fact that the same author offers two differing explanations on separate occasions.

Charlap: This name (widely known, incidentally, as the name of a street in Jerusalem) is interpreted in two essays in the *JFF*[70] as an abbreviation of "Chiya Rosh L'galil Polen" ("Chiya, district leader of Poland"). As is expounded there at some length, the Charlap family is a clan of the Spanish-Portuguese House of Ibn-Jachya who consider themselves descendants of King David, the lineage going back through Gaonim, Exilarchs, Amoraim and Tannaim. According to those *JFF* contributions, this Chiya lived during the eleventh and twelfth centuries and could well have emigrated from the Iberian Peninsula to Poland. The author of both essays, Benzion Don Jachia-Donchin, is inclined to the view, however, that a migration to Poland was hardly likely; instead, he suggests reading "Portugal" in place of "Polen" in the abbreviation. But elsewhere in the *JFF*[71] Otto Neumann proposes the abbreviation "Chiya Rosh *L'goley* (not L'galil) Polen" – that is, "leader of the *exiles* to Poland". Kessler does not mention the name at all.

Ginsberg, Günzburg, etc.: This is commonly held to be a place-name (name of origin), i.e., from Günzburg on the Danube (near Augsburg); thus Kessler,[72] and Otto Neumann in the *JFF*[73] agrees with it "in many cases". But then he adds that Königsberg in East Prussia was, in former times, colloquially called Ginsberg, and therefore that town could also be considered the place of origin. In a later reader's letter in the *JFF*[74] the same author adduces a further source in support of a derivation from Königsberg. From this follows this "hierarchy" of the name in jargon: Königsberg – Kinsberg – Ginsberg. The connection with Königsberg finds the agreement of Dr. Wilfred Cohn Hulse,[75] is rejected in a

[66] *Op. cit.*, p. 18.
[67] *JFF*, Issue 49, pp. 914 and 916.
[68] *JFF*, Year II, No. 1, p. 112.
[69] *JFF*, Issue 48, p. 893, n. 2.
[70] *JFF*, Issue 11, pp. 262–263; and Double Issue 30/31, p. 458.
[71] *JFF*, Issue 32, p. 494.
[72] *Op. cit.*, pp. 35 and 49.
[73] *JFF*, Issue 32, p. 495, n. 1.
[74] *JFF*, Issue 36, p. 624.
[75] *JFF*, Issue 47, p. 869.

reader's letter,[76] and is then, once more, taken up by Otto Neumann in a further reader's letter.[77] He insists on Königsberg, but then he does admit: "Thus Ginsburg belongs to those names which have a double origin." Members of the family can, therefore, "choose" whence they hail.

Heschel: The *"Sefer Even Meir"* [78] sees this name as a cognomen (Kinnui) for "Joshua" (acc.), and this is confirmed by Kessler.[79] It is, in fact, a diminutive form of "Joshua"; and it might be explained, here, that in a number of diminutive names, where the suffix "el" or simple "l" was added, the first syllable of the original name was omitted ("swallowed"). In this case, the syllable "Jo" – more exactly: "Jeho" – was dropped; other similar examples would be "Seckel" for "(I)saac" and "Koppel" for "(Ja)kob". Yet, as regards this "Heschel" a further hypothesis ought to be mentioned, viz., that it could also have developed from "Heskel"; this latter name is derived by Kessler [80] from "Jecheskiel" – to which finally must be added his derivation [81] of "Haskel" from "Hoshea".

London: This is indeed to be found among Jewish family names, and the obvious suggestion is to link it with the British metropolis. Kessler does not list it. Nevertheless, a different suggestion in the *JFF* [82] should also be noted, according to which the name could also have derived from "Lamdam" ("teacher" or "scholar"). And yet, this is rejected out of hand in a reader's letter in the *JFF*,[83] which states: "Demonstrably there exist connections with London." Besides this one, the Jewish surname *Landy* occurs not infrequently in England and America; again, this does not appear in Kessler's lists. I am inclined to see it as an "anglicised" version of "Landau" (the town in the Palatinate).

Rothensüss: This is a strange name, very occasionally to be found among Hessian Jews. Not surprisingly, Kessler does not list it. It is an arbitrary or chance-name, pure and simple. I was once given its history by one of its bearers. Subsequently I discovered that the story is told by Heinrich Loewe in the *JFF*,[84] and as a good illustration of what was actually possible, it may be quoted here in a literal translation: "There, in Witzenhausen, one Moshe or Avrom was obliged, after all, to go to the Maire, in order to be allocated a family name. But however much he racked his brains as to what to call himself, no nice name would occur to him. Then he had an idea. The head of the commission was an educated man. When this person would ask him how he wanted to be called, he would reply that the other should make a guess. He would then hear from him a number of different names, and he would pick the nicest of them, saying that 'this is the one I have chosen'. So, after his arrival and on being asked the expected question, he said: '*Herr Landrat, roten Sie's*' (in Hessian jargon: 'Sir, you guess it'). To this the official immediately replied 'Rothensüss, ah well, that is a nice name'; and in this way the family received the name of Rothensüss." Thus Heinrich Loewe. This story reminded me of an uncle of mine called *Lindenbaum* whom I had, as a youngster, once questioned as to the origin of his name; he, too, was a native of Hessen. The explanation was a similar one, though not quite so "funny": Again, one Jacob was summoned to appear before the

[76]*JFF*, Issue 48, p. 912.　[77]*JFF*, Issue 49, p. 936.　[78]See above, n. 17.

[79]*Op. cit.*, p. 22.　[80]*Op. cit.*, p. 18.　[81]*Op. cit.*, p. 22.

[82]*JFF*, Issue 46, p. 862.　[83]*JFF*, Issue 47, p. 888.　[84]*JFF*, Issue 12, p. 275.

commission, and he, too, could not think of a suitable name at all. Helplessly, he looked about him, until he beheld, through the window of the room, the big linden tree which stood in the courtyard of the town hall; and with a sigh of relief he quickly answered: "Lindenbaum".

Schick, Schik, Schück: None of these names has an entry in Kessler's book. Lavoslav Sik explains in the *JFF*[85] that we have here an abbreviation for "Shem Yisrael Kodesh" ("a name in Israel is hallowed"), because once a pious Jew had refused to adopt a civic name; he did not wish to bear a name other than the one given him at his circumcision. Consequently, he replied to the messengers of the authorities: "Schik – Shem Yisrael Kodesh", and those messengers took the acrostic to be the answer. In a reader's letter elsewhere in the *JFF*,[86] however, the name is explained – on the authority of the *Jewish Encyclopedia* – as an abbreviation of "Schemuel Juda Katzenellenbogen".[87] A further reader's letter,[88] for its part, rejects both abbreviations, for "the family name of Schik has existed in Prague already in 1552"; but no different explanation is suggested by the writer of that letter.

Spitz, Spitzer: Three readers' letters in the *JFF*[89] vouchsafe varying explanations for these names, as follows: (a) After the pointed hat ("*Spitzhut*") which Jews in Germany were forced to wear during the Middle Ages, as is clearly shown in a number of contemporary illustrations; (b) as a name of origin, from Spitz on the Danube; (c) as a name of origin from Spitz in Lower Austria (the same place?): "These families have since their expulsion from Lower Austria (in 1671) resided in Moravia and Hungary, but not in Steiermark; the Spitzers of Croatia can be traced back to Hungary." Kessler[90] on the one hand derives the name, without specifying details, from the "East German-Slavonic Colonial Regions and Poland" and, on the other hand, from the Polish word "Zips" (what does it mean?), but this would only be possible as a result of a shifting of the consonants (or reading the word backwards).

Seligmann: In one respect this kind of shifting of consonants could, equally, have occurred in this widespread Jewish name; at least, it might be a matter for debate. To begin with, Kessler must again be consulted; according to him,[91] this "Germanised Hebrew Name" stands for "Baruch", "Ascher" and "occasionally also for Abieser, Gerson, Isaac, Josua and Pinchas". The derivation of "Seligmann" from "Isaac" has become widely known for one particular reason, which was that the famous "Würzburger Rav", R. Seligmann Bär Bamberger (1807–1878) bore the Hebrew names Yitzchak Dov. Only the derivation from Isaac can be briefly touched upon here, because it might be concluded from a statement in the previously quoted *Sefer Even Meir*[92] that a shifting of consonants might indeed have happened here, following this line of development: Isaac – Seckel[93] – Seleck (at this stage the shift of consonants occurs) – Seligmann. No final decision seems, however, to be indicated.

---

[85]*JFF*, Issue 13, p. 6. [86]*JFF*, Issue 42, p. 783.
[87]On Katzenellenbogen, see *LBI Year Book XIX* (1974), pp. 234–235. R. Schemuel Juda Katzenellenbogen was the father of the Jewish "King for One Night" of Poland, Saul Wahl.
[88]*JFF*, Issue 44, p. 815. [89]*JFF*, Issue 26, p. 375.
[90]*Op. cit.*, pp. 42 and 57. [91]*Op. cit.*, p. 20.
[92]See above, n. 17. [93]See above, under "Heschel".

Selka, Seldis: Kessler[94] derives "Selka" and "Selke" from "Salomon", and for "Selka" alone he offers[95] the alternative derivation from "Seligmann". However, Heinrich Loewe's references to this matter in the *JFF*[96] are noteworthy: Firstly, as he reports, a family tradition traces the name "Selka" back to an ancestress named "Suleika". Admitting that this would not be impossible, he nevertheless points out that the Old German word "Salida", meaning "good fortune", had been used, like Glückel or Glückchen, as a Jewish female name. In Middle High German, "Salida" developed into "Selde", the corresponding Slavonic form of endearment being "Selka" or "Sylka", and in this manner Heinrich Loewe offers an entirely different explanation for "Selka", as well as for the surname "Seldis".

Wasserzug: Kessler[97] sees this as a designation of a trade, i.e., "like Badeknecht (servant in baths)". In a reader's letter in the *JFF*[98] the question is put (which then remained unanswered) whether in relation to this name it would be right to think of Moses ("For I pulled him from the water"[99]). It is further asked there whether the name *Wassermann* could have the same origin. Kessler explains the latter name, of course; additionally he has[100] *Wasserreich* as a "Galician Derogatory Name".

Weil: In this as well as in slightly deviating spelling, this name has been normally considered as one of origin, namely, from Weilderstadt; even though not expressly so related, this seems to be also Kessler's view.[101] A tradition among some families of this name who are Levites tends, however, towards an entirely different explanation. Dr. Julius Pfeiffer, Montreal, writes in his letter: "My late father-in-law, Rav Dr. H. L. Weyl, Düsseldorf, mentioned often that, especially in Alsace, 'Levi' became 'Weil' by means of metathesis." This, then, is again a shifting of consonants. Arthur Bab in the *JFF*[102] puts forward a similar opinion: "Weil or Weill has nothing to do with a Weiler ('hamlet') but must be seen as developing out of the second syllable of Lewi, with the first syllable then attached to it in a reversed order of letters." The same is stated by Gustav Samuel elsewhere:[103] "By changing the order of letters 'Lewie' became Weile in Schlochau (West Prussia) and Weil in Cologne." He adds this relevant information: "These Cologne Weils, who are Levites, are to be clearly distinguished from the widespread South German family of the same name, whose uninterrupted descent can be traced through seventeen generations, right up to their ancestor, R. Jaakov Weil from Weilderstadt on the Neckar, 1380–1456."

Wollheim: Kessler does not list this name. He only has[104] "Wollmann" and "Wollner" as tradesmen's names (i.e., "wool man" and "wool dealer") and[105] "Wollstein(er)" as a name of origin from Eastern Germany. About *Wollheim* Otto Neumann writes in a reader's letter in the *JFF*:[106] "At first sight one is

[94]*Op. cit.*, p. 23.   [95]*Op. cit.*, p. 20.
[96]*JFF*, Issue 12, pp. 276–277.
[97]*Op. cit.*, p. 70 ("Wasserzug"); also as an "environmental name" ("Wassermann"), p. 59.
[98]*JFF*, Issue 34, p. 560.   [99]Exodus 2:10.
[100]*Op. cit.*, p. 79.   [101]*Op. cit.*, p. 36.
[102]*JFF*, Issue 14, p. 53.   [103]*JFF*, Issue 46, p. 845.
[104]*Op. cit.*, p. 73.   [105]*Op. cit.*, p. 42.
[106]*JFF*, Issue 34, p. 560.

almost sure that this is a place-name; but this is not the case, there is no place called Wollheim. What could, therefore, be the origin of the name? My assumption is that it derives from the Russian district of Wolhynia which borders on Galicia. It was difficult to form a name out of the strangely sounding Wolhynia (Wolhynien). Wollheim was made out of it, for this was easier to pronounce."

Hahle, Hahlo: Kessler[107] derives this name from the town of Halle, basing himself on the book, well known at the time, by Dr. Rudolf Hallo which deals with the history of his family.[108] But a completely different view is put forward by Gustav Samuel in his specific essay already quoted above;[109] he considers the name "Hahlo" to be an "amalgamation" of "Heinemann Salomon" by means of swallowing whole syllables, as was not unusual in Westphalia. As another example of this sort he cites "Benfey", as a fusion of "Benedikt Feybusch", and this latter theory finds its confirmation by Kessler.[110] Whether the fairly frequent Jewish surnames *Heller* and *Hellmann* are related to the ones just examined is a moot point. As to *Heller*, one immediately tends to think of the famous *Tossafot Yomtov*, R. Yomtov Lipmann Heller (born 1579), whose family bore this surname already in the sixteenth century. However, Kessler[111] does not derive this surname *Heller* from Halle, but from Hall (Schwäbisch-Hall?), while for *Hellmann* he offers two different alternatives,[112] both of which remain to be proven: On the one hand, he sees this as a Germanised "Samuel", on the other hand as a mutilated place-name, viz., "Hamburg".

Kugelmann: Kessler[113] groups this under "Nicknames or Derogatory Names", whereas Gustav Samuel[114] plumps for a connection with the Kugelsberg, near Volkmarsen, Westphalia. Quite a difference of opinion here!

Robitschek: This is an infrequent name, and Kessler does not give it. A member of this family once told me that the name had developed out of "Reb Yitzchak".

And this brings the further investigation of individual names to an end, for the present. May it be emphasised once more that, of course, there can never be a real "end" to it. Numerous other names, some no less fascinating, have again remained unmentioned, because they have long since received adequate explanation.

III

To conclude, some further remarks about the Jewish "King for One Night", Saul Wahl,[115] seem indicated. As regards his family name *Katzenellenbogen*, which originates from the township of Katzenelnbogen (meaning: "Melibocus of the Chatten"), Gustav Samuel[116] observes that this place was called "Catti-melibocus" in certain Latin documents. Katz Castle ("Burg Katz") on the

[107]*Op. cit.*, p. 49.
[108]Dr. Rudolf Hallo, *Geschichte der Familie Hallo*, Kassel 1930.
[109]See above, n. 40.
[110]*Op. cit.*, p. 60.
[111]*Op. cit.*, p. 35.
[112]*Op. cit.*, pp. 21 and 96.
[113]*Op. cit.*, p. 75.
[114]See above, n. 40.
[115]See above, n. 87.
[116]See above, n. 40.

Rhine, not very far away, is similarly named after the Germanic tribe of the Chatten. I did not know the meaning of the name of the mountain – Melibocus – until yet another correspondent, Dr. Alfred E. Laurence, Isle of Wight, wrote to me as follows: ". . . I am an old Melibocus admirer and was told – some 45 years ago – that this old name goes back to the days of the Roman Limes and stands for 'Black Forest', deriving from a Greek and Roman melange of terms as possibly used by legionnaires."

The *JFF* has two contributions on the subject of Saul Wahl's "kingship", one from the pen of Max Wollsteiner[117] – who later, in 1930, published in book form a genealogical survey and summary of the whole Katzenellenbogen clan – and in a later issue by Arthur Kronthal.[118] Their versions of the story concerning this "kingship" diverge only in minor details; the major (legendary) episode is described alike by both of them. As a contribution to the question – so far unsolved – whether the story could be true, the following may be quoted from Wollsteiner's article: "Professor Berschadski, of Petersburg University, basing himself on documents, some of them written, others printed, has shown that Saul Wahl was without doubt the most important Jew of Lithuania and Poland . . . Berschadski asserts that Saul's 'kingship for one day' belongs to the realm of legend. Yet there exist a large number of very solid publications in which the contrary is being asserted." Wollsteiner is not inclined to accept the negative conclusion out of hand, and therefore he continues: "A great-grandson of Saul Wahl, Moses Katzenellenbogen, Rabbi of Schwabach in Bavaria, born 1670, died 1733, in a manuscript which is now in the Oxford Royal Library,[119] has described the circumstances attending the election as king in great detail and very vividly. It goes without saying that there must be some truth in this 'election' " – but here his own conclusion is not absolutely convincing, rather is his reasoning as follows: "For otherwise the great-grandson would not have been in a position to describe so thoroughly the exact circumstances of the election. Not so many years had yet elapsed since Saul Wahl's death that a legend could already have arisen. Apart from this manuscript, the definitive work about Saul Wahl is presumably a publication in Hebrew by Hirsch Edelmann which appeared in London in the fifties of the last century; its title is *Gedullath Shaul*, and it gathers together everything that has become known about Saul Wahl. In general, I may say that the Christian historians do not mention Saul Wahl at all, whilst the Jewish historians make at least some mention of him . . ."

The editor of the *JFF*, Arthur Czellitzer, adds the following by way of supplement:[120] "Already in 1884 I heard from an old lady who was a descendant of Saul Wahl on her mother's side, to my great amazement, the story of his election as King of Poland; and I was impressed by her pride in the role which her ancestor had played, a role that, after all, was only that of a stop-gap, provided that the events were, altogether, in accordance with what has been claimed by tradition."

[117] *JFF*, Year I, No. 4, pp. 74 ff.
[118] *JFF*, Issue 6, pp. 1 30 ff.
[119] Max Wollsteiner refers here, of course, to the Bodleian Library.
[120] *JFF*, Year I, No. 4, p. 77.

Arthur Kronthal writes in a footnote to his own article:[121] "In the course of the years, the writer has been apprised of close on six different versions of the story of Saul Wahl. He has been most deeply impressed by the above quoted version, which he first heard in 1867 from Mr. Merzbach, a teacher of religion in Posen. This version may also be found in the excellent critical collection of all the most important legendary material concerning Saul Wahl from the pen of Rabbi Professor Dr. Philipp Bloch, an eminent authority in the fields of both philosophy and Jewish history. His work appeared, under the title of 'Die Sage von Saul Wahl, dem Eintagskönig von Polen', in the *Zeitschrift der Historischen Gesellschaft für die Provinz Posen*.[122]

An intriguing story like this legend of Saul Wahl might tempt certain romanticists to accept it as truth, and some of his descendants might be forgiven if they follow a similar line. However, nothing so far produced or discovered enables us to take the episode of his "kingship" out of the realm of legend. When I, personally, first dealt with this subject in 1970[123] I relied, in addition to Max Wollsteiner, on *De'ath K'doshim*, a work by Israel Tobia Eisenstadt, a nineteenth-century cantor, researcher and author in Rozana. He, too, was not able to adduce any proof, whereas the fact that Saul Wahl was highly esteemed and a great scholar and leader has been established – but this alone does not constitute secular "kingship".

[121]*JFF*, Issue 6, p. 131, n. 1.

[122]Vol. IV, pp. 234–258 (1889). Cf. also: Rychlicki, 'Zur Sage von Saul Wahl', *ibid.*, vol. V, p. 194 (1890).

[123]In: *Allgemeine jüdische Wochenzeitung*, Düsseldorf, 30th January 1970.

Gottfried Semper and German Synagogue Architecture

BY HELEN ROSENAU

Gottfried Semper (1803–1879)[*] was a great, versatile and internationally minded architect and writer. Born in Altona, he moved to Dresden where he lived from 1834 to 1849 and there got involved in the Revolution of 1849, fighting on the barricades. In this way his fate was similar to Richard Wagner's who was also one of the Dresden revolutionaries. Both friends were forced to leave Germany. Semper fled, stayed some time in Paris and then worked in London from 1851 to 1855. He became Professor of Architecture at the Zürich Eidgenössische Technische Hochschule from 1855 to 1871, a progressive poly-technic-like institution, and then lived in Italy until his death in Rome.[1] A Protestant, he was commissioned in 1838 to build the Dresden Synagogue in 1839 and 1840, the rabbi in charge of the congregation being the famous Zach-arias Frankel who kept a middle course between Reformers and Conservatives.[2] The synagogue was built in a prominent position near the Elbe, outside the ancient Jewish quarter. It was destroyed by the Nazis in 1938.

In Semper's period Jewish architects were exceptional. This was due to the fact that, although Jews had excelled in the crafts during the Middle Ages and up to the Emancipation, the guilds remained closed to them.[3] It was a big step to enter a profession that required specialised training and wide social contacts.

One such Jewish architect was Albert[4] (possibly the equivalent of Abraham) Rosengarten (1809–1893) who was an assistant to the Christian architect

[*]It is a pleasant duty to thank the authorities of the Semper Archiv of the Eidgenössische Technische Hochschule Zürich, Professor A. M. Vogt, Mr. Martin Fröhlich and Mrs. Christina Reble. I also wish to thank Hanspeter Rebsamen for his generous help, as well as the authorities of the various Zürich Archives. Mrs. Zipora Halpern of the Israelitische Kultusgemeinde in Zürich, Mr. D. L. Paisey of the British Library and Mr. Helmut Eschwege, Dresden, were most helpful and the Wiener Library and the British Library were as usual the source for study of the relevant books. Without them the present essay could not have been undertaken. I am also indebted to Miss Bertha Cohn, London, for help in deciphering some difficult words and to the Zürich and Dresden authorities for providing photographs.

Part of this study has been delivered as a paper at the Conference of the Association of Art Historians in London in March 1977.

[1]The literature on Semper is immense. The most important recent publication is Martin Fröh-lich, *Gottfried Sempers Zeichnerischer Nachlass an der ETH Zürich*, 1974. On Dresden the thorough work of F. Löffler, *Das alte Dresden*, Dresden 1955, is to be recommended. On Dresden Jewry see A. Diamant, *Chronik der Juden in Dresden*, Darmstadt 1973. Cf. also Adolf Max Vogt, Christina Regle, Martin Frohlich (eds.), *Gottfried Semper und die Mitte des neunzehnten Jahrhunderts*, Basel–Stuttgart 1976.

[2]Harold Hammer-Schenk, *Untersuchungen zum Synagogenbau in Deutschland*, Diss. Tübingen 1974, is excellent and supersedes the relevant parts of Rachel Wischnitzer, *The Architecture of the European Synagogue*, Philadelphia 1964, *passim*. On the intellectual background see D. Philipson, *The Reform Movement in Judaism*, New York 1907.

[3]Mark Wischnitzer, *A History of Jewish Crafts and Guilds*, New York 1965.

[4]On names cf. Georg Herlitz and Bruno Kirchner, *Jüdisches Lexikon*, Berlin 1930, under 'Namen der Juden' and 'Namensgesetzgebung der Juden', pp. 383 ff.

August Schuchardt (1820–1889) although his senior by eleven years. This may well reflect the sociological situation in Germany, where it was easier for a Jew to work as an assistant than as a principal. Rosengarten had decided views on synagogue architecture, pointing out that the association between Jews and Egyptians had not been all that happy in the past and therefore Egyptian forms should be avoided. (They had earlier been introduced by Weinbrenner into his Karlsruhe Synagogue.) More important, Jews now lived in modern times and a new approach to synagogue architecture had to be developed. This led to a modest but pleasing synagogue building in Kassel between 1834 and 1839, erected in a semi-Classical style combined with semi-Gothic ornamentation.[5]

In England the situation was different: David Mocatta (1806–1882) is well remembered as a builder of railway stations and as an expert connected with the building of the West London Synagogue between 1866 and 1870. As to George Basevi, a Christian convert (1794–1845), he became a church architect and was to die as the result of an accident, falling from the spire of Ely Cathedral.[6]

To return to Semper: his Dresden Synagogue developed a new type, which moulded the public image of synagogues for at least a century. The building was flanked by two towers in front, surmounted at a later date by the Star of David, and had a tower in the centre which was covered by a tent-like octagonal roof, a form not to be confused with a dome. To gain space the Synagogue was provided with double galleries and for reasons of economy it had a timber ceiling. The centralised shape of the structure made it particularly fitting for Jewish worship around a central *bimah* or platform and allowed easily for galleries for women. Although he was not averse to using historical forms, he believed in adapting them to new usages. He felt that a tower over the crossing, influenced by Byzantine or Romanesque art, would be suitable for synagogue building. Furthermore, several drawings exist in Dresden,[7] which show elevations and the side tower in a more monumental form, reminiscent of a campanile. It is surmounted by the Star of David, which gained popularity in Jewish religious decoration at this time, thus foreshadowing Semper's later Paris synagogue designs.

The architect felt that these designs combined aesthetic satisfaction with religious solemnity. Semper's interest in the scheme was such that he personally designed all the fittings: a drawing for a lamp, a free adaptation of the Moorish style, is preserved in the Semper Archive of the Eidgenössische Technische Hochschule in Zürich; and one for the Ark in the Institut für Denkmalspflege, Dresden.[8] The latter shows the two Tablets of the Law as well as a surmounting Star of David. Enclosures and a gateway were added on the South side of the

[5]Hammer-Schenk, *op. cit.*, *passim*. See the present writer in 'German Synagogues in the Early Period of Emancipation', in *LBI Year Book VIII* (1963), pp. 214 ff.
[6]V. D. Lipman (ed.), *Three Centuries of Anglo-Jewish History*, Cambridge 1961, p. 74 on Mocatta. Cf. also the pamphlet by A. S. Diamond, *The Building of a Synagogue*, London 1970, p. 7, and H. M. Colvin, *A Biographical Dictionary of British Architects*, London 1954, p. 63.
[7]Kind information from Mr. Martin Fröhlich, Zürich and Mr. Helmut Eschwege, Dresden. There are prints and drawings for the Paris synagogue also in Dresden.
[8]Gottfried Semper, *Der Stil in den Technischen und Tektonischen Künsten*. Frankfurt and Stuttgart 1860–1863. The lamp is reproduced in vol. II, p. 57.

synagogue at a later date. The latter bears the inscription: "Mine house shall be called an house of prayer for all peoples" (Isaiah 56:7).

Semper's Synagogue foreshadows some ideas expressed in his writings on the theme of Protestant church architecture: Protestantism was for him akin to Judaism, while Catholic architecture, based on the basilica, was opposed to the ideal of a place of worship concentrated on the sermon.[9] For this reason he advocated a square plan and a large narthex or ante-nave suitable for worship.

The Dresden Synagogue influenced many other synagogue buildings that adopted the "Roman-Moorish" decorations, the centralised plan and the low tent-like roof. They thus seemed vaguely, though not specifically, ancient and oriental, reminiscent of the eastern origin of the Jewish religion. This is a significant fact in a period of political and social emancipation, as it expresses self-assurance and communal pride.[10]

Semper's Synagogue was popular with the Jews in Dresden and widely acclaimed. It was not so much copied as used as a partial model. Otto Simonson, Semper's pupil, built the well-known Leipzig Synagogue dedicated in 1855; it incorporated a timber ceiling, two tiers of galleries, side towers and Moorish detailing. Several letters by Simonson are found in the Semper Archive in Zürich. They request Semper's professional patronage; one, of the 22nd September 1853, states that the fact that he was incidentally (*zufälligerweise*) Jewish did not help him with the Jewish community, and that he had beaten four competitors; this, we may add, in spite of, or perhaps because of, his Jewishness.[11]

Among Semper's patrons had been the banker Martin Wilhelm or Wilhelm Martin Oppenheim (*c.* 1800–1863), who had come from Berlin to Dresden, according to the Dresden Directory of 1840. At any rate, he lived in Dresden and Semper executed for him two important buildings in a Neo-Renaissance style, the Villa Rosa of 1839 and a city mansion, the Palais Oppenheim, of 1845–1848. The name Wilhelm, so popular in the Prussian Royal family, suggests Oppenheim's Prussian origin. That he was on intimate terms with the Foulds and acquainted with the Rothschilds in Paris is attested by his letters to Baron James de Rothschild and to Semper of 1849, printed below. The fact that Oppenheim mentions the two buildings of which he was the patron, without revealing to the Rothschilds that they were built for him, may be due to the fact that the former were noted for their Jewish loyalties and that both Oppenheim and his wife Rosa were converts to Protestantism. With regard to Rosa Oppenheim this is clear from the inscription on her funerary monument in the Protestant Trinitatis Cemetery of Dresden, designed by Gottfried Semper, which states that she was born on Good Friday 1792 and died on 4th June 1849. The monument is adorned by a medallion in Neo-Classical style with a portrait in profile by the

---

[9]See Gottfried Semper, *Kleine Schriften*, Basel and Stuttgart 1884, especially 'Über den Bau Evangelischer Kirchen', pp. 443 ff., Leipzig 1845, and 'Noch etwas über den St. Nikolai-Kirchenbau', pp. 468 ff. (*Neue Hamburgische Blätter*, 1845.) On the importance of the sermon in Judaism in the nineteenth century cf. Alexander Altmann, 'Zur Frühgeschichte der jüdischen Predigt in Deutschland: Leopold Zunz als Prediger', in *LBI Year Book VI* (1961), pp. 3–59.
[10]Hammer-Schenk, *op. cit.*, p. 392 and *passim*.
[11]Cf. O. Simonson, *Der Neue Tempel in Leipzig*, Berlin 1858.

then famous sculptor Ernst Rietschel. It shows an intelligent and distinctly Jewish-looking profile.[12]

At any rate the relationship with the Baron de Rothschild, who seems to have been quite unmoved by the appeal, appears cool, while the tone with regard to the Fould banking family is friendly. Members of that family, like the Heines, were highly assimilated and some had either embraced, or were to embrace, Christianity.

When Semper had to leave Dresden he tried to settle in Paris and also contemplated emigrating to the United States. This is corroborated by the letter written by the banker Martin Wilhelm Oppenheim to Semper in 1849 (see Appendix). Oppenheim wrote a rather cool note of introduction to Baron James de Rothschild and an accompanying letter to Semper himself, explaining that he also wrote to the banker Ber Leon Gould whose granddaughter, Cécile Heine, had seen Semper's buildings for Oppenheim in Dresden.

In both letters the project of a Paris Synagogue is mentioned and patronage requested. This shows that Semper did not easily give up his plans for synagogue architecture. The Synagogue of the Ashkenazi Jews in Paris, the Temple in the Rue Notre-Dame-de-Nazareth, built by Sandrié and Silveyra from 1820 to 1822, was then regarded as unsafe and closed in 1850. It was rebuilt by the architect Jean Alexandre Thierry in 1851, a smallish building in conventional style possessing two tiers of galleries in order to accommodate more congregants.[13]

A project existed to build a synagogue on a site near the Rue Chauchat. Here Semper produced one of his most dramatic schemes, a vast building with double entrance towers, a tower over the centre and a monumental double flight of frontal stairs, surpassing the one found before the church of St. Vincent de Paul by Jakob Ignaz Hittorff, his friend and colleague. The synagogue was to be surmounted by a star of David on its central tower and in the final version of the scheme also by the star of David on the side towers. In a letter from Paris of 21st March 1850, presumably to an artist or fellow architect, Semper speaks about his artistic contacts and worries. He also expresses his wish to be considered as a competitor for the project, although, as he says himself, the architect had already been appointed. If Semper's professional ethics are here doubtful, there can be no doubt that the Paris Jewish community was the loser, because he failed to receive the commission and therefore never built this potential masterpiece.

In trying to assess Semper's contribution to synagogue architecture, a short consideration of previous types is called for. The synagogues in Antiquity were mostly derived from the basilica, in the Middle Ages from the double-aisled hall. During later periods they were clearly influenced by the Protestant church and Neo-Classical models, until Semper created a novel type. This happened not only because he was a gifted architect, but, more significantly, because in his period a feeling for the aesthetic value of historical forms was prevalent, and could lead to a conscious selection and adaption of such forms.

[12]See Löffler, *op. cit., passim.*
[13]See Rachel Wischnitzer, *passim* and Thieme-Becker, *Allgemeines Lexikon der Bildenden Künstler.*

In the case of synagogue architecture this was extraordinarily fruitful, combining a certain strangeness with associations from the East and allowing a
functional approach, with regard to the arrangement of the pulpit, the galleries
and the detailing which created a new tradition. In Synagogue architecture,
"historicism" revealed itself as creative rather than imitative, suggesting utopian
dreams of a better future.[14]

It is significant of the tradition set by Semper that most readers of this short
study will be able to recall many synagogues which reveal at least some Semper-
like features. His original prototype in Paris was relatively unknown and also too
rich to invite slavish copy. Instead Semper set standards which led to creative
adaptations and proved an inspiration to others. In the words by his friend and
disciple Friedrich Pecht in the Appendix of the second edition of *Der Styl*[15]:
"Style is the accordance of an art form with the history of its origin." This
definition clearly applies to Semper's synagogues.

[14]Historicism played an important and positive part in the history of Synagogue architecture.
On the evaluation of historicism and utopias generally cf. *Historismus und Bildende Kunst*, ed.
L. Grote, Munich 1965 and H. Bauer, *Kunst und Utopie*, Berlin 1965.
[15]Vol. II, Munich 1879, pp. 565ff.

APPENDIX

I

Copy of a letter by the Banker Martin Wilhelm Oppenheim to Baron James de Roth-schild, dated 30th July 1849. Oppenheim states that Semper had to leave Dresden for political reasons and that he wished to be considered for the erection of a new Temple by the Jewish community. (Project connected with the Ashkenazi Temple of the Rue Notre-Dame-de-Nazareth in Paris.) Oppenheim gives a positive assessment of Semper's standing as an architect, and mentions a variety of buildings by him in Dresden, among them the Jewish Temple "in oriental taste".

Herren Baron Gebrüder von
   Rothschild in Paris   Dresden, d. 30. Juli 1849

Hierdurch erlaube ich mir Herrn Baumeister und Professor G. Semper bey Ihnen einzuführen. Derselbe war veranlaßt, politischer Zustände wegen, Dresden zu verlassen und seinen hiesigen bedeutenden Wirkungskreis, aufzugeben. Bey Ihnen angelangt, erfährt derselbe durch seine Freunde, die ihn zugleich auffor-dern, sich als Candidat zu melden, daß die dortige jüdische Gemeinde beab-sichtige, einen neuen Tempel zu erbauen. Da es Hr. Semper ebenso erwünscht als beehrend wäre, mit einem solchen Auftrag betraut zu werden, so hat er sich an mich gewendet, um ihn bey Ihnen einzuführen, da es Ihrem mächtigen Einfluß, falls Sie ihn anzuwenden die Güte haben wollen, gewiß gelingen würde, ihm diesen Auftrag ertheilen zu laßen. Ich kann Ihnen nur sagen, daß Pf. Semper wohl Einer der ersten Baumeister Deutschlands ist, daß sein Genie und Erfin-dungsgabe unerschöpflich sind, und daß er hier bereits durch öffentliche und private Bauten dieselben aufs Glänzendste bewährt hat. So will ich nur anfüh-ren, das neue Theater, ein Hospital, eine Villa und ein Stadthaus und neuer jüdischer Tempel im orientalischen Geschmack, der von allen Kennern so wohl als auch von Laien, ganz besonders bewundert u. hervorgehoben wird. Endlich auch noch das neue Museum, an dessen Vollendung er leider durch die letzten politischen Verwicklungen verhindert worden ist. Ich bin überzeugt, geben Sie meiner Empfehlung Gehör, Sie werden sich freuen, ein Talent, wie das des Prof. Semper, in Paris zur Geltung gebracht zu haben. Verzeihen Sie, die Ihnen hierdurch verursachte Belästigung.

Ihr ganz ergebener
M. W. Oppenheim

Chef von Oppenheim & Marquand [?]
in Königsbau [?][16]

[16]A Königstrasse is indicated in Löffler's Dresden map of 1837–1852.

II

Letter by the Banker Martin Wilhelm Oppenheim to Gottfried Semper, connected with the first document. Oppenheim refers to a previous letter by Semper, and states that he is sending two letters of introduction, one to Baron de Rothschild, and the other to Mr. B. L. Fould, the head of the French ¡ banking family, and Fasche Oppenheim.[17] Oppenheim rightly does not consider Rothschild to be a "native", and seems to be on cool terms with him, as suggested above. Oppenheim thinks that Fould may be of greater use. With regard to the villa and the town mansion built for him in Dresden, Oppenheim suggests that this should be mentioned orally, particularly to Fould who is acquainted with these facts, especially as the buildings have been seen by Fould's granddaughter, Madame Heine.[18] Oppenheim also mentions letters of introduction to America, to be sent shortly.

Ihr werthes Schreiben vom 24. d. beeile ich mich, dadurch zu beantworten, daß ich Ihnen meine 2 Empfehlungs Briefe an den Baron v. Rothschild und an Hr. B. L. Fould & Fasche Oppenheim übersende. Da ich eines Theils glaube, daß Hr. von Rothschild nicht einheimisch ist, andern Theils aber Hr. Fould Ihnen auch sehr nützlich seyn könnte, so habe ich dies Letzterem noch hinzugefügt. Der Himmel gebe daß sie Ihnen von Nutzen seyn mögen. Ich habe in den Briefen nicht erwähnt, daß die Villa und das Stadthaus für mich waren. Es würde aber gut seyn, wenn Sie dies mündlich thun, besonders bey Fould, da diese bereits davon gehört haben und sogar eine Enkelin Mad. Heine beides selbst gesehen hat. Die Empfehlungen nach America hat mir Herr von Lenzentin, der verreist ist versprochen, baldigst zuzusenden. So wie ich sie empfange, erhalten Sie sie.

Ergebenst
M. W. Oppenheim

III

Draft of a letter by Gottfried Semper to an anonymous friend, probably an artist or architect, dated 21st March 1850. Semper states that his situation is still precarious, and this is why he has not written earlier. He is involved in decorations for the Paris opera house; Semper states that he is friendly with the decorator Diéterle and lodges with Sechan.[19] He is dissatisfied but doubtful about a possible removal to London which actually came about one year later. He expresses worry about his work, referring to the completion of his *magnum opus: Der Stil in den Technischen und Tektonischen Künsten*, first

---

[17]On the Foulds see *Encyclopaedia Judaica* with bibliography. Fasche, a diminutive form, is perhaps connected with Fanny. On banking see Paul H. Emden, *Money Powers of Europe in the Nineteenth and Twentieth Centuries*, London [1938].

[18]F. H. Eisner, 'Four Heine Letters (From the Collection of the Leo Baeck Institute, New York)', in *LBI Year Book VI* (1961), pp. 280 and 283. Cécile Heine lived in Hamburg and was the poet's cousin by marriage. On the Rothschilds see Egon Caesar Conte Corti, *Die Rothschilds*, new edn., Frankfurt a. Main 1962.

[19]Charles Diéterle and Jules Pierre Michel Séchan were well-known Paris artists. See Thieme-Becker, *op. cit.*

published in two volumes in 1860 and 1863.[20] (The third volume planned by him has so far not reached publication, and may be only fragmentary.) Although Semper knew that the Israelitic Community had already commissioned an architect for its new synagogue he nevertheless wished to be considered as a competitor for the commission.

Paris, 21. März 1850

Geehrter Freund!

Schon längst hätte ich Ihnen auf Ihr freundschaftliches Schreiben vom ers. Sept. vorigen Jahres antworten sollen, aber Ihr Wunsch, Ihnen Bestimmtes über meine Lage melden zu können, ist noch immer unerfüllt geblieben und [*erasures*] somit unterblieb bis jetzt meine Antwort.

Ihr Brief traf mich in Gent, wohin mich eine falsche Aussicht gebracht hatte. In Brüssel überfiel mich bald nachher eine ernsthafte Krankheit, an welcher ich mehrere Wochen danieder lag. Hieher zurückgekehrt schlug mir Dieterle vor, an seiner Decoration für die Oper mitzuarbeiten. Ich nahm diese Arbeit gerne an und sie wird nach der von mir ausgeführten Einpunkte [?] jetzt gemacht. Ich wohne seitdem bei Séchan, das heißt seit dem December vorigen Jahres.

Manche andere Pläne hatte ich seitdem, die aber alle zu nichts führten. Dieterle's von mir bis jetzt zu wenig befolgten Bevormundungen haben mich von meiner Hauptaufgabe, das Werk zu vollenden, abgelenkt und in tausend fruchtlose Allotria hineingelockt. Neuestens habe ich eine sehr rauhe Zeichnung, das Innere eines Saales für einen Englischen Tapezier verfertigt, der sich bei Dieterle um meinen Zeichner gemeldet hatte. Ich bereue aber die Zeit, die ich darauf verwendete; denn erstens (weiss ich noch [*erased*] erhalte ich gar keine Antwort und zweitens finde ich nach reiflicher Überlegung, daß eine Stellung als Zeichner bei einem Londoner Decorateur für mich keine besonderen Aussichten einer glänzenden Zukunft darbietet. Die hiesige Israelitische Gemeinde beabsichtigte früher ihren alten Tempel durch einen dazu schon erkorenen Architecten erneuern zu lassen. Neulich erfuhr ich zufällig, daß sie nun ihre Absicht geändert haben und einen ganz neuen Tempel an einer anderen Stelle erbauen wollten. Ich begab mich daher zu einem Gönner Herrn Kohen um das Nähere zu erfahren, der mir sehr große Hoffnungen machte, daß ich wenigstens als Concurrent zu dieser Arbeit berücksichtigt werden. (Sic.)

Hochachtungsvoll
Semper

[20]*Der Stil, op. cit.*, shows great interest and knowledge of ancient Near Eastern art, and advances theories on textile values in the Tabernacle and the Temple. Semper recognises the relationship between the two Biblical descriptions. He indulged, however, in rather fantastic reconstructions in order to suit his theories.

Semper: Funerary Monument and portrait medallion of Rosa Oppenheim by
Ernst Rietschel, 1849

By courtesy of the Deutsche Fotothek, Dresden

Semper: Dresden Synagogue, South side,
from an old photograph

Semper: Dresden Synagogue, Exterior, West side,
shortly before final destruction

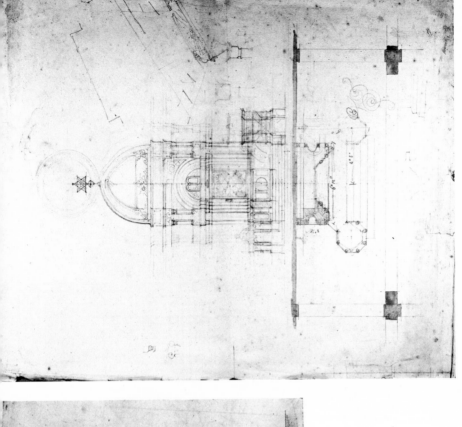

Semper: Dresden Synagogue, Preliminary Drawing for the
Torah shrine by the Architect

Semper: Dresden Synagogue, Project, Section

Semper: Paris Synagogue, Project, Completed version, 1850

By courtesy of the Semper-Archiv, Zürich

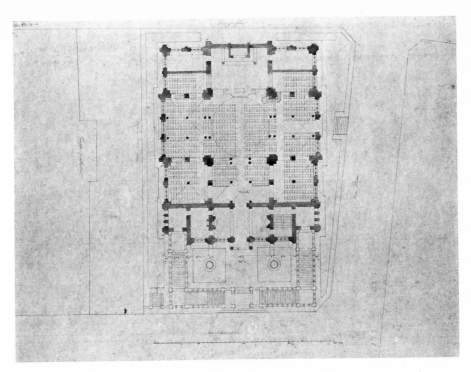

Semper: Paris Synagogue, Project, Ground Plan

Semper: Paris Synagogue, Project, Section

The Prague Origins of the Güntherian Converts (1800–1850)

BY THOMAS W. SIMONS, JR.

I

Converts from Judaism played significant roles in both the major movements for Catholic renewal in Vienna during the first half of the nineteenth century.

The circle which gathered around Klemens Maria Hofbauer[1] in the years 1808–1820 was composed of German publicists and Austrian officials on the one hand, and of Vienna university students on the other. Of the publicists, none was more prominent than Friedrich Schlegel, whose wife Dorothea was Moses Mendelssohn's daughter. It was an age when the salon and the restaurant provided the twin poles of social and intellectual life outside the stultifying First Society of the Court, and if the Schlegel salon was more modest, in the galaxy which made the Vienna Congress famous, than those of the great Jewish banking families like the Arnsteins and the Eskeles', it was at least as lively. Hofbauer was a kind of house chaplain at the Schlegels'.[2] The students around Hofbauer tended to congregate in restaurants, in what might be called a "third society", and it had no more promising member than Johann Emanuel Veith, son of a Jewish tobacco monopolist in Western Bohemia, studying veterinary medicine.

The second circle, which was thrust into prominence a generation later in the Revolution of 1848, centred on Veith and Anton Günther, whom Hofbauer had called the Augustine of the group in testimony to his philosophical talents.[3] After Hofbauer's death in 1820 the disciples went their separate ways, and it was only in the course of the decade that Günther began to publish works of original speculation. At the end of the decade he and Veith renewed their friendship, and a new, younger circle gathered around them, joined by attachment to Günther's "system" and to each other. When the Old Régime collapsed – for a moment – in 1848, this Güntherian circle became a movement, the motor of Catholic defence and Catholic reform, and it founded institutions – the Catholic press and the Catholic laymen's association – which were to remain important long after reaction in Church and State had disposed of the founders. The role

---

[1] The standard work on this circle, with older bibliography, is Rudolf Till, *Hofbauer und sein Kreis*, Vienna 1951.

[2] *Ibid.*, p. 61.

[3] A scholarly renaissance concerning Günther is currently underway. The earlier literature is cited in my 'Vienna's First Catholic Political Movement: The Güntherians, 1848–1857', in *Catholic Historical Review*, LV (July 1969–January 1970), pp. 173–194, 377–393, 610–626; and more recent works are listed on p. 7 of Joseph Pritz, *Wegweisung zur Theologie. Briefe Anton Günthers an Johann Nepomuk Ehrlich mit einer Einleitung*, Vienna 1971. On Veith, the basic works are Johann Heinrich Loewe, *Johann Emanuel Veith. Eine Biographie*, Vienna 1879; and now Eduard and Maria Winter, *Domprediger Johann Emanuel Veith und Kardinal Friedrich Schwarzenberg. Der Günther-Prozeß in unveröffentlichten Briefen und Akten*, Vienna 1972.

of converts in the movement was positively striking: upwards of a third of the most important Güntherian activists and of the more or less supportive group members in the Austrian lands (Vienna, St. Pölten, Salzburg) were born as Jews. Such men played substantial and often key roles in the Viennese secular revolution too, but nowhere were they as numerous, relatively, as in the leadership of this Catholic movement.

Veith was the central figure. He edited the newspapers of the Catholic Union founded on Güntherian initiative, he preached continually and he was a prime mover in the Union itself. Carl Ferdinand Hock[4] assisted Veith as editor and was also a leader of the Union, but he was most valuable for his connections. He was the trusted confidant of the Bishop of Salzburg (and Primate of Germany), Friedrich Prince Schwarzenberg, and as a senior civil servant, Director of the Main Customs Bureau, he was influential in government. From March to May 1848 he edited the semi-official *Constitutionelle Donau-Zeitung* for Minister Pillersdorf; he had been a member of the Juridical–Political Reading Association before 1848, with most of the prominent liberals of the day, and was a member of the liberal Monarchical–Constitutional Association in 1848; and he was to spend his last years till 1869 as a Life Member of the Upper Chamber (*Herrenhaus*). Veith's nephews Johann Heinrich and Joseph Loewe[5] played subordinate but practical roles. The first was editor of Schwarzenberg's paper in Salzburg and advisor to Schwarzenberg both in Salzburg and after he became Prince-Archbishop of Prague in 1850. The second was a businessman who contributed financial support. Franz Kalmus[6] taught religion at the Vienna Engineering Academy and was spiritual adviser to many (presumably well-connected) families. Moritz Bermann,[7] an art dealer, drafted the initial programme of the Catholic Union along with Veith and another convert, Ignaz Bondi,[8] director of an unnamed institute. Bondi was one of the Union's leaders, and he also enjoyed a brief and forgotten prominence in city government. With three other Güntherians he was elected to the Municipal Council in October 1848, but he also had the distinction of serving as its chairman – the formal Mayor of Vienna – during and after the reconquest of the city by Imperial troops, until December. Finally, Johann Georg Schwarz,[9] acclaimed first chairman of the Union at its

[4]On Hock, Erwin Mann's 'Die philosophisch-theologische Schule A. Günthers. Der Literat, Philosoph und Nationalökonom Carl Ferdinand Hock', in Viktor Flieder, ed., *Festschrift Franz Loidl zum 65. Geburtstag*, II, Vienna 1970, pp. 228–257, lists what must be all the published sources.

[5]On the Loewe brothers, in addition to Johann Heinrich's biography of Veith cited in n. 3 above (where he refers to Joseph on p. 264), see Joseph Pritz, 'Zur Geschichte der philosophisch-theologischen Schule Anton Günthers. Briefe A. Günthers an den Philosophen J. H. Löwe', in Viktor Flieder, ed., *Festschrift Franz Loidl zum 65. Geburtstag*, I, Vienna 1970, pp. 204–254; and 'Löwe, Heinrich, auch Johann Heinrich', in Constant von Wurzbach, *Biographisches Lexikon des Kaiserthumes Oesterreich*, XV, Vienna 1866, pp. 419–420.

[6]On Kalmus, see Loewe, *op. cit.*, pp. 175 and 264.

[7]On Bermann, who was Viennese-born, see S. Wininger, ed., *Grosse Jüdische National-Biographie*, I, Czernowitz (n.d.), pp. 335–336.

[8]On Bondi, see especially Rudolf Till, 'Theologen in der Wiener Stadtverwaltung', in *Jahrbuch des Vereines für Geschichte der Stadt Wien*, XIII (1957–1958), pp. 203–206.

[9]On Schwarz, see Eduard Winter, *Die geistige Entwicklung Anton Günthers und seiner Schule*, Paderborn 1931, pp. 170–171; Joseph Pritz, *Mensch als Mitte. Leben und Werk Carl Werners*, I, Vienna

founding session in his house on the Graben, was also the American Consul. In radical August, acting quite without instructions, he accepted the Papal Nunciature's request that the United States take the Nunciature palace under its protection, and sent an American flag to be unfurled in case of need.

Six of these Catholic activists – Veith, the Loewe brothers, Hock, Bondi and Kalmus – almost certainly came to Vienna from the Prague Jewish community of the first quarter of the century. It may be of more than antiquarian interest to trace their personal paths back to the Prague milieu, to suggest what it was about the Prague ghetto and their new Viennese environment which could account for their surprising emergence as Catholic reformers, and along the way to identify a source for further research on the Prague community which is available in Prague itself today.

II

With about 10,000 Jews, the Prague community was the largest in the world, and its unusual metropolitan character gave it an uncommon sensitivity to new developments elsewhere. Around 1800 it was the scene of novel and substantial tensions which have been defined in some detail by modern research.[10] The most important new element was a strong Jewish Enlightenment movement, but at the same time Prague witnessed a last surge of Frankist millenarianism. The presence in force of both Enlighteners and Frankists gives the Prague situation its special significance for historians, and has made Prague a particularly interesting subject for recent study of the interrelationships of the two currents. There were basic differences, and Frankists and Enlighteners quarrelled with each other, as well as with the traditional milieu surrounding them both. But it is unnecessary to draw these distinctions too finely, since they also shared certain traits: both received impulses from outside; were orientated towards the Germanies; accepted the necessity of a rapprochement with the Gentiles. Towards mid-century both currents flowed into modernism.

In terms of the Güntherian phenomenon, the most significant features of the Prague situation were the intermingling of the two currents and the fact that both were drawn from the élite, from a few of the wealthier and better-educated

---

1968, p. 52 (on the founding meeting of the Union); and the correspondence about the flag in the United States Archives, Vienna Consular Despatches, Microfilm Copy T-243, Roll T-1, cited in my article, *loc. cit.*, p. 338.

[10] The basic works are Ruth Kestenberg-Gladstein, *Neuere Geschichte der Juden in den böhmischen Ländern*, I: *Das Zeitalter der Aufklärung 1780–1830*, Tübingen 1969 (Schriftenreihe wissenschaftlicher Abhandlungen des Leo Baeck Instituts 18/1); Gershom Scholem, *Major Trends in Jewish Mysticism*, New York 1969; and Gershom Scholem, 'Redemption through Sin', in *The Messianic Idea in Judaism and Other Essays on Jewish Spirituality*, New York 1971, pp. 78–141, 346–353. On Frankism in Prague, see also Václav Žáček, 'Zwei Beiträge zur Geschichte des Frankismus in den böhmischen Ländern', II: 'Die Frankisten in Prag und ihre Verfolgung um das Jahr 1800', in *Jahrbuch der Gesellschaft für Geschichte der Juden in der Čechoslovakischen Republik*, IX (1938), pp. 358–410; and Scholem, 'A Sabbatian Will from New York', in *The Messianic Idea, op. cit.*, pp. 167–175, 355–359.

families. In a community of 10,000, the élite is small: these families quarrelled but they also knew each other, intermarried and fought each other and the traditional society with the same weapons. Identifying the Prague roots of these converts throws light both backward and forward: on the complexities of Prague, and on the role the converts were to assume in Vienna.

The evidence is partly direct, partly circumstantial. There is biographic material on Veith, Hock and Johann Heinrich Loewe. It proves Veith's personal involvement in the Prague Enlightenment of the early years of the century and his kinship with the Loewe brothers and Hock. It also shows that Hock and Johann Heinrich Loewe were born in Prague, as Jews, in 1808. The rest must be inferred from the Jewish birth records for 1770–1820 preserved in the Birth Registration Section (*Matriční oddělení*) of the Prague First District National Committee, read in conjunction with the incidental biographic data in secondary works.[11]

The birth records give date of birth, house number, name of child and of both parents. There is also a column for *Partheyen*. For most (but far from all) male children, this contains two signatures, the first without qualification and the second "as circumciser". A house number indicates that the child was actually born there, and probably that the parents resided there, but houses in old Prague were numbered consecutively by the date of construction, so that it is necessary to establish proximity and neighbourhood by the use of late nineteenth-century maps.[12] While the German word *Parthey*, commonly meaning "house-owner", has no equivalent in Jewish custom, it is almost certain that the first, unqualified *Parthey* in the records denotes the *sandek*, and it is certain that the circumciser himself performed the operation. In the families of interest here – Löwy, Bondi, Hock, Kalmuss – *Partheyen* were very frequently of the same family, and even when they were not, *Partheyen* for these families were not normally inscribed for births in other families, which had other favourite *Partheyen*. Since

---

[11] I am indebted to a number of most helpful people in the National Committee (*Obvodní národní výbor*, Prague 1), the Marxism–Leninism Institute attached to the Central Committee of the Communist Party of Czechoslovakia, and the National Archives for permission to use these birth records during a brief visit to Prague in January 1971, at an evidently difficult time. I am also grateful to the staff of the Jewish State Museum in Prague for use of its library then and for indispensable clarifications on Prague religious and administrative custom in subsequent correspondence.

The documents themselves are of two kinds: four stout volumes, covering the years 1779–1822 and identified only as 1R, 2R, 3R and 4R, in which all Jewish births are entered in order of registration (usually some weeks after the birth); and a single register of all live, legitimate male births for the years 1780–1865 (*Matrik-Register N^ro I. vom Jahre 1780–1865*), in which the names of family, son and father are entered alphabetically by month and year of registration (e.g., 1808, April, all Hirschmanns, then all Hocks, etc.). Birth dates of the newly-born listed in the register can be ascertained only by reference to the line-entry in the relevant registration volume. For instance, Simon Hock (later Carl Ferdinand), born 27th March 1808, appears under April in the register. Since only five documents are involved, I shall simply refer to these sources in the text, which would be overwhelmed by elaborate footnote references and cross-references to volume and page number.

[12] Letter from Dr. Vilém Benda, Director of the Jewish State Museum in Prague, dated 3rd August 1971. In the main I have used the map entitled 'Plán asanačnich obvodů v Praze', between pp. 186–187 of Joseph Erben, ed., *Verwaltungsbericht der königlichen Haupstadt Prag . . . für die Jahre 1893 u. 1894*, Prague 1896.

some of the circumcisers were quite rich, it can be assumed further that those dealt with here were not professionals but were performing the function as a *mitzva*. And since they did so only in a relatively few family circles, it can be concluded that participation in the circumcision ceremony signified an honour for the father and was based on more or less close ties of kinship or affinity, a link beyond mere community spirit or neighbourliness.[13] Evidence of such participation will here suggest links between the Güntherian converts and the Prague Enlightenment or Prague Frankism.

Johann Emanuel Veith was the eldest of the group, and the only one known to have been involved personally, rather than by inheritance, in the cross-currents stirring the Prague community. He was born Mendel Veith in Kutten-plan (Chodová Planá) in Western Bohemia, on 10th July 1787. His father Baruch was a teacher of religion in the small Jewish community there, but presently, following his successful defence of a neighbouring community against an arbitrary tax-farmer, which had included several trips to the Court in Vienna, he was granted the lease for the government tobacco monopoly in the Klattau (Klatovy) district south of Pilsen. This was a profitable business, and further evidence of prosperity is the move to Klattau the family made when Mendel was six: the town was closed to Jews by imperial decree between 1747 and 1848, and thus presumably accessible only to the rich.

Mendel was given a Hebrew teacher who read the Old Testament with him; he studied Talmud; and he was expected to become a rabbi. But his father also had "progressive" views, for that time, on education. Baruch Veith brought back piles of secular books from his frequent business trips to Prague for Mendel to read, and he gave his son a secular education, first at the school in Klattau, then as an external student at the Pilsen *Gymnasium*, and finally, beginning in 1801, at the Academic *Gymnasium* in Prague.[14]

There Mendel came in contact with the Jewish Enlightenment. He was in correspondence at this time with his elder brother Joseph. Joseph remained a Jew, but a non-traditional one. He became a teacher at the Jewish religious school in Vienna in 1812, and a contributor to "enlightened" periodicals, and at the time of his death in 1834 was Secretary of the Vienna Community. He was buried under a tombstone provided by his converted brothers, alongside such prominent Prague Enlighteners as Juda Jeitteles, in Vienna's Währing Cemetery.[15] In these earlier letters to Joseph and others, Veith wrote very harshly of the Enlighteners. He was also in conflict during these years with his parents and with Joseph over moving to Vienna himself and later over bringing still another brother, Elias, with him. He went to Vienna in 1808; Elias came in 1812.

---

[13]These details on custom are from Dr. Benda's letter cited above and a letter dated 28th May 1971 from Dr. Ruth Kestenberg-Gladstein.
[14]Professor Rabbi Alfred Schapirnik (Kuttenplan), 'Geschichte der Juden in Kuttenplan und Umgebung', in Hugo Gold, ed., *Židé a židovské obce v Čechách v minulosti i v přitomnosti*, Brno–Prague 1934, pp. 340, 336; František Teplý, 'Geschichte der Juden in Schwihau', in *ibid.*, pp. 345, 347n; and Loewe, *op. cit.*, pp. 1–4.
[15]G. Wolf, *Geschichte der Juden in Wien (1156–1876)*, Vienna 1876, p. 126; Max Grunwald, *Vienna* ('Jewish Communities Series'), Philadelphia 1936, pp. 251, 504.

However passionately he opposed the Enlightenment in Prague, in Vienna Veith was part of the most emancipated wing of the Jewish community, in a social if not religious sense. He wrote poems to the glory of Bernhard von Eskeles and Fanny von Arnstein, representatives of the great banking families whose salons brightened the Vienna Congress, and a hymn celebrating the return of Kaiser Franz, for the Vienna synagogue. The poems were probably gentle pleas for patronage from a young man in a strange city without powerful connections of his own, but the implication is modernist, for the Eskeles' and Arnsteins were far from traditional families. The Arnsteins in particular, whose Berlin relatives were enthusiastic Enlighteners, provided most of the Viennese subscribers to Mendelssohn's Pentateuch translation and the "enlightened" Hebrew periodical *Hame'assef*.[16]

There may also have been a family connection with the Enlightenment. Veith went to Prague from Pilsen at the urging of his maternal uncle. The Loewe brothers were Veith's nephews; Johann Heinrich Loewe was born in Prague in 1808; the only family name in the birth records resembling Loewe is Löwy: it follows that the uncle was a Löwy, as Veith's "godfather" in Kuttenplan, the retail merchant Samuel Löwy, had been. Löwys were prosperous and prominent in both Kuttenplan and Klattau then and later, and there were several in Prague too.[17] By chance, however, there was only one male Löwy born in Prague in 1808, according to the birth records. His name was Wilhelm, born 15th September to Simon Elias and Iphigenia. It follows that Wilhelm Löwy became Johann Heinrich Loewe on conversion. And Wilhelm's first *Parthey* was none other than Juda Jeitteles, the most prominent Enlightener in Prague. Juda's father Jonas had been the man who did most to introduce the new ideas into the community, and Juda and his brother Baruch were the prime movers of the second, post-1800 phase.[18] Other members of this great Enlightened house participated in the circumcisions of other Löwy boys in the same period. Jeitteles and Löwy therefore seem to have been on good and familiar terms. Loewe claimed in his biography of Veith that the latter accepted no help from his family during his student days. None the less he came to Prague at his uncle's behest and was close to his nephews all his life,[19] and this would imply close personal ties to the family as well, at least during this period.

[16]Ludwig Bato, *Die Juden im alten Wien*, Vienna 1928, pp. 185–186. In Prague, the subscription list was composed of employees of the Jewish school, of students from good families, and of wealthy tobacco families with known Frankist sympathies: Kestenberg-Gladstein, *op. cit.*, p. 125.

[17]These details are from Loewe, *op. cit.*, pp. 3, 9, 21 and 34; Mann, *op. cit.*, p. 230; Pritz, 'Briefe ... Günthers an ... Löwe', *loc. cit.*, p. 204; and Schapirnik, *op. cit.*, p. 340. On p. 337 Schapirnik writes that in 1770 Wenzel Count von Sinzensdorf leased his brewery to the Kuttenplan Jew Lazar Löw. Gold's 1934 collaborative work has no written contribution on Klattau, but among the fourteen Klattau Jewish notables whose photographs appear on p. 265, three were Löwys.

[18]On the Jeitteles', see Kestenberg-Gladstein, *op. cit.*, pp. 118–124 (Jonas), 125–146 (Baruch), 259–263 and 292–309 (Juda).

[19]Loewe, *op. cit.*, pp. 23, 117 and 201, where he cites letters from Veith to himself and his brother Joseph from as late as the 1850s.

The evidence for a link between Veith and Frankism is weaker, but still intriguing.

Firstly, there is a curious story preserved that in 1804, long before Veith or his younger brother converted but not long after he moved to Prague, his mother asked the parish priest of a town near Kuttenplan to make a hole in the wall of the church so as to provide a view of the altar, in order that she could worship from without.[20] This is implausible as it stands, since the family was then living in Klattau. On the other hand, Bräundl Veith died in 1824 away from Klattau, in Brzeznitz;[21] as the wife of a prosperous tobacco monopolist she may have had occasion to travel; and she appears to have had a brother to visit in Kuttenplan, the retail merchant Samuel Löwy. Further, it is hard to imagine why such a story should have been fabricated. If true, however, it is nevertheless perplexing. A sincere interest in Christianity was quite rare among either traditional or Enlightened families at this early date, and Frankist conversions were uncommon, at least in Prague. Still, Frank himself converted, and Frankist propaganda from his daughter Eva's "court" in Offenbach was, in the late 1790s, urging conversion.

Secondly, Veith's father was a tobacco monopolist, and while most tobacco monopolists were probably not Frankist, many Frankists seem to have been tobacco monopolists, or connected with families of tobacco monopolists. The great Prague Frankist houses of Wehle and Bondi both included men of this profession.[22] The sect's leader at this time, Jonas Wehle, was accompanied on pilgrimages to Offenbach by his son-in-law Enoch Löw Hönig von Hönigsberg, grandson of the greatest of them all, Israel Hönig from Kuttenplan (1724–1808), Maria Theresa's army supplier, monopolist in all the Habsburg hereditary lands.[23] As men who moved about freely for professional reasons, and were rich, tobacco monopolists were attractive recruits for a missionary sect. Veith was born into this small society.

Thirdly, the Löwys had Frankists among their *Partheyen*. The family was not numerous in Prague: between 1798 and 1812 there were only seventeen Löwy boys born to nine fathers, in a period when there were around 250–300 male births in the ghetto every year. Juda Jeitteles stood *Parthey* to little Wilhelm Löwy, but Wilhelm's elder brother Ignaz was circumcised in 1805 by Jonathan Herz Bondi, identified as a Frankist in an anonymous denunciation of 1799, and between 1803 and 1807 four other Löwy boys were circumcised by Aaron Beer Wehle, brother of Jonas and like him a pilgrim to Offenbach, and one was held by Enoch Hönig von Hönigsberg.[24]

[20]Schapirnik, *op. cit.*, p. 340, citing the local history of G. Weidl, L. Hammer and M. Urban.
[21]Loewe, *op. cit.*, p. 89.
[22]Kestenberg-Gladstein, *op. cit.*, pp. 125, 175, 184n, and (on the retired tobacco monopolist Samuel Bondi) Jonas Marcus Bondi, *Zur Geschichte der Familie Jomtob-Bondi in Prag, Dresden und Mainz*, Frankfurt a. Main 5681, pp. 10, 16–17 and family tree.
[23]On the Hönigs, see Kestenberg-Gladstein, *op. cit.*, pp. 104–109, 183, and Žáček, *op. cit.*, pp. 362, 383–389, 396. Veith's personal secretary during the last years of his life was Toni Hönig. Cf. Winter, *Domprediger, op. cit.*, p. 18.
[24]On Jonathan Herz Bondi, see Žáček, *op. cit.*, p. 362. On Aaron Beer Wehle, see *ibid.*, pp. 362–367, and Scholem, 'Sabbatian Will', *op. cit.*, *passim*: Aaron Beer is the father of the Gottlieb Wehle who emigrated to New York in 1849 and died there in 1881, leaving the will.

It would be wrong to push this type of evidence too far, and unnecessary to do so. It is enough to remember that Frankism and Enlightenment together formed the non-contradictory poles of Veith's generation in Prague, and to note the overlap between Veith's experience and the contemporary tensions in the Prague community.

The world Veith entered when he came to Prague in 1801 was the world into which the other Güntherian converts were born. The Loewe brothers, as noted, were his nephews, and inherited the problems he lived at first hand. After studying at the Old City *Gymnasium* and reading law for a year in Prague, Johann Heinrich moved to Vienna in 1825–1826 and converted shortly thereafter, almost certainly under Veith's influence.[25]

There is no biographic material on Ignaz Bondi, and there is no Ignaz among the male Bondis born in Prague between 1788 and 1820. But he was born in this generation – as Mayor of Vienna in 1848 he was unlikely to have been over sixty or under twenty-eight – and he was almost certainly born in Prague. The Bondis were a very large and old Prague family, and although they were also prominent in Dresden, Mainz and smaller Bohemian communities, Prague was the family seat. They had arrived in that city round about 1600, probably from Upper Italy, and they had produced what appears to be a practically unbroken line of scholars, businessmen and community notables. In the first quarter of the nineteenth century the house provided the head of one of the leading Frankist families, a community treasurer, two community elders (*Vorsteher*), a retired tobacco monopolist, a director of a private yeshiva and publisher of Talmudic texts, and a rabbi and preacher.[26] What proportion was Frankist, or Enlightened, is difficult to determine. Some sources give the impression that most Bondis had been Sabbatian and then Frankist;[27] Gershom Scholem states that a majority were not Frankist;[28] of the fifty-two male Bondis born consecutively between 1788 and 1808, twenty-two had Jonathan Herz Bondi, Emanuel Bondi, Aaron Beer Wehle or Salomon Zerkowitz, all identified Frankists, as *Partheyen*. Enlightenment influences seem to have been much weaker. Jonas Jeitteles was first *Parthey* for one Bondi (but with Jonathan Herz Bondi as circumciser), and his son Juda stood as first *Parthey* for another, as he had for little Wilhelm Löwy. But Frankists thus outnumber Enlighteners by more than ten to one. It is true that Juda Jeitteles' sister was married to the Frankist Jonathan Bondi, but she apparently quarrelled with him over his Frankism.[29]

[25]Mann, *op. cit.*, pp. 228–229.

[26]On the Bondi family, see Bondi, *op. cit.*, *passim*; Wininger, *op. cit.*, I, pp. 421, 483; and *Encyclopaedia Judaica. Das Judentum in Geschichte und Gegenwart*, VII, Berlin 1929, pp. 938–940.

[27]Dr. Klein, 'Zuschrift an Herrn Moses Mendelsohn in Hamburg, die Zusammenstellung der rabbinischen Autoritäten im vorigen Jahrhundert betreffend', *Literaturblatt des Orients* (Leipzig), 33 (12th August 1848), col. 525–526.

[28]In a letter dated 2nd September 1971. After reading an earlier draft of this article, Professor Scholem was rather sceptical as to any of the Güntherian converts having had Frankist backgrounds.

[29]On this marriage, see Kestenberg-Gladstein, *op. cit.*, p. 184n, and Žáček, *op. cit.*, p. 406. In the letter cited above, Professor Scholem pointed out that marriage did not necessarily assure ideological harmony.

The conclusion must be tentative: while it is entirely possible that Ignaz Bondi grew up outside the ebb and flow of Enlightenment or Frankist currents or countercurrents, it is improbable.

Carl Ferdinand Hock presents a different kind of problem, for there are biographic notices about him. They state that he was born a Jew in Prague in March 1808, and on this basis the birth records show that he was born on 27th March 1808, as Simon, son of Joseph and Sara Hock, in House No. 271. A younger brother was born in the same house two years later, on 4th July 1810, so the family almost certainly resided there. Two and perhaps three Frankist families lived in the same house. Six months after Hock's birth, on 16th September 1808, Dr. Med. David Porges' son Joseph was also born in No. 271. This Dr. Porges was the son of Gabriel Porges, a distiller and alcohol merchant, one of Prague's most prominent Frankists and most frequent pilgrims to Offenbach. Two younger brothers of David Porges had travelled to Offenbach in 1798 and later when they fled, gave an account which is one of the best sources on Prague Frankism.[30] A year earlier, on 12th October 1807, a son, also named Joseph, had been born to Jonas Porges at No. 271: it is doubtful that this Jonas would have been unrelated to the Frankist family. And during these same years, on 4th September 1809 and 25th January 1812, a son and a daughter were born in the house to Elias Simon Eger. Jonas Wehle's sister Rösel, who was known in Prague as a Sabbatian seeress until her death from cholera in 1831, had married a Simon Eger, and although his refusal to contribute to the sect's treasury leaves his Frankist enthusiasm open to doubt,[31] there is none when it comes to hers. Whether or not they were the Egers in No. 271, the house was steeped in Frankism.

What influence this ambiance had on the Hocks is uncertain. Hock's father, a merchant who was related in some unspecified way to Veith and thus to the Löwy family, moved to Vienna for better business opportunities in 1822. There the family mixed in Christian circles, including Veith's, and converted as a family, under Veith's influence, in 1823, when Hock was fifteen. Hock had already been a classmate of Johann Heinrich Loewe at the Old City *Gymnasium* in Prague, and now rejoined him as a student in the Vienna Law Faculty, after having graduated in philosophy along with Friedrich Schwarzenberg in 1826. When Veith joined Günther after 1828 he brought the two younger men with him. Thus the core of the Günther circle was prepared by school and family ties reaching back to Prague.[32]

On Franz Kalmus, finally, there is nothing beyond the multiplicity of Kalmusses (as they are entered in the birth records) in Prague, and their location. There is no Franz among the thirty-three male Kalmusses born between 1791 and 1819. It was a fairly numerous family, and it had its share of Frankist *Partheyen*: Aaron Beer Wehle thrice and Löw Wehle and Salomon Zerkowitz

---

[30]Dr. Med. David Porges is identified in Kestenberg-Gladstein, *op. cit.*, p. 177. On Gabriel Porges and the younger sons, Moses and Leopold, see Žáček, *op. cit.*, pp. 364–368.
[31]On Rösel Eger and her husband, see Scholem, 'Sabbatian Will', *loc. cit.*, pp. 172, 357; Klein, *op. cit.*, col. 528; and Žáček, *op. cit.*, p. 363.
[32]Mann, *op. cit.*, pp. 228–232, and Winter, *Domprediger*, *op. cit.*, pp. 16, 39.

once each. More suggestive is the fact that although Kalmusses (like the Bondis) lived all over the ghetto, they tended to concentrate (like the Löwys) in the streets around the Old–New Synagogue. Two-thirds of the Kalmuss boys and half the Löwys lived in this area, together with a quarter of the Bondis (and another 30 per cent of the Bondis were born in two houses, Nos. 196 and 198, facing each other across the central street north of the Synagogue). In the two groups of houses facing each other South of the Synagogue there were at least seven Bondis, three Löwys and eleven Kalmusses born and presumably growing up together in these decades. The Kalmus of contemporary note, Seligmann (present at four Kalmuss circumcisions), was a signer of the "conservative" counter-petition of 1790 asking the Emperor to re-establish pre-Toleration Patent privileges for the Jews,[33] and there is nothing to indicate that the Kalmusses were anything but traditional. Nevertheless, it was probably in these streets that Franz Kalmus began his spiritual journey to the Güntherian camp.

III

In conclusion, it may be worthwhile to ask how the Prague background and the new Vienna setting converged to thrust these men into their novel historical role.

The Güntherian converts shared the formative experience of living in a community where ideological conflict using certain kinds of weapons was part of the atmosphere. Enlightenment and Frankism were ideological movements struggling for public influence within a small community. This was true, first, because the notion of community is a religious one in Judaism, inseparable from theology. In this community it was also true in fact, for the struggle in Prague involved convincing other members of an élite in face-to-face argument, in little magazines and in community institutions.

"Society" in Vienna at the turn of the nineteenth century extended beyond the Court, but not very far, and the Court had a monopoly on politics. It may be far-fetched to compare the "community institutions" of the Vienna Court and the Prague ghetto, since their structures and purposes were so different. But it is worth pointing out that both these élite societies were relatively small, that both were permeable, that – despite the devotion to the written word which the Habsburg bureaucracy and the Prague Jewish community shared – politics was still primarily oral in both milieux, but that this primacy was being eroded.

In Prague, personal contact, say through emissaries from and pilgrimages to Offenbach in the case of the Frankists, remained the chief vehicle of outside influence, as it remained the touchstone of standing within the community. However, it was now challenged by the printed word, in the form of books and magazines from the Germanies which also swayed opinion, especially among the young. Similarly, at the Vienna Court, Hofbauer was expert in the traditional modes of personal and bureaucratic influence which were still dominant. He himself worked by word of mouth, and his specific goals were eminently bureaucratic: to secure imperial approval for establishment of his Redemptorist order

[33]On Seligmann Kalmus, see Kestenberg-Gladstein, *op. cit.*, p. 334.

in the Habsburg lands, and to compete in the various Church-political struggles of the day. What was novel about Hofbauer was his appeal to and use of writers, established publicists of petty noble (and Protestant) origin from the Germanies, who addressed themselves to the German reading public, characteristic of urban, middle-class society, and necessarily distinct from the multinational, polyglot nobility which had borne the burden of empire for two centuries.

Partly, perhaps, this new strand can be explained by the pronounced German and even European phase the Vienna Court passed through during the Napoleonic Wars. It ended after the Vienna Congress, when Austria became the China of Europe, and by the late 1820s, when Veith joined Günther to form a new circle, Austrian isolation was such that the constituency was restricted to the Germanies – since Günther's philosophy was directed straight at educated middle-class men – while the recruitment base was restricted to Austria. Günther's "system" revolved around the selfconsciousness of the free individual and was highly speculative, and while it had many adherents in German universities it had few in Vienna, because Habsburg higher education was designed to produce functionaries and treated religion as a form of civics. Without Hofbauer's German immigrants and with limited appeal to that large portion of the native-born stamped in a bureaucratic mould, Günther's circle much more than Hofbauer's was composed of converts from Judaism.

The weapons of ideological struggle which characterised the Prague ghetto were not of much use in Metternich's Austria. Face-to-face argument was the traditional politics of the Vienna Court, but for the Güntherians the competition there was too stiff. Polemics in little magazines were of very little influence. There were no institutions that counted outside the Court, which for practical purposes included the Church.

All this changed in 1848, when the integument of Viennese politics burst asunder. The Press was suddenly a power, and institutions – unions, associations, commissions, the Municipal Council – were springing up everywhere. When the Court and the Prince-Archbishop left the city, what remained – or so it appeared – were the middle class and the proletariat, as in the Prague community. In addition, revolutionary Vienna was a self-consciously German city, basking in an all-German ambiance for the first (and last) time between Hofbauer's days and the end of the monarchy. It now seemed that the time had come for the Güntherians' specific talent, publicistic excellence directed towards the German middle classes.

This was the situation where the converts of the Günther circle came into their own. The goal of the Güntherian movement in Vienna was quite consciously a Church equipped to retain or regain the secularised middle classes, the "natural leaders" of the Catholic community. The converts threw themselves into the task of reforming a community from above the better to preserve it. But in the heat of action they found themselves organising from below, and they demonstrated a flair for sustained organisational work in public, a sense of the social aspect of ideological struggle, more striking even than the publicistic skill they shared with other members of the movement. And to this task they brought the habits of group politics in the community they had forsaken.

They failed – for the traditional structure of politics was quickly reimposed, if in streamlined form and only for a little while – but their experience suggests that their background shaped the talents they brought to the novel task of organising from below, of organising in the broader arena of politics beyond the Court and the bureaucracy which was just beginning to take shape at this moment in Central European history. And these talents, this background, did not disappear with the advent of mass politics – quite the contrary.

Julius Preuss: Father of Hebrew Medical Research

BY FRED ROSNER

The oldest known Hebrew medical writing* is that of Asaph which dates from the seventh century.[1] Since the ancient Hebrews left us no specific medical texts, our only sources of knowledge on this subject are the medical and hygienic references found in the Jewish sacred, historical and legal literatures.[2] It is from these that the fragments of our knowledge of their medical views and practices have been gathered. The difficulty has been great, for the material is scant and its meaning often uncertain; the period which these sources cover is very long. Much of the material is "popular medicine"; most, if not all, was transmitted by laymen.

The first systematic studies of the medicine of the Bible were published early in the seventeenth century, among the first fruits of the study of the Bible awakened by the Reformation. The earlier books dealt only with the Old and the New Testaments (with the single exception of the dissertation of Gintzburger of 1743). It was not until the nineteenth century that studies included the Talmud and other ancient Hebraic writings.[3]

The literature that has grown up during the past three centuries is very extensive; much of it deals with special subjects, much embraces studies limited to single works such as the Talmud. As would be expected, these studies reflect the scientific spirit of their period, the uncritical or the critical attitude of the Biblical scholars, and the current views on medicine.

The writers have, for the most part, been Biblical students; others were students of medical history; there are a few who were both.

Thus, for instance, of the two most important works on Biblical and Talmudical medicine until recently, one published in 1860 was by a layman, R. J. Wunderbar, and the other which appeared in 1901–1903 was by a great physician, Wilhelm Ebstein, but one unfamiliar with the Semitic language and literature. What this means can hardly be appreciated by someone who knows nothing of the Hebrew or Arabic tongues – their briefness, conciseness and force.[4] It was not until the publication of Julius Preuss's *Biblisch–Talmudische Medizin* in 1911 that we acquired a reliable, comprehensive and scholarly exposition of the subject by one who was a first-class physician and a thorough semitic philologist, who made the history of medicine his life's study.[5]

---

*A part of this essay was delivered as a lecture at the New York Leo Baeck Institute on 20th February 1975.

[1] Suessman Muntner, *Introduction to the Book of Asaph the Physician* (in Hebrew), Jerusalem 1957.
[2] Harry Friedenwald, *The Jews and Medicine*, Baltimore 1944, vol. 1, pp. 99–145.
[3] *Ibid.*, p. 99.
[4] David Israel Macht, 'In Memoriam – Dr. Julius Preuss', in *Johns Hopkins Hospital Bulletin*, 25, No. 277 (March 1914).
[5] *Ibid.*

Julius Preuss was born on 5th September 1861 in the small village of Gross-Schönbeck near Potsdam in Uckermark. His was the only Jewish family in the village. He attended primary schools in the town of Angermünde and then entered the *Gymnasium* in Prenzlau, where he distinguished himself by his brilliant scholarship. Upon graduation, he went to study medicine at the University of Berlin. There, he completed the course of study in 1886. Preuss's doctoral thesis was entitled *Concerning Syphilis as the Etiology of Tabes Dorsalis and Dementia Paralytica.* The newspapers contained an interesting account of the brilliant young doctor who had achieved the rare feat of having passed Rudolf Virchow's examination with the highest marks.[6] Virchow, the founder of cellular pathology, was a highly versatile personality known for his uncompromisingly exacting standards. He paid Preuss the extreme compliment of telling him that his way of thinking was that of a true physician: *Sie können medizinisch denken.* Preuss returned to his native town to practise medicine, but in 1891 went back to Berlin where he worked as a general medical practitioner and where he studied and wrote.

According to Muntner,[7] Preuss lived in an age which saw the resurgence of the critical approach in scientific as well as historical research. He was a part of the century which gave to the Jewish world Salomo Juda Rapoport, Leopold Zunz, Leopold Dukes, Abraham Berliner, David Cassel, Abraham Geiger, Moritz Güdemann and Heinrich Graetz. Towering above all these luminaries was Moritz Steinschneider, the Orientalist and bibliographer who, in addition to other ancient source material, unearthed a wealth of data on the history of Jewish research in the sciences, including medicine.

Historical literature in the field of medicine could boast of a number of impressive works, including those of Heinrich Haeser, August W. E. Theodor Henschel, Max Neuburger and Julius Pagel. Sadly lacking, however, was reliable and critical research in the field of Jewish medicine. To be sure, continues Muntner, there was no dearth of general essays on medicine in Biblical and even Talmudic times, but most of these were superficial, unscientific and, occasionally, like those written by Eliakim Carmoly (1802–1875), of dubious authenticity. Even the few outstanding works that appeared such as those of F. Bergel, David Holub, Rabinowitz, Wunderbar and Ebstein, fell far short of the analytical approach which characterised the writings of Julius Preuss.[8]

Preuss was a physician of fine training and wide experience, a learned scholar in Hebrew literature as well as in medical and general history. He studied Talmud with Rabbi Eduard Biberfeld and the famous Rabbi Dov Ritter, later Chief Rabbi of Rotterdam, never having attended a Jewish school in his youth. Preuss's unusual Hebraic background, his vast knowledge of Jewish thought and

---

[6]Karl Sudhoff, *Essays in the History of Medicine*, New York 1926, pp. 351–353.

[7]Suessman Muntner, 'Julius Preuss. Father of Hebrew Medical Research', in *Julius Preuss' Biblisch–Talmudische Medizin*, New York 1971, pp. vii–xii; *idem.*, 'Julius Preuss as a Founder of Research on the Field of the Ancient Hebrew History of Medicine', in *Koroth* (A Quarterly Journal Devoted to the History of Medicine and Science – in Hebrew), Jerusalem–Tel Aviv, X, vol. 2, No. 9–10 (May 1961), pp. 410–413.

[8]Muntner, *Preuss. Father of Hebrew Medical Research* . . ., *op. cit.*, p. viii.

Hebrew literature and his scientific method makes his book *Biblisch–Talmudische Medizin* the authoritative work on the subject to this very day.

In 1961, to commemorate the one-hundredth anniversary of the birth of Julius Preuss and the fiftieth anniversary of the appearance of his *magnum opus*, a variety of meetings and lectures were held, and numerous articles and essays published.[9] Leibowitz[10] decries the lack of available detailed information concerning the life of Preuss. He points out that Rabbi Joseph Carlebach, last Chief Rabbi of Hamburg and the son-in-law of Preuss, said that Preuss used to read the book of Psalms and study the *Mishnah* when he travelled to and from his patients in neighbouring towns, so that after a while he learned them by heart. Preuss turned to the renowned Rabbi Hildesheimer for legal Judaic opinions concerning medical matters, such as remuneration for Sabbath visits to the sick. Preuss's return to Berlin in 1891 was precipitated either by his desire to be surrounded by learned scholars and academicians[11] or by the great difficulties in the observance of traditional Judaism which he encountered in his small native village.

Preuss was a very successful physician and his practice grew considerably. He married Martha (Rachel) Halberstadt from Hamburg late in 1899 or early in 1900. His wife Martha was an enormous help to her husband in proof-reading all his writings and in assisting in any other possible way. The Preusses had three children, two daughters and one son. One daughter and her husband Rabbi Joseph Carlebach were killed in the holocaust of the Second World War.

Preuss himself became ill in 1911 when his *Biblisch–Talmudische Medizin* first appeared, although he had already written to Immanuel Löw in 1898 expressing his fear that he would not be able to complete his work because of ill health.[12] His illness is variously described as "a lung abscess which probably could have been controlled by chest surgery and/or antibiotics which were not available in his lifetime"[13] or "cancer of the throat, complicated by tuberculosis and bronchiectasis".[14] Details of his fatal illness are described by Leibowitz. Preuss died on 23rd September 1913 at the early age of fifty-two and was buried in the "Adath Israel" cemetery in Berlin. He was not eulogised at his funeral, according

[9]Hirsch Leib Gordon, 'The Centenary of the Birth of Dr. Julius Preuss', in *Harofe Haivri* (The Hebrew Physician – in Hebrew), vol. 1–2 (1961), pp. 196–204; Muntner in the Hebrew quarterly *Koroth* (see n. 7); Joshua O. Leibowitz, 'Julius Preuss and the Medico-Historical Research in Bible and Talmud', in *Koroth, loc. cit.*, pp. 414–425 (Hebrew) and pp. i–iii (English); J. Moeller, 'My Memories on Julius Preuss', *ibid.*, pp. 404–406; Karl Sudhoff, 'Julius Preuss', *ibid.*, pp. 407–409; David Margalith, Obituary. Dr. Yitzhak (Yulius) Preuss. 5th September 1861 to 23rd September 1913, *ibid.*, pp. 479–480. The following works have likewise been consulted: Solomon R. Kagan, *Jewish Medicine*, Boston 1952, p. 562; David Margalith, *Physician Forerunners of Modern Israel*, Jerusalem Academy of Medicine, Tel Aviv 1973, pp. 163–164; idem., *The Way of Israel in Medicine* (in Hebrew), Jerusalem Academy of Medicine, Jerusalem 1970, pp. 348–349; Julius L. Pagel, *Biographisches Lexicon hervorragender Ärzte des neunzehnten Jahrhunderts*, Berlin–Vienna 1900–1901.
[10]*Loc. cit.*, p. 3.
[11]Macht, *loc. cit.*, p. 92.
[12]See the facsimile of the letter between pp. 260–261.
[13]Leibowitz, *loc. cit.*, p. 9.
[14]Muntner, *Preuss. Father of Hebrew Medical Research . . ., op. cit.*, p. x.

to his own wishes. In his last Will and Testament dated 18th May 1905[15] Preuss said, "No one should deliver a funeral oration, memorial address or the like for me, not at home nor at the cemetery, not at the interment nor later, not a paid speaker nor anyone else. No one should be motivated to fast on the day of my death . . . the grave should not be preserved with any type of ornament or ivy or the like." His tombstone bears the simple epitaph: *rophé, velo lo*, "physician, but not for himself". The humility of Preuss is also exemplified by the title which appears beneath his name in all editions of his book: "Arzt in Berlin". Lengthy eulogies did appear in the Press, however, following Preuss's death including those of Karl Sudhoff,[16] Eduard Biberfeld,[17] Joseph Carlebach,[18] David Macht[19] and many others.

Sudhoff said the following about Preuss:[20]

> "In the one hour we were together, Preuss permitted me, the non-Jew, to see so deeply into his soul, that I knew his wish was to be a classical philologist – this man, whose practical course of life made his dream impossible because he was a Jew. He had become a physician and his remarkable talent for historical and philological investigation directed him to the study of the history of his specialty as an avocation and in particular to that branch which inevitably attracts every Jewish physician of the old stamp, namely, Biblical and Talmudic medicine.
> . . . Julius Preuss never lacked in his work either the inspiration or the devotion so essential to thorough accomplishment. But from inspiration he derived only the incentive which spurred him on to the mastery of difficulties. Never did he permit it to obscure his historical judgement in its incorruptible service toward the establishment and enunciation of truth. Cool to the very heart as he was; love of the people of Israel did not cloud his view. Enthusiasm for their superior viewpoint did not make him see straight lines as crooked. For these very reasons, Dame History has laid laurels upon his grave, as a memorial to him, the master of historic criticism . . ."

The original manuscript of Preuss's *magnum opus* is today housed in the manuscript and archives section of the Hebrew University library[21] in Jerusalem. In the Friedenwald collection of medica-judaica in the same library, one finds an item called 'Notes on Preuss'[22] in which the late Harry Friedenwald of Baltimore took copious notes in English on Preuss's book, chapter by chapter. Interesting is Friedenwald's assertion near the end of his notes that: "I find no chapter on senility in Preuss, not even a paragraph."

Preuss's writings on Biblical and Talmudical medicine began with an article entitled 'Der Arzt in Bibel und Talmud' which was published in 1894 in the prestigious *Virchow's Archiv* and was soon reprinted in Hebrew translation in the periodical *Hame'asef*. Numerous other essays on various aspects of Biblical and Talmudical medicine followed in a variety of scientific and literary journals.

---

[15]See the facsimile of the last Will and Testament between pp. 260–261.
[16]*Münchener Medizinische Wochenschrift*, 13th January 1914.
[17]*Der Israelit*, 1st October 1913.
[18]'Sanitätsrat Dr. Julius Preuss', in *Jüdische Presse*, 1913, pp. 395 ff.
[19]*Loc. cit.*, p. 92.
[20]Sudhoff, *Essays . . ., op. cit.*, pp. 351–353.
[21]Ms. Var 443, No. 13–14, two pages of which are reproduced between pp. 260–261.
[22]Rare book division, Fr. 812B.

JULIUS PREUSS
(1861–1913)

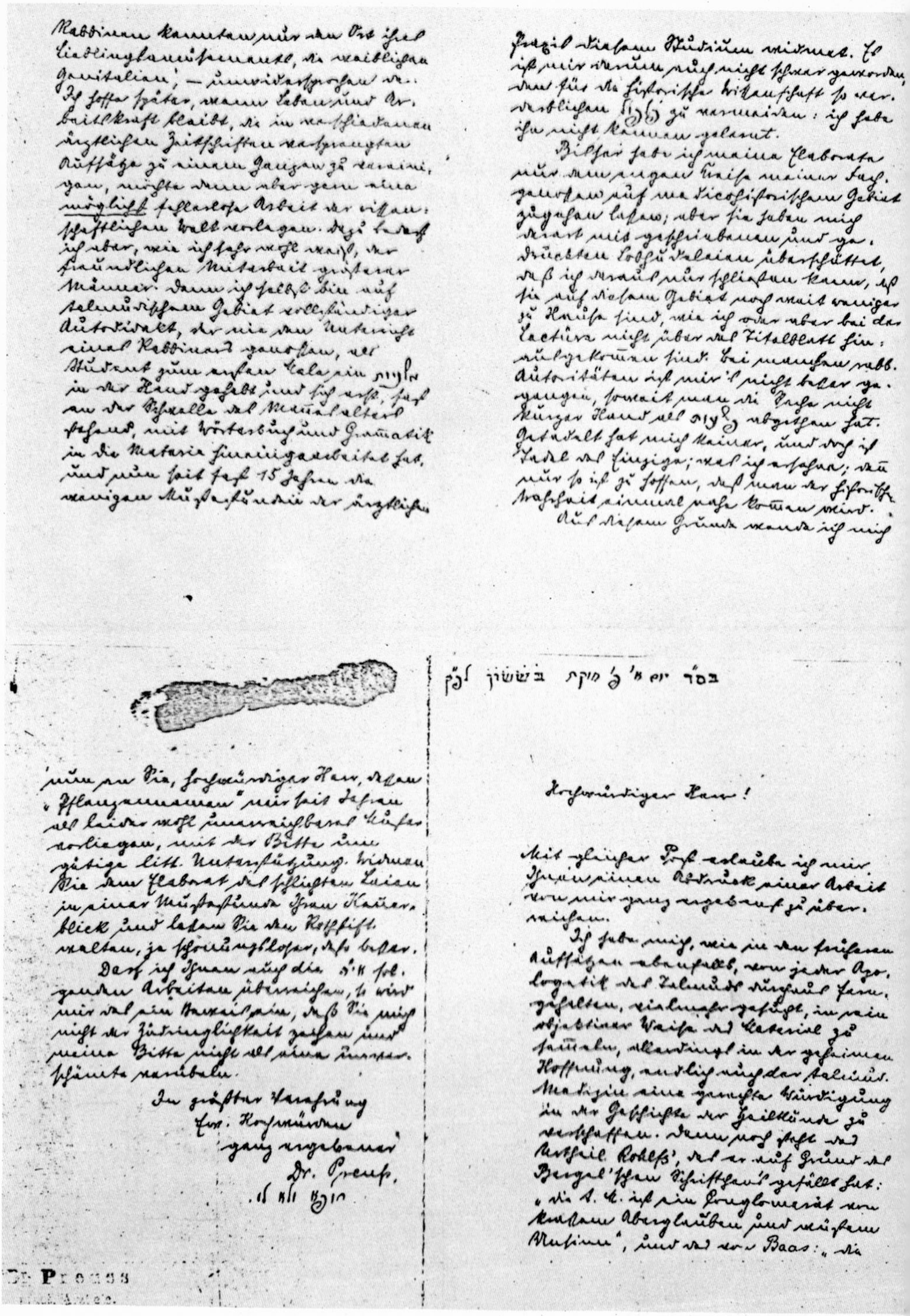
בס״ד יום א׳ פ׳ חקת בששון לפ״ק
Hochwürdiger Herr!
Dr. Preuss.
Dr. Preuss

Letter written by Julius Preuss in 1898 to Immanuel Löw

By courtesy of Mr. Jacob Preuss, Herzliya, Israel

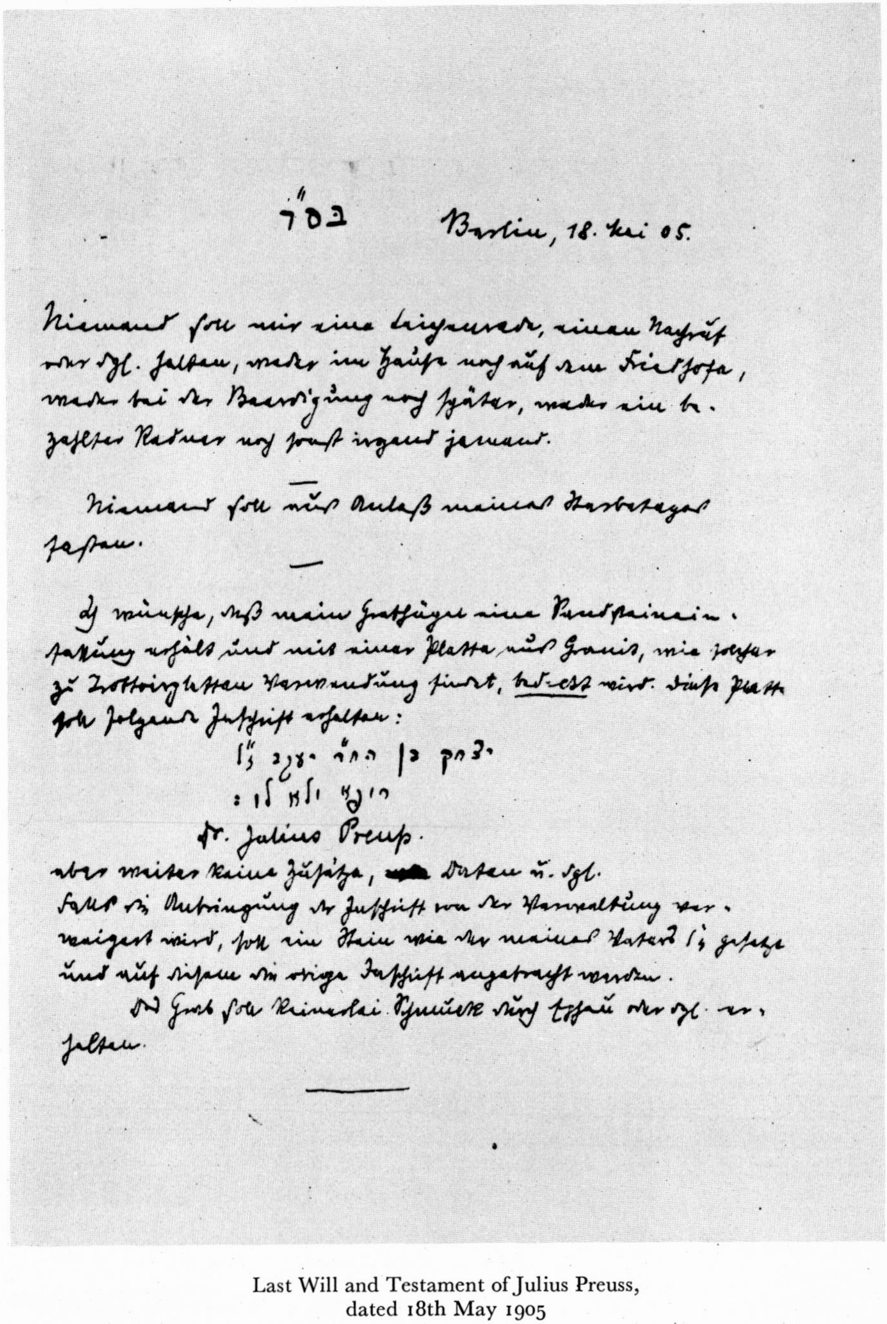

בס״ד Berlin, 18. Mai 05.

Niemand soll mir eine Leichenrede, einen Nachruf oder dgl. halten, weder im Hause noch auf dem Friedhofe, weder bei der Beerdigung noch später, weder ein bezahlter Redner noch sonst irgend jemand.

Niemand soll aus Anlaß meines Sterbetages fasten.

Ich wünsche, daß mein Grabhügel eine Randsteineinfassung erhält und mit einer Platte aus Granit, wie solcher zu Trottoirplatten Verwendung findet, bedeckt wird. Diese Platte soll folgende Inschrift erhalten:

יצחק בן הה״ר יעקב ז״ל

רופא ולא לו :

Dr. Julius Preuss.

aber weiter keine Zusätze, [illegible] Daten u. dgl.

Falls die Anbringung der Inschrift von der Verwaltung verweigert wird, soll ein Stein wie der meines Vaters s. A. gesetzt und auf diesem die obige Inschrift angebracht werden.

Das Grab soll keinerlei Schmuck durch Efeu oder dgl. erhalten.

Last Will and Testament of Julius Preuss,
dated 18th May 1905

By courtesy of Mr. Jacob Preuss, Herzliya, Israel

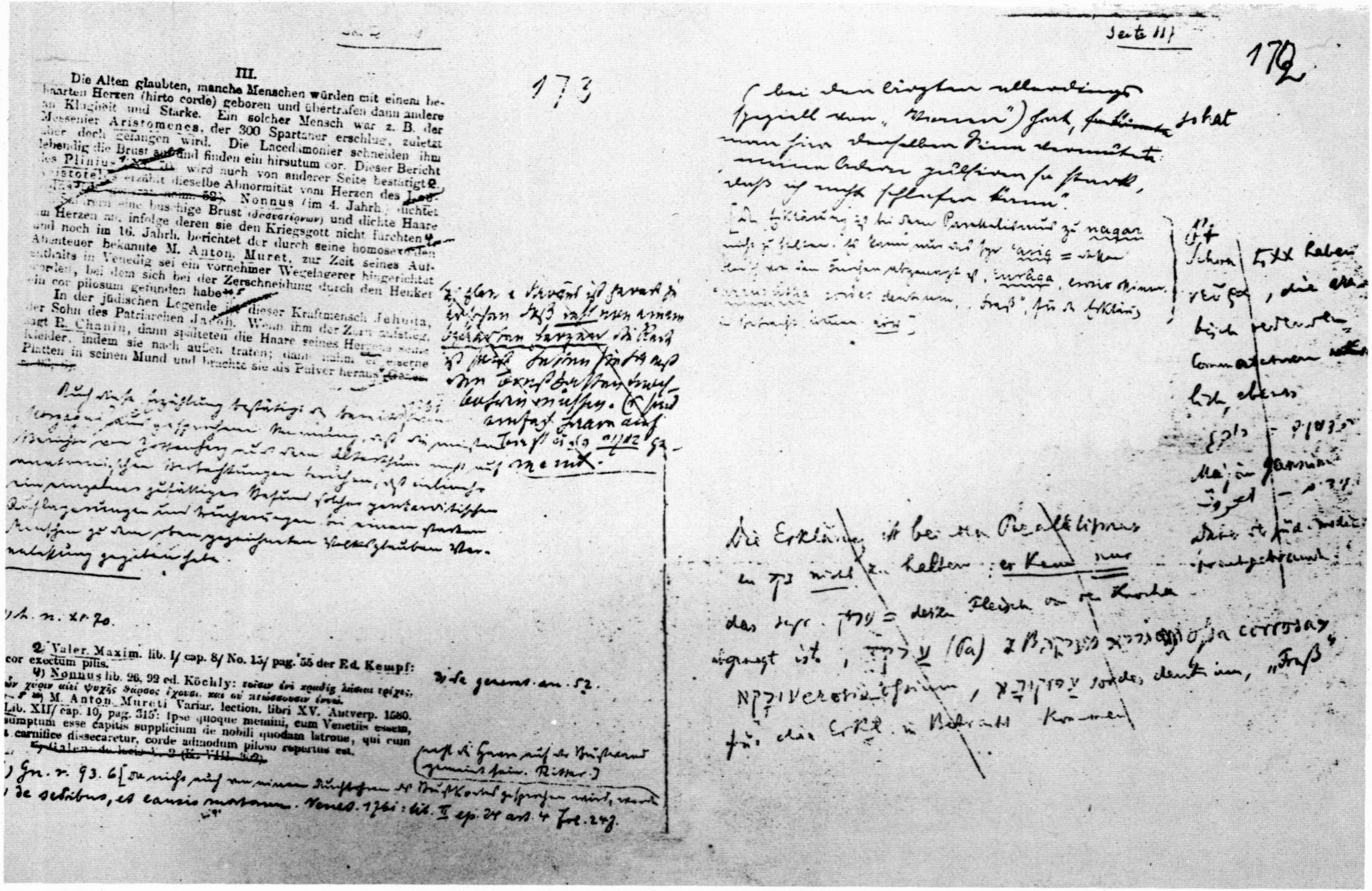

III.

Die Alten glaubten, manche Menschen würden mit einem behaarten Herzen (hirto corde) geboren und übertrafen dann andere an Klugheit und Stärke. Ein solcher Mensch war z. B. der Messenier Aristomenes, der 300 Spartaner erschlug, zuletzt aber doch gefangen wird. Die Lacedämonier schneiden ihm lebendig die Brust auf und finden ein hirsutum cor. Dieser Bericht des Plinius [illegible] wird auch von anderer Seite bestätigt.[2] [illegible] Nonnus (im 4. Jahrh.) dichtet [illegible] eine buschige Brust (δασυστέρνων) und dichte Haare am Herzen an, infolge deren sie den Kriegsgott nicht fürchten.[4] Und noch im 16. Jahrh. berichtet der durch seine homosexuellen Abenteuer bekannte M. Anton. Muret, zur Zeit seines Aufenthalts in Venedig sei ein vornehmer Wegelagerer hingerichtet worden, bei dem sich bei der Zerschneidung durch den Henker ein cor pilosum gefunden habe.[5]

In der jüdischen Legende [illegible] dieser Kraftmensch Jehuda, der Sohn des Patriarchen Jacob. Wenn ihm der Zorn aufstieg, sagt R. Chanin, dann spalteten die Haare seines Herzens seine Kleider, indem sie nach außen traten; dann nahm er eiserne Platten in seinen Mund und brachte sie als Pulver heraus.

2) Valer. Maxim. lib. I/ cap. 8/ No. 15/ pag. 55 der Ed. Kempf: cor exectum pilis.

4) Nonnus lib. 26, 92 ed. Köchly: [illegible]

5) M. Anton. Mureti Variar. lection. libri XV. Autverp. 1580. Lib. XII/ cap. 10, pag. 315: Ipse quoque memini, cum Venetiis essem, sumptum esse capitis supplicium de nobili quodam latrone, qui cum a carnifice dissecaretur, corde admodum piloso repertus est.

Pages 117 and 118 of the original manuscript of Preuss's
Biblisch-Talmudische Medizin

The two previously published bibliographies of Preuss's writings already quoted[23] are incomplete and contain several errors. Both Friedenwald and Muntner cite an anonymously written English article entitled 'The Medicine of the Bible' published in *Medical Magazine*.[24] It seems highly unlikely that Preuss wrote this paper, since he did not write in English[25] and the article was published a year after he died. Furthermore an article entitled 'Über die Veränderungen der Zähne bei der Kieferrachitis des Schweines' published in the *Archiv für Wissenschaftliche und Praktische Tierheilkunde*[26] was actually written by a Dr. Julius Preuss who was a veterinarian.[27]

Preuss's book is not without imperfections. Gordon[28] points out that the Jerusalem Talmud was not compiled by Rabbi Yochanan as Preuss asserts because many sages therein lived much later than Rabbi Yochanan. Rav Ashi is also not the last of the compilers of the Babylonian Talmud, as stated by Preuss. The listing of physicians of the Talmud enumerated by Preuss is incomplete. Numerous other "minor" criticisms are cited by Gordon. For certain errors Preuss is not to be blamed. For example, he states that the earliest Hebrew medical writing is that of Donnolo from the tenth century. Recent research by Muntner[29] has shown that the text of Asaph Harofe antedates Donnolo by several centuries. The indices in Preuss's book, particularly the general index, are very sparse.

In preparing an English translation of Preuss's classic book, the present author, too, has found numerous minor errors. For example, in chapter 12, Preuss states that Tractate Negaim has ten chapters whereas in fact there are fourteen. In chapter 17, he erroneously attributes a Talmudic statement to Rabbi Akiba instead of Rabbi Eleazar and, in chapter 6, Preuss does the reverse. In the first appendix to chapter 5, Preuss gives the dates of birth and death of Maimonides as 1131 and 1205. The correct dates are, of course, 1135 and 1204. In chapter 4, Preuss incorrectly speaks of the "daughter" of the Shunamite woman instead of her "son". He says the Hebrews have no word for coughing like the *su'al* of the Arabs; yet he overlooked the Hebrew word for cough which is *she'ul*. He says that *yerakon* and *shiddaphon* always occur together in Bible and Talmud. There is an exception, however, in Jeremiah 30:6. Numerous other minor errors of this nature could be cited. Furthermore, there are more than a score of incorrect bibliographic citations from Bible and Talmud (for example, Ecclesiastes 13:2 instead of 12:2 and Genesis 32:36 instead of 32:25). These amount, however, to less than a fraction of 1 per cent of the many thousands of references which Preuss quotes.

The above shortcomings do not detract from the classic and enduring value of

---

[23]Friedenwald, *op. cit.*; Muntner, *Preuss. Father of Hebrew Medical Research . . ., op. cit.*, 'Bibliographie der Schriften von Julius Preuss', *ibid.*, pp. xxiii–xv.
[24]London, vol. 23, No. 4 (April 1914), pp. 232–244.
[25]Personal communication of 31st August 1974 from Jacob Preuss, the son of Julius Preuss, now living in Herzliya.
[26]Berlin, vol. 35, No. 6 (27th September 1909), pp. 561–581.
[27]See n. 25.
[28]*Loc. cit.*, p. 200.
[29]Muntner, *Introduction . . ., op. cit.*, p. 1 ff.

Preuss's work. Every major medical library, public or private, possesses at least one copy of *Biblisch–Talmudische Medizin*. The creation of the state of Israel in 1948 and the renaissance of the Hebrew language have awakened new interest in Biblical and Talmudical writings. The grandeur of Preuss's contribution to medical research from Bible and Talmud is being more and more appreciated by modern scholars. An updating and revision with correction of errors of Preuss's *magnum opus* remains a *desideratum* to this very day. Only four pages of Preuss's work (pages 515 to 519) and a few excerpts[30] have ever been published in English translation.[31] The inaccessibility of Preuss's classic book to the non-German reader has now been overcome with the imminent publication of an English translation. Karl Sudhoff, the most illustrious figure in the field of the history of medicine during the era of Preuss, hailed Preuss's work as one of the most important contributions to the history of medical scholarship in the preceding half century.[32] Nothing has happened in the nearly seven decades since then to change that assertion. It remains an indispensable work for the student of Hebrew medicine.

Attention should also be drawn to several little-known yet important articles by Preuss which antedated his Biblical–Talmudical compositions. The first, which was never published, was written in 1885 and is entitled *Über Untersuchungen des Blutes zu Diagnostischen Zwecken* (concerning the examination of blood for diagnostic purposes). In this paper, Preuss gathered material from the major books and medical journals on pathology, therapy and diagnosis. His purpose was to provide practical diagnostic guidance to the practising physician about bleeding from any orifices of the body.

This lengthy paper already shows systematic organisation of source material and its presentation in a clear and lucid manner, qualities characteristic of Preuss's subsequent writings including his classic *Biblisch–Talmudische Medizin*.

Another major but little-known article entitled 'Vom Versehen der Schwangeren' was published in two different periodicals in 1892. In this detailed critical-historical study with 211 references, Preuss discusses the possible effect of psychic or psychological impressions of a woman during coitus on her child. Can such psychic influences partially or completely alter the development of the unborn foetus?

This erudite paper was published in 1892 and already clearly demonstrated the depth and precision with which Julius Preuss approached a subject. Preuss begins by citing the classic Biblical example of the story of Jacob and the spotted sheep (Genesis 30:37–39). His scholarship was extraordinary and it was the lucidity of his presentation that made Rudolf Virchow say of him "he knew how to think medically".

Another brief article entitled 'Zur Pathologie der Zunge' (On the pathology

[30]Jacob Snowman, *A Short History of Talmudic Medicine*, London 1935, p. 1 ff.
[31]R. Rosenthal, 'The Care of the Sick in the Bible and the Talmud'. Translated from Julius Preuss (1861–1913), in *Victor Robinson Memorial Volume*, edited by Solomon R. Kagan, New York 1948, pp. 353–358.
[32]Sudhoff, *Essays . . .*, *op. cit.*, pp. 351–353.

of the tongue) describes two patients, one of whom was a baby with a tumour of the lingual frenulum and the other a woman with chronic superficial glossitis.

Other unpublished articles by Preuss include papers on quackery and secret remedies, domicile hygiene, the position of the woman in Judaism and the duty of Jewish physicians.

Preuss's classic book *Biblisch–Talmudische Medizin* was a book which has indelibly recorded Preuss's name for posterity as a giant in Biblical and Talmudic medical scholarship. Muntner seems fully justified in calling Preuss "the father of Hebrew medical research", from whence the title of this essay. Preuss's book was originally published in Berlin by S. Karger in 1911; it was reprinted unchanged in 1921 and 1923 by the original publisher and in 1969 by Gregg Publishers in England. In 1971, the Ktav Publishing Company in New York reprinted the book unchanged for the fourth time but added an introduction, biographical sketch and bibliography of Julius Preuss by Suessmann Muntner, and a Hebrew and Aramaic register which was prepared in handwritten copy by Adolph Löwinger several years after the original 1911 publication. An English translation of this register by Samuel Paley is also included.

Preuss's work is an anthology of all his articles published over many years in a variety of scholarly journals beginning with his pioneering study entitled 'Der Arzt in Bibel und Talmud' which appeared in *Virchow's Archiv* in 1894. In the preface to his book, Preuss points out that the number of commentaries, textbooks and individual works on the Bible is greater than the number of letters contained in the Bible. Preuss's book, covering the entire subject of Biblical and Talmudical medicine, is the first composed by a physician in which the material is derived directly from the original sources. Wunderbar, who completed his *Biblisch–Talmudische Medizin* in 1860, was a layman. Ebstein, whose writings appeared in 1901 (*Die Medizin im Alten Testament*) and 1903 (*Die Medizin im Neuen Testament und im Talmud*) was dependent upon the use of available fragmentary translations. Other works concerning the totality of Biblical–Talmudical medicine did not exist.

In chapter 1, entitled 'The Physician and Other Medical Personnel', Preuss defines the term physician, *rophé* in Hebrew and *asya* in Aramaic. He describes the position of the physician in antiquity, his fees and his responsibilities to his patients. In Judaism, a physician is regarded as a messenger of God. If he intentionally injures a patient, the physician is obviously liable; otherwise he is held blameless. Physicians served as expert witnesses in civil court cases and in the evaluation of a criminal in terms of his capacity to tolerate disciplinary flogging. The physician was and still is consulted regarding the severity of an illness which involves the need to desecrate the Sabbath or the Day of Atonement for the patient.

Preuss describes the education of a physician in ancient times which was accomplished either by the apprenticeship method or in official schools of medicine. He also lists some of the physicians mentioned in the Talmud such as Theodoros, Tobiya, Bar Girnte, Bar Nathan, Rabbi Ammi and, of course, Mar Samuel, the most illustrious of all.

Preuss cites a very interesting homiletical exposition (*Midrash* Psalms 6:3) which seem to accurately depict a twentieth-century scene:

> "A patient being treated by a physician waited: when will the physician come? At 4 or 5 or 6 or 7 o'clock – he did not arrive, however. It is 8, 9 and 10 o'clock and he still has not arrived. Finally, at dawn, his wagon was heard in the distance. Then the patient said to the physician: had you tarried just a little bit longer, my soul would have left me."

The "other medical personnel" described in this chapter are the blood-letter, the ritual circumciser, the midwife and the veterinarian. Preuss points out that a blood-letter, of whom very few complimentary things are said in the Talmud, is an artisan and not a scholar, and hence on a lower social scale than the physician.

In chapter 2, Preuss describes the anatomy and physiology of the various body organs and limbs as mentioned in the Bible and Talmud by dividing them into external organs (head, face, chin, neck, shoulder, axilla, elbow, forearm, hand, fingers, thumb, fist, nail, foot, heel, toes, knee, thigh, hips, back and abdomen), organs of sensation (eye, nose, ear, skin) and internal organs. The latter include organs of the digestive system (lips, teeth, œsophagus, stomach, liver, gall bladder and spleen), respiratory system (lung and voice box), circulatory system (heart and aorta), genito-urinary system (kidneys, urinary bladder and male and female genitalia) and nervous system (brain and spinal cord). Preuss attempts to identify the 248 limbs mentioned throughout early Jewish writings which are said to correspond to the 248 positive commandments of Judaism.

In chapter 3, Preuss begins by defining a patient. He then discusses the belief in ancient Judaism that demons cause illness. For example, the Talmud states that a mad dog is possessed by an evil spirit. Preuss talks of astrology and the evil eye, of magic and incantations and amulets to ward off disease. Astrological reasons were especially decisive for the selection of days appropriate for blood-letting, not only in Talmudic times, but throughout the centuries and millennia. Rarely found in Talmudic writings is the medieval concept of the four body humours (black bile, yellow bile, phlegm and blood) whereby diseases are thought to occur by a dysequilibrium of these humours with one or the other predominating in the body or in a specific organ.

The fourth chapter, called 'Sicknesses and Their Treatment', begins with a lengthy discussion of plague or pestilence. Preuss lists all the epidemics described in the Bible and Talmud, and concludes that it is not possible, because of the dearth of symptomatology mentioned, to establish with certainty whether or not the numerous Biblical and Talmudical diseases referred to as *megepha*, *deber*, *nega* or *negeph* represent bubonic plague, cholera, dysentery, typhus or some other epidemic illness. *Askara* seems to be epidemic diphtheria since it afflicts primarily children, and the major symptoms are referable to the throat.

Preuss discusses acute and chronic fevers and describes various remedies, mostly from folk medicine, for quotidian, tertian and quartan fevers. He also lists the causes and remedies for hydrops (dropsy), podagra (gout), heatstroke, and *yerakon* which is the Biblical and Talmudical expression for jaundice and/or anaemia.

Biblical and Talmudic descriptions of lung maladies such as perforations, defects, lumps, cysts, fistulae and adhesions, as well as citations of digestive tract illnesses such as dysentery, colic, bulimia, haemorrhoids and intestinal worms are provided by Preuss in this chapter. In the section on illness of the oral cavity including mouth odours and abscesses, Preuss cites the following interesting Talmudic passages:

> "one should not converse with people who eat raw vegetables before the fourth hour of the day because they emit a bad odour from the mouth. (Berachoth 44b). If one doesn't walk at least 4 ells after eating before one lies down to sleep, the food putrefies without being digested, and this is the beginning of a bad mouth odour. (Shabbath 41a)."

Finally, the five types of heart ailments are discussed: pain, weakness, heaviness, palpitations and pressure of the heart. For example, the following are the Talmudic assertions concerning weakness of the heart or *chulsha de libba*: Rabbi Chisda and Rabbi Huna sat all day engaged in Judgements and their "hearts grew weak" (Shabbath 10a). Perhaps hunger pangs or hypoglycemia are meant here. Rabbi Zera was unable to teach because his "heart felt faint or weak" (Taanith 7a). Rabbi Awia had "weakness of the heart" and did not go to hear the lecture of Rabbi Joseph (Berachoth 28b).

Chapter 5 is devoted to surgery and deals primarily with injuries and malformations. Preuss begins with a discussion of surgical instruments such as the small drill for opening the skull, the knife for circumcision, needles to remove splinters, and others. He then describes various types of injuries such as sword or other stab or puncture wounds, burn wounds, broken bones, dislocations and sprains, and amputations for gangrene. Also described are injuries inflicted by animals such as the bite of a mad dog, snake bites, insect bites and worm infestation. The signs of a mad dog as mentioned in the Talmud are as follows: its mouth is open, its saliva is dripping, its ears flap, its tail hangs between its thighs and it walks on the edge of the road.

There are two appendices to this chapter. The first deals with circumcision. Preuss discusses some of the boundless literature on the theories of the origin of circumcision, the covenant of Abraham, the importance and technique and timing of circumcision and reasons for its postponement, i.e., illness, the instrumentation used and circumcision practised by other peoples. Astounding is the recognition by the sages of the Talmud of a bleeding disorder, probably haemophilia, and its genetic transmission. The Talmud rules that if two children of a woman be exsanguinated as a result of circumcision, the third child should not be circumcised. Furthermore, if two sisters each had a son who died of bleeding following circumcision, then the third sister should not circumcise her son. Although later Jewish codes assumed that haemophilia can also be transmitted through the baby's father, the second-century Talmud correctly recognised the sex-linked nature of this disease, i.e., only males have the disease but females are carriers and transmit it to their male offspring.

The second appendix deals with blood-letting, either for therapeutic reasons or as a preventive measure. The Talmud discusses the frequency, amount, site of blood-letting and the instrumentation used including a lancet, a nail or other pointed objects and cupping glasses. Dietary factors in relation to blood-letting are considered important. Mar Samuel said that a person to be bled should be fasting; after the blood-letting, the patient should tarry a little, then arise and eat a little before going out. The consumption of nourishing foods after blood-letting is essential. Venesection on animals is also discussed.

Surgery on the eye is not considered at all in the Bible or Talmud. Preuss cites several instances from the New Testament of miraculous healing of the blind by placing one's hands on the patient or his eyes. Eye-glasses, eye prostheses, artificial eyes and eye make-up are described in some detail.

In chapter 7, which deals with dentistry, Preuss discusses toothaches, cavities, loose teeth and artificial teeth. Sour fruit is said to be good for toothache. The vapours of a bathhouse are harmful to the teeth. Vinegar causes loosening of teeth. Preuss points out the emphasis which oriental people place on beautiful teeth.

In the very brief chapter on otology, Preuss describes anatomical defects of the ears, piercing of ears and other injuries, whether intentionally inflicted or not, pain in the ear, remedies for ear ailments, and deafness and its causes.

In an equally brief chapter on disorders of the nose, Preuss describes various abnormal shapes and disfigurements of the nose, as found in the Bible and Talmud, mostly secondary to leprosy. Nasal polyps are discussed, as well as remedies for nosebleeds, mostly from folk medicine.

Chapter 10 is devoted to neurological disorders. About a third of the chapter deals with epilepsy and hysteria. Love-sickness was thought in antiquity to be a type of hysteria. Also discussed in this chapter are headache, plethora and migraine, paralysis, strokes (apoplexy), sciatica and the tremor of old age. The Talmud recommends that one rub the head with wine, vinegar or oil to treat a headache. Numerous remedies are prescribed for migraine including many from folk medicine.

Mental disorders are covered in chapter 11. Preuss discusses in detail the mental illness of King Saul of Israel. After considerable deliberation, Preuss concludes that Saul was a "melancholic in the psychiatric sense"; today we would say that he suffered from a paranoid psychopathia. His raving and ranting, his affliction with evil spirits and the stripping off of his clothes, are interpreted by Preuss to represent epilepsy or an epileptic equivalent. Visual and auditory hallucinations, insanity, "possession by demons or spirits" and exorcism are all described by Preuss from Bible and Talmud. An imbecile is considered to be mentally deficient and is equated with a minor and a deaf-mute in Jewish law: he cannot testify in court, his contracting of marriage is invalid, etc. The Talmud defines someone who is mentally ill: "He who goes out at night alone, and he who spends the night in a graveyard, and he who tears his garments, and destroys everything that is given to him" (Chagigah 3b).

Someone mentally ill is distinguished from a drunk or intoxicated person in that the latter behaves like a madman.

In the chapter on skin diseases, Preuss points out that an enormous number of books and treatises have been written about the thirteenth chapter of the book of Leviticus which deals with an illness called *tzaraath*, probably leprosy. As a result, says Preuss: "one might think that every detail would have been clarified and every linguistic and archaeological problem solved. However, just the opposite is the case."

Preuss discusses the fundamental law of *tzaraath*, and describes the various skin lesions, scabs, boils, scars, eczema, burn wounds and the like as mentioned in the Bible and Talmud. The diagnosis, treatment and cure of leprosy are discussed. Leprosy was thought to represent punishment for the sin of slander. The illness *shechin* and its various forms, the *shechin* of Egypt, and the sicknesses of Job and King Hezekiah (possibly leprosy, elephantiasis, syphilis, diphtheria, variola or other malady) are also discussed. Preuss concludes that *shechin* is a collective name comprising many types of skin diseases including inflammatory and traumatic lesions.

There are two appendices to this chapter. The first deals with gonorrhoea, its causes and mode of transmission, and the Jewish ritual laws pertaining to someone afflicted with it. In the second appendix, which concerns cosmetics in the Bible and Talmud, Preuss describes hair-cutting instruments, haircuts and hair styles for both men and women, hair hygiene, depilatories and wigs. Also discussed are embrocations, oils, perfumes, cosmetics, soaps and facial make-up.

A brief chapter on gynaecology deals primarily with menstruation and its ritual implications, vaginal bleeding and its causes and treatment, and castration in the female. Most remedies are from folk medicine; for example, "give the woman with vaginal bleeding Persian onions boiled in wine or cumin, safflower and fenugreek boiled in wine, and exclaim to her: cease your discharge!"

Chapter 14 is devoted to obstetrics. The first half of the chapter deals with normal physiological events surrounding pregnancy including the recognition and duration of pregnancy, the foetus and foetal development, sex determination, multiple births, premature births, parturition, the birthstool, the placenta, postpartum ritual purification, the newborn infant, washing, salting and swaddling of the newborn, lactation and suckling, wet-nurses and nursing from an animal or bottle. Of particular interest is the recognition by Mar Samuel in the Talmud that a foetus begins to assume form and shape at forty days after conception. Prior to that time, it is "mere fluid". Also of interest is the "preserving stone" which women carried with them to insure normal pregnancies. Furthermore, the concept of superfecundity, that is one woman becoming pregnant from two men, was accepted in the Talmud.

The second half of the chapter on obstetrics deals with pathological occurrences. Among the subjects discussed are sterility, oral contraception by means of a "potion of herbs", abortion and the abortus, moles, monster births and the "sandal" foetus, false pregnancy, difficult labour and embryotomy, sorcery in obstetrics, caesarian sections and puerperal illnesses. Numerous methods of contraception are discussed in the Talmud but perhaps the most interesting is the "potion of herbs", also known as the "cup of roots". This remedy is prepared from Alexandrian gum, liquid alum and garden crocus, powdered and mixed with beer or wine (Shabbath 110a).

In chapter 15, which is entitled 'Materia Medica', Preuss first discusses the plant remedies which the Talmud recommends as abortifacients, emetics, purgatives, digestives, etc., as well as various types of plasters, compresses, poultices, and bandages and the like, and their various medicinal ingredients. Also discussed are animal remedies such as honey, goat's milk, crushed pearl, animal dung and urine, and the great theriac. Non-medicinal remedies can be exemplified by the Talmudic suggestion that for abdominal pain, one should place warm clothes on the abdomen or a hot cup or bottle on the navel. Sun-bathing is said to heal a variety of ailments. Certain foods should be avoided for certain illnesses. The final part of this chapter is devoted to a discussion of Jewish hospitals in antiquity (or lack thereof) and the visiting of the sick. The tradi-tional Jewish concept of visiting the sick is that it is not a social call but a visit in which to help the patient by cooking or cleaning for him, or by assisting him in any other manner.

Chapter 16 is very lengthy and deals with sex ethics in the Bible and Talmud. The subjects discussed by Preuss in this chapter are: chastity, marriage, pro-creation, genealogy in marriage, conjugal duties, cohabitation, impotence, un-natural coitus, *coitus interruptus*, abstention from procreation, times when cohab-itation is prohibited, cohabitation and sexual desire, aphrodisiacs, the *duda'im* or mandrakes, conception *sine concubito*, proscribed marriages, punishment for incest, rarity of punishment infliction, the incest of Lot and his daughters, Amnon and Tamar, Levirate marriage, adultery, lustful thoughts, the *sotah* or suspected adulteress, rape, seduction, virginity, prostitution, the street of harlots, harlots in Biblical times, their skills, their attire and their hire, the *jus primum noctis*, Hegemonian coitus, masturbation, pederasty and homosexuality, transvestism, sodomy and bestiality, tribady and lesbianism.

In chapter 17, Preuss discusses the Jewish dietary laws, ritual slaughtering, and the Biblical prohibitions of blood and certain fat. He then describes the laws of ritual purity and impurity known as *tumah* and *taharah* of the human body, utensils and clothing; and the rules of defilement relating to the Temple, priests, cadavers, people afflicted with leprosy and/or gonorrhoea, and the purification process including the ritual immersion. Even though these rules may serve a hygienic purpose, they are not meant to be "hygienic laws" but are Divine commands. The importance of washing and bathing in ancient times is empha-sised by Preuss.

Preuss also discusses death and dying in this chapter. In Jewish law, a dying person may not be touched or moved lest his death be hastened. The recognition of death required the cessation of respiration and the absence of a heartbeat. Furthermore, one must be certain that the person has not just fainted or fallen in a swoon. The perfuming and embalming of the dead are then described. The five Biblical cases of suicide are mentioned including those of Saul, Ahitophel and Omri. Remarkable are the Biblical and Talmudic descriptions of marble and wooden coffins. Graves were either in the ground or in natural or man-made caves. Biblical and Talmudic discussions of the sepulchres of the Patriarchs and of burial, cremation and the decomposition of bodies, conclude the section on death and dying.

The final chapter, entitled 'Dietetics', deals with the rules which a healthy person should follow in order not to become ill. Preuss asserts that dietetics refers not only to nutrition, as the modern usage of the word connotes, but also includes the entire mode of life of an individual, since residence and clothing and sports and work and many other things have certain influences on health, and hence belong in the word "diet".

The general rules of health and nutrition, among others, are: eat moderately, eat simply, eat slowly and eat regularly. Chronic alcoholism, a rare disorder among Jews, is mentioned because of the juridical difference in Jewish law between a *shattuy* (tipsy or fuddled) and a *shikkor* (drunk or intoxicated). Regarding exercise, Rabbi Yohanan said: "do not sit too much, for sitting provokes haemorrhoids; do not stand too much, for standing is harmful to the heart (or stomach); do not walk too much, for (excessive) walking is harmful to the eyes" (Kethuboth 111a).

With regard to domicile, it is said that it is healthy to live in an open city, and harmful to live in a fortified or closed city. In the latter, houses are built close together, but in the former there are gardens and parks and the air is good.

How does one find words to emphasise the immensity of the contribution to medicine and Judaica of Preuss's book, of which I have made but a brief summary here? It was perhaps best expressed by Leibowitz in 1961 in his editorial in *Koroth*:[33]

> ". . . Preuss was one of the greatest Jewish historians of medicine; endowed with intimate insight in the field of early Hebrew medicine; outstanding in his critical approach, wide knowledge and unbiased honesty. Dear to our heart, his memory may serve as a shining and stimulating example for present and future historians."

[33]Leibowitz, *loc. cit.*, p. 1.

Post-War Publications on German Jewry

A Selected Bibliography of Books and Articles 1976

Compiled by
BERTHA COHN

Leo Baeck Institute
4 Devonshire Street
London W.1.

CONTENTS

BIBLIOGRAPHY 1976

I. HISTORY

A. General

13383. ANGRESS, WERNER T.: *Das deutsche Militär und die Juden im Ersten Weltkrieg.* Dokumentation. [In]: Militärgeschichtliche Mitteilungen. Hrsg. vom Militärgeschichtlichen Forschungsamt durch Friedrich Forstmeier und Manfred Messerschmidt u.a. Jg. 19, Nr. 1. Freiburg i. Br. 1976. Pp. 77–146, notes pp. 130–146.

13384. CECIL, LAMAR: *Wilhelm II. und die Juden.* [In]: Juden im Wilhelminischen Deutschland 1890–1914. Pp. 313–347. [See No. 13387.]

13385. EKSTEINS, MODRIS: *The Limits of Reason.* The German Democratic Press and the Collapse of Weimar Democracy. London: Oxford University Press, 1975. xv, 337 pp., tabs., bibl. (pp. 315–325). (Oxford Historical Monographs.) [Incl. chaps.: Liberalism and the Press in Germany in 1918. The Press in the Weimar Republic. The Firms of Mosse, Ullstein and Sonnemann. The Eclipse of Liberalism. Odd Bedfellows: The Frankfurter Zeitung and I.G. Farben. Ullstein v. Ullstein. Gleichschaltung, Phase One: The Elimination of Opposition. Gleichschaltung, Phase Two: The End of Ullstein, Mosse and Sonnemann. A revised version of No. 12638/YB. XXI.]

13386. *Juden im Mittelalter.* Eingel. und zusammengestellt von Dieter Berg und Horst Steur. Göttingen: Vandenhoeck & Ruprecht, 1976. 87 pp., bibl. (pp. 85–87). (Historische Texte: Mittelalter, Bd. 17).

13387. *Juden im Wilhelminischen Deutschland 1890–1914.* Ein Sammelband. Hrsg. von Werner E. Mosse unter Mitwirkung von Arnold Paucker. Tübingen: J. C. B. Mohr (Paul Siebeck), 1976. xiv, 786 pp. tabs., bibl. (pp. 703–754). (Schriftenreihe wissenschaftlicher Abhandlungen des Leo Baeck Instituts, 33.) [Cont.: Vorwort von Werner E. Mosse und Arnold Paucker. Emanzipation und Krise – Zur Geschichte der 'Judenfrage' in Deutschland vor 1890 (Reinhard Rürup, pp. 1–56). Die Juden in Wirtschaft und Gesellschaft (Werner E. Mosse, pp. 57–113). Die Rathenaus. Zwei Generationen jüdischen Anteils an der industriellen Entwicklung Deutschlands (Ernst Schulin, pp. 115–142). Die jüdische Beteiligung an der Politik (Peter Pulzer, pp. 143–239, tabs.). Begegnung mit der Moderne. Deutsche Juden in der deutschen Kultur (Peter Gay, pp. 241–311). Wilhelm II. und die Juden (Lamar Cecil, pp. 313–347). Die gesellschaftliche Bedeutung der christlich-jüdischen Differenz. Zur Situation im deutschen Katholizismus (Herman Greive, pp. 349–388). Struktur und Funktion des deutschen Antisemitismus (Werner Jochmann, pp. 389–477). Zur Problematik einer jüdischen Abwehrstrategie in der deutschen Gesellschaft (Arnold Paucker, pp. 479–548). Die geistigen und religiösen Strömungen in der deutschen Judenheit (Pinchas E. Rosenblüth, pp. 549–598). Theologische Debatte um das 'Wesen' des Judentums (Uriel Tal, pp. 599–632). Die umkämpfte nationaljüdische Idee (Yehuda Eloni, pp. 633–688). Die schleichende Krise der jüdischen Identität. Ein Nachwort (Robert Weltsch, pp. 689–702). Bibliographie. Register.]

13388. KALLNER, RUDOLF: *Herzl und Rathenau.* Wege jüdischer Existenz an der Wende des 20. Jahrhunderts. Stuttgart: Klett, 1976. 446 pp., bibl. (pp. 432–438).

13389. KEMPNER, ROBERT M. W.: *When Democracy Failed.* From Weimar to Hitler. [In]: AJR Information. February. London, 1974. Pp. 6–7. [Author was chief adviser to the Police Dept. of the Prussian Ministry of the Interior when the Nazis came to power. After the war, he was Deputy US Chief Prosecutor at the Nuremberg Trials.]

13390. KISCH, GUIDO: *Research in Medieval Legal History of the Jews.* Studies in Political and Social History. [In]: American Academy for Jewish Research. Medieval Jewish Life. Studies from the Proceedings of the American Academy for Jewish Research, selected, and with an introduction by Robert Chazan. New York: Ktav, 1976. xiv, 463 pp.

13391. KÜTHER, CARSTEN: *Räuber und Gauner in Deutschland.* Das organisierte Bandenwesen im 18. und frühen 19. Jahrhundert. Göttingen: Vandenhoeck & Ruprecht, 1976. 197 pp., map, notes pp. 151–175, bibl. (pp. 176–190). (Kritische Studien zur Geschichtswissenschaft, Bd. 20.) [Part II: Die soziale Herkunft der Räuber. Zigeuner und Juden.]

273

13392. LOWENSTEIN, STEVEN M.: *The Pace of Modernisation of German Jewry in the Nineteenth Century.* [In]: LBI Year Book XXI. London, 1976. Pp. 41–56, facsims., tabs.

13393. MOSSE, GEORGE L.: *Towards the Final Solution.* The European Experience of Race. London: Dent, 1976. 256 pp., 16 pp. illus.

13394. PAZI, MARGARITA: *Die Juden in der Ersten Deutschen Nationalversammlung, 1848/49.* [In]: Jahrbuch des Instituts für Deutsche Geschichite. Bd. V. Tel Aviv, 1976. Pp. 177–209. [See No. 13481.]

13395. POIS, ROBERT A.: *The Bourgeois Democrats of Weimar Germany.* Transactions of the American Philosophical Society. New Series, vol. 66, part 4, July. Philadelphia: The American Philosophical Society, 1976. 117 pp., bibl. (pp. 113–114). [Chap. VI: The German Democrats and the Jews. VII: The Democratic Reaction to Nazism.]

13396. PULZER, PETER: *Die jüdische Beteiligung an der Politik.* [In]: Juden im Wilhelminischen Deutschland 1890–1914. Pp. 143–239, tabs. [See No. 13387.]

13397. RICHARZ, MONIKA, ed.: *Jüdisches Leben in Deutschland.* Selbstzeugnisse zur Sozialgeschichte 1780–1871. Hrsg. und eingel. von Monika Richarz. Stuttgart: Deutsche Verlags-Anstalt, 1976. 499 pp., ports., illus., facisms. (Veröffentlichung des Leo Baeck Instituts). [Cont.: Vorwort von Reinhard Rürup. Einführung. I. Die Quellen. 1. Die Memoirensammlung des Leo Baeck Institutes. 2. Auswahl und Edition. II. Zum Verständnis der Selbstzeugnisse. Quellentexte. I. Händler in Napoleonischer Zeit. II. Landjudentum. III. Handwerker. IV. Kaufleute und Bankiers. V. Textilindustrie. VI. Lehrer, Schächter, Vorsänger. VII. Akademiker und Beamte. VIII. Milieu der Kindheit. IX. Auswanderung.]

13398. SCHORSCH, ISMAR: *On the History of the Political Judgement of the Jew.* New York: Leo Baeck Institute, 1976. 23 pp., biogr. notes pp. 21–23. (The Leo Baeck Memorial Lecture, 20).

13399. SÖSEMANN, BERND: *Das Ende der Weimarer Republik in der Kritik demokratischer Publizisten.* Theodor Wolff, Ernst Feder, Julius Elbau, Leopold Schwarzschild. Berlin: Colloquium-Verlag, 1976. 256 pp., notes pp. 182–231, bibl. (pp. 232–245). (Abhandlungen und Materialien zur Publizistik, Bd. 9). [Theodor Wolff, chief ed. of the Berliner Tageblatt (1868 Berlin–1943 Berlin), Ernst Feder, journalist, (1881 Berlin–1964 Berlin), Julius Elbau, journalist, last chief ed. of the Vossische Zeitung, (1881 Stuttgart–1965 New York), Leopold Schwarzschild, ed. of 'Das Tagebuch', 1891 Frankfurt/M.–1950 Santa Margherita, Italy.]

13400. STERN, FRITZ: *Gold and Iron: Bismarck, Bleichröder and the Building of the German Empire.* New York: Knopf, London: Allen and Unwin, 1976. 620 pp., ports. [Cf. also No. 10884/YB. XVIII: The Collaboration and Friendship of Gerson Bleichröder and Otto von Bismarck. [And]: The Jew behind the Junkers (Hugh Trevor-Roper) in: Sunday Times, 1st May, London 1977, port. See also No. 13758.]

13401. VIERHAUS, RUDOLF, ed.: *Das Tagebuch der Baronin Spitzemberg geb. Freiin von Varnbüler.* Aufzeichnungen aus der Hofgesellschaft des Hohenzollernreiches. Ausgew. u. hrsg. von Rudolf Vierhaus. 4. Aufl. Göttingen: Vandenhoeck & Ruprecht, 1976. 612 pp., port. (Deutsche Geschichtsquellen des 19. und 20. Jahrhunderts. Hrsg. von der Histor. Kommission bei der Bayerischen Akademie der Wissenschaften, Bd. 43). [1. Aufl. 1961, 3. Aufl. 1963. Contains many references to Jews.]

Linguistics

13402. ALTHAUS, HANS PETER: *Die Kunst der Paraphrase.* Otto F. Best über das Jiddische. [In]: ZDL (Zeitschrift für Deutsches Altertum und Deutsche Literatur), 41, Wiesbaden: Steiner, 1974. Pp. 318–337.

13403. COPELAND, ROBERT M. and NATHAN SÜSSKIND, eds.: *The Language of Herz's Esther.* A Study in Judeo-German Dialectology. Birmingham: University of Alabama Press, 1976. 439 pp. [Linguistic analysis of Joseph Herz's nineteenth-century Yiddish comedy 'Esther oder die belohnte Tugend'. A facsim. of the title page of the second edition (Fürth, 1854), in: LBI Year Book XXI, London, 1976, between pp. 46 and 47. See No. 13482.]

13404. DREESSEN, WULF-OTTO, WALTER RÖLL, ERIKA TIMM: *Jiddische Drucke vor 1800.* Hilfen für den Umgang mit einem neuen Quellenverzeichnis. [In]: ZDL (Zeitschrift für

Deutsches Altertum und Deutsche Literatur. Bd. 105, H. 4. Wiesbaden: Franz Steiner, 1976. Pp. 310–317.

13405. *Jiddisch Kolloquium an der Universität Trier*, 29, u. 30. Juli 1976. [A report in]: Unijournal. Zeitschrift der Universität Trier. Jg. 2, Nr. 4, 28. Okt. 1976, facsim. [And in]: AJR Information, Oct. London, 1976. [Papers read incl.: Sepher ha-Gan by Isaac b. Eliezer (Walter Roell), Florus and Blanchefleur (Theresia Friderichs), Glosses of the Bernese Small Aruch (Erika Timm), Synonymic Problems in Old Yiddish (Wulf-Otto Dreessen), Yiddish Letters of the Period and Environment of Glueckel von Hameln (Günter Marwedel), Did Jews in Zuerich read and speak Yiddish by the end of the fourteenth century? (Florence Guggenheim), The Influence of the Netherland Culture on the Yiddish Literature in the Seventeenth and Eighteenth Century (L. Fuks), The State and Development of Yiddish in the Course of the Sixteenth Century (J. Maitlis).]

13406. RÖLL, WALTER: *Man hört wenig sagen von Frieden.* Ein jüdisches Lehrgedicht aus dem Mayen des 17. Jahrhunderts. [In]: Kurtrierisches Jahrbuch. 16. Jg. Hrsg. von der Stadtbibliothek Trier und dem 'Verein Kurtrierisches Jahrbuch'. Trier, 1976. Pp. 40–42.

B. Communal and Regional History

1. Germany

13407. ALLENSTEIN. TRUNZ, ERICH: *Frieda Strohmberg: Erinnerungen.* [In]: Bausteine zur Kultur Allensteiner Profile. Sonderdruck des 'Allensteiner Briefes', hrsg. von Msgr. Paul Kewitsch 1975.

13408. ALTONA. BRILLING, BERNHARD: *Zur Geschichte der Hebräischen Buchdruckereien in Altona.* 1. Zur Vorgeschichte des Druckereiprivilegs von Jacob Emden (1743). [In]: Studies in Bibliography and Booklore. Vol. XI (Centennial Issue). Publ. by the Library of Hebrew Union College – Jewish Institute of Religion. Winter, 1975/76. No. 1–2. Cincinnati, 1976. Pp. 41–56, documents, notes pp. 54–56. [See No. 9249/YB. XVII: Die Privilegien der hebräischen Buchdruckereien in Altona (1726–1836), by the same author.]

13409. FREIMARK, PETER: *Zu den Judentoren in Altona.* [In]: 'Die Heimat', Monatsschrift des Vereins zur Pflege der Natur – und Landeskunde in Schleswig Holstein, Hamburg und sein Umland. 83. Jg., H. 1, Januar. Kiel: Wachholz, 1976. Pp. 1–5. [Cf. No. 12661/YB. XXI.]

13410. MARWEDEL, GÜNTER: *Die Privilegien der Juden in Altona.* Hrsg. und eingel. von Günter Marwedel. Hamburg: Hans Christians, 1976. 432 pp., cover, facsim., facsims., bibl. (pp. 30–41), list of names. (Hamburger Beiträge zur Geschichte der Deutschen Juden, Bd. V.)

13411. ALZEY. BÖCHER, OTTO: *Die Geschichte der Alzeyer Juden.* Festvortrag anlässlich der Gedenkfeier für die jüdischen Mitbürger am 30. Sept. 1973 im Musiksaal des Staatl. Aufbaugymnasiums Alzey. [In]: Alzeyer Geschichtsblätter, Bd. 10. Alzey: Rheinhessische Druckwerkstätte, 1974. Pp. 37–43.

13412. BÖCHER, OTTO: *Zur Geschichte der Alzeyer Juden.* Pp. 196–206. [In]: 1750 Jahre Alzey. Festschrift. Hrsg. im Auftrag der Stadt Alzey von Friedrich Karl Becker u.a. Alzey: Rheinhessische Druckwerkstätte, 1973. xii, 384 pp., ports., illus.

13413. BADEN. RIFF, MICHAEL ANTHONY: *The Anti-Jewish Aspect of the Revolutionary Unrest of 1848 in Baden and its Impact on Emancipation.* [In]: LBI Year Book XXI. London, 1976. Pp. 27–40.

13414. BAVARIA. GEISSLER, KLAUS: *Die Juden in Deutschland und Bayern bis zur Mitte des 14. Jahrhunderts.* München: Beck, 1976. ix, 240 pp. (Zeitschrift für bayerische Landesgeschichte, Beih. Reihe B, 7). Zugl. Philos. Diss., Univ. München 1974.

13415. BERLIN. BLOCH, PETER: *Grabmäler in Berlin.* [In]: Berliner Forum. Hrsg. vom Presse- und Informationsamt des Landes Berlin. Sept. 1976. 112 pp. illus. [Incl. the tombs of David Kalisch, Leopold Kronecker, Alfred Messel, B. Henry Strousberg, Ludwig Dessoir – all baptised Jews buried in the cemetery of the Matthäus–Gemeinde in Berlin–Schöneberg.]

13416. JAMESON, EGON: *Berlin – so wie es war*. Ein Bildband. 4. Aufl. Düsseldorf: Droste, 1973. 128 pp., 216 illus. [1969 ed. see No. 7631/YB. XV.]

13417. KIAULEHN, WALTHER: *Berlin – Schicksal einer Weltstadt*. Unveränd. Nachdr. München: Beck, 1976. 596 pp., 67 ports. and illus., maps, bibl. (pp. 580–583). (Beck'sche Sonderausgaben). [First publ. 1958. See No. 1609/YB. V. With numerous references to Berlin Jews.]

13418. LIANG, HSI-HUEY: *Die Berliner Polizei in der Weimarer Republik*. Aus d. Amerik. übers. von Brigitte und Wolfgang Behn. Berlin–New York: de Gruyter, 1976. xx, 233 pp., ports., illus., maps, bibl. (Veröffentlichungen der Histor. Kommission zu Berlin, Bd. 47). [Incl. numerous references to Jews, in particular to Dr. Bernhard Weiss (1880 Berlin–1951 London) who was Deputy Police President from 1927–1932 when he had to resign. For the orig. see No. 8430/YB. XVI.]

13419. MACHOW, MAX: *Die Ost- und Westpreussen in Berlin*. Ein Beitrag zur Bevölkerungsgeschichte der Stadt. Berlin: Haude & Spener, 1975. 114 pp. (Berlinische Reminiszenzen, Nr. 48). [Incl. Johann Jacoby, physician and politician, 1805 Königsberg–1877 Königsberg. B. Henry Strousberg, industrialist, 1823 Neidenburg–1884 Berlin. Hugo Haase, politician, 1863 Allenstein–1919 Berlin. Hugo Heimann, politician, 1859 Konitz–1951 New York. Erich Mendelssohn, architect, 1887 Allenstein–1953 San Francisco. Leopold Jessner, theatre producer, 1878 Königsberg–1945 Los Angeles.]

13420. OSCHILEWSKI, WALTHER G.: *Zeitungen in Berlin im Spiegel der Jahrhunderte*. Berlin: Haude & Spener, 1975. 326 pp., ports., illus., facsims., bibl. (pp. 300–302). [Incl. chaps.: Rudolf Mosse tritt auf den Plan. Leopold Ullstein begründet sein zukünftiges 'Imperium'. Georg Bernhard, Theodor Wolff.]

13421. RHEINISCHES LANDESMUSEUM BONN, ed.: *Klima einer Hauptstadt. Jüdische Maler im Berlin der Jahrhundertwende*. Veranstalter der Ausstellung: Gesellschaft f. Christl.-Jüdische Zusammenarbeit Bonn in Verbindung mit der Ostdeutschen Galerie Regensburg, 11. März bis 4. April 1976. (Katalog). 32 pp., illus. [Incl. Charlotte Berend-Corinth (painting of Max Pallenberg). Emil Orlik, Ernst Stern, Ludwig Meidner, Michel Fingesten, Lesser Ury, Friedrich Feigl, Rudolf Levy, Eugen Spiro, Hugo Steiner-Prag, Jakob Steinhardt, Heinrich Tischler, Walter Trier.]

13422. BONN. *Bonner Juden und ihre Nachkommen bis um 1930*. Eine familien- und sozialgeschichtliche Dokumentation. Zusammengestellt, eingeleitet und kommentiert von Klaus H. S. Schulte. Bonn: Röhrscheid, 1976. 724 pp., tabs., plans, bibl. (pp. 20–31). (Veröffentlichungen des Stadtarchivs Bonn, Bd. 16.)

13423. BREMEN. SCHROETER, WILLY: *Die Juden in der Hansestadt Bremen*. [In]: 'Allgemeine'. 7. Mai, Düsseldorf, 1976. illus. [the new Synagogue Schwachauser Heerstr. 117]. Appr. 2,000 Jews lived in Bremen in 1933.]

13424. BRESLAU. RABIN, ESTER: *Schattenbilder*. Massada, 1975. 148 pp. [Memories of an orthodox Jewess whose husband, at the beginning of the Nazi régime, was Rabbi and lecturer at the 'Jüdisch-Theologisches Seminar' in Breslau.]

13425. FRANKFURT A./O. GOTTGETREU, ERICH: *Juden aus dem anderen Frankfurt*. [In]: 'MB', 20. Februar. Tel Aviv, 1976. Pp. 3–4. [The archaeologist Prof. Yohanan Aharoni (orig. Aronheim), born 1919 in Frankfurt a./O. died in Jerusalem 1976.]

13426. FRIEDRICHSTADT. (Nordfriesland). HANSEN, HERMANN: *Unsere Friedrichstädter Juden*. 2254 Friedrichstadt: Selbstverlag H. Hansen, Am Mittelburgwall 7, 1976. 119 pp., ports., illus., tabs., facsims.

13427. GOSLAR. MAIMON, ARYE (orig. Herbert Fischer): *Die Flucht der Juden aus Goslar im Jahre 1414 und ihre Folgen*. [In]: 'Harz-Zeitschrift', Jg. 24/25, 1972/73, i.e., Jg. 105/106-der Zeitschrift des Harz-Vereins für Geschichte und Altertumskunde. Goslar, 1974. Pp. 113–119.

13428. GRIESHEIM. ARNSBERG, PAUL: *Der vergessene Friedhof von Griesheim*. [And]: Ein Leserbrief von Adolf Diamant. [In]: 'Allgemeine', 23. Jan. und 6. Februar. Düsseldorf, 1976.

13429. LAHR. KATTERMANN, HILDEGARD [née Becker]: *Geschichte und Schicksale der Lahrer Juden*. Eine Dokumentation. Lahr: Stadtverwaltung, 1976. 43 pp. + 4 pp. bibl., + 39 pp. lists of names. [Mimeog.]

13430. MANNHEIM. GÖRLER, INGEBORG, ed.; *So sahen sie Mannheim*. Stuttgart: Theiss, 1974. 204 pp., ports., illus., bibl. (pp. 201–204). [Incl. chaps. on Hermann Broch, Hugo Wolf, Rahel Straus, Hugo Marx, Vicki Baum, Max Oppenheimer and others.]

13431. MARBURG. Mack, Rüdiger: *Jüdische Universitätsverwandte und Studenten in Marburg im 18. Jahrhundert.* [In]: Hessisches Jahrbuch für Landesgeschichte. Vol. 24. Wiesbaden 1974. Pp. 191–227.

13432. PADERBORN. (Westphalia). Brilling, Bernhard: *Zur Geschichte des Rabbinats von Paderborn (1809–1869): 1. Kapitel (1809–1826).* [In]: 'Udim', Zeitschrift der Rabbiner-konferenz in der Bundesrepublik Deutschland. Bd. VI. Frankfurt a.M. 5736/1975–1976. Pp. 19–32.

13433. PRUSSIA. *Sammlung der die religiöse und bürgerliche Verfassung der Juden in den königlich preussischen Staaten betreffenden Gesetze, Verordnungen, Gutachten, Berichte und Erkenntnisse.* Mit e. Anhang, welcher Gesetze fremder Staaten enthält. Hrsg. von Jeremias Heinemann. Reprogr. Nachdr. d. 2. Aufl. Glogau 1831. Hildesheim: Gerstenberg, 1976. xvi, 522 pp.

13434. RHEDA. (Westphalia). Brilling, Bernhard: *Zur Erinnerung an die Synagoge von Rheda/ Westfalen (1805–1938).* [In]: 'Allgemeine', 24./31. Dez. Düsseldorf, 1976. [See also No. 12689/YB. XXI.]

13435. Weinberg, Werner: *Tale of a Torah Scroll.* Geschichte einer Thora-Rolle. Cincinnati (Ohio): Hebrew Union College – Jewish Institute of Religion, 1976. [The chronicle of a Torah which originally belonged to the author's family in Rheda where he was the last Jewish teacher of the Community, and which he has now given to the Synagogue in Cincinnati.]

13436. RIETBERG. Barlev, Jehuda: *Die Judengemeinde der Grafschaft Rietberg.* Dokumente aus einer langen Geschichte. [In]: 'Allgemeine', 12. März. Düsseldorf, 1976. Pp. 15, 16, 19, 21, illus.

13437. SEESEN/HARZ. *175 Jahre Jacobson-Gymnasium in Seesen.* Hrsg. von der Schule. Seesen, 1976. 40 pp. [Israel Jacobson (Halberstadt 1768–1828 Berlin) founded the school in 1801. Cf. No. 11955/YB. XX: Die Jacobson-Schule in Seesen (Gerhard Ballin).]

13438. SILESIA. '*Mitteilungen des Verbandes ehemaliger Breslauer und Schlesier in Israel*'. Hrsg. Erich Lewin. Nr. 39–40, Apr.–Sept. Tel Aviv, 1976. [2 vols.] Nr. 39 incl.: Die Provinz Schlesien in jüdischer Geschichte und Folklore (A. Tobias). Schlussstein der Emanzipation. Zum 100. Geburtstag von Ismar Freund (Max P. Birnbaum, port.). Zur Geschichte der Juden in Konstadt, Kreuzburg und Pitschen O/S. (Aus dem Nachlass Louis Lewin). Nr. 40 incl.: Über die Anfänge des Zionismus in Breslau, 1897 (Bernhard Brilling). Erinnerungen von Hans Margolius [continued from No. 39]. Martin Bielski (Marol) s. A. (Alice Perez-Tichauer, port.). Rabb. Bernhard Brilling 70 Jahre (Erich Lewin). Felix Daniel Pinczower zum 75. Geburtstag (Erich Lewin, port.). Paul Mühsam zum 100. Geburtstag des Dichter-Philosophen (Annie Loewenstein-Pribatsch). Briefe aus dem Breslauer Rabbinerseminar von Isaak Prager (contin. from No. 39). Zum Gedenken an Otto Hecht (Frieda Hebel. Cf. Nos. 12534 and 12627/YB. XX.). Geschichte der Familie Nothmann (contin. from Nos. 38 and 39).]

13439. WESTPHALIA – NOTTULN nr. Münster. Brilling, Bernhard: *Zur Geschichte der Juden in Nottuln bei Münster.* [In]: Nottulner Weihnachtsmarkt, hrsg. vom Männerge-sangverein Nottuln 1860. Weihnachten 1976. (Auch als Sonderdruck): Nottuln: Druckerei Niemann, 1976. 8 cols., illus.

13440. WORMS. Huttenbach, Henry R.: *The Reconstruction and Evaluation of a Social Calendar as a Primary Source for the History of the Jewish Community of Worms (1933–1938).* [In]: Proceedings of the Sixth World Congress of Jewish Studies. Vol. 2. Jerusalem, 1975. Pp. 367–397. [See also No. 12792/YB. XXI.]

13441. Reuter, Fritz: *Leopold Levy und seine Synagoge von 1875.* Ein Beitrag zu Geschichte und Selbstverständlichkeit der Wormser Juden im 19. Jahrhundert. [In]: Der Wormsgau. Bd. 11, 1974/75. Worms a.Rh.: Stadtbibliothek, 1975. Pp. 58–68, illus.

1a. Alsace

13442. Blumenkranz, Bernhard and Albert Soboul, eds.: *Les Juifs et la Révolution Française.* Problèmes et Aspirations. Toulouse: Edouard Privat, 1976. 231 pp., ports., illus., facsims. (Collection Franco-Judaica, 4ᵉ vol.). [Incl.: *Les Juifs de Metz et De Lorraine (1791–1795)* par Henri Tribout de Morembert, pp. 87–104, illus., facsim. *La Régénération Économique des Juifs d'Alsace. A L'Époque Révolutionnaire et Napoleonienne* (Roland Marx, pp. 105–120, illus.), *Les Juifs D'Alsace et la Conscription au Dix-Neuvième Siècle* (Freddy Raphaël, pp. 121–142, illus.).]

2. Austria

13443. *Austrian History Yearbook.* Published by Rice University in Cooperation with the Conference Group for Central European History. Vol. XI, 1975. Houston, Texas: Rice University, 1976. vi, 389 pp. [Incl. *The Migration of Galician Jews to Vienna, 1857–1880* (Anson G. Rabinbach, pp. 44–54). Comments (Karl R. Stadler and Wolfgang Häusler, pp. 55–56, 57–58). *Galician Jews as Migrants: An Alternative Hypothesis* (Scott M. Eddie, pp. 59–63).]

13444. GAISBAUER, ADOLF: *Eine Jugendbewegung.* Zur Geschichte der jüdisch-nationalen Studentenbewegung in Österreich 1882–1914. [In]: Zeitgeschichte. Jg. 2, H. 6, März. Wien: Geyer Edition, 1975. Pp. 135–147, notes p. 147.

13445. MICHEL, BERNARD: *Banques et Banquiers en Austriche au Début du 20ᵉ Siècle.* Paris: Presse de la Fondation Nationale des Sciences Politiques, 1976. 404 pp., tabs., bibl. (pp. 377–397). (Cahiers de la Fondation . . . No. 199). Édition abrégée de la thèse de doctorat d'État soutenue le 27 juin 1970 à la Sorbonne.

13446. *Phantastisches Österreich.* Eingel. u. hrsg. von Jean Gyory. Wien: Zsolnay, 1976. 432 pp., 23 ports. [Texts by twenty-three authors incl. Kafka, Stefan Zweig, Freud, Schnitzler, Wittgenstein.]

13447. VIENNA. *150 Jahre Wiener Stadttempel.* Wien: Selbstverlag der Israelit. Kultusgemeinde (1190 Wien, Bauernfeldgasse 4), 1976. 64 pp., illus.

13448. FAERBER, MEIR: *Zur 200-Jahr-Feier des Burgtheaters.* [In]: 'Das Neue Israel', 28. Jg., H. 9, März. Zürich, 1976. Pp. 497–499. [On the manifold relations between Jewish authors and actors with the Burgtheater.]

13449. PICHLER, WALTHER: *Von der Synagoge zur Kirche.* Zur Entstehung der Pfarre St. Leopold. Geleitwort von Franz Loibl. Wien: Dom Verlag, 1975. 164 pp., illus., bibl. (Veröffentlichungen des kirchenhistorischen Instituts der Universität Wien, Bd. 15). [On 24th June, 1670 the last Jews were forced to leave Vienna, and only two months later a church was built on the site of the former synagogue.]

3. Czechoslovakia

13450. *Jan Masaryks Gedanken über das Judentum.* Aufgezeichnet von Dr. Avigdor Dagan (orig. Viktor Fischl), Israels Botschafter in Wien. [In]: 'Isr. Wochenblatt', 76. Jg., Nr. 39, 24. Sept., Zürich, 1976. Pp. 35 and 37, ports. [Dagan was a close friend of J.M. This is a chapter from the 'Gespräche mit Jan Masaryk', which will be publ. in German translation by 'Konfrontation' in Zürich.]

13451. '*Judaica Bohemiae*'. Vol. XII, Nos. 1–2. Chief ed.: Erik Klima. Praha: Statui Zidovské Muzeum, 1976. 52 + 4 pp. illus., résumé in French; Pp. 55–127, illus. [2 vols.] [No. 1 incl.: Kommentare zu den ausgewählten Grabinschriften vom Alten Jüd. Friedhof in Prag (comp. by Otto Muneles, pp. 3–30), De la collection, des manuscrits de Musée Juif d'État de Prague (Vladimir Sadek-Jiřina Šedinová, pp. 31–36 in Czech). Sippurim. Legenden der alten Judenstadt Prags (Jana Dolezelová). No. 2 incl.: The Restorations of the Old Jewish Cemetery in Prague were started (Vladimir Sadek). Soziale Differenzierungen und Streitigkeiten in jüdischen Kultusgemeinden der Böhmischen Länder im 17. Jahrhundert und Entstehung der 'Landesjudenschaft' (Bedřich Nosek, pp. 59–92). De la collection des manuscrits du Musée Juif d'État de Prague (Vladimir Sadek-Jiřina Šedinová, pp. 93–125).

13452. MUNELES, OTTO: *Bibliographical Survey of Jewish Prague.* Ed. by Hana Volavkova. London: Pordes, 1975. 562 pp. (Jewish Monuments in Bohemia and Moravia Series.)

13453. '*Zidovska Rocenka*'. Das jüdische Jahrbuch 5737. Ed.: Rudolf Iltis. Prag: Kirchenzentral Verlag, 1976. [Incl. Orthodox oder zeremoniell, eine Betrachtung aus dem Nachlass von Leo Baeck. Der ewig junge Heinrich Heine (Jindřich Flusser). Eine Würdigung des Schaffens des Schriftstellers Leopold Kompert (Marie Štemberková).]

4. Hungary

13454. PÁKOZDY, LADISLAUS MARTIN: *Der siebenbürgische Sabbatismus.* Seine Entstehung und seine Entwicklung vom Unitarismus zum Judentum sowie sein Untergang. Stuttgart: Kohlhammer, 1973. 67 pp., notes pp. 56–67. (Franz Delitzsch-Vorlesungen 1969 an der Universität Münster, hrsg. von Karl Heinrich Rengstorf.)

13455. *Pinkas Hakhillot.* Encyclopaedia of Hungarian Jewish Communities. Jerusalem: Yad Vashem, 1976. 557 pp., illus., bibl. [Register of Hungarian Jewish communities with a history from the middle ages to 1939 by Nathaniel Katzburg, and the Holocaust period by Livia Rothkirchen. Text in Hebrew.]

13456. *Studien zum ungarischen Judentum.* Hrsg.: Institut für Judaistik der Universität Wien. Eisenstadt: Roetzer, 1976. 79 pp., bibl. (Studia Judaica Austriaca, 3).

5. Switzerland

13457. GUGGENHEIM-GRÜNBERG, FLORENCE: *Wörterbuch zu Surbtaler Jiddisch.* Die Ausdrücke hebräisch-aramäischen und romanischen Ursprungs. Einige bemerkenswerte Ausdrücke deutschen Ursprungs. Zürich: Juris, 1976. 49 pp. (Beiträge zur Geschichte und Volkskunde der Juden in der Schweiz, 11.)

13458. HÄSLER, ALFRED A. and RUTH K. WESTHEIMER: *Ruth K.: Die Geschichte der Karola Siegel.* Ein Bericht. Bern: Benteli, 1976. 128 pp., front., port., ports., illus., facsims., chronology. [Ten-year-old Karola Siegel came with a children's transport to Switzerland in Jan. 1939 through 'SHEK', Schweizer Hilfswerk für Emigrationskinder. Prof. Westheimer, formerly Karola Siegel, is a sociologist and psychologist at a New York university.]

13459. LANG, EMANUEL: *Zur Geschichte der jüdischen Presse in der Schweiz.* Separatdruck aus 'Jüdische Rundschau Maccabi'. Basel, Nr. 21, 20. Mai 1976. Beilage zum Delegiertentag des Schweizerischen Israelitischen Gemeindebundes, 16 pp., facsims., bibl.

13460. *Pferdehandlung Lob.* Seltene Familientradition. In Bern kann die Pferdehandlung Lob in diesem Jahr auf eine 150-jährige Geschichte zurückblicken. [In]: 'Isr. Wochenblatt', 13. Aug., Zürich, 1976. Pp. 19 and 22, ports. [Founder of the firm was Joseph Lob (1792–1863) who came with his family to Avenches (Switzerland) in 1826. The firm, in the fifth generation, is the oldest in Switzerland and the biggest in Europe.]

C. German Jews in Various Countries

13461. BEIT, ALFRED. ARONSFELD, C. C.: *Founding Father of Rhodesia.* The remarkable career of Alfred Beit. [In]: 'AJR Information', Sept. London, 1976. [Sir Alfred Beit, diamond magnate, 1853 Hamburg–1906 Tewin Water (England).]

13462. FEINGOLD, HENRY L.: *The Success Odyssey of German Jews in America.* [Chap. in]: Zion in America. The Jewish Experience from Colonial Times to the Present. New York: Hippocrene Books, 1974. xiv, 357 pp., bibl. (pp. 343–348). [Incl. also: The Elaboration of Jewish Organizational Life 1900–1920). Jews in American Foreign Affairs, 1900–1920. American Jewry and the Holocaust.]

13463. GREBLER, LEO: *German Jewish Immigrants to the United States during the Hitler Period.* Personal Reminiscences and General Observations. Los Angeles, California 90024: Privately printed (832 Glenmont Avenue), 1976. iv, 128 pp., biogr. sketches of the author and his wife Anne Marie née Gerson, a child psychologist and educational therapist, and bibls. of both their writings. [Typescript.] [Born 1900 in Berlin, Dr. Grebler was prior to his emigration (1935 to Switzerland, 1937 to USA) staff writer and Berlin correspondent of the Frankfurter Zeitung.]

13464. HIBBERT, CHRISTOPHER: *Edward VII.* A Portrait. London: Allen Lane, 1976. 339 pp. [Incl. The King's outstanding financial advisers Sir Ernest Cassel (1852 Cologne–1921 London), Baron Maurice (Moritz) Hirsch (1831 Munich–1896 O'gyala, Hungary). See also No. 4614/YB. X.]

13465. HIRSCHBERG, ALICE IRENE com a colaboração de Eva Hirschberg e Gabriela Wilder:

Desafio E Resposta. A História da Congregação Israelita Paulista desde a sua Fundação. Prefácio do Rabino. Fritz Pinkuss. Capa: Hanna Brandt. Edição Especial Por Ocasião Do Quadrigenário Da Congregação Israelita Paulista – São Paulo. 5736–1976. 238 pp.

13466. Howe, Irving with the assistance of Kenneth Libo: *The Immigrant Jews of New York, 1881 to the Present.* London: Routledge and Kegan Paul, 1976. 714 pp., ports., illus. (The Littman Library of Jewish Civilization.)

13467. Jick, Leon A.: *The Americanization of the Synagogue, 1820–1870.* Hanover, N.H.: Brandeis Univ., 1976. 247 pp. [Describes efforts of Jewish immigrants from Germany in the first half of the nineteenth century to reconstruct their communal life in the new environment.]

13468. MAYER, ROBERT, SIR. Holden, Anthony: *Sir Robert Mayer.* Once more with feeling. [In]: The Sunday Times Magazine. 8th August London, 1976. port. [Born 5th June, 1879 in Mannheim, came to England in 1896. Organises and finances concerts for children.]

13469. MEYER, CARL, SIR. Aronsfeld, C. C.: *A Jewish Patron of the National Theatre.* [In]: 'AJR Information'. May. London, 1976. [Born 1851 Hamburg–1922 London. A banker associate of N. M. Rothschild, came to England in 1872, was naturalised 1877 and knighted in 1911.]

13470. Meyer, Michael A.: *The Refugee Scholars Project of the Hebrew Union College.* [In]: A Bicentennial Festschrift for Jacob Rader Marcus. Waltham, Mass.: American Jewish Historical Society. New York: Ktav, 1976. Pp. 359–375, bibl. (pp. 373–375).

13471. NAMIER, LEWIS, SIR [orig. Lewis Bernstein Namierowski]. Kenyon, John: *Namier – Outsider who loved England.* [In]: Observer Magazine. 19th December, London, 1976. Pp. 28–35, ports. (The Great Historians). [Born 1888 in Austrian Galicia–1960 England.]

13472. Rabinowitz, Dorothy: *New Lives.* Survivors of the Holocaust living in America. New York: Knopf, 1976. viii, 242 pp.

13473. Schwarz, Stefan: *Juden in Amerika.* Der Beitrag der Juden aus Deutschland zur Entwicklung der Vereinigten Staaten. Teil I–II. [In]: 'MJN', 9. Juli und 24. Sept. München, 1976.

13474. Simmonds, Lionel: *Refugees.* From Germany, with Honour. [In]: Jewish Chronicle Colour Magazine, 26th November. London, 1976. Pp. 46–56, ports., illus. [Some 50,000 German and Austrian Jews found refuge in Gt. Britain from Nazi persecution and became British citizens.]

13475. Stokes, Lawrence D.: *Canada and an Academic Refugee from Nazi Germany.* The Case of Gerhard Herzberg. [In]: The Canadian Historical Review. Vol. 57, No. 2, June. Toronto: University of Toronto Press, 1976. Pp. 150–170.

13476. SULZBACH, HERBERT. Sulzbach, Herbert: *Inside Featherstone Park.* Pp. 10–32 in: Total War to Total Trust. Personal accounts of thirty years of Anglo-German relations – the vital role of non-governmental organisations. Ed. by Rolf Breitenstein. Introd. by Lothar Kettenacker. London: Oswald Wolff in cooperation with the Embassy of the Federal Republic of Germany, 1976. 92 pp. [Herbert Sulzbach, born 1894 in Frankfurt/M. republished his war diaries in English translation: 'With the German Guns', see No. 11753/YB. XIX.]

13477. Wilk, Gerard: *Americans from Germany.* New York: German Information Center, 1976. xii, 81 pp., ports. [Biographical sketches of only a few of those who played a special role in America and/or in German–American relations. Incl. are: Albert Einstein, Manfred George, Oskar Hammerstein I, Ernst Lubitsch, Abraham Jacobi, Henry A. Kissinger, Erwin Panofsky, Martin Schwarzschild (astro physicist), Levi Strauss (blue jeans manufacturer), University in Exile 'The New School' established by German refugees in 1933, Bruno Walter, Kurt Weill a.o.]

II. RESEARCH AND BIBLIOGRAPHY

A. Libraries and Institutes

13478. DEUTSCHE AKADEMIE FÜR SPRACHE UND DICHTUNG, DARMSTADT, ed.: *Jahrbuch 1975.* Heidelberg: Schneider, 1976. 226 pp., bibl. (pp. 189–199). [Incl. Reden der Preisträger: M. Sperber (Georg-Büchner-Preis). E. Bloch (Sigmund-Freud-

Preis). Laudatio auf Ernst Bloch (Dolf Sternberger, pp. 61–66). Gedenkworte für Robert Neumann (Hilde Spiel, pp. 157–159.]

13479. *Jahrbuch der Deutschen Schillergesellschaft, Marbach.* Hrsg. von Fritz Martini. Walter Müller-Seidel, Bernhard Zeller. Bd. 19. Stuttgart: Kröner, 1976. 550 pp. [Incl. Masse, Macht und Tod im Werk Elias Canettis (Dagmar Barnouw). Gedenkrede für Kurt Pinthus (Bernhard Zeller). Briefe und Postkarten von Hugo von Hofmannsthal an Hannibal Karg von Bebenburg (1874–1940), geschrieben in den Jahren 1895 bis 1905, mitgeteilt von Mary E. Gilbert. 'Rühmen, Das Ists!' Zur Eröffnung der Rainer Maria Rilke-Ausstellung in Marbach a.N. am 10. Mai 1975 (Käte Hamburger, pp. 501–509).]

13480. *Jahrbuch des Freien Deutschen Hochstifts.* Tübingen: Niemeyer, 1975. [Incl. Das Grauenhafte im lachenden Spiegel des Witzes. Untersuchung des Humors bei Heinrich Heine (Horst Schillemeit). 'Konflikt zweier Welten. Kafkas Triadik und "Der Bau" ' (Ralf R. Nicolay).]

13481. *Jahrbuch des Instituts für Deutsche Geschichte.* Hrsg. u. eingel. von Walter Grab. Bd. 5. Tel Aviv. Universität, Institut für Deutsche Geschichte. Ramat Aviv, 1976, 620 pp., xvi pp. Hebrew résumés. [Incl.: Hegemonialbestrebungen der deutschen Aussenpolitik während der Weimarer Republik. Gustav Stolpers 'Dienstag-Kreis' (Harro Molt, pp. 419–448). 'Anklage gegen den Volksverderber Hitler'. Ein Beitrag zur Geschichte der Oppositionen im Dritten Reich. Ein noch nicht veröffentlichtes Dokument (Haim Shamir, pp. 448–466), Dokumentenanhang. Some selected contributions are listed according to subject.]

13482. LEO BAECK INSTITUTE. *Year Book XXI.* The Jewish Question and Antisemitism II. An annual Collection of Essays on the history and activity of Jews in Germany during the past century. Ed. Robert Weltsch. London: Secker & Warburg, 1976. xviii, 379 pp., front., port. [of S. Adler-Rudel], ports., illus., facsims., bibl. (pp. 297–367). [Individual contributions are listed according to subject.]

13483. LBI NEW YORK. *Inventory List of Archival Collections.* Catalog. Number II. New York, 1976. iv, 31 pp.

13484. *Library and Archives News.* Ed.: Gabrielle Bamberger. No. 4 (May). New York: Leo Baeck Institute, 1976. [8 pp.]

13485. *LBI News.* Ed.: Gabrielle Bamberger. Vol. XVII, Spring–Summer 1976, Winter 1976/77. New York: Leo Baeck Institute, 1976/77. 12 pp., front., illus., port. [of Ernest Hamburger], illus.; 12 pp., front., port. [of Paula Beer-Hofmann], ports., illus., facsim. [2 vols.] [No. 1 incl.: Report on a Gertrud Kolmar Evening: Survival through Art: Getrud Kolmar (1894–1943). Significant Freud Letters donated to the LBI. The Jews in Germany's Social Upheaval (1850–1914), a lecture by Fritz Stern. The German-Jewish Immigrant in America. Excerpts from four Memoirs: Rudolf Brach, Carl Dernburg, Abraham Kohn, Edmond Uhry, pp. 5–8, illus. Rilke, Judaism and Jews (Ilse Blumenthal-Weiss). No. 2 incl.: Schlaflied für Miriam. A Postcard View of Jewish Life. Eva Reichmann: A Birthday Tribute. German Synagogues – A Historical Record in Word and Picture. The Infamous Judenzaehlung of 1916. The Story behind an Opera ['Der Kaiser von Atlantis']. The composer Viktor Ullmann and the librettist Peter Kien wrote the opera in Theresienstadt, both were murdered in Auschwitz. The world première took place in Amsterdam, December 1975.]

B. Bibliographies and Catalogues

13486. *Bibliographie zur Geschichte der deutschen Arbeiterbewegung.* Hrsg.: Bibliothek des Archivs der sozialen Demokratie (Friedrich Ebert Stiftung). Comp.: Horst Ziska u.a. Jg. 1, H. 1–2. Bonn–Bad Godesberg: Verlag Neue Gesellschaft, 1976. xvi, 69, xxix pp.; xvii, pp. 70–156, xxix pp. [2 vols.]

13487. *Concise Encyclopaedia of Jewish Music.* Comp. by Macy Nuhman. New York: McGraw Hill, 1975. 276 pp., 500 entries. [Musicological and historical facts about Jewish music with biographies of composers and musicians and descriptions of their works.]

13488. *Demography and Statistics of Diaspora Jewry, 1920–1970.* A Bibliography. Comp. by U[siel] O[skar] Schmelz, Sergio Della Pergola a.o. Vol. I: World and Intercontinental, America, Africa, Asia, Oceania, Europe (Albania to France). Jerusalem: The Hebrew University, The Institute of Contemporary Jewry, 1976. xxiii, 391 pp. [mimeog.] (Jewish Population Studies).

13489. *Encyclopaedia Judaica Year Book 1975/6.* Events of 1974/5. Jerusalem: Encyclopaedia Judaica, 1976. 472 pp., ports., illus. [Continuation volume]. [Feature articles incl.: Chaim Weizmann – Thoughts for a Centenary (Chaim Raphael). Jewish Faith after the Holocaust: Four Approaches (Steven T. Katz). Anti-Semitism and Jewish Uniqueness (Arthur Herzberg).] [16 vols. were publ. 1971/2. See No. 9350/YB. XVII. Continuation vols.: No. 11161/YB XIX, 11993/YB. XX.]

13490. *Encyclopedia of the Third Reich.* Comp. by Louis L. Synder. New York: McGraw-Hill, 1976. 410 pp., ports., illus., facsims., tabs., bibl. (pp. 389–410).

13491. *Grosses Lexikon der Musik.* Comp.: Norman Lloyd. Aus dem Engl. von Alfred Baumgartner. Deutsche Bearbeitung: Franz Grasberger. Gütersloh: Bertelsmann, 1974. 752 pp., ports., illus., music.

13492. *Guide to unpublished materials of the Holocaust period.* Ed. Yehuda Bauer. Comp. by Esther Blumenzweig, Emmanuel Brand, Chasia Turtel-Aberzhanska. Introd. by Joseph Kermisch. Vol. III. Jerusalem: The Hebrew University, The Institute of Contemporary Jewry, Division of Holocaust Studies, Yad Vashem Martyrs' and Heroes' Remembrance Authority, 1975. 413 pp. [Vol. I see No. 8559/YB. XVI, vol. II, No. 10261/YB. XVIII.]

13493. *International Bibliography of Jewish Affairs, 1966–1967.* A select annotated list of books and articles published outside Israel. Comp. and ed. by Elizabeth E. Eppler. Publ. for the Institute of Jewish Affairs in Ass. with the World Jewish Congress. London: Deutsch, 1976. ix, 401 pp. [New York edition: Holmes & Meier, 1975.] [The items listed cover international Jewish affairs. Religious studies and belles lettres (excepting documentary novels and memoirs) are excluded.]

13494. *'Neue Deutsche Blätter', Prag 1933–1935.* Bibliographie einer Zeitschrift. Comp. by Helmut Praschek. Mit e. Vorw. von Wieland Herzfelde. 1. Aufl. Berlin [East]: Aufbau, 1973. 100 pp. (Analytische Bibliographien deutschsprachiger literarischer Zeitschriften, 6).

13495. *The Picture Researcher's Handbook.* Comp. by Hilary and Mary Evans and Andra Nelki. London: David & Charles, 1975. 365 pp., ports., illus. [The handbook lists nearly 600 sources for the supply of book illustrations incl. The Wiener Library and the Central Zionist Archives.]

13496. *Post-War Publications on German Jewry.* A Selected Bibliography of Books and Articles 1975. Compiled by Bertha Cohn. [In]: LBI Year Book XXI. London, 1976. Pp. 295–367.

13497. *Survey of Research in Jewish Subjects in Europe.* Comp.: Sarah Lock, London: The Institute of Jewish Affairs, 1976. 61 pp., 310 entries. [Covers research now in progress for books and articles, theses and dissertations registered since 1970. Britain is not included as this was covered by a similar study of the Oxford Centre for Postgraduate Hebrew Studies. East European countries are included, but not the Soviet Union.]

III. THE NAZI PERIOD

General

13498. ARNDT, INO and WOLFGANG SCHEFFLER: *Organisierter Massenmord an Juden in nationalsozialistischen Vernichtungslagern.* Ein Beitrag zur Richtigstellung apologetischer Literatur. Mit einer Vorbemerkung von Martin Broszat. [In]: Vierteljahrshefte für Zeitgeschichte. 24. Jg., H. 2. Stuttgart: Deutsche Verlags-Anstalt, 1976. Pp. 105–135. [See also No. 14117.]

13499. AUSCHWITZ. *From the History of KL-Auschwitz.* Ed.: Kazimierz Smolen. Transl. from the Polish Text by Krystyna Michalik. Publ. by Panstwowe Muzeum W Oświęcimin. Vol. I: 1967. 225 pp., ports., illus., facsims.; vol. II: 1976. 299 pp., illus., maps, facsims. [2 vols.]

13500. *Hefte von Auschwitz.* Nr. 15. Berater der deutschen Ausgabe: Stefan Popiolek. Auschwitz: Staatl. Auschwitz Museum, 1975. 279 pp., port., illus., facsims. [Cont. Die Rolle des Häftlingskrankenbaulagers im KL Auschwitz II. (D. Czech). Organisation, Entwicklung und Tätigkeit des Häftlings-Krankenhaus in Monowitz (KL Auschwitz III) (A. Makowski). Das Nebenlager Jawischowitz (A. Strzelecki).]

13501. HOESS, RUDOLF: *Commandant of Auschwitz.* Transl. from German by Constantine Fitzgibbon, with an introduction by Lord Russell of Liverpool. London/Sydney: Pan Books, 1974. 283 pp., ports., illus. [Paperback ed. of the commandant's autobiography.]

13502. LANGBEIN, HERMANN, comp. and ed.: *Genocid im 20. Jahrhundert*. Bericht über eine Internationale Podiumsdiskussion anl. des 30. Jahrestages der Befreiung von Auschwitz, veranstaltet vom Intern. Verbindungskomitee der Überlebenden von Auschwitz an der Johannes-Kepler-Universität Linz am 20. Jänner 1975. Sonderdruck der Frankfurter Hefte, Jg. 31, H. 5, Mai, 1976. 16 pp. (Dokumentationsarchiv des österr. Widerstandes, Wien 1, Altes Rathaus.)

13503. BADEN. SCHADT, JÖRG, ed.: *Verfolgung und Widerstand unter dem Nationalsozialismus in Baden*. Die Lageberichte der Gestapo und des Generalstaatsanwalts Karlsruhe, 1933–1940. Hrsg. vom Stadtarchiv Mannheim. Stuttgart: Kohlhammer, 1976. 354 pp., diagrs., bibl. (pp. 15–21). (Veröffentlichungen des Stadtarchivs Mannheim, Bd. 3).

13504. BAVARIA. LAAK, URSULA VAN, comp.: *Bibliographie zu Widerstand und Verfolgung in Bayern 1933–1945*. o.O., [1974]. iii, 72 pp. Typescript.]

13505. BERLIN. KARDORFF, URSULA VON: *Berliner Aufzeichnungen 1942–1945*. Erw. u. bebilderte Neuausg. München: Nymphenburger Verlag, 1976. 335 pp., ports., illus. [For 1st ed. see No. 3075/YB. VIII.]

13506. BRATISLAVA. EHRENREICH, YARON, comp.: *Documentation Centre of the Central Union of Jewish Communities in Bratislava* (Record Group M-5). Jerusalem: Yad Vashem Central Archives, 1975. vii, 87 pp., bilingual index (Slovak and Hebrew) for persons, places, organisations and institutions (pp. 80–87). (Guides of the Yad Vashem Archives, Catalogue No. 2). [In Hebrew with an English introduction.]

13507. BUCHENWALD. HARTUNG, HANS-JOACHIM: *Signale durch den Todeszaun*. Histor. Reportage über Bau, Einsatz und Tarnung illegaler Rundfunkempfänger und -Sender im Konzentrationslager Buchenwald. Berlin [East]: Verlag Technik, 1974.

13508. CARSTEN, F[RANCIS] L[UDWIG]: *Die historischen Wurzeln des Nationalsozialismus*. [In]: Deutschland. Wandel und Bestand (Edgar Josef Feuchtwanger). München: Desch, 1973. Pp. 134–158. [The work incl. also: Soziale und psychologische Grundlagen des Nationalsozialismus (Martin Broszat, pp. 159–190).]

13509. DACHAU. SHALIT, LEVI: *The Road from Dachau*. Thirty years after the liberation. Publ. by the S.A. Jewish Board of Deputies as a commemorative supplement to 'Jewish Affairs'. June. Johannesburg, 1975. 23 pp.

13510. DAHM, VOLKER: *Das 'jüdische' Buch im Dritten Reich unter besonderer Berücksichtigung des Schocken Verlages*. Frankfurt a.M.: Buchhändler-Vereinigung, 1976. [Cont.: Teil I: Die Ausschaltung des 'jüdischen' Buches im Dritten Reich. 1. Das 'jüdische' Buch als Volksfeind – eine Einleitung. 2. Die Ausschaltung der jüdischen Autoren und Buchhändler durch Berufsverbot. 3. Die Ausschaltung des 'jüdischen' Schrifttums durch Buchverbot. Teil II: 1. Salman Schocken als Unternehmer, Bibliomane und Zionist. 2. S. Sch. als Herausgeber und Mäzen bis zur Gründung des Schocken Verlages (1914–1931). 3. Der Schocken Verlag (1931–1939). 4. Das 'jüdische' Buch als Volksliteratur – eine Schlussbemerkung. 5. Bibliographie des Schocken Verlages.]

13511. DAWIDOWICZ, LUCY S., ed.: *A Holocaust Reader*. New York: Behrman House, 1975. 416 pp. [Anthology of Nazi documents and personal memoirs forming a companion volume to 'The War against the Jews'.]

13512. DAWIDOWICZ, LUCY S.: *The War against the Jews 1933–1945*. London: Weidenfeld and Nicolson, 1976. xviii, 460 pp., tabs., maps, notes, pp. 404–436, bibl. (pp. 437–450). [For American ed. see No. 12763/YB. XXI. Cf. History and the Holocaust (Leon Wieseltier) in: TLS, 25th February, London, 1977. Pp. 220–221.]

13513. DES PRES, TERRENCE: *The Survivor*. An Anatomy of Life in the Death Camps. New York: Oxford University Press, 1976. 218 pp. [Study of the behaviour-patterns of inmates in concentration camps in situations of extremity.]

13514. EISENBACH, ARTUR: *Les Déportations de la Population Juive pendant la IIe Guerre Mondiale*. [In]: Studia Historiae Oeconomicae UAM, Vol. 8. Poznań: Nadbitka, 1973. Pp. 117–146.

13515. GRUNFELD, FREDERIC V.: *Die deutsche Tragödie*. Adolf Hitler und das deutsche Reich 1918–1945 in Bildern. Nachwort: Hugh Trevor-Roper. Aus d. Engl. von Wolfgang Eisermann und Martin Speck. Hamburg: Hoffmann und Campe, 1975. 384 pp., mostly illus. [For English original see No. 12018/YB. XX.]

13516. HAREL, ISSER: *The House on Garibaldi Street*. The Capture of Adolf Eichmann. London.

Andre Deutsch, 1975. 288 pp., map. [German ed.]: *Das Haus in der Garibaldi Strasse.* Aus d. Engl. von Marianne Lipcowitz. Frankfurt/M.: Ullstein, 1976. 287 pp., ports., illus., map. [French ed.]: *La Maison de la Rue Garibaldi.* Trad. par Robert Laffont. Paris: Laffont, 1976, 298 pp. [Report on the capture by the former chief of the Israeli secret service.]

13517. HAUSER, MARTIN: *Auf dem Heimweg.* Aus den Tagebüchern eines deutschen Juden 1929–1945. Vorbemerkung von Jutta Bohnke-Kollwitz. Bonn: Bundeszentrale für Politische Bildung, 1975. 228 pp. + [16 pp.] ports., illus., facsims. (Schriftenreihe der Bundeszentrale . . . Bd. 109).

13518. HESSE. MORITZ, KLAUS und ERNST NOAM, eds.: *Die Ahndung von NS-Verbrechen gegen Juden nach 1945.* Eine Dokumentation aus hessischen Justizakten. Wiesbaden: Kommission für die Geschichte der Juden in Hessen, 1976. (Schriften der Kommission für die Geschichte der Juden in Hessen II, Justiz und Juden Verfolgung, Bd. 2). [For vol. I see No. 12768/YB. XXI.]

13519. HILLEL MARC und CLARISSA: *Lebensborn e.V.* Im Namen der Rasse. Wien: Zsolnay, 1975. 351 pp., ports., illus., facsims., bibl. [Cf. Der Strom des guten Blutes. Rassenwahn im eingetragenen Verein (François Bondy) in: 'Zeit', 28th November, Hamburg, 1975. [Also]: 'Lebensborn' (Richard Grunberger) [In]: Wiener Library Bulletin, XVI, No. 3 (July), London, 1962, Pp. 52–53, bibl.]

13520. HITLER. FEST, JOACHIM C.: *Hitler.* Eine Biographie. Ungek. Ausg. Bd. 1: Der Aufstieg mit 99 z.T. unbekannten Bild- und Textdokumenten. Bd. 2: Der Führer mit 112 Bild- und Textdokumenten. Berlin–Frankfurt/M.: Ullstein, 1976. 529 pp., pp. 533–1190, ports., illus., bibl. (Ullstein Buch Nr. 3273 u. 3274). [2 vols.] Transl. from German by Clara und Richard Winston. London: Weidenfeld and Nicolson, 1974. 928 pp. [and] Penguin edition, London, 1976.

13521. *Hitlers Weg zur totalen Macht: 1933–1938.* (Ausstellung). Vorw. von Charles Bloch. Hrsg. von der Stadt Oberhausen aus Anlass der Ausstellung, die von d. Intern. Komitee zur Wissenschaftl. Erforschung der Ursachen u. Folgen des 2. Weltkrieges (Luxemburg) u.d. Kulturamt d. Stadt Oberhausen gestaltet wurde. Oberhausen: Laufen, 1974. 289 pp., 30 pp. ports., illus. [Incl.: Was, du lebst noch immer? (Hans Hinrich Flöter).]

13522. LANG, JOCHEN VON, ed.: *Adolf Hitler: Gesichter eines Diktators.* Eine Bilddokumentation. Psychogramm des Diktators von Joachim Fest. Die Fotos stellte d. Zeitgeschichtliche Bildarchiv Heinrich Hoffmann zur Verfügung. München: Herbig, 1975. 16 pp. text, 80 pp. ports., illus.

13523. STERN, JOSEPH PETER: *Hitler, the Führer and the People.* London: Fontana/Collins, 1975. 254 pp. (Fontana, 3674). [Author, philologist, originally from Prague, lives in London.]

13524. TOLAND, JOHN: *Adolf Hitler.* Garden City, New York: Doubleday, 1976. xx, 1035 pp, ports., illus., facsims., geneal. table, bibl. (pp. 906–923). [Cf. Hitler Rediscovered (Prittie and Nelson), in: Jewish Observer and Middle East Review, 24th March, London, 1977.]

13525. HOLLAND. JONG, SALOMON DE: *Joodse Oorlogsherinneringen (1940–1945).* Franeker: Wever, 1975. 175 pp., ports., illus., facsims.

13526. MOORE, ROBERT G.: *The Jewish Refugee Committee in Amsterdam.* One aspect of refugee relief work in the Netherlands 1933–1940. A Thesis [pres. to] University of Manchester, 1976. 75 pp , bibl. (pp. 74–75).

13527. SIJES, B. A., ed.: *Studies over Jodenvervolging.* Assen: Van Gorzum, 1974, viii, 184 pp., ports., tabs., bibl. notes (pp. 170–180).

13528. VETH, D. GILTAY and A. J. VAN DER LEEUW: *Rapport door het Rijksinstituut voor Oorlogs-documentatie uitgebracht aan de minister van justitie inzake de activiteiten van drs. F. Weinreb gedurende de jaren 1940–1945, in het licht van nadere gegevens bezien.* 's-Gravenhage: Staatsuitg., 1976. xlii + xi + 1,683 pp., facsims. [In 2 vols.]

13529. WARMBRUNN, W.: *Die niederländischen Juden unter deutscher Besatzung.* Pp. 75–86 [In]: Diktaturen im Nacken. Hrsg. von Rolf Italiaander. München: Delp, 1971. 358 pp. (Disput, Bd. 10).

13530. HOLOCAUST. ECK, NATHAN: *The Holocaust of the Jewish People in Europe.* Jerusalem: Yad Vashem, 1975. 451 pp., bibl. (pp. 359–419), cover maps. [In Hebrew.]

13531. *The Holocaust – a Generation After.* Conference sponsored by The World Federation of Bergen–Belsen Survivors, The International Committee of the Institute of Contemporary Jewry and the International Remembrance Award Committee. New York, 1975. 2 vols., various pagings.

13532. KATZ, JACOB: *Was the Holocaust Predictable?* [In]: Commentary, Vol. 59, No. 5 (May). New York: American Jewish Committee, 1975. Pp. 41–48.

13533. MELTZER, MILTON: *Never to Forget: The Jews of the Holocaust.* New York: Harper & Row, 1976. 217 pp. [A survey of the organisation and dimensions of the Holocaust based on eye witness reports.]

13534. ROBINSON, JACOB and HENRY SACHS, eds.: *The Holocaust. The Nuremberg Evidence.* Part 1: Documents: Digest, Index and Chronological Tables. Jerusalem: Yad Vashem Martyrs' and Heroes' Memorial Authority, YIVO Institute for Jewish Research, 1976. 370 pp. (Yad Vashem and YIVO Bibliographical Series, Vol. 13.)

13535. RUTTIE, A.: *When Millions Screamed.* Stories of the Holocaust. Chatsworth, Cal.: Barclay House, 1974. 192 pp.

13536. YAD VASHEM MARTYRS' AND HEROES' REMEMBRANCE AUTHORITY, eds.: *The Holocaust.* Jerusalem, 1975. 79 pp., ports., illus., facsims.

13537. *Justiz und NS-Verbrechen.* Sammlung deutscher Strafurteile wegen nationalsozialistischer Tötungsverbrechen 1945–1966. Bearb. von Irene Sagel-Grande, H. H. Fuchs, C. F. Rüter. Bd. XIV: Die vom 27. 06. 1956 bis zum 04.07.1958 ergangenen Strafurteile. Lfd Nr 438–465. Bd. XV.: Die vom 4.7.1958 bis zum 8.7.1959 . . . Lfd. Nr. 465–480. Bd XVI: Die vom 8.7.1959 bis zum 4.11.1960 . . . Lfd. Nr. 480–500. Amsterdam: University Press, 1976. v, 832 pp.; 851 pp., tabs.; v, 843 pp. [3 vols.] [For previous vols. see No. 12771/YB. XXI.]

13538. KARESKI, GEORG. LEVINE, HERBERT S.: *A Jewish Collaborator in Nazi Germany: The Strange Career of Georg Kareski, 1933–1937.* [In]: Central European History. Vol. VIII, No. 3, September. Atlanta, Ga.; Emory University, 1975. Pp. 251–281.

13539. KLEPPER, JOCHEN: *Unter dem Schatten deiner Flügel.* Aus den Tagebüchern der Jahre 1932–1942. Vollständige Ausgabe mit einem Geleitwort von Reinhold Schneider. Stuttgart: Deutsche Verlags-Anstalt, 1976. 1,172 pp. [J.K., born 1903, committed suicide in 1942 together with his wife and her daughter from her first marriage because he saw no help for them as both were Jewish. – See also No. 13546.]

13540. KULKA, ERICH: *Die Massenvernichtung der Juden wird geleugnet.* Eine Studie über die beunruhigenden Perspektiven der Vergangenheit. Jerusalem: Yad Vashem, 1975. 20 pp., facsim.

13541. LANGER, LAWRENCE L.: *The Holocaust and the Literary Imagination.* New Haven and London: Yale University Press, 1975. xiii, 300 pp. [Confronted with the undescribable, the author analyses the imaginative works of writers on the Holocaust like Paul Celan, Nelly Sachs, Ernst Wiechert, Charlotte Beradt, Primo Levi, Ladislav Fuks, Jacov Lind, André Schwarz-Bart, George Steiner, Heinrich Böll, Elie Wiesel a.o. Cf. Beyond Imagination (Vera Elyashiv) in: The Jewish Quarterly, Vol. 24, No. 1–2, London, 1976. Pp. 35–39.]

13542. MORSE, ARTHUR D.: *While Six Million Died.* A Chronicle of American Apathy. New York: Hart Publishing Co., 1975. 420 pp. [Paperbound reprint. For 1st eds. in German, English, French and Dutch see No. 7737/YB. XV.]

13543. NOAKES, JEREMY and GEOFFREY PRIDHAM, eds.: *Documents on Nazism, 1919–1945.* Introduced and edited by . . . London: Cape, 1974. 704 pp., bibl. (pp. 698–702). [Chap. 15: Antisemitism 1933–1945.]

13544. PAPANEK, ERNST and EDWARD LINN: *Out of the Fire.* New York: Morrow, 1975. 299 pp. [The work of the O.S.E. organisation in the rescue of Jewish children and refugees during the Second World War.]

13545. PICK, ALBERT and CARL SIEMSEN: *Das Lagergeld der Konzentrations- und DP-Lager, 1933–1945,* München: Battenberg, 1976. 56 pp., illus.

13546. RIEMSCHNEIDER, ERNST G.: *Der Fall Klepper.* Eine Dokumentation. Stuttgart: Deutsche Verlags-Anstalt, 1975. 142 pp., front., illus., facsims. [See also No. 13539.]

13547. 'ST. LOUIS'. THOMAS, GORDON and MAX MORGAN-WITTS: *Das Schiff der Verdammten. Die Irrfahrt der St. Louis.* Zug: Edition Sven Erick Bergh im Ingse Verlag, 1976. 382 pp., illus. [The ship sailed from Hamburg on 13th May 1939 with 937 Jews on board. They were refused permission to land in Cuba and were returned to Germany. For English original see No. 12037/YB. XX.]

13548. SHAMIR, HAIM: *Be-terem shoah. Before the Holocaust.* Jews in the Third Reich and Western

European Public Opinion, 1933–1939. Tel Aviv: Sifriat Poalim, 1974. 367 pp., bibl. [In Hebrew.]

13549. SHANGHAI. KRANZLER, DAVID: *The History of the Jewish Refugee Community of Shanghai, 1938–1945.* Diss., pres. to Yeshiva University. New York, 1971. xl, 519 pp., facsims., plans, bibl. (pp. 397–434). [Photocopy.] [Cf. Nos. 10314–10315/YB. XVIII, 12039/YB. XX, 12784/YB. XXI.]

13550. KRANZLER, DAVID: *Japanese, Nazis and the Jews.* The Jewish Refugee Community of Shanghai, 1938–1945. Foreword by Abraham G. Duker. New York: Yeshiva University Press, 1976. 644 pp., ports., illus., maps, facisms., graphs, notes, pp. 567–577. bibl. (pp. 583–604).

13551. SMITH, BRADLEY und AGNES F. PETERSON, eds.: *Heinrich Himmlers Geheimreden.* Mit einer Einführung von Joachim Fest. Berlin: Ullstein/Propyläen Verlag, 1975. 320 pp. + 240 ports., illus. and text documents. [Cf. Entlarvung einer Ideologie (Rolf Krüger) in: 'Allgemeine', 4. Sept. Düsseldorf, 1975.

13552. *Verfehmte Kultur.* 29. Folge. Proszenium Katalog Nr. 75: *Filmschauspieler – Verfolgt. Vertrieben. Ermordet.* Eine Bilddokumentation. Kemnath-Stadt: Theater- und Film-Fachantiquariat, 1975. 22 pp., ports.

13553. WIESENTHAL, SIMON. WIESENTHAL, SIMON: *Naziprozesse heute?* Rede vom 25.2.1969 anlässlich der Jahreshauptversammlung der Gruppe der NS-Verfolgten im öffentlichen Dienst bei der Stadtverwaltung München u.a. München, 1969. 16 pp., port., chron., bibl. [S.W., born 1908 in Buczacz (then Austria), architect, survivor of concentration camps, head of the 'Dokumentationszentrum des Bundes jüd. Verfolgter des Nazi-Regimes' in Wien. His book 'Sonnenblume' was publ. in German and English, see No. 8570/YB. XVI. A New York ed., Schocken, 1975.]

13554. WIESENTHAL, SIMON: *The Murderers among us.* The Simon Wiesenthal Memoirs. Ed. and with an Introductory Profile by Joseph Wechsberg. New York: Bantam Books, 1973. 346 pp., ports., illus., facsims. (Bantam Books Q 7593). [For previous German and English eds. see No. 6359/YB. XIII.]

13555. *Nemesis on a Card Index.* David Pryce-Jones questions Mr. Wiesenthal about his life's work. [In]: 'The Daily Telegraph Magazine' No. 538, 21st March, London, 1975. Pp. 34–36, 38, 42, ports., illus.

13556. SPEIJERS, SIMON, comp.: *Essays über Nazi-Verbrechen.* Simon Wiesenthal gewidmet. Verlegt unter Auspizien des Wiesenthalfonds in Amsterdam und des Bundes jüd. Verfolgter des Nazi-Regimes in Wien. Amsterdam: Wiesenthal Fonds, 1973. 295 pp., front., port., bibl. (pp. 169–175). [Incl.: Zur Genesis der 'Endlösung' der Judenfrage (N. Blumenthal). Die Endlösung der Judenfrage (B. A. Sijes). Die Juden in national-sozialistischen Zwangslagern (historisch und soziologisch betrachtet) (H. G. Adler). Die Verfolgung der 'Zigeuner' (Lau C. Mazirel). Vom Menschen im KZ und vom KZ im Menschen (J. Bastiaans). Für und Wider die NS-Prozesse in der Bundesrepublik Deutschland (A. Rückerl). Die Verjährung der NS-Gewaltverbrechen (J. Baumann). Anmerkungen zur Sprache der Diktatur in Deutschland (Harry Pross).]

13557. WIESFLECKER, OSKAR, ed.: *Das Urteil.* Eine Dokumentation zum 30. Jahrestag des Urteilsspruchs im Nürnberger Prozess gegen die nazistischen Hauptkriegsver-brecher. Zusammengestellt und hrsg. von der Internationalen Föderation der Wider-standskämpfer (FIR). Wien, 1976. 64 pp., ports., illus., bibl. [In French]: *Le Verdict.* Une Documentation à l'occasion du 30ᵉ anniversaire du verdict du Procès de Nurem-berg . . . Wien: FIR, A 1021 Castellezgasse 35.

13558. *Yad Vashem Studies on the European Jewish Catastrophe and Resistance.* Ed. by Livia Roth-kirchen. Vol. XI. Jerusalem: Yad Vashem Martyrs' and Heroes' Remembrance Authority. 1976. 383 pp. [Incl.: An Overall Plan for Anti-Jewish Legislation in the Third Reich? (Uwe D. Adam, pp. 33–55). The Zionist Character of the 'Self-Govern-ment' of Terezin (Theresienstadt). A study in Historiography (Livia Rothkirchen, pp. 56–90, bibl. (pp. 88–90). The Last Letters of the Brandt-Meyer Family from Berlin (John S. Conway, pp. 91–130, facsims.). The Impact of the Nazi Racial Decrees on the University of Heidelberg. A Case Study (Arye Carmon, pp. 131–163). American Non-Sectarian Refugee Relief Organizations (1933–1945) (Haim Genizi, pp. 164–220). The Plight of Jewish Refugees from Czechoslovakia in the USSR. (Research based on Survivors' Testimony) (Erich Kulka, pp. 298–328). 'The War Against the Jews 1939–1945' (Yisrael Gutman, pp. 329–343). [Review article on Prof. Lucy S. Dawidowicz's book, see No. 13511–13512]. Kristallnacht at the Dinslaken Orphanage. Reminiscences (Yitzhak S. Herz, pp. 344–368, facsims.]

IV. POST WAR

A. General

13559. BERG, JAN: *Hochhuths 'Stellvertreter' und die 'Stellvertreter'*–Debatte: Vergangenheitsbewältigung in Theater und Presse der sechziger Jahre. Kronberg/Ts.: Scriptor, 1976. 260 pp. (Scriptor Hochschulschriften: Literaturwiss., 17.)

13560. BERLIN. *Jahresbericht.* Hrsg. vom Vorstand der Jüdischen Gemeinde zu Berlin. Sept. 1976. [16 pp.], ports., illus.

13561. CZECHOSLOVAKIA. *'Informationsbulletin'.* Gesamtgestaltung und Übersetzung: Rudolf Iltis. Hrsg.: Rat der Jüd. Religionsgemeinden in d. Tschechischen Sozialist. Republik und vom Zentralverband d. Jüd. Religionsgemeinden in d. Slowakischen Sozialist. Republik. Nr. 1–4. Prag: Kirchenzentral-Verlag, 1976. [4 vols.] No. 1 incl.: Gedenkstunde für 3,800 am 8./9. März in Auschwitz ermordete Juden aus Böhmen und Mähren. No. 3: Kever Avot in Theresienstadt, pp. 1–14.

13562. GERMAN DEMOCRATIC REPUBLIC. *'Nachrichtenblatt'* d. Jüd. Gemeinde von Gross-Berlin und d. Verbandes d. Jüd Gemeinden in der Deutschen Demokratischen Republik. Eds.: Helmut Aris, Peter Kirchner, Herbert Ringer. Nr. 1–4. Berlin-Dresden, 1976. 26, 24, 21, 31 pp., illus. [4 vols.] [Nr. 1 incl.: Jizchok Leib Perez zum 125. Geburtstag (Helmut Eschwege). Berühmte jüd Ärzte. 1. Der Philosoph und Arzt Maimonides und seine Zeit (Erich Cohn). Zum jüd.-christl. Dialog (Josef Bor). Nr. 2: Zur Situation auf den Friedhöfen d. Jüd. Gemeinde von Gross-Berlin (Peter Kirchner). Nr. 3: Aus der Geschichte der Berliner Jüd. Gemeinde (Hanns Reissner, reprinted from 'Jüd. Rundschau', Berlin, 25.Aug. und 23.Sept.1936). Die jüd. Zeremonialkunst (Peter Kirchner). Nr. 4: Das kolossale leise Rascheln der Blätter eines grünen Baumes. Freimütige Reminiszenzen an die 100-Jahr-Feierlichkeiten des Bukarester Jüd. Staatstheaters (August 1976) (Jürgen Rennert, pp. 5–9).]

13563. GOSHKO, JOHN: *West Germany's reborn Jewish community numbers no more than 27,000 – one twentieth of one per cent of the population.* [In]: The Guardian, 18th December, London, 1974. [Reprinted from Washington Post – no date.]

13564. KNÜTTER, HANS-HELMUT: *Emigration und Emigranten als Politikum im Nachkriegsdeutschland.* [In]: 'Politische Studien'. 25, München, 1974. Pp. 413–426.

13565. MUNICH. GAY, RUTH: *Reichenbachstrasse 27: The Jews of Munich Today.* [In]: 'Midstream', vol. XXI, No. 8 (October), New York: The Theodor Herzl Society, 1975. Pp. 40–49. [The site of one of Munich's four synagogues and of the Isr. Kultusgemeinde.]

13566. PRESSE- UND INFORMATIONSAMT DER LANDESHAUPTSTADT MÜNCHEN, ed.: *Heimweh nach München.* Das Schicksal der emigrierten jüdischen Bürger Münchens. Text: Gerd Thumser. Illus.: Josef Blaumeiser, Rudolf Dix u.a. 2. Aufl. München: Wurm, 1967. 23 pp., ports., illus. (München im Blickpunkt, H.3). [1st ed. 1965. See No. 5106/YB. XI.]

13567. NEUBERGER, JOSEF. NEUBERGER, JOSEF: *Moderner Strafvollzug in Nordrhein-Westfalen.* Düsseldorf: Presse- und Informationsamt d. Landesregierung Nordrhein-Westfalen, 1971. 26, illus. [Prof. Neuberger who, from 1966–1972, was Minister of Justice in Rheinland Westfalen, was born 1902 in Antwerp. He died January 1977 in Düsseldorf. Obituaries: Er war deutscher Jude und israelischer Patriot. Zum Tode von Staatsminister a.D. Dr. Josef Neuberger (Hans Lamm) in: 'Isr. Wochenblatt', Nr. 3, 21. Jan., Zürich 1977. In: 'Allgemeine' (Hermann Lewy), 11./12. Jan. Düsseldorf, 1977. 'deutschland-berichte' (Rolf Vogel), Febr., Bonn 1977, pp. 10–12. 'Jewish Chronicle', 21st January, London, 1977., 'NJN', Nr.1, 4. Febr., München 1977.

13568. *Reports on Jewish Communities in Central Europe: Federal Republic of Germany* [and] *German Democratic Republic* (Friedo Sachser). [In]: American Jewish Year Book 1977. Vol. 77. Eds.: Morris Fine, Milton Himmelfarb, Martha Jelenko. New York: The American Jewish Committee, Philadelphia: The Jewish Publication Society of America, 1976. Pp. 428–451, 452–453.

13569. SILBERMANN, ALPHONS and HERBERT A. SALLEN: *Latenter Antisemitismus in der Bundes-*

republik Deutschland. [In]: Kölner Zeitschrift für Soziologie und Sozialpsychologie. H. 4. Opladen/Köln: Westdeutscher Verlag, 1976. Pp. 706–723, tabs.

13570. *Antisemitismus Heute.* Eine empirisch-soziologische Untersuchung in der Bundesrepublik Deutschland über die Latenz eines Voruteils. Durchgeführt im Forschungsinstitut für Soziologie der Universität zu Köln, Abtlg. Massenkommunikation. Direktor Prof. Dr. Alphons Silbermann. Projektleitung Herbert A. Sallen. Wiss. Mitarbeit Albin Hänseroth, Klaus Hang. Juli. Köln, 1975. 86 pp.

13571. SILBERMANN, ALPHONS: *Minoriätenforschung.* Antisemitismus in der Bundesrepublik Deutschland. [In]: bild der wissenschaft, Nr. 6. Stuttgart, 1976. Pp. 68–74. [A gallup poll on Antisemitism among 2,000 West Germans. For its result see 'Umfrage über den Antisemitismus' in: 'MB', 11. Juni, Tel Aviv, 1976 and 'Allgemeine', 16. Juli, Düsseldorf, 1976.]

13572. TENNENBAUM, SILVIA: *Return to Germany.* [In]: 'Midstream', Vol. XXII, No. 10, December. New York: The Theodor Herzl Society, 1976. Pp. 39–45. [Thoughts of the author (a cousin of Anne Frank) when she visited Germany which she had left as a child in 1936.]

13573. WILDER-OKLADEK, F.: *Young Persons in Migratory Conflict.* The Case of Young Adult Post War Jewry in Germany. [In]: International Migration and Adaptation in the Modern World. Papers presented at the 8th World Congress of Sociology, held in Toronto, Canada, August 1974. Ed.: Anthony H. Richmond. Toronto: Research Committee on Migration, International Sociological Association, 1976. Pp. 113–136, tabs., notes and bibl. pp. 133–136. [Mimeog.]

B. Restitution

13574. MAY, KURT. TRAMER, HANS: *Kurt May – der Grandseigneur der Wiedergutmachung* (aus Anlass seines 80. Geburtstages am 15. August 1976) in: 'MB', 13th August, Tel Aviv, 1976. Pp. 3–4. Another tribute in: 'AJR Information', August, London, 1976.

13575. OBERSTES RÜCKERSTATTUNGSGERICHT, ZWEITER SENAT: *Ausgewählte Entscheidungen des Obersten Rückerstattungsgerichts.* Auswahl der zwischen dem 1.7.1971 und 30.6.1976 erlassenen Entscheidungen. Veröffentlicht im Auftrage: Edward A. Marsden. Bd. IX. Herford/Westf. 1976 [In German and English.] [For Vol. VIII see No. 9459/YB. XVII.]

13576. *Rentenwegweiser für Deutsche in Übersee* [from]: Renten-Sozialbetreuung. P.O. Box 1758, Div. 16. Santa Monica, Cal. 90406.

C. Antisemitism, Judaism, Nazism in Education and Teaching

13577. BÖING, AXEL: *Auschwitz.* Unterrichtseinheit für den Schulgebrauch. Erprobt im Deutschunterricht einer 10. Hauptschulklasse. Frankfurt a.M.: Röderberg Verlag, 1976. 38 pp., illus. bibl., mit 5 herausnehmbaren Fotos in der Umschlagklappe. [Author is a member of 'Aktion Sühnezeichen'.]

13578. GIES, HORST: *Zeitgeschichte im Unterricht.* Ein didakt. Grundriss zur Geschichte im 20. Jahrhundert. Mit e. Geleitwort von Otto Büsch. Berlin: Colloquium Verlag, 1976. 170 pp., bibl. (pp. 167–170). (Historische und pädagogische Studien, Sonderreihe Bd. 1.)

13579. GITTLEMAN, SOL: *A Sociological Approach for the Classroom:* Confronting the Image of the Jew in German Studies. [In]: Die Unterrichtspraxis. Vol. VII, No. 1, Spring. Philadelphia, Pa., 1974. Pp. 32–38, bibl., notes. [Image of the Jew in the work of Annette Droste-Hülshoff, Georg Büchner, Felix Dahn, Gustav Freytag, Wilhelm Raabe u.a.]

13580. PILCH, JUDAH, ed.: *The Jewish Catastrophe in Europe.* [And]: *Guide to Teachers and Group Leaders* (Leon H. Spotts). New York: The National Curriculum Research Institute, Sponsored by the American Association for Jewish Education, 1968. 182 pp., bibl. (pp. 177–182).

13581. POST, ALBERT, comp.: *Teaching Guide on Holocaust.* Ed.: The New York Board of Education. New York, 1975. 66 pp. [The guide contains a course outline, model lessons, suggested teaching strategies, case studies of several camps. Attention is also given to Jewish heroism and resistance in various ghettoes.]

13582. ROTH, HEINZ: *Auf der Suche nach der Wahrheit.* Bd. 1: Wieso waren wir Väter Verbrecher? 3., unv. Aufl., 1972. 171 pp. Bd. 2: Was hätten wir Väter wissen müssen? Teil I, 1933–1939. Bd. 3: Teil 2: 1939–1945. 192, 190 pp. Bd. 4: Was geschah nach 1945? Teil 1: Der Zusammenbruch. 3., unv. Aufl. 1976. 186 pp. Odenhausen/Lumda: Postfach H. Roth, Selbstverlag, 1972/1976. [4 vols.]

13583. ROTHSCHILD, ELI: *Brückenschlag.* [In]: Schulbuchanalyse und Schulbuchkritik. Im Brennpunkt: Juden, Judentum und Staat Israel. Hrsg. von Gerd Stein und E. Horst Schallenberger. Duisburg, 1976. Pp. 199–207.

13584. SCHALLENBERGER, E. HORST and GERD STEIN: *Jewish History in German Textbooks.* [In]: Patterns of Prejudice. Vol. 10, No. 5, September/October London, 1976. Pp. 15–17 and 21, bibl. [See No. 14132.]

13585. SCHATZKER, CHAIM: *Das Deutschlandbild in den israelischen Geschichtsbüchern.* [In]: Aus Politik und Zeitgeschichte. Beilage zu 'Das Parlament'. 9. Okt. Bonn: Bundeszentrale für politische Bildung, 1976. Pp. 3–11. [An edited English version of this article: '*The German Image in Israeli Textbooks*' [in]: Patterns of Prejudice, Vol. X, No. 6, London, 1976. Pp. 21–24 and 35. See No. 14132.]

13586. SCHATZKER, CHAIM: *Die 'Schoah'.* Das Schicksal des europäischen Judentums im Dritten Reich als didaktisches Problem in der israelischen Schule. [In]: 'neue sammlung', 17. Jg., H. 1, Jan.-Febr. Göttingen: Vandenhoeck & Ruprecht, 1977. Pp. 95–101, bibl.

13587. SCHICKEL, ALFRED: *Die Darstellung der nationalsozialistischen Judenverfolgung in neueren Geschichtsbüchern der Bundesrepublik Deutschland.* [In]: Emuna-Israel Forum, H. 4, 1976. Pp. 21–28. [See No. 14089.]

13588. SEUBERT, JOSEF: *Judenverfolgung im Dritten Reich.* Kosmos-Wandbilder für den Unterricht. Stuttgart: Verlag Der Neue Schulmann, 1976. Lieferung 67, Nr. 4279, pp. 1–8, illus.

V. JUDAISM

A. Jewish Learning and Scholars

13589. BEN SASSON, H[AIM] H[ILLEL], ed.: *A History of the Jewish People.* Cambridge, Mass.: Harvard University Press, London: Weidenfeld and Nicolson, 1976. 1,170 pp., + 38 pp. illus., maps. [Originally publ. in Hebrew in 1969. Cf. The Texture of Jewish History (Chaim Raphael), in: Commentary, vol. 63, No. 1 (January), 1977. Pp. 64–69]

13590. BERGMAN[N], S. HUGO. BERGMAN[N], S. HUGO: *Die dialogische Philosophie von Kierkegard bis Buber.* Hrsg. von Moshe Barasch. Hebräische Universität Jerusalem, Heidelberg: Lambert Schneider, 1976. 283 pp., port. (Phronesis. Eine Schriftenreihe, Bd. 1.)

13591. BERGMAN[N], SHMUEL HUGO: *Toldot Haphilosophia Hachadashah.* Bd. III: The Philosophy of Dialogue from Kierkegaard to Buber. Jerusalem: Mossad Bialik, 1974. 283 pp., port. [Franz Rosenzweig, pp. 199–245. Haphilosophia Hadialogit shel Martin Buber, pp. 246–269. For vols. I-II see No. 12077/YB. XX.]

13592. GRANACH, YOCHANAN: *In Memory of S. H. Bergman.* The Philosopher as a Man. [In]: Ariel. No. 41. Jerusalem, 1976. Pp. 95–98, port. [S. H. Bergman, 1883 Prag–1975 Jerusalem.]

13593. BERKOVITS, ELIEZER: *Major Themes in Modern Philosophies of Judaism.* New York: Ktav, 1974. vii, 248 pp. [Cont.: Hermann Cohen's Religion of Reason. Franz Rosenzweig's Philosophy of Judaism. Martin Buber's Religion of the Dialogue. Faith and Law. Reconstructionist Theology, a critical evaluation. Dr. A. J. Heschel's Theology of Pathos.]

13594. BIBERFELD, EDUARD. ROSENBAUM, JACOB: *Dr. Eduard Biberfeld – Ein Wort der Erinnerung.* [In]: 'Mitteilungen des Verb. ehemaliger Breslauer und Schlesier. Nr. 40, Tel Aviv, 1976. [See No. 13438.] [E.B. gründete 1906 den 'Verband der Sabbath Freunde'.]

13595. BREUER, ISAAC: *Concepts of Judaism.* Selected and edited by Jacob S. Levinger. Jerusalem: Israel University Press, 1974. v, 348 pp., front., port. [A grandson of Samson Raphael Hirsch, I.B. was born 1883 in Hungary and died 1946 in Jerusalem.]

13596. BUBER, MARTIN. BUBER, MARTIN: *Zwanzig chassidische Erzählungen.* Mit 20 Orig.-

Radierungen von Erich Brauer. Frankfurt/M.: Editeuropa-Anstalt und Galerie Sydow, 1973. 89 pp., 20 illus.

13597. FRIEDMAN, MAURICE S.: *Martin Buber. The Life of Dialogue.* Chicago: University of Chicago Press, 1975. xvii, 322 pp., bibl. (pp. 283–309). [First publ. 1955. See No. 392/YB. I.]

13598. GOLDSTEIN, WALTER B.: *Der Glaube Martin Bubers.* Jerusalem: Rubin Mass, 1969. 186 pp. [Cont.: Der Glaube M.B., M.B. und das Böse. M.B., der Sozialist.] [Enlarged entry of No. 7790/YB. XV.]

13599. GORDON, HAIM: *A Method for Clarifying Buber's I–Thou Relationship.* [In]: Journal of Jewish Studies. Ed. Geza Vermes. Vol. XXVII, No. 1, Spring. Oxford: The Oxford Centre for Postgraduate Hebrew Studies, 1976. Pp. 71–83.

13600. ILLMAN, KARL JOHAN: *Leitwort – Tendenz – Synthese.* Programm und Praxis in der Exegese Martin Bubers. Abo: Abo Akademie, 1975. 308 pp., bibl. (pp. 302–308). (Meddelanden fran Stiftelsens för Abo Akademi Forsknings institut, No. 2). Diss.-Turku. [Cont.: Tradition und Methode (Stilanalyse), Traditionskritik, Historische Darstellung. Der methodologische Standort. Ergebnisse.]

13601. KOHANSKI, ALEXANDER S.: *An Analytical Interpretation of Martin Buber's I and Thou.* New York: Barron's Educational Series, Inc., 1975. 176 pp.

13602. KOHANSKI, ALEXANDER S.: *Martin Buber's Philosophy of Judaism.* [In]: Judaism. Vol. 24, No. 1, Winter. New York: American Jewish Congress, 1975. Pp. 69–81.

13603. *Martin Buber zum Gedächtnis.* Was kann uns Martin Buber heute lehren? Eine vorläufige Bilanz. Vorträge und Berichte in der Universität Frankfurt anlässlich des Symposions zum 10. Todestag. [In]: DZ-Information. Nr. 11. Hrsg. Didaktisches Zentrum der Johann Wolfgang Goethe-Universität Frankfurt am Main. Bearb.: Arbeitsstelle Fernstudium und Weiterbildung im Didakt. Zentrum. 1976. 92 pp., bibl. M.B. pp. 91–92. [Incl.: Worte Martin Bubers verlesen von Erica Futran am 10. Juni 1975 in der Univ. Frankfurt anlässlich seines 10. Todestages. Ein Votum (D. Albrecht Goes). Martin Bubers lebendiges Erbe (Ernst Simon, pp. 17–51). Das dialogische Prinzip Martin Bubers und das erzieherische Verhältnis (Werner Faber, pp. 53–61). Dialogik-und das konkrete Leben (Hans Michael Elzer, pp. 63–74). Zur Arbeit des M.B.-Zentrums für Erwachsenenbildung an der Hebr. Universität Jerusalem (Hans-Henning Kappel, pp. 75–84). Die 'Freunde der Hebr. Universität' und ihre Beziehungen zum Buber-Zentrum (Bertold Simonsohn). Bericht: Symposion zum Gedenken Martin Bubers (Roland Schüssler).]

13604. MENDES-FLOHR, PAUL R.: *Martin Buber's Concept of the Centre and Social Renewal.* [In]: The Jewish Journal of Sociology. Vol. XVIII. No. 1, June. London: World Jewish Congress, 1976. Pp. 23–26.

13605. SPEAR, OTTO: *Martin Buber's Dialogue – Topics and Partners.* [In]: Universitas. Vol. 18, No. 1. Stuttgart: Wissenschaftliche Verlagsgesellschaft, 1976. Pp. 75–83. (A Quarterly English Language Edition.)

13606. TALMON, SHEMARYAHU: *Martin Buber's Ways of Interpreting the Bible.* [In]: Journal of Jewish Studies. Ed. Geza Vermes. Publ. by the Oxford Centre for Postgraduate Hebrew Studies. Vol. XXVII, No. 2, Autumn. Oxford, 1976. Pp. 195–209.

13607. TIMMERMANN, HERBERT: *Aufhebung der Gottesfinsternis – Religiöser Sozialismus bei Martin Buber.* Diss., Philos. Fak., Univ. Wien, 1975. 130 pp., bibl. (pp. 119–130). [Mimeog.]

13608. CARLEBACH, JOSEPH TZVI. GILLIS-CARLEBACH, MIRYAM: *The Educational Precepts of Joseph Tzvi Carlebach. Theory and Practice.* Ramat Gan: Bar Ilan University, 1975.

13609. COHEN, HERMANN, JOSPE, EVA: *Hermann Cohen's Judaism: A Reassessment.* [In]: Judaism. Vol. 25, No. 4. New York: American Jewish Congress, 1975. Pp. 461–472.

13610. KLEIN, JOSEPH: *Die Grundlegung der Ethik in der Philosophie Hermann Cohens und Paul Natorps.* Eine Kritik des Marburger Neukantianismus. Göttingen: Vandenhoeck und Ruprecht, 1976. 298 pp., bibl. (pp. 296–298). (Abhandlungen der Akademie der Wissenschaften in Göttingen, Philologisch-Historische Klasse, Folge 3, Nr. 100). Zugl. Kath. Diss., Univ. Bonn, 1942. [The work incl. certain passages about Hermann Cohen which had to be omitted from the original dissertation.] [Paul Gerhard Natorp, 1854–1924.]

13611. MOOS, P.: *Hermann Cohen als Musikästhetiker.* Pp. 88–91 [In]: Festschrift Hermann Kretzschmar zum 70. Geburtstage. Hildesheim: Olms, 1973. vi, 184 pp., music.

13612. SCHMIDT, WINRICH De: *Psychologie und Transzendentalphilosophie.* Zur Psychologie-Rezeption bei Hermann Cohen und Paul Natorp. Bonn: Bouvier, 1976. 208 pp., bibl. (pp. 179–186). (Abhandlungen zur Philosophie, Psychologie und Pädagogik, Bd. 105).

13613. FACKENHEIM, EMIL L.: *From Bergen–Belsen to Jerusalem.* Contemporary Implications of the Holocaust. Jerusalem: World Jewish Congress and Institute of Contemporary Jewry, The Hebrew University, 1975. 45 pp., bibl. (Study Circle on Diaspora Jewry under the Auspices of the President of Israel).

13614. HIRSCH, SAMSON RAPHAEL. HIRSCH, SAMSON RAPHAEL: *From the Wisdom of Mishle.* New York: Feldheim, 1976. 260 pp. [Essays on various themes in the biblical book Mishle, originally publ. in the German language periodical 'Jeschurun'.]

13615. ASARIA, ZVI (i.e., Helfgott): *Samson Raphael Hirsch* – seine rechtliche Stellung als Landesrabbiner und sein segensreiches Wirken im Lande Niedersachsen. Hameln: Sponholtz, 1970. 71 pp., ports., facsims. [A much extended version of No. 8639/YB. XVI.]

13616. GILLIS-CARLEBACH, MIRYAM: *The Meaning of Derekh Eretz.* Tel Aviv: Friends of the Midrashia, 1976. Pp. 105–112. (Reprinted from NIV, a journal devoted to Halacha, Jewish Thought and Education.)

13617. ROSENBLOOM, NOAH H.: *Tradition in an Age of Reform.* The Religious Philosophy of Samson Raphael Hirsch. Philadelphia: Jewish Publication Society of America, 1976. xv, 480 pp., front., port., bibl. (pp. 455–470).

13618. JAY, MARTIN: *Politics of Translation.* Siegfried Kracauer and Walter Benjamin on the Buber–Rosenzweig Bible. [In]: LBI Year Book XXI. London, 1976. Pp. 3–24, ports., facsims.

13619. KISCH, ALEXANDER. KISCH, GUIDO: *Alexander Kisch, 1848–1917.* Biographische Übersicht. [In]: 'Udim', Zeitschrift der Rabbinerkonferenz in der Bundesrepublik Deutschland. Bd. VI. Frankfurt a.M., 5736/37–1975/76. Pp. 33–45. [See also No. 13299/YB. XXI: Die Familie Kisch.]

13620. MAIMON, SALOMON. MAIMON, SALOMON: *Gesammelte Werke, Bd. 7.* Hrsg. von Valerio Verra. Mit einem Nachw. des Hrsgs. und einem Gesamt-Inhaltsverzeichnis. Reprogr. Nachdr. Hildesheim–New York: Olms, 1976. 729 pp. [Incl. Ideen und Pläne zu neuen Untersuchungen. S. Maimons Geschichte seiner philosophischen Autorschaft, in Dialogen. Ideen und Pläne aus hinterlassenen Papieren. S. Ms. kritische Gutachten über die Kantische Philosophie. Maimoniana oder Rhapsodien zur Charakteristik Salomon Maimons. Aus seinem Privatleben gesammelt von Doct. Med. Sabattia Joseph Wolff (Berlin, 1813). For vols. 1–6 see No. 9492/YB. XVII.]

13621. HAREL, AZA: *Das Problem der Wahrheit bei Salomon Maimon.* Diss., Univ. München, 1969. xii, 158 pp.

13622. MAYBAUM, IGNAZ, RABBI. *In Memory of Rabbi Maybaum.* 2nd March 1897, Vienna– 24th March 1976, London. Obituaries: The Thinker and Teacher (Rabbi Dow Marmur). The Guardian of our Heritage (Werner Rosenstock). [In]: 'AJR Information', May, London, 1976. Pp. 8–9. Albert H. Friedlander [in]: European Judaism, Vol. 10, No. 2, Summer, London, 1976. [In]: 'Jewish Chronicle', 2nd April, London, 1976, port. Robert Weltsch [in]: 'MB', 18th March, Tel Aviv, 1977.

13623. MENDELSSOHN, MOSES. MENDELSSOHN, MOSES: *Briefwechsel.* Gesammelte Schriften. Hrsg. von Alexander Altmann. (1), Bd. 11: 1754–1762, 1974. xiv, 574 pp.; (2), Teilbd. 12/I: 1763–1770. 1976, x, 332 pp.; Teilbd. 12/II: 1771–1780, 1976, 276 pp. Stuttgart– Bad Cannstatt: Frommann–Holzboog, 1974/1976. (Jubiläumsausgabe. In Gemeinschaft mit F. Bamberger, H. Borodianski (Bar-Dayan), S. Rawidowicz, B. Strauss, L. Strauss. Begonnen von I. Elbogen. J. Guttmann, E. Mittwoch, fortgesetzt von Alexander Altmann). [In preparation is vol. 13 which will contain the correspondence from 1781 until Mendelssohn's death.]

13624. BACH, HANS I.: *Moses Mendelssohn.* [In]: 'European Judaism'. Vol. 10, No. 2 (Summer). London, 1976. Pp. 24–30.

13625. JAKOB, LUDWIG HEINRICH: *Prüfung der Mendelssohnschen Morgenstunden oder aller spekulativen Beweise für das Daseyn Gottes.* Nebst einer Abhandlung von Herrn Prof. Immanuel Kant. Neudr. d. Ausg. Leipzig 1786. Hildesheim: Gerstenberg Reprints, 1976. LX, 334 pp.

13626. PRINZ, JOACHIM: *The Secret Jews.* New York: Random House, 1974. 207 pp. [An account of the Marranos who converted to Christianity to escape the tortures of the Inquisition, but continued to practise secretly the rituals of Judaism as they were dispersed through many lands, incl. Germany.]

13627. ROSENBLÜTH, PINCHAS E.: *Die geistigen und religiösen Strömungen in der deutschen Judenheit.* [In]: Juden im Wilhelminischen Deutschland 1890–1914. Pp. 549–598. [See No. 13387.]

13628. SALZBERGER, RABBI DR. GEORG. *In Memory of Rabbi Salzberger:* A Guide to Searching Minds (Eva G. Reichmann). Memories from Frankfurt (Erwin Seligmann). The Teacher (C. H. Guttmann), and further tributes by Margaret Jacoby and K. G. von Hase, Botschafter der Bundesrepublik Deutschland [In]: 'AJR Information,' February, London, 1976. Pp. 6–7. Rabbi Dr. Albert H. Friedlander [In]: 'Jewish Chronicle', 2nd January, London, 1976. [Rabbi Salzberger, born 23rd December 1882 in Culm (West Prussia) died 1975 in London aged 92.]

13629. SCHOLEM, GERSHOM. SCHOLEM, GERSHOM: *Jugenderinnerungen.* [In]: 'Neue Rundschau'. H. 4. Frankfurt/M.: Fischer, 1976.

13630. SCHOLEM, GERSHOM: *On Jews and Judaism in Crisis.* Selected Essays. New York: Schokken, 1976. [Incl. essays on Buber, Agnon, Zionism, the diaspora, Jewish Theology.]

13631. SAHM, URI: *Gerschom Scholem, die Kabbalah und der Zionismus.* [In]: 'Tribüne', 15. Jg., H. 59, 1976. Pp. 7114–7118. [See No. 14072.]

13632. STEINSCHNEIDER, MORITZ: *Bibliographisches Handbuch über die theoretische und praktische Literatur für hebräische Sprachkunde.* Mit Zusätzen und Berichtigungen von M. Steinschneider, A. Freimann, Nathan Porges u.a. Nachdr. d. Ausgabe Leipzig 1859–1917. Hildesheim-New York: Olms Reprints, 1976. xxxvi, 295 pp.

13633. TAL, URIEL: *Theologische Debatte um das 'Wesen' des Judentums.* [In]: Juden im Wilhelminischen Deutschland 1890–1914. Pp. 599–632. [See No. 13387.]

13634. '*Tradition und Erneuerung*', Zeitschrift d. Vereinigung für Religiös-Liberales Judentum in der Schweiz. Begr. von Lothar Rothschild. Ed.: Lutz O. Zwillenberg. Nr. 41, September. Bern, 1976. [Incl. Die Erhaltung und Wiederbelebung des Judentums in der modernen Welt (John D. Rayner, pp. 1–17, with an English summary).]

13635. TREPP, LEO: *Judaism. Development and Life.* 2nd. ed. Encino, Cal.: Dickenson, 1974. 294 pp., bibl. (Paperbound). [Deutsche Erstausg. Das Judentum. Geschichte und lebendige Gegenwart, see No. 8670/YB. XVI.]

13636. WILHELM, KURT, ed.: *Jüdischer Glaube.* Eine Auswahl aus zwei Jahrtausenden. Nachdr. aus der Sammlung Dietrich. Bonn: Bouvier, 1975. xix, 524 pp. (Zeugnisse jüd. Glaubens. Eine Quellenauswahl vom Talmud bis Martin Buber, jeweils mit geistesgeschichtlichen und biographischen Einführungen). [First publ. 1961. See No. 2634/YB. VII.]

13637. ZIMMELS, H[IRSCH] J[AKOB]: *The Echo of the Nazi Holocaust in Rabbinic Literature.* London: Marla Publications, 1976. xxiii, 372 pp. [Responses of Rabbis to agonising questions on Jewish Law raised by sufferers from Nazi persecution.] [The late rabbi Dr. Zimmels was lecturer at the Jewish Theological Seminary in Breslau from 1929 to 1933.]

13638. ZINBERG, ISRAEL: *A History of Jewish Literature.* Transl. from the Yiddish by Bernard Martin. Vols. 1–7. Cincinnati: Hebrew Union College Press, New York: Ktav, 1973–1975. 231, 257, 323, 232, 224, 324, 403 pp. [7 vols.]

13639. ZUNZ, LEOPOLD: *Gesammelte Schriften.* Hrsg. vom Curatorium der 'Zunzstiftung'. 3 Bde. in 1 Bd. Nachdr. d. Ausgabe Berlin 1875/76. Hildesheim-New York: Olms Reprints, 1976. 354, 304, 301 pp. [959 pp., 3 vols. in one.]

13640. ZUNZ, LEOPOLD: *Zur Geschichte und Literatur.* Bd. 1. Nachdr. d. Ausg. Berlin 1845. Hildesheim-New York: Olms Reprints, 1976. viii, 607 pp. [Incl. Zur Literatur des jüd. Mittelalters in Frankreich und Deutschland. Bibliographisches. Die jüdischen Dichter der Provence. Geschichte der Juden in Sicilien.] [L. Zunz, scholar, historian, 1794 Detmold–1886 Berlin. Mitbegründer der Wissenschaft des Judentums.]

B. The Jewish Problem

13641. DEUTSCHER, ISAAC: *Die ungelöste Judenfrage.* Zur Dialektik von Antisemitismus und Zionismus. Mit einem Vorwort von Mario Offenberg. Berlin: Rotbuch Verlag, 1976. 120 pp. (Rotbuch, 159). [Incl. chaps.: Was prägt jüdische Identität: Religion, Sprache, Kultur oder Antisemitismus? Über die internationalistische Tradition unter den Juden. Hat die russische Revolution das jüdische Problem gelöst? Zur Fortdauer von Antisemitismus in nachkapitalistischen Gesellschaften. Zur Entwicklung der gesellschaftlichen Konflikte in Israel. Kann der Zionismus als anti-arabische Strategie überleben?]

13642. FRYE, BRUCE B.: *The German Democratic Party and the 'Jewish Problem' in the Weimar Republic.* [In]: LBI Year Book XXI. London, 1976. Pp. 143–172.

13643. RÜRUP, REINHARD: *Emanzipation und Krise.* Zur Geschichte der 'Judenfrage' in Deutschland vor 1890. [In]: Juden im Wilhelminischen Deutschland 1890–1914. Pp. 1–56. [See No. 13387.]

13644. TALMON, J. L.: *Reflections of an Historian in Israel.* [In]: 'Encounter'. XLVI, No. 5 (May). London, 1976. Pp. 82–90.

13645. TOURY, JACOB: *Die Behandlung jüdischer Problematik in der Tagesliteratur der Aufklärung (bis 1783).* [In]: Jahrbuch des Instituts für Deutsche Geschichte. Bd. V, Tel Aviv, 1976. Pp. 13–47. [See No. 13481.]

13646. [TOYNBEE, ARNOLD] LIEBESCHÜTZ, HANS: *Arnold Toynbee (1889–1975).* [In]: LBI Year Book XXI. London, 1976. Pp. 289–292.

13647. RABINOWICZ, OSKAR K.: *Arnold Toynbee on Judaism and Zionism.* A Critique. London: W. H. Allen 1974. 372 pp. notes pp. 323–366. (Posthumously publ. ed. by John M. Shaftesly. [O. K. Rabinowicz (1903–1969) devoted many years of study to the examination of Toynbee's 'A Study of History' which became almost from the outset the centre of controversy, particularly among Jewish scholars, because of his treatment of Jewish history and his indictment of Judaism.]

13648. WELTSCH, ROBERT: *Die schleichende Krise der jüdischen Identität.* Ein Nachwort. [In]: Juden im Wilhelminischen Deutschland 1890–1914. Pp. 689–702. [See No. 13387.]

C. Jewish Life and Organisations

13649. ADLER-RUDEL, SHALOM. (23rd June, 1894 Czernowitz–14th November, Jerusalem). *In Memoriam Shalom Adler-Rudel* (Robert Weltsch) [In]: LBI Year Book XXI London, 1976. Pp. xiii–xvi. A Life for the Jewish People (Robert Weltsch). Co-Founder of AJR (Werner Rosenstock) [In]: 'AJR Information', London, January 1976. Schalom Adler-Rudel zum Gedenken (Hans Tramer). Am Grabe unseres alten Freundes (Ernst Simon) [in]: 'MB', 21st November and 12th December, Tel Aviv, 1975. Zum Tode S. Adler-Rudels (E. G. Lowenthal) [in]: 'Allgemeine', November 28th, Düsseldorf, 1975. 'Jewish Chronicle', 28th November, 1975.

13650. BARLEV, JEHUDA: *'Wir wollen eine Bahn euch ebnen'.* Die Anfänge handwerklicher Ausbildung deutscher Juden. [In]: 'Allgemeine', 23rd September, Düsseldorf, 1976. Pp. 17 and 19.

13651. BEHR, WERNER M., OBE. *Werner M. Behr zum Gedenken* (Heinz Gerling) [In]: 'MB', 3rd September, Tel Aviv, 1976. Devoted Worker for Jewish Causes. AJR's Indebtedness (Werner Rosenstock). A Loss for the Council of Jews from Germany (Curt C. Silberman, New York and Heinz Gerling, Jerusalem). Tribute by British Academy (Neville Williams). A Personal Appreciation (H. Oscar Joseph) [In]: 'AJR Information', October, London, 1976. 'Jewish Chronicle', 3rd September, London, 1976. [Werner B. Behr died on 22nd August 1976, aged 73.]

13652. BREßLAU, HARRY. KISCH, GUIDO: *Harry Breßlau – Historiker der Juden in Deutschland.* Ein verspätetes Gedenkblatt zum 50. Todestag. [In]: 'Allgemeine', 24./31. Dez. Düsseldorf, 1976. [H. B., father-in-law of Albert Schweitzer, 1848 Dannenberg (Hanover)–1926 Heidelberg.]

13653. FREUND, ISMAR. BIRNBAUM, MAX P.: *Die Endphase der Emanzipation.* Zum 100. Geburtstag von Dr. Ismar Freund. [In]: 'MB', 14. April und 7. Mai, Tel Aviv, 1976. Pp. 9–10 und 5–6. [Also]: *Schlussstein der Emanzipation* (Max P. Birnbaum) [In]: 'Mitteilungen d. Verbandes ehemaliger Breslauer und Schlesier in Israel', Nr. 39, Tel Aviv, 1976, port. [See No. 13438.] [And in]: 'Allgemeine' (Ernst G. Lowenthal), 11. Juni, Düsseldorf, 1976. [Ismar Freund, 1876 Breslau–1956 Jerusalem. Freund's main work: Die Emanzipation der Juden in Preussen (1912).]

13654. FRIEDLANDER, FRITZ. *Gruss nach Melbourne zum 75. Geburtstag des Historikers.* (E. Gottfried). [In]: 'Allgemeine', 21. Mai, Düsseldorf 1976. West Berlin Colleague (E. G. Lowenthal) [and] A Local Tribute (Samuel Billigheimer) [In]: 'The Australian Jewish News', 14th May, Melbourne, 1976, port. [And in]: 'AJR Information' (Eva

G. Reichmann), June, London, 1976. [Dr. Fritz Friedlander was born on 17th May 1901 in Berlin.]

13655. *The Hill–Page Collection.* Ed. by Maurice Spertus, Museum of Judaica. With Introductory Remarks by Arthur M. Feldman. Chicago: Spertus College of Judaica Press, 1976, n.p., ports., illus. (Catalogue). [This publication documents a collection of seventy Jewish ceremonial objects and memorabilia representing the totality of traditional life in a German-Jewish home during the late nineteenth and early twentieth centuries, providing an historical record and an insight into the German-Jewish life-style of that time. The objects were given to the Museum by Ann E. Cohn Hirschland (Hill), Eleanor A. Cohn-Pagener (Page) and Ernest J. Cohn Hirschland (Hill) in memory of their parents Julius Cohn and Bertha Cohn Hirschland (Hill) and Mrs. Cohn-Pagener's husband, Max Pagener (Page), whose parents lived in Epe, Westphalia.]

13656. KAPLAN, MARION A.: *German-Jewish Feminism in the Twentieth Century.* [In]: Jewish Social Studies. Vol. XXXVIII, No. 1 (Winter) New York: Conference on Jewish Social Studies, 1976. Pp. 39–53. [On the aims and activities of the 'Jüdischer Frauenbund' (League of Jewish Women) and its founder Bertha Pappenheim (1859 Vienna–1936 Neu Isenburg).]

13657. PASCHELES, W[OLF], ed.: *Sippurim.* Eine Sammlung jüdischer Volkssagen, Erzählungen, Mythen, Chroniken, Denkwürdigkeiten und Biographien berühmter Juden. 5 Teile in 2 Bden. Nachdr. d. Ausgabe Prag 1854–58. (Volkskundliche Quellen. Reihe IV). Hildesheim-New York: Olms Reprints, 1976. 1477 pp. [Wolf Pascheles, author, publisher, bookseller, 1814 Prague–1857 Prague].

13658. PRESTON, DAVID L.: *The German Jews in Secular Education, University Teaching, and Science: A Preliminary Inquiry.* [In]: Jewish Social Studies. Vol. XXXVIII, No. 2 (Spring). New York: Conference on Jewish Social Studies, 1976. Pp. 99–116, tabs.

13659. RINOTT, MOSHE: *The Zionist Organisation and the Hilfsverein.* Cooperation and Conflict (1901–1914). [In]: LBI Year Book XXI. London, 1976. Pp. 261–278. [Incl. a letter by Arthur Hantke to Arthur Ruppin, dated 22nd January 1914].

13660. ROSENSTEIN, NEIL: *The Unbroken Chain.* Biographical Sketches and the Genealogy of Illustrious Jewish Families from the fifteenth to twentieth Centuries. New York: Shengold Publishers, 1976. xii, 716 pp., gen. tables. [The author presents 400 years of genealogical history from the Rabbi of Padua, who was the founder of the Katzenellenbogen family to such varied personalities as Martin Buber and Helena Rubinstein, themselves cousins, Moses and Felix Mendelssohn, Rabbi Jonathan Eybeschütz, Karl Marx, whose nephew, Sir Harry Juta, was the Attorney General to Prime Minister Cecil John Rhodes.]

13661. *Zeitschrift für die Wissenschaft des Judenthums.* Hrsg. von dem Verein für Cultur und Wissenschaft der Juden. Red. L[eopold] Zunz. Nachdr. d. Ausg. Berlin 1823. Hildesheim-New York: Olms reprints, 1976. viii, 539 pp.

D. Jewish Art and Music

13662. BROD, MAX: *Die Musik Israels.* Revidierte Ausgabe mit einem zweiten Teil: *Werden und Entwicklung der Musik in Israel* von Yehuda Walter Cohen. Kassel: Bärenreiter, 1976. 164 pp., illus., music, biographical register. ['Israel's Music' was publ. by Brod in Tel Aviv in 1951, later also in German. Now brought up to date and supplemented by Y. W. Cohen.]

13663. FRAUBERGER, HEINRICH: *Objects of Ancient Jewish Ritual Art and Illuminated Hebrew Script and Ornaments of Printed Books.* With a new introduction by Hermann M. Z. Meyer. Jerusalem, 1970. viii, 104 pp. + 271 illus., facsims. (Reprinted by order of the Universitas Booksellers). [The vol. incl.: Über alte Kultusgegenstände in Synagoge und Haus [and] Verzierte hebräische Schrift und jüdischer Buchschmuck [originally publ. in]: Mitteilungen der Gesellschaft zur Erforschung jüdischer Kunstdenkmäler. Frankfurt a.M., H. III-IV (Okt.) 1903 [and] H. V–VI (Okt.) 1909.]

13664. GRADENWITZ, PETER: *Klänge und Echo.* Testimonium: Zeugnisse jüdischer Geschichte in Wort und Musik. [In]: 'MB', 27th February, Tel Aviv, 1976. (Ein Bericht über die 4. Serie der von Recha Freier begründeten 'Testimonium'-Werke als Zeugnis für Leiden und Streben des jüdischen Volkes im Laufe seiner Geschichte.)

13665. HOFMAN, SHLOMO: *Mikra'ei Musica*. A Collection of Biblical References to Music. Tel Aviv: Israel Institute, 1974. 184 pp. [See also]: Wandel in der Kunstliteratur (Heinrich Strauss) [and]: 'Mikra'ei Musica'. Zur Geschichte der Musik Israels (Peter Gradenwitz) [In]: 'MB', 14th April, Tel Aviv, 1976.

13666. ROSENAU, HELEN: *A Short History of Jewish Art*. London: Pordes, 1975. 78 pp.

13667. ROTHMÜLLER, ARON MARKO: *The Music of the Jews*. A historical appreciation. Transl. from the German by H. C. Stevens. New and revised edition. Cranbury, N.J.: Barnes, 1975. 320 pp., illus., music (Paperbound). [For previous English and German eds. see No. 5808/YB. XII.]

13668. WERNER, ERIC: *A Voice Still Heard* . . . The Sacred Songs of the Ashkenazic Jews. University Park, Pa.: The Pennsylvania State University Press, 1976. xiii, 350 pp., front., illus., port., music samples, notes pp. 285–324, index of names. (A Publication in the Leo Baeck Institute Series). [In addition, a cassette of Synagogal music from the text selected by the author and chanted by Cantor Erwin Hirsch, Congregation Habonim, New York City, has been issued.]

13669. WERNER, ERIC, ed.: *Contributions to a Historical Study of Jewish Music*. New York: Ktav, 1976. 287 pp., ports., illus., music. [12 essays. Incl. Gustav Mahler and Arnold Schoenberg by Peter Gradenwitz, reprinted from LBI Year Book V, London 1960. Pp. 262–284.]

VI. ZIONISM AND ISRAEL

13670. BEN-CHORIN, SCHALOM: *Siebzig Jahre Bezalel*. Zur Geschichte der ältesten Kunstschule Israels. [In]: 'Allgemeine', 12. Dez., Düsseldorf, 1975. [The sculptor Prof. Boris Schatz (1866–1932) founded the school in Jerusalem in 1906.]

13671. BLUMENFELD, KURT: *Im Kampf um den Zionismus*. Briefe aus fünf Jahrzehnten. Hrsg. von Miriam Sambursky und Jochanan Ginat. Stuttgart: Deutsche Verlags-Anstalt, 1976 311 pp. (Veröffentlichung des Leo Baeck Instituts). [Vorwort: Kurt Blumenfeld und der deutsche Zionismus, pp. 7–37.]

13672. COH[E]N, BENNO. CAPELL, HANS: *Ein Leben für zionistische Verwirklichung*. Benno Cohen s.A. zu den Schloschim. [In]: 'MB', 26. Dez., Tel Aviv, 1975. [Benno Cohn, 30th September 1894 Labischin b. Bromberg–24th November 1975 Tel Aviv.]

13673. ELONI, YEHUDA: *Die umkämpfte nationaljüdische Idee*. [In]: Juden im Wilhelminischen Deutschland 1890–1914. Pp. 633–688. [See No. 13387.]

13674. GOLDMANN, NAHUM: *Israel muss umdenken*. Die Lage der Juden 1976. Mit einem Gespräch zum deutsch-jüdischen Verhältnis. Deutsche vom Autor besorgte Erstausgabe. Reinbek: Rowohlt, 1976. 121 pp. (rororo Bd. 4061). ['French edition]: *Où va tu Israel?* Paris: Calmann-Lévy, 1975. 189 pp. ('Diaspora'). [English translation of a chap. from the French]: *Israel cannot be a country like all others*. [In]: 'The Jewish Quarterly'. Ed. Jacob Sonntag. XXIV, No. 1–2 (87–88, Spring/Summer). London: Jewish Literary Trust, 1976. Pp. 3–9. [Cf. Israel – die unvollendete Erneuerung. N. Goldmanns Mahnungen an den jüdischen Staat (Nachum Orland) in: 'FAZ', 3. Dez. Frankfurt/M. 1976.]

13675. GOLDMANN, NAHUM: *Le paradoxe Juif*. Paris: Édition Stock, 1976. 261 pp.

13676. HERZL, THEODOR. BRUDE-FIRNAU, GISELA: *Vision und Politik*. Die Tagebücher Theodor Herzls. Auswahl und Nachwort von . . . Frankfurt/M.: Suhrkamp, 1976. 344 pp., bibl. Th. H. und bibl. (pp. 336–338). (Suhrkamp Taschenbuch, 374).

13677. ELON, AMOS: *Herzl*. London: Weidenfeld and Nicolson, 1976. xi, 448 pp., ports., illus., bibl. (pp. 413–417), notes pp. 419–432. [For American and German eds. see No. 12915/YB. XXI.]

—— KALLNER, RUDOLF: *Herzl und Rathenau*. Wege jüdischer Existenz an der Wende des 20. Jahrhunderts. [See No. 13388.]

13678. HESS, MOSES. AVINERI, SHLOMO: *Socialism and Nationalism in Moses Hess*. [In]: 'Midstream'. Vol. XXII, No. 4, April. New York: The Theodor Herzl Foundation, 1976. Pp. 36–44.

13679. BOYER, ALAIN: *Du Socialisme Vrai au Sionisme Socialiste*. L'Itinéraire d'un Prophète: Moise Hess. [In]: Le Mouvement Social. Vol. 95, Avril–Juin. Paris, 1976. Pp. 25–52.

13680. NA'AMAN, SHLOMO: *Moses Hess in der deutschen Arbeiterbewegung*. Zum 100. Jahrestag seines Todes am 6. April 1975. [In]: Jahrbuch d. Instituts für Deutsche Geschichte. Bd. V. Tel Aviv, 1976. Pp. 247–297. [See No. 13481.]

13681. KANAAN, HAAVIV: *Die fünfte Kolonne – Die Deutschen in Erez Israel, 1933–1945.* Vorwort von Gideon Hausner. Tel Aviv: Hakibbuz Hameuchad, 1976. [A study on the last years of the Templars in Palestine.]

13682. KLAUSNER, MARGOT. CZERSKI, ALEXANDER: *Margot Klausner – ein Leben für Israel und die Kunst.* [In]: 'Allgemeine', 28th November, Düsseldorf, 1975. [Margot Klausner (1905 Berlin–1975 Tel Aviv) played a prominent part in the development of the Habima Theatre. In 1974 she publ. a biography of her father Julius Klausner, who was the founder of 'Schuhhaus Leiser' in Berlin. See No. 12348/YB. XX.]

13683. LAQUEUR, WALTER: *A History of Zionism.* New York: Schocken Books. 1976. 640 pp. (Paperbound Reprint). [For London ed. see No. 10448/YB. XVIII, German ed.: Der Weg zum Staat Israel see No. 12922/YB. XXI.]

13684. MA'OZ, MOSHE, ed.: *Studies on Palestine during the Ottoman Period.* Jerusalem: Magnes Press, 1975. xix, 582 pp., geneal., table, maps. (This vol. is an outcome of an international conference held in Jerusalem, in 1970, on the history of Palestine and its Jewish population during the Ottoman period.) [Incl. German interests and the Jewish Community in nineteenth-Century Palestine (M. Eliav). The German settlers in Palestine and their relations with the local Arab population and the Jewish community, 1868–1918 (A. Carmel). Documentary material in Austrian and German Archives relating to Palestine during the period of Ottoman rule (A. Carmel).]

13685. RUPPIN, ARTHUR. BEIN, ALEX: *Der Vater der jüdischen Siedlung.* Zum 100. Geburtstag von Arthur Ruppin (1. März 1876 Rawitsch–1. Januar 1943 Jerusalem). [In]: 'MJN', 26. März, München, 1976. [In]: 'Das Neue Israel', 28. Jg., H. 11, Mai. Zürich, 1976, port. [And]: Father of Jewish Settlement. The Centenary of Dr. Arthur Ruppin falls this Month [In]: 'Jewish Observer and Middle East Review', 19th March, London, 1976.

13686. KROLIK, SCHLOMO: *Arthur Ruppin – ein humanistischer Zionist.* Zu seinem 100. Geburtstag. [In]: 'MB', 27th February, Tel Aviv, 1976. Pp. 5–7.

13687. WALK, JOSEPH: *'Der Zionist'.* Zur Geschichte der ältesten zionistischen Zeitung Deutschlands. [In]: 'MB', Nr. 15/16, 14th April, Tel Aviv, 1976. Pp. 11 and 16. [The four numbers of the paper, edited by Hugo Schachtel, Breslau, appeared in 1901.]

13688. WELTSCH, ROBERT. *Robert Weltsch zum 85. Geburtstag* (am 20. Juni 1976): Lehrer und Warner, Publizist und Prophet (Moshe Tavor, Hans Tramer). Religiös fundierter Humanismus (Pinchas Rosenblüth). Reminiszenzen aus der Frühzeit des Zionismus, entnommen dem Briefwechsel zwischen Robert Weltsch und seinem Freunde Hugo Bergman s.A., mitgeteilt von dessen Witwe Escha Bergman. [In]: 'MB', 18. Juni. Tel Aviv, 1976. Pp. 5–8. port. [Further Tributes]: Historian of a stormy century (Max Gruenewald). Homage to a great writer (Margot Pottlitzer). Robert Weltsch: A Thought and a Word (Albert H. Friedlander). Erinnerungen an Prag (Nelly Engel-Thieberger). Berlin 1933 (Walter Breslauer). Vom Zusammenfall der Gegensätze (Ernst Simon). Robert Weltsch and the LBI Year Book (Werner Rosenstock). [In]: 'AJR Information', XXXI, No. 6 (June), London, 1976. Pp. 1–2, 6–8, port. Aus der Geschichte lernen (E. G. Lowenthal [In]: 'Allgemeine', 18. Juni, Düsseldorf, 1976 [and in]: 'Aufbau', 11th June, New York, 1976.

13689. WISTRICH, ROBERT S.: *German Social Democracy and the Problem of Jewish Nationalism 1897–1917.* [In]: LBI Year Book XXI. London, 1976. Pp. 109–142.

13690. YISRAELI, DAVID: *The German Reich and Palestine.* The Palestine Problem in German Politics in the Years 1889–1945. Ramat Gan: Bar Ilan University, 1974. 334 pp. [In Hebrew.]

VII. PARTICIPATION IN CULTURAL AND PUBLIC LIFE

A. General

13691. 'DIE AKTION'. Wochenschrift für Politik, Literatur, Kunst. Hrsg. von Franz Pfemfert. Bd. 1–22, 1911–1932 (alles Ersch.) Nendeln (Liechtenstein): Kraus Reprint, 1976. [For a 1961 reprint see No. 3219/YB. VIII.]

13692. PETER, LOTHAR: *Literarische Intelligenz und Klassenkampf 'Die Aktion' 1911–1932.* Köln:

Pahl-Rugenstein, 1972. 221 pp., biogr. notes, bibl. (pp. 215–221). Zugl. Gesellschafts-wiss. Diss., Univ. Marburg, 1971 u.d.T. Das Verhältnis von Schriftstellern zum politischen Engagement am Beispiel 'Die Aktion'. 1918–1925. [Many Jews were closely connected with paper.]

13693. ALTHAUS, HORST: *Zwischen Monarchie und Republik* – Schnitzler, Kafka, Hofmannsthal, Musil. München: Fink, 1976. 188 pp.

13694. ARONSFELD, C. C.: *Jewish Bankers and the Tsar*. [In]: 'Jewish Social Studies', Vol. XXXV, No. 2 (April). New York: Conference on Jewish Social Studies, 1973. Pp. 87–104. [Incl. German-Jewish bankers.]

13695. BENZ, WOLFGANG und HERMANN GRAML, eds.: *Die revolutionäre Illusion*. Zur Geschichte des linken Flügels der USPD. Erinnerungen von Curt Geyer. Mit e. Vorw. von Robert F. Wheeler. Stuttgart: Deutsche Verlags-Anstalt, 1975. 303 pp., bibl. C.G. pp. 297–299. (Schriftenreihe der Vierteljahrshefte für Zeitgeschichte, Nr. 33). [Incl. Friedrich and Victor Adler, Eduard Bernstein, Oskar Cohn, Kurt Eisner, Ruth Fischer, Hugo Haase, Walter Hasenclever, Hilferding, Otto Landsberg, Paul Levi, Rosa Luxemburg, Willi Münzenberg, Karl Radek, Kurt Rosenfeld, Friedrich Stampfer and others.]

13696. BOSCH, MICHAEL: *Liberale Presse in der Krise*. Die Innenpolitik der Jahre 1930 bis 1933 im Spiegel d. 'Berliner Tageblatts', d. 'Frankfurter Zeitung' und der 'Vossischen Zeitung'. Bern/Frankfurt M.: Lang, 1976. ix, 343 pp. (Europ. Hochschulschriften, Reihe 3, Bd. 65).

13697. BRAUNTHAL, JULIUS: *Geschichte der Internationale*. Bd. 1: Von den Anfängen bis 1914. Bd. 2: 1914–1943. Bd. 3: 1943–1969. Bonn–Bad Godesberg: Dietz. 1971/74. 404 pp., ports.; 617 pp., ports.; 750 pp., ports. [3 vols.] [For previous German and English eds. see No. 9593/YB. XVII. – Julius Braunthal died 1972.]

13698. DÖNHOFF, MARION GRÄFIN: *Menschen, die wissen, worum es geht*. Politische Schicksale 1916 bis 1976. Hamburg: Hoffman und Campe, 1976. 259 pp., ports. [Incl.: Bewundert viel- und viel gescholten: Henry Kissinger. Der Basler Gelehrte: Verzauberer und Entzauberer zugleich: Edgar Salin. Die Schule der Selbstbewährung: Kurt Hahn. Ein Kolleg über Inflation und Deflation: L. Albert Hahn (1889 Frankfurt/M.–1968 Zürich.]

13699. EHRLICH, LEONARD H.: *Karl Jaspers: Philosophy as Faith*. Amherst: University of Massachusetts Press, 1975. xii, 287 pp., port., bibl. K.J. pp. 231–235. [Chap.: Dialogue and Communication – Buber and Jaspers, pp. 77–97.]

13700. EXILE LITERATURE. BERENDSOHN, WALTER A.: *Die humanistische Front*. Einführung in die deutsche Emigranten-Literatur. Zweiter Teil: *Vom Kriegsausbruch 1939 bis Ende 1946*. Worms: Heintz, 1976. xii, 236 pp., list of names pp. 196–224, facsims. (Eine Schriftenreihe hrsg. von Georg Heintz, Bd. 6). [Part I: Von 1933 bis zum Kriegsausbruch 1939 was publ. Zürich, 1946.]

13701. *Deutsche Exilliteratur seit 1933. I. Kalifornien*. Teil 1 hrsg. von John M. Spalek und Joseph Strelka. Teil 2 hrsg. von John M. Spalek, Joseph Strelka und Sandra H. Hawrylchak. Bern: Francke, 1976. 868 pp., 216 pp., bibls. [2 vols.] [Incl. chaps. on Günther Anders (i.e., orig. Günther Stern), Raoul Auernheimer, Vicki Baum, Emil Bernhard (Cohn), Döblin, Paul Elbogen, Lion Feuchtwanger, Bruno Frank, Hans Habe, Oskar Jellinek, Stephan Lackner, Ludwig Marcuse, Alfred Neumann, Alfred Neumeyer, Alfred Polgar, Wilhelm Speyer, Friedrich Torberg, Joseph Wechsberg, Franz Werfel, Victoria Wolff née Victoria Trude Victor, Paul Frank, George Froeschel, Leopold Jessner, Gina Kaus, Henry Koster (orig. Hermann), Bob Kosterlitz, Max Reinhardt, Walter Reisch, Curt Siodmak, Billy Wilder. Vol. II contains the bibliographies of the authors dealt with in vol. I.]

13702. *Exil in der Sowjetunion*. Beiträge von oder über Jiri Weil, Herwarth Walden, Carola Neher, Heinrich Kurella, Werner Hirsch, Alexander Granach, Siňa Walden u.a. Briefe Heinrich Kurellas an Margret Boveri und Alexander Granachs an Lotte Lieven. Akten der Geh. Staatspolizei, der SS und zahlreiches bisher unveröffentlichtes Fotomaterial. Berlin: Verlag europäische ideen, 1976. 160 pp., illus.

13703. MAAS, LIESELOTTE: *Handbuch der deutschen Exilpresse, 1933–1945*. Hrsg. von Eberhard Lämmert. Bd. 1: Bibliographie A–K. München: Hanser, 1976. 352 pp., text of preface and introd. in German and English. (Sonderveröffentlichungen der Deutschen Bibliothek, Nr. 2).

13704. MÜSSENER, HELMUT: *Deutschsprachige Emigration nach 1933 in Schweden*. Die Bestände d.

Stadtbibliothek Västeras. Ein Verzeichnis. Stockholm, 1975. 29 pp. (Veröffentlichung, Stockholmer Koordinationsstelle zur Erforschung der deutschsprachigen Exil-Literatur, Deutsches Institut, Universität Stockholm, Nr. 18). [Cf. also No. 9607/YB. XVII and No. 12170/YB. XX.]

13705. ROLOFF, GERHARD: *Exil und Exilliteratur in der deutschen Presse 1945–1949.* Worms: Heintz, 1976. x, 313 pp. (Schriftenreihe Deutsches Exil 1933–1945, Bd. 10).

13706. SANDQVIST, GISELA: *Johannes Urzidil Prag, New York: Vom Untertan d. österr. Monarchie zum amerikanischen Staatsangehörigen.* Stockholm, 1975. 18 pp. (Veröffentlichung, Stockholmer Koordinationsstelle zur Erforschung der deutschsprachigen Exil-Literatur, Deutsches Institut, Universität Stockholm, Nr. 19).

13707. STOCKHOLMER KOORDINATIONSSTELLE Z. ERFORSCHUNG D. DEUTSCHSPRACHIGEN EXILLITERATUR, ed.: *Rechenschaftsbericht.* Universität Stockholm. Deutsches Institut, 1975. 22 pp.

13708. FENSKE, HANS, ed.: *Vormärz und Revolution 1840–1849.* Aufsätze. Darmstadt: Wiss. Buchgesellschaft, 1976. (Quellen zum politischen Denken der Deutschen im 19. und 20. Jahrhundert). [Incl. Moses Hess, Marx, Friedrich Julius Stahl.]

13709. FLECHTHEIM, OSSIP K.: *Der Januskopf des Rechtes.* Zur Rechtstheorie von Marx, Kelsen und Freud. [In]: Die Zukunft. Sozialistische Zeitschrift für Politik, Wirtschaft und Kultur. H. 6/7, Wien, 1976. Pp. 12–15.

13710. THE FRANKFURT SCHOOL. JAY, MARTIN: *Dialektische Phantasie.* Die Geschichte der Frankfurter Schule und des Instituts für Sozialforschung 1923–1950. Mit e. Vorw. von Max Horkheimer. Aus d. Amerik. von Hanne Herkommer und Bodo von Grieff. Frankfurt a.M.: Fischer, 1976. 432 pp., bibl. (pp. 405–422). [For the original 'The Dialectical Imagination' see No. 11394/YB. XIX.]

13711. SLATER, PHIL: *Origin and Significance of the Frankfurt School.* A Marxist Perspective. London: Routledge & Kegan Paul, 1976. 185 pp. (International Library of Sociology).

13712. FRASER, ANTONIA: *Love Letters.* London: Weidenfeld & Nicolson, 1976. 200 pp. [Incl. love letters of Rosa Luxemburg and Franz Kafka.]

13713. GAY, PETER: *Begegnung mit der Moderne.* Deutsche Juden in der deutschen Kultur. [In]: Juden im Wilhelminischen Deutschland 1890–1914. Pp. 241–311. [See No. 13387.] [For an English version see No. 12947/YB. XXI.]

13714. *Germanistische Streifzüge.* Festschrift für Gustav Korlén. Hrsg. von Gert Mellbourn *et al.* Stockholm: Almqvist & Wiksell International, 1974. 288 pp., port. (Acta Universitatis Stockholmiensis, Stockholmer germanistischer Forschungen, 16). [Incl.: W. A. Berendsohn: 'Es waren ihrer sechs' von Alfred Neumann. E. Lämmert: Peter Weiss – ein Dichter ohne Land. Hans Mayer: Ernst Bloch, Utopie, Literatur. M. Reich-Ranicki: Flucht ins Märchen oder Kakanien als Wille und Vorstellung: Die Erzählungen Joseph Roths.]

13715. HERBIG, JOST: *Kettenreaktion.* Das Drama der Atomphysiker. München: Hanser, 1976 514 pp., ports., illus., bibl. (pp. 503–506). [Chap.: Juden, Nationale, Kommunisten, Liberale und 'Parteigenossen'. Incl. Einstein, Lise Meitner, Niels Bohr, Enrico Fermi (husband of the Jewish physicist Laura Fermi), J. Robert Oppenheimer, Edward Teller, Arnold Sommerfeld, Leo Szilard, Isidor Isaac Rabi, Max Born, Wolfgang Pauli, Sir Francis Eugen Simon.]

13716. KEEN, HARRY, JOHN JARRETT and ARTHUR M. LEVY, eds.: *Triumphs of Medicine.* London: Elek, 1976. 193 pp., ports., illus. [Ehrlich, Freud, Selman Abraham Waksman, Sir Hans Adolf Krebs, Sir Ernst Boris Chain, Albert Bruce Sabin, Jonas Edward Salk and other Jews have contributed to advances in medicine.]

13717. LAQUEUR, WALTER: *Weimar.* Die Kultur der Republik. Aus dem Engl. von Otto Weith. Bilddokumentation: Hermann Haarmann. Berlin: Ullstein Propyläen, 1976. 391 pp., ports., illus., facsims., bibl. (pp. 353–368). [For English original see No. 12187/YB. XX.]

13718. LEHRMANN, CHARLES C[UNO]: *Jewish Influences on European Thought.* Transl. from the French by George Klin and from the German by Victor Carpenter. Cranbury, N.J.: Fairleigh Dickinson Press, 1976. 323 pp. [Essays originally publ. in German under the title: Das jüdische Element in der europäischen Geisteswelt. – Author was from 1960– 1971 Rabbi in West Berlin.]

13719. MOSSE, WERNER E.: *Die Juden in Wirtschaft und Gesellschaft.* [In]: Juden im Wilhelminichen Deutschland 1890–1914. Pp. 57–113. [See No. 13387.]

13720. PULZER, PETER: *Die jüdische Beteiligung an der Politik*. [In]: Juden im Wilhelminischen Deutschland 1890–1914. Pp. 143–239, tabs. [See No. 13387.]

13721. SCHUSTER, THEO: *Die grossen Schachmeister der zwanziger Jahre*. Schicksale berühmter Schachmeister, wie sie kämpften, siegten und unterlagen. Die Neuromantiker von Reti bis Niemzowitsch. Stuttgart: Franckh, 1976. 109 pp., 66 ports., illus. [Richard Reti, 1889 Slovakia–1929 Prague. Aron Niemzowitsch, 1887–1935. See also Nos. 13907 and 14017.]

13722. VILLIERS, DOUGLAS, ed.: '*Next Year in Jerusalem*'. Jews in the Twentieth Century. Essays. London: Harrap, 1976. 352 pp., ports., illus. [The impact made by Jews on modern Western society in many and quite different fields is analysed by various contributors. Cf. A People with so much Talent (David Astor) [In]: Jewish Observer and Middle East Review, 11th June, London, 1976. Contributors incl. Stephen Aris, Isaac Bashevis Singer, Chaim Bermant, Richard Crossman, David Daiches, Arthur Koestler, Yehudi Menuhin, Sir Rudolf Peierls, Leo Rosten, George Steiner, Elie Wiesel, Isaiah Berlin a.o.]

13723. WEISSENBERGER, KLAUS: *Zwischen Stein und Stern*. Mystische Formgebung in der Dichtung von Else Lasker-Schüler, Nelly Sachs und Paul Celan. Bern-München: Francke, 1976. 339 pp.

13724. WISTRICH, ROBERT S.: *Revolutionary Jews from Marx to Trotsky*. With a Foreword by James Joll. London: Harrap, New York: Barnes & Noble, 1976. 254 pp., ports., maps, notes pp. 208–239, bibl. (pp. 240–243). [The remarkable role played by individual Jews in modern European socialist movements, the effect of their Jewish identity upon their politics and Marxist attitudes towards the Jewish minority. Cf. The Great Paradox. Early Marxists and Judaism (Eva G. Reichmann) [In]: 'AJR Information', December London, 1976. Pp. 1–2.]

13725. ZAHN, LOTHAR: *Die letzte Epoche der Philosophie*. Kommentare zu 'Texte von Hegel bis Habermas'. Stuttgart: Klett, 1976. 320 pp. [Incl. Marx, Freud, Horkheimer, Adorno, Wittgenstein, Popper, Helmut Schelsky, Herbert Marcuse.]

B. Individual

13726. ABRAHAM, KARL. ABRAHAM, HILDA: *Karl Abraham*. Sein Leben für die Psychoanalyse. Eine Biographie. Aus d. Engl. übertragen von Hans-Horst Henschen. Ergänzt durch eine Aufzeichnung Karl Abrahams über einen Kindheitskonflikt seiner Tochter Hilda. München: Kindler, 1976. 191 pp., facsim., bibl. K.A. u. bibl. pp. 183–190. [Engl. orig.]: An Unfinished Biography, ed. by Tom and Marion Burgner. [In]: International Review of Psychoanalysis, I, 17, 1974. [Karl Abraham, psychoanalyst, 1877 Bremen–1925 Berlin. Written by his daughter Hilda (1907 Zurich–1971 London).]

13727. ADLER, ALFRED. ADLER, ALFRED: *Kindererziehung*. Mit einer Einführung von Wolfgang Metzger. Aus d. Amerik. von Willi Köhler. Frankfurt/M.: Fischer-Taschenbuch-Verlag, 1976. xii, 179 pp. (Fischer Tb. 6311; Bücher des Wissens).

13728. SPERBER, MANES: *Masks of Loneliness*. Alfred Adler in Perspective. Transl. from the French by Krishna Winston. London: Macmillan, 1974. 245 pp. [Alfred Adler, 1870 Vienna–1937 Aberdeen/Scotland.]

13729. ADLER, HANS GÜNTHER. ADLER, H. G.: *Die Freiheit des Menschen*. Aufsätze zur Soziologie und Geschichte. Tübingen: Mohr (Paul Siebeck), 1976. 358 pp. [Incl. essays: Zur Morphologie der Verfolgung. Die Erfahrung der Ohnmacht/Zur Soziologie der Verfolgung. Utopie und Zwang/Gefahr politischer Illusionen.]

13730. *H. G. Adler – Buch der Freunde*. Stimmen über den Dichter und Gelehrten. Mit unveröffentlichter Lyrik. Zum 65. Geburtstag am 2. Juli 1975. Hrsg. von Willehad P. Eckert und Wilhelm Unger. Köln: Wienand, 1975. 170 pp., ports., chronol. notes, bibl. H.G.A. pp. 152–168, bibl. (pp. 169–170).

13731. ADORNO, THEODOR W. ADORNO, THEODOR W.: *Prismen*. Kulturkritik und Gesellschaft. Frankfurt/M.: Suhrkamp, 1976. 342 pp. (stb. wiss. Nr. 178). [First publ. 1955. 1969 ed. see No. 7944/YB. XV. Engl. ed.: Prisms, see No. 6464/YB. XIII.]

13732. JABLINSKI, MANFRED: *Theodor W. Adorno: 'Kritische Theorie' als Literatur- und Kunstkritik*. Bonn: Bouvier, 1976. 256 pp. (Abhandlungen zur Kunst-, Musik- und Literaturwissenschaft, Bd. 221).

13733. AMÉRY, JEAN. Améry, Jean: *Hand an sich legen.* Diskurs über den Freitod. Stuttgart: Klett, 1976. 150 pp. (Edition Alpha). [Cf. Manchmal hat das Unglück recht. Ein Gespräch mit Jean Améry über sein neues Buch (Christian Schultz-Gerstein) [In]: 'Zeit', 13. Aug., Hamburg 1976. Pp. 30–31]. [Jean Améry, orig. Hans Mayer, born 1912 in Vienna, received the Lessing Preis 1977.]

13734. ARENDT, HANNAH. Arendt, Hannah: *Eichmann in Jerusalem.* Ein Bericht von der Banalität des Bösen. Aus d. Amerik. von Brigitte Granzow. Von der Verf. durchges. u. ergänzte deutsche Ausg. 4. Aufl. München: Piper, 1976. 345 pp., bibl. (pp. 330–333). (Piper-Paperback). [Cf. The Hannah Arendt Controversy. Nos. 3790–3793/YB. IX and 4433-4465/YB. X.]

13735. Arendt, Hannah: *Die verborgene Tradition.* 8 Essays. 1. Aufl. Frankfurt/M.: Suhrkamp, 1976. 125 pp. (stb. Nr. 303). [Cont.: Zueignung an Karl Jaspers. Über den Imperialismus. Organisierte Schuld. Die verborgene Tradition. Juden in der Welt von gestern. Franz Kafka. Aufklärung und Judenfrage. Der Zionismus aus heutiger Sicht. Six of these essays were first publ. 1947.] [Cf. Manipulation mit einer Toten (Hans Lamm) [In]: 'Allgemeine', 2. April. Düsseldorf, 1976.]

13736. BARON, SALO W.: *Hannah Arendt.* (*1906–1975*). [In]: Jewish Social Studies. Vol. XXXVIII, No. 2 (Spring). New York, 1976. Pp. 187–189.

13737. CRANSTEN, MAURICE: *Hannah Arendt.* [In]: 'Encounter'. Vol. XLVI, No. 3 (March). London, 1976. Pp. 54–56.

13738. *Hannah Arendt in Memoriam:* Handeln, Erkennen, Denken (Hans Jonas über ihr philosophisches Werk, pp. 921–935). Die versunkene Stadt (Dolf Sternberger über ihre Idee der Politik, pp. 935–945). Jürgen Habermas über ihren Begiff der Macht, pp. 946–960. Erich Heller über ihre Vorstellung von Literatur, pp. 996–1000. [In]: 'Merkur', 30. Jg., H. 10 (341), Okt. Stuttgart: Klett, 1976.

13739. KRIEGER, LEONARD: *The Historical Hannah Arendt.* Review Article. [In]: 'Journal of Modern History'. Vol. 48, No. 4, December. Chicago: University of Chicago, 1976. Pp. 672–684. [In slightly different form, this paper was delivered at a memorial colloquium on the work of Hannah Arendt, held at Bard College, 26th April, 1976.]

13740. REIF, ADELBERT, ed.: *Gespräche mit Hannah Arendt.* München: Piper, 1976. 127 pp., names index, bibl. (Serie Piper. 138). [Cont.: Was bleibt? Es bleibt die Muttersprache (Gespräch mit Günter Gaus 1964). Der Fall Eichmann und die Deutschen (mit Thilo Koch). Politik und Revolution (mit Adelbert Reif 1970). Diskussionen mit Hans Dichgans, Arnold Gehlen, Werner Maihofer, Dolf Sternberger, Sebastian Haffner, Bernhard Vogel, Hans-Friedrich Hölters.] [Cf. Die Anstössigkeit Hannah Arendts (Joachim Fest). Zu zwei Sammelbänden mit Essays [see No. 13735] und Gesprächen [In]: FAZ, 12. März, Frankfurt/M. 1977, port.]

13741. SCHWARTZ, BENJAMIN I.: *The Religion of Politics,* Reflections on the Thought of Hannah Arendt. [In]: 'Dissent', 17, 1970. Pp. 144–161.

13742. SONTHEIMER, KURT: *Mit ungetrübten Augen.* Gespräche über Eichmann und den Studentenprozess. In memoriam Hannah Arendt. [In]: 'Zeit', 3. Dez. Hamburg, 1976.

13743. AŠKENAZY, LUDVÍK. Schmid, Regula: *Ludvík Aškenazy.* Studien zu seinem Prosawerk. Bern: Lang, 1975. 155 pp. (Europ. Hochschulschriften, Reihe 16, Bd. 7). [L.A. emigrated from Czechoslovakia in 1968.]

13744. BAMBERGER, LUDWIG. Zucker, Stanley: *Ludwig Bamberger.* German Liberal Politician and Social Critic. Pittsburgh, Pa.: University of Pittsburgh Press, 1975. 343 pp. [L.B. 1823 Mainz–1899 Berlin.]

13745. BAUER, OTTO. Bauer, Otto: *Werkausgabe in 7 Bänden.* Mit e. Vorw. von Bruno Kreisky. Bd. 1–3. Wien- Europaverlag, 1976.

13746. BEER-HOFMANN, RICHARD. Jonas, Klaus W.: *Richard Beer-Hofmann and Rainer Maria Rilke.* [In]: Modern Austrian Literature. Vol. 8, No. 3/4. Ashland, Pittsburgh, Pa., 1975. pp. 43–73, notes pp. 67–73. [See also No. 14157]. [R.B.-H. 1866 Vienna–1945 New York.]

13747. LIPTZIN, SOL: *Richard Beer-Hofmann and Joseph Viktor Widmann.* [In]: 'Modern Austrian Literature'. Vol. 8, No. 3/4, Ashland, Pittsburgh, Pa. Pp. 74 *et seq.* [J. V. Widmann writer, 1842 Moravia–1911 Bern.]

13748. BEKKER, PAUL [orig. Baruch]. Bekker, Paul: *Musikgeschichte als Geschichte der musikalischen Formwandlungen.* Nachdr. d. Ausg. Stuttgart–Berlin 1926–1928. Hildesheim-

New York: Olms Reprints, 1976. v, 237 pp. [P.B. musicologist, conductor, 1882 Berlin–1937 New York.]

13749. BENJAMIN, WALTER. GEBHARDT, P., N. GRZIMEK, D. HARTH, M. RUMPF, U. SCHÖDLBAUER, B. WITTE: *Walter Benjamin – Zeitgenosse der Moderne.* Kronberg: Scriptor, 1976. 200 pp. (Monographien Literaturwiss., Bd. 30.)

13750. KURZ, GERHARD: *Benjamin – Kritischer gelesen.* [In]: Philosophische Rundschau. Eine Zeitschrift für philosophische Kritik. Hrsg. in Verbindung mit Hans-Georg Gadamer und Helmut Kuhn von Rüdiger Bubner und Bernhard Waldenfels. 23. Jg., H. 3/4. Tübingen: Mohr (Paul Siebeck), 1976.

13751. WITTE, BERND: *Walter Benjamin, der Intellektuelle als Kritiker.* Unters. zum Frühwerk Walter Benjamins. 1. Aufl. Stuttgart: Metzler, 1976. xii, 244 pp. (Metzler-Studienausgabe). Zugl. Philos. Diss., Techn. Hochschule Aachen.

13752. BERNAYS, KARL LUDWIG. HIRSCH, HELMUT: *Die Tätigkeit des emigrierten deutschen Demokraten Karl Ludwig Bernays während des amerikanischen Bürgerkrieges.* [In]: Jahrbuch des Instituts für Deutsche Geschichte, Bd. V. Tel Aviv, 1976. Pp. 227–245. [See No. 13481.] [Cf. also No. 12984/YB. XXI.]

13753. BERNFELD, SIEGFRIED. KOCH, ANNETTE: *Siegfried Bernfelds Kinderheim Baumgarten.* Voraussetzungen jüdischer Erziehung um 1920. Diss., Univ. Hamburg, 1974. 215 pp.

13754. BERNSTEIN, ARON [Pseud. Rebenstein]. SCHOEPS, JULIUS H.: *Aron Bernstein – ein liberaler Volksaufklärer, Schriftsteller und Religionsreformer.* [In]: Zeitschrift für Religions- und Geistesgeschichte. Hrsg. von E. Benz und Hans-Joachim Schoeps in Verbindung mit der Klopstockstiftung Hamburg. Bd. XXVIII, H. 3. Köln: Brill, 1976. Pp. 223–244. [A.B., 1812 Danzig–1884 Berlin. Founder of the 'Berliner Volkszeitung'.]

13755. BERNSTEIN, EDUARD. BERNSTEIN, EDUARD: *Ein revisionistisches Sozialismusbild.* Drei Vortäge. Hrsg. u. eingel. von Helmut Hirsch. 2., erw. u. überarb. Aufl. (1. Aufl. 1966). Bonn–Bad Godesberg: Dietz, 1976. 167 pp. (Intern. Bibliothek, Bd. 95.)

13756. KAUTSKY, KARL: *Bernstein und das sozialdemokratische Programm.* Eine Antikritik. 2. Aufl. Nachdr. d. 1. Aufl. 1899. Mit einer Einführung von Hans-Josef Steinberg. Bonn–Bad Godesberg: Dietz, 1976. 230 pp. (Internationale Bibliothek, Bd. 97).

13757. BLANKENSTEIN, BARON VON [orig. Aaron Löb (Levi) Wetzlar]. SCHWARZ, WALTER: *Baron von Blankenstein – The Career of an Early Nineteenth-Century Impostor.* [In]: LBI Year Book XXI. London, 1976. Pp. 229–245, facsim.

13758. BLEICHRÖDER, GERSON VON. STERN, FRITZ: *Bismarck and his Banker.* [In]: 'TLS', 5th November, London, 1976. Pp. 1389–1390, port. [Gerson v. Bleichröder, 1822–1893 Berlin. Cf. The Bleichröder Bank. An Interim Report (David S. Landes) [In]: LBI Year Book V, 1960. Pp. 211–220, port. See also No. 13400.]

13759. BLOCH, ERNST. BLOCH, ERNST: *Zwischenwelten in der Philosophiegeschichte.* Aus Leipziger Vorlesungen. Frankfurt/M.: Suhrkamp, 1976. 374 pp. (Gesamtausgabe in 16 Bänden, Bd. 12).

13760. BAHR, EHRHARD: *Ernst Bloch.* Berlin: Colloquium, 1974. 94 pp., bibl. (pp. 90–91). (Köpfe des 20. Jahrhunderts, Bd. 76).

13761. WIEGMANN, HERMANN: *Ernst Blochs ästhetische Kriterien und ihre interpretative Funktion in seinen literarischen Aufsätzen.* Bonn: Bouvier, 1976. 185 pp., bibl. (pl. 172–181). (Abhandlungen zur Philosophie, Psychologie und Pädagogik, Bd. 110).

13762. BÖRNE, LUDWIG. KAHN, LOTHAR: *Ludwig Börne. First Jewish Champion of Democracy.* [In]: 'Judaism', Vol. XXV, Issue No. 100, No. 4 (Fall). New York: American Jewish Congress, 1976. Pp. 420–434.

13763. MAYER, THOMAS MICHAEL: *Ludwig Börnes Beziehungen zu Hessischen Demokraten.* [In]: Jahrbuch des Instituts für Deutsche Geschichte. Bd. V. Tel Aviv, 1976. Pp. 101–123. [See No. 13481.]

13764. REICH-RANICKI, MARCEL: *Bruchstücke einer grossen Rebellion.* Der Literaturkritiker Ludwig Börne war ein toleranter Fanatiker. [In]: 'FAZ', 10. April. Frankfurt/M., 1976, port. [Shortened version of a lecture delivered February 1976 on receiving the Heinrich-Heine-Plaquette. The full text will appear in the Heine Yearbook 1977.]

13765. SCHLAIFER, SERGE, ed.: *Von der Literaturkritik zur Gesellschaftskritik: Ludwig Börne.* Stuttgart: Klett, 1975. 120 pp. (Literaturwissenschaft–Gesellschaftswissenschaft. Materialien und Untersuchungen zur Literatursoziologie, Bd. 2).

13766. BORN, MAX. BORN, MAX: *Vorlesungen über Atommechanik.* Bd. 1. Reprint d. Ausg. Berlin 1925. Berlin–Heidelberg–New York: Springer, 1976. ix, 358 pp., 43 graphics. [M.B. (1882–1970), received the Nobel Prize in 1954.]

13767. BROCH, HERMANN. LÜTZELER, PAUL MICHAEL, ed.: *Hermann Broch – Kommentierte Werkausgabe in 16 Bänden.* Bd. 3: Die Verzauberung. Roman. 415 pp., bibl. Bd. 4: Der Tod des Vergil. Roman. 520 pp., bibl. Bd. 5: Die Schuldlosen. Roman in 11 Erzählungen. 352 pp., bibl. Bd. 9/1: Schriften zur Literatur. 1. Kritik. 422 pp. bibl. Bd. 9/2. 2. Theorie. 318 pp., bibl. Frankfurt/M.: Suhrkamp, 1976. [5 vols.] [H.B., 1886 Vienna–1951 New Haven.]

13768. CANETTI, ELIAS. CANETTI, ELIAS: *Der Beruf des Dichters.* Essay. München: Hanser, 1976. 28 pp.

13769. CANETTI, ELIAS: *Dramen:* Hochzeit. Komödie der Eitelkeit. Die Befristeten. München: Hanser, 1976. 256 pp.

13770. CANETTI, ELIAS: *Komödie der Eitelkeit.* Drama in drei Teilen. Neuausg. Wien-München: Sessler, 1976. 102 pp., port.

13771. CURTIUS, MECHTHILD: *Kritk der Verdinglichung in Elias Canettis Roman 'Die Blendung'.* Eine sozialpsychologische Literaturanalyse. Bonn: Bouvier, 1973. 212 pp. (Abhandlungen zur Kunst-, Musik- und Literaturwissenschaft, Bd. 142). ['Die Blendung' see No. 11458/YB. XIX.]

13772. GRETSKY, LAURENCE ARTHUR: *Sprachverzerrung und Sprachüberwindung als Themen in Elias Canettis Roman 'Die Blendung'.* Bern-München: Francke, 1976, 120 pp.

13773. CASSIRER, ERNST; *Substanzbegriff und Funktionsbegriff.* Untersuchungen über die Grundfragen der Erkenntniskritik. 4., unv. Aufl., reprogr. Nachdr. d. 1. Aufl. Berlin 1910. Darmstadt: Wissenschaftl. Buchgesellschaft, 1976. xv, 459 pp.

13774. CASSIRER, ERNST: *Wissen und Wirkung des Symbolbegriffs.* 5., unv. Aufl. Darmstadt: Wissenschaftl. Buchgesellschaft, 1976. 230 pp., graphic.

13775. CASTONIER, ELISABETH: *Das Gesicht am Fenster.* Roman. München: Herbig, 1976. 248 pp. [E.C., born in Dresden, died 1975 in Munich. She publ. her Memoirs 'Stürmisch bis heiter' in 1964. See No. 4840/YB. X.]

13776. CELAN, PAUL. CELAN, PAUL: *Breath Crystal.* Twenty-One Late Poems. Transl. by Walter Billeter. Ivanhoe, Victoria (Australia): Rigmarole of the Hours, 1976.

13777. CELAN, PAUL: *Die Niemandrose.* 3. Aufl. Frankfurt/M.: Fischer, 1976. 94 pp.

13778. CELAN, PAUL: *Speech-Grille and Selected Poems.* Transl. by Joachim Neugroschel. New York: Dutton, 1976. 225 pp.

13779. CELAN, PAUL: *Von Schwelle zu Schwelle.* Gedichte. Frankfurt/M.: Suhrkamp, 1976. 65 pp. (stb. Nr. 301).

13780. CELAN, PAUL: *Zeitgehöft.* Späte Gedichte aus dem Nachlass. Frankfurt/M.: Suhrkamp, 1976. 68 pp. [Cf. An Enclosure of Time (George Steiner) [In]: 'TLS', 4th February, London, 1977.]

13781. BEESE, HENRIETTE: *Paul Celan.* Nachdichtung als Erinnerung. Allegorische Lektüre einiger seiner Gedichte. Darmstadt: Agora, 1976. 221 pp., illus. (Canon-Literaturwiss. Schriften, Bd. 3).

13782. BUHR, GERHARD: *Celans Poetik.* Göttingen: Vandenhoeck & Ruprecht, 1976. 207 pp., bibl. P.C. u. bibl. pp. 204–207.

13783. GLENN, JERRY: *Paul Celan.* New York: Twayne, 1976. 174 pp. [A critical study of the poet in English.]

13784. JANZ, MARLIES: *Vom Engagement absoluter Poesie.* Zur Lyrik und Ästhetik Paul Celans. 1. Aufl. Frankfurt/M.: Syndikat, 1976. 253 pp. zugl. Diss., FU Berlin, 1974.

13785. SCHULZE, JOACHIM: *Celan und die Mystiker.* Motivtypologische und quellenkundliche Kommentare. Bonn: Bouvier, 1976. vi, 115 pp. (Abhandlungen zur Kunst-, Musik- und Literaturwissenschaft, Bd. 190).

13786. CHAIN, SIR ERNST BORIS. LOWENTHAL, E. G.: *Sir Ernst Boris Chain.* Versuch eines Lebensbildes. [In]: 'Das Neue Israel'. 29. Jg., H. 3, September, Zürich, 1976. [E. B. Chain was born 1906 in Berlin.]

13787. DEHMEL, PAULA: *Fitzebutze.* Mit Bildern von Ernst Kreidolf. Faks.-Druck d. Original Ausgabe aus dem Jahre 1900. Frankfurt/M.: Insel, 1976. 38 pp. mostly illus. [P. Dehmel née Oppenheimer (1862–1918), writer of children's books.]

13788. DÖBLIN, ALFRED. DÖBLIN, ALFRED: *Ein Kerl muss eine Meinung haben.* Berichte und Kritiken 1921–1924. Olten: Walter, 1976. 287 pp. [Cf. Der Theaterkritiker, der keiner sein wollte. Rezensionen von und über Alfred Döblin (Günter Blöcker) [In]: 'FAZ', 26. Juni, Frankfurt/M., 1976, port.]

13789. DÖBLIN, ALFRED: *Wallenstein*. Roman. Nachwort von Walter Muschg. Olten: Walter, 1976. 751 pp. [For a Berlin [East] edition see No. 9727/YB. XVII.]

13790. *Alfred Döblin im Spiegel der zeitgenössischen Kritik*. Hrsg. von Ingrid Schuster und Ingrid Bode in Zusammenarbeit mit dem Deutschen Literaturarchiv Marbach a.N. Bern: Francke, 1976. 485 pp., bibl. A.D. pp. 451–476. [Cont. a representative selection of all the criticism of Döblin's works that were publ. between 1912 and 1958. – For a 1973 ed. see No. 11481/YB. XIX.]

13791. DOLBIN, B[ENEDIKT[F[RED]. SCHABER, WILL: *B. F. Dolbin – Der Zeichner als Reporter*. München: Verlag Dokumentation, 1976. 177 pp., ports., illus. (Dortmunder Beiträge zur Zeitungsforschung, Bd. 23). [Cf. No. 12262/YB. XX.] [1883 Vienna–1971 New York.]

13792. EINSTEIN, ALBERT. CLARK, RONALD W.: *Albert Einstein. Leben und Werk*. Dt. Übers. von Monika Raeithel-Thaler. München: Heyne, 1976. xv, 507 pp., ports., illus., bibl. (pp. 484–498). (Heyne Biographien, Taschenbuch Bd. 30). [For earlier eds. in German and English see No. 9731/YB. XVII and 11489/YB. XIX.]

13793. HOFFMANN, BANESH: *Albert Einstein*. [In]: LBI Year Book XXI. London, 1976. Pp. 279–288.

13794. HOFFMANN, BANESH/HELEN DUKAS: *Albert Einstein. Schöpfer und Rebell*. Biographie. Aus. d. Engl. von Jeanette Zehnder. Stuttgart: Belser- Dietikon-Zürich: Stocker-Schmid, 1976. 320 pp., 135 ports., illus. [For Engl. orig. see No. 10606/YB. XVIII. French ed.]: *Albert Einstein, créateur et rebelle*. Tr. de l'américain par Maurice Manly. Paris: Editions du Seuil, 1975. 298 pp., ports., illus., facsims.

13795. EINSTEIN, CARL. OEHM, HEIDEMARIE: *Die Kunsttheorie Carl Einsteins*. München: Fink, 1976. 248 pp., bibl. (pp. 240–243). [Art historian, 1885 Neuwied–1940, committed suicide in the South of France.]

13796. EISLER, HANNS. EISLER, HANNS: *Gespräche mit Hans Bunge: Fragen Sie mehr über Brecht*. Übertr. u. erl. von Hans Bunge. Leipzig: Dt. Verlag für Musik, 1975. 433 pp. (Ges. Werke Hanns Eisler, Serie 3, Bd. 7. hrsg. von Stephanie Eisler und Manfred Grabs für Akademie der Künste der DDR, Hanns-Eisler-Archiv). [See also No. 8863/YB. XVI.]

13797. BETZ, ALBRECHT: *Hanns Eisler. Musik einer Zeit, die sich eben bildet*. München: Edition Text + Kritik, 1976. 252 pp., port., illus., bibl. (pp. 235–242). [An analysis of Eisler's work showing the relation between his music and politics.] [H.E., 1898 Leipzig–1962 Berlin [East].]

13798. ERFURTH, HUGO. LOHSE, BERND, ed.: *Hugo Erfurth (1874–1948)*. Der Fotograf der Goldenen Zwanziger Jahre. Seebruck: Verlag Heering, 1976. 208 pp., ports. [Incl. portraits of Franz Blei, Alfred Flechtheim, Marc Chagall and other Jews.]

——— FELIX, RACHEL. FALK, BERNARD: *Rachel the Immortal*. [See No. 13960.]

13799. FEUCHTWANGER, LION. FEUCHTWANGER, LION: *Die Füchse im Weinberg*. Roman. Mit e. Einf. von Willi Meinek und e. Nachw. von Karl Heinz Berger. Illustrationen: Volker Pfüller. Berlin: Verlag Neues Leben, 1976. 926 pp., 22 illus. [Also Berlin [East]: Aufbau, 1976. 913 pp.]

13800. FEUCHTWANGER, LION: *Die Geschwister Oppermann*. Berlin [East]: Aufbau, 1976. 374 pp. (Ges. Werke in Einzelausgaben, Bd. 11).

13801. FEUCHTWANGER, LION: *Goya oder der arge Weg der Erkenntnis*. Roman. 5. Aufl. Berlin [East]: Aufbau, 1975. 657 pp. (Ges. Werke in Einzelausgaben, Bd. 7).

13802. FEUCHTWANGER, LION: *Die hässliche Herzogin Margarete Maultasch*. Roman. Mit 13 Zeichnungen von Michael Matthias Prechtl. Köln: Kiepenheuer & Witsch, 1976. 312 pp., illus. (Lizenz d. Aufbau-Verl., Berlin [East].) [The novel was first publ. 1923.]

13803. FEUCHTWANGER, LION: *Jud Süss*. Roman. Ungek. Ausg. Frankfurt/M.: Fischer Taschenbuch Verlag, 1976. 525 pp. (Fischer Tb., 1748). Lizenz d. Aufbau-Verl., Berlin [East]. [First publ. 1925.]

13804. FISCHER-VERLAG: *Almanach*. Das Neunzigste Jahr. 1886–1976. Ein Rechenschaftsbericht in Bildern. Hrsg. und mit e. Geleitwort von Gottfried und Brigitte Bermann Fischer. Beiträge zur Chronik – Abbildungen – Lyrik im S. Fischer Verlag. Frankfurt/ M.: Fischer, 1976. 300 pp., ports., illus.

13805. FRANK, BRUNO: *Der Reisepass*. Roman. Hrsg. und mit e. Nachw. von Martin Gregor-Dellin. München: Nymphenburger Verlag, 1975. 359 pp. [Based on his own experiences in exile, this novel was first publ. in Amsterdam, in 1937. It appears now for the first time in Germany.]

13806. FRANK, BRUNO: *Tage des Königs und andere Erzählungen.* Hrsg. und mit e. Nachw. von Martin Gregor-Dellin. Mit einer Einführung 'Politische Novelle' von Thomas Mann. Ungek. Ausg. Frankfurt/M.: Fischer-Taschenbuch-Verlag, 1976. 191 pp. (Fischer Tb., 1708). [First publ. 1924.] [Bruno Frank, 1887 Stuttgart–1945 Beverly Hills (Calif.]

13807. FREUD, ANNA. FREUD, ANNA: *Das Ich und die Abwehrmassnahmen.* München: Kindler, 1976. 182 pp. (Paperback). [First publ. in 1936.]

13808. FREUD, SIGMUND. FREUD, SIGMUND: *Eine Kindheitserinnerung des Leonardo da Vinci.* Frankfurt/M.: Suhrkamp, 1976. 110 pp., illus. (BS Bd. 514).

13809. BARTELS, MARTIN: *Selbstbewusstsein und Unbewusstes.* Studien zu Freud und Heidegger. Berlin–New York: de Gruyter, 1976. x, 201 pp. (Quellen und Studien zur Philosophie, Bd. 10).

13810. BITTER, WILHELM, ed.: *Freud, Adler, Jung.* Neuaufl. München: Kindler, 1976. (Geist und Psyche, Bd. 2091).

13811. BRANDELL, GUNNAR: *Sigmund Freud, Kind seiner Zeit.* Aus. d. Schwed. übers. von Detlef Brennecke. Dt. Erstausgabe. München: Kindler, 1976. 84 pp. (Kindler-Taschenbücher, 2163: Geist und Psyche).

13812. EISSLER, KURT R[OBERT]: *Freuds 'Zerstreute Gedanken'* [and]: *Psychoanalytische Einfälle zu Freuds 'Zerstreute Gedanken'.* [In]: Jahrbuch der Psychoanalyse, Beiheft 2. Bern: Huber, 1974. Pp. 101–128, bibl. (pp. 127–128).

13813. EISSLER, KURT R[OBERT]: *Über Freunds Freundschaft mit Wilhelm Fliess.* Nebst einem Anhang über Freuds Adoleszenz und einer historischen Bemerkung über Freuds Jugendstil. [In]: Jahrbuch der Psychoanalyse, Beiheft 2. Bern: Huber, 1974. Pp. 39–100, bibl. (pp. 98–100). [For Freud's 'Briefe an Wilhelm Fliess' see No. 13288/YB. XXI.]

13814. FREUD, MARTIN: *Freud, mon père.* Tr. de l'ámericain par Philippe Rousseau. Présentation par Marie Bonaparte. Préf. de Jacques Trilling. Paris: Denoël, 1975. xxi, 274 pp. (Freud et son temps). [Engl. ed.: Glory Reflected. London/New York, 1958. See No. 1474/YB. IV.]

13815. GLASER, HERMANN: *Sigmund Freuds Zwanzigstes Jahrhundert.* Seelenbilder einer Epoche. Materialien und Analysen. München: Hanser, 1976. 512 pp.

13816. GMELIN, OTTO: *Anti Freud.* Freuds Folgen in der bildenden Kunst und Werbung. Mit einem Beitrag von Helene Saussure. Köln: DuMont Schauberg, 1975. 164 pp., illus. (DuMont Kunst-Taschen-bücher, 21).

13817. MORRIS, NAT: *A Man Possessed.* The Case History of Sigmund Freud. Los Angeles: Regent House, 1974. 160 pp.

13818. PLÉ, ALBERT: *Freud und die Religion.* Eine kritische Bestandsaufnahme für die Diskussion der Zeit. Aus. d. Franz. übers. von Eva M. Kittelmann mit Augustinus Wucherer. 2., neugestaltete Aufl. Wien: Cura, 1976. 126 pp. [For 1st ed. see No. 8033/YB. XV, French orig. No. 7247/YB. XIV.]

13819. RAINEY, REUBEN M.: *Freud as Student of Religion.* Perspectives on the Background and Development of his Thought. Missoula, Mont.: American Academy of Religion, 1975. 174 pp., bibl. (pp. 159–174). (Dissertation Series, 7). [Cont.: The Judaism of Freud's Family. Freud's Instruction in Judaism. Freud's Jewish Identity. His 'Superstitions' and his Interest in the 'Occult'. Freud's Resources for the Study of Religion and his Scholarly Style. Freud's Early Ideas on Religion, 1882–1898.]

13820. REIK, THEODOR: *Dreissig Jahre mit Sigmund Freud.* Mit bisher unveröffentlichten Briefen von S.F. an Theodor Reik. München: Kindler, 1976. 128 pp. (Kindler Taschenbuchreihe 'Geist und Psyche', Bd. 2172). [Theodor Reik, psychologist, 1888 Vienna –1969 USA.]

13821. ROAZEN, PAUL: *Sigmund Freud und sein Kreis.* Eine biographische Geschichte der Psychoanalyse. Aus. d. Amerik. von G. H. Müller. Bergisch-Gladbach: Lübbe, 1976. 559 pp., ports., illus., bibl. [For the orig. 'Freud and his Followers' see No. 13040/YB. XXI.]

13822. SCHARFENBERG, JOACHIM: *Sigmund Freud und seine Religionskritik als Herausforderung für den christlichen Glauben.* 4. Aufl. Göttingen: Vandenhoeck und Ruprecht, 1976. 221 pp. [Habil. – Schrift Tübingen, see No. 7250/YB. XIV. and 3. Aufl. No. 11853/YB. XIX.]

13823. *Sigmund Freud.* Sein Leben in Bildern und Texten. Hrsg. von Ernst Freud, Lucie Freud und Ilse Grubrich-Simitis. Mit e. biogr. Skizze von K. R. Eissler. Gestaltet von Willy Fleckhaus. Frankfurt/M.: Suhrkamp, 1976. 352 pp., 357 ports., illus., facsims. [Cf. Freuds Wien (Nicolaus Sombart) Aus Anlass des grossen Bildbandes über Sigmund Freud. [In]: 'Merkur', H.2(345), Febr. Stuttgart: Klett, 1977. Pp. 185–190.]

13824. FRIED, ERICH. FRIED, ERICH: *Die Beine der grösseren Lügen* (1969). *Unter Nebenfeinden* (1970). *Gegengift* (1974). Drei Gedichtsammlungen. Berlin: Wagenbach, 1976. 168 pp. (Political Lyric). (Quartheft Nr. 83).

13825. FRIED, ERICH: *Höre Israel.* Gedichte und Fussnoten. Hamburg: Verlag Association, 1974. 154 pp., ports., illus., facsims. [Anti-Zionist. see also No. 14110.]

13826. FRIEDENTHAL, RICHARD. . . . *und unversehens ist es Abend.* Von und über Richard Friedenthal: Essays, Gedichte, Fragmente, Würdigungen, Autobiographisches. Hrsg. von Klaus Piper. München: Piper, 1976. 304 pp., ports., bibl. (pp. 293–298).

13827. *Humanist im Geiste Stefan Zweigs.* (Erich Gottgetreu). Glückwunsch für Richard Friedenthal [In]: 'MB', 2. Juli. Tel Aviv, 1976. [And]: *Salute to Richard Friedenthal on his 80th Birthday* (Egon Larsen) [In]: 'AJR Information', June. London, 1976. [R.F., born 9th June 1896 in Munich, publisher (founder of Knaur) and author.]

13828. FROMM, ERICH. FROMM, ERICH: *Beyond the Chains of Illusion.* My Encounter with Marx and Freud. Transl. into Hebrew by Aharon Amir. Jerusalem: Rubinstein, 1975. 183 pp [German ed.: Jenseits der Illusionen, transl. from the English original by Harry Maor, see No. 6798/YB. XIII.]

13829. FROMM, ERICH: *Haben oder Sein.* Die seelischen Grundlagen einer neuen Gesellschaft. Aus d. Engl. von Brigitte Stein. Stuttgart: Deutsche Verlags-Anstalt, 1976. 212 pp., bibl. (pp. 202–206). (Weltperspektiven). [English title: To Have or to Be.]

13830. GIEHSE, THERESE: *'Ich hab nichts zum Sagen.'* Gespräche mit Monika Sperr. Gütersloh: Bertelsmann, 1973. 232 pp., ports., illus., chronology. [Actress, 1898–1975 Munich.]

13831. GLASER, EDUARD: *Skizze der Geschichte und Geographie Arabiens von den ältesten Zeiten bis zum Propheten Muhammed.* Nebst e. Anhang zur Beleuchtung der Geschichte Abessyniens im 3. u. 4. Jahrhundert n. Chr. Auf Grund der Inschriften, der Angaben der alten Autoren und der Bibel. 2. Bd. Berlin 1890. Hildesheim–New York: Olms Reprints, 1976. iii, 575 pp. [E.G., explorer, 1855 Bohemia–1908 Munich.]

13832. GOLDSCHMIDT, ADOLPH: *Die Elfenbeinskulpturen aus der Zeit der karolingischen und sächsischen Kaiser, VIII.–IX. Jahrhundert.* Unter Mitwirkung von P. G. Hübner und Otto Homburger. Bd. 2. *Aus der romanischen Zeit, XI.–XIII. Jahrhundert.* Bd. 3. Unv. Nachdr. d. Ausgabe Berlin, Cassirer, 1918. Berlin: Deutscher Verlag für Kunstwissenschaft, 1976. LXX pp., illus.; 57, LX pp., illus. [2 vols.] (Denkmäler der deutschen Kunst, Sekt. 2, Plastik Abtlg. 4). [For vols. I and IV see No. 13051/YB. XXI.] [A.G., art historian, an authority on the art of the Middle Ages, 1863 Hamburg–1944 Basle.]

13833. GOLL, YVAN [orig. Lang]: *Gedichte, 1924–1950.* Auswahl und Nachwort von Horst Bienek. München: Dt. Taschenbuch-Verlag, 1976. 132 pp. (dtv, 5437, Sonderreihe).

13834. GROSSER, ALFRED: *In wessen Namen?* Worte und Wirklichkeit in der Politik. Übers. von Ruth Groh. Ungek. Ausg. Berlin–Frankfurt: Ullstein, 1976. 331 pp. (Ullstein Buch Nr. 3247). [French orig.: Au nom de quoi?] Lizenz d. Hanser-Verl., München. [A.G., born 1935 in Frankfurt/M.]

13835. GRÜNBERG, CARL. NENNING, GÜNTER: *Biographie von Carl Grünberg.* [In]: Indexband zum Nachdruck des Grünberg Archivs, Wien, 1973. Pp. 1–214. [C.G., political scientist, 1861 Romania, was murdered by Nazis in Frankfurt in 1940. In 1911 he founded the 'Archiv für die Geschichte des Sozialismus und der Arbeiterbewegung, ('Grünberg-Archiv') and in 1924 he opened as its first director the 'Institut für Sozialforschung' (The Frankfurt School) in Frankfurt/M.]

13836. GUGGENHEIM, KURT; *Alles in Allem.* Roman. Frauenfeld: Huber, 1976. 1111 pp. [First publ. in 4 vols. 1952–1955. Re-publ. on the occasion of the author's 80th birthday.] [The novel describes Zürich's history in this century.] [K.G. born 14th January 1896 in Zürich. Kurt Guggenheim 80 Jahre. (Ruth Binde). 'Zum Lob der Schweizer' [In]: Börsenblatt f.d. Dt. Buchhandel, Nr. 13, 13. Febr., Frankfurt/M., 1976, p. 211, port. [and] Zürcher Schriftsteller. Schriftsteller Zürichs. K.G. zum 80. Geburtstag [In]: 'NZZ', 15. Jan., Zürich 1976, port.]

13837. HAASE, HUGO. CALKINS, KENNETH R.: *Hugo Haase: Demokrat und Revolutionär.* Aus d.

Amerik. übers. von Arthur Mandel. Berlin: Colloquium, 1976. 244 pp., port., bibl. H.H. u. bibl. pp. 236–241. (Köpfe des XX. Jahrhunderts). [Cf. Porträt eines zu Unrecht Vergessenen (Ernest Hamburger) [in]: 'Aufbau', 10th December, New York, 1976.] [H.H. 1863 Allenstein–1919 Berlin.]

13838. HABE, HANS: *Leben für den Journalismus.* Bd. 1: Reportagen und Gespräche. Bd. 2: Meilensteine. Bd. 3: Artikel und Glossen. Bd. 4: Reden und Antworten. München: Droemer/Knaur, 1976. 1216 pp. [4 vols.]

13839. HABE, HANS: *Staub im September.* Roman. Olten u. Freiburg i. Br.: Walter, 1976. 364 pp. (Ges. Werke in Einzelausgaben). [First publ. 1939 under the title 'Tödlicher Friede', Europa Verlag, Zürich. Engl. transl.: Sixteen Days. Cf. Ein Liebesroman, vor dem Goebbels zitterte (Hermann Lewy) in: 'Allgemeine', 23. Sept., Düsseldorf, 1976.]

13840. CRAMER, ERNST: *Hans Habe – Ein Romancier, der ein Journalist bleiben wird . . .* [In]: 'Welt am Sonntag', 8. Febr., Berlin–Hamburg, 1976, illus. [H.H., orig. J. Bekessy, born 12th February 1911 in Budapest.]

13841. HAHN, KURT. BYATT, D. A., comp.: *Kurt Hahn, 1886–1974.* An Appreciation of his Life and Work. Foreword by the Duke of Edinburgh. Aberdeen: Gordonstoun School, 1976. 147 pp., front., port., ports., illus., facsim.

13842. MINER, JOSHUA: *Unforgettable Kurt Hahn of Gordonstoun.* [In]: Reader's Digest. January, London, 1976. Pp. 72–82, port. [K.H., educationist, 1886 Berlin–1974 Salem/Bodensee. Obituaries: Die Befreiung der 'giftlosen Leidenschaften'. Kurt Hahn zum Gedächtnis (Brigitte Beer) [In]: 'FAZ', 28. Dez., Frankfurt/M., 1974. Erziehung zur Verantwortung. Zum Tode von Prof. Kurt Hahn (E. G. Lowenthal) [In]: 'AWZ', 3. Jan., Düsseldorf, 1975. [In]: 'Isr. Wochenblatt', 3. Jan., Zürich, 1975.]

13843. HALLGARTEN, GEORGE W. F. RADKAU, JOACHIM and IMANUEL GEISS, eds.: *Imperialismus im 20. Jahrhundert.* Gedenkschrift für W. F. Hallgarten. München: Beck, 1976. 281 pp., front., port., notes pp. 250–264, bibl. G.W.F.H. pp. 279–281. [Incl.: Die Juden im englisch-deutschen imperialistischen Konflikt vor 1914 (Alfred Vagts, pp. 113–143, notes pp. 134–143). Auszug aus dem Briefwechsel zwischen George W. F. Hallgarten und Eckart Kehr 1931–1933.] [The historian, born January 1901 in Munich died there January 1976.]

13844. HAMBURGER, KÄTHE: *Kleine Schriften zur Literatur- und Geistesgeschichte.* Stuttgart: Akademischer Verlag Hans-Dieter Heinz, 1976. 282 pp.

13845. HANSLICK, EDUARD; *Vom Musikalisch-Schönen.* Ein Beitrag zur Revision der Ästhetik der Tonkunst. Unveränd. reprogr. Nachdr. d. 1. Aufl. Leipzig 1854. Darmstadt: Wiss. Buchgesellschaft, 1976. 104 pp. (Reihe Libelli, Bd. 131). [Musicologist, 1825 Prag–1904 Wien.]

13846. HEARTFIELD, JOHN [ie., Helmut Herzfelde]. HERZFELDE, WIELAND: *John Heartfield.* Leben und Werk. Dargestellt von seinem Bruder. 3. Aufl. Dresden: Verlag der Kunst, 1976. 376 pp., front., port., ports., illus., facsims. [First publ. in 1962. For 2nd. ed., 1971, see No. 9767/YB. XVII.] [John Heartfield (1891–1968), the pioneer of photomontage, publicist, writer and initiator of the Malik Verlag in Berlin.]

13847. HEINE, HEINRICH. HEINE, HEINRICH: *Jüdisches Manifest.* Eine Auswahl aus seinen Werken, Briefen und Gesprächen. 2., erw. Aufl. der 'Confessio Judaica'. Hrsg. von Hugo Bieber. New York: Mary S. Rosenberg, [1976]. 320 pp. [Excerpts from Heine's works, letters and conversations concerning Judaism. First publ. New York, Rosenberg, 1946.]

13848. HEINE, HEINRICH: *Ludwig Börne.* Eine Denkschrift und kleinere politische Schriften. Bearb. von Helmut Koopmann. Hamburg: Hoffmann und Campe, 1976. 920 pp. (Historisch-kritische Gesamtausgabe der Werke in 16 Bden. Düsseldorfer Ausgabe. Hrsg. von Manfred Windfuhr. Bd. 11).

13849. HEINE, HEINRICH: *Sämtliche Schriften.* Sechster Band, zweiter Teilband: *Gedichte.* Hrsg. und kommentiert von Walter Klaar. München: Hanser, 1976. 886 pp., bibl. [With vol. 6 is this ed. of Heine's writings in chronological order of their appearance, ed. by Klaus Briegleb, complete. For vols. 1–5 see No. 12300/YB. XX.]

13850. GREINER, MARTIN, ed.: *Heinrich Heine.* Werkausgabe im Taschenbuch. Bd. 1: Gedichte. Bd. 2: Gedichte und Prosa. Bd. 3 u. 4: Prosa. Bergisch-Gladbach: Lübbe, 1976. 465 pp., pp. 468–844, 852–1275, 1284–1659. [4 vols.] Lizenz d. Verl. Kiepenheuer u. Witsch, Köln.

13851. *Heine-Jahrbuch 1976.* Hrsg.: Heinrich-Heine-Institut Düsseldorf. Schriftleitung Eberhard Galley. 15. Jg. Hamburg: Hoffmann und Campe, 1976. 237 pp., front., port. [of

E. Galley], port., illus., facsim., Heine-Literatur 1974/75 mit Nachträgen pp. 216–231. [Incl. Indifferentismus. Bemerkungen zu Heines ästhetischer Terminologie (F. Mende, pp. 11–22). The image of Russia in Heines Reisebilder (Clara Hollosi, pp. 23–37). Über die strukturelle Einheit von Heines Fragment 'Der Rabbi von Bacherach' (Margaret A. Rose, pp. 38–51). Die Götter im Exil – Heine und der europäische Symbolismus (Lia Secci, pp. 96–114). Konservativ oder liberal? Heine und die Droste (Wilhelm Gössmann, pp. 115–139). Zweimal deutsche Kulturgeschichtsschreibung. H. H. und Hugo Ball (Volker Knüfermann, pp. 140–165).]

13852. HERMAND, JOST: *Der frühe Heine*. Ein Kommentar zu den 'Reisebildern' mit einer Einführung, einem bibliographischen Anmerkungsteil und einem Namensregister. München: Winkler, 1976. 226 pp., notes pp. 200–220.

13853. KLEINKNECHT, KARL THEODOR: *Heine in Deutschland*. Dokumente seiner Rezeption. 1833–1956. Mit einer Einleitung hrsg. von . . . München: Deutscher Taschenbuch-Verlag und Tübingen: Niemeyer, 1976. xxxii, 176 pp., bibl. (Deutsche Texte, Bd. 36 – dtv Wissenschaftliche Reihe, 4190). [Twenty-two texts on Heine by Börne, Gutzkow, Treitschke, Kraus, Kerr and Adorno's essay: Die Wunde Heine, written in 1956, and other articles.]

13854. WIESE, BENNO VON: *Signaturen*. Zu Heinrich Heine und seinem Werk. Berlin: Erich Schmidt, 1976. 251 pp. [Incl.: Heines politische Dichtung. Goethe und Heine als Europäer.]

13855. ZIEGLER, EDDA: *Julius Campe*. Der Verleger Heinrich Heines. Hamburg: Hoffmann und Campe, 1976. 382 pp., ports., illus., facsims., bibl. (pp. 329–337). (Heine-Studien. In Verbindung mit dem H.H. Institut Düsseldorf hrsg. von Manfred Windfuhr). [Cf. Heine und Campe. Szenen einer literarischen Ehe. [In]: Börsenblatt für d. Deutschen Buchhandel, Nr. 4, 14. Jan., Frankfurt/M., 1977. Pp. 115–117.]

13856. HELLER, ERICH. HELLER, ERICH: *The Poet's Self and the Poem*. Essays on Goethe, Nietzsche, Rilke and Thomas Mann. University of London: The Athlone Press, 1976. 96 pp. [Four Lord Northcliffe Lectures given at University College London in 1975 and repeated at the Van Leer Foundation in Jerusalem.]

13857. DÜRR, VOLKER and GÉZA V. MOLNÁR, eds.: *Versuche zu Goethe*. Festschrift für Erich Heller. Zum 65. Geburtstag am 27.3.1976. Heidelberg: Stiehm, 1976. 380 pp., front., port., illus., notes, bibl. E.H. pp. 363–380. [Twenty-one contributions partly in German, partly in English.]

13858. HERMLIN, STEPHAN [orig. Rudolf Leder] ed.: *Deutsches Lesebuch*. Von Luther bis Liebknecht. München: Hanser, 1976. 577 pp. [Incl. texts by Börne, Heine, Marx, Hofmannsthal, Heym, Kafka, Lasker-Schüler, Luxemburg, Kraus.] Cf. Ein wahrhaft deutsches Lesebuch (Golo Mann) [In]: 'FAZ', 11. Dez., Frankfurt/M., 1976. [St. Hermlin, born 1915 in Chemnitz (Karl-Marx-Stadt) lives in the GDR.]

——— HESS, MOSES. NA'AMAN, SHLOMO: *Moses Hess in der deutschen Arbeiterbewegung*. Zum 100. Jahrestag seines Todes am 6. April 1975. [See No. 13680.]

13859. HEYM, STEFAN [orig. Hellmuth Fliegel]: *Der Fall Glasenapp*. Roman. München: Bertelsmann, 1976. 384 pp. [First publ. in English in New York in 1942. Transl. into German by the author and publ. 1956 in Leipzig.]

13860. HEYM, STEFAN: *Fünf Tage im Juni*. Roman. Frankfurt/M.: Fischer-Taschenbuch-Verlag, 1976. (FTB Bd. 1813). [First German ed. 1974. See No. 12316/YB. XX. English ed.]: *Five Days in June*. London: Hodder & Stoughton, 1976. 352 pp. [A fictional analysis of those days in June 1953 when workers in East Berlin went on strike for the first time in twenty years.] [The author, born 1913 in Chemnitz, lives in the GDR where the novel has not yet been publ.]

13861. HILDESHEIMER, WOLFGANG. HILDESHEIMER, WOLFGANG: *Hörspiele:* Das Opfer Helena. Herrn Malsers Raben. Unter der Erde. Monolog. Frankfurt/M.: Suhrkamp, 1976. 157 pp. (stb Bd. 363).

13862. HILDESHEIMER, WOLFGANG: *Theaterstücke:* Die Verspätung. Nachtstück. Pastorale. Über das absurde Theater (Rede). Frankfurt/M.: Suhrkamp, 1976. 185 pp. (stb Bd. 362).

13863. HILFERDING, RUDOLF. KURATA, MINORU: *Rudolf Hilferding*. Bibliographie seiner Schriften, Artikel und Briefe. [In]: IWK (Intern. Wissenschaftl. Korrespondenz), Jg. 10, Berlin 1974. Pp. 327–346.

13864. PIETRANERA, GIULIO: *Rudolf Hilferding und die ökonomische Theorie der Sozialdemokratie*.

Berlin: Merve, 1974. 103 pp. (Internationale Marxistische Diskussion, Bd. 48). [This essay was first publ. as the introduction to the Italian ed. of Hilferding's Finanzkapital (publ. 1910). R.H., 1877 Vienna–1941 in a Paris Gestapo prison.]

13865. HOCHWÄLDER, FRITZ: *Can Freedom Survive?* Graz-Wien: Styria, 1976. [Hochwälder gave the speech at the 'Association of Friends of the Burgtheater' in Vienna, on 29th October 1974. On the occasion of his sixty-fifth birthday, on 28th May 1976, this special edition is publ. by Styria.]

13866. HUSSERL, EDMUND. HUSSERL, EDMUND: *Erfahrung und Urteil.* Unters. zur Genealogie d. Logik. Redigiert und hrsg. von Ludwig Landgrebe. Mit Nachw. und Reg. von Lothar Eley. 5. Aufl. mit erg. Reg. Hamburg: Meiner, 1976. xxvi, 532 pp. (Philos. Bibliothek, Bd. 280).

13867. SCHAPP, WILHELM: *Erinnerungen an Edmund Husserl.* Ein Beitrag zur Geschichte der Phänomenologie. Wiesbaden: Heymann, 1976. 32 pp. [E.H., 1859 Prossnitz (Moravia)–1938 Freiburg i. Br.]

13868. JACOB, DANIEL LOUIS. LÜTH, ERICH: *Daniel Louis Jacob und seine Nachbarn.* Die Geschichte eines Weinrestaurants. Hrsg. zur Wiedereröffnung des Weinhauses Jacob im 180. Jahr seines Bestehens von Armin Gustav. Hamburg: Christians, 1971. 36 pp., cover illus. [by Max Liebermann], ports., illus., facsims. [One of the guests of the wine restaurant in the Elb-chaussee of Hamburg was Salomon Heine.]

13869. JACOB, HEINRICH EDUARD: *Mozart, Geist, Musik, Schicksal.* Zeittafel, Stammtafel, Bibliographie und Werkverzeichnis (comp. by) Günter Pössiger, Genehmigte, ungek. u. erw. Taschenbuchausg. München: Heyne, 1976. 479 pp., ports., illus., notes. (Heyne Biographien, 22). Lizenz d. Societäts-Verl., Frankfurt/M. [H.E.J., writer, 1889 Berlin–1967 Salzburg.]

13870. JACOBSOHN, SIEGFRIED. RÜHLE, GÜNTHER: *Eine Schule der Kritik.* Siegfried Jacobsohn, ein Gedenkblatt. [In]: 'FAZ', 3. Dez. Frankfurt/M., 1976. [Theatre critic 28.1.1881 Berlin–3. Dez. 1926 Berlin. Founder and editor of 'Die Schaubühne' (later 'Die Weltbühne').]

13871. JACOBY, JOHANN. SILBERNER, EDMUND: *Johann Jacoby.* Politiker und Mensch. Bonn-Bad Godesberg: Verlag Neue Gesellschaft, 1976. 647 pp., ports., illus., bibl. J.J. u. bibl. pp. 567–622. (Veröffentlichungen des Instituts für Sozialgeschichte Braunschweig). [J.J., 1805 Königsberg–1877 Königsberg.]

13872. JELLINEK, HERMANN. HÄUSLER, WOLFGANG: *Hermann Jellinek (1823–1848).* Ein Demokrat in der Wiener Revolution. [In]: Jahrbuch des Instituts für Dt. Geschichte. Bd. V. Tel Aviv, 1976. Pp. 125–175. [See No. 13481.]

13873. KAFKA, FRANZ. KAFKA, FRANZ: *Gesammelte Werke.* Taschenbuchausgabe in 7 Bänden. Hrsg. von Max Brod. 1. Amerika. Roman, 262 pp.; 2. Der Prozess. Roman, 230 pp.; 3. Das Schloss. Roman, 357 pp.; 4. Erzählungen. 244 pp.; 5. Beschreibung eines Kampfes. Novellen, Skizzen, Aphorismen aus d. Nachlass, 268 pp.; 6. Hochzeitsvorbereitungen auf dem Lande und andere Prosa aus d. Nachlass, 358 pp.; 7. Tagebücher 1910–1923, 575 pp. Frankfurt/M.: Fischer-Taschenbuch-Verlag, 1976. [7 vols.] [The work ed. by Max Brod 1950–1954.]

13874. BINDER, HARTMUT: *Kafka in neuer Sicht.* Mimik, Gestik und Personengefüge als Darstellungsform des Autobiographischen. Stuttgart: Metzler, 1976. xxiv, 680 pp., 21 ports., illus., bibl. (pp. 651–660).

13875. BINDER, HARTMUT: *Kafka-Kommentar.* 1. Zu sämtlichen Erzählungen. Mit einer Einführung, einem Lebensgang und einer Zeittafel. 2. Zu den Romanen, Rezensionen, Aphorismen und zum 'Brief an den Vater'. Mit einer Einführung, einer Bibliographie und einem Gesamtregister. München: Winkler, 1975. 346 pp., bibl.; 1976. 491 pp., bibl. [2 vols.] [Vol. 2 incl.: 'Rede über die jiddische Sprache'.]

13876. FRIEDLANDER, ALBERT H.: *Kafka's Ape.* A Meditation on Religious Dialogue. [In]: 'European Judaism'. Vol. 10, No. 1, Winter 1975/76. London, 1976. Pp. 30–36, notes pp. 35–36.

13877. HELLER, ERICH: *Franz Kafka.* Übers. von Gerhart Kindl. München: Dt. Taschenbuch-Verlag, 1976. 123 pp., chron., bibl. F.K. pp. 122–123. (dtv Nr. 580). (Modern Theoretiker).

13878. HOFFMANN, WERNER: *Kafkas Aphorismen.* Bern u. München: Francke, 1974. 128 pp. [Cf. 'Ich hätte ein kleiner ostjüdischer Junge sein wollen!' Franz Kafka und das Judentum (Hermann Lewy) [In]: 'Allgemeine', 28. Nov., Düsseldorf, 1975.]

13879. KUNA, FRANZ, ed.: *On Kafka*. Semi-Centenary Perspectives. London: Elek, 1976. xi, 196 pp., notes pp. 184–196. [Nine essays incl.: Rage for Verification: Kafka und Einstein (Franz Kuna). The Great Wall of China: The Elaboration of an Intellectual Dilemma (Christian Gooden). Kafka: A Critical Essay (Ronald Grey).]

13880. SHNEIDERMAN, S. L.: *Franz Kafka y su mundo judío*. Trad. del idisch por Isidoro Niborski. Buenos Aires: Congreso Judío Latinoamericano, 1973. 48 pp., illus., ports. (Biblioteca popular judía. colección Grandes figuras del Judaísmo, 86).

13881. SOKEL, WALTER HERBERT: *Franz Kafka*. Tragik und Ironie. Zur Struktur seiner Kunst. Ungek. Ausg. Frankfurt/M.: Fischer-Taschenbuch-Verlag, 1976. 636 pp., bibl. (pp. 630–632). (Fischer-Taschenbücher, 1790). [First publ. 1964. See No. 4717/YB. X.]

13882. TISMAR, J.: *Kafkas 'Schakale und Araber' im zionistischen Kontext betrachtet*. [In]: Jahrbuch der Deutschen Schillergesellschaft. Hrsg. Fritz Martini, Walter Müller-Seidel, Bernhard Zeller. 19. Jg. Stuttgart: Kröner, 1975. Pp. 306–323. (vii, 548 pp.)

13883. KALÉKO, MASCHA: *Feine Pflänzchen: Rosen, Tulpen, Nelken und nahrhaftere Gewächse*. Mit 12 Zeichnungen von Helga Gebert. Düsseldorf: Eremiten Presse, 1976. 51 pp. [Written shortly before her death in January 1975, posthumously publ.]

13884. KAUFMANN, WALTER: *Am Kai der Hoffnung*. Stories. Mit e. Nachw. von Joachim Schreck. Aus d. Engl. übers. von Elga Abramowitz u.a. 1. Aufl. Berlin [East]: Verlag der Nation, 1974. 365 pp. [Born 1924 in Berlin author emigrated as a child to Australia and has been living in East Berlin since his return in 1955.]

13885. KELSEN, HANS: *The Communist Theory of Law*. Reprint of the edition London 1955. Aalen: Scientia, 1976. viii, 203 pp. (The Library of World Affairs, 26). [H.K., 1881 Prague–1973 USA.]

13886. KOESTLER, ARTHUR. KOESTLER, ARTHUR: *The Heel of Achilles*. Essays 1968–1973. London: Pan Books, 1976. 256 pp. [Paperback ed. of essays and book reviews, incl. several of Jewish interest, first publ. in 1974.]

13887. KOESTLER, ARTHUR: *The Thirteenth Tribe*. The Khazar Empire and its Heritage. London: Hutchinson, 1976. 255 pp. [Cf. Chosen peoples (Chaim Raphael) [In]: 'TLS', 11th June, London, 1976. History or Fiction? Marginal Notes on K.'s . . . (J. J. Maitlis) [In]: 'AJR Information', November, London, 1976, pp. 5–6. Dreizehn – wer weiss es? Altneuer Chasaren-Mythos (A. Tobias) [In]: 'MB', 11. Febr., Tel Aviv, 1977, pp. 5–6. Who are the Jews? (Philip Toynbee) in: 'Observer', 4th April, London, 1976.]

13888. GROSSMAN, EDWARD: *Koestler's Jewish Problem*. [In]: Commentary, Vol. 62, No. 6, December. New York: The American Jewish Committee, 1976. Pp. 59–64.

13889. KOLMAR, GERTRUD [orig. Chodziesner]: LEUTENEGGER, BEATRICE: '*Aus dem Dunkel komme ich . . .*' Die unbekannte Dichterin Gertrud Kolmar. Eine Einführung. [In]: 'NZZ', 7. Mai. Zürich, 1976. port., bibl. G.K.

13890. ZOHN, HARRY: *The Poetry of Gertrud Kolmar*. [In]: 'The Jewish Quarterly'. Vol. 24, No. 1–2 (87/88), Spring–Summer, London, 1976. Pp. 26–28. [G.K., 1894 Berlin–1943 Auschwitz.]

13891. KRACAUER, SIEGFRIED: *Das Ornament der Masse*. Essays. Mit e. Nachw. von Karsten Witte. Frankfurt/M.: Suhrkamp, 1976. (stb Bd. 371). [S.K., author, sociologist, 1889 Frankfurt/M.–1966 New York.]

13892. KRAFT, WERNER. KRAFT, WERNER: *Der Chandosbrief und andere Essays über Hugo v. Hofmannsthal*. Mit einer Gesamtbibliographie aller Bücher und Einzelaufsätze des Autors anlässlich seines 80. Geburtstages und in Ergänzung der zu Anfang 1976 erschienenen Kassette. Darmstadt: Agora, 1976. 110 pp. (Erato Druck, Bd. 16).

13893. SIMON, ERNST: *Verantwortung vor dem Geist*. Werner Kraft zum 80. Geburtstag. [In]: 'MB', 30th April, Tel Aviv, 1976. Pp. 5–6 and 9. [Tributes also in]: 'Allgemeine' (Istor), 21. Mai, Düsseldorf, 1976. Deutsche Tradition in Jerusalem (Ernst-Peter Wieckenberg) [In]: 'FAZ', 6. Mai. Frankfurt/M., 1976. [W.K., writer, essayist, 4. Mai 1896 Braunschweig, since 1934 in Jerusalem.]

13894. KRAUS, KARL. PFABIGAN, ALFRED: *Karl Kraus und der Sozialismus*. Eine politische Biographie. Mit e. Vorwort von Norbert Leser. Wien–Zürich: Europaverlag, 1976. 364 pp., Register.

13895. SCHEICHL, SIGURD PAUL, comp.: *Bibliografie Karl Kraus*. Kommentierte Bibliografie. München: edition text+kritik, 1975. 88 pp. [This bibliography is also included in: Karl Kraus, ed. by Heinz Ludwig Arnold. See No. 13115/YB. XXI.]

13896. STIEG, GERALD: *Der Brenner und die Fackel*. Ein Beitrag zur Wirkungsgeschichte von Karl

Kraus. Salzburg: Müller, 1976. 379 pp., ports., illus., facsims., bibl. (pp. 363–374). (Brenner-Studien, Bd. 3).

13897. SZASZ, THOMAS: *Karl Kraus and the Soul-Doctors*. London: Routledge, 1976. 180 pp.

13898. ZOHN, HARRY, ed.: *In these great times*. A Karl Kraus Reader. With translations by Joseph Fabry and others. Montreal: Engendra Press, 1976. 263 pp., ports., illus., facsims., bibl. (pp. 261–263).

13899. ('Die) KREATUR'. MICHEL, CHRISTOPH: *Die Kreatur*. Eine Zeitschrift 1926–1929/30. 1. Die Vorgeschichte. Florens Christian Rang und Martin Buber. 2. Der Name 'Kreatur'. Franz Rosenzweig. 3. Die Mitherausgeber: V[iktor] v. Weizsäcker und J[osef] Wittig. 4. Autoren. 5. Nachgeschichte. 'Die Wandlung'. E[ugen] Rosenstock. [In]: 'Tribüne'. 15. Jg., H.59. 1976. Pp. 7078–7092. [See No. 14082.]

13900. KREBS, SIR HANS A. *Birthday Tributes to Sir Hans A. Krebs;* True to his origin (Werner Rosenstock). Scientist and Friend. Refugees' Impact on Biochemistry (Sir Ernst Chain) [In]: 'AJR Information', August, London, 1975. [And]: Der Nobelpreisträger aus Hildesheim. Zum 75. Geburtstag von Sir Hans A. Krebs (E. Gottfried). [In]: 'Allgemeine', 22nd August, Düsseldorf, 1975.

13901. (Der) KURT WOLFF VERLAG. GÖBEL, WOLFRAM: *Der Kurt Wolff Verlag 1913–1930*. Expressionismus als verlegerische Aufgabe. Mit einer Bibliographie des Kurt Wolff Verlages und der ihm angeschlossenen Unternehmen, 1910–1930. Frankfurt/M.: Buchhändler-Vereinigung, 1976/77, cols. 521–1456, ports., illus., bibl. (cols. 921–937), bibl. d. K.W. Verlages cols. 1299–1456. (Sonderdruck aus dem 'Archiv für Geschichte des Buchwesens', Bd. XV, Lieferungen 3 und 4 und Bd. XVI, Lieferung 6, Frankfurt/M. 1976/77).

13902. LANDAUER, GUSTAV. LANDAUER, GUSTAV: *Erkenntnis und Befreiung*. Ausgewählte Reden und Aufsätze. Hrsg. und mit einem Nachw. versehen von Ruth Link-Salinger (Hyman). Frankfurt/M.: Suhrkamp, 1976. 106 pp., bibl. p. 106. (es Bd. 818).

13903. LINK-SALINGER, RUTH (HYMAN): *Oeuvres Gustav Landauer*. [In]: Proceedings of the American Academy for Jewish Research. Vol. 43. New York, 1976. Pp. 209–234, bibl.

13904. LANDMANN, MICHAEL: *Anklage gegen die Vernunft*. 1. Aufl. Stuttgart: Klett, 1976. 230 pp. (Edition Alpha).

13905. LANG, FRITZ. EISNER, LOTTE H.: *Fritz Lang*. Transl. by Getrud Mander and ed. by David Robinson. London: Secker and Warburg, 1976, 416 pp. [Cf. The cost-effective visionary (S. S. Prawer) [In]: 'TLS', 21st January, London, 1977.]

13906. JANSEN, PETER W./WOLFRAM SCHÜTTE, eds.: *Fritz Lang*. Mit Beiträgen von Frieda Grafe, Enno Patalas, Hans Helmut Prinzler und Peter Syr (Fotos). München: Hanser, 1976. 176 pp., ports., illus., bibl. F.L. and bibl. pp. 144–176. (Reihe Hanser, 208, Reihe Film, 7). [F.L., film director, 1890 Vienna–1976 Beverly Hills.]

13907. LASKER, EMANUEL: *Gesunder Menschenverstand im Schach*. 4., unveränd. Auflage. Düsseldorf, Kempten/Allgäu: Rau, 1976. 64 pp., illus. [See also Nos. 13721 and 14017.] [E.L., 1868 Berlinchen–1941 New York. World chess master, mathematician, philosopher.]

13908. LASKER-SCHÜLER, ELSE LASKER-SCHÜLER, ELSE: *Mein Herz*. Ein Liebesroman mit Bildern und wirklich lebenden Menschen. Mit Zeichnungen der Autorin aus der Ausgabe von 1912. Frankfurt/M.: Suhrkamp, 1976. 165 pp. [BS Nr. 520.] Lizenz d. Kösel-Verl., München.

13909. HESSING, JAKOB: *Else Lasker-Schüler and her People*. [And]: Israel Eliraz: 'Else' (Homage). [Excerpts from I. Eliraz and Joseph Tal's 'Opera' which sets some of E.L.-Sch.'s poems about Jerusalem to music] [and]: J. Hirschberg: Joseph Tal's Homage to Else [which incl. also a description of Tal's meetings with her in Jerusalem during the Second World War]. [In]: 'Ariel', No. 41, Jerusalem, 1976. Pp. 61–76, port., illus.; pp. 77–82, illus.; pp. 83–93, illus., music.

13910. LASSALLE, FERDINAND. DAYAN-HERZBRUN, SONIA: *Le socialisme scientifique de Ferdinand Lassalle*. [In]: 'Le Mouvement Social', No. 95, April–Juni, Paris, 1976. Pp. 53–70.

13911. WISTRICH, ROBERT S.: *Ferdinand Lassalle: The Gladiator*. [In]: European Judaism. Vol. X, No. 1, Winter 1975/76. London, 1976. Pp. 15–23, notes pp. 22–23.

13912. LISSITZKY, EL[IEZER]. *El Lissitzky*. Ausstellung vom 9. April–Ende Juni 1976. Galerie Gmurzynska, Köln. Katalog, bearb. von Krystyna Rubinger. Köln: Galerie Gmurzynska, 1976. 164 pp., mostly illus., bibl. (pp. 91–94). [Texts in German and

English. E.L., painter, 1890 Smolensk. He studied in Darmstadt until 1914, lived in Hanover to 1928. In 1941 he was one of Stalin's victims.]

13913. LÖWENSTEIN, KURT: *Sozialismus und Erziehung*. Eine Auswahl aus den Schriften 1919–1933. Neu hrsg. von Ferdinand Brandecker und Hildegard Feidel-Mertz. Bonn–Bad Godesberg: Dietz, 1976. 446 pp., bibl. K.L. pp. 427–430, bibl. (pp. 431–436). (Internationale Bibliothek, Bd. 91). [Incl. Kurt Löwenstein–Eine biographische Skizze by his son Dyno Löwenstein (New York), pp. 363–377.] [K.L., political educationalist, 1885 Bleckede/Elbe–1939 Paris.]

13914. LUBLINSKI, SAMUEL: *Der Ausgang der Moderne*. Ein Buch der Opposition (1909). Mit einer Bibliographie von Johannes J. Braakenburg neu hrsg. von Gotthart Wunberg. Tübingen: Niemeyer, 1976. x, 412 pp., bibl. (Ausgewählte Schriften, Bd. 2. Deutsche Texte Bd. 41). [Vol. 1: Die Bilanz der Moderne (written 1904), see No. 12382/YB. XX.] [S.L. scholar, 1868 Johannisburg (Ostpr.)–1910 Weimar.]

13915. LUDWIG, EMIL [orig. Cohn]: *Wilhelm II*. Autoris., textl. ungekürzte, durch Zeittafeln, Literaturverzeichnis und Personenregister erw. Neu-Ausgabe. München–Berlin: Herbig, 1976. 510 pp., ports., illus., bibl. E.L. pp. 507–509. [E.L., 1881 Breslau–1948 Ascona (Schweiz).]

13916. LUKÁCS, GEORG [orig. Löwinger]: Lukács, Georg: *Ästhetik*: in 4 Teilen. Teil 2. Vom Autor in dieser selbständigen Gestalt gewünschte, auf Grund der Originalfassung von Ferenc Fehér in Übereinstimmung mit dem Autor gek. Ausgabe. Neuwied: Luchterhand, 1976. 298 pp. (Sammlung Luchterhand, 64).

13917. Lukács, Georg: *Entwicklungsgeschichte des modernen Dramas*. Neuwied: Luchterhand, 1976. 600 pp. (Werke, Bd. 15).

13918. Lukács, Georg: *Geschichte und Klassenbewusstsein*. Studien über marxistisches Denken. Sonderausg. Neuwied: Luchterhand, 1976. 518 pp. (Sammlung Luchterhand, Bd. 11). [1971 ed. see No. 10761/YB. XVIII.]

13919. Lukács, Georg: *Politische Aufsätze*. Bd. 1: Taktik und Ethik, 1918–1920. Bd. 2: Revolution und Gegenrevolution, 1920–1921. Hrsg. von Jörg Kammler und Frank Benseler. Übers. aus dem Ungar. von Janos Györkös. Neuwied: Luchterhand, 1976. 293 pp., 272 pp. [2 vols.]

13920. Grunenberg, Antonia: *Bürger und Revolutionär*. Georg Lukács, 1918–1928. Vorw. von Frank Benseler. Frankfurt/M.: Europäische Verlagsanstalt, 1976. 300 pp. (Studien zur Gesellschaftstheorie). Zugl. Diss., FU Berlin, 1975 u.d.T.: Der Zusammenhang zwischen Linksradikalismus und Geschichtsphilosophie in Praxis und Theorie von Georg Lukács.

13921. LUXEMBURG, ROSA. Geras, Norman: *The Legacy of Rosa Luxemburg*. London: New Left Books (NLB), 1976. 210 pp., bibl. R.L. pp. 205–206, bibl. (pp. 206–208). [Cf. Socialism or Barbarism (E.H. Carr) [In]: 'TLS', 17th September, London, 1976.]

13922. Hetmann, Frederick, (pseud.) [i.e., Hans-Christian Kirsch]: *Rosa L. . . .* Die Geschichte der Rosa Luxemburg und ihrer Zeit. Mit dokumentarischen Fotos. 1. Aufl. Weinheim–Basel: Beltz & Gelberg, 1976. 312 pp., ports., illus., bibl. (pp. 297–302).

13923. *Rosa Luxemburg in Selbstzeugnissen und Bilddokumenten*. Dargestellt von Helmut Hirsch. Den Anhang besorgte der Autor. 6. Aufl. Reinbek b. Hamburg: Rowohlt, 1976. 157 pp., ports., illus., facsims., bibl. R.L. und bibl. pp. 148–154. (Rowohlts Monographien, Bd. 158). [1st. ed. 1969. See No. 8142/YB. XV.]

13924. MAHLER, GUSTAV. Blaukopf, Kurt, ed.: *Mahler*. Sein Leben, sein Werk und seine Welt in zeitgenössischen Bildern und Texten. Eine Dokumentarbiographie. Mit Beiträgen von Zoltan Roman u.a. Wien: Universal Edition, 1976. 287 pp. with 36 ports. and illus., facsims. [English edition]: *Mahler – A Documentary Study*. Comp. and ed. by Kurt Blaukopf with contributions by Zoltan Roman a.o. London: Thames & Hudson, 1976. [For a biographical study of Mahler by the compiler see No. 11651/YB. XIX (in English) and No. 8143/YB. XV for the German ed.] [G.M., 1860 Bohemia–1911 Vienna.]

13925. Danuser, H.: *Zwischen Nostalgie und Moderne*. Gedanken über den gegenwärtigen Erfolg Gustav Mahlers. [In]: Universitas, Zeitschrift für Wissenschaft, Kunst und Literatur. H.10. Stuttgart: Wissenschaftliche Verlagsgesellschaft, 1976.

13926. *Gustav Mahler und Wien*. Texte von Pierre Boulez, Henry Louis de la Grange, Friedrich C. Heller, Marcel Prawy, Wolf Rosenberg, Gottfried Scholz, Hilde Spiel und Sigrid

Wiesmann. Gestaltung: Jaroslav Krejci. Stuttgart: Belser, 1976. 168 pp., ports., illus. [Engl. ed.]: *Gustav Mahler in Vienna*. New York: Rizzoli International Publications, 1976.

13927. MARTNER, K[NUD], ed.: *Gustav Mahler*. Eindrücke und Erinnerungen aus den Hamburger Jahren. Hamburg: Musikverlag J. Schubert, 1976. 85 pp.

13928. WALTER, BRUNO: *Gustav Mahler*. London: Severn, 1975. 176 pp. [The German original 'Gustav Mahler: Ein Porträt' was first publ. in 1957. See No. 1240/YB. III.]

13929. MARCUSE, HERBERT: *Der eindimensionale Mensch*. Studien zur Ideologie der fortgeschrittenen Industriegesellschaft. Übers.: Alfred Schmidt. 8. Aufl. Neuwied: Luchterhand, 1976. 282 pp. (Sammlung Luchterhand, 4). [Engl. ed.]: [One-Dimensional Man, see No. 4747/YB. X.]

13930. MARCUSE, HERBERT: *Wider eine bestimmte marxistische Ästhetik*. Essay. Erstausgabe. München: Hanser, 1976. (Reihe Hanser, Bd. 206).

13931. MARCUSE, LUDWIG. FISCHER, KLAUS-UWE: *Ludwig Marcuses schriftstellerische Tätigkeiten im französischen Exil, 1933–1939*. Kronberg/Ts.: Scriptor, 1976. 164 pp., bibl. L.M. pp. 148–161. (Scriptor-Hochschulschriften, Literaturwiss., 16). Zugl. Philos. u. Sozialwiss. Diss., Univ. Hamburg.

13932. MARGOLIUS, HANS: *Werte und Wege*. Aphorismen zur Ethik. Mit Holzschnitten von Willy Thaler. Zürich: Stro., 1976. 146 pp., illus. [Author born 1902.]

13933. MARX, KARL. MARX, KARL: *Differenz der demokratischen und epikureischen Naturphilosophie*. Eine Documentation hrsg. von der Friedrich-Schiller-Universität Jena, 1976. [Marx wrote his Dissertation in 1841. The original could not be traced but has now been made available by the Moscow Institute for Maxism-Leninism.]

13934. MARX, KARL/FRIEDRICH ENGELS: *Über Religion*. 2., überarb. u. erw. Aufl. Hrsg.: Institut f. Marxismus-Leninismus beim ZK der SED. Berlin [East]: Dietz, 1976. 328 pp., bibl. (pp. 300–307). [Cf. Nos. 13161–13162/YB. XXI.]

13935. DRAHN, ERNST, comp.: *Marx-Bibliographie*. London: Carl Slienger, 1976.

13936. HANISCH, ERNST: *Karl Marx und die Berichte der österreichischen Geheimpolizei*. Trier: Karl-Marx-Haus, 1976. 30 pp. (Schriften aus dem Karl-Marx-Haus Trier, H.16).

13937. LÖWENSTEIN, JULIUS I[SAAK]: *Marx contra Marxismus*. 2. Aufl. Tübingen: Mohr, 1976. xiv, 262 pp. (Uni-Taschenbücher UTB 631). [1. Aufl. u.d.T. 'Vision und Wirklichkeit' see No. 9023/YB. XVI.]

13938. KAPP, YVONNE: *Eleanor Marx*. Vol. I: Family Life, 1855–1887. Vol. II: The Crowded Years, 1884–1898. London: Lawrence and Wishart, 1972/1976. 317 pp., ports., illus.; 738 pp., ports., illus., facsims. [2 vols.] [Eleanor (Tussy) Marx committed suicide at forty-three. But up to the end, her identification as a Jewess was uncompromising (W. J. Fishman) [In]: 'Jewish Chronicle', 25th February, London, 1977.]

13939. PRAWER, S. S.: *Karl Marx and World Literature*. London: Clarendon–Oxford University Press, 1976. 446 pp. [Cf. Karl Marx: The revolutionary from the world of epic (George Steiner) [In]: Sunday Times, 21st November, London, 1976, port. [and]: The Books that Marx read (Hugh Lloyd-Jones) [In]: 'TLS', 4th February, London, 1977, pp. 118–119.]

13940. MAYER, HANS, ed.: *Deutsche Literaturkritik im 19. Jahrhundert*. Von Heine bis Mehring. Frankfurt/M.: Goverts, 1976. 1041 pp., bibl. (pp. 1022–1024). [Four vols. cont. twenty-seven contributions.] (Neue Bibliothek der Weltliteratur.)

13941. MENDELSSOHN, ERICH. BERCKENHAGEN, EKHART, ed.: *Fünf Architekten aus fünf Jahrhunderten*. Zeichnungen von Hans Vredeman de Vries, Francesco Borromini, Balthasar Neumann, Hippolyte Destailleur, Erich Mendelssohn. Katalog zur Ausstellung in Berlin, Staatl. Museen Preuss. Kulturbesitz. Berlin: Mann, 1976. 212 pp., mit 143 illus. (Sammlungskataloge der Kunstbibliothek Berlin, 11).

13942. NEUMEISTER, DOROTHEA: *Der zeichnerische Nachlass des Architekten Erich Mendels[s]ohn*. [In]: Aus dem Antiquariat, Börsenblatt für den Dt. Buchhandel, Nr. 96, 30. Nov., Frankfurt/M., 1976. Pp. A384–A385. [In 1955 the 'Berliner Kunstbibilothek' acquired some 2,300 sketches and drawings from the architect's widow, a number of which are incl. in the illus. catalogue, see No. 13941.] [E.M., 1887 Königsberg–1953 San Francisco.]

13943. MENDELSSOHN, HENRIETTE. REISSNER, H. G.: *Henriette Mendelssohn*. Unresolved Conflicts of Integration. [In]: LBI Year Book XXI. London, 1976. Pp. 247–258, port. [H.M. née Meyer, daughter-in-law of Moses Mendelssohn.]

13944. (The) MENDELSSOHNS. Kupferberg, Herbert: *Die Mendelssohns.* Aus dem Amerik. von Klaus Leonhardt. Tübingen: Wunderlich, 1972. ii, 302 pp., ports., illus., facsim., gen. table, music. [For orig. English ed. see No. 10804/YB. XVIII.]

13945. MISCH, GEORG: *Geschichte der Autobiographie.* (Vier Bände in 8 Halbbänden). Bd. 1: Das Altertum. Unveränd. Nachdr. der 3., verm. Aufl. von 1949. Bd. 2: Das Mittelalter. Teil I: Die Frühzeit. photomech. Nachdr. d. 2. Aufl. 1970. Pp. 306–666. Frankfurt/M.: Schulte-Bulmke, 1976. xiii, 354 pp., bibl. [For Bd. 4, Teil 1–2, see No. 8178/YB. XV.] [G.M., philosopher, 1878 Berlin–1965 Göttingen.]

13946. MORUS (*i.e. Richard Lewinsohn*]. Obry, Olga: *Abenteuer des Geistes.* Gedächtnisausstellung Richard Lewinsohn – Morus – zum 80. Geburtstag in der Zentralbibliothek Zürich vom 11. bis 30. November 1974. 10 pp., port., bibl. R.L.M.

13947. MÜHSAM, ERICH: *Fanal.* Zum Alltag der Weimarer Republik. Hrsg. von Peter Hamm. Berlin: Wagenbach, 1976. 192 pp. (Wagenbachs Taschenbücher, 22).

13948. Mühsam, Erich: *Von Eisner bis Leviné:* Die Entstehung und Niederlage der bayerischen Räterepublik. Ein Bericht. Repr. d. Orig. Ausg. 1. Aufl. Hamburg: MaD-Verlag Schulenburg, 1976. 90 pp. (MaD-Flugschrift Nr. 17).

13949. NELSON, LEONARD: *System der philosophischen Rechtslehre und Politik...* 2., durchges. Aufl. Hamburg: Meiner, 1976. 566 pp. (Ges. Schriften in 9 Bden. Hrsg. von Paul Bernays, Bd. 6). [For previous vols. see Nos. 12425–12426/YB. XX.] [L.N., philosopher, 1882 Berlin–1927 Göttingen.]

13950. NEUMANN, ALFRED: *Der Teufel.* Roman. Vollst. Taschenbuchausg. München-Zürich: Droemer-Knaur, 1976. 314 pp. (Knaur Tb. Bd. 345). [The novel was written in 1926. A.N., 1895 Lautenburg (Westpr.)–1952 Lugano.]

13951. NEUMANN, ROBERT: *Die Kinder von Wien.* Roman. Bergisch-Gladbach: Lübbe, 1976. (Bastei-Lübbe-Taschenbücher, 14041). [The novel was originally publ. in English 'The Children of Vienna', in 1946. Transl. into German by the author and publ. in 1974 by Piper, Munich.] [R.N., 1897 Vienna–1975 Munich.]

13952. NISSEN, RUDOLF: *Randbemerkungen.* Bern: Huber, 1974. [The musings of a surgeon who, born 1896 in Neisse (Silesia) worked from 1933–1939 in Turkey, until 1952 in USA and from then until his retirement in 1967 as the director of the 'Chirurgische Universitätsklinik in Basle'. In 1975 he received the highest award of the 'Deutsche Gesellschaft für Chirurgie'. For his Memories 'Helle Blätter – Dunkel Blätter see No. 8294/YB. XV.]

13953. OPPENHEIM, HEINRICH BERNHARD. Hentschel, Volker: *Nationalpolitische und sozialpolitische Bestrebungen in der Reichsgründungszeit.* Das Beispiel Heinrich Bernhard Oppenheim. [In]: Jahrbuch des Instituts für Dt. Geschichte. Bd. V. Tel Aviv, 1976. Pp. 299–345. [See No. 13481.] [H.B.O., politician, 1819 Frankfurt/M.–1880 Berlin.]

13954. PHILIPP, HUGO WOLFGANG. Philipp, Hugo Wolfgang: *Lehmanns Flohzirkus.* Ein heiterer Berlin Roman. Posthum hrsg. von Lee van Dowski. Mit Umschlagzeichnung von Heinrich Zille. Darmstadt: Bläschke, 1973. 174 pp. [A selection from the first three vols. of the author's octology 'Auf den Hintertreppen des Lebens'.]

13955. Heuer, Renate: *Hugo Wolfgang Philipp.* Bern: Francke, 1973. 106 pp., bibl. H.W.P., comp. by Elazar Benyoetz.

13956. *Hugo Wolfgang Philipp. 2.2.1883 in Dortmund–18.3.1969 in Zürich.* Eine Bibliographie von Elazar Benyoetz. Mit e. Geleitwort von Lee van Dowski. Dortmund: Stadtbücherei, 1975. 23 pp. (Dortmunder Autoren und Künstler. Eine Verzeichnisreihe. Folge 2, hrsg. von Hedwig Bieber). [Offprint from Renate Heuer's work, see No. 13955.]

13957. PLESSNER, HELMUTH: *Die Frage nach der Conditio humana.* Aufsätze zur philosophischen Anthropologie. Frankfurt/M.: Suhrkamp, 1976. 198 pp. (st Bd. 361).

13958. POLAK, JACOB EDUARD: *Persien, das Land und seine Bewohner.* Ethnographische Schilderungen. Leipzig 1865. Hildesheim–New York: Olms Reprints, 1976. xix, 769 pp. [2 vols. in one.] [J.E.P., 1818 Bohemia–1891 Vienna. From 1855–1860 court physician to the Shah of Persia. He organised the Persian Medical School, founded a hospital and compiled a medical dictionary in Persian, Arabic and Latin. This book and other of his writings contain much of interest on the Jews.]

13959. PREUß, HUGO. Schnur, Roman: *Hugo Preuß und die Weimarer Republik.* Erinnerung an den Staatsrechtslehrer und Politiker. [In]: 'NZZ', Nr. 189, 14./15. Aug., Zürich, 1976, port. [H.P., 1860–1925 Berlin.]

13960. RACHEL, ELISA [*orig. Rachel Felix*]. Falk, Bernard: *Rachel the Immortal.* Stage-queen, grande amoureuse, street urchin, fine lady. A frank biography. 12 special plates by Frank C. Papé. Bath: Cedric Chivers, 1974. 334 pp., front., port., ports., illus., facsims. [Actress, 1821 Mumpf (Switzerland)–1858 Cannes.] [The monument erected on the Pfaueninsel nr. Potsdam in memory of her performances at the Prussian Court in 1852, was destroyed by the Nazis in 1935.]

13961. RADEK, KARL [*i.e., Sobelsohn*]. MÖLLER, DIETRICH: *Karl Radek in Deutschland.* Revolutionär, Intrigant, Diplomat. Köln: Verlag Wissenschaft und Politik, 1976. 303 pp., bibl. K.R. pp. 285–298, bibl. (pp. 299–301). [K.R. 1855 Lemberg–1939 [?], a victim of the Stalinist purges.]

13962. RAPHAEL, MAX: *Arbeiter, Kunst und Künstler.* Beiträge zu einer marxistischen Kunstwissenschaft. Mit e. Nachw. von Norbert Schneider. Frankfurt/M.: Fischer, 1975. 296 pp.+18 pp. illus., bibl. (pp. 275–276). (Reihe Fischer Format). [Cf. Kunst als Weg vom Schein zum Sein (Manfred Bosch) [In]: Tribüne, H.59, 1976. Pp. 7132–7133. See No. 14082.] [M.R., 1889 Schönlanke (Posen)–1952 USA.]

13963. (Die) RATHENAUS. FELIX, DAVID: *Walther Rathenau.* The Bad Thinker and his Uses. [In]: 'European Studies Review'. Vol. 5, No. 1, January. London: Sage Publications, 1975. Pp. 69–79, notes.

13964. FREEDEN, HERBERT: *Der letzte der Rathenau-Mörder.* Ein Brief bewirkte die Wandlung. [In]: 'Allgemeine', 7. März. Düsseldorf, 1975. [Also in]: 'Isr. Wochenblatt', 4. Juli, supplemented by Kurt Kaiser-Blüth in 'I.W.', 18. Juli. Zürich, 1975. [On the death of Werner Techow, one of the three assassins who shot Walter Rathenau on 24th June 1922 in Berlin.]

——— KALLNER, RUDOLF: *Herzl und Rathenau.* [See No. 13388.]

13965. SCHULIN, ERNST: *Die Rathenaus.* Zwei Generationen jüdischen Anteils an der industriellen Entwicklung Deutschlands. [In]: Juden im Wilhelminischen Deutschland 1890–1914. Pp. 115–142. [See No. 13387.]

13966. ZUNKEL, FRIEDRICH: *Die gemeinwirtschaftliche Konzeption Richard von Moellendorffs und Walther Rathenaus.* Pp. 56–68 [In]: Industrie und Staatssozialismus. Der Kampf um die Wirtschaftsordnung in Deutschland 1914–1918. Düsseldorf: Droste, 1974. 227 pp., bibl. (pp. 207–220). (Tübinger Schriften zur Sozial- und Zeitgeschichte, 3).

13967. REICH, WILHELM. REICH, WILHELM: *Charakteranalyse.* Das letzte Kapitel 'Die schizophrene Spaltung' wurde aus d. Amerik. übers. von Karl H. Bönner. Ungek. Ausg. Frankfurt/M.: Fischer-Taschenbuch-Verlag, 1976. 508 pp., graphic. (Fischer Tb., 6197, Bücher des Wissens). Lizenz d. Verl. Kiepenheuer & Witsch.

13968. OLLENDORFF-REICH, ILSE: *Wilhelm Reich.* Das Leben des grossen Psychoanalytikers und Forschers, aufgezeichnet von seiner Frau und Mitarbeiterin. Aus d. Amerik. übertragen von Manfred Kluge. Vorw. von A. S. Neill. München: Kindler, 1975. 214 pp., ports., illus., bibl. [For Engl. original see No. 8199/YB. XV.] [W.R., born 1897 in Galicia, died 1957 in an American prison.]

13969. REINHARDT, MAX. FUHRICH-LEISLER, EDDA and GISELA PROSSNITZ, comps.: *Max Reinhardt in Amerika.* Text- und Bilddokumentation. Salzburg: Otto Müller, 1976. 456 pp., 60 ports., illus., bibl. (pp. 435–441). (Schriftenreihe der Gesellschaft für Max-Reinhardt-Forschung.)

13970. LÖDEN, BRIGITTE: *Max Reinhardts Massenregie auf der Guckkastenbühne von 1905 bis 1910.* Ein Versuch zu Darstellungsmitteln und Regieintention. Bern/Frankfurt/M.: Lang, 1976. 176 pp., graphics. (Europ. Hochschulschriften, Reihe 30, Film- und Theaterwiss. Studien, Bd. 3.) Zugl. Kunstwiss. Diss., F.U. Berlin.

13971. *Max Reinhardt in Europa und Amerika.* Ausstellung der Max-Reinhardt-Forschungs- und Gedenkstätte, Salzburg unter Mitwirkung der Botschaft der Vereinigten Staaten von Amerika in Wien und dem Kulturamt der Stadt Wien, 9. Nov.–7. Dez. 1976. Zusammenstellung der Ausstellung und Bearb. des Katalogs: Edda Fuhrich-Leisler und Gisela Prossnitz. Salzburg: Reischl-Druck, 1976. 26 pp., pp. 27–74 ports., illus.

13972. RODA RODA, ALEXANDER FRIEDRICH [orig. Ladislaus Rosenfeld]: *Wilde Herren, wilde Liebe: die Panduren.* Roman. Bergisch-Gladbach: Bastei Verlag, 1975. 204 pp. (Bastei-Lübbe, 16008: heiterer Roman). [Satirical writer, 1872 Slawonien–1945 New York.]

13973. ROSENAU, HELEN: *The Ideal City.* Its Architectural Evolution. New Edition. London: Studio Vista, 1976. 176 pp., illus. [First ed. 1959.]

13974. ROSENBERG, LUDWIG: *Kommentare zur Zeit.* Aufsätze. Köln: Bund Verlag, 1976.

244 pp. [L.R., born 1903 in Berlin, former chairman of the DGB (Deutsche Gewerkschaftsbund.]

13975. ROTH, JOSEPH. ROTH, JOSEPH: *Flight Without End*. Novel. London: Peter Owen, 1976. 144 pp.

13976. ROTH, JOSEPH: *Hiob*. Roman eines einfachen Mannes. Reinbek: Rowohlt, 1976. 154 pp. (Rororo Taschenbuch Nr. 1933). [Publ. 1974 by Kiepenheuer & Witsch, see No. 12456/YB. XX.]

13977. ROTH, JOSEPH: *Legende vom heiligen Trinker*. Frankfurt/M.: Suhrkamp, 1976. 71 pp. (BS, Bd. 498).

13978. ROTH, JOSEPH: *Der Leviathan*. Erzählungen. Mit e. Nachw. von Hermann Kesten. München: Dt. Taschenbuch-Verlag, 1976. 207 pp. (dtv Bd. 1127). Lizenzausg. Kiepenheuer & Witsch, Köln und de Lange, Amsterdam. [Cont. eight essays incl. 'Der Vorzugsschüler'.]

13979. ROTH, JOSEPH: *Werke*. In 4 Bänden, hrsg. und eingel, von Hermann Kesten. Bd. 1 u. 2: Romane. Bd. 3: Die Erzählungen, die Essays 'Juden auf Wanderschaft', 'Der Antichrist', 'Clemenceau' und die kleine Prosa 'Panoptikum', Reisebilder. Bd. 4: Weitere kleine Prosa, Porträts, literarische Aufsätze, Buchbesprechungen, Beiträge zu Theater und Film, polemische Aufsätze, Texte zu 'Österreich und Habsburg', Feuilletons und ein Nachwort des Hrsgs. Köln: Kiepenheuer & Witsch, 1975/76. 980, 1148, 1114, 932 pp. [4 vols.]

13980. HACKERT, FRITZ: *Kaddisch und Miserere*. Untergangsweisen eines jüdischen Katholiken. Joseph Roth im Exil. Stuttgart: Reclam, 1975.

13981. ROTHFELS, HANS. ERDMANN, KARL DIETRICH: *Hans Rothfels*. [In]: 'Geschichte in Wissenschaft und Unterricht'. Jg. 27, H.9, Sept. Stuttgart: Klett, 1976. Pp. 521–523. [Historian, died 22nd June 1976 in Tübingen.]

13982. RUBINER, LUDWIG: *Der Dichter greift in die Politik*. Ausgew. Werke 1908–1919. Hrsg. und mit e. Nachw. von Klaus Schuhmann. 1. Aufl. Frankfurt/M.: Röderberg Verlag, 1976. 381 pp., notes, bibl. (pp. 372–380). (Röderberg-Taschenbuch, Bd. 44). [L.R., expressionist writer, 1881–1920.]

13983. SACHS, CURT: *Eine Weltgeschichte des Tanzes*. Nachdr. d. Ausg. Berlin 1933. Hildesheim: Olms Reprints, 1976. xi, 325 pp., ports., illus., music, bibl. (pp. 302–317). [The musicologist Curt Sachs (1881 Berlin–1959 New York) publ. the first history of world dancing. His work was immediately destroyed by the Nazis but several editions appeared in America. This Olms ed. is the first reprint of the original.]

13984. SACHS, NELLY. KELLER, BRIGIT (STOCKER): *Die Lyrik von Nelly Sachs*. Entwicklung und Grundstruktur anhand von Interpretationen. Zürich: Zentralstelle der Studentenschaft, 1973. 197 pp. Diss. Univ. Zürich, 1972. Microfilmcopy, Zürich, Zentralbibliothek.

13985. SAHL, HANS: *'Wir sind die Letzten'*. Gedichte. Mit e. Nachw. von Fritz Martini und einer Hans Sahl-Bibliographie. Heidelberg: Schneider, 1976. 87 pp., bibl. H.S. pp. 85–87. (Deutsche Akademie für Sprache und Dichtung, Darmstadt, 50. Veröffentlichung.) [Lyric poet, born 1902 in Dresden.]

13986. SAMBURSKY, SHMUEL: *Der Weg der Physik*. Texte von Anaximander bis Pauli. Zürich: Artemis, 1975. 760 pp., ports.

13987. SALOMON, ERICH. SAGER, PETER: *König der Neugierigen*. Wer war Erich Salomon? [In]: 'Zeit-Magazin'. Nr. 38, 10. Sept. Hamburg, 1976. Pp. 16–22, port., illus. [E.S., photographer, 1886 Berlin–1944 Auschwitz. His album 'Berühmte Zeitgenossen in unbewachten Augenblicken' (1931) contains 170 photos of important people of his time.]

13988. SCHELER, MAX. SCHELER, MAX: *Erkenntnis und Arbeit*. Hrsg. von Manfred S. Frings. Frankfurt/M.: Klostermann, 1976. xxii, 266 pp.

13989. SCHELER, MAX: *Logik*. Mit e. Nachw. von Jörg Willer. Amsterdam: Rodopi, 1975. 295 pp., bibl. (Elementa. Bd. 3).

13990. SCHELER, MAX: *Späte Schriften*. Mit e. Anhang hrsg. von Manfred S. Frings. Bern-München: Francke, 1976. 384 pp., bibl. (Ges. Werke, Bd. 9.) [Incl. essays written between 1922–1928: 'Die Stellung des Menschen im Kosmos'. 'Philosophische Weltanschauung'. 'Idealismus–Realismus'. For other vols. see No. 13224/YB. XXI.] [M. Sch., 1874–1928.]

13991. SCHNITZLER, ARTHUR. SCHNITZLER, ARTHUR: *Anatol. Anatols Grössenwahn. Der grüne Kakadu*. Mit e. Nachw. von Gerhart Baumann. Nachdruck. Stuttgart:

Reclam, 1976. 173 pp. (Universal-Bibliothek, Nr. 8399.) Lizenz d. Fischer-Verl., Frankfurt/M.

13992. SCHNITZLER, ARTHUR: *Traumnovelle.* Mit e. Nachw. von Hilde Spiel. Frankfurt/M.: Fischer, 1976. 152 pp. (Fischer Bibliothek). [Cf. Reclam ed. 1975 mit e. Nachw. von Hartmut Scheible. See No. 13227/YB. XXI.]

13993. *Arthur Schnitzler in Selbstzeugnissen und Bilddokumenten.* Dargestellt von Hartmut Scheible. Reinbek: Rowohlt, 1976. 158 pp., ports., illus., facsims., chronol., bibl. A. Sch. u. bibl. pp. 145–154. (rororo, bild monographien, Bd. 235).

13994. GLASER, H[ORST] A[LBERT]. ed.: *Wollüstige Phantasie.* München: Hanser, 1974. (Reihe Hanser, Bd. 147). [Incl. Arthur Schnitzler und Frank Wedekind.]

13995. SEIDLER, HERBERT: *Die Forschung zu Arthur Schnitzler seit 1945.* [In]: 'Zeitschrift für deutsche Philologie'. Vol. 95, No. 4. Berlin, 1976. Pp. 567–595. [A. Sch., 1862–1931 Vienna.]

13996. SCHOENBERG, ARNOLD. LIPMAN, SAMUEL: *Schoenberg's Survival.* [In]: 'Commentary'. Vol. 62, No. 5, November, New York: American Jewish Committee, 1976. Pp. 69–75, music.

13997. MACDONALD, MALCOLM: *Schoenberg.* London: Dent, 1976. (The 'Master Musicians' Series.) [Incl. previously unpublished letters.]

13998. ROSEN, CHARLES: *Schoenberg.* London: Fontana/Collins, 1976. 124 pp., music, notes pp. 117–120, chronology pp. 121–122, bibl. (pp. 123–124). (Fontana Modern Masters.) [Hardback ed.: London: Marion Boyars.]

13999. SEGHERS, ANNA. SEGHERS, ANNA: *Glauben an Irdisches.* Essays aus vier Jahrzehnten. Hrsg. von Christa Wolf. 2. Aufl. Leipzig: Reclam, 1974. 398 pp. (Reclam Universal-Bibliothek, Sprache und Literatur, 469).

14000. SEGHERS, ANNA: *Die Hochzeit von Haiti.* Karitische Geschichten. Darmstadt: Luchterhand, 1976. 245 pp. (Sammlung Luchterhand, 193.) [Cont. Die Hochzeit von Haiti. Wiedereinführung der Sklaverei in Guadeloupe. Das Licht auf dem Galgen.]

14001. SEGHERS, ANNA: *Der Kopflohn.* Roman aus einem deutschen Dorf im Spätsommer 1932. Erstausg. Neuwied: Luchterhand, 1976. 182 pp. (S.L. Bd. 234.)

14002. SEGHERS, ANNA: *Die schönsten Sagen vom Räuber Woynok.* Sagen und Legenden. Frankfurt/M.: Suhrkamp, 1975. 105 pp. (Bibliothek Suhrkamp, Bd. 458.)

14003. SEIDLIN, OSKAR. GILLESPIE, GERALD and EDGAR LOHNERT, eds.: *Herkommen und Erneuerung.* Essays für Oskar Seidlin. Fest und Dankesgabe zum 65. Geburtstag. Tübingen: Niemeyer, 1976. 434 pp., port., bibl. O.S. pp. 415–426. [Twenty-six contributions incl. Übersicht über Leben und Werk des Jubilars und seine Ansprache bei der Entgegennahme des Oberschlesischen Kulturpreises des Landes Nordhein-Westfalen 1975 und eine Tabula gratulatoria. [The literary historian was born on 17th February 1911 in Königshütte.]

14004. SILVERBERG, PAUL. STEGMANN, DIRK: *Die Silverberg-Kontroverse 1926.* Unternehmerpolitik zwischen Reform und Restauration. [In]: Sozialgeschichte heute. Festschrift für Hans Rosenberg zum 70. Geburtstag. Hrsg. von Hans-Ulrich Wehler. Göttingen: Vandenhoeck und Ruprecht, 1974. Pp. 594–610. [Paul Silverberg, industrialist (1876 Bedburg nr. Köln–1959 Lugano in exile) was from 1903–1933 second chairman of the 'Reichsverband der Deutschen Industrie'. For other contributions to the 'Festschrift' see No. 11925/YB. XX.]

14005. SINZHEIMER, HUGO: *Arbeitsrecht und Rechtssoziologie.* Gesammelte Aufsätze und Reden. Hrsg. von Otto Kahn-Freund und Thilo Ramm. Köln: Europäische Verlagsanstalt, 1976. 457, 355 pp., biogr. and bibl. H.S. pp. 323–341. [2 vols.] (Schriftenreihe der Otto-Brenner-Stiftung, 4.) [Incl. Wesen und Entwicklung des Arbeitsrechts. Das Koalitionsrecht. Die Räte. Biographische Würdigungen und Rezensionen. Zur Rechtssoziologie und Rechtstheorie.] [H.S., socialist politiker, 1875 Worms–1945 Bloemendaal, Holland.]

14006. SOMMER, ERNST: *Der Aufruhr und andere ausgewählte Prosa.* Mit e. Einführung und einer Bibliographie von Věra Macháčková-Riegerová. Wiesbaden: Steiner, 1976. 170 pp., port. (Verschollene und Vergessene.) [E.S., poet and writer, 1889 Iglau (CSR)–1955 London.]

14007. SONNENSCHEIN, HUGO [pseud. SONKA]. SPICKER, FRIEDEMANN: *Hugo Sonnenschein – Sonka.* Der Vagant. Pp. 220–246, bibl. (pp. 311–313). [In]: Deutsche Wanderer-Vagabunden- und Vagantenlyrik in den Jahren 1910–1933. Wege zum Heil – Strassen der Flucht. Berlin–New York: de Gruyter, 1976. xi, 346 pp., bibl. (pp. 291–338). (Quellen und Forschungen zur Sprach- und Kulturgeschichte der germanischen Völker. Neue Folge, Bd. 66 (190).) [The poet was born 1889 in Moravia, liberated by the Russians in Auschwitz but denounced as a Nazi collaborator and sentenced to twenty years hard labour. He died 1953 in a Prague prison. For one collection of his poems 'Schritte des Todes', written in Auschwitz, see No. 4991/YB. X.]

14008. SPERBER, MANÈS. SPERBER, MANÈS: *Wie eine Träne im Ozean*. Romantrilogie. Neuausgabe. Wien: Europaverlag, 1976. 1035 pp. [Cont.: Der verbrannte Dornbusch (1949). Tiefer als der Abgrund (1950). Die verlorene Bucht (1953).]

14009. DOVSKI, LEE VAN: *Zum 70. Geburtstag von Manès Sperber*. Versuch einer Würdigung. [In]: 'Allgemeine', 5. Dez., Düsseldorf, 1975. [M.Sp. born 12th December 1905 in Zablotow.]

14010. KRAUS, WOLFGANG, ed.: *Schreiben in dieser Zeit*. Für Manès Sperber. Wien: Europaverlag, 1976. 197 pp., bibl. M.S. pp. 195–197. [Tributes on his 70th birthday by Jean Améry, Heinrich Böll, François Bondy, Eugène Ionesco, Hermann Kesten, Siegfried Lenz, Carlo Schmid, Friedrich Torberg, Raymond Aron, André Malreaux.]

14011. SPIEL, HILDE: *Kleine Schritte*. Berichte und Geschichten. München: edition spangenberg im Ellermann Verlag, 1976. 254 pp.

14012. SPITZER, LEO: *Romanische Literaturstudien 1936–1956*. 2., unv. Aufl. Tübingen: Niemeyer, 1976. ix, 944 pp. [L.S., romanic scholar, 1887 Vienna–1960 Forte dei Marmi.]

14013. STEINTHAL, HEYMANN. *Die Classification der Sprachen*, dargestellt als die Entwicklung der Sprachidee, von H. Steinthal. Unv. Nachdr. der Ausg. Berlin 1850. Frankfurt/M.: Minerva, 1976. 91 pp. [H.St., 1823 Gröbzig (Anhalt)–1899 Berlin.]

14014. STERN, CLARA und WILLIAM: *Die Kindersprache*. Eine psychologische und sprachtheoretische Untersuchung. Unv. reprogr. Nachdr. d. 4., neubearb. Aufl. Leipzig 1928. Darmstadt: Wissensch. Buchgesellschaft, 1975. 436 pp., bibl. (pp. 423–432). Lizenz d. Barth-Verl., Leipzig. Ursprünglich als Stern, Clara: Monographien über die seelische Entwicklung des Kindes, Bd. 1.

14015. STERNHEIM, CARL: *Gesamtwerk*. Hrsg. von Wilhelm Emrich unter Mitarb. von Manfred Linke. Bd. 10/1: Spätwerk: unveröffentlichte Dramen. Kurzfassung 'Europa', Autobiographie. Bd. 10/2: Nachträge: Anm. zu d. Bd. 1 bis 9. Texte zu den Bd. 6 u. 7. Lebenschronik. Neuwied: Luchterhand, 1976. 614 pp., pp. 623–1358. [2 vols.]

14016. STERNHEIM, CARL: *Napoleon*. Erzählung. 12 Original-Holzschnitte von Gerhard Grimm. Düsseldorf: Eremiten Presse, 1976. 45 pp., 12 illus. [C.St. 1878 Leipzig–1942 Brüssel.]

14017. TARRASCH, SIEGBERT: *Das Schachspiel*. Systematisches Lehrbuch für Anfänger und Geübte. Neu bearb. im allgemeinen Teil von Karl Junker. Eröffnungen von Rudolf Teschner. Ungek. Ausg., 4. Aufl. Reinbek: Rowohlt, 1976. 406 pp., illus. (rororo-Sachbuch Bd. 6816). Lizenz d. Habel-Verl., Darmstadt. [The physician and chess champion (1862 Breslau–1934 München) had a great influence on the development of the game.]

14018. TOLLER, ERNST. BÜTOW, THOMAS: *Der Konflikt zwischen Revolution und Pazifismus im Werk Ernst Tollers*. Mit e. documentarischen Anhang: Essayistische Werke Tollers, Briefe von und über Toller. Hamburg: Lüdke, 1975. 426, 75 pp. (Geistes- und Sozialwiss. Dissertationen, Bd. 36.) Zugl. Diss. Philos. Fak., Univ. Freiburg/Br., 1975. [E.T., 1893 Samotschin b. Bromberg–1939 New York, suicide.]

14019. TORBERG, FRIEDRICH [i.e., Kantor Berg, Friedrich]: *PPP: Pamphlete, Parodien, Post Scripta*. Neuaufl. München: Langen-Müller, 1976. 514 pp. (Ges. Werke in Einzelausgaben, Bd. 3.) [1964 ed. see No. 4818/YB. X.]

14020. TORBERG, FRIEDRICH: *Der Schüler Gerber*. Roman. 3. Aufl. München: Dt. Taschenbuch-Verl., 1976. 291 pp. (dtv, 884). Lizenz d. Zsolnay Verl., Wien, Hamburg.

14021. TUCHOLSKY, KURT: *Deutschland, Deutschland über alles*. A picture-book by Kurt Tucholsky. Photographs assembled by John Heartfield. Transl. from the German by Anne Halley. Afterword and notes by Harry Zohn. Amherst: University of Massachusetts Press, 1972. 245 pp., ports., illus. [For German ed. see No. 11759/YB. XIX.]

14022. TUCHOLSKY, KURT: *Die Laternenanzünder*. Zeichnungen von Kurt Steinel. Mainz: Eggebrecht-Presse, 1975. 16 pp., illus. (Spitze–Feder–Reihe Eggebrecht, 3.) Lizenz d. Rowohlt-Verl., Reinbek.

14023. *Kurt Tucholsky, 1935–1975*. Eine Ausstellung der Deutschen Bibliothek, Frankfurt am

Main, Jan.–Feb. 1976. Ausstellung und Katalog: Werner Berthold. Frankfurt/M.: Dt. Bibliothek, 1976. 78 pp., front., port., illus., facsims., tabs.

14024. WALDINGER, ERNST. KAUF, ROBERT: *Ernst Waldinger im Exil.* [In]: Literatur und Kritik. Österr. Monatsschrift. H.108 (September), Wien, 1976. Pp. 474–489. [E.W., 1896 Wien–1970 USA.]

14025. WALTER, BRUNO [orig. Bruno Walter Schlesinger]: *Von der Musik und vom Musizieren.* Sonderausg. Frankfurt/M.: Fischer, 1976. 254 pp. [First publ. 1957, see No. 1296/ YB. III.] [B.W., 1876 Berlin–1962 Beverly Hills, Calif.] [Bruno Walter called this work his 'musical will'.]

14026. (M. M.) WARBURG & CO., BANKHAUS. ROSENBAUM, E[DUARD] and A. J. SHERMAN: *Das Bankhaus M. M. Warburg & Co. 1798–1938.* Hamburg: Hans Christians, 1976. 235 pp., ports., illus., facsims., bibl. (pp. 215–222).

14027. WEICHMANN, HERBERT. WEICHMANN, HERBERT: *Gefährdete Freiheit.* Hamburg: Hoffmann und Campe, 1976. [Cont. thirteen speeches made during 1973 and 1974 after his retirement from office.]

14028. *Herbert Weichmann 80 Jahre.* [A few of the many appreciations]: Ein kämpferischer Demokrat und Gentleman der Politik (Bundeskanzler Helmut Schmidt). [In]: Sozialdemokratischer Pressedienst, 24. Febr., Hamburg 1976. Anwalt für den gerechten Staat. Hamburgs Bürgermeister Hans-Ulrich Klose würdigt seinen Vorgänger [In]: 'Zeit', 20. Febr., Hamburg 1976. port. Ansprache von Bürgermeister Klose anlässlich der Überreichung der Hamburgischen Ehrendenkmünze in Gold an Bürgermeister a.D. Professor Dr. Weichmann am Freitag, 23. April, im Rathaus [In]: Staatliche Pressestelle Hamburg, 23. April 1976. Pp. 1–11. [Und]: Ansprache von Bundeskanzler Helmut Schmidt, 7 pp. [Typescript.] Verfechter der Humanität (Hans Tramer) [In]: 'MB', 20. Febr., Tel Aviv, 1976. [H.W., born 23rd February, Landsberg/Upper Silesia. Lord Mayor of Hamburg 1965–1971.]

14029. WEIGEL, HANS: *Antiwörterbuch.* Zürich: Artemis, 1974. 161 pp. [Cf. Die Leiden der jungen Wörter. Hans Weigels Attacke gegen Halbbildung (Werner Ross) [In]: 'FAZ', 18. Mai 1974, port.]

14030. WEIGEL, HANS: *Der grüne Stern.* Ein satirischer Roman. Neuauflage. Wien: Molden, 1976. 248 pp. [Publ. 1943 in a Swiss paper, as a book in 1946.]

14031. WEISS, PETER. WEISS, PETER: *Stücke.* Bd. I. Frankfurt/M.: Suhrkamp. 1976. 465 pp. (Edition Suhrkamp. Bd. 833.) [Incl.: 'Der Turm', 'Die Versicherung', 'Nacht mit Gästen', 'Mockinpott', 'Verfolgung und Ermordung Jean Paul Marats', 'Die Ermittlung'.]

14032. BOHRER, KARL HEINZ: *Katastrophenphantasie oder Aufklärung?* Zu Peter Weiss' 'Die Ästhetik des Widerstands'. [In]: 'Merkur', 30. Jg., H.1 (332). Januar. Stuttgart: Klett, 1976. Pp. 85–90. [See No. 13271/YB. XXI.]

14033. WERFEL, FRANZ: *Zwischen Oben und Unten.* Prosa, Tagebücher, Aphorismen, Literarische Nachträge. Sammelband. Aus dem Nachlass hrsg. von Adolf D. Klarmann. München-Wien: Langen-Müller-Herbig, 1975. 918 pp., ports. (Gesammelte Werke, Abschlussband.) [F.W., 1890 Prag–1945 Beverly Hills, Calif.] [Enl. entry No. 13272/ YB. XXI.]

14034. ZUCKMAYER, CARL. ZUCKMAYER, CARL: *Aufruf zum Leben.* Porträts und Zeugnisse aus bewegten Zeiten. Frankfurt/M.: Fischer, 1976. 347 pp. [The thirty-four writings incl.: Ein Brief an Friderike Zweig (1944). Für Gottfried Bermann Fischer zum 60. Geburtstag (1957). Memento zum 20. Juli 1969. Gedächtnisrede für Julius Elias, gesprochen an seinem Sarg, am 5. Juli 1927. Ein Nachruf wie zu Lebzeiten (1970)-auf Ludwig Berger, 1890–1969. Tischrede zu Max Reinhardts 70. Geburtstag (1943). Berthold Viertel (28. Juni 1885–24. Sept. 1953). Versuch einer Porträtskizze (1953). Heinrich Heine und der liebe Gott und ich (written 1972 when receiving the Düsseldorf Heine Prize).]

14035. ZUCKMAYER, CARL: *Die Fastnachtsbeichte.* Mit einem Nachw. von Alice Herdan-Zuckmayer. Frankfurt/M.: Fischer, 1976. 224 pp. (Fischer-Bibliothek). [First publ. 1959.]

14036. ZUCKMAYER, CARL: *Lesebuch.* Frankfurt/M.: Fischer, 1976. 471 pp. [Incl.: Der fröhliche Weinberg. Der Hauptmann von Köpenick. Des Teufels General. Die Geschichte eines Bauern aus dem Taunus. Eine Liebesgeschichte. Der Seelenbräu. Engele von Loewen.]

14037. ZUCKMAYER, CARL: *Der Rattenfänger*. Eine Fabel. [In]: 'Neue Rundschau'. 85. Jg., H.4. Frankfurt/M.: Fischer, 1974. Pp. 547–567.
14038. ZUCKMAYER, CARL: *Werkausgabe in Zehn Bänden: 1920–1975:* Bd. 1–2: Als wär's ein Stück von mir. Bd. 3: Gedichte. Bd. 4–6: Erzählungen. Bd. 7–10: Stücke. Frankfurt/ M.: Fischer Taschenbuch Verlag, 1976. [10 vols.]
14039. STADT MAINZ und CARL-ZUCKMAYER-GESELLSCHAFT, eds.: *Festschrift für Carl Zuckmayer zum 80. Geburtstag am 27. Dez. 1976.* Mainz: Hanns Krach. 1976. 152 pp. [Thirty-one contributions.]
14040. *Carl Zuckmayer*, born 27th December 1896 in Nackenheim/Rhein, died 18th January 1977 in Visp, Switzerland. Some of the many tributes on his 80th birthday and obituaries on his death, which followed only three weeks later: 'Als wär's ein Stück von mir'. C.Z. zum 80. Geburtstag. Gespräch mit Regisseur Everding [In]: 'Allgemeine', 24./31. Dez., Düsseldorf, 1976. – C.Z. zum 80. Geburtstag. Sein Werk in deutschsprachigen Literatur- und Theatersammlungen (Barbara Glauert) [In]: Aus dem Antiquariat, Börsenblatt für den Dt. Buchhandel, Nr. 12, 29. Dez., Frankfurt/M., 1976. Pp. A419– A427, port., facsims. – C.Z. zum 80 Geburtstag (Alexander Hildebrand) [In]: Blätter der Carl Zuckmayer-Gesellschaft, Jg. II, H.2. Mainz: Carl-Zuckmayer-Gesellschaft, 1976. Pp. 31–91. – Ein Zeitgenosse, kein Prophet. Eine Würdigung des grossen alten Mannes der deutschen Literatur (Walther Killy) [In]: 'Die Zeit', 24. Dez., Hamburg, 1976, port.
14041. *Obituaries:* Carl Zuckmayer (Egon Larsen) [In]: 'AJR Information', March, London 1977. – Carl Zuckmayers versöhnende Weisheit. Zu seinem Tode (Günther Rühle) [In]: 'FAZ', 20. Jan., Frankfurt/M., 1977, port. – Herr Carl Zuckmayer. A distinguished German dramatist [In]: Times, 20th January, London, 1977. – Carl Zuckmayer 1896–1977 (Hans Tramer) [In]: 'MB', Nr. 5, 4. Febr., Tel Aviv, 1977, pp. 5–6.
14042. ZWEIG, ARNOLD. ZWEIG, ARNOLD: *Die Zeit ist reif*. Roman. Berlin [East]: Aufbau, 1976. 663 pp. [Obtainable also from IBV (Intern. Buch-Versand, 1 Berlin 19, Eschenallee 21.]
14043. KAMNITZER, HEINZ: *Der Tod des Dichters*. Berlin [East]: Der Morgen, 1974. 144 pp. [Cf. Erinnerungen an Arnold Zweig. Gedanken zu einer Biographie (Gabriele Tergit) [In]: 'AJR Information', May, London, 1976. Pp. 13–14. See also No. 12521/YB. XX.]
14044. RIEDEL, VOLKER, ed.: *'Orient'*. Haifa 1942–1943. Bibliographie einer Zeitschrift. Mit einem Vorwort von Rudolf Hirsch. Berlin [East]: Aufbau, 1973. 97 pp., tabs. (Analytische Bibliographien deutschsprachiger Zeitschriften, hrsg. von der Akademie der Künste der DDR.) [Co-editor of the paper was Arnold Zweig.]
14045. WIZNITZER, MANUEL: *Spuk, Hybris und linker Kurs.* Arnold Zweigs drei Begegnungen mit Vertretern westlicher Demokratien. Aus dem Französ. übersetzt von A. Tobias. [In]: 'MB', 20. Aug., Tel Aviv, 1976. [Some transl. extracts from the forthcoming biography 'Arnold Zweig et le Pays d'Israel – Patrie ou Exil?']
14046. ZWEIG, MAX: *Die Entscheidung Lorenzo Morenos und andere Dramen*. [And]: *Frühe Dramen*. Heidelberg: Selbstverlag G. Müller (Jahnstr. 28), 1976. 279, 314 pp. [2 vols.] [Born 1892 Prossnitz (Moravia).]
14047. ZWEIG, STEFAN. ZWEIG, STEFAN: *Erstes Erlebnis*. Vier Geschichten aus Kinderland. Mit e. Nachw. von Richard Friedenthal. Frankfurt/M.: Fischer, 1976. 224 pp. (Fischer-Bibliothek. [First publ. 1911.]
14048. ZWEIG, STEFAN: *Die Monotonisierung der Welt*. Aufsätze und Vorträge. Ausgew. u.m.e. Nachw. von Volker Michels. Frankfurt/M.: Suhrkam, p. 1976. 254 pp. (BS, Bd. 493). [The title essay was written in 1925.]
14049. ZWEIG, STEFAN: *Vierundzwanzig Stunden aus dem Leben einer Frau*. Novellen. Berlin [East]: Aufbau, 1974. 306 pp. (Lizenz d. Fischer-Verl., Frankfurt/M.).
14050. STEIMAN, LIONEL B.: *The Agony of Humanism in World War I*. The Case of Stefan Zweig. [In]: 'Journal of European Studies', VI, Chalfont St. Giles, Bucks. (England), 1976. Pp. 100–124, notes pp. 119–124.

VIII. AUTOBIOGRAPHY, MEMOIRS, LETTERS, GENEALOGY

14051. BEER-HOFMANN, RICHARD. *Herbert Steiner an Richard Beer-Hofmann*. Eine Auswahl unveröffentlichter Briefe. Mitgeteilt und eingeleitet von Walter Grossmann. [In]:

'NZZ', FA Nr. 223, 24. Sept. Zürich, 1976. [A selection from 145 letters in the possession of the Harvard's Houghton Library. They concern Steiner's preparation of B-H.'s
lectures in Switzerland, and Steiner's publication of some of B-H.'s works.]

14052. BERNAUER, RUDOLF: *Das Theater meines Lebens*. Erinnerungen. Berlin: Arani, 1976.
412 pp., ports., illus. [First publ. by Blanvalet, Berlin, 1955. See No. 740/YB. I.] [R.B.,
theatre director, stage manager, 1880–1953.]

14053. BLUMENFELD, ERWIN: *Durch tausendjährige Zeit*. Frauenfeld: Huber, 1976. 428 pp.
[Cf. Autobiographie eines Stehaufmännchens (Robert Jungk) [In]: 'Zeit', 5. Nov.,
Hamburg, 1976.]

14054. CANETTI, ELIAS: *Die gerettete Zunge*. Geschichte einer Jugend. München: Hanser,
1976. 384 pp.

14055. (The) EPHRAIM FAMILY. MICHAELIS, DOLF: *The Ephraim Family*. [In]: LBI Year
Book XXI. London, 1976. Pp. 201–228, illus., facsims.

14056. FÜRST, MAX: *Gefilte Fisch*. Eine Jugend in Königsberg. Mit e. Nachw. von Helmut
Heissenbüttel. Ungek. Ausg. München: Dt. Taschenbuch-Verlag, 1976. 279 pp. (dtv
Bd. 1187). Lizenz d. Hanser-Verl., München. [First publ. 1973. See No. 11097/YB.
XIX.]

14057. FÜRST, MAX: *Talisman Scheherezade*. Die schwierigen zwanziger Jahre. München: Hanser, 1976. 447 pp. [In this vol. Fürst talks of his years in Berlin giving a picture of Germany at the time of the Weimar Republic.]

14058. GOLDSCHMIDT, DIETRICH: *'Ein Fisch mit vielen Köpfen. Jeder Kopf möchte erzählen'*. Die
Erinnerungsbücher von Max Fürst. [In]: neue sammlung. Göttinger Zeitschrift für
Erziehung und Gesellschaft. 17. Jg., H.1 (Jan.–Feb.) Göttingen: Vandenhoeck und
Ruprecht, 1977. Pp. 102–106.

14059. HAMBURGER, MICHAEL: *A Mug's Game*. Intermittent Memoirs, 1924–1954.
Cheadle Hulme: Carcanet Press, 1973. 301 pp., front., port., ports., illus. [M.H., born
1924 in Berlin.]

14060. HAY, JULIUS: *Born 1900*. Memoirs. Transl. from the German by J. A. Underwood.
London: Hutchinson, 1974. 384 pp. [The Hungarian Communist writer died 1974 in
Switzerland. For German ed. see No. 10031/YB. XVII.]

14061. HEINE, HEINRICH. WOESLER, WINIFRED, ed.: *Briefe an Heine*, 1852–1856. Bd. 27.
(Die Briefe Campes an Heine wurden bearb. von Nicole Bandet und Paul Laveau.)
Berlin [East]: Akademie Verlag, Paris: Editions du CNRS (Centre National de la Recherche Scientifique), 1976. 398 pp. (Säkularausg., Werke, Briefwechsel, Lebenszeug-
nisse. Hrsg. von den Nationalen Forschungs- und Gedenkstätten d. Klass. Dt. Literatur
in Weimar u.d. Centre National de la Recherche Scientifique in Paris). [For 'Briefe an
Heine', vols. 24, 25 and 26 see No. 13292/YB. XXI.]

14062. JACOBY, JOHANN. GRAB, WALTER: *Johann Jacobys Briefwechsel im Vormärz und in der
Revolution von 1848/49*. [In]: IWK (Intern. Wissenschaftliche Korrespondenz zur Ge-
schichte des deutschen Arbeiterbewegung). Hrsg. von der Historischen Kommission zu
Berlin. Jg. XII, H.1. Berlin: Colloquium Verlag, 1976. Pp. 2–18. [See also No. 12537/
YB. XX.]

14063. KAFKA, FRANZ: *Briefe an Felice und andere Korrespondenz aus der Verlobungszeit*. Hrsg.
von Erich Heller und Jürgen Born. Ungek. Ausg. Frankfurt/M.: Fischer-Taschenbuch
Verlag, 1976. 783 pp., illus. (F Tb. Bd. 1697). [For Engl. ed. see No. 12539/YB. XX.
For the German 1967 ed. No. 6802/YB. XIII.] [The envelopes in which the letters were
sent, addressed in Kafka's handwriting, are in the Leo Baeck Institute Archives, New
York, presented by Dr. Henry Manasse, Felice's son.]

14064. KAFKA, FRANZ: *Briefe an Milena*. Hrsg. u.m.e. Nachw. versehen von Willy Haas. Zürich:
Ex-Libris-Verlag, 1976. [First publ. 1952. See No. 761/YB. I. English ed. (1953) see No.
2913/YB. VII. Also as Fischer-Taschenbuch, Bd. 756.]

14065. KORTNER, FRITZ: *Aller Tage Abend*. Ungek. Ausg., 5. Aufl. München: Dt. Taschenbuch-Verlag, 1976. 367 pp. (dtv Bd. 556). Lizenz d. Kindler-Verl., München. [The
autobiography was first publ. 1959. See No. 1856/YB. V.]

14066. LASKER-SCHÜLER, ELSE: *Lieber gestreifter Tiger – Wo ist unser buntes Theben?* Briefe
von Else Lasker-Schüler, hrsg. von Margarete Kupper. 2 Bände. München: Kösel,
1976. 344 pp., 16 pp. facsims.; 398 pp., drawings [by E.L.Sch.], biogr. and bibl. notes.
[2 vols.] [Paperback Edition.] [Orig. publ. 1969. See No. 8285/YB. XV.]

14067. LENHOFF, FRED G.: *The First Thirty Years*. An Autobiographical Study. Harmer

Hill, Shrewsbury, England: Shotton Hall Publications, 1975. 162 pp. [Lenhoff born 1903 in Berlin, emigrated to England in 1937. After the war he opened a school for maladjusted children. For his social work he was awarded the O.B.E. He finished this autobiography shortly before his death.]

14068. LUXEMBURG, ROSA: *Briefe an Freunde*. Nach dem von Luise Kautsky fertiggestellten Manuskript hrsg. von Benedikt Kautsky. Überarb. Neuauflage. Köln: Europäische Verlagsanstalt, 1976. 177 pp., ports.

14069. MENDELSSOHN-BARTHOLDY, FELIX. ROTHE, HANS-JOACHIM und REINHARD SZESKUS, eds.: *Felix Mendelssohn-Bartholdy: Briefe aus Leipziger Archiven*. 2. Aufl. Leipzig: Dt. Verlag für Musik, 1976. 290 pp., bibl., music. [First ed. 1972. See No. 10940/YB. XVIII. Among the recipients of letters were the painter Eduard Bendemann (1811–1889) and the violinist Ferdinand David (1810–1873).]

14070. POPPER, KARL R.: *Unended Quest*. An Intellectual Autobiography. London: Fontana, 1976.

14071. REINEMANN, JOHN OTTO: *Carried Away* . . . Memoirs. Ed. by Hertha Reinemann. Philadelphia: Priv. Printed [Pa., 21 West Phil Ellena Street], 1976. 216 pp., port., list of names. [J.O.R., criminologist, 1902 Frankfurt/M.–1976 USA. Cf. Geschichte eines reichen Lebens (Robert M. W. Kempner) [In]: 'Allgemeine', 2. Juli, Düsseldorf, 1976].

14072. SCHWIEFERT, PETER. LANZMANN, CLAUDE, ed.: *L'oiseau n'a plus d'ailes* . . . Les Lettres de Peter Schwiefert présentées par Claude Lanzmann. Paris: Gallimard, 1974. 181 pp., ports., facsims. [Engl. edition]: *The Bird has no Wings*. Letters of Peter Schwiefert. Ed. by Claude Lanzmann. Transl. by Barbara Lucas. London: Search Press, 1976. [A selection of these letters also in]: 'Encounter', Vol. XLVI, Nos. 5 and 6, May, London, 1976. Pp. 15–31 and 34–46. [Letters to his Jewish mother from a young German who tried to solve the problem of being half German, half Jewish by emigration and by committing himself to Judaism. He was killed fighting with the Free French forces in 1944. His mother took the opposite way out of the predicament by emigrating to escape persecution and converting to Catholicism.]

14073. STEIN, EDITH: *Selbstbildnis in Briefen*. Teil I: 1916–1934. Freiburg i. Br.: Herder, 1976. 167 pp. (Edith Steins Werke, hrsg. von L. Gelber, Bd. 8).

14074. TEMIANKA, HENRI: *Respektlose Erinnerungen aus einem Leben mit der Musik*. Rüschlikon: Albert Müller, 1976. [The violinist, born in Holland, remembers his teacher Carl Flesch and meetings with Bronislaw Hubermann, Leonard Bernstein, Rudolf Bing, Artur Schnabel, Arthur Rubinstein.]

14075. TREPPER, LEOPOLD: *The Great Game*. The Story of the Red Orchestra. London: Michael Joseph, 1976. 442 pp., ports., illus. [French original]: *Le Grand Jeu*. Paris: Editions Albin Michel, 1975. [German ed.]: *Die Wahrheit*. Autobiographie. München: Kindler, 1975. 440 pp., ports., illus. [The 'Chef der Roten Kapelle', born 1904 in Neumarkt (Nowy Targ), Galicia, states that he became a Communist, 'because I am a Jew', hoping that Marxism would put an end to racism and antisemitism.]

14076. WERFEL, FRANZ. GOLDSTÜCKER, EDUARD: *Ein unbekannter Brief von Franz Werfel*. [In]: Austriaca. Beiträge zur österr. Literatur. Tübingen: Niemeyer, 1975. Pp. 370–375. [Werfel sent the letter from Santa Margherita Ligura to his parents in Prague on 24th March 1933.]

14077. WOLFSKEHL, KARL/FRIEDRICH GUNDOLF. *Karl und Hanna Wolfskehl/Friedrich Gundolf: Briefwechsel 1899–1931*. Hrsg. von Karlhans Kluncker. Amsterdam: Castrum Peregrini Presse, 1976. 320, 350 pp., ports., illus., facsims. [2 vols.] (Castrum Peregrini, 123/125.)

14078. ZWEIG, STEFAN: *Die Welt von gestern*. Erinnerungen eines Europäers. 58.–65. Tsd. Frankfurt/M.: Fischer-Taschenbuch Verlag, 1976. 317 pp. (Fischer Tb. Bd. 1152). [First publ. Stockholm, Bermann Fischer, 1941.]

14079. ZWEIG, STEFAN: *Briefe an Freunde*. Hrsg. von Richard Friedenthal. Genie der Freundschaft – Briefe eines Europäers. Frankfurt/M.: Fischer, 1976. 304 pp.

Bibliography

IX. GERMAN-JEWISH RELATIONS

A. General

14080. Lüth, Erich: *Die Friedensbitte an Israel 1951*. Eine Hamburger Initiative. Mit Beiträgen von Rudolf Küstermeier, Moshe Tavor und Norbert Wollheim. Hamburg: Hans Christians, 1976. 160 pp., ports., illus., facsims., bibl. E.L. und bibl. pp. 152–155. [The Hamburg 'Aktion Friede mit Israel' began on 31st August 1951. Erich Lüth with Rudolf Küstermeier, one of the two initiators, reviews the movement and shows examples of efforts of German-Jewish reconcilation.]

14081. Tramer, Hans: *Erich Lüth und seine Israel-Friedensaktion*. [In]: 'MB', 28. Jan., Tel Aviv, 1977. [Written on the occasion of Erich Lüth's 75th birthday who, together with Rudolf Küstermeier commenced the 'Aktion Friede mit Israel' in August 1951. See Nos. 308 and 309/YB. I.]

14082. '*Tribüne*', Zeitschrift zum Verständnis des Judentums. Hrsg. von Elisabeth Reisch. 15. Jg., H. 57–60, pp. 6655–6784. Frankfurt/M.: Tribüne Verlag, 1976. [4 vols.] [Nr. 57 incl.: Juden in München. Die Entwurzelten (Ursula v. Kardorff). Juden in der DDR. Lippenbekenntnisse erwünscht (Uwe Siemon-Netto). Ein Vertrauter des Lesers. Kurt Tucholsky, 1935 bis . . .? (Eberhard Seybold). Nr. 59: Quo vadis Israel? Auswirkungen des Generationenwechsels auf Israels Gesellschaft und Politik (Rolf W. Schloss). Über den Zionismus (Manfred Dörr). Lebendiges Judentum (Peter Stiegnitz). Sigmund Freud und der Erste Weltkrieg (Hermann Glaser). Filmkunst im Dritten Reich. Ein Mythos für die Demontage (Hilmar Hoffmann). Bericht über mich selbst (Robert Neumann, aus dem Nachlass). Nr. 60: Israel und das jüdische Dilemma (Joseph Dan). Friedrich Dürrenmatts Israel-Buch (Ernst-Peter Wieckenberg). Some selected contributions are listed according to subject.]

14083. Uthmann, Jörg von: *Doppelgänger – du bleicher Geselle*. Zur Pathologie des deutsch-jüdischen Verhältnisses. Stuttgart: Seewald, 1976. 189 pp. [The title of the book is a Heine-quotation. – Author, a German diplomat, born in 1936, served in the German Embassy in Israel. Cf. Some Passover Meditations. Eschatological Pitfalls (Robert Weltsch) [In]: 'AJR Information', Vol. XXXI, No. 4, April, London 1976.]

B. German-Israeli Relations

14084. 'deutschland-berichte'. Hrsg. Rudolf Vogel. 12. Jg., Nr. 1–12. Bonn, 1976. [12 vols.]

C. Church and Synagogue

14085. '*Christian Attitudes on Jews and Judaism*'. A Bi-Monthly Documentary Survey. Ed. C. C. Aronsfeld. No. 46 (Febr.), No. 47 (Apr.), No. 48 (June), No. 49 (Aug.), No. 50 (Oct.), No. 51 (Dec.) London: Institute of Jewish Affairs in Association with the World Jewish Congress, 1976. [6 vols.] [No. 46 incl.: Jews and Catholics since 'Nostra Aetate' (Charles Angell). Meaning and Purpose of the Jewish-Christian Dialogue (II) (Jean Radermakers, see No. 13333/YB. XXI). Teaching Christians about Judaism (Harriet L. Kaufman). No. 48: All Christians are Antisemitic (Fr. Edward H. Flannery). No. 49: Jesus the Jew (Don Cupitt). Israel – Significance and Realities (W. W. Simpson). No. 50: Shalom (Bishop George Appleton). No. 51: Judaism and Christianity, Prophecy and Fulfilment (John Barton). Dialogue must not blur differences (Charlotte L. Klein). See also No. 14090.]

14086. Eckert, Willehad Paul/Hans-Hermann Henrix, eds.: *Jesu Judesein als Zugang zum Judentum*. Eine Handreichung für Religionsunterricht und Erwachsenenbildung. Aachen: Einhard Verlag. [Obtainable from: Bischöfliche Akademie des Bistums Aachen, 5100 Aachen, Leonhardstr. 18–20], 1976. (Aachener Beiträge für Pastoral- und Bildungsfragen, Bd. 6.) [Incl. Jesus und das heutige Judentum (W. P. Eckert). Betrachtung des Problems, welche Stellung Juden zu Jesus einnehmen (E. L. Ehrlich). Jesus von Nazaret und sein Verhältnis zum Judentum (J. Maier).]

14087. Ehrlich, Ernst Ludwig: *Begegnungen, die zu Stationen des christlich-jüdischen Dialogs wur-*

den. [Speech made on receiving the Buber-Rosenzweig-Medal 1976.] [In]: 'Emuna-Israel Forum', H.2, 1976. Pp. 28–33. [Incl. meetings with Leo Baeck, Walter Baumgartner, Martin Buber, Karl Thieme, Augustin Kardinal Bea, Robert Raphael Geis, Max Horkheimer.]

14088. *'Emuna'*. Horizonte zur Diskussion über Israel und das Judentum. X. [last] Jg. Supplementheft 1: Frau im Judentum [see No. 13335/YB. XXI]. Sonderh. 2: Venedig, Geschichte und Gestalt seines Ghettos. Frankfurt/M., 1975. 60, 94 pp. [Two Supplement vols. For continuation see No. 14089.]

14089. *'Emuna-Israel Forum'*. Vereinigte Zeitschriften über Israel und Judentum. Hrsg.: Deutscher Koordinierungsrat der Gesellschaften f. Christl.-Jüdische Zusammenarbeit. Deutsch-Israelische Gesellschaft (DIG). Verlag Israel-Forum, Landsberger u. Co. Eds.: Willehad Paul Eckert, Hans Landsberger, s.A. [with] Reiner Bernstein, Michael Brocke, Ernst-Ludwig Ehrlich, N. Peter Levinson, Hermann Meier-Cronemeyer, Rolf Rendtorff, Martin Stöhr. H.1–4. Rothenburg ob der Tauber: Emuna-Israel Forum, 1976. 84, 72, 72, 72 pp., ports., illus. [4 vols.] [H.1 incl.: Martin Buber und die jüdische Kunst (Monika Becker). Jüdische Identität und Assimilation (Agnes Viest). Aus meinem Tagebuch 1937–1946 [continued in H.2] (Erna Becker-Kohn). Ein Pionier deutsch-israelischer Verständigung. Zum Tod von Propst Heinrich Grüber (Heinz Elsberg). Gib deine Münzen dem Sand . . . Zum Tod von Paul Schallück (Bernhard Doerdelmann). H.2 incl.: '. . . dann wollen wir das Fest des Lebens feiern!' Zum Tode von Max Tau (Bernhard Doerdelmann, port.) Der deutsche Jude in Israel – wie ist es ihm ergangen? (J. H. Roman). Nr. 3: Ernst Ludwig Ehrlich, ein Vorkämpfer der christl.-jüd. Bewegung. Laudatio auf E.L.E. anlässlich der Verleihung der Buber-Rosenzweig Medaille 1976 (W. P. Eckert). Reformjudentum und Zionismus (Wolfgang Hamburger, pp. 14–30, bibl.) [see also No. 13335/YB. XXI]. Meine Erfahrungen in Posen, Antoniek und Theresienstadt bis zur Rettung in der Schweiz (I) (Edith Kramer, continued in H.4). 'Ich vertrau auf die Jugend der Welt . . .' Hans Landsbergers Tod löste Erschütterung aus (Cornelius Streiter). Nr. 4: Vom Antisemitismus zum Antizionismus – oder: Wie die Linke das Erbe der Rechten übernommen hat (Henryk M. Broder).] [Some slected contributions are listed according to subject.]

14090. EVERETT, ROBERT: *Christian Theology after the Holocaust*. [In]: 'Christian Attitudes on Jews and Judaism'. Nos. 50 and 51. London, 1976. Pp. 10–12, 11–12 and 17.) [See No. 14085.] [This paper was originally read under the title 'James Parkes and the Quest for a Christian Theology without Antisemitism'. Publ. here as a tribute to Dr. James Parkes on his 80th birthday on 18th December 1976.]

14091. FLEISCHNER, EVA: *Judaism in German Theology since 1945*. Christianity and Israel considered in Terms of Mission. Metuchen, N.J.: Scarecrow Press, 1975. 205 pp., bibl. (pp. 181–192). [Study of Christian Thought concerning Israel and Judaism, the Synagogue and the Jewish experience.]

14092. FLUSSER, DAVID: *Jesus in Selbstzeugnissen und Bilddokumenten*. Dargestellt von David Flusser. 7. Aufl. Reinbek: Rowohlt, 1976. 154 pp., ports., illus., bibl. (pp. 150–153). (Rowohlts Monographien Bd. 140.)

14093. *'Freiburger Rundbrief'*. Beiträge zur christlich-jüdischen Begegnung. Hrsg. (mit Unterstützung der Deutschen Bischofskonferenz und des Deutschen Caritasverbandes) von Willehad Paul Eckert, Rupert Giessler, Georg Hüssler, Ludwig Kaufmann. XXVIII. Folge 1976. Nr. 105–108. Dez. Freiburg i./Br. Freiburger Rundbrief, 1976. 176 pp., Literaturhinweise pp. 76–137, facsims. [1 vol.] [Incl. Zehn Jahre kath.-jüdische Beziehungen: Eine Neubesinnung. Der jüd.-christl. Dialog. Eine Herausforderung für die Theologie? David Flusser zum 60. Geburtstag. Partikularismus und Universalismus aus jüd. Sicht. (Shemaryahu Talmon). Offenbarung, Judentum und Christentum im Denken Franz Rosenzweigs. Juden und Judentum im christl. Religionsunterricht. Aussprache: Replik an David Flusser von Johannes M. Oesterreicher.] [See also No. 14099.]

14094. GOLDSCHMIDT, HERMANN LEVIN: *Weil wir Brüder sind*. Biblische Besinnung für Juden und Christen. Mit e. Geleitwort von Klaus Hemmerle. Stuttgart: Verlag Katholisches Bibelwerk, 1975. 199 pp.

14095. GREIVE, HERMANN: *Die gesellschaftliche Bedeutung der christlich-jüdischen Differenz – Zur Situation im deutschen Katholizismus*. [In]: Juden im Wilhelminischen Deutschland 1890–1914. Pp. 349–388. [See No. 13387.]

14096. GUTTERIDGE, RICHARD: *Open Thy Mouth For The Dumb!* The German Evangelical

Church and the Jews, 1879–1950. Oxford: Blackwell, 1976. New York: Harper and Row, 1976. 374 pp., bibl. (pp. 358–370). [Incl. The roots of 'Christian' antisemitism, 1879–1918. Anti-Jewish sentiment in the Weimar Period. Hitler, the Church and the Jews, January–April 1933. Appendix I: Luther and the Jews. App. II: Judenmission. App. IV: Die Ostjuden.]

14097. HAMMERSTEIN, FRANZ VON, ed.: *Von Vorurteilen zum Verständnis.* Dokumente zum jüdisch-christlichen Dialog. Frankfurt/M.: Lembeck, 1976. 165 pp.

14098. HOMMEL, GISELA: *Der siebenarmige Leuchter.* Erster Blick aufs Judentum für Christen. Ein Erfahrungsbericht. München: J. Pfeiffer, 1976. 156 pp., bibl. [Cf. Erlebtes Judentum (E. L. Ehrlich) [In]: 'Allgemeine', 23. Juli. Düsseldorf, 1976. Pp. 5 and 8.]

14099. *'Immanuel'.* Dokumente des heutigen religiösen Denkens und Forschens in Israel. Hrsg.: Ökumenisch-Theologische Forschungsgemeinschaft in Israel und Freiburger Rundbrief. V, 1976. Jerusalem–Freiburg i. Br., 1976. Pp. 146–176 im Freiburger Rundbrief. [See No. 14093.] (Hebräische Veröffentlichungen aus Israel in deutscher Übersetzung). [Incl.: Shmuel Hugo Bergman (Nathan Rotenstreich, pp. 147–149). Der Gekreuzigte und die Juden (David Flusser, pp. 152–157). Der Sabbat im Staat Israel (Eliezer Schweid, pp. 165–172).]

14100. INSTITUT KIRCHE UND JUDENTUM BEI DER KIRCHLICHEN HOCHSCHULE BERLIN, ed.: *Treue zur Thora.* Beiträge zur Mitte des christlich-jüdischen Gesprächs. Festschrift zum 75. Geburtstag von Prof. D.Dr. Günter Harder. H.3. Berlin, 1976. 223 pp., bibl. G.H. for the years 1933–1975. [Prof. Harder was a leading member of the 'Bekennende Kirche' and co-founder of 'Dienst an Israel'.]

14101. *Jewish-Christian Dialogue.* Six years of Christian-Jewish consultations. The Quest for world community. Jewish and Christian perspectives. Publ. by the International Jewish Committee on Interreligious Consultations and The World Council of Churches' Subunit on Dialogue with the People of Living Faiths and Ideologies. Geneva, 1975. 72 pp. [Contributions by Uriel Tal, Shemaryahu Talmon, Norman Lamm, Ellen Flessman-van Leer, Krister Stendahl.]

14102. KÜNG, HANS/PINCHAS LAPIDE: *Jesus im Widerstreit.* Ein jüdisch-christlicher Dialog. München: Kösel, Stuttgart: Calwer, 1976. 51 pp., bibl.

14103. LAPIDE, PINCHAS: *Ist das nicht Josephs Sohn?* Jesus im heutigen Judentum. München–Stuttgart: Kösel-Calwer, 1976. 167 pp. [Jesus in Hebrew literature. Jesus in Israeli school books. Rabbis on Jesus.]

14104. LITTELL, FRANKLIN H.: *The Crucifixion of the Jews.* New York–London: Harper and Row, 1976. 153 pp. [The Failure of Christians to Understand the Jewish Experience. Chap. 2: Christian Antisemitism. Chap. 3: The Church Struggle and the Jews. 4: The Meaning of the Holocaust. 5: Israel: The Crisis of Christianity. Cf. Die Kreuzigung der Juden (Pinchas Lapide) [In]: 'Allgemeine', 23. Sept., Düsseldorf, 1976. Pp. 34 and 37.]

14105. MAYDELL, BODO FREIHERR VON: *Das Volk der Völker.* Lehren aus jüdischem und christlichem Schrifttum in Versen. Karlsruhe: Karlsruher Bote, 1976. 28 pp., gen. table. [Stammbaum Heinrich Heines und seine Gemeinsamkeit mit dem Stammbaum des Verfassers.]

14106. POLIAKOV, LEON: *The Catholic Church and the Jews.* The Vatican's New Guidelines. [In]: 'Midstream'. Vol. XXII, No. 8, October. New York: The Theodor Herzl Society, 1976. Pp. 29–35.

14107. PRÖPPER, THOMAS: *Der Jesus der Philosophen und der Jesus des Glaubens.* Ein theologisches Gespräch mit Jaspers, Bloch, Kolakowski, Gardavsky, Machovec, Fromm, Ben Chorin. 1. Aufl. Mainz: Matthias-Grünewald-Verlag, 1976. 148 pp. (Grünewald-Reihe.)

14108. *Richtlinien und Hinweise für die Konzilserklärung 'Nostra aetate', Artikel 4.* Von den deutschen Bischöfen approbierte Übersetzung. Päpstl. Komm. für die Religiösen Beziehungen zu dem Judentum. Eingel. von Willehad Paul Eckert. Trier: Paulinus-Verlag, 1976. 40 pp. (Nachkonziliare Dokumentation, Bd. 49.)

D. Antisemitism

14109. AMÉRY, JEAN: *Der ehrbare Antisemitismus.* [In]: 'Merkur'. 30. Jg., H.6 (Juni). Stuttgart: Klett, 1976. Pp. 532–546.

14110. Améry, Jean: *Der neue Antisemitismus.* [In]: 'Tribüne'. 15. Jg., H.59, 1976. Pp. 7010–7014. [See No. 14082.]

14111. Aretz, Emil: *Hexen Einmal-Eins einer Lüge.* Paehl b. Weilheim: Verlag Hohe Warte, 1976. 392 pp., bibl. [Elaborate effort to dispute the figure of six million Jews killed by the Nazis.]

14112. Aris, Helmut: *Kampf gegen Rassismus und Antisemitismus.* Auftrag und Verpflichtung. [Chap. in]: Antirassismus–Antiimperialismus. Der Beitrag der Christen zum Kampf gegen rassistische und kolonialistische Unterdrückung. Hrsg. vom Sekretariat des Hauptvorstandes der Christlich-Demokratischen Union Deutschlands. Berlin [East]: Union Verlag, [1971]. 132 pp. [Helmut Aris is president of the Union of Jewish Communities in the DDR.]

14113. Baron, Salo W.: *Changing Patterns of Antisemitism.* [In]: Jewish Social Studies. Vol. No. XXXVIII No. 1 Winter. New York: Conference on Jewish Social Studies, 1976. Pp. 5–38.

14114. Bethge, Eberhard: *Versuchung des Glaubens.* Zur Kritik des christlichen Antijudaismus. 1. Aufl. Neukirchen-Vluyn: Neukirchener Verlag, 1976. 16 pp. (Erbauliche Reden, 1).

14115. Bieberstein, Johannes Rogalla von: *Die These von der Verschwörung, 1776–1945.* Philosophen, Freimaurer, Juden, Liberale und Sozialisten als Verschwörer gegen die Sozialordnung. Bern/Frankfurt/M.: Lang, 1976. 292 pp., bibl. (pp. 236–284). (Europäische Hochschulschriften, Reihe III: Geschichte und ihre Hilfswirtschaften, Bd. 63). [Pp. 156–169: Funktion und geschichtliche Bedeutung der Verschwörungsthese. 1. Die Rolle der Juden im Rahmen der Verschwörungsthese.]

14116. Broder, Henryk M.: *Antizionismus – Antisemitismus von links?* [In]: 'Aus Politik und Zeitgeschichte'. B24/76, 12. Juni. Bonn: Bundeszentrale für Politische Bildung, 1976. Pp. 31–46.

14117. Broszat, Martin: *Zur Kritik der Publizistik des antisemitischen Rechtsextremismus.* [Introduction to]: Organisierter Massenmord an Juden in national-sozialistischen Vernichtungslagern (Ino Arndt und Wolfgang Scheffler) [In]: Aus Politik und Zeitgeschichte, 8. Mai, B19/76). Bonn: Bundeszentrale für Politische Bildung, 1976. Pp. 3–7, 8–22. [See also No. 13498.] [An English translation of the introduction]: On the Whitewashers of Nazi Crime [In]: 'Patterns of Prejudice', Vol. 10, No. 5, September–October, London, 1976. Pp. 11–14. [See No. 14132.]

14118. Butz, Arthur R.: *The Hoax of the Twentieth Century.* Richmond, Surrey: Historical Review Press, 1976. 315 pp., notes pp. 291–299, bibl. (pp. 300–304). [Author attempts to "prove" that not a single Jew was ever exterminated! Cf. Hoax of the Century (C. C. Aronsfeld) [in]: 'Patterns of Prejudice', Vol. X, No. 6, 1976. Pp. 13–16. See No. 14132.]

14119. *European Antisemitism 1890–1945.* [In]: 'The Wiener Library Bulletin'. Ed. Robert S. Wistrich. Vol. XXIX. New Series, Nos. 39/40. London, 1976. 62 pp., facsims., bibls. [Incl.: Czech Antisemitism and the Jewish Response before 1914 (Michael A. Riff, pp. 8–20, notes pp. 19–20). Georg v. Schoenerer and the Genesis of Modern Austrian Antisemitism (Robert S. Wistrich, pp. 20–29, bibl., pp. 28–29). Blood on the Ringstrasse: Vienna's Students 1918–33 (John Haag, pp. 29–34, notes pp. 33–34). National Socialist Vienna: Antisemitism as a Housing Policy (Gerhard Botz, pp. 47–55, notes pp. 54–55. [Cf. No. 12752/YB. XXI.] Völkisch Idealism and National Socialism: The Case of Friedrich Lienhard (Roderick Stackelberg, pp. 34–41, notes). Julius Streicher and the Impact of Der Stürmer (Randall T. Bytwerk, pp. 41–46, facsims., notes p. 46).]

14120. Fried, Erich: *Ist Antizionismus Antisemitismus?* [In]: 'Merkur', 30. Jg., H.6 (337), Juni. Stuttgart: Klett, 1976. Pp. 547–554. [See also No. 13825.]

14121. Ginzel, Bernd: *Gegen Antisemitismus und Antizionismus.* Aus der Arbeit der Bundeszentrale für Politische Bildung, Bonn. Ein Bericht [In]: 'Allgemeine', 23. Sept. Düsseldorf, 1976.

14122. Goldhagen, Erich: *Weltanschauung und Endlösung.* Zum Antisemitismus der nationalsozialistischen Führungsschicht. [In]: Vierteljahrshefte für Zeitgeschichte. 24. Jg., H.4 (Okt.). Stuttgart: Deutsche Verlags-Anstalt, 1976. Pp. 379–405.

14123. Härtle, Heinrich: *Deutsche und Juden.* Studien zu einem Weltproblem. Leoni am Starnberger. See: Druffel, 1976. 325 pp., ports., illus., notes pp. 310–318.

14124. Heinen, Ernst: *Antisemitische Strömungen im politischen Katholizismus während des Kultur-*

kampfes. Pp. 259–299 [In]: Geschichte in der Gegenwart. Festschrift für Kurt Kluxen zu seinem 60. Geburtstag. Hrsg. v. Ernst Heinen und Hans Julius Schoeps. Paderborn: Schöningh, 1972. x, 339 pp., front., port., bibl. K.K. pp. 337–339. [Corrected entry No. 11864/YB. XIX.]

14125. JOCHMANN, WERNER: *Struktur und Funktion des deutschen Antisemitismus*. [In]: Juden im Wilhelminischen Deutschland 1890–1914. Pp. 389–477. [See No. 13387.]

14126. KATER, MICHAEL H.: *Studentenschaft und Rechtsradikalismus in Deutschland 1918–1933*. Eine sozialgeschichtliche Studie zur Bildungskrise in der Weimarer Republik. Hamburg: Hoffmann und Campe, 1975. 361 pp., tabs., notes pp. 225–308, bibl. (pp. 309–344). [Incl. chap.: Der Antisemitismus der Studenten: Das Ergebnis sozial-ökonomischer Verunsicherung.]

14127. KATZ, JACOB: *The 'Hep-Hep' Disturbances of 1819 in Germany and their Historical Background*. [In]: Zion, 38. Jerusalem, 1973. Pp. 62–115. [In Hebrew, quotations in the German original.]

14128. KÜHNER, HANS: *Der Antisemitismus der Kirche*. Essenz und Evidenz. Genese, Geschichte und Gefahr. Zürich: Verlag Die Waage, 1976. 215 pp., bibl. (pp. 207–215). [Cf. Wie christlich war und ist die Kirche? (Pinchas Lapide) [In]: 'Allgemeine', 23. Sept., Düsseldorf, 1976.]

14129. KWIET, KONRAD: *Historians of the German Democratic Republic on Antisemitism and Persecution*. [In]: LBI Year Book XXI. London, 1976. Pp. 173–198.

14130. LOWENFELD, DAVID: *A Futile Defense: Jewish Responses to German Anti-Semitism 1879–1914*. [In]: Olam. Jewish Themes and World Issues. Spring. London: World Union of Jewish Students, 1976. Pp. 38–47, facsims.

14131. MORAIS, VAMBERTO: *A Short History of Anti-Semitism*. New York: Norton, 1976. x, 300 pp., notes pp. 255–280, bibl. (pp. 281–286). [Orig. publ. in Portuguese under the title Pequeña Historia do Anti-Semitisme, Sao Paulo, 1972.] [A study dealing with the psychological, moral and philosophical aspects of antisemitism.]

14132. *'Patterns of Prejudice'*. Ed. C. C. Aronsfeld. Publ. Bi-Monthly. Vol. 10, Nos. 1–6. London: Institute of Jewish Affairs, 1976. [6 vols.] [No. 3 incl. Lessons of the Past Lost on the Present. Jews and other Scapegoats. – See Nos. 13584, 13585, 14117, 14118.]

14133. PAUCKER, ARNOLD: *Zur Problematik einer jüdischen Abwehrstrategie in der deutschen Gesellschaft*. [In]: Juden im Wilhelminischen Deutschland 1890–1914. Pp. 479–548. [See No. 13387.]

14134. PAUL, INGRID: *Zur Entstehungsgeschichte des politischen Antisemitismus*. [In]: 'Tribüne'. 15. Jg., H.59, 1976. Pp. 7016–7030, bibl. [See No. 14082.]

14135. PFISTERER, RUDOLF: *Die christliche Gesellschaft und ihr Judenbild*. [In]: 'Tribüne'. 15. Jg., H.60, 1976. Pp. 7220–7231. [See No. 14082.]

14136. POLIAKOV, LÉON: *Geschichte des Antisemitismus*. I. Von der Antike bis zu den Kreuzzügen. Deutsch von Rudolf Pfisterer. Worms: Georg Heintz, 1976. 93 pp.

14137. RAPHAËL, F[REDDY]: *Conditionnements Socio-Politiques et Socio-Psychologiques du Satanisme*. [In]: Revue des Sciences Religieuses, Tome 50, No. 2. Strasbourg, 1976. Pp. 112–156. [The devilish image of the Jew as depicted in history.]

14138. ROSENBERG, HANS: *Moderner Antisemitismus und vorfaschistische Strömungen*. Pp. 88–117. [In]: Grosse Depression und Bismarckzeit. Wirtschaftsablauf, Gesellschaft und Politik in Mitteleuropa. Ungek. Ausg. Frankfurt/M.: Ullstein, 1976. xiv, 301 pp., bibl. (pp. 274–287). (Ullstein Buch Bd. 3239). Lizenz d. Verl. de Gruyter. [First publ. 1967. See No. 9186/YB. XVI.]

14139. ROSENSAFT, MENACHEM Z.: *Jews and Antisemites in Austria at the End of the Nineteenth Century*. [In]: LBI Year Book XXI. London, 1976. Pp. 57–86.

14140. *Ursachen, Formen und Folgen der Judenfeindschaft im 19. Jahrhundert*. Hrsg. vom Institut Kirche und Judentum bei der Kirchlichen Hochschule. H.4. Berlin, 1976, 54 pp.

14141. WHITESIDE, ANDREW G.: *The Socialism of Fools*. George Ritter von Schönerer and Austrian Pan-Germanism. Berkeley, Cal.: University of California Press, 1975. x, 404 pp., front., port., notes pp. 327–369, bibl. (pp. 371–396). [Schönerer's antisemitic ideas had great influence on Lueger's Christian-Socialist and Hitler's national-socialist movements.] [Correction to 13354/YB. XXI.]

14142. WISTRICH, ROBERT S.: *German Social-Democracy and the Berlin Movement*. [In]: IWK (Intern. Wissensch. Korrespondenz) zur Geschichte der deutschen Arbeiterbewegung). 12. Jg., H.4, Dec. Berlin, 1976. Pp. 433–442. [The attitude adopted by German Social

Democracy towards Adolf Stoecker's Berlin Movement, and organised 'political anti-semitism' in the early 1880s.]

14143. ZISENWINE, DAVID W., ed.: *Anti-Semitism in Europe: Sources of the Holocaust*. Introduction by Robert Chazan. New York: Behrman House, 1976. ix, 110 pp. (The Jewish Concepts and Issues Series.)

E. Noted Germans and Jews

14144. ADENAUER, KONRAD. *Konrad Adenauer und seine Zeit*. Politik und Persönlichkeit des ersten Bundeskanzlers. Festschrift Bd. 1. Im Auftrag der Adenauer-Stiftung. Stuttgart: Deutsche Verlagsanstalt, 1976. [Incl. Beiträge von Weg- und Zeitgenossen. Adenauer und das jüdische Volk (Nahum Goldmann). Über den Abschluss des Luxemburger Wiedergutmachungsvertrag (Franz Böhm).]

14145. BÖHM, FRANZ. GÖTZ, HANS HERBERT: *Architekt der Freiheit*. Rechtslehrer, Parlamentarier und Moralist. Franz Böhm zum 80. Geburtstag. [In]: 'FAZ', 15. Febr. Frankfurt/M., 1975, port. [In 1952 Franz Böhm negotiated with the Jewish Claims Conference, and the restitution treaty with Nahum Goldmann.]

14146. BRANDT, WILLY. BRANDT, WILLY: *Begegnungen und Einsichten*. Die Jahre 1960–1975. Hamburg: Hoffman und Campe, 1976. [Incl. his attitude to Zionism and Israel, Nazi persecution of Jews, restitution, and his meetings with various Jewish personalities.]

14147. FONTANE, THEODOR: *Briefe 1833–1860*. Hrsg. und mit e. Nachw. von Helmuth Nürnberger und Otto Drude. München: Hanser, 1976. 752 pp. (Werke, Schriften und Briefe. 4. Abtlg., Bd. 1). [One of the two most important correspondents during this very difficult period in Fontane's life was the Jewish progressionist Wilhelm Wolfsohn (1820–1865). The vol. contains also a section of letters to Paul Heyse.]

14148. GEORGE, STEFAN. LANDFRIED, KLAUS: *Stefan George*. Politik des Unpolitischen. Mit e. Geleitwort von Dolf Sternberger. Heidelberg: Stiehm, 1975. 290 pp. (Literatur und Geschichte, Bd. 8). Zugl. Hist. Diss., Univ. Heidelberg 1969/70. [An examination of the political and social aspects of George and his work.]

14149. LANDMANN, GEORG PETER: *Stefan George und sein Kreis*. Eine Bibliographie. 2. Aufl. Mit der Hilfe von Gunhild Günther erg. und nachgeführt. Hamburg: Hauswedel, 1976. 452 pp.

14150. JASPERS, KARL. PIPER, KLAUS und HANS SANER, eds.: *Erinnerungen an Karl Jaspers*. München: Piper, 1974. 333 pp. [Incl. contributions by Hannah Arendt, Heinrich Liepmann, Edgar Salin, Friedrich Gundolf, Michael Landmann.]

14151. MANN, THOMAS. GOTTGETREU, ERICH: *Zwei vergessene Äusserungen Thomas Manns über den Zionismus*. [In]: 'MB', Nr. 48, 12. Dez. Tel Aviv, 1975. [See also No. 13362/YB. XXI: Thomas Mann über den Zionismus (Walter A. Berendsohn).]

14152. MIETH, DIETMAR: *Epik und Ethik*. Eine theologisch-ethische Interpretation der Josephsromane von Thomas Mann. Tübingen: Niemeyer, 1976. x, 237 pp. (Studien zur deutschen Literatur, Bd. 47).

14153. RÖHN, GISELA: *Joseph*. Bilder und Gedanken zu dem Roman 'Joseph und seine Brüder' von Thomas Mann. Hamburg: Friedrich Wittig, 1976. 152 pp., illus.

14154. RILKE, RAINER MARIA. RILKE, RAINER MARIA: *Zwei Prager Geschichten*. [Und] *Ein Prager Künstler*. Mit Illustrationen von Emil Orlik. Hrsg. von Josef Mühlberger. Frankfurt/M.: Insel, 1976. (it Bd. 235).

14155. GLAUERT, BARBARA: *'Liliane'*. Rainer Maria Rilke und Claire Studer in ihren Briefen, 1918–1923. [In]: Aus dem Antiquariat. Börsenblatt für den Dt. Buchhandel. Nr. 7. 23. Jan. Frankfurt/M., 1976. Pp. A1–A11, ports., notes, bibl. (pp. A9–A11). [Liliane, i.e., Claire Studer (born 1891 in Nuremberg), in 1929 married Ivan Goll.]

14156. HAMBURGER, KÄTE: *Rilke*. Eine Einführung. 1. Aufl. Stuttgart: Klett, 1976. 199 pp.

14157. JONAS, KLAUS W.: *Rainer Maria Rilke und Richard Beer-Hofmann*. [In]: Philobiblon, XVII, Hamburg, 1973. Pp. 156–177. [See also No. 13746.]

14158. ROSENBERG, ALFONS: *An Unknown Rilke Correspondence*. [In]: 'AJR Information'. April. London, 1976. [Recipient of the unpubl. letters was Margarete Rosenberg (pen name Henriette Hardenberg), born 1895 in Berlin. She was married to the writer Alfred Wolfenstein through whom she met Rilke in Munich, in 1916. A vol. of her poems 'Neigungen' was publ. 1919, reprinted in 1974.]

14159. SOMBART, WERNER. MENDES-FLOHR, PAUL R.: *Werner Sombart's: The Jews and Modern Capitalism.* An Analysis of its Ideological Premises. [In]: LBI Year Book XXI. London, 1976. Pp. 87–107.
14160. WAGNER, RICHARD. WAGNER, RICHARD: *Mein Leben.* Vollständige, kommentierte Ausgabe. Hrsg. und mit e. Nachw. von Martin Gregor-Dellin. München: List, 1976. 845 pp., facsims., Nachw. pp. 771–837.
14161. GRADENWITZ, PETER: *Richard Wagners Feinde und Freunde.* Gedanken anlässlich der Veröffentlichung einer hebräischen Übersetzung der Schrift 'Vom Judentum in der Musik'. [In]: 'MB', Nr. 40, 29. Okt., Tel Aviv, 1976. Pp. 4–5 and 8.
14162. GRÜNEWALD, H. I.: *Richard Wagner und das Judentum.* [In]: 'Allgemeine'. XXXI, Nr. 37, 10. Sept. Düsseldorf, 1976.
14163. ZELINSKY, HARTMUT: *Richard Wagner – ein deutsches Thema.* Frankfurt/M.: Verlag Zweitausendeins, 1976. 292 pp. [Incl. the essay: Judentum in der Musik. The book deals mainly with the effects of his work and of his Weltanschauung.]
14164. WEGNER, ARMIN T. STECKEL, RONALD, ed.: *Odyssee der Seele.* Ausgew. Werke von Armin T. Wegner. Wuppertal: Hammer, 1976. 396 pp. [Cf. Verschollen für ein Menschenalter. Porträt des Dichters und Widerstandskämpfers Armin T. Wegner anlässlich einer Werkauswahl (Thomas B. Schumann) [In]: 'Tribüne', H.61, 16. Jg. Frankfurt/M., 1977. Pp. 123–130. [Also]: Tragik des Alterns. Zum 90. Geburtstag des Dichters Armin T. Wegner [In]: 'MB', 28. Jan., Tel Aviv, 1977. – Ungebeugter Armin T. Wegner zum Neunzigsten [am 16. Okt. 1976] (Walter Jens) [In]: 'FAZ', 16. Okt. Frankfurt/M., 1976. – In 1933 Wegner wrote his 'Open Letter to Hitler' asking him to stop the persecution of the Jews, for which he was sent to a concentration camp.]

X. FICTION, POETRY AND HUMOUR

14165. AUERBACH, BERTHOLD: *Barfüssele.* Roman. München: Heyne, 1976. 189 pp. (Heyne-Nostalgie-Bibliothek, 19). [Written 1856. B.A., 1812–1882.]
14166. AUSLÄNDER, ROSE: *Gesammelte Gedichte.* Hrsg. von Hugo Ernst Käufer und Berndt Mosblech. Holzschnitte: HAP Grieshaber. Mit e. Nachw. von Walter Helmut Fritz. Leverkusen: Literarischer Verlag Braun, 1976. 424 pp., ports., illus., facsims., 1 record, bibl. [Cont. the collections of poems: Blinder Sommer (1965), 36 Gerechte (1967), Inventar (1972), Andere Zeichen (1974), Ohne Visum (1974). Ninety-eight hitherto unpubl. poems. – Cf. An mein Gedächtnis. Anmerkungen zu den 'Gesammelten Gedichten' (Günter Lanser) [In]: 'Emuna-Israel Forum', H.4, 1976. Pp. 71–72, port. See No. 14089.] [Rose Ausländer, born 1905 in Czernowitz.]
14167. AUSLÄNDER, ROSE: *Selected Poems.* Transl. by Ewald Osers. London: London Magazine Editions, 1976. [Cont. the German poems and their transl. into English.]
14168. BEREND, ALICE: *Spreemann & Co.* Frankfurt/M.: Fischer, 1976. 288 pp. (Im Fischernetz). [A success story of three generations. The novel was first publ. 1916. – A.B., 1878 Berlin–1938 Florence.]
14169. MARX, LEOPOLD: *Es führt eine lange Strasse.* Gedichte. Berlin: Friedrich Nolte, 1976. 135 pp. [Cf. Wegzeichen des Lebens (Ernst Simon) [In]: 'MB', 15. Apr., Tel Aviv, 1977. – L.M., born in Cannstadt, has been for forty years a farmer in Israel.]
14170. REMARQUE, ERICH MARIA: *Die Nacht von Lissabon.* Roman. Berlin [East]: Aufbau, 1976. 320 pp. [The novel, publ. 1964, deals with the fate of German refugees in 1942.]
14171. ROKEAH, DAVID: *Wo Stachelrosen wachsen.* Gedichte. Aus dem Hebräischen unter Mitwirkung des Autors übertragen von Paul Celan, Benigna Chilla, Erich Fried, Gerhard Schoenberner, Walter Helmut Fritz. Frankfurt/M.: Fischer, 1976. 71 pp. [D.R., born 1916 in Lemberg.]

Index to Bibliography

List of Contributors

ANGRESS, Werner T., Ph.D., b. 1920 in Berlin. Professor of History, State University of New York at Stony Brook, N.Y. Author of *Stillborn Revolution. The Communist Bid for Power in Germany 1921–1923* (1963); 'Juden im politischen Leben der Revolutionszeit', in *Deutsches Judentum in Krieg und Revolution 1916–1923* (1971); 'Das deutsche Militär und die Juden im Ersten Weltkrieg. Dokumentation' in *Militärgeschichtliche Mitteilungen* (1976); and of articles and book reviews in scholarly journals in USA and Germany. Fellow of the LBI, New York, and Member of its Board. (Contributor to Year Books X and XVII.)

GLATZER, Nahum N., Ph.D., Dr. h.c., b. 1903 in Lemberg (Austria). 1950–1973, Professor of Jewish History and Social Ethics, Brandeis University. Now Professor of Judaica and Religion, Boston University. Author of a.o. *Franz Rosenzweig: His Life and Thought* (1953); *Leopold and Adelheid Zunz. An Account in Letters* (1958); *Leopold Zunz: Jude – Deutscher – Europäer* (1964); *The Dimensions of Job; Essays in Jewish Thought*. Editor of *The Judaic Tradition; I am A Memory Come Alive: Kafka* (1974); *Modern Jewish Thought*. Member of the New York Board of the LBI. (Contributor to Year Books I and V.)

GRUNWALD, Kurt, Dr. rer. pol., b. 1901 in Hamburg. Now lives in Jerusalem. Formerly Manager of Union Bank of Israel. Author of a.o. *Türkenhirsch. A Study of Baron Maurice de Hirsch* (1966); co-author of *Industrialization in the Middle East* (1961), and author of numerous articles in economic and historical periodicals. (Contributor to Year Books XII, XIV and XVII.)

MENDES-FLOHR, Paul R., Ph.D., b. 1941 in New York. Lecturer in Modern Jewish Thought, The Hebrew University of Jerusalem. Editor (with Michael A. Fishbane) of (and contributor to) *Texts and Responses. Studies Presented to Nahum N. Glatzer on the Occasion of His Seventieth Birthday* (1975); of *Wissenschaft des Judentums. An Anthology* (1977, in Hebrew); and author of various essays on Martin Buber, Franz Rosenzweig and other topics in sociological, literary and historical journals. (Contributor to Year Book XXI.)

MORK, Gordon R., Ph.D., b. St. Cloud, Minnesota. Associate Professor of History, Purdue University. Author of *Modern Western Civilization. A Concise History* (1976); and of various essays on nineteenth-century German history in American historical journals.

PELLI, Moshe, Ph.D., b. 1936 in Haifa (Israel). Associate Professor of Hebrew Literature, Cornell University. Formerly editor, *NIV, Literary Quarterly* and *Lamishpahah* (Hebrew monthly). Author of *Moses Mendelssohn: Bonds of Tradition* (1972, in Hebrew); and of novels, short stories and many papers on the Hebrew Enlightenment and modern Hebrew literature. (Contributor to Year Book XX.)

PETUCHOWSKI, Jakob J., Ph.D., b. 1925 in Berlin. Research Professor of Jewish Theology and Liturgy, Hebrew Union College, Cincinnati, Ohio. Author of a.o.

349

The Theology of Haham David Nieto (1954, ²1970); *Ever Since Sinai* (1961, ²1968); *Contributions to the Scientific Study of Jewish Liturgy* (1970); *Understanding Jewish Prayer* (1972); *Beten im Judentum* (1976). Co-Editor of a.o. *Literature of the Synagogue* (1975); *Drei Wege zu dem Einen Gott* (1976). Author of numerous articles on Rabbinics, Jewish Theology, and Jewish Liturgy in periodicals and encyclopaedias.

REINHARZ, Jehuda, Ph.D., b. 1944 in Haifa. Associate Professor of History, University of Michigan. Author of *Fatherland or Promised Land: The Dilemma of the German Jew 1893–1914* (1975); Editor of Volume IX of the *Letters and Papers of Chaim Weizmann* (1977); Co-Editor of (and contributor to) *Essays in Jewish Thought and History* (1977). Currently editing *Dokumente zur Geschichte des deutschen Zionismus* to be published by the Leo Baeck Institute. Author of reviews and articles in scholarly periodicals.

RONALL, Joachim O., F.R.A.S. (London), b. 1912 in Berlin and educated at the Universities of Berlin, Marburg and Paris. Professor of Economics, Fordham University, New York. Author of a.o. *Industrialization in the Middle East* – with Kurt Grunwald (1960, 1975); and of numerous contributions on banking history, economics and related topics to scholarly journals in Europe and the USA. Economic Editor, *Encyclopedia Judaica*.

ROSENAU, Helen, Ph.D., b. in Monte Carlo. Formerly Reader in the History of Art, University of Manchester. Now Lecturer for University of London and Central Polytechnic, London. Author of a.o. *A Short History of Jewish Art* (1948); *Boullée's Treatise on Architecture* (1953); *The Ideal City* (1959, 2nd edn. 1974); *Boullée and Universal Architecture* (1974); *The Image of the Temple in Judaism and Christianity* (1977); and of numerous essays, pamphlets, etc. (Contributor to Year Book VIII.)

ROSENBLÜTH, Pinchas E., Dr. phil., b. 1906 in Berlin. Lecturer in Political Science at Bar Ilan University, Ramat Gan, Israel. Author of *Martin Buber. Sein Denken und Wirken* (1968); 'Die geistigen und religiösen Strömungen in der deutschen Judenheit', in *Juden im Wilhelminischen Deutschland 1890–1914* (1976); 'Samson Raphael Hirsch. Sein Denken und Wirken', in *Das Judentum in der Deutschen Umwelt 1800–1850* (1977); and of studies on civic education, Jewish political thought and modern history.

ROSNER, Fred, M.D., F.A.C.P., b. 1935 in Berlin. Director of Hematology of the Queens Hospital Center, New York, and Associate Professor of Medicine, State University of New York College of Medicine at Stony Brook. Author of a.o. *The Medical Aphorisms of Moses Maimonides* (1970–71); *Sex Ethics in the Writings of Moses Maimonides* (1974); *Modern Medicine and Jewish Law* (1972); *Medicine in the Bible and Talmud* (1977); and of numerous articles on hematology, Jewish medicine and medical history.

SCHORSCH, Ismar, Ph.D., b. 1935 in Hanover. Professor of Jewish History and Dean of Graduate School, Jewish Theological Seminary of America, New York.

Author of *Jewish Reactions to German Anti-Semitism 1870–1914* (1972); Editor of Heinrich Graetz, *The Structure of Jewish History and other Essays;* and author of numerous articles in scholarly journals. Fellow of the LBI New York and Member of its Board. (Contributor to Year Books XI and XIX.)

SIMONS, Thomas W., Jr., Ph.D., b. 1938 in Crosby, Minnesota. Diplomat (Foreign Service Officer of the United States). Author of essays on political and theological subjects and of book reviews in American and Austrian publications.

STERN, William G., b. 1915 in Cologne. Formerly a teacher, now journalist and translator. Author of numerous essays and articles on Jewish and general subjects and of regular contributions to the Jewish press in Austria, Germany and Switzerland. (Contributor to Year Book XIX.)

TOURY, Jacob, Ph.D., b. 1915 in Beuthen. Professor of Jewish History at the Diaspora Research Institute, Tel Aviv University. Author of a.o. *Die politischen Orientierungen der Juden in Deutschland. Von Jena bis Weimar* (1966); *Turmoil and Confusion in the Revolution of 1848* (1968, in Hebrew); 'Der Eintritt der Juden ins deutsche Bürgertum' and 'Die Revolution von 1848 als innerjüdischer Wendepunkt', in *Das Judentum in der deutschen Umwelt 1800–1850* (1977); *Zwischen Revolution, Reaktion und Emanzipation* (1977); of textbooks and of numerous contributions to learned periodicals, encyclopaedias, etc. in English, German and Hebrew. (Contributor to Year Books XI, XIII and XVI.)

WISTRICH, Robert Solomon, Ph.D., b. 1945 in Lenger-Ugol, USSR. Editor of *The Wiener Library Bulletin* and lecturer in history. Author of *The Myth of Zionist Racism* (1976); *Revolutionary Jews from Marx to Trotsky* (1976); *Marxists against Zion* (1977); *Austrian Social Democracy and the Rise of Anti-Semitism 1880–1914* (1977); Co-editor – with Walter Laqueur and George Mosse – of *Theories of Fascism* (1976); and author of articles in historical and literary journals. Member of the London Board of the LBI. (Contributor to Year Book XXI.)

Correction
to the Bibliography of Year Book XXI

13168: The Editor regrets the occurrence of a misstatement in this entry due to an oversight The former German finance minister Schwerin von Krosigk, who served the Nazi government to the end, though – as he claims – with considerable reservations, cannot, of course, be described as an opponent of Nazism.

Abstracts of articles in this Year Book are included in *Historical Abstracts* and *America: History and Life.*

General Index to Year Book XXII
of the Leo Baeck Institute

Just published

Das Judentum in der Deutschen Umwelt 1800–1850

Studien zur Frühgeschichte der Emanzipation
herausgegeben von

HANS LIEBESCHÜTZ
und
ARNOLD PAUCKER

(Schriftenreihe wissenschaftlicher Abhandlungen des Leo Baeck Instituts 35) 1977. XIII, 444 Seiten

INHALT

J. C. B. MOHR (PAUL SIEBECK), TÜBINGEN

PUBLICATIONS OF THE
LEO BAECK INSTITUTE

Juden im Wilhelminischen Deutschland 1890–1914

Ein Sammelband herausgegeben von WERNER E. MOSSE unter Mitwirkung von ARNOLD PAUCKER

(Schriftenreihe wissenschaftlicher Abhandlungen des Leo Baeck Instituts 33)
1976. XIV, 786 Seiten

INHALT

J. C. B. MOHR (PAUL SIEBECK), TÜBINGEN